Personnel Management
and Industrial Relations

PRENTICE-HALL INDUSTRIAL RELATIONS AND PERSONNEL SERIES

Dale Yoder, *Editor*

BELCHER   *Wage and Salary Administration, 2nd Ed.*
BELLOWS   *Creative Leadership*
BELLOWS   *Psychology of Personnel in Business and Industry, 3rd Ed.*
BELLOWS, GILSON AND ODIORNE   *Executive Skills*
CARPENTER   *Case Studies in Collective Bargaining*
DANKERT   *Contemporary Unionism in the United States*
DANKERT   *Introduction to Labor*
DAVEY   *Contemporary Collective Bargaining, 2nd Ed.*
DUBIN   *Human Relations in Administrations, 2nd Ed.*
DUBIN   *Working Union Management Relations*
ECKER, MACRAE, OUELLETTE AND TELFORD   *Handbook for Supervisors*
GOMBERG   *Trade Union Analysis of Time Study, 2nd Ed.*
LINDBERG   *Cases in Personnel Administration*
MAHONEY   *Building the Executive Team*
MILLER   *American Labor and the Government*
OTIS AND LEUKART   *Job Evaluation, 2nd Ed.*
PFIFFNER   *Supervision of Personnel, 2nd Ed.*
SHARTLE   *Executive Performance and Leadership*
SHARTLE   *Occupational Information, 3rd Ed.*
STONE AND KENDALL   *Effective Personnel Selection Procedures*
THOMPSON   *Personnel Management for Supervisors, 2nd Ed.*
YODER   *Personnel Management and Industrial Relations, 5th Ed.*
YODER   *Personnel Principles and Policies, 2nd Ed.*

FIFTH EDITION

Personnel Management and Industrial Relations

DALE YODER
Director, Division of Industrial Relations
Graduate School of Business
Stanford University

SIR ISAAC PITMAN & SONS LTD.

London

PERSONNEL MANAGEMENT AND INDUSTRIAL RELATIONS
FIFTH EDITION

(First Edition: *Personnel and Labor Relations*)

© COPYRIGHT 1938, 1942, 1948, 1956, 1962 by
PRENTICE-HALL, INC.
ENGLEWOOD CLIFFS, N. J.

LIBRARY OF CONGRESS
CATALOG CARD NO: 62-18304

First Published in Great Britain
1958
By Sir Isaac Pitman & Sons Ltd.
39 Parker Street, London, W.C.2

Reprinted 1960, 1962
Revised Edition 1963
Reprinted 1965

MADE AND PRINTED BY OFFSET IN GREAT BRITAIN BY
WILLIAM CLOWES AND SONS, LIMITED
LONDON AND BECCLES

F.5—(B.611)

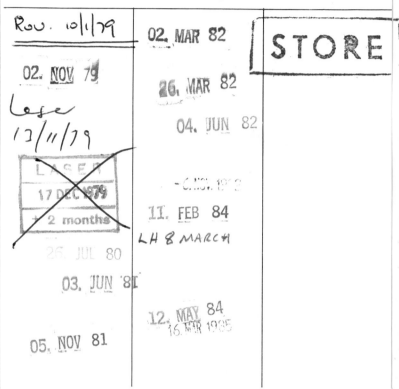

To

M.N.Y.

Preface to the Fifth Edition

Preparation of this fifth edition of *Personnel Management and Industrial Relations* has been more challenging than that of any previous revision, mainly because of recent, far-reaching changes in collegiate education for management—changes that reflect new and different approaches, designed to improve both the policy and practice of managers.

The industrial relations field has grown, both in scope and in sophistication. Like all management education—which has moved toward a closer relationship with the behavioral sciences and incorporated new views of organization and administration—today's courses in personnel and industrial relations must give more attention to theory, policy, and relevant research. The present edition is designed to facilitate these developments. In particular, it places greater emphasis on the growing body of theory that seeks explanations for satisfaction, enthusiasm, and contribution in work. It stresses the responsibility of all managers to maintain an appropriate setting and climate for work and to help their assistants and successors in preparing for similar responsibilities.

Throughout this edition, emphasis is placed on employment relationships as a field of major interest and concern for all students of management, not merely for those who contemplate careers as staff managers in personnel or labor relations. Decisions with respect to manpower policies are recognized as inescapable responsibilities of *all* managers. Only when all managers understand the philosophical and theoretical foundations of modern employment policy can industrial relations staff managers function effectively. To encourage such understanding, the new edition gives added attention to theory and policy, with less detailed descriptions of practice than earlier editions. (Extensive footnote references, however, suggest convenient sources of information on current practice.) Theory is recognized as providing the essential bridges that connect the basic goals of working organizations to appropriate policies. It also permits managers to make rational choices among programs designed to implement selected policies. Professional competence for managers requires an understanding of both theory and practice.

Today's management education should also orient students toward research, for research is the shortcut to progress in management, the pathway to continued improvement. It is the most efficient means of testing theories and developing more dependable explanations of working behavior. Accordingly, this edition continues a persistent emphasis on developing a research orientation for students and helping them achieve some sophistication in appraising reported research. Students are aided in becoming familiar with research-reporting journals to facilitate their continuing awareness of current research.

This fifth edition presents an extensive reorganization of material, shifting the order as well as the content of the chapters. Following an introductory section, a second section is devoted to the organizational setting, with special attention to theories of work, organization, and administration. The third section is concerned with general labor policy, emphasizing its tripartite development and implementation, and serves as an introduction to the more specific policies, discussed in the chapters that follow, underlying programs in the functional or activity areas.

The text has been prepared for use with or without supplementary readings and cases. Each chapter includes a list of carefully selected supplementary readings and short case problems. A new instructor's manual has been developed as the text was written and is available directly from the publishers.

By the time any text has reached its fifth edition, the author is so widely indebted that an attempt to acknowledge individual obligations for contributions is futile. Most of the changes that mark this fifth edition should be credited to faculty members in various schools, colleges, and universities who have commented on earlier editions, advanced suggestions, discussed objectives and methods of presentation and provided the author with their favorite examples, cases, and other materials. Ideas presented in conferences of the Industrial Relations Research Association, the Academy of Management, the Society for Personnel Administration, and the American Society for Personnel Administration have influenced the text on many points.

To all those whose ideas have been so helpful, the author wishes to express his sincere appreciation. It would be far more of a chore and much less rewarding to prepare or revise a text without these exchanges. It should be apparent that whatever usefulness the volume has must be credited in large measure to fellow-teachers and unofficial collaborators rather than to the author.

The author is particularly indebted to his colleagues at the University of

Minnesota and to Professors John P. Troxell, Karl M. Ruppenthal, and Thomas W. Harrell at Stanford University for valuable suggestions, insights, and teaching materials. Miss Jane Packard and Mrs. Connie McKeague deserve special mention for their preparation of the manuscript.

The author wishes particularly to express his appreciation to Professor Donald S. Holm, Jr., of the University of Missouri for his thoughtful, helpful criticism of the entire manuscript.

DALE YODER

Stanford, California

Table of Contents

III. TRILATERAL MANPOWER POLICY

V. MANPOWER TRAINING
AND DEVELOPMENT

VI. INCENTIVES IN WORK

holidays; 2.4. Paid vacations; 2.5. Rest pauses and coffee breaks; 2.6. Standby, downtime, and reporting pay; 2.7. Leaves of absence. **3.0. Morale: Personal Identification:** 3.1. Employee counseling; 3.2. Legal aid; 3.3. Food services; 3.4. Recreational programs; 3.5. Housing and transportation; 3.6. Credit for employees; 3.7. Stores, discounts; 3.8. Music and work. **4.0. Employment Security:** 4.1. Severance pay; 4.2. Unemployment insurance; 4.3. Supplemental unemployment benefits; 4.4. Retraining and TAP. **5.0. Health and Welfare:** 5.1. Safety programs and workmen's compensation; 5.2. Compensation for illness; 5.3. Temporary disability insurance; 5.4. Paid sick leave; 5.5. Group health programs. **6.0. Old Age and Retirement:** 6.1. OASDI; 6.2. Old age assistance; 6.3. Private pensions; 6.4. Retirement programs. **7.0. Summary.**

23. *Employee Morale* 526

1.0. Morale, Attitudes and Behavior: 1.1. Individual and group morale; 1.2. Indicators of morale. **2.0. Policy on Employee Morale:** 2.1. Development and maintenance of high morale; 2.2. Continuing appraisals of morale. **3.0. The Syndrome of Negative Morale:** 3.1. Lack of interest; 3.2. Labor turnover; 3.3. Grievances; 3.4. Work stoppages; 3.5. Absenteeism; 3.6. Disciplinary problems; 3.7. Restriction of output. **4.0. Surveys of Morale:** 4.1. Preliminary questions; 4.2. Dimensions: subscales; 4.3. Items or questions; 4.4. Analysis and interpretation. **5.0. Summary.**

24. *Employment Communications* 556

1.0. Problems and Definitions: 1.1. Problems in communications; 1.2. Varying perceptions; 1.3. Definitions; 1.4. Active participation; 1.5. Channels, media, and structures. **2.0. Theory and Policy in Communications:** 2.1. Two-way communication; 2.2. Semantics in communications; 2.3. Factor in morale; 2.4. Skill and attitude of transmitter; 2.5. Interest and attitude of receivers; 2.6. Differences in media; 2.7. Barriers to communication; 2.8. Rumor, gossip; 2.9. Current policy. **3.0. Media and Practice:** 3.1. Face-to-face exchange; 3.2. Handbooks and house organs; 3.3. Financial reports; 3.4. Bulletin boards; 3.5. Information racks; 3.6. Suggestion systems; 3.7. Audio-visual supplements; 3.8. Other media. **4.0. Checks on In-Plant Communications:** 4.1. Morale studies; 4.2. Reading ease and interest; 4.3. Communication audits. **5.0. Summary.**

VII. INSIGHT, PERSPECTIVE AND EVALUATION

25. *Industrial Relations Research* 584

1.0. Nature of Research: 1.1. Essentials in research; 1.2. Background; 1.3. Co-disciplinary approach; 1.4. Pure, basic and applied

*Personnel Management
and Industrial Relations*

I. INTRODUCTION

1. The Industrial
Relations Field

This is a book about the management of people in their work in free, democratic societies. The objective of such management has been defined as "guiding human and physical resources into dynamic organization units which attain their objectives to the satisfaction of those served, and with a high degree of morale and sense of attainment on the part of those rendering the service."[1]

The process of managing free, mobile "managees" in societies where work organizations are rapidly changing is more complicated than manpower management in earlier, simpler societies (see Chapter 2). Today's manager must recognize numerous expressions of employee desires for their own development and for participation in management decisions. He must direct a wide range of special personnel programs. He may have to negotiate with unions of employees. The modern manager must understand the managees' expectations regarding wages, hours, security, and other working conditions. The present-day manager in American industry faces varied and complex problems in managing the people on whom his success depends.

Providing *leadership* for working men and women is, of course, only a part of the total function and responsibility of the manager. It is, however, widely recognized as the most important and the most difficult managerial task. People are the one essential resource in all working organizations. Whatever the other resources to be combined, people must control the combining. People alone can provide the thinking required to get the job done. No fore-

[1] Unpublished report of the Personnel Round Table.

1

seeable technological developments in automation or electronic brains can entirely eliminate the necessity for personal decisions and direction.

Management of people represents the most difficult managerial responsibility, because free people insist on exercising a considerable degree of *self-management*. They have their own ideas about working and make many decisions about when and where to work, whether to operate their own business or to work for others, and what they consider adequate and fair compensation for their contributions. Moreover, free workers change their minds on these questions, so that what they decided a year ago may not seem to them an appropriate answer today or tomorrow. Free workers may want to change jobs or the localities in which they work or the employers with whom they are associated. They may conclude that they want more or different opportunities for their own development, with a chance to try learning new skills. They may conclude that present managers are not as resourceful or as well-informed as they should be. All in all, therefore, free, mobile men and women in modern democratic societies pose complex and ever-changing problems for their managers and employers. Management must recognize the propriety of these personal decisions and take them into account in planning and directing the work of their organizations.

Today's industrialized societies have developed a distinctive system of management. It has been shaped by experience in the three hundred years since the earlier argricultural and handicraft systems began to give way to factories and mass employment. It is a system that has worked and is working. Indeed, the changing system of management has played an important role, together with growing capital and material resources and the increased skill of workers, in facilitating the productivity of modern industrial societies.

This book is designed to help its readers understand today's system of management, particularly the management of people. The purpose of such a presentation is not to suggest how to *manipulate* employees. Neither is the purpose to encourage "soft" management in a sentimental sense, nor a thin facade or veneer of shallow consideration from those to whom workers entrust positions of leadership and direction in their working lives.

The purpose here is to help those who plan to work in manager positions attain that competence—that special skill and knowledge—which can justify their designation and support in these positions.

1.0 MANAGEMENT OF PEOPLE AT WORK

The heart of employment relationships and the setting for all problems of management is the process of employment. This is, in itself, a unique and distinctive process. In it, politically free citizens voluntarily work for other free citizens, performing operations in which they may have relatively little personal interest, as a means of "making a living." These free workers accept the leadership of managers they may not respect, recognizing that such managers may have appointed themselves to positions of leadership. The process thus creates some relationships that are not readily explainable in terms of the other common associations of free people.

As will be noted, many explanations of these relationships have been advanced. Both leaders and followers have had to accept one or another of these explanations as a basis for their collaboration. None, however, avoids today's common problems of management. Can men and women who may have little personal interest in the jobs which they are performing be expected to work efficiently? Can leaders of working organizations expect free workers to work effectively under their leadership? What sort of employment relationships make sense in societies of free men and women?

1.1 Problems and practice. This is a book about modern management in all free societies, with special reference to the management of people. It is a book about managerial policies, practices, and problems. Attention usually turns first to problems, since they demand consideration. In a sense, every managerial practice is designed to solve a problem. Problems arise, however, because the practice of management fails to attain the goals set for it.

Problems, as the term is used here, represent situations in which we fail to achieve the goals we have set for ourselves. We regard them as problems because the reality of day-to-day working relationships is not consistent with the ideals and objectives we seek to achieve in these relationships.

A few examples may help to clarify this viewpoint and this definition of problems. One common managerial goal is to maintain stable employment and steady earnings. When people who want to work cannot find jobs or are frequently laid off or are unemployed because of labor disputes, we recognize their idleness as an important problem. Again, employment in jobs that create serious health hazards represents a problem because we seek to avoid such dangers. Employment in jobs that fail to use the finest talents and skills of workers represents a measure of wasted manpower, which we regard as a problem because we want to minimize such waste.

Public expectations give the manager heavy responsibilities. We expect him to be effective in leading, planning for, and directing his working organization. Our customs and traditions make him responsible for avoiding waste in his combination of the factors of production; he is expected to make the best possible combinations. In private industry, he must achieve a level of profit or of prospective earnings that will encourage investors to provide such capital as is required. In public organizations, we expect him to provide a continually improving service to citizens.

1.2 Modern employment goals. About three-fourths of the American labor force (adults who are working as well as those who are available for work) are employees. We are not satisfied that they simply have jobs. Generally, we expect their jobs to make possible their enjoyment of life and their active, intelligent participation as citizens in a free, democratic society. One summary of modern employment objectives follows:[2]

2 "Manpower Blueprint for a Free Economy," *Staff Report to the Sub-committee*

(1) We want to maintain an even balance of jobs and jobholders, with enough manpower working to raise living scales for all our citizens and permit us to help the less fortunate in other nations to improve their living and working conditions.

(2) We want to help all our men and women, now and in the future, to have the best, most productive, most profitable jobs they can fill. We want them to find the jobs in which they can be most happy, enthusiastic, and effective.

(3) We want to assist every member of our labor force team in maximizing his contribution and his reward for that contribution, by developing and applying his highest talents in his chosen career with the latest and best in tools and equipment.

(4) We want to insure the careful protection and conservation of all our manpower, to avoid its waste or careless use, to eliminate any semblance of a human scrap pile.

(5) We want to accomplish all these objectives in a free society in which men and women make their own decisions with a minimum of dictation and enforced direction and in which personal advancement is limited only by insistence that considerations of general welfare shall always hold top priority.

These are what may be described as basic goals. They represent long-term, over-all objectives of our American society. The goals of individual citizens and of special groups do not always coincide with these social goals. The individual may be so interested in his own personal advancement and welfare as to ignore his fellows. Many groups may seek special advantages for their members. For this reason, problems of regulation and control cannot be avoided. As a nation, we must reconcile these conflicting objectives, prevent unfair advantages to individuals or groups, and help individuals do their part toward attainment of social goals.

Although these generally accepted social ideals represent a synthesis and a balancing of the personal goals of employees and those of employers, the minority of workers who hold positions as managers have been given major responsibility for working toward and achieving these goals. The manager's job is one of providing leadership, guidance, direction, and control in a group endeavor. The manager's job is to insure an effective, satisfying setting and atmosphere for work. His function is much the same, whether he works for a private firm or a public agency. It is a complicated assignment. Management means much more than merely making impersonal decisions and issuing instructions designed to get a job done. Management means finding people who can work together toward the common objective or mission of the organization, leading them in the accomplishment of this objective, developing their interest and enthusiasm in common tasks, and offering opportunities for the accomplishment of personal objectives and goals through employment.

1.3 Progress by trial and error. It is not surprising that we have continuing problems, that we fail to attain our goals. In part, such problems persist because we continue to advance our objectives. Our ideals and goals change. In part, our problems result from our heavy dependence on trial and

on Labor and Labor-Management Relations, Washington, D.C.: Government-Printing Office, 1953, p. 8.

error in attempting improvements in management. Our current practice always represents many tentative, experimental solutions.

This current practice has had to be experimental, because our understanding of human behavior in work is so limited. We cannot be sure that new practices or modifications of older practice will achieve the desired results. Trial and error is necessarily a slow route toward progress. We need much more understanding of working behavior as a basis for improvements in our management of people. We need carefully planned research to provide such understanding. Research offers a much more rapid route to progress.

Throughout the chapters that follow, frequent references will indicate that we are using this "research route" more than in the past. We have found that research can provide solutions for many of the problems of manpower management. We have also discovered, however, that many of these problems extend beyond the boundaries of any individual behavioral science. Hence they do not yield to the approach of any single discipline. Their solutions require a many-sided analysis that must frequently combine the insights of several disciplines.

Much current practice must be regarded as tentative, because it is based on traditional but dubious folklore, impression, and opinion. Also, many current solutions and related practices represent emergency measures; for example, when a strike in the steel or transportation industries threatens public health or safety or prosperity, emergency solutions for immediate relief must be quickly found. In such crises, time does not permit a comprehensive analysis in depth. One of our favorite devices in such situations, local as well as national, is to "pass a law." If it gives temporary relief, we may easily lean and depend on it, postponing any further attempt to understand the basic problem. In less spectacular examples, we develop stop-gap means for *training* employees for new jobs, for *selecting* employees or managers, or for *negotiating* a labor agreement. If these practices work fairly well, they tend to become established, even though they are not perfect solutions. Like the leaky roof that doesn't get repaired between rains, problems may be forgotten and neglected until another crisis appears.

1.4 Changing employment relationships. Meanwhile, it is clear that employment relationships and the problems in these relationships are constantly changing. Those who work are changing: each year more than a million new workers enter our labor force, while a smaller number of workers withdraw from it. New entrants—threshold workers—have different values and attitudes.

Meanwhile, *employment opportunities change* as old jobs disappear and new, different jobs are created. Unskilled jobs have become much less common than they were a generation ago. Semiskilled jobs have become particularly vulnerable to the impact of modern technology, widely described as *automation*. A variety of new jobs has appeared in semiprofessional and service occupations.

All these changes affect employment. Some changes should make it possible for us to come closer to our ideals. They may provide at least partial solutions to problems. Other changes create new gaps between the actual and the ideal, which means that we have new, different problems. As the problems change, solutions must also change.

2.0 RESPONSIBILITY FOR MANPOWER MANAGEMENT

In managing people, as in raising a family, almost every adult citizen considers himself something of an expert. When unemployment rises to 6 or 7 per cent of the labor force, for example, many citizens propose special legislation ranging from made-work programs to adjustments in tariffs and taxes. Union leaders may advance still other suggestions. The Chamber of Commerce and the National Association of Manufacturers can generally be counted on to propose something opposed to the most common union suggestion, and union spokesmen react similarly to the proposals of employer organizations. Taxicab drivers, ministers, teachers, television comedians, and rank and file employees all have their own solutions for employment problems.

2.1 **Agency management.** Managers, however, have a special responsibility for finding satisfactory solutions. They must recruit, employ, and retire employees who will work under their management. They must provide satisfactory working conditions to gain and hold essential manpower. They cannot continue to manage unless they find reasonably satisfactory solutions to emerging problems. In a very real sense, ours is a system of *agency management,* in which managers coach and direct employees, acting as their agents. Managers must provide a service that is satisfactory if they are to get the manpower they require. This agency responsibility is nowhere more evident than in the recruitment of college graduates. Every up-to-date advertisement promises to help the recruit grow, develop, and become an all-American worker or manager. Meanwhile, of course, managers must also satisfy their employers.[3]

For most managers, managing people is their "crucial task"—the most difficult and critical of their assignments. No matter how skillful they may be in solving mechanical, sales, or financial problems, their value and effectiveness are severely limited if they cannot lead and direct their associates. Indeed, management has been defined as getting things done through people. As every student of economics has been told, management requires the com-

---

[3] How can a manager be the agent of employees when he is already the agent of his employers? Doesn't he thus involve himself in a serious conflict of interest? To some degree at least, his action as an agent for employees, aiding them in achieving their personal goals, is entirely consistent with owner interests in getting and retaining superior people. Perhaps more important is the tendency of public opinion to expect something approximating professional management, which means that managers are expected to give a heavy weight to the public interest. The public interest requires an effort to employ individuals at their highest potential.

bination and application of the "four M's"—men, materials, machines, and money. Leadership of men or people is an essential ingredient. In a society that is committed to a national policy of full employment—which means tight labor markets, with demands in excess of supplies—the agency management responsibility is and must be crucial.

2.2 The manager job. Managing people is an integral part of every major element in the manager job. Studies of managerial jobs have generally described five principal responsibilities, including:

1. *Planning*—preparing for future action, both immediate and long-term, with reference to what, when, where, and by whom action is to be taken.
2. *Organizing*—finding appropriate help and dividing the work to be done among those who are to do it.
3. *Directing*—providing leadership and guidance with clear assignments of responsibilities to all who are to have a part in the work of the organization.
4. *Coordinating*—maintaining effective relationships among the contributions of participants in terms of timing and of balance in the total operation.
5. *Controlling*—maintaining a clear view of the entire organizational operation and continually comparing the actions and results with assignments and expectations.

Managing people is an important element in each of these managerial assignments. Time-budget studies show that "directing subordinates" requires a major share of a supervisor's time, that the higher the manager in the management bureaucracy, the more time devoted to these personnel problems. We may state, as a general principle, that each time an additional employee is hired, the manager adds new problems and complicates those with which he is already concerned.

Managers may also be seriously frustrated in managing people. The complexities of the manager-managee relationship and the resulting uncertainties about employee reactions appear to be the areas in which managers are least sure of themselves. For this reason, many managers are unsure about their acceptance by and status in the work society.

2.3 Staff assistance. Many business organizations maintain special "employee relations" or "personnel" divisions to provide special technical and professional assistance to all "line" or unspecialized managers. These divisions help supervisors, managers, and executives in their relationships with employees. Their staff members may direct programs of recruitment, hold preliminary employment interviews, give selective tests, negotiate with union representatives, and administer benefit programs. They cannot, however, relieve supervisors and managers of their basic responsibility for managing the people who work under their direction.

2.4 Small-firm practice. What of the manager of the small firm, in which no personnel or labor relations manager can be justified? To some degree, his problems may be simpler because of the close personal relationships between himself and the employees. He may, also, employ independent industrial relations consultants to provide special know-how and experience. On the other hand, such a manager, since he cannot avoid responsibilities in this area, may need to know *more* about policies, practices, and problems in manpower management than his counterpart in the large firm.[4]

3.0 DIMENSIONS OF MANPOWER MANAGEMENT

Current usage describes "manpower management" variously as *personnel management, labor management, employee relations,* and *industrial relations.* The considerable variation in terminology used in reference to manpower management often creates confusion in determining its scope or dimensions. Fortunately, however, a standardization of terminology is appearing.[5] "Industrial relations" or "employee relations" is becoming widely accepted as the most inclusive of these terms, with "personnel management" and "labor relations" as the two major subdivisions.

3.1 Current terminology. Although the title of this book has been accepted for more than twenty years, it does not clearly fit this growing practice, for it suggests that personnel management and industrial relations are two distinct fields. Actually, however, present usage defines "personnel management" as being *one of the two major parts of industrial relations*—the other being what is now described as "labor relations." Nevertheless, the book's title does have significance: it combines the two most common designations for the specialized staff divisions, or departments, that have been created to assist managers in handling the problems of manpower management. The older designation for this division is "personnel department." The newer designation is "industrial relations." Many firms still describe their specialized manpower-management programs as "personnel management" or "personnel administration."

With the expansion of collective bargaining after the enactment of the National Labor Relations Act in 1935, however, managers found their problems and programs more complicated. Specialists for *dealing with unions* and *the administration of collective agreements* became a necessary addition to earlier personnel departments. In some cases, these specialists were made a part of established personnel divisions. In others, new labor relations units were created. As it became clear that problems in personnel and labor relations were inseparable, the two functions were frequently combined in an *industrial relations* or *employee relations* department.

---

[4] See Frances Torbert, *Personnel Management in Small Companies,* Los Angeles: University of California Institute of Industrial Relations, 1959; James M. Black and J. G. Piccoli, *Successful Labor Relations for Small Business,* New York: McGraw-Hill Book Company, Inc., 1953.

[5] See Dale Yoder and Roberta J. Nelson, "Jobs in Employee Relations," *Research Study No. 38,* American Management Association, 1959.

In today's technical terminology, therefore, personnel management refers to managerial approaches to problems in which managers deal with employees as individuals. In contrast, *labor relations* refers to problems of management-union relationships in which managers negotiate agreements with groups of employees and administer these "labor contracts."

Manpower management or *labor management,* although these terms are not widely used, are probably the most realistic descriptions of this whole area of employment problems. They clearly distinguish *in-plant, managerial problems* from the broader social problems of *manpower allocation* or *manpower marketing.* The latter process—the disposition of human resources—takes place largely in the labor markets of free economies. It is influenced by education, counseling, employee mobility, and many other variables that are not ordinarily subject to managerial control.

Manpower management includes leadership in both group and individual relationships, both labor relations and personnel management. It effectively describes the processes of planning and directing the application, development, and utilization of human resources in employment. Employers, employees, unions, and public agencies all have important roles to play in these processes. In the pages that follow, another term—*employee relations*—will be used as a synonym of *manpower management* and of *industrial relations.*

3.2 Major functions or activities. For convenience in exploring, outlining, and explaining manpower management, its principal activities and types of problems may be classified as follows:

1. Setting general and specific management policy for employment relationships and establishing and maintaining a suitable organization for leadership and cooperation.
2. Collective bargaining.
3. Staffing the organization: finding, getting and holding prescribed types and numbers of workers.
4. Aiding the self-development of employees at all levels: providing opportunities for personal development and growth as well as requisite skills and experience.
5. Incentivating: developing and maintaining the motivation in work.
6. Reviewing and auditing manpower management in the organization.
7. Industrial relations research: carrying out studies designed to explain employment behavior and thereby to improve manpower management.

From the manager's viewpoint, these dimensions may be graphically sketched as shown in Figure 1.1. In the figure, these major functional or activity divisions are listed at the left of the chart.

3.3 Levels of attention. The chart, it will be noted, has a second, horizontal, dimension. Columns in the chart describe the major activities in terms of levels of managerial attention. To understand the job of the man-

Major Dimensions of Manpower Management

Activity or Function	Problems	Practices & Programs	Policies	Theories & Philosophy
1. Policy, organization and administration				
2. Labor Relations: Negotiation Administration				
3. Staffing: Job analysis Recruiting Selecting Orientation Promoting Transferring Releasing				
4. Developing: Training Personal appraisal Counseling				
5. Incentivating: Wage and salary administration Benefits and services Maintaining interest and morale Maintaining in-plant communications				
6. Audit and review				
7. Research				

Figure 1.1   Major Dimensions of Manpower Management

ager, each functional area must be approached *in depth,* for problems arise in each distinctive level.

Most managers give top priorities to the problems they face. The manager notes industrial unrest, requests for transfer, employee criticisms of policy and practice, grievances, labor turnover, absenteeism, difficulties in recruiting, disciplinary cases, and other indications of unsatisfactory employment relationships. This view is sometimes described as that of the firewarden, and resulting programs are seen as putting out fires.

The *problems column* in Figure 1.1 represents all those situations in which current practice fails to achieve a perfect score. Thus, for example, selection practice still results in hiring some misfits, and training programs do not completely meet the needs for which they were designed.

The second column shifts attention from the problems to the programs and detailed practices currently used in each major activity area. At this level, managerial concern centers on what is now being done in staffing, collective bargaining, and the other major areas. Programs represent planned courses of action designed to solve specific problems. Thus a firm might have a variety of job-training or selection programs. Programs include specific and detailed *practice* and *procedure*.

A third and deeper level of managerial concern looks to the policies behind each program. *Policy* refers to intentions, what we want to do and intend to do or accomplish in our management of people. At this level, the question is: What are we trying to do? What are our intentions in the programs we provide? What course have we adopted and proposed to follow? For example, assume that the problems column notes some failure to select employees regarded as satisfactory. Roots of the problem may appear in an analysis of *practice*. Perhaps the current program is misusing tests or relying too heavily on interviews. Someone with responsibilities for screening applicants may be reading character from the handwriting of applicants.

It may be, however, that the difficulty arises at the *policy* level. Policy may, for example, propose that first opportunity in every vacancy shall be given to present employees. Such a policy could be quite inappropriate if some jobs to be filled require special talent or education or experience not necessary for any other jobs in the organization.

3.4 Theory and philosophy in management. Consideration of policies tends to raise additional questions. Why is policy what it is? Why, for example, does policy prescribe promotion from within? Most of the answers to such questions are to be found in the theories and philosophy of management. Managerial *theories* represent *explanations and rationalizations that managers accept and use* to guide them in their selection of policies and programs. Thus a theory that all workers want promotion may encourage a policy of promotion from within. Another theory may lead to a policy of racial or religious discrimination in hiring or to the practice of requiring that all applications for employment be handwritten by the applicant.

Managerial philosophy—the pattern or system of beliefs, attitudes, ideas, and values—is basic to the whole combination of theories, policies, and programs in management. Thus, for example, a problem in the form of continually high labor turnover might be traceable to policies and practices indicating a lack of management interest in such employee problems as unemployment or irregular wages. Again, a philosophy that gives little weight to managerial ethics may readily express itself in practice that misrepresents jobs or opportunities for advancement.

Students generally have little difficulty in recognizing problems in each of the several functional areas. They readily understand most of the common programs, practices, and procedures. Techniques, even though they may be complex, are tangible and meaningful. Understanding policies, theory, and philosophy requires a more probing type of analysis.

No superficial understanding of the techniques of manpower management can be regarded as adequate for managers in the years ahead. Competent managers must understand policy as well as practice and the relevant theory underlying both. They must give as much attention to the "why" of management as to the "how" of program and practice. They need to recognize the necessity for continuing change in both policy and practice. Just as historic practice may be irritating and frustrating to modern workers, historic assumptions and theories may be obsolete or inadequate. Modern management must express and implement modern theory.

Managerial philosophy must also change and grow. Socially acceptable values with respect to employment relationships are by no means set and unchanging. Modern industrialized societies expect, for example, much more stable employment and more economic security for workers than was expected in past generations. Modern society places heavier responsibilities on managers, as is evident in the common tendency to hold them responsible for the waste of resources in strikes and for the economic security of retired workers. Several states are presently contemplating legislation that would charge firms with responsibility for retraining employees displaced by technological change. Negotiated agreements in several industries have already created similar managerial obligations, in addition to responsibilities for a wide range of employee benefits and services. The captains of industry and empire builders of a generation past might have found real difficulty in fitting such responsibilities into their philosophies of management.

4.0 PREVIEW AND OUTLINE

Students who plan to specialize in the personnel or industrial relations field may have somewhat greater interest in the details of common practice than those whose major interests are in other fields. It is well to remember, however, that both the greatest challenge and the deepest satisfactions for *all managers* frequently grow out of their management of others. All students of management should understand both the principal functional areas and the levels of managerial concern pictured in Figure 1.1. Table 1.1 may be helpful in providing more detail with respect to the broad categories of activities or functions. All students need to recognize the continuing importance of policy.

As a guide to modern management, with major emphasis on the management of people, this textbook must give adequate attention to all levels of managerial concern—problems, practice, programs, theory, and philosophy. In the past, both managerial and student attention has frequently concen-

Table 1.1 Details of Industrial Relations Practice

[Adapted from the questionnaire used by the University of Minnesota Industrial Relations Center in periodic surveys of industrial relations ratios and budgets.]

I. General Administration of the Industrial Relations Department
1. Formulation of industrial relations policy
2. Planning, coordinating IR activities
3. Planning, recommending revisions in company organization structure
4. Selection, promotion, transfer of IR staff members
5. Work assignments for IR staff members
6. Supervision of IR staff
7. Employee records
8. Records on specific phases of IR program
9. Reports of activities
10. Review and evaluation of IR programs and practices
11. Budgeting for IR programs

II. Recruitment, Employment, Placement
1. Forecast of personnel requirements
2. Manning tables; personnel inventories
3. Labor market studies: sources of employees
4. Recruitment: recent college graduates
5. Recruitment: non-supervisory production employees
6. Recruitment: non-supervisory office employees
7. Recruitment: supervisory, managerial, executive
8. Recruitment: sales
9. Recruitment: professional and technical
10. Pre-employment testing program
11. Pre-employment interviewing
12. Reference and experience checking
13. Pre-employment physical examinations
14. Placement: referring selected applicants to job openings
15. Coordination of promotions, transfers, demotions
16. Coordination of layoffs, recalls
17. Coordination of quits, discharges
18. Exit interviews

III. Training and Development
1. Orientation and induction of new employees
2. On-the-job training: shop, office, sales
3. Apprenticeship and other craft training
4. Out-of-hours vocational courses
5. Tuition refunds
6. Scholarship programs
7. Supervisory training
8. Management training
9. Graduate training for professional and scientific personnel
10. Conferences and short courses: inside company
11. Conferences and short courses: outside company
12. Job rotation program
13. Internship trainees—cooperative arrangements with schools
14. Educational and vocational counseling
15. Appraisals of employee potential and performance
16. Appraisals of supervisory and managerial potential performance

IV. Labor Relations
1. Collection of information preparatory to contract negotiations
2. Preparation of company briefs
3. Contract negotiations
4. Contract interpretation and day-by-day administration

    5. Dealing with union representatives in administration of contract
    6. Grievance handling
    7. Preparation and presentation of cases for arbitration, mediation, NLRB, government agencies
    8. Check-off
    9. Union-management committees: e.g., health and welfare

V. Wage and Salary Administration
    1. Job analysis and description
    2. Job evaluation and grading
    3. Establishment of wage rates and rate structures
    4. Rate review and adjustment
    5. Wage and salary surveys
    6. Wage incentive plans
    7. Profit sharing plans
    8. Stock purchase plans
    9. Bonus plans

VI. Administering of Benefits and Services Programs, Including Health and Safety
    1. Life insurance
    2. Medical and hospital care insurance
    3. Unemployment compensation; supplementary unemployment benefits
    4. Severance pay
    5. Disability pay
    6. Workmen's compensation
    7. Rehabilitation of handicapped workers
    8. Sick leave
    9. Leaves of absence (military and other)
   10. Vacations
   11. Recreation programs, social events
   12. Food services
   13. Employee newspapers, magazines
   14. Informational booklets: handbooks, policy manuals
   15. Annual reports to employees
   16. Bulletin boards
   17. Music
   18. Thrift and savings programs
   19. Credit union
   20. Counseling
   21. Awards for long service
   22. Suggestions systems
   23. Periodic physical examinations
   24. First aid and dispensary service
   25. Preventive medicine and health education
   26. Occupational hygiene
   27. Safety inspections
   28. Accident investigations
   29. Accident control activities
   30. Safety training and safety promotion campaigns
   31. Safety equipment: machine guards, personal protective equipment

VII. Research
Plan and conduct research studies within company on:
    1. measurement devices: tests, weighted application blanks, rating scales, etc.
    2. interviewing
    3. supervision, leadership
    4. supervisory and employee attitudes
    5. job satisfaction
    6. training needs

7. training techniques
8. training subject matter
9. motivation
10. employee-management communications
11. turnover, absenteeism
12. methods of wage payment
13. techniques of recruitment
14. employee benefit plans
15. records design and control
16. Participate in studies conducted by outside research groups
17. Maintain library of pertinent industrial relations materials

---

trated on practice and neglected policy and theory. Today's alert managers realize that such a focus permits only a superficial analysis of problems. Program and practice should be expressions of policy. Philosophy sets the goals that become the objectives in policy. In addition, theory largely determines the development or selection of policy, practice, and procedure.

This outline of modern manpower management begins with the widely-accepted assumption that the major responsibility of every manager is to provide a satisfactory setting for work. He must create and maintain working conditions and relationships that encourage his colleagues and assistants to perform the tasks that will together accomplish the objectives of the organization. His contribution may be measured by his success in blending individual goals with those of the working organization.

To that end, he must sense and control the factors that influence the will to work among his associates. He must use the tool of *organization* in setting the stage and maintaining an effective tone and climate for work. He must assume responsibility for leading in the development of management *policies* that are acceptable as a basis for collaboration.

The chapters that follow have been arranged to facilitate an understanding of these responsibilities. This chapter and the two that follow in Section I provide historic perspective for viewing the complex relationships of employment and management. Chapter 2 emphasizes the concept of *systems* of employment relationships and the major *variables* in these systems. Chapter 3 notes current *trends* in each of these variables.

Section II, consisting of four chapters, introduces the major *theoretical bases* for manpower management, with special emphasis on changing theories of work and of working organizations. Section III is concerned with *general manpower policy*—selected intentions in employment relationships—and the tripartite determination of this policy in modern societies. It notes the prominent roles of both unions and government in policy-making and the pervasive influence of general policy as a guide for detailed policies and programs in all functional phases of manpower management.

The remaining sections consider problems, practice, policy, and theory in the major functional areas of staffing, employee and management development, incentivation, industrial relations research, and auditing.

16   *Introduction*

SELECTED SUPPLEMENTARY READINGS

Baker, Alton W., *Personnel Management in Small Plants.* Columbus, Ohio: Bureau of Business Research, Ohio State University, 1955.
Bellows, Roger M., *Case Problems in Personnel Management,* Case 1. Dubuque, Iowa: William C. Brown Co., 1955.
Chruden, Herbert J., and Arthur W. Sherman, Jr., *Personnel Management,* Chaps. 1, 2. Cincinnati: South-Western Publishing Company, 1959.
Condon, Justin J., "A General Management View of the Personnel Function," *Business Topics* (Michigan State University), Vol. 9, No. 3, pp. 65–73, Summer 1961.
"Industrial Relations Here and Now," *Report Number 34.* New York: American Management Association, 1960.
Jucius, Michael J., *Personnel Management,* Chaps. 1, 2. Homewood, Ill.: Richard D. Irwin, Inc., 1959.
Lipstreu, Otis, "Personnel Management in the Automated Company," *Personnel,* Vol. 38, No. 2, pp. 38–44, March-April 1961.
Malm, F. T., "The Development of Personnel Administration in Western Europe," *California Management Review,* Vol. 3, No. 1, pp. 69–83, Fall 1960.
McCrensky, Edward, "Personnel Management—Soviet Style," *Personnel Administration,* Vol. 23, No. 5, pp. 44–51, September-October 1960.
Personnel Administration, Vol. 24, No. 5, September-October, 1961. (Entire issue features a "Reappraisal of the Personnel Job.")
Pigors, Paul, and Charles A. Myers, *Personnel Administration,* Chaps. 1, 2. New York: McGraw-Hill Book Company, Inc., 1961.

SHORT CASE PROBLEM 1.1

Management Tests Own Management
by Arthur C. Prendergast*

Suppose you have just been appointed manager of a plant. You sit down at your new desk for the first time, feeling a nice glow.

Then you look at the stack of papers before you.

The industrial-relations manager submits a memo reporting a rumor that one of your key men is planning to leave.

The plant manager wants authorization for a new $90,000 boiler, quick, because the old one is likely to blow up.

A big customer is unhappy about delivery of his order.

The accounting manager wants to know why the budget hasn't been turned in.

Your predecessor has left behind a request for a speech to be made next week.

Also, the boss wants a report on the efficiency of a shipping package and a revision of the benefits program, both for the bimonthly meeting a week away.

An injured employee is suing the company. What action should be taken?

The annual fund drive is coming up. How should it be organized?

The plant superintendent wants time to go over a big operating problem with you thoroughly.

Oh, yes, the boss also wants an evaluation of the supervisory training problem. And that's only part way down the pile.

Phone Interrupts

What a big job ahead! But you're ready for it.

* From the *Christian Science Monitor* (Boston), February 13, 1959.

Just then the telephone rings. The president hurriedly orders you to catch the first plane to the home office. All plant managers in for an emergency conference. Be prepared to stay at headquarters a week.

It's just an hour until plane time. How do you handle all these things lying on your desk?

Do you start according to the age of each? Do you consult your secretary for precedents? Do you phone people in some of the other plants for advice? Do you call in the department heads and start delegating responsibilities? Which matters should you handle yourself?

Problem: Which of these pressing questions would you regard as "manpower management"? How should the new manager establish priorities for action in this situation? Could you properly send some of these problems to staff advisors? Would you be willing to direct some of them to a union of your employees?

SHORT CASE PROBLEM 1.2

Indexes of Employee Relations Health

The Cellex Company (electronics, adhesives, missiles) employed a consulting firm to work with its Industrial Relations Division in an extensive evaluation of employee relations. In a summary of findings, the Industrial Relations Audit Report listed some 50 "indexes" and, in the body of the report, commented on them individually and in various combinations. Among these indexes were the following:

1. Labor costs as a proportion of total costs: 38 per cent
2. Annual factory labor turnover rate: hiring, 27 per 100
3. Annual factory labor turnover rate: replacement, 27 per 100
4. Annual factory labor turnover rate: separations, 22 per 100
5. Scores on consultant's morale scale: hourly rated employees, 73
6.   supervisory, 64
7.   middle management, 70
8. Personnel ratio: 0.75 (number of I.R. staff per hundred employees)
9. Per employee cost, annual, Industrial Relations Division: $103.67
10. Selection ratio (hired per 100 applicants): 14
11. Average recruitment time lag: 24 days
12. Average hourly rates, factory employees: $2.35
13. Average annual increase in hourly rates, five years: 9.3 cents
14. Ratio of highest to lowest factory rates: 1.5 to 1.0
15. Fringe costs as percentage of wage costs: 23.2 per cent
16. Training division, annual budget per employee: $14.93
17. Suggestions: annual: 1 per 4.6 employees.
18. Grievances: settled at first stage: 17 per cent
19.   per cent arbitration awards for management: 34
20. Salary of Director of Industrial Relations; per cent of president: 21.

Problem: On the basis of this excerpt of indexes: (1) Do you conclude that industrial relations in the firm are essentially healthy? (2) Summarize the reasons for your conclusion by reference to these symptoms.

2. Changing Industrial Relations Systems

Chapter 1 has suggested the range and the complexity of problems in today's management of people. This chapter is designed to provide *perspective* in appraising these problems.

Are today's problems of employment relationships more serious than those of earlier periods? Are solutions more difficult? Why have these problems attracted more popular attention and concern? What is different about employment relationships today? What has changed since men worked together in the ancient agricultural economies, or the later handicraft system, or early industrial societies? Thoughtful consideration of such questions raises others. Are there discernible trends that suggest further changes in employment relationships? Will the problems of managing people in 1975 or in 2000 be different from those we now face? If so, can we forecast the more important changes? How can today's educational programs anticipate these future managerial problems and prepare students to meet them?

1.0 INDUSTRIAL RELATIONS SYSTEMS

People have always worked and organized for work and allowed themselves to be managed in work. In every type of society, some members of the working group have been held responsible for leadership and direction. Nevertheless, no single, simple plan or arrangement has achieved universal acceptance. A variety of arrangements persists in the world today. Societies have tried many plans to provide leadership, gain individual acceptance of group goals and insure effective if not enthusiastic cooperation in the work to be done. They have, in other words, developed a variety of "systems" of employment relationships.[1]

1.1 Major variables. Students who have examined the long evolution in employment relationships have found it helpful to note a number of variables that appear to be prominent in all stages throughout this historic process. Changes in these variables distinguish the *stages* and mark the continuing change in industrial relations systems. Edward Gross, for example, notes four major variables in these systems: (1) the institutional setting, (2) the pattern of status and authority, (3) the careers of individuals, and (4) the nature of face-to-face work groups.[2] With this model, he analyzes the industrial relations systems of societies, from those of primitive groups to modern industrialized nations.

Dunlop describes a somewhat different model in which he identifies three principal "groups of actors" in changing industrial relations systems. Each system, he says, includes (1) employees and their organizations, (2) managers and their organizations, and (3) governmental agencies with responsibilities for working conditions and the work community.[3]

Such a model outlines, pictures or diagrams an area of interest, spotlighting or emphasizing what are regarded as the more important features. Used in study or investigation, it focuses attention on the portions in which the investigator has major interest. Orcutt defines a useful model as a representation "designed to incorporate those features deemed to be significant for one or more specific purposes." He notes that "maps are models of geographic areas and they incorporate spatial, topological features of the areas represented."[4] A useful model of industrial relations systems is thus a portrayal of employment relationships that highlights and emphasizes what are regarded as the most interesting features of the whole.

1.2 A management model. What are the principal items in a useful model depends, as has been said, on the purpose of the model builder. The political scientist investigating employment relationships might give great emphasis to the roles played by various public agencies. The student of cultural anthropology might emphasize the cultural setting in which working organizations are created and maintained. For the special purposes of the economist, a model might highlight labor markets, wage structures, and changing demands for workers. For the student of management, a somewhat different model is appropriate.

Managerial interest centers on possibilities of control to create the best

[1] The term "industrial relations system" is used to describe a systematic organization of recognized major variables that exert controlling influences in working relationships.
[2] Edward Gross, *Work and Society*, New York: Thomas Y. Crowell Company, 1958.
[3] John Dunlop, *Industrial Relations Systems*. New York: Holt, Rinehart & Winston, 1958, Preface, p. VII.
[4] Guy H. Orcutt, "Simulation of Economic Systems," *American Economic Review*, Vol. 50, No. 5, December 1960, p. 897.

possible setting for work. The student of management constructs a model that highlights the variables that appear most influential in the attainment of this objective. A useful model for the student of manpower management would highlight three types of major variables, including:

1. *Workers and working careers.* Emphasis here is on the personal characteristics of workers, their cultural attainments, educational levels, skills, and attitudes toward work and on typical or common patterns of working careers.
2. *Working organizations.* Here, the spotlight turns on work groups or teams, their variations in size, composition and the extent of specialization they impose. It notes provisions for internal communications in such groups, the structures of authority and status they create, and such ancillary organizations as unions and employer associations.
3. *Role of government.* The model also highlights the part played in employment by various agencies of government and the nature and extent of public intervention, assistance, and regulation.

Such a generalized management model of industrial relations systems has been sketched in Figure 2.1, where these principal variables are identified as resting in the basic cultural setting of every society.

2.0 EARLY INDUSTRIAL RELATIONS SYSTEMS

Modern industrial relations represent a blending of older systems with innovations introduced as societies have changed through the ages. Some features of early systems show great persistence—the practice of seniority, for example, may to some extent express the tradition of deference to elders found in many early systems. Other features of modern industrial relations, on the contrary, represent sharp breaks with tradition. Such breaks often create problems for managers, for their newness may occasion resentment on the part of some workers.

Every manager needs to realize that employment relationships are dynamic. Perhaps their most obvious characteristic is the persistence of change. They have changed, are changing, and will presumably continue to change. It is helpful, both in understanding today's industrial relations and in forecasting the changed systems to be expected in the future, to review the major stages in earlier systems.

Although all early civilizations included some type of organizations for work, early systems show little resemblance to today's models. In most primitive societies, all members of the small tribes or clans expected to work throughout their active lives.

Specialization was not impressive, although some specialization based on sex was common. Groups were so small that no formal structure for communications would have been useful. Members communicated on a face-to-face basis. Authority structures varied, with a generally high regard for age

MAJOR VARIABLES
in
INDUSTRIAL RELATIONS SYSTEMS

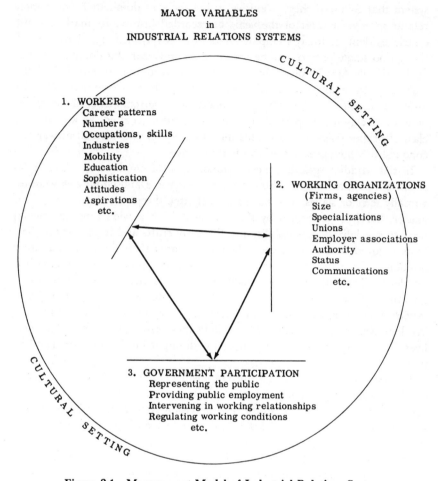

Figure 2.1   Management Model of Industrial Relations Systems

and seniority but frequent references to physical prowess. Government was not a separate structure.

In early hunting and fishing and pastoral economies no clear line distinguishes employers from employees. Almost all members of these relatively small groups frequently worked side by side, with only the minimal specialization required by physical differences between sexes. Supervisory specialization and authority might be recognized in such work groups, with age, experience, and sex as important factors in status and authority systems. Since social, economic, and political organizations were combined, no special influence can be ascribed to government. Within the tribe or clan, senior patriarchs or matriarchs exercised the basic authority in decision making. Careers followed the simple lines thus prescribed.

2*

2.1 Industrial relations in the agricultural period. The agricultural system that followed these primitive, tribal societies dominated employment relationships over most of the years of recorded history. Its marks are still clearly evident in today's employee-employer-government relationships. Although no single pattern can be described as universal, this dominant system of the Middle Ages involved significant changes from the earlier tribal system. Generally, for example, the tribal view of property as a common, collective asset was modified to identify real property as a personal asset of the prince or lord. A class of propertied individuals was thus created, as was another class of property-less workers. This transition was in part a result of war and conquest in which prisoners of war became slaves.

In the Middle Ages, the most common type of employee-employer relationship was that in which employers were masters and employees were essentially serfs or slaves. The slave was a chattel, the personal property of his master. Services performed by slaves ranged from a wide range of menial tasks to specialized responsibilities in the early crafts and in military service. Serfs enjoyed a somewhat more favorable status than slaves in that their position in the manorial system entitled them to certain fairly well-established privileges. Their duties and obligations were defined largely in terms of quantities of produce they must give to the master and of possible military service. Worker careers were, for the most part, narrowly defined and limited. Workers were born to their jobs and held these same jobs throughout their lives. They were generally not provided with opportunities for formal education.

The structure or organization of employment might be large in terms of numbers, especially on the manorial estates and principalities, but it was generally simple. Levels or strata of supervision were few. As years passed, a small but growing group of artisans or skilled craftsmen developed and added some complications to this earlier, more simple structure.

Authority and status centered in the lord or master and his family. Their residual and unlimited authority was justified by assumptions of inborn superiority and by their ownership of property. Managers or owners were regarded as being intellectually and morally superior to their workers. Masses of slaves and serfs were regarded as unfortunates who were fallen from grace and born to a lifetime of servitude. They were of limited intellect, ignorant, depraved and were without personal ethics and hence subject to complete direction and domination. They were what Burke described as the "Swinish herd." This view of worker status was clearly recognized and is still observable in remnants of the caste system.[5]

Government was not a divergent influence in employment relationships. Rather simple political organizations resulted from the alliances and conquests of the period and supported the authority of owners. Some masters

---

[5] For more detail, see Reinhard Bendix, "A Study of Managerial Ideologies," *Economic Development and Cultural Change*, Vol. 5, No. 2, January 1957, p. 120.

became subordinates as others achieved dominant positions. Otherwise, political institutions confined their activities largely to military and related operations.

2.2 Free artisans. In the latter part of this period, two changes deserve special mention. In many of the embryo nations that were appearing, the Church became affiliated with government by lords and princes. The status and authority of ruling families gained added sanction by virtue of this alliance. The Church, in turn, was granted authority to regulate some basic working conditions, especially those affecting the growing class of free artisans.

The second major change was that in which increasing numbers of artisans achieved freedom and became independent, specialized and mobile workers. They were skilled as workers in wood, textiles, leather, stone, metals, and other materials. Their careers varied sharply from those of serfs and slaves, permitting greater independence and personal choice and much greater mobility. Their freedom created an important innovation in employer—wage-earner relationships. It modified the established exercise of authority by owners and permitted a new regulatory role for Church and government.

This change was slow. It can be traced to a growing specialization and recognition of special skills. As individual skills and crafts became more important, some artisans were able to purchase or otherwise establish their independence. Then they sold their services or the products of their work in somewhat the same manner as do today's independent craftsmen—shoemakers, blacksmiths, building tradesmen, and others—in modern society.

The status of these early artisans differed essentially, however, from that of modern, free employees, for they were specifically limited with respect to the wage they could charge. Wages were neither strictly competitive nor freely set by the employee and his employer. They were subject to regulation, in part by Church authorities. These authorities developed a *fair-price criterion,* which they applied to personal services as well as to commodities. For the former, they held that a fair wage was one that permitted the wage earner to live, to raise his family, and to maintain his customary scale of living. Wages of artisans were frequently fixed at levels that were believed adequate in these terms.

Application of these rules by Church and government assumed increasing importance as numbers of free artisans continued to grow. In England, where these changes were accelerated—as compared with European principalities— local as well as national governments assumed responsibilities and exercised authority in regulating wages. As early as 1351, when the Black Death reduced numbers of workers by half, Parliament restricted wages and required artisans to accept work at approved rates.

2.3 The handicraft system. Another major step in the evolution of industrial relations systems introduced an important innovation in the careers of workers—one in which they could actually move from the ranks of employees to those of employers. It created *the handicraft system*. The change began as artisans developed facilities for selling their products rather than their services. They established home workshops and salesrooms. They performed the hand tasks that gave the new production system its name. Many of them trained their own or other children to learn the craft. Some of them found markets large enough to justify hiring other craftsmen to work for them. Still others found new opportunities in selling the products of such workshops, rather than in creating them.

Within this home-workshop system, new careers, new employment structures, and new patterns of authority and status appeared. Government developed new alliances with master craftsmen. Artisans began their careers as apprentices, bound to work for master craftsmen for stipulated periods in which they could learn the craft. When apprenticeships were finished, the artisans emerged as free journeymen, available for employment. They were highly mobile workers, who could sell their services as they wished. If they were fortunate, they might marry, inherit, or buy a shop of their own and become masters. This career pattern was a distinct innovation.

Similarly new was the structure of relationships within the handicraft shop and among the master, one or more journeymen, and apprentices. The new structure was smaller and more personal than the earlier manorial system. Master craftsmen worked side by side with those they directed. Only one or, at most, two levels of supervision were involved.

The handicraft system created new structures of authority and status. Within the shop or store, the dominance and acceptance of the master craftsman was impressive. Both his authority and that of the journeyman were based in part on demonstrated skill. For the master, this sanction was reinforced by ownership. Lowly as was the status of the apprentice, it was definitely superior to that of the earlier slave or serf. The apprentice was an embryo journeyman and master.

The master's authority was supplemented and modified by a new institution—*the guild*. Early guilds grew slowly. A specialization of two types appeared. *Merchant guilds* were made up of local distributors who banded together to set standards of quality, improve their competitive position, and seek assistance from government. *Craft guilds* were composed of craftsmen who sought to control admissions to their ranks and to maintain standards of craft performance.

Within craft organizations, a strong status structure accorded top recognition to master craftsmen (the entrepreneurs of the system). Journeymen (its wage earners) held a secondary but clearly defined position. Wages, hours, and other conditions of employment were determined by guild regulations. Many of the organizations provided various fraternal benefits. The origins of modern trade-union benefits for death, disability, and unemployment may be traced to these practices of the guilds.

Masters' guilds were influential in obtaining the cooperation of government in their control of wages, prices, and working conditions. For the period dominated by these organizations of masters, an important role of government was that of supporting and enforcing guild decisions and regulations.

2.4 Yeomanry or journeyman guilds. Further modifications in the industrial relations systems of the handicraft period were introduced by the development of *yeomanry or journeyman guilds*. They became prominent during the later years of the handicraft period, although some of them had appeared much earlier. Their emergence is generally attributed to changes that, by preventing the journeymen's progress into ranks of masters, tended to block their careers. These new organizations of journeymen introduced another important variable in the structure of employment relationships: a bargaining organization of employees.

Technological change played an important part in this development. As more complicated tools were perfected, competition made this new equipment essential. It became necessary for most journeymen to remain longer as journeymen and to save more of their earnings for the capital necessary to set themselves up in business. At the same time, master craftsmen in many trades sought to limit the admission of new establishments by regulations that prevented journeymen from advancing to the master craftsman ranks. Many journeymen concluded that the craft guilds, in which masters, journeymen, and apprentices were members, failed to meet their economic needs. Journeymen needed an association to deal for them with masters, rather than one in which masters, journeymen, and apprentices joined to protect common interests.

Yeomanry guilds are of particular interest because they represent an early form of what is now generally described as "the labor movement." They signaled further changes in the prevailing industrial relations system. They indicated a changing view of workers' careers, in which the likelihood of attaining employer status was reduced. The most common career pattern for most workers became one of continuing employee status. Yeomanry guilds also introduced the practice of negotiating for and promoting public intervention with respect to working conditions. They spoke for journeymen in attempts to change the attitude and action of government, although the evidence of their influence in such efforts is not impressive.

3.0 THE FACTORY SYSTEM

The next great change, the Industrial Revolution, shifted production from the former home workshops to new mills and factories. Steam and water power supplemented or were substituted for the effort and energy of people. Guilds lost much of their influence in this transition, as many master craftsmen and merchants became employees in the new industrial units. At the same time, skill lost much of its market value as machines standardized processes and products.

New factories developed as a result of both technological changes and the expansion of markets and trade. Shops could become more specialized as they produced for wider markets. They required larger supplies of raw materials. Even in occupations where handwork or tasks involving simple, personally owned tools continued to be feasible, traveling traders undertook to finance larger-scale production. They brought the raw materials to the homes of the craftsmen, hired the latter to process them, and then collected and sold the finished products. This arrangement was known as the "putting-out system."

This system of *trader capitalism,* so-called because traders supplied the capital necessary to provide adequate quantities of raw materials and to hold finished products until they could be sold, was only a short step from *industrial capitalism,* commonly called the "factory system." Trader capitalists, realizing the possibility of increasing economies in production attainable from newly perfected machines, developed larger workshops and provided power tools and equipment. Instead of "farming out" production to numerous small establishments, they installed machinery and offered employment at the factory. The home as a unit in the productive process was thus displaced by the factory, and the homeworker became a factory "hand."

The factory style of production with its associated growth of larger plants introduced important changes in several elements in industrial relations systems. Moreover, as that process expanded then and continues even now to spread throughout the so-called less-developed nations, these changes affected and are still affecting employment relationships throughout the world. Industrialization everywhere occasions a complicated revision in patterns of employment relationships.[6]

3.1   Industrialized employee relations. The pattern of these changes is not identical in all societies. In part, this is true because industrialization *has* moved into varying cultures and economies with different histories and traditions. As a result, the impact of industrialization has been somewhat diverse. In some nations, the process has been more rapid than in others. In some, also, the existing political order has dominated industrialization and has limited or directed the changes. In the Communist nations, for example, the careers of workers, organizations for work, and assignments of authority have been powerfully influenced by the totalitarian authority and influence of the state.

3.11   Careers. In the non-communist nations, one preliminary effect of industrialization was to limit shifts from journeyman to master status. The transition from employee to employer became more difficult than in handicraft production because of the requirement of large amounts of capital. For this reason, it has been said that the most impressive creation of the Industrial Revolution was a new class of citizens, the *industrial proletariat.* Mem-

---

[6] See, for more detail on this point, Reinhard Bendix, *Work and Authority in Industry,* New York: John Wiley & Sons, Inc., 1956. See also Clark Kerr, John T. Dunlop, Frederick H. Harbison, and Charles A. Myers, *Industrialism and Industrial Man,* Cambridge, Mass.: Harvard University Press, 1960, chap. 2.

bers of this new class, industrial employees, were doomed, in this view, to a lifetime as wage workers. Requirements of capital, powered equipment, and organizing ability have presumably made survival in the ranks of large-scale employer-proprietors more difficult. To a large degree, therefore, prospective careers for workers are those of non-proprietors who sell their personal skill, talent, and effort to employers. The latter provide the resources of materials and facilities that have become essential to competitive production and distribution.

On the other hand, the new factory system gave greater mobility to employees and thus broadened potential careers within their own group. Reduced skill requirements facilitated shifts from one job to another. The same change created new, industrial working careers for vast numbers of former agricultural workers.

3.12 Work Organizations. The new system also created distinctively changed working organizations. The most obvious change was the growth or expansion of productive units. Whereas employees in the handicraft shop knew all their co-workers personally, industrial employees found themselves working beside dozens or hundreds of others, including many newcomers, threshold or beginning workers. Where they had formerly worked in a cottage or home workshop, they now came to work in much larger factories.

The new working organization permitted more *specialization* and thus a more extensive range of occupations. Specialization divided employees and, in a sense, related them to their machines more closely than to their fellows.

3.13 Manager groups. Earlier employers were individual master craftsmen. In the new establishments, employers might be individuals or a group of partners. Employees were recruited and paid to contribute their effort and talent to the purpose of the enterprise. In many plants, a new class of *managers* represented employers and directed the work of employees. This new managerial group was interposed between owner-employers and rank and file employees. Personal relationships and direct communications between employer-proprietors and employees were reduced.

3.14 Employee unions. A new industrial *labor movement* soon became an important element in this structure. Membership in unions was more inclusive than that in the earlier yeomanry guilds. The new unions included unskilled and semi-skilled as well as skilled employees. The unions emerged in the early stages of industrialization as means of protesting the changing career opportunities open to employees and questioning the concentration of power and authority in the hands of owners. They expressed the concern of industrial employees about working conditions—levels of wages, stability of employment, and status in the new industrial society of work. They sought, also, to represent industrial employees in relationships with government.

3.15 Authority and status structures. These structures were drastically changed from those of the handicraft system. To replace the authority of master chaftsmen and their guilds, merchant and industrial capitalists became the source of power and direction. Authority flowed from the owners of capital. They appointed managers to represent them and to direct the hired workers needed to carry out the mission of the enterprise.

Status, under the handicraft system, had been closely identified with *skill* and *ownership*. Masters held highest status because they combined both. Journeymen enjoyed a relatively high status because of their skill and related mobility and independence. Apprentices occupied the lowest position in the structure. However, their status included an important element of security and acceptance because of their prospective advancement.

In industrialized employment, working skill became less important if not unimportant in determining status. In some jobs, unskilled women and children were as productive and earned as much as former craftsmen or journeymen. New skills, useful in planning and organizing the work of larger crews of employees, became an important basis for status. At the same time, status in these industrialized working groups was related to the obvious power that flowed from the ownership of capital. The new capitalist proprietors, as the source of authority, gained top status in the organizations they developed. Those to whom the merchant or trader capitalist delegated major responsibilities for management ranked high in the status hierarchy.

3.16   Government. In the early stages of industrialization, government became closely identified with the new entrepreneurs and venturers. Many of the early trading companies were chartered and sponsored by public officials, who thus became personally interested in their success. National welfare was identified with the success of trader capitalism, as a growing group of political economists emphasized the national gains to be achieved through colonization and foreign trade.

Although new unions of employees tried to enlist government support for their campaigns for higher wages and improved working and living conditions, they were generally unsuccessful. On the other hand, employers sought and secured public intervention to restrict the activities of unions, to restrain their demands for higher wages and to maintain and justify the full authority of owners. Unions were politically and economically weak. Because they encouraged united action that interfered with what were regarded as the rights of employers, unions were frequently held to be conspiracies and hence illegal.

Development of the factory system was accompanied by widespread acceptance of the *physiocratic* or *laissez-faire viewpoint*. That school of political and economic thought was popularized by Rousseau, Bentham, and Hobbes and was further advanced by Malthus, Adam Smith, and others of the so-called classical school of economists. The laissez-faire viewpoint proposed a *minimum of public intervention or control in economic activity,* holding that any such control is a "crutch with which the sound limb dispenses," and a handicap to the national economic welfare.

Early working conditions were strongly influenced by this laissez-faire viewpoint. Governmental regulation was minimized, on the theory that the greatest social benefits required a hands-off policy on the part of government. Employment was irregular. Women and children were employed, often for long hours, because machine production simplified operations and reduced skill requirements. In many cases, inexperienced employees were preferred to more experienced craftsmen, because the latter found it difficult to adapt themselves to machine methods. Whole families moved to the locations in which employment opportunities appeared most promising. At the same time that geographic mobility (place-to-place) was thus facilitated, occupational and industrial mobility (changing tasks and jobs) increased greatly. Jobs were simplified, so manpower was readily adapted to a variety of positions instead of to a single craft or trade.

Living conditions in the early factory cities were socially objectionable if not deplorable. Both living and working conditions were frequently unsanitary. Housing was inadequate for the sudden concentrations of population around sources of power and jobs. Children were put to work at the age we now regard as appropriate for grade-school education. Efforts to band employees together for purposes of collective bargaining were opposed by employers and outlawed by governments friendly to employers.

3.2 Continuing development. A dozen generations, in the industrialized nations, have sought to adapt themselves to the changes introduced by the industrial revolution. With growing prosperity and rising real wages, workers have gained higher living scales, more education and sophistication, and generally greater mobility. Career patterns have changed, as growing proportions have left the farms and become wage and salary workers. The working organizations in which they are employed have become larger and shifted from individual to corporate ownership. Employees have formed and joined powerful unions, and employers have formed bargaining associations to balance the power of local, national, and international labor organizations. Government has played a growing role in industrial relations, in part by becoming the employer for millions of workers and in part by regulating working conditions in private employment.

Industrial relations continue to change. Technological advances eliminate long-established jobs and create opportunities that require sharply different patterns of experience and education. Higher living scales encourage demands for new products and services. Economic prosperity permits greater economic security, and public regulation makes the assurance of that security a problem for managers. All of these changes seem to make our system of employment relationships more complex. Yet collaboration in work is more essential than ever before, for relatively few workers can work alone and mass production is a necessity to support the populations of modern nations.

Faced with similar problems, half the world has relinquished much of its freedom to gain the advantages of rapid industrialization. In our half, we seek to preserve and enhance our gains while insuring a maximum of individuality and personal choice. Our success will be largely determined by the insight, understanding, and competence of managers. Their most crucial task is likely to be that of managing people at work.

4.0 SUMMARY

Such a brief, descriptive, "horseback" survey of historic stages in industrial relations provides clear evidence of persistent change. It identifies many of the most important changes with one or another of the principal variables in our management model of industrial relations systems—with workers and their careers, working organizations, and governmental participation and intervention.

While the speed of such changes is not readily measured, initial stages of the industrial revolution seem to have been one period of unusually rapid change. The shift from earlier agricultural and handicraft systems to the age of factories was drastic. That stage is being reenacted today in many of the less developed nations of the world. In them, new and inexperienced managers face problems similar to those encountered in our society more than a hundred years ago. Their problems—in which we cannot avoid great interest—are complicated by popular desires to achieve quickly the economic benefits and advantages we have gradually gained through industrialization.

Meanwhile, in our own society, many observers conclude that we are in the midst of another period of accelerated change, a *second industrial revolution,* sparked by automation and the age of the computer. The next chapter provides some evidence with respect to current changes in our system of industrial relations and the trends apparent in them.

SELECTED SUPPLEMENTARY READINGS

Bendix, Reinhard, *Work and Authority in Industry.* New York: John Wiley & Sons, Inc., 1956.

Dunlop, John, *Industrial Relations Systems.* New York: Holt, Rinehart & Winston, 1958.

Jucius, Michael J., *Personnel Management,* chap. 2. Homewood, Ill.: Richard D. Irwin Inc., 1959.

Kerr, Clark, John T. Dunlop, Frederick H. Harbison, and Charles A. Myers, *Industrialism and Industrial Man,* chap. 2. Cambridge, Mass.: Harvard University Press, 1960.

"Perspective in Public Personnel Administration," *Public Personnel Review,* Vol. 17, No. 4, pp. 178–338, October 1956.

Scott, Walter Dill, Robert C. Clothier, and William R. Spriegel, *Personnel Management,* chaps. 1, 15. New York: McGraw-Hill Book Company, Inc., 1954.

SHORT CASE PROBLEM 2.1

Responsibility for Manpower Management

"In the free nations, managers of private firms should quit trying to determine working conditions for free citizens," said Frank Knox, in a prepared statement to the Nisswa chapter of the National Managers' Club. Speaking at a noon luncheon meeting in the Moose Hall, Knox justified this conclusion by reference to long-term trends he described as inevitable and by what he called the philosophy of personal sovereignty.

Knox said that managers have consistently lost in arguments with government and unions over the determination of working conditions. "Look at the expansion of legislation on hours of work, workmen's compensation, unemployment insurance, and benefits of all kinds," he said. "Look at the coverage of collective-labor contracts in this country. Compare them with the one page contracts of a generation ago. Can anyone doubt that managers are on the outside looking in?"

In part, according to Knox, these changes have occurred because managers simply haven't developed and probably can't develop the professional competence necessary to leadership in managing people. In part, also, it is philosophically inconsistent to allow any small group such as managers to decide questions of such vital importance as wages, promotions, and discharges for other free men. To do so, according to Knox, is as unreasonable as to allow free citizens to sell themselves into slavery.

The Knox statement was not accepted by all members of the group with enthusiasm. "How can we manage the creamery?" asked Peter Rundquist, local superintendent of the Nisswa Cooperative Marketing Association, "if we surrender control of working conditions?"

Knox replied that in his opinion, managerial decision-making should be confined to problems of financing, buying, selling, and processing, areas in which managers "can hope to achieve some special competence." Actually, he concluded, "Management will be much simpler when managers quit trying to be all-powerful in deciding the fates and futures of all their employees. Let the public agencies and the unions worry about such matters, so that we can give our attention to things we know about."

Problem: Do you agree with the Knox viewpoint? Why do you think some members did not accept Knox's conclusions? Are the arguments on which Knox based his conclusion sound?

SHORT CASE PROBLEM 2.2

Savings from Payroll Dollars

President Gross of the McConnell Company was much impressed by a conference of presidents arranged by a large, national management group. In one session, the leader introduced the subject, "Savings in Payroll Dollars," referring to the viewpoint of Frederick W. Taylor.

"More than fifty years ago," said the leader, "Frederick W. Taylor attracted wide and frequently critical attention by his description of the multi-million dollar savings that could be made by more effective direction of manpower in industry and government. Taylor based his argument on the observation that some workers and groups of workers were much more productive than others in similar jobs. In essence, he proposed that the less productive workers be managed in such a way that they would perform at the level of their more effective counterparts."

"In the years since Taylor sought to popularize this viewpoint," he continued, "many managers have accepted such practices as time study and work simplification as means of helping the less efficient become more efficient. Some managers, however, have recognized the much broader implications of the Taylor viewpoint. They have noted that wide variations in worker productivity continually point to opportunities for superior management. As long as some workers are more effective than others in similar assignments, alert managers can gain competitive advantage by adapting their manpower management to the example set by the most efficient firms." The leader concluded his introduction with the observation that savings of 10 to 20 per cent of labor costs may be attainable through this process.

In the session that followed, members of the group were asked to mention their own experiences in discovering improved ways of managing employees and the savings gained through such improved practice. They described such programs as suggestion systems, special training programs, incentive wage and bonus systems, company housing for employees, consultative supervision and Scanlon plans, and other arrangements with which they had experimented.

President Gross concluded that this particular session was meant for him. Immediately upon his return, he reported the session in some detail to his own management group. He repeated the general position expressed by Taylor. He raised the question: What can we learn here at McConnell from the experience of other firms that will improve our practice in managing our manpower?

The company employs 1,810 workers in two plants in the Mid-West. The business is that of grain processing. Products include oils, fats, starch and stockfeeds. Labor costs represent approximately 40 per cent of total costs.

The organization of the firm is simple, with a top management consisting of the president, a vice president for production and one for sales, and a secretary-treasurer. The management group includes an industrial relations director with two assistants. Production workers are organized and are represented by two locals of the Grain Millers. Processing equipment consists principally of elevators, pressure cookers, presses, oil extractors and mixers. Employment has been stable; employees have averaged 2,044 hours per year. Wages are negotiated annually and follow a national pattern. They are calculated on an hourly basis and paid every two weeks. The firm has been profitable, with earnings of about 3 per cent of sales. Management has made generous gifts to the two communities in which plants are located. The firm assists employees in the purchase or building of homes with funds available at a low interest rate. The firm has never had a strike.

Problem: Assume that you are an assistant to President Gross. He has asked you, during the next several weeks, to look into the possibilities thus suggested and to make recommendations to be considered by the management group. Summarize your recommendations in 500 words, briefly describing the possible improvements you regard as worthy of serious consideration. Attach an appendix with references that explain and justify your recommendations. In the appendix, list other possible innovations you considered but discarded.

3. Current Trends in Industrial Relations

If conditions with which a manager must deal are changing, much of his success will depend on his ability to forecast and anticipate significant changes. Perhaps his most frequently useful approach to this forecasting responsibility is the analysis and evaluation of *significant trends*.

Trends in industrial relations are particularly important because of the dynamic nature of employment relationships, illustrated in the preceding chapter. Managers must be especially sensitive to changes in working relationships, in part because they may be rapid, as illustrated by the almost spectacular development of collective bargaining in the years following passage of the National Labor Relations Act in 1935. Growing demands for a variety of employee benefits and services and increased acceptance of arbitration as a means of resolving issues and public regulations of minimum wages and working hours illustrate the appearance and development of significant trends.

Managers translate their appraisals of trends into guides for their managerial policy and practice. In the management of people, for example, trends in the characteristics and careers of workers may have important managerial impacts on recruitment, selection, training, or compensation. Again, trends toward larger working organizations and more powerful unions might suggest modifications in employment communications or in the process in which many policies are developed. Trends toward increased public intervention in collective bargaining, to take another example, might suggest a critical review of both policy and practice in negotiation.

In short, manpower managers need to be constantly alert to trends in the whole system of employment relationships.

This chapter, as a part of the introductory section of the book, examines several trends of particular importance to manpower management. As a guide in the identification of such trends, it uses the model of industrial relations systems described in Chapter 2. Attention is directed to what appear to be continuing changes in each of the three major variables identified there.

In essence the questions for which answers are sought can be stated as follows: What are the major changes that appear to persist in our industrial relations system? What are the implications of their extrapolation for the industrial relations of the future?

Some notion of the importance of these changes to managers may be gained from a brief preview of the discussion that follows. Figure 3.1 raises a number of questions about trends in industrial relations. It is a device, developed in a conference of managers, for comparing their predictions. You may wish to try your hand in similar forecasts before reading further.

DIRECTIONS: Mark with an arrow to indicate the direction of expected trend.

I. WORKERS AND WORKING CAREERS

1.........Labor force size	12.........Proportions of white-collar
2.........Proportion of males in labor force	13.........Working hours
3.........Proportion of females over 35 yrs.	14.........Cost of living
4.........Proportions of older workers	15.........Real wages
5.........Participation rate: % over 14	16.........Education of employees
6.........Proportions of unskilled	17.........Worker mobility
7.........Proportions of semi-skilled	18.........Man-hour productivity
8.........Proportions technical and prof.	19.........
9.........Proportions in agriculture	20.........
10.........Proportions in manufacturing	21.........
11.........Proportions in services	22.........

II. WORKING ORGANIZATIONS

1.........Size, numbers of employees	12.........Range or scope of bargaining
2.........Proportions non-productive wkrs.	13........."Positive" bargaining by mgrs.
3.........Ratios of middle managers	14.........Membership in employer assns.
4.........Ratios of staff managers	15.........Employer strike-aid plans
5.........Specialized competence of mgrs.	16.........Works councils-represent'n plns.
6.........In-firm management dev. progs.	17.........Use of arbitration
7.........University management dev. progs.	18.........Area of manager prerogatives
8.........Professional management assocns.	19.........Negotiated benefits and services
9.........Security and tenure of managers	20.........
10.........Union membership	21.........
11.........White collar unions	22.........

III. GOVERNMENT ROLE IN EMPLOYMENT

1.........Public employment—proportion	8.........Compulsory arbitrat'n-labor crts.
2.........Coverage of social security	9.........Public regulation of unions
3.........Coverage of unemployment ins.	10.........Limitations on manager actions
4.........Amounts of pub. old age pensions	11.........
5.........Level of unemployment benefits	12.........
6.........Level of minimum wages	13.........
7.........Public health benefits	14.........

Figure 3.1   Check-List of Trends in Industrial Relations

1.0   TRENDS IN WORKING CAREERS

Impressive changes—with significant trends that are influencing present and prospective systems of industrial relations—are evident in the careers of employees. In part, such changes have affected labor-force dimensions, the numbers and types of citizens working or available for work. These changes are in part a result of *population growth*. They have been influenced, also, by the changing *age distribution* of populations and varying *participation rates*. Meanwhile, workers are themselves changing, with increasing mobility and levels of formal *educational attainment* and knowledgeability and sophistication as perhaps the most obvious of these developments.

While today's employees have the same basic physical and mental abilities and still contribute their effort and talent as they did when their assignments were hunting, fishing, or tending children and herds, their numbers, skills, experience, education, sophistication, opportunities, and aspirations have changed and are changing. Their points of view and attitudes toward work and working relationships have changed. Cultural levels, educational achievement, and general sophistication of employees are far different from what they were in earlier periods. Many of these trends can be expected to continue far into the future.[1]

1.1   Population and labor force. Perhaps the most obvious and impressive changes are those in the continuing growth and expansion of the labor force. In part, these changes reflect the continued growth of population.

In the United States rapid population growth is not a recent development. Although our citizens frequently express concern over the *population explosion* in other nations, few of them realize how our own changes may appear to citizens elsewhere. Figure 3.2 provides information for such a comparison. In it, the growth of the United States is combined with that of Canada and Mexico to show the rapid expansion in all North American nations since the 17th Century.

In the United States, population has grown from 5,308,000 in 1800 to 179,773,000 in 1960. Estimated population for 1970 is 208,199,000 and for 1975 about 220 million.

A study undertaken under United Nations auspices forecasts a world population in 2000 that is 2½ times that in 1950. Largest increases are expected in Asia, Latin America, Europe and Africa.

Not all of our people work or are available for work. Our measure of workers is the *labor* force. It is composed of all those 14 years of age and over who are working or available for paid work. Calculations do not include, as members of the labor force, women who keep house or children who work without formal pay on family farms or other enterprises. In 1960, when the population was approximately 180 millions, some 127 millions were 14 years of age or older. Approximately 2 millions of these could not accept employment because they were confined in hospitals and penal institutions. Of the

---

[1] See the very interesting forecasts outlined in *U.S. Industrial Relations—The Next 20 Years,* East Lansing, Michigan: Michigan State University Press, 1958.

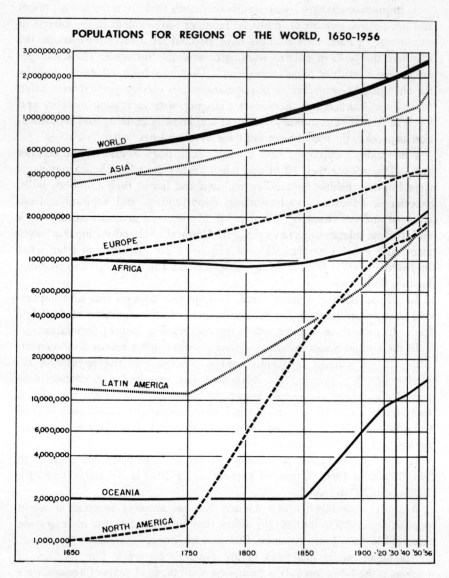

Figure 3.2   Population Growth by Regions of the World, 1650–1956
sources: *Health and Demography,* U.S. Department of Health, Education and Welfare, 1956, p. 25; Statistical Office of the United Nations.

Table 3.1   Labor Force Participation Rates by Age Groups and Sex, 1960

Age Group	Participation Rates	
	Males	Females
14 Years and Over	80.9	36.4
14 through 19	47.9	28.6
20 through 24	88.1	45.4
25 through 34	96.5	37.9
35 through 44	96.9	43.0
45 through 54	95.1	48.2
55 through 64	86.4	37.4
65 and over	36.0	11.0

SOURCE: Adapted from Bureau of Labor Statistics, *Monthly Report on the Labor Force,* continuing series.

remaining 125 millions, some 74 millions were members of the labor force. The remaining 51 millions were potential labor force members. Many of them were *secondary workers,* that is, they could work and did at times seek work, but they were not usually available for employment. They may be, for example, housewives or retired persons or college students.

1.2   Participation rates. The labor force was about 58 per cent of the population 14 years of age and older in 1960. In other words, the general *participation rate* was about 58 per cent. That level may be regarded as normal, in that it is a common or modal rate. This participation rate was 57.7 in 1950 and the Department of Labor forecast for 1970 is 57.8.[2] Figure 3.3 shows changes in population, labor force, and the general participation rate over a 50-year period.

Participation rates show short-term as well as long-term fluctuations. Perhaps the most obvious of these is the seasonal pattern, in which young workers from high school and college move into the labor force during summer months. Recessions sometimes increase these participation rates, as secondary workers seek jobs to supplement reduced family incomes. Also, when wage rates are rising, some secondary workers may be enticed into the labor force.[3]

Participation rates vary with sex and age. Much larger proportions of men seek paid employment than women, although this difference is declining. The normal participation rate for men, in recent years, has been about 83 per cent, while that for women has been about 33 per cent. However, the predicted rates for men in 1960 and 1970 are 80.9 and 78.4, while those for women are 36.4 and 38.3.[4]

[2] *Guide to Manpower Challenge of the 1960's,* U. S. Department of Labor, 1960, p. 35.

[3] See Gladys Palmer, *Labor Mobility in Six Cities,* New York: Social Science Research Council, 1954; Herbert J. Parnes, "Research on Labor Mobility," *Bulletin 65,* New York: Social Science Research Council, 1954.

[4] *Guide, op. cit.,* p. 35.

As a result of changing participation rates for women, the labor force has become increasingly feminine; its members include growing proportions of women. In 1870, women made up about one-seventh of the labor force. In 1960, they were more than one-third of the total. (See Figure 3.4.)

1.3 The working life. Sex differences in participation rates are complicated by the influence of age. Highest participation rates for males are those

POPULATION, LABOR FORCE AND LABOR FORCE PARTICIPATION RATE, 1900-1970

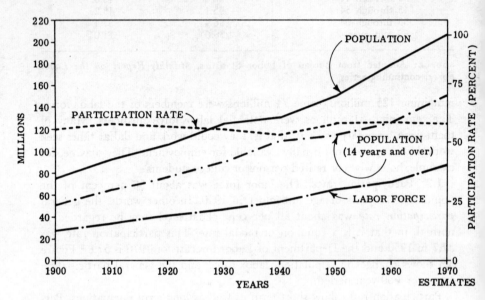

Figure 3.3 U.S. Population, Labor Force and Labor Force Participation Rates, 1900–1970
SOURCES: Gertrude Bancroft, *The American Labor Force,* New York: John Wiley and Sons, 1959, pp. 28 and 202; U.S. Department of Labor, *Guide to Manpower Challenge of the 1960's,* 1960, pp. 6, 8, 33, 34, 35.

of the 25- to 54-year age groups. For females, age groups with highest rates are 18–24 and 45–54. For both sexes, the highest rate is that of the 35–44 year age group. These comparisons are summarized in Table 3.1.

One recent trend that deserves special mention is the increasing participation of women 35 years of age and over. The mechanization of household duties and availability of wider employment opportunities for women have encouraged this trend. By 1970, it is expected that nearly half of all women aged 35 to 64 will be in the labor force.

Another significant change has been the growing tendency of older workers to withdraw or to be forced out of the labor force. This change is clearly evident in time-to-time comparisons of participation rates for these older-age groups. To a considerable degree, it can be attributed to the growing provision of pensions, coupled with requirements of compulsory retirement. The pattern appeared to be similar for women until 1940. Since then, it has been reversed.

Age differences in participation rates emphasize the importance of the changing age distribution of our population and labor force. The average age of American workers has been increasing since the 1920's. Proportions of workers in the older-age groups have grown, which means, of course, that

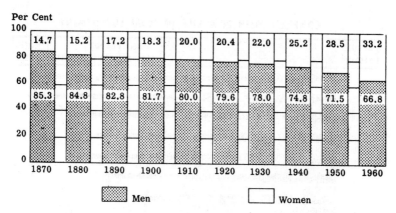

Figure 3.4   Women in the Labor Force, 1870–1960
SOURCES: Bancroft, *op. cit.,* p. 137; and continuing releases from the U.S. Bureau of the Census.

proportions of workers in younger-age groups have declined. While several factors exert powerful influences on these participation rates, the most obviously influential factor in the changing age distribution is the birth rate. In earlier years, immigration also played a prominent part, but restrictions imposed in the 1920's have largely eliminated this factor. Relatively low birth rates in the 1930's meant that numbers and proportions of threshold workers twenty years later would inevitably be relatively smaller. The persistence of low birth rates until the close of World War II indicated that this condition will continue at least until 1965.

The years immediately ahead will see a rather impressive shift in the age distribution of our labor force. Numbers of young workers, under 25 years of age, will increase by about 6.5 millions in the decade from 1960 to 1970. Those from 25 to 34 will increase, but only by about 1.8 million. Those from

35 to 44 will actually decline in numbers, and those 45 and over will increase by 5.5 millions.[5]

1.4 Changing opportunities for work. Worker careers have been and are being influenced by changing demands for their services. Industrial and occupational demands have been changing. Continued shifts appear certain.

These changing opportunities for work have influenced the careers of workers. They have planned their working careers to fit what they anticipate as opportunities for long-term participation. Most younger workers know that *raw labor*—untrained and uneducated—finds fewer opportunities for

INDUSTRIES WILL VARY WIDELY IN THEIR RATE OF GROWTH

COMPARED WITH 20% RISE IN TOTAL EMPLOYMENT

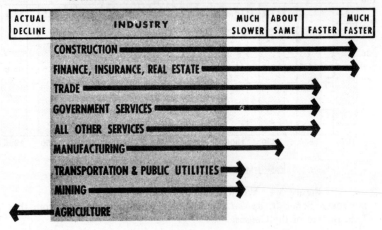

Figure 3.5 Employment Changes by Industry Groups, 1960–1970
SOURCE: *Guide to Manpower Challenges of the 1960's,* Washington: U.S. Department of Labor, 1960, p. 13.

employment. In part, this is true because industries that formerly provided such opportunities have become less important sources of jobs. Agriculture shows the most impressive decline in this respect. Even manufacturing, which has expanded since the early years of the nation, has started to decline as a source of employment. The United States Department of Labor has noted these trends and developed the forecast for 1960–1970 shown in Figure 3.5.

Occupational changes parallel those in various industries. Long-term trends—from 1900 to 1960—have shown a continuing decline in farmers and farm managers and workmen and in nonfarm unskilled labor. Semiskilled operatives have maintained their relative position in this period. Meanwhile, professional and technical workers, managers, officials and proprietors, crafts-

[5] *Guide, op. cit.,* p. 10.

men, and employees in the service industries (filling stations, beauty parlors, hotels, and others) have become a larger part of the labor force.

Looking ahead, most forecasts conclude that farmers and farm workers will become less prominent in the labor force than they were in earlier years. Farm owners and managers, who made up 7 per cent of the labor force in 1955, will probably decline to about 3 per cent by 1975. Farm laborers are expected to decline from 3 per cent to 2 per cent in the same period. The service occupations will decline from 12 to 11 per cent. Meanwhile, the unskilled will continue to decline, from 7 per cent to 3 per cent.

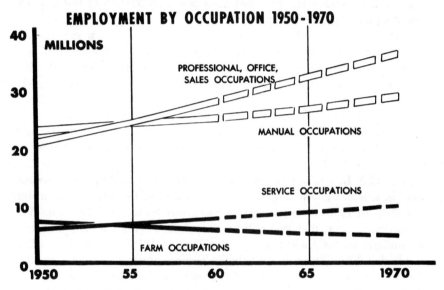

Figure 3.6   Changing Occupations in the U. S., 1960–1970
SOURCE: *Guide, op. cit.,* p. 14.

On the other hand, skilled craftsmen, 13 per cent in 1955, are estimated at 14 per cent in 1975. Proportions of semiskilled workers may grow slightly from 21 to 22 per cent. The growth of white-collar workers is most impressive. While proprietors and managers remain at about 10 per cent of the labor force, clerical workers and salesmen are expected to increase from 19 to 22 per cent, and professional workers from 8 to 12 per cent. This change in occupations passed a significant milepost in 1956, when numbers of white-collar workers exceeded those of blue-collar employees for the first time. Labor Department studies suggest that this trend will be accelerated in the years immediately ahead. By 1965, professional, clerical, and sales workers will number about 37 millions. One forecast of such future changes is illustrated in Figure 3.6.

1.5   Manpower Mobility. Industrialization has mobilized workers. They have greater opportunity to change employers, localities, industries, and occupations. Their careers show no such patterns of permanent attachment to starting jobs as was characteristic of earlier periods and industrial relations systems. This mobility involves about one-fourth as many changes of jobs as members of our labor force each year. It means that workers can and do shift from being employers to being employees and vice versa and that they make frequent moves among employers, regions, industries, and occupations. They move into and out of the labor force and from employment to unemployment and back.

Edward L. Maher has provided the graphic illustration of this aspect of workers careers shown in Figure 3.7.

It should, however, be noted that the process of technical specialization encouraged by industrialization has limited the mobility of some employees. Some current employment practice—seniority, private pensions and retirement provisions, and the extension of profit sharing—may have exerted a similar influence.

Workers as a whole, the members of the labor force, have more formal education than ever before. This shift is clearly evident in comparisons of older and younger workers. For those 65 and over, the median years of formal schooling are 8.3. For those from 45 to 54, this median is 10. For those 25 to 29, it is 12.3. In 1947, of all young men 18 and 19 years of age, 25.1 per cent were in school. For the same ages, 18.4 per cent of the young women were in school. In 1956, these percentages had grown to 35.7 and 32.2. For 1975, predictions suggest that they will be 52 and 35. High school enrollments of 9.2 millions in 1960 will reach 13.7 millions in 1970, and college students numbering 3.8 millions in 1960 should number about 6.4 millions in 1970, according to the U. S. Department of Health, Welfare and Education.

Meanwhile, the general level of knowledge, understanding, and sophistication is probably rising more rapidly than ever before, as a result of better mass communications, including the wider circulation of books and of newspapers, travel, and the availability of radio and television.

1.6   Productivity and living scales. Workers' careers are changing, and a firm foundation for such change is provided by the rising productivity, real earnings and family and individual incomes of workers.

Productivity changes show great variation by industry and from time to time. It is possible, however, to make some generalizations. In the 50-year period from 1909 through 1959, the average annual increase in output per manhour was approximately 2.2 per cent. Details are shown in Figure 3.8. Meanwhile, per capita shares of the gross national product have grown from $2,300 in 1950 to $2,800 in 1960. They will probably approximate $3,500 in 1970 (all based on 1958 price levels).[6]

All such calculations may be confused because of the persistent inflation that reduces the value of the dollar. It can be said, however, that, in the past,

[6] *Guide, op. cit.,* p. 5.

MILLION OF JOB CHANGES EVERY MONTH

AVERAGE CHANGE, FROM ONE MONTH TO THE NEXT, DURING THE YEAR, 1952
(Thousands of persons)

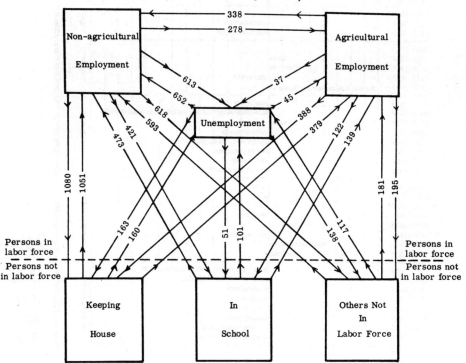

Total number of shifts 8,333,000
Number of persons entering labor force 3,193,000
Number of persons leaving labor force 3,174,000

Figure 3.7 Worker Mobility Illustrated
SOURCE: Edward L. Maher, *Automation: A Background Memorandum,*
National Association of Manufacturers, 1960, p. 9.

real wages have increased about 1 per cent per year.[7] This persistent increase
in real wages has been a result, in part, of reduced compensation for the other
factors of production.

[7] See, for additional discussion of these changes, Dale Yoder and Herbert G.
Heneman, Jr., *Labor Economics and Industrial Relations,* Cincinnati: South-Western
Publishing Company, 1959, pp. 285, 454, and 578.

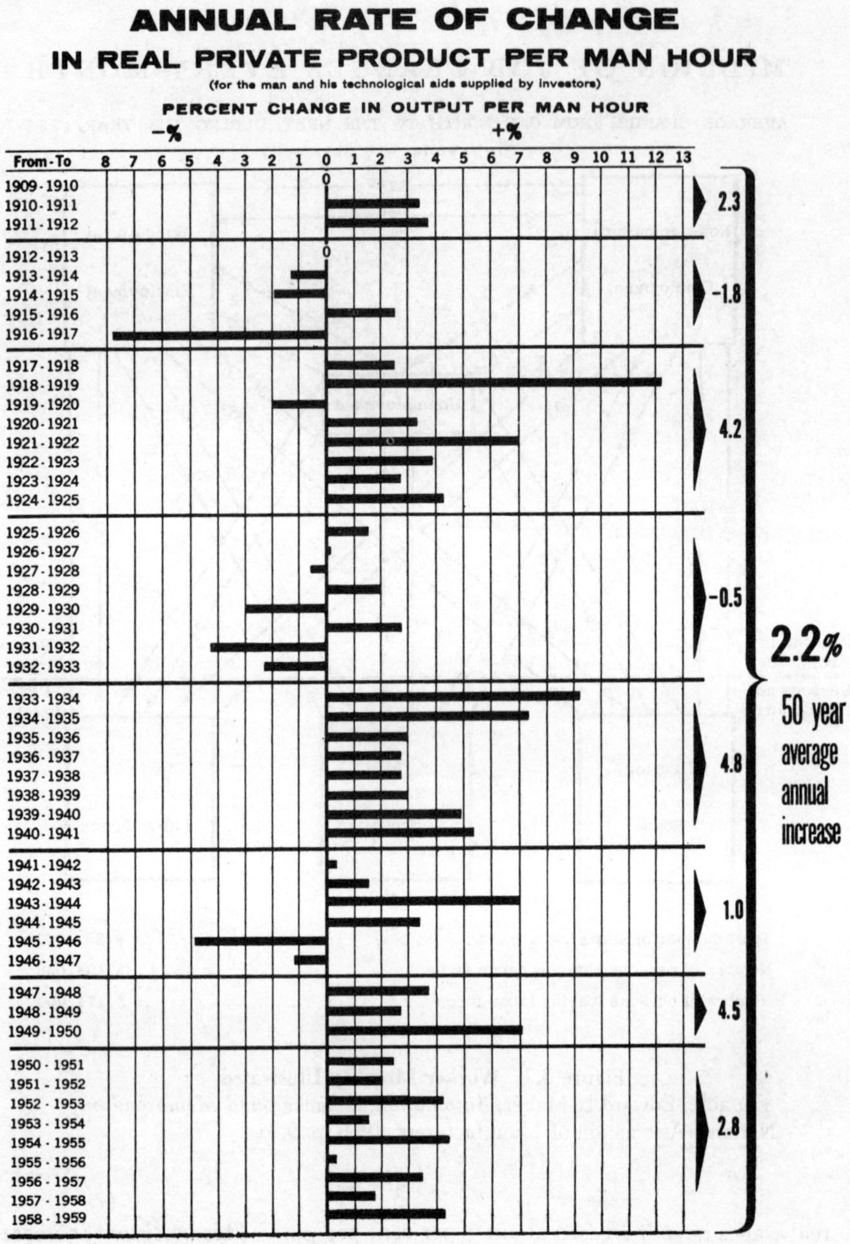

ANNUAL RATE OF CHANGE
IN REAL PRIVATE PRODUCT PER MAN HOUR
(for the man and his technological aids supplied by investors)

PERCENT CHANGE IN OUTPUT PER MAN HOUR

Figure 3.8   Annual Rate of Change in Output Per Man Hour
SOURCE: *Productivity and Wage Settlements*, Chamber of Commerce
of the United States, 1961, p. 7.

A parallel trend is that in which wage structures have narrowed. Rising wages, including real wages, have given a continually greater proportion of these increases to low-wage workers. *Across-the-board* raises, frequent in the rounds of wage increases since the war, have tended to reduce differentials between low- and high-skilled workers. This leveling process is continuing.[8]

It should be noted that these gains have been made in the face of a long-term, persistent trend toward shorter working hours. The historic facts are widely recognized. If the long-term trend continues, hours per week would approximate 35 in 1975 and 30 by 1995. In general, workers have absorbed about one-fourth of their increases in productivity by reducing hours of work.

2.0 TRENDS IN WORKING ORGANIZATIONS

Working organizations show significant changes in recent years, many of which may be expected to continue. They are becoming larger, including more workers in individual firms and agencies. Corporations continue to replace individual proprietors. As they have grown, they have also become more complex, with additional specialization. Their direction has required several levels of supervision and management. The roles of owners and managers have been modified to provide for increasing numbers of non-owner, employee, managers. Authority structures are changing, with a somewhat subtle change in the source of ownership authority from owners to directors and managers. Structures of status and communications have been modified to accompany these changes.

Meanwhile, unions have grown in numbers and in influence and employer associations have assumed an active part in both negotiation and administration of agreements with unions.

2.1 Growing complexity. Today's working organizations are becoming larger. More employees are working in large business units than were before. While small business firms persist, the trend toward merger and combination is evident.[9]

At the same time, working organizations continue to become more complicated. Specialization increases with size and affects not only job assignments to production workers but also the jobs of supervisors and managers. Growth interposes additional levels of supervision in a *layering process* which creates new relationships of authority and status. This process of complicating work relationships is widely recognized. It is frequently alleged that each addition to the payroll creates demands for more workers. The process has been described in a cynical but perspicacious essay, *Parkinson's Law.*[10]

[8] See Lloyd G. Reynolds and Cynthia Taft, *The Evolution of Wage Structures*, New Haven, Conn.: Yale University Press, 1956.

[9] Students will enjoy two essays on the implications of increasing size, Kenneth E. Boulding, "The Jungle of Hugeness," *Saturday Review*, Mar. 1, 1958; and Harlan Cleveland, "Dinosaurs and Personal Freedom," *Saturday Review*, Feb. 28, 1959.

[10] See Cyril N. Parkinson's *Law and Other Studies in Administration*, Boston: Houghton Mifflin Company, 1957.

The pyramid of the employment structure has grown taller, with larger numbers of levels, ranks, supervision, and management. This layering is one of the most impressive trends in modern structures of employment. It is closely related to one of the most widely recognized problems for today's management—that of effective communication in employment.

2.2 Specialization of management. The participation of owners and employers in employment relationship has become less personal and less influential. Corporate enterprise increases the numbers of owners, but large-scale corporate enterprise may give owners a minor role in day-to-day operations. Most of them become almost forgotten men. Meanwhile, those who play the role of individual proprietors become a smaller proportion of the labor force. The continuing growth of the labor force does not create a proportional expansion in numbers of employer-proprietors. In part, this trend results from the decline of agriculture, with its many small, independent farmers. At present slightly more than three-fourths (about 76 per cent) of all labor force members are employees. Employers make up about 11 per cent, and self-employed the remaining 13 per cent. Managers and officials are included as employers in these calculations, even though many of this group are in a very real sense employees.

Meanwhile, hired-employer managers become the leaders and directors of employment. Corporate stockholders, through their boards of directors, employ managers to take over direction of the enterprise. Managers gain power and influence in part because changes in ownership through sales of stock result in extensive turnover among owners. Many stockholder owners have never seen the plants they own, nor met an employee or an executive or manager in the firms whose stock they hold. They may be owners two or three times removed through their purchase of stock in investment funds.

Numbers and proportions of managers—as distinguished from proprietors—have grown and are growing. At the same time, managers have become specialized. This differentiation of managerial jobs is evident in such titles as "general manager," "production manager," "vice-president for finance" or "vice-president, industrial relations." The process has increased the numbers of specialized *staff* or advisory managers as distinguished from *line* or operating managers (see Chapter 6). As a result, the simple *line organization* of early periods has been replaced with one that includes a variety of specialists to supplement management by supervisors, foremen, and other line managers.

The ratio of *non-production, indirect workers* to production workers is growing. Hill and Harbison found, for example, that from 1947 to 1957, while production workers increased by about 1 per cent, non-production workers increased 55 per cent. Overhead costs are rising because of this trend. Thus, while the salaries of professional and managerial employees were about one-fourth of total manufacturing costs in 1947, they amounted, according to

Hill and Harbison, to about one-third of these costs in 1957.[11]

Implications of this trend for the future of organization are by no means clear. The trend may be influenced by the development of data-processing and computer equipment. Most forecasters predict continuing increases in proportions of staff managers. Some of them suggest that ranks of middle managers will be reduced, as electronic data-processing equipment becomes available to all firms. The resulting organization would appear like a church steeple surmounted by a football, rather than as the conventional organization pyramid.[12] A change of this type would have highly significant implications for the education of future managers.

2.3   Staff managers. Growth in numbers of managers is but one means of meeting the managerial requirements of larger working organizations. At the same time, as noted, managers have been increasingly specialized. Numerous *staff* managers—specialists in marketing, finance, engineering, law, and industrial relations, for example—have been provided as counselors and assistants to *line* or *general managers*. This specialization is readily illustrated by reference to the industrial relations field. Particularly in recent years, working organizations in the United States have leaned heavily on specialized *staff* personnel and *industrial relations divisions*. Common practice provides a staff based on a minimum personnel ratio of .75. That means there is at least one such staff member for each 133 employees (the *ratio* is the number of professional and technical industrial relations staff members per 100 employees).

In earlier practice, these special personnel managers were expected to manage the firm's employment offices as well as to bridge the gap between employers and employees. Sometimes their assignment was described as "representing employee interests." They were often expected to know employees by their first names, to remember birthdays and family occasions, and to try to impress employees with employer interest in their welfare. Many of them were essentially employment clerks. Others were sometimes cynically described as handshakers, backslappers, and fanny-patters.

In current practice, they work with other managers and perform many specialized functions for them. They suggest, recommend, and evaluate policies affecting employees. They frequently recruit new workers, interview and test candidates, and direct training programs. They assist in transfers, promotions, demotions, penalties, and discharges. They may take the lead in negotiations with unions and in contract administration, including the han-

[11] Samuel E. Hill and Frederick Harbison, *Manpower and Innovation in American Industry,* Industrial Relations Section, Princeton University, 1959, pp. 63–65. See also Frederick Harbison, "American Management in Perspective, *Personnel Administration,* Vol. 19, No. 3, May-June 1956; Edwin E. Witte, "The Evolution of Managerial Ideas in Industrial Relations," *Bulletin No. 27,* New York State School of Industrial and Labor Relations, November 1954.

[12] See Harold J. Leavitt and Thomas L. Whisler, "Management in the 1980's," *Harvard Business Review,* Vol. 36, No. 6, November-December 1959, p. 41.

dling of grievances. They may administer programs of benefits and services (hospitalization, unemployment insurance, retirement, etc.). They may be responsible for wage and salary administration. In all of these and other tasks, they are expected to provide special technical competence, with professional training, knowledge, and skill.

2.4 Authority and status. Meanwhile, the divorcement of ownership from management is creating new systems of authority and status for managers. Traditions extending far back into the agricultural stage in economic evolution related authority directly to ownership and proprietorship. In the handicraft stage that authority was augmented by a high regard for the skill of the master craftsman. All through the period dominated by modern industrialism, authority has been regarded as flowing by delegation from owner-proprietors to managers and their assistants and throughout the ranks of supervision, thus creating the familiar scalar structure and hierarchy.

Status relationships in employment have tended to parallel this hierarchy of authority. Ownership was a recognized basis for high office and position. Managers and supervisors were accorded a high status, corresponding to the authority they exercised. In addition, skill and experience have been highly regarded, so that status was scaled to match the popular impression of what each owner, manager, and foreman was qualified to do and could do.

Current attitudes and opinion accord ownership no unrestricted authority for direction and control of working organizations. A trend toward further limitations on ownership-based authority and control has been evident for many years. In part, this trend is expressed in the growing acceptance of *bilateral policy making* through collective bargaining. In this practice, authority is shared with employees and their unions. At the same time, owner authority has been limited by increased government intervention in employment.

2.41 Salaries as status symbols. A major mark of status, in the older, traditional viewpoint, was the salary or wage level. Indeed, the distinction between salaried and hourly rated workers has been, in itself, an important basis for status. Salaried employees were regarded as more closely identified with propertied proprietors and owners.

The narrowing process in wage and salary structures, already noted, is reducing the significance of this distinction and of salary levels as status symbols. The formerly distinctive perquisites of salaried employees—paid vacations, sick leave, more stable employment, and others—have now been extended to hourly rated employees. The latter have also benefited from transfer payments, income taxes, unemployment insurance, public pensions, and the general extension of public services. As a result of such changes, many wage workers live in the same neighborhoods as salaried employees and own comparable automobiles—also a common status symbol. They send their children to the same schools. The dollar sign on wages and salaries has thus lost much of its significance as a symbol of status, both in the workshop and in the working community.

2.42 Participative management. This trend has been strengthened by growing acceptance of what is usually described as a *participative* rather than an *authoritative attitude* for managers and supervisors. To that end, they seek to enlist the interested participation of employees, to encourage their expression of opinions and their decision-making in areas in which they are competent. This point of view stresses the common goals of employees and their organizations as a basis for active participation and collaboration.

2.43 Specialized competence. In this transition, newer status symbols are typified by the college degree and the certificate or license. They imply that specialized skill and competence should be accorded high recognition in working associations. Those who have made the most of their talents are regarded as deserving special recognition for that accomplishment.

2.44 Professional management. Managers have not escaped the impact of these changes. They have felt the need for more indicators of their own competence. These pressures have been largely responsible for the rapid growth of supervisory training and management development programs (see Chapters 18 and 19). They have created a wide interest in professional qualifications for management.

Staff managers, specialized in engineering, marketing, industrial relations, and other managerial fields, have pointed the general direction of this change. As the dollar-mark of wages and salaries has become less impressive, specialized competence, as exemplified in staff management and engineering and scientific specialization, has achieved greater influence. Educational attainment appears to be increasingly influential. Staff managers, in part on this account, have been accorded a higher status than in earlier years. General managers, particularly in middle management and supervisory positions, may have suffered by comparison.

Pressures for *professional competence* in general management have been magnified by the rising educational attainments of employees. Hill and Harbison forecast a continuing trend in this direction. They conclude that:[13]

> It should be almost blindingly obvious to most companies that the greater employment of brainpower in industry will demand smarter and much more thoroughly and broadly trained top executives. It will not be possible for a top manager to learn by experience alone what he must know to direct the affairs of tomorrow's enterprises. Even today, large companies are too complicated to be understood by the too narrowly educated pragmatist. The top executive must coordinate the activities, inspire the enthusiasm, and command the respect of highly educated technical specialists in virtually every branch of the business.

These changes have encouraged a clearcut trend toward *professional education* for management (see Chapter 20) and *research* as a means of finding better solutions for managerial problems. A sample of firms participating in frequent surveys of personnel ratios and budgets reports average annual expenditures of approximately one dollar per employee for private research in

[13] Samuel E. Hill and Frederic Harbison, "The Changing Composition of American Manpower," *Manpower and Innovation in American Industry,* Princeton, N.J.: Princeton University Press, 1959, p. 65.

manpower management.[14] More than thirty American universities have created special industrial relations research centers, institutes, and divisions. In 1947, a national *Industrial Relations Research Association* was formed, with members from management, unions, and academic groups.

2.45 Certification for status. Licensing and certification of managers have been frequently proposed. Some local associations of managers have attempted to establish membership requirements that approximate certification. On the other hand, many present managers have expressed themselves as opposed to licenses or certificates. They argue that (1) there is no well-defined common body of knowledge that all managers should know; (2) management is essentially an art, so unmeasurable skills are of major importance; and (3) the movement to license is simply a step toward monopolistic, restrictive marketing practice, not unlike practices they associate with unions.

On the other hand, proponents of the movement insist that managerial incompetence can not be tolerated, so that more effective, speedy means of eliminating inadequate managers must be found. They suggest that employee and public as well as owner pressures make provisions for licensing or certification essential.[15] It is notable that current practice uses degrees from universities for somewhat the same purpose. Similarly, the public service system of job classification provides for examinations and for identification by level of specialized knowledge and skill.[16]

2.5   Unions in the work organization. Meanwhile, modern working organizations have been affected by the growing size and power of unions. The management of employment is becoming increasingly complicated because of the active intervention of today's unions. The small, local labor organizations characteristic of our colonial period and first century as a nation have been supplanted by national and international unions and federations. Union membership has grown, especially since the great depression of the 1930's and the changed public policy signaled by the National Labor Relations Act of 1935. Earliest unions were largely composed of craftsmen. Later, industrial unionism expanded membership to include semiskilled operatives in mass-production industries. Today's unions also include at least 3 million white-collar clerical and sales workers.

The few, small local unions characteristic of the pre-Civil War period have expanded to include more than 60,000 locals, 150 national and international unions, and some 17 million individual members. At the present time, these members represent approximately 34 per cent of all non-agricultural employees, as compared with 12 per cent in 1930.

[14] See continuing reports from the University of Minnesota Industrial Relations Center.

[15] See Lawrence A. Appley, "Manager Certification," *Management News,* Vol. 32, No. 9, September 1959, pp. 1–2.

[16] See "Perspective in Public Personnel Administration," *Public Personnel Review,* Vol. 17, No. 4, October 1956, pp. 178–338; William G. Torpey, *Public Personnel Management,* Princeton, N.J.: D. Van Nostrand Company, Inc., 1953.

The trend in union membership is by no means clear. Long-term growth is evident. So is the relative decline in membership since the middle fifties. To grow, unions must enlist white-collar workers in ever-greater proportions. Whether they can do so is presently a matter of sharply differing opinions.

Meanwhile, the range of union influence has expanded. American unions have discarded the non-political policy of the early A. F. of L. and now exert powerful pressures on local, state, and federal governments. They have widened their concern about working conditions, which now extends far beyond the earlier concept of wages and hours. They negotiate on managerial policy and practice, from bulletin boards to wage increases and differentials. They enjoy several types of union security, assuring the continued membership and support of the employees they represent.

Public policy on unions has changed greatly since they were small local fraternities of craftsmen. Both federal and state legislation has given unions much more responsibility in working organizations. The area of approved bargaining has been expanded. In this expansion, unions have demanded and secured a voice with respect to what some managers regard as elementary management prerogatives. In the opinion of such managers, unions have made it almost impossible for managers to manage. Union demands for even wider opportunities for policy making suggest a continuing trend.[17]

These developments are described in detail in Chapters 6, 7 and 8.

3.0 PUBLIC INTERVENTION: THE ROLE OF GOVERNMENT

Current trends include significant changes in the part played by public agencies in the employment process. Despite vocal opposition on the part of both managers and unions, public regulation of employment relationships has tended to increase. Many conditions have influenced this development, including the growth of unions, international competition with Iron Curtain nations, the fear of bigness in business, and general recognition that employable manpower is a scarce resource. A public policy of *full employment,* growing demands by unions for minimum labor standards, and public concern about obvious *waste* in industrial unrest and conflict are other proximate factors in this change.

As has been noted, modern industrial capitalism was born in an era dominated by a laissez-faire philosophy. Supplies of labor were generally in excess of demands. Government intervention was regarded as an evil to be avoided. Today's industrial relations system shows little resemblance to this earlier model. Federal, state, and local governments play a large part in regulating all employment. The nation is committed to a full-employment policy that proposes a long-term choice of jobs. Public policy also guarantees employees the right to bargain through unions with respect to employment

---

[17] For an interesting case study of these changes, see John A. Garraty, "The United States Steel Corporation *versus* Labor: The Early Years," *Labor History,* Vol. 1, No. 1, Winter 1960, pp. 3–38.

conditions. Government agencies police this right and regulate negotiations. Federal regulations set minimum wages and regulate working hours and the employment of children. State and local governments provide similar regulations for intrastate industries.

Government has taken the lead in providing a vast system of social security provisions that affect all employers and employees. Federal and state agencies provide unemployment insurance, old-age and survivers' pensions and benefits, workmen's compensation, free public-employment services, aid to areas of persistent unemployment, and other similar assistance.

Government has developed rules of fair employment practice, not only to prevent discrimination against individual applicants or employees based on race, religion, nationality, or age but also to reduce the waste of special talents and skills. Public concern about the waste of human resources and the public inconvenience, if not hazard, in strikes and lockouts has encouraged extensive intervention in collective bargaining and dispute settlement. Numerous proposals for compulsory arbitration, public disability insurance, and aid in the relocation of unemployed workers forecast a growing role for government in industrial relations systems of the future.

Meanwhile, government has become the employer for growing numbers and proportions of employees. Government employment of civilian employees has grown from about 8 per cent of all employment in 1940 to 11 per cent in 1960. Both federal agencies and state and local governments have increased their work forces, but state employment has provided the principal increase since World War II.

What do these developments suggest with respect to the management of the future and the part to be played by government in management? One of the most intriguing forecasts has been provided by four students of world-wide industrialization. Kerr, Dunlop, Harbison, and Myers conclude that:

> All these responsibilities mean the state will never "wither away"; that Marx was more utopian than the despised utopians. It will be the dominant organization in any industrial society. . . . The productive enterprise under pluralistic industrialism, whether it is private or public, will be in a dominant position. It will often be large and it must always have substantial authority in order to produce efficiently. This authority will not be complete for it will be checked by the state, by the occupational association, by the individual employee; but it will be substantial.
>
> The managers, whether private or public, will be professionals, technically trained and carefully selected for their tasks. They will be bureaucratic managers, if private, and managerial bureaucrats, if public; each responding to the rules and the technical requirements of the job. The distinction between the private and the public manager will decrease just as the distinction between the private and the public enterprise. . . .[18]

4.0 SUMMARY

This chapter has suggested the nature and the general direction of cur-

[18] Clark Kerr, John T. Dunlop, Frederick Harbison, and Charles A. Myers, *In-*

rent trends in industrial relations systems. Discussion has been organized about the three major variables described in the preceding chapter.

It is apparent that the process of industrialization has not ended, even in the most industrialized societies. Indeed, some of the changes it occasions appear to be gaining in acceleration. Working careers are changing, with a clear trend toward more non-agricultural employment and larger proportions of technical and professional workers. As could be expected, workers will require and are acquiring more and different education for the jobs of the future. They may and do anticipate higher real wages and living scales.

Within working organizations, the specializing process continues to exert an almost overwhelming influence. It has occasioned a significant increase in proportions of managers or indirect workers in modern work teams. How far this trend may go in modifying the organizational structures of the future is not at all clear, although predictions are essential in planning education for future managers.

Meanwhile, authority and status structures based on ownership are being sharply modified. Most current theory holds that proprietary authoritarian leadership is inappropriate in modern democracies. A trend toward more participation by employees has gained wide acceptance. Salaries are less widely accepted as symbols of status, and evidences of specialized competence have gained wider acceptance.

These changes are creating strong pressures for evidence of the specialized competence of managers. Staff managers have tended to achieve recognition and status more readily than unspecialized general managers in this change. Individual firms and universities are offering new management development programs to assist general managers in developing required knowledge and skills. Questions are being raised about the professionalization of management and perhaps the licensing or certification of managers. Interest in management research is growing, and research reporting is improving.

These trends have been encouraged by the growth of unions and their increased influence. They have been accompanied by a notable extension in the role played by government in the industrial relations of our democratic society.

In the next four chapters, attention is directed to reflections of these trends on employment theory. What changes can be noted in current theories of work and organization and administration? How do managers propose to use these tools of organization and administration in performing the management assignment?

SELECTED SUPPLEMENTARY READINGS

Dodge, Joseph M., "Some Special Characteristics of Successful Management," *Advanced Management*. Vol. 20, No. 4, pp. 5–8, April 1955.

dustrialism and Industrial Man, Cambridge: Harvard University Press, 1960, p. 291; see also a summary of their viewpoint in "Industrialism and the Industrial Man," *International Labour Review*, Vol. 32, No. 3, September 1960, p. 249.

Drucker, Peter F., "Thinking Ahead: Potentials of Management Science," *Harvard Business Review,* Vol. 37, No. 1, pp. 25ff. January-February 1959.

Harbison, Frederick, "American Management in Perspective," *Personnel Administration,* Vol. 19, No. 3, pp. 9–18, May-June 1956.

Hill, Samuel E., and Frederick Harbison, *Manpower and Innovation in American Industry.* Princeton, N.J.: Princeton University Industrial Relations Section, 1959.

Hauser, Philip M., "Business Implications of Population Growth," *Business Horizons,* pp. 87–96. Bloomington, Ind.: University of Indiana, Vol. 3, No. 2, Summer 1960.

Kerr, Clark, John T. Dunlop, Frederick Harbison, and Charles A. Myers, "Industrialization and Industrial Man," *International Labour Review,* Vol. 32, No. 3, pp. 249ff. September 1960.

Maher, Edward L., "Automation: A Background Memorandum." New York: National Association of Manufacturers, 1960.

Parkinson, Cyril N., *Law and Other Studies in Administration.* Boston: Houghton Mifflin Company, 1957.

Selekman, Benjamin, *A Moral Philosophy for Management.* New York: McGraw-Hill Book Company, Inc., 1959.

SHORT CASE PROBLEM 3.1

Status for Managers

"The greatest weakness in the current management system in the United States," declared Mr. MacKenzie, noted international management consultant, "is the absence of a status system in American industry and business. In every other industrialized nation, supervisors and managers have a well-recognized status structure. They know where they stand. Everyone else in the organization knows, too. For many, their status is related to family ownership. For others, status is a matter of long service and successful performance. In the United States, this basis for effective organization and cooperation is missing. You have put so much emphasis on political democracy and the equality of all men that the short roots of your traditions provide no security in the status structure for managers. As a result, rank-and-file as well as supervisors recognize no clear-cut status distinctions. Most of your managers are insecure and unsure of their futures.

"I know your arguments that such democracy and insecurity are precisely what have made you great. My point, however, is that you have destroyed the old status systems without creating anything to take their place. I know, too, that you have tried. You have developed a host of symbols to reinforce a "dollar" status system. You have sought to relate status to salary and income and wealth. The point is, however, that such a system is directly contrary to your national traditions. It cannot achieve persistent acceptance.

"I have been asked many times to prescribe for the ills of individual managements in your great nation. In almost all of them, I find myself thwarted by this vast vacuum, this chaos of work status. There is no simple remedy. You must, and reasonably promptly if you are to meet today's international competition, create a distinctively American status system for your work groups. You can build it around the values your people regard as important and permanent and enduring and appropriate. My opinion is that it must probably combine some of these values, especially those of specialized competence and public responsibility. If this means that the American status system must be based on professional management, that would not surprise me."

Problem: Be prepared to comment on this viewpoint. Do you regard it as sound? Is the diagnosis realistic? Can you cite evidence on this point? Is a status structure appropriate in democratic societies? How do you regard this consultant's prescription? How could we move in this direction if we regarded it as appropriate?

SHORT CASE PROBLEM 3.2

George Hackett, Manpower Manager

Part I

When George Hackett graduated from the University of Missouri, he intended to work his way to the top of a small manufacturing firm. He was quite clear about plans for his career. He had his degree in Business Administration; he intended to become a professional manager.

George had several opportunities; recruitment was active when he graduated in 1960. He accepted a job with Southern Pump Company because it was small and he saw in it the kind of organization he regarded as promising. His job was at the bottom of the chart in the industrial sales division. The assignment, for the first year, was to learn all about the business while working in the sales office of the firm.

During September of his first year with the firm, he was assigned to attend the regular weekly meetings conducted by the Personnel Department and attended by one representative from each of the firm's seven departments. The group, known as the Personnel Council, met to discuss long- and short-term personnel problems and to develop personnel policy for meeting such problems. As the representative of his department, George was expected to participate in the discussions and to report them and the tentative conclusions to the manager of his department. This responsibility was rotated among members of the department who were assigned to the central office.

During the first of these meetings George felt somewhat lost and ineffective. Attention centered on the question of retraining employees. He was not sufficiently familiar with present jobs or prospective changes to make much of a contribution. However, at the third meeting, the Personnel Director presented several charts representing nationwide forecast of changes in the labor force and suggested that members of the Council consider their implications for policy in Southern Pump. He called on George to comment on them, suggesting that his newness in the firm should not be too great a handicap, while his recent University experience might be a distinct advantage. The charts are those shown as figures 3.3, 3.4, 3.5, and 3.6.

Problem: In this situation, what comments would you have made?

II. THEORY IN MANPOWER MANAGEMENT

4. Theories in Management: Work Theory

The four chapters in this second section of the book are designed to help you understand your reactions and those of others to past and future changes in industrial relations. They point to the key importance of theories as explanations of managerial actions and reactions. They redirect attention to the "dimensions" chart in Chapter 1, with special emphasis on the column headed "Theories and Philosophy."

A manager's theories represent explanations he accepts for the behavior he seeks to understand. His theories of industrial relations explain the behavior of employment. A theory is a plausible explanation. It may, for example, provide an explanation as to why some employees work with more zeal and enthusiasm or more effectiveness than others. It may explain why some organizations seem to gain unusual levels of employee good will or loyalty.

The management of people in working organizations requires a wide range of theories. It turns to theories to provide clues as to what workers want and expect from their work. Because management uses the tools of *organization* and *administration* to set the stage for work, it requires theories that explain behavior in these areas. It is not enough for the manager to know about historic or current practices and techniques. Just as the medical practitioner needs to know the theory behind his diagnosis and prescription, managers need to understand theories of management.

The four chapters in this section provide an introduction to what may be regarded as basic theories in manpower management. Many other theories of great importance—theories of personality, of learning and of leadership, for example—require attention in later discussions of particular types of problems and managerial activities.

1.0 THEORY AND PHILOSOPHY IN MANAGEMENT

Every manager is something of a philosopher and theorist. Spokesmen for modern management and professional associations of managers have frequently urged managers to give more attention to their theories and philosophies.

One basic and persistent influence of management theories is exerted through their impact on and interaction with the personal philosophies of managers. Theories influence the manager's perception of values. They color and focus his views, screening what he sees. At the same time, a manager's philosophy monitors his acceptance of theories. The manager, for example, whose theory holds that power and authority in work reside in and flow from ownership is likely to be philosophically opposed to both union and government interference in management. On the other hand, the manager whose philosophy places a top value on personal freedom will be concerned about regimentation whether imposed by government, unions, or fellow managers.

Theories and philosophy, although interacting and modifying each other, are not the same. The manager's philosophy gives system and order to his thinking. His philosophy of management creates a hierarchy of values, identifying for him what is most important and what is less important. It creates a persistent frame of reference and system of values to which managerial problems are related. Some of these values have moral connotations and thus shape the ethical principles the manager applies to his own behavior as well as that of others.

Public interest in the philosophy of management has grown as managers have gained greater power and influence. In some earlier periods, the manager could insist that he didn't make the rules; he just enforced them. When widely accepted theories explained the social benefits of unrestricted enterprise, neither owner nor manager philosophies appeared as appropriate subjects for public investigation or concern.

In today's working organization, it is evident that managers exercise great influence with wide discretion. Public reaction seems to expect something approximating professional standards of responsibility and ethics in management, with a high regard for the public welfare. Recent corporate campaigns to avoid managerial conflicts of interest are reactions to this viewpoint and suggest a growing concern over manager philosophies. Widely publicized AFL-CIO Codes of Ethical Conduct for union leaders (to be noted in Chapter 10) have frequently occasioned questions about the absence of similar codes for managers.

One study of the "basic factors" about which managerial philosophies must be concerned lists them as follows: the economic system, the system of ownership, government, community, unions, the motive of business, the problems of growth, customers, and employees.[1] Although the list closes with "employees," there is no implication that they are least important.

Establishment of priorities and hierarchy or system among values is presumably a result of the manager's basic intelligence, formal education, and his whole lifetime of experience.

Professor Ralph C. Davis has provided an excellent summary of the pervasive influence of management philosophies in the practice of modern management.[2]

> The problem of greatest importance in the field of management is and probably will continue to be the further development of the philosophy of management. A philosophy is a system of thought. It is based on some orderly, logical statements of objectives, principles, policies and general methods of approach to the solution of some set of problems. . . . A managerial philosophy cannot supply a basis of effective thinking for the solution of business problems if it is satisfactory only to owners and employees. A managerial philosophy that is commonly accepted is a requisite for a common scale of values in an economy. It is necessary, therefore, for unity of thought and action in the accomplishment of economic objectives. We cannot have an effective industrial economy without effective industrial leadership. We cannot have an effective leadership without a sound managerial philosophy.
>
> Industrial leaders without such a philosophy are business mechanics rather than professional executives. . . .

Professor Waldo Fisher has tersely summarized the fundamental importance of managerial philosophy in the management of people.[3]

> This presentation of the role and basic functions of industrial relations in the business enterprise will have little value unless it has conveyed the primary importance of a workable philosophy of human relations. Successful industrial relations is not brought into being by programs and techniques but by the spirit, attitudes, and appreciation of human values that executives and supervisors bring to the task of managing the enterprise. Once a constructive philosophy of human relations permeates the organization and is accepted by its participants, it will become much easier to convince individuals and groups in the organization that the enterprise is a cooperative undertaking in which all participants must recognize the rights and responsibilities of every other functional group, that want-satisfaction must be attained by means of increased productivity, and that the gains obtained by the redistribution of existing income are seldom substantial. It is in the minds of men and women that harmonious and cooperative human relations must be built.

[1] Julius Rezler, "The Meaning and Elements of the American Business Philosophy," *Iowa Business Digest,* Vol. 29, No. 5, May 1958; see also Marshall E. Dimock, *A Philosophy of Administration,* New York: Harper & Brothers, 1958.

[2] "Research in Management During the '50's" in *Research Needs in Business during the '50's* (Indiana Business Reports, Report No. 13), Bloomington, Indiana: The School of Business, Indiana University, 1959, p. 32.

[3] "The Role and Functions of Industrial Relations in the Business Organization," *Bulletin No. 34,* Industrial Relations Center, California Institute of Technology, 1961, p. 36. See also Richard Eells, *The Meaning of Modern Business,* especially Chapter 1, "The Search for a Philosophy of Business," New York: Columbia Universtiy Press, 1960.

It may be added that a sound management philosophy is largely dependent on the development and wide acceptance of sound management theory. No appropriate system of managerial values is to be expected when managers misunderstand (i.e., hold inadequate theories about) the processes and behavior they seek to influence. No manager, for example, is likely to attach a high priority to the development of employee personalities if he theorizes that his employees want only more wages. To a large extent, therefore, the development of sound managerial philosophy hinges on the understanding of the best in relevant theory.

2.0 THEORY, POLICY AND PRACTICE

The impact of theories is by no means limited to the level of philosophy. *Theories* are *tentative but plausible explanations,* representing the thinking man's answer to many of the questions of "Why" in the universe. They are explanations of impersonal as well as personal relationships. Some theories seek to explain the behavior of things; others, the behavior of people. In a sense, being tentative and not conclusively proved, they are hypotheses.

Theories differ from *principles* mainly in the degree to which they have been verified and have achieved acceptance. Both represent generalizations. The *principle* may, however, have wider general acceptance; also, the term frequently implies a rule governing practice rather than simply an explanation of observed phenomena or behavior. Thus we may speak of a theory of wages, a theory of individual differences, and a principle of learning or teaching, or a principle in leading a conference or reprimanding an employee.

Laws, in this usage, represent a further degree of certainty and acceptance. A law in this sense describes what is regarded as a certainty about relationships, as the law of falling bodies, or Gresham's law (bad money drives out good).

All managers base many of their most important decisions on theories. They must do so, simply because present-day knowledge of management processes is limited. Theories provide *tentative explanations* to supplement what is known. They thus facilitate planning and action in the absence of full knowledge and understanding.

Thus a manager may favor a proposal for a public address system because his theories about working organizations emphasize the part played by communications. The same manager may also favor guaranteed annual wages for employees because he accepts theories that relate economic security positively to employee working efficiency. Again, this manager may insist on regular measures of employee attitudes because he accepts the theory that high employee morale is an important factor in high output or productivity.

Managers can base their decisions and action only to a limited degree on demonstrated laws and principles. Thus a manager can recognize the *principle* of individual differences, certain *principles* of learning, such *economic principles* as those of diminishing utility and marginality and others. The same manager, however, must accept something less certain than a law or principle as a basis for many of his decisions. He must act "on the theory that" some particular relationship prevails. He recognizes that this relationship is not certain or conclusive.

Theories play an especially important part in the complex problems and difficult decisions involved in managing people. Recognition and understand-

PHILOSOPHY	PRIORTIES IN GOALS	POLICIES	PROGRAMS	PRACTICES	PERFORMANCE
	Objectives End	Considered intentions, courses, routes	Planned, systematic action	Procedures, techniques	
	Examples	Examples	Examples	Examples	
Personal and organization value systems	Long-term continuation	Stabilized employment	Selection: job analysis, recruitment, interviewing, testing	Seniority Bumping Buzz sessions Role playing Job rotation Wage survey Severance pay Escalators Job engagement Pirating Profit-sharing Suggestion system Vesting	Success in attaining the goals of the organization
Patterns and hierarchies of values	Perpetuation Reputation for leadership	Economic security for employees High employee participations	Employee development, training		
Basic viewpoint: guiding principles.	Employee loyalty, enthusiasm Stability of profit levels World-wide example	Effective in-plant communications Promotion on merit	Collective bargaining Job evaluation		

THEORY BRIDGES
Work organization Leadership

THEORY BRIDGES
Administration Learning Communication

Figure 4.1   Theory Bridges in Management

ing of the most widely accepted theories of work, organization, administration, and public intervention are essential to an understanding and evaluation of current policy and practice.

2.1   Theory bridges. Perhaps the importance of theories can be clarified by a modification of the chart on "Dimensions of Manpower Management," introduced in Chapter 1. Figure 4.1 is entitled "Theory Bridges in Management." The drawing is designed to suggest that the way in which we move from one of the columns to the next is largely determined by our theories. Theories lead us from goals to policies, from policies to programs, and so on across these columns. In other words, we select our policies because of our theories about how they will implement goals. We develop practices on the basis of theories about how they can put policies into effect. On the basis of such a chart, we might create a new management game called "What's your theory?" or we might state an axiom: A manager is known by the theories he holds. In discussions of the merits of various policies and programs, it might be appropriate to observe to participants that their theories are showing![4]

At the same time, recognition of theories facilitates a research approach to managerial problems. Research flows from theories, for the latter state problems that deserve investigation. Theory is the major source of hypotheses to be tested in research. Management will expand its background of knowledge and understanding as students recognize its theories and attempt to check on their validity.

2.2 Theories and practice. The range of theories on which managers lean is very broad. Political theories, economic and psychological and sociological and educational theories, all contribute to the viewpoints and attitudes of managers and to their philosophies. Managers design training and developmental programs to fit their theories of learning. They create and modify wage and salary and benefit plans according to their theories of work or motivation. They negotiate with unions according to their theories of social and political organization and economic behavior.

Employees also lean heavily on theories as guides in their reactions to managerial policy and practice. They appraise job opportunities and offers of employment in part in terms of their theories about what jobs should offer job-holders. They select jobs in part because of their theories about work as a source of wages or of interesting experience or social satisfaction. They react to managerial directions according to theories of authority and status. They may form or join unions as an expression of other theories about the role of workers in democratic societies.

2.3 Historic interest in theories. Although discussions of theory in management has attracted increasing attention in recent years, questions of theory have been widely discussed since the earliest formal industrial relations and personnel programs appeared. Theoretical considerations received extensive attention from the early industrial psychologists. In the years following World War I, several attempts to explain industrial unrest and the motivations of workers received wide attention. In 1919, Carleton Parker's *The Casual Laborer and Other Essays* outlined what is essentially an instinct theory of on-the-job frustration and personal disorganization. By implication, it suggested that such current practices as job-enlargement and attitude surveys were steps toward more effective organization and job performance. A year earlier, in 1918, Helen Marot published *The Creative Impulse in Industry*, and Ordway Tead released his *Instincts in Industry*. Other theorists of this period include Whiting Williams, Richard T. Dana, and A. W. Kornhauser.[5]

Management has always had its theories; many historic theories of management may have been valid for their times. One basic question in all

---

[4] See in this connection Victor M. Victoroff, "The Assumptions We Live By," *ETC, A Review of General Semantics*, Vol. 16, No. 1, Autumn 1958, pp. 17–30; Douglas McGregor, *The Human Side of Enterprise*, New York: McGraw-Hill Book Company, Inc., 1960, preface and p. 6.

[5] Carleton Parker, *The Casual Laborer and Other Essays*, New York: Harcourt

theories of work and working organizations is, How far can we generalize about human behavior? First, we can be sure that all workers will not respond uniformly to financial incentives, or to the rules-of-the-game in working organizations, or to opportunities to express their opinions and to assist in planning. Secondly, we can generalize as far as we can see reasonably established, significant patterns among workers or smaller sub-groups or types of workers. Theories of working behavior have assumed that there are such patterns and that they are reasonably persistent and can be identified.

2.4 Areas of basic theory. Two broad, fundamental areas of theory play a prominent part in all employee relations. One may be described as the area of *work theory*. Such theories advance tentative answers to questions about why people work as they do. The theories play an important part in the answers that both managers and employees give to these questions. These tentative explanations seek to explain why people work. Why do they accept particular jobs? Why do they favor some opportunities over others? Why do they join some work groups and remain in them, and why do they leave others? Why do they sometimes work hard and enthusiastically and at other times appear to resist each task? Why is output from work so variable, both in quantity and quality? How can work be expected to develop and utilize the highest skills of workers? How can it minimize the toil and drudgery associated with working?

A second major area of theory in labor management reflects the necessity, in most modern employment, of *organizing* for work and of managing organized groups of workers. What are the effects of organizing on the behavior of work? What characteristics of *organization* and *administration* are related to efficient work or interesting work or work that satisfies workers? Why do workers enjoy their participation in some organizations and find the experience personally pleasing and satisfying, while they react less favorably to other organizations? Why are some organizations more successful in their missions than others?

2.5 Theories and models. Theories suggest relationships and create or may be expressed in models. As noted, such models identify major variables and suggest relationships among them. Perhaps the simplest of such models is one in which one variable is regarded as a function of another, as when we theorize that worker mobility is to some degree a function of age. Such a model can be expressed in mathematical symbols, and many models are developed as mathematical expressions of theories or hypotheses.

Although the term "model" has not been widely used in management and in the underlying behavioral sciences until recently, the idea of developing abstract statements of assumed relationships to describe a theory or test an

Brace & World, Inc. 1919; Helen Marot, *The Creative Impulse in Industry*, New York: E. P. Dutton and Co., 1918; Ordway Tead, *Instincts in Industry*, Boston: Houghton Mifflin Company, 1918; Whiting Williams, *Mainsprings of Men*, New York: Charles Scribner's Sons, 1925; Richard T. Dana, *The Human Machine in Industry*, New York: Codex Book Company, 1927; A. W. Kornhauser, "The Motives in Industry Problem," *Annals of the American Academy*, Vol. 110, 1923, pp. 113–116.

hypothesis is not new. In economics, for example, the model of a labor market can be readily traced as far back as Adam Smith. Every economics text has included charts of such markets, in which the marketing process is over-simplified for purposes of emphasis and explanation. Sociology, psychology, and other disciplines have described a great many similar models.

3.0 THEORIES OF WORK

Work theory may be regarded as a special case of what psychologists call *motivation theory*. The questions with which work theory is concerned involve explanations of on-the-job motivation. Work theory, however, is concerned only with behavior in work, as distinguished from the many other activities in which all workers take part.

Theories about why people work as they do or why their working behavior shows widely different patterns require careful consideration of (1) what is meant by work and (2) the dimensions of working behavior. It is quite clear that work is activity, but by no means that all activity is work. People do many of the same things in work as in other behavior that they regard as "play." Playing baseball, for example, is recreation for most of us and for the whole unpaid Nisswa Nailers' team, but it is work for members of the Los Angeles Dodgers and the Milwaukee Braves. Building bookcases is work for the employees of the Curtis Furniture Company but play for Mr. and Mrs. Canoyer in their new home.

3.1 Essentials of work. What is the distinction between work and non-working activity and endeavor? Certainly not the intensity of effort: many men put more of that into their golf than into their jobs. Sometimes it is argued that the distinctive character of work is its arduous nature. Work, it is said, is irksome and unpleasant. Further, we do it when we don't want to do it. Play, on the other hand, is pleasure-giving and satisfying. We play because, and when, it gives us satisfaction to do so. Only a little consideration, however, will indicate the limitations of this distinction. It is clear that we often want to work, that we are unhappy without it. Further, it is clear that for many workers, work is not entirely unpleasant. To many observers who generalize from their own experience—including college professors and text-book writers—work is quite interesting if not fascinating. It includes continuing elements of adventure—not unlike travel and recreation. They identify themselves with their products. They can scarcely find enough time for work and are likely to work even when they should perhaps forget their work in the interest of playing and socializing with their families and friends. Most professional workers, for example, insist on setting their own hours. While they may limit the hours they are available for consultation or office duties, they tend to live with their work.

Large numbers of non-professional workers appear to find no such fascination in their daily tasks. Even when their duties are not routine nor particularly monotonous, they carry no special promise of adventure. They cannot readily identify themselves with their products. The one effect of their effort that appears to be directly related to it is their pay. They may conclude therefore that work is essentially a way of earning a living—and very little more than that.[6]

Although management may benefit from study of independent, *self-employed* workers, it is clear that most managerial problems center in another group—the worker in the team, the employee in the organization, in short, what has been called in Chapter 1 the "managee." He is the problem worker for the manager. Work theory must focus on him.

For managees, the distinctive characteristics of work appear to be that (1) it is a means to ends desired by someone other than the worker, rather than an end in itself for the worker, and (2) it is something the worker feels compelled to do, so he does it because he has to, not because he wants to. Work is thus a service performed to attain satisfactions other than those that may be generated in its performance. It is undertaken to satisfy employers by creating products or services that can be used or exchanged by managers. Further, work is distinguished as being done under some obligation or compulsion. The worker regards work as necessary or compulsory for living.[7]

3.2 Related variables. Thus defined, work is by no means simple behavior. It is not merely "doing something." To the manager, trying to achieve certain objectives, the worker should do more than simply be present and working at a given job. We all note that some workers are much more effective than others on the same jobs. We note that some jobs make use of the top skills of workers; others use only a portion of these skills. Some workers accomplish much with a minimum of effort and energy. Some workers appear to get real pleasure from their jobs. Others appear much less satisfied with what they are doing.

Thus, while all work involves doing something someone wants done and exchanging time, effort, and skill for some form of "pay," work shows widely varying degrees of effort, energy, aptitudes, skill, efficiency or productivity, and worker satisfaction. These differences suggest the principal variables in work. They are not mutually independent; one may influence or be influenced by others. There may be persistent relationships among them. Perhaps the higher the inherent satisfaction, the more efficient the worker. This is a common assumption. Again, perhaps satisfaction in work varies directly with the extent to which work assignments utilize top talents. The toil in work may vary with the use of highest skills and job satisfaction. These are, in themselves, expressions of widely-held work theories.

    [6] See Chris Argyris, "The Individual and Organizational Structure," *Personnel,* Series No. 168, American Management Association 1956; Frederick Herzberg, Bernard Mausner, and Barbara Bloch Snyderman, *The Motivation to Work,* 2nd ed., New York: John Wiley & Sons, Inc., 1959.
    [7] Mortimer J. Adler, "Labor, Leisure and Liberal Education," in *Toward the Liberally Educated Executive,* New York: Fund for Adult Education, 1959, pp. 75–76.

Important *variables* in work in the working organization may be outlined as follows:

1. *Output or productivity.* This is the resultant of work, usually expressed in terms of the mission of the organization. It may vary in both *quantity* and *quality,* sometimes called the "q and q" of work.
2. *Input.* The extent to which employment develops and utilizes the highest aptitudes, talents, and skills of workers.
3. *Work satisfaction.* The degree of satisfaction developed by employees in performance on the job.
4. *Disutility.* The level of pain, discomfort, irksomeness, and dissatisfaction occasioned by work.

Managers may place varying degrees of priorities on each of these variables. They may regard output as dominant, having little concern for other variations. They may see important relationships among the variables. Societies may impose prescribed patterns of objectives. For example, for American industry, our current social goals seek to minimize the fourth of these variables.

3.3 Historic theories of work. Early theories of work expressed comparatively little concern about the full utilization of skills and aptitudes, job satisfaction, and the limitation of pain and disutility. Developed in periods of labor surplus, theories saw little relationship between job satisfaction and either quantity or quality of output. Some attention had to be given to the development of skills. Managers had a responsibility to make decisions, tell workers what to do and how, and administer penalties for failure to follow orders.

Reinhard Bendix has illustrated the early conception of "labor" by reference to Tsarist Russia.[8]

> The doctrines of autocratic rule assumed the total depravity of workers and serfs. An ethic of work was not expected of the laboring masses; it was assumed, rather, that they needed to be punished severely if they failed in their obligations. Autocratic rule relied upon the omnipresence of fear and coercion to make workers and serfs act as they ought to act, and its ideological appeals exclusively stressed the sacred duty of submission.

Since workers were regarded as irresponsible, only the most detailed and arbitrary direction could be expected to maximize their contribution in work. And, since they could be expected to exhibit no ethical sense, they must be controlled in minute detail. In addition, of course, workers must be given essential physical necessities at the subsistence level or their effort would be impaired; that subsistence must permit them to raise families, or else supplies of workers would be depleted.

3.4 Market theories. Emergence of a class of free artisans required a new viewpoint toward work and workers. The artisan marketed his services,

---

[8] "A Study of Managerial Ideologies," *Economic Development and Cultural Change,* Vol. 5, No. 2, January 1957, p. 124 (see also pp. 118–128).

setting many of his own standards of performance. The handicraft system, based largely on the skills of craftsmen, advanced this market theory of work at the same time that it relied on the offer of subsistence to secure apprentices.

The market theory held that employers bid for and bought the quantity and quality they wanted. Employers set the specifications for work. Workers had a simple choice: either accept the work—as defined by employers—at the market price or be unemployed.

Early stages in industrialization encouraged wide acceptance of this market theory of work. That point of view recognized the importance of both effort and skill as sub-variables in work. However, it showed little concern for the "job satisfaction" of workers, for it tended to regard the opportunity to work as a creation of employers, generously tendered to workers. The theory saw little need to reduce toil and disutility, except as such changes could be translated into advantages in recruitment and retention of better workers. Generally, however, manpower was available in large quantities. Labor was a relatively cheap resource. Workers often exchanged skill and effort for little more than the means of subsistence. Since employers created the opportunity and offered the jobs, they could stipulate quantity and quality, prescribing standards of output. The worker who didn't do enough to satisfy his employer could be discharged. Policing as well as directing the work was a proper function of authoritarian employers.

This early viewpoint has been described both as a subsistence theory and a marketing theory. As it developed, the theory found further explanations of employers' wage offers in the well-known subsistence, wages fund, and marginal productivity theories of wages, familiar to all students of labor economics.

This market theory of work still has wide acceptance, although various amendments have been developed to modify the explanation. Growing specialization is recognized as reducing the mobility of many workers and their choice of opportunities to work. On the other hand, higher real wages, more education, and the growth of unions have tended to counteract this limitation and to permit more worker control of effort and productivity. Growing public intervention, with special attention to the distribution of national income, has helped to make labor an expensive and limited, rather than a cheap, resource. Public programs designed to insure full employment propose to maintain a choice of jobs for all workers.

The theory still regards employer-imposed controls as major conditioners affecting quantity and quality of work. It often concludes that workers "work hard" when jobs are scarce and employers require hard work. It may suggest that "hard times"—business recession and wide unemployment—may be the most effective forces in causing employees to apply their effort and talent more diligently.

3.5 Early union influences. In the early years of industrialization, unions appeared to those who held a market theory of work to be improperly interfering with the job-creating, work-offering, employee-directing functions of employers by seeking to influence basic conditions of employment, especially wages. In doing so, they were generally regarded as invading the area of what were described as employer or management prerógatives.

Later, as unions gained political power and acceptance, work theory was further modified to account for union participation. Unions were regarded as agents of workers in the wage or price-setting process. They influenced the quantities of workers available at various prices according to what became known as the *bargaining theory* of wages. They also influenced the variables in work by setting standards of performance, restricting output, and creating bogies and quotas for various jobs. Union organizers were frequently accused of influencing workers' attitudes and output and of encouraging discontent and criticism of managers and their policies.

Simple market theories of work still have followers. They may be heard forecasting that workers will "change their tune" when the next big depression comes or demanding that employers have a free hand to hire and fire, or protesting the provision of unemployment benefits or the power and influence granted unions in current employment relationships. They argue that work would be regulated by the market for services if government and unions would allow the natural laws of supply and demand to operate. Those who hold this view are becoming fewer, however, for most citizens conclude that modern social ideals and goals would not tolerate a perfectly free market for human services.

4.0 MODERN WORK THEORY

It is apparent that no market theory can accurately and adequately describe all the major factors affecting work in today's industrial relations systems. In many societies, people do not actually have to work to live and raise their families; public relief programs would assure subsistence. Employers and managers cannot unilaterally set and maintain whatever standards of quality and quantity of work they choose. They must be realistic and sensitive in their requirements if they are to get the workers they require. They find many marketing and working conditions set by *collective agreements* with unions. Others are regulated by public agencies. Public opinion places a powerful emphasis on the *conservation of human resources,* their development and efficient application and utilization. Simple economic incentives alone cannot be expected to stimulate high levels of effectiveness in the application of effort and skill. However realistic the market analysis may have been in earlier periods, it is not adequate today.

4.1 Changing goals. Modern theories of work begin by noting that work is activity performed to attain ends other than activity in itself and under the pressure of some compulsion. Workers recognize that they must work to attain the ends or goals they have set for themselves. These ends or goals have changed and are changing. On this point, analysis follows the economic logic of diminishing utilities. As various levels of human needs are satisfied, the means of attaining that particular satisfaction appear less attractive and valuable. Such needs become less pressing and, therefore, the possibility of satisfaction is less of a stimulant. Basic physical needs—food and clothing, for example—become less motivating when they are reasonably certain. Hence a subsistence theory of work that might be appropriate in a period when scales of living are very low becomes quite inappropriate when subsistence can be taken for granted.[9]

As elementary physical needs are satisfied, the worker's "search level" changes. When food, clothing, housing, and the other subsistence elements are practically assured, other types of needs become the object of his search. For example, the desire to achieve the respect and regard of one's fellows, to be socially accepted and approved, may become a major attraction. The subsistence variable may be supplemented and largely replaced by such considerations as the opportunity to gain recognition, to exercise one's judgment, to be accepted as a leader, and to participate in a joint undertaking with coworkers who are admired.

The concept of a changing need or search level has had wide acceptance. Workers vary in the levels at which they seek satisfaction. Levels for individual workers presumably vary with time. As "lower" levels of need are satisfied, "higher" levels become more important. If, however, circumstances change in a manner threatening the persistence of more elementary satisfactions, individual emphasis will return to the latter.[10]

In current theory, physiological needs represent the lowest level. With physical welfare reasonably assured, motivation becomes more closely identified with social needs. At that level, the worker seeks "belonging," that is, association with and acceptance by fellow workers. A still higher level, which McGregor describes as egotistic, includes needs relating to self-confidence, independence, and self-esteem and those relating to status, recognition, and the appreciation of fellow workers. A final level, sometimes described as *self-actualization,* involves needs for self-fulfillment, in which the individual seeks to develop fully his personal potentialities and to be expressive and creative.

In current thinking, the individual is seen as seeking work that appears to him to be "satisfactory" as measured against his current level of aspiration. In other words, he strives hard to attain a solution that he regards as appropriate at the time; he does not go all out to maximize utility. This is a theory of *optimizing* or satisficing which appears to be a much more realistic view of current employee negotiations with employers than the earlier theory of economic maximizing.

[9] See Frederick Hertzberg, Bernard Mausner, and Barbara Bloch Snyderman, *The Motivation to Work,* New York: John Wiley & Sons, Inc., 1957.

[10] See Abraham Maslow, *Motivation and Personality,* New York: Harper & Brothers, 1954, pp. 80–106; Douglas M. McGregor, "The Human Side of Enterprise," *Proceedings,* Fifth Anniversary Convocation of the School of Management, Massachusetts Institute of Technology, April 9, 1957, pp. 6ff.

It suggests that numerous working conditions, in addition to wages or earnings, enter into employer-employee participation in the labor marketing and the subsequent employment processes. It explains how the employment relationship inevitably involves a many-sided adjustment, in which the current ideas and aspirations of employees influence a wide range of working conditions as well as day-to-day job performance. This viewpoint is in sharp contrast to the older notion that an employee simply takes or leaves a job offer, basing his decision on the price or wage. Obviously, this viewpoint has significant implications for recruitment, selection, labor relations, wage and salary administration, and productivity in work.

4.2 Controls. To attain the goal of effective self-satisfying work, which means making work represent a means of fulfillment of what has been called the whole man, modern work theory proposes careful regard for several types of related factors or working conditions. Current analysis of work notes that it is not simple but complex behavior. It suggests that the factors exerting major influence on work are also multiple rather than simple. Among the most important of these are four, which may be described as follows: [11]

4.21 Security-contribution complex. The lowest level among worker's needs, the requirement of subsistence together with protection against arbitrary mistreatment, gives rise to a continuing concern about security. In part, this factor involves what is usually described as economic security, the bread and butter, food and clothing and housing and normal living needs of modern society. It includes protection against unemployment, accidents, illness, and other serious economic hazards. In addition, security includes personal security and protection against discrimination in work. Security may be related to contribution, but the question as to how is widely and inconclusively discussed. In general, our social goals prescribe a rising level of minimum security regardless of the level of contribution.

Most, but not all, employees may take economic security for granted. Most of them have wages and benefits and services that provide a considerable degree of economic security. Many employees, however, are still insecure with respect to catastrophe, disabilities, and discriminatory practices.

4.22 Personal "appreciation." The need here is for an opportunity to grow, to improve one's self, to develop highest aptitudes and thus to become more valuable. Many workers in today's industrial relations system see themselves as facing long careers as employees. They are investing their working lives; they want to have a fair chance of personal "appreciation" comparable to the appreciation in financial investments. This concept of *appreciation* is the individual reflection of the economic investment in human capital that has achieved growing recognition in recent years. [12]

---

[11] See, also, Robert Saltonstall, "What Employees Want From Their Work," *Harvard Business Review*, Vol. 31, No. 6, November-December 1953, pp. 72–78. Saltonstall notes three levels of concern about each: (1) as an individual worker, (2) as a member of a work group, and (3) as an employee in an organization.

[12] For a classic statement on this point, see Theodore Schultz, "Investment in Human Capital," *American Economic Review*, Vol. 51, No. 1, March 1961, pp. 1–17.

Within this broad variable is the need for freedom to differ, to avoid detailed conformity. It seeks the chance to hold and express ideas that do not conform to any superimposed pattern. Today's more sophisticated workers may rebel at requirements that restrict what they regard as their personal freedom. They may want to be able to disagree and to be original. In one simple example, many workers resent pace-setting by supervisors. They often work harder when relieved of such controls. Likert reports that "the only situation we have found where freedom did not bring high performance is one where the job is poorly defined and the person has not been well-trained."[13]

4.23 Organizational orientation and identification. This is a complex factor including both recognition and status in the organization, on the one hand, and an opportunity to influence day-to-day working decisions, on the other.

In part, the need is for status in the work group. Most workers want to feel that they are identified with and accepted into the society of their fellow workers. This variable has been widely described as reflecting the desire for belonging and for active acceptance in the work group. It poses special problems in certain types of operations, notably those associated with assembly-line production, as noted by Turner.[14]

> One of the most difficult problems is that for the average assembly worker there is little in the way of a group to which he can belong in a meaningful way. Perhaps the most important counterweight to anonymity and lack of belonging or purpose, if they exist in a factory, is the sense of belonging to a small work group.

In working organizations, recognition and status are closely related to opportunities for expression and especially for participation in decisions. Hence work behavior may be influenced by the presence or absence of opportunities for participation. Creating opportunities can encourage a higher level of identification with the working organization, in which its mission and goals become more closely associated with the individual goals of member-workers. Vroom found that participation in decision-making affected worker attitudes favorably among workers who sought greater independence of action. The attitudes of less independent employees were unaffected by the opportunity. In general, he concluded that participation generally has positive effects on motivation.[15]

Modern managers have become concerned about the worker's acceptance and approval of and identification with the working organization. How does he regard the whole? How does he appraise the organization's mission and

[13] See Rensis Likert, "How to Raise Productivity by 20%," *Nation's Business,* Vol. 47, No. 8, August 1959, pp. 30ff.

[14] Arthur N. Turner, "Management and the Assembly Line," *Harvard Business Review,* Vol. 33, No. 5, September-October 1955, p. 40.

[15] Victor H. Vroom, "Some Personality Determinants of the Effects of Participation," Englewood Cliffs, N.J.: Prentice-Hall, Inc., 1960.

purpose? What does he think of its managerial leadership? Is the mission of the organization one in which the worker can take pride?

This question has attracted increasing attention as modern industry has come to employ large numbers of scientists and engineers. In one study of the attitudes of such workers, more than half of them indicated their dissatisfaction with their employer's emphasis on sales and profits. More than two-thirds felt that their talents were not well used. In general, they were not satisfied with the employer's idea of the organization's mission or with their own contribution to it.[16]

At the same time, this identification may be related to the social acceptance of the mission or purpose of both the job and the enterprise as a whole. Studies have shown that higher productivity and more efficient work are associated with a feeling of pride in the worth and importance of the organization. This need may also be viewed as a form of group loyalty.[17]

One of the important interests of many modern workers concerns their confidence in the adequacy of leadership. They want to feel that they are being led by competent supervisors, foremen, managers, and executives. They are interested in the adequacy of the whole organization. They may be quite critical of its mission, its structure, its policies and practices, and its leaders. There is probably no greater source of frustration for many sophisticated workers than that of being directed by supervisors and managers they regard as incompetent.

Union insistence on bargaining on details of working conditions may express a lack of confidence in managerial policy and competence. Union demands for participation in decision-making, especially on questions of production, scheduling, plant location, farming-out work, and other such issues is a rather obvious reflection of critical attitudes toward the judgment of managers.

4.24 Limitation of disutility. Managers cannot ignore the influence of unpleasant working conditions, which may influence each of these other variables.

Figure 4.2 is a graphic representation of these important variables in modern work theory.

5.0 SUMMARY

The philosophies with which managers approach their jobs—their systems of values and their viewpoints and frames of reference—are the foundations on which managers build managerial policy and practice. Theories play an important role in all managerial philosophies. These plausible but inconclusive explanations provide usable guides to thought and action. They bridge the gaps between philosophy and policy and between policy and practice. Two areas of theory are especially prominent: (1) theories of work and (2) theories of organization and administration.

[16] Reported in *Industrial Relations News,* Vol. 9, No. 4, October 31, 1959, p. 4.
[17] See Rensis Likert, "How to Raise Productivity by 20%," *op. cit.,* pp. 30ff.

Modern work theory recognizes that the behavior of work is not simple. It varies most obviously in terms of the quantity of output. Quality of output also varies. In addition, work varies in terms of its input, the level of skills and aptitudes it expresses, the work satisfaction it creates and the pain, toil, and distress it occasions.

GENERAL THEORY OF WORK
(in organizations)

INPUT	CONTROLLABLES:	WORK
A. Manpower Varying interests, aptitudes, goals	1. Security: adequacy for individual needs, demands	1. Productivity, contribution, output--quality and quantity.
B. Management Knowledge, skill, technology	2. Opportunity for investment, development, appreciation in human capital	2. Development and application of highest aptitudes
C. Cultural setting Organization, Economic, political, etc.	3. Organizational orientation: Personal adjustment; identification, participation	3. Satisfaction, fulfillment, self-actualization, enthusiasm.
	4. Limitation of toil, drudgery, unpleasantness	

Figure 4.2   General Model for Work Theory

Traditional theories of work largely ignored these internal variables, assuming that employers prescribed what was to be done and could set such standards as they wished. Modern thinking, however, recognizes interrelationships among these characteristics of work and seeks to increase work satisfaction and reduce disutility, in part as means of maximizing quantity and quality of output.

How are these results to be achieved in working organizations? Early theory concluded that order-giving and penalties for failure were an adequate answer. Later, as industrialization emphasized marketing processes, work theories concluded that basic needs, together with competition in labor markets, would insure efficient, socially satisfactory work.

Modern theory prescribes a more complicated formula. Work is viewed as motivated by several levels of individual needs. Workers have different and changing search levels. Variables in work are regarded as reacting to several important characteristics of working situations. Controls can be classified as including four major areas: (1) the security-complex; (2) opportunity for personal appreciation and development; (3) organizational orientation and adjustment; and (4) limitation of discomfort and disutility.[18]

From this outline, it is apparent that modern work theory proposes no simple model. It sees work, which takes such a large part of all waking hours,

[18] For an interesting test of some parts of current theory see A. Zalesnick, C. R.

as a way of life rather than simply a means of making it possible to live. For this reason, modern theory has sometimes been described as a "whole man" theory. In it, no single key opens the door to ideal working performance. Rather, expert managerial practice seeks to control the whole complex to provide the best possible blend for effective work. Moreover, managers must realize that this blend can be expected to change as personal and social goals change.

Modern theory provides challenging problems for all managers. They can get ahead of their competitors by shaping work in their organizations to the demands of today's workers and citizens. One suggested pattern has been described by Saltonstall.[19]

> Our goal cannot be to provide the kind of empty satisfactions that lead to complacency, laziness, and lack of responsibility for results. Instead, our goal should be to provide a well-organized working environment where physical and mental obstacles to production are removed and where people are challenged to optimum effort because they see this as worthwhile and soul-satisfying for them. This implies aggressive and inspired and sensitive leadership, high standards of performance, and adequate discipline which leads to mutual respect. In such an environment employees see management creating opportunities for them to grow and to utilize their physical and mental skills in meaningful work under good supervision. Employees should be expected and will like to assume responsibility and to participate in the planning and achievement of goals which they understand and helped to formulate.

The third area of controllable factors in the model of work theory relates to the organizational setting in which work takes place. Managers must use the tools of organization and administration to facilitate the development and maintenance of effective working relationships. The next chapter directs attention to working organizations and especially to theory that explains major variations in the effectiveness of working organizations.

SELECTED SUPPLEMENTARY READINGS

Argyris, Chris, "The Individual and Organizational Structure," *Personnel Series No. 168,* American Management Association, 1956.

Barkin, Solomon, "A Trade Unionist Appraises Management Personnel Philosophy," *Harvard Business Review,* Vol. 38, No. 5, pp. 59–64, September, 1950.

Karsh, Bernard, "The Meaning of Work in an Age of Automation," *Bulletin,* University of Illinois Institute of Labor and Industrial Relations, Vol. 55, No. 5, pp. 13, August 1957.

Likert, Rensis, and Stanley E. Seashore, "Increasing Utilization through Better Management of Human Resources," in William Haber and others, *Manpower in the United States,* pp. 23–39, New York: Harper & Brothers, 1954.

Christensen, and F. J. Roethlisberger, *The Motivation, Productivity and Satisfaction of Workers: A Predictive Study,* Boston: Harvard University Graduate School of Business Administration, 1958.
[19] Robert Saltonstall, *Human Relations in Administration,* New York: McGraw-Hill Book Company, Inc., 1959, p. 177.

Litwin, G. L., and J. A. Ciarlo, "Achievement Motivation and Risk-Taking in a Business Setting," Relations Services, General Electric Company, New York 22, March 1961.

McGregor, Douglas, "The Human Side of Enterprise," *Proceedings,* Fifth Anniversary Convocation of the School of Management, Massachusetts Institute of Technology, 1957, pp. 23–30; also, *The Human Side of Enterprise.* New York: McGraw-Hill Book Company, Inc., 1960.

Piel, Gerard, "Consumers of Abundance," *Occasional Paper,* Center for the Study of Democratic Institutions, Santa Barbara, Calif., June 1961.

Toedt, Theodore A., "The Modern Philosophy of Personnel Administration," *Personnel Journal,* Vol. 52, No. 5, pp. 178–180, October 1953.

SHORT CASE PROBLEM 4.1

LeBlanc Separator Company

The Separator Company, located in Chicago, is small and, as firms go, a young firm. With approximately five-hundred employees at the present time, it has grown rapidly. It is owned by two men, both of whom gained their experience as assistant general foreman in the much larger Fairchild Governor Company, which is still the dominant firm in the neighborhood. Many of the firm's employees have been former Fairchild workers.

All production employees of both firms are members of the same local of the International Association of Machinists. Relations between the managers of LeBlanc and the union have been friendly since the firm was started. Negotiations have been fairly easy, for they have followed the pattern established at Fairchild.

In 1958, the employer proposed to the union that the firm engage a consulting firm to make time-and-motion studies of all production jobs. The owners suggested that all could benefit from resulting work simplification. They said there was no implication whatever that employees were not working hard enough, but that it was possible that productivity on some jobs might be increased.

The union's three spokesmen replied that their members were against this innovation. They had talked the proposal over at the most recent union meeting and members were practically unanimous in opposition to the time and work study.

The spokesmen were frank in their explanation of the union's position. They regarded the costs of consultants as an unnecessary expense. They would rather, they said, see the amount involved added to wages. They did not think the studies would benefit anyone. In a friendly discussion with the firm's labor relations director, one of the negotiators said, "If what you want to know is whether we could get out more work, we already know the answer. We can. We could do 20 to 25 per cent more each day without any strain." When asked why the men didn't do that much, the union spokesman replied, "We are already doing enough. We are doing more here on the same job than the fellows are doing at Fairchild. We are working for the same pay [as at Fairchild]. We don't want to throw anybody out of work."

After this negotiating session, the labor relations director called for a meeting of the management negotiating commitee. He reported the siuation and asked for suggestions. Several committee numbers were quite critical of the union position. One argued that the union's position was completely unreasonable. He felt that the decision as to what constitutes a fair day's work on each job is a management responsibility. The meeting adjourned without a decision on next steps.

Problem: Assume that you were a member of the management committee. What philosophy and theory would seem to you to be helpful?

How do you evaluate the union's position? What philosophy—system of values— is evident in it? What work theory? Who is right? Why?

SHORT CASE PROBLEM 4.2

The Airline Pilots

Read the interesting story of "What's Eating the Airline Pilots?" in *Fortune,* April 1959, pp. 122ff.

Problem: How would you explain the attitudes of the pilots in terms of modern theory?

SHORT CASE PROBLEM 4.3

An Acid Test for Modern Work Theory

Charlie Johnson graduated in 1949 from the University of S., School of Management and Administration. He was fourteenth from the top in a class of several hundred. His subsequent business experience has been one of great success and rapid advancement. In 1958, he moved to the Saybrook Manufacturing Company, a steel- and aluminum-fabricating firm with approximately 2100 employees. He was employed as vice-president in charge of production. Six months later he became executive vice-president.

In the spring of 1959, orders declined. Although the Saybrook employees were not involved in the nationwide steel strike, they could not be fully employed, and this low level of activity became worse during the summer months. The sales department reported that orders were scarce and small, that usual customers feared to maintain normal inventories because they believed the country was in for a serious recession. Salesmen were encouraged to offer special inducements in the form of extensions of credit, but sales continued to lag. Several salesmen inquired about the possibility of cutting prices, expressing the opinion that they could get additional business if prices were reduced.

Johnson recognized the situation as a real crisis in his career. He discussed the firm's problem with other executives. Most of them took the position that the industry was and always had been one of feast or famine. They felt that little could be done, that the best policy was to lay off more men and to sit tight until the storm blew over. Johnson was not satisfied with these prospects. He felt a strong obligation, both to stockholders and employees, to find ways of maintaining normal levels of activity. He was convinced that more efficient operations would permit price reductions that could make profitable business.

He was familiar with the details of the manufacturing operations and concluded that only a few technical changes offered possibilities of economies. On the other hand, he felt strongly that few of the employees were working at their top efficiency. He concluded that the best interests of the organization and of the employees would be served by several changes in work rules and by appreciable increases in individual employee productivity.

The man who had suggested Johnson to officials of the firm was its Director of Human Relations, George Paterson. For several years, he had worked on a long-term program that involved improving internal communications, developing consultative supervision, and encouraging employee participation in day-to-day planning. Paterson had majored in psychology as an undergraduate and had taken a master's degree in the same field. He also had attended the same university as Johnson at the same time.

Johnson and Paterson discussed the situation at Saybrook and agreed that improved individual productivity could reduce costs, permit price cuts, and might restore business to something like a normal level. Paterson joined Johnson in preparing several letters to employees in which this development was proposed. When employees appeared to ignore these letters, Johnson advanced an additional proposal. "You agree," he said to Paterson, "that our normal wages and earnings are far above the levels of actual needs for employees. You also argue that wages are only one of many incentives to work. You have developed effective communications and a good deal of employee understanding of management problems. Let's propose that the men agree to a temporary 15 per cent wage cut. That would give us a big advantage in today's market."

"Moreover," Johnson observed, "this will give us a real test of whether this human relations program is worth what it costs."

Problem: Try to put yourself in Paterson's position. How would you reply to this proposal?

SHORT CASE PROBLEM 4.4

*Absence Because of Jail Term**

The background: A worker had to serve a jail term for operating a motor vehicle while intoxicated, and also for child neglect. The company fired him because he had been absent three consecutive days without a justifiable reason. The contract made this just cause for discharge. The union maintained that his incarceration was an adequate reason for not being on the job.

The issue: Was the employee's jail sentence a justifiable excuse for being absent from work?

The company argues: The employee was discharged solely because he picked up three consecutive A.W.O.L.'s The contract defines A.W.O.L. as an employee failure to report his intention to be absent, or an absence without excuse, or an absence without a justifiable reason for being absent. It was this last reason that made the employee subject to discharge. The contract provision that an absence was excusable if for justifiable reason did not have a hard and fast interpretation. It took its color from the circumstances surrounding each individual case. The employee had a very poor attendance record. He had also been absent previously because of being in jail, and the company had warned and excused him. Therefore, this second absence because of jail confinement was not justifiable.

The union argues: Confinement in jail was a justifiable reason for being absent from work. The company had excused him for the identical reason in 1953. It had also excused other jailed employees. When the contract excuses absences for circumstances under which employees cannot reasonably be expected to be present, it does not mean circumstances acceptable to the company. Certainly, an employee in jail cannot be expected to be at work. The company cannot use the employee's previous jail record in 1953 as a basis for discharge since the employee's record is cleared

* *Employee Relations and Arbitration Report,* Vol. 22, No. 7, Pages 5 and 6, October 2, 1961.

if he has not been guilty of an infraction for a period of a year or more. The employee had a justifiable reason for being absent and is entitled to his job back without loss of seniority.

Problem: Use the arbitration case summarized here to check your theories and philosophy in such employment relationships. What are the appropriate responsibilities of employers and employees in such situations? Decide on a reasonable, nontechnical resolution of the issue.

5. Theories of Working Organizations

In industrialized societies, work takes place largely in working organizations that combine the contributions of dozens, hundreds, or thousands of workers. About three-fourths of all labor force members in the United States are members of such work groups or teams. Some organizations are very small, with only a single manager and one or more employees. Most working organizations are small in terms of the usual definitions of "small business." On the other hand, many working organizations include thousands of members.

Working organizations exert powerful influences on work and on the whole way of life of citizens. They set the stage and define the roles of all workers. Organization is a powerful tool of all managers.

This chapter is titled "Theories of Working Organizations." It directs attention to the part played by the organizational setting for work and outlines current thinking about how organizations condition and influence work.

It is apparent that some working organizations are more successful than others, when measured by common yardsticks such as profits, rapid growth and expansion, rising stock values, team member enthusiasm, and service to clients and customers. Some organizations appear to get more and better work from employees than others, to stimulate more effort and output, to engender more enthusiasm, personal interest, and what is frequently called loyalty.

What explains these differences in working organizations? Some of the variation is presumably explained by the differences in the problems they must solve. Some of it may be attributed to their size. Our interest centers on their varying success in providing an effective setting for work. The primary question to be considered is: What variables within working organizations appear to exert greatest influence on their success in facilitating work?

1.0 ORGANIZATION FOR WORK

Managers must continually strive to create a tone, atmosphere and climate that is conducive to work. That is their primary and indispensable contribution. They must provide direction, leadership, and inspiration. They must set the stage for the effective work of others in attaining the organization's mission. Managers must, therefore, plan, create, and maintain effective working organizations.[1]

Organization is thus a major tool of the manager in controlling and manipulating the principal variables associated with excellence in work. Organization theory—like work theory—begins by recognizing that most employees are brought together by an employer to help him do what he wants done. Recruits are not usually consulted in advance about what the organization they are joining should undertake, what its goals should be. They have not had any part, in most cases, in creating the firm or agency, establishing its mission or purpose, or selecting managers and supervisors. They may have little direct, personal concern in the success of the venture. They sell their services, somewhat as they might sell their homes or their cars—except that in joining the organization they have to go with and stay with the services they deliver.

In the minds of some managers, theories of work and organization stop at this point. Managers may conclude that acceptance of the job offer includes an implicit agreement by the employee to become a "doer" rather than a thinker or planner. They have bought the worker; he is theirs for eight hours per day.

Other managers recognize that the services delivered may vary widely in their usefulness and contribution. They recognize the necessity to gain a sanction to lead from those who are led. They want a justification for their leadership assignments that will secure a maximum of contribution from employees.

1.1 "Organization" defined. The term "organization" is commonly used with at least two meanings. In one, an "organization" is regarded *as a* long-term association created and maintained to attain certain objectives and to perform a particular mission. In the other meaning, "organization" refers to *the process* in which such structures are created and maintained. Thus organizing—the process of organization—is used to institute, create, modify, expand, and otherwise maintain the working organization. The process of

---

[1] See Marshall E. Dimock, *A Philosophy of Administration*. New York: Harper & Brothers, 1958, especially chap. 12; also his *Administrative Vitality*, New York: Harper & Brothers, 1959.

organization is often described as the systematic arrangement of parts in a working whole. The *structure* of an organization is the formal expression of that systematic arrangement. The structure prescribes relationships among parts of the organization and, as a result, among the people who are members of the organization.

A working organization is essentially a means of getting and allocating or assigning and keeping help. Organizations begin with goals or objectives, recognized and expressed by the organizers. They seek associates, helpers, to join them in carrying out these missions. For each organization, they recruit co-workers, each to be fitted into the whole, each to be given a role to play, an assignment to perform. All assignments presumably contribute to the total mission.

Like other institutions, organizations may also be described in terms of their *concepts*. The concept indicates the purpose or objective.

1.2 Models for organization theory. How can an organization create and control working conditions that will maximize its success in its mission, that will encourage effective participation by all the people on all levels and divisions in the organization. What major differences in organizations exert most effect on the contributions and cooperation of members? Does the size of the organization encourage or exclude such participation? What other conditions deserve consideration and attention? *Models* help to answer these questions and to express theories of organization.

Organization theory proposes plausible answers to all these questions— answers based on experience, experiment, and research. Theories become guides to action for managers at the same time that they are being rechecked in such action programs. As in work theory, this type of analysis creates models that serve as tentative explanations pending further study and greater understanding. These models focus attention on what are regarded as the most significant and influential variables.[2] Models may suggest *sequential relationships,* in which a given pattern of independent variables is followed or accompanied by particular patterns of the behavior to be understood and controlled. In describing relationships, they imply methods of control. They suggest what appear to be *causal relationships,* or explanations of cause and effect in organizational behavior.

In today's societies, organizations are used to accomplishing a wide range of objectives. Although interest here centers on organization for work, we all recognize that churches, political units, schools, military services use similar organizing processes to create and maintain organizations.

Analyses have sought explanations for the varying effectiveness of organizations. Some investigators have focused attention on the organization of small groups in individual work crews or a single shop. In contrast with this "micro" approach, others have looked for principles of organization in large structures, throwing the spotlight of inquiry on complex bureaucracies with extensive hierarchies of supervisors, managers, and executives. Some

[2] See the discussion of *models* in Chapter 4.

theory has emphasized the personal attributes of leadership in organizations; other theories are impressed with the influence of institutional, traditional, and other cultural variables.[3]

2.0 CHANGING THEORIES OF ORGANIZATION

Theories change, and theories of organization provide excellent examples of this tendency. The influence of theory is, however, persistent—it may hold popular acceptance long after a theory has been seriously questioned or discredited. To understand current organization theory, it is helpful, therefore, to note its background and development. Several fairly distinct stages may be noted. Early theory has been described as autocratic and authoritarian, because it generally emphasized a rather simple delegation of force and power. Later, with the spread of industrialization and democratic political philosophies, theory tended to emphasize the mechanics of organization and the influence of economic factors and of marketing processes. In more recent modifications, theories show increasing concern about the acceptance of authority and leadership by free, mobile workers.

Modern theory has benefited from increasing research in all the behavioral sciences. It reflects, also, the application of mathematical models to human behavior in modern theories of games and decision-making.[4]

2.1 Early authoritarian theory. While the basic questions concerning success in the organization's mission have remained the same, specific questions have changed with changing times. Early theories generally took for granted the propriety and social acceptability of the mission of business units. They assumed the basic right of leaders and managers to define these missions and to direct their organizations. As in early theories of work, theories of organization regarded the masses of people as born to work. They saw the primary problem of organization for work as one of manipulating this "help" to do what leaders wanted done. This was an understandable viewpoint in the late years of the agricultural stage and in the subsequent period of handicraft production. It fitted the historic master-serf relationship as

---

[3] For examples, see Richard N. Adams and Jack J. Preiss, *Human Organization Research*, New York: The Dorsey Press, 1960; E. Wight Bakke and Chris Argyris, *Organizational Structure and Dynamics: A Framework for Theory*, New Haven: Yale University Labor and Management Center, 1954; H. J. Leavitt, "Small Groups in Large Organizations," *Journal of Business*, Vol. 28, No. 1, Universtiy of Chicago, January 1955, pp. 8–17; Mason Haire, "Toward a Theory of Industrial Organization," *General Management Series No. 182*, New York: American Management Association, 1956, pp. 30–38; Edward H. Litchfield, "Notes and General Theory of Administration," *Administration Science Quarterly*, Vol. 1, No. 1, June 1956, pp. 3–29; W. W. Haynes, "Toward a General Approach to Organization Theory," *Journal of the Academy of Management*, Vol. 2, No. 2, August 1959, pp. 75–88.

[4] See Arthur L. Swenson, "Development of Management Organization Theory," *Western Business Review*, Vol. 3, No. 2, University of Denver, May 1959, pp. 26–29; Mason Haire, *Modern Organization Theory*, New York: John Wiley & Sons, Inc., 1959.

well as the pressing organizational problems introduced by preliminary stages in the Industrial Revolution.

The question of how to secure compliance in the behavior of participants in an organization was answered in terms of a rather simple structure in which all authority flowed downward from the proprietor. Since all authority resided in the ruling classes, they could—and indeed were obligated to—order and compel performance. They delegated authority to their appointed subordinates. They could enforce severe penalties against any who refused to accept orders or to perform at the level of standards set by leaders.

To attain more than a crude application of the brute force of manpower, early theory noted some differences in aptitudes among workers and the advantages to be gained from specialization of functions. This process, in which the total mission of the organization is divided into parts, is said to have been carefully described and evaluated by the Chinese as early as 1644 and was the subject of a notable essay by Charles Babbage in 1832.

Specialization created problems of coordination, for performance in the specialized processes must be controlled to fit the pace of the total organization. The solution to that problem was coordination through authoritarian delegation, in which some authority was granted by top leaders to those who were assigned leadership and control in each specialized section and echelon or level of the organization.

These rudiments of organization theory suggested a structure for employment that created a *chain of command*. They raised questions about relationships with subordinates and about what is usually called the *span of control*. Fayol, Sheldon, and others have described this delegation theory. Largely by reference to military organization, these students of organization popularized the familiar view of the employment structure as a hierarchy of workers, supervisors, and managers, gradually converging with the leader at the top of a pyramid. They described this structure as a means of delegating authority from the top downward through the chain of command to accomplish the mission of the organization. They noted the formal scalar status system in which status in these structures was defined by the level of delegated authority or proximity to the leader.[5]

As viewed by most of those who studied early industrial relations systems, most large-scale employment assumed a fairly simple, authoritarian theory of organization. Employment structures were also simple, although larger organizations might require some specialization and layering. The typical structure could be illustrated by a relatively low pyramid. Status and authority assignments were dictated by the powerful owner employer, who delegated throughout his chain of command. Work theory, noted in the preceding chapter, emphasized the necessity for rigorous and unquestioning acceptance of the employer's instructions. Organization theory emphasized the dominant

---

[5] See, for example, Henri Fayol, *Industrial and General Administration*, London: Sir Isaac Pitman & Sons, Ltd., 1930, pp. 43ff. Oliver Sheldon, *The Philosophy of Management*, London: Sir Isaac Pitman & Sons, Ltd., 1923, pp. 119ff.

influence of order-giving managers and assistants, who told workers what to do and how to do it and compelled performance by imposing severe penalties for failure to satisfy the employer or his assistants. Organizational success depended on getting enough workers, dividing them to create whatever specialized parts were required, telling them what to do and enforcing these orders. Some early theories considered the comparative advantages of rewards and penalties in this process, but most thinking took power, force, and penalties for granted.

2.2 Economic and mechanistic modifications. Increasing industrialization introduced changes and suggested modifications in the early theories of organization. The rapid expansion of industrialization throughout the 18th and 19th centuries created a new class of wealthy traders and industrialists. They appeared as residual holders and sources of authority in the firms, partnerships, and stock companies that dominated this expansion. The organizations they led undertook complicated and varied missions in which important advantages appeared attainable through extensive specialization.

Continued specialization, however, created more complex problems of coordination. Recruitment became more complicated, as the free and more mobile employees of industrialized societies had to be brought together for the growing variety of occupations.

Industrialization introduced masses of wage earners and created competition for their services. Manpower, accustomed to the traditions of agricultural workers, had to be committed to new careers as employees. Industrialization created no inclusive employer associations comparable to the guilds.

Ideas of compensation appropriate to fairly simple handicraft operations were inadequate in early industrialized societies. More complicated wage structures developed as managers sought to entice employees into jobs that were new, different, and frequently more routine or otherwise unattractive. Industrialization increased the importance of wages and differentials in wages as factors in recruitment and in retaining members of work forces.

Emergence and expansion of unions added further complications. Their role was not simple. They protested the demands of industrial employers that workers accommodate themselves to the new machines. Unions frequently protested the displacement of workers by machines. Early union spokesmen frequently talked of revolution and of future socialistic and classless societies.

Industrialization made its early impact in societies dominated by a laissez-faire political philosophy. That viewpoint emphasized the virtue of allowing natural processes to take their course. Within industrial organizations, the most obvious forces were economic. Capitalists invested to gain financial returns. Employees joined or left organizations to increase their earnings. Owners and managers secured and retained the workers they needed through their wage offers.

This viewpoint suggested a theory of organization that linked organizational success to compliance with "natural laws" such as those of supply and demand. The most successful organizations, in this view, were those that facilitated the operation of such natural processes. This approach has been described as *mechanistic,* since it emphasizes the force of basic natural processes that manipulate people in organizations.

The mechanistic theory was supported by the economic philosophy in which industrialization developed. It was further advanced by the scientific-management movement that appeared in the late 19th and early 20th century. Economists had suggested that the compensation of workers was set by natural market forces that reflected the likely contribution of each type of labor. Compensation was thus related to and explainable in terms of supplies of workers and demands for their services. The latter represented manager's estimates of worker's contributions. Further, in this view, varying wages could insure maximum worker performance—in terms of organizational objectives—by wage payment plans that sharply emphasized payment for results. Illustrative of this thinking are the early wage incentive, bonus, and premium plans advanced by Halsey, Rowan, Emerson, Gilbreth, Gantt, and others. (See Chapter 21.)

This economic relationship could and should, according to the *laissez-faire* view, modify earlier status assignments and establish a system based on earnings. Wage and salary levels would identify similar levels of status within and outside working organizations.

Frederick W. Taylor's contribution of what he described as *functional management* gave further impetus to this market-oriented, mechanistic viewpoint. Taylor proposed further specialization in supervision and management with added restrictions on the thinking of subordinates. He suggested superimposing a third dimension of functional management on the established pyramid, with more complicated delegation based on technical competence in management. Organizational relationhips were describable in principles that could become the basis for an almost mechanical control of the organization.

In mechanistic theories of organization, dominated by natural laws, the dependent variable was the attainment of the organizational mission. Independent variables included the mechanistic market forces of labor supplies and demands, the basic authority system imposed by ownership and delegation, and a status system that combined delegated authority and earnings as major factors.

Employee reactions to these theories and associated practices were not uniform. In many situations, both functionalization and incentive wage programs, for example, appeared to be at least temporarily effective in stimulating improved performance. In others, employees became highly critical of these programs. Mechanistic analysis tended to identify unions as unnecessary at best and more often as barriers to effective administration. To many, unions appeared to interfere with management. Their participation in the labor-marketing process tended to prevent its simple operation and its accurate appraisal of worker contributions, according to this analysis.

Union leaders and members concluded that this mechanistic approach represented a threat to the labor movement as well as a hazard to their employment and earnings. In the historic Hoxie investigation of union attitudes toward scientific management, leaders criticized the separation of "brain and brawn," in which decision-making was largely reserved for supervisors and managers. Many workers interpreted Taylor's suggestion of economizing by *scientific management* as evidence that jobs would be scarcer and wages lower if practice were based on these marketing, mechanistic theories of organization.

2.3 Humanitarian and behavioral contributions. Earlier theories could scarcely be expected to fit the social and political philosophies of modern society. Two World Wars expressed growing popular resentment toward political authoritarianism. Growing interest in political democracy created questions about authority, status and participation in working organizations. Popular discussions raised the question whether free men and women could be first class citizens in the community while they were second class citizens in their work.

Especially since World War II, the free nations have found themselves in direct competition with Russia and Russian satellites in speeding the trend toward industrialization and political independence in the less-developed nations. Missions have visited the far corners to explain our system of employment relationships. They have frequently encountered the charge that our political democracy is not paralleled by a similar philosophy in industry and that we have neglected human values in the struggle for competitive advantage.

Meanwhile, growing separation of ownership and management, paralleling the growth of corporations, has reduced the earlier acceptance of proprietary authority. Now, managers, in many modern employment structures, hold a position only a little different from that of non-managerial employees. The old viewpoints that made ownership and management the same and gave managers a mandate to make all rules and decisions no longer apply.

Meanwhile, also, the education and sophistication of employees have increased, as noted in Chapter 3; moreover, modern societies have become increasingly concerned about the interests of individual workers. The spread of democracy and continuing struggles between democracies and totalitarian states have re-emphasized the high value democratic societies place on the dignity of the individual citizen. The rise of Communism and its competition for support by the peoples of less-developed nations have forced free nations to re-evaluate their attitudes toward economic security and job satisfaction. Communist critics of what is widely described as the American System have argued that it has been economically efficient but ignores human values. They charge that it is unconcerned about the "little people." Such criticism has unquestionably encouraged advances in social security, public intervention in employment relationships and wide public interest in human values in working relationships.

3.0 MODERN ORGANIZATION THEORY

Most current thinking about organizations of free citizens emphasizes the theme that organizational behavior is largely shaped by the attitudes with which an organization's people regard and treat each other. Theories point to the importance of attitudes between individual worker and manager in day-to-day contacts.

3.1 Human relations. The emphasis on attitudes and reactions has encouraged numerous studies of small group behavior, frequently described as *human relations* or as *group dynamics*. These studies have indicated the inadequacy of earlier theory, which emphasized only economic motivation and assumed that employer and employee interests coincide and that both groups act in a relatively simple but rational manner to maximize their rewards. A growing literature, highlighted by the widely described Western Electric or Haythorne Studies of the 1930's, has reported on these investigations. Leadership in this approach may be traced to Elton Mayo, Kurt Levin, their followers, and the British Tavistock Institute of Human Relations.[6]

3.2 Leadership in employment. Another viewpoint in recent thinking has been impressed with the dominating influence of successful leadership. In its simplest form, it has used what is often described as a *trait approach,* assuming that major clues to organizational behavior are to be found in the distinctive personal traits of leaders. More sophisticated analysis has recognized the difficulties in generalizing about leadership qualities in organizations that vary so widely in size and in the problems they face from time to time. It proposes, by typing the changing circumstances and problems of organizations, to define effective combinations of leadership attributes and particular situations and problems. A simplified illustration from political life notes that a nation at war requires military leaders, while the same nation in peace needs statesmen as leaders.[7]

These newer insights into the nature of organizations have been encouraged by the growing volume of theory and research in the behavioral sciences. The frames of reference of psychology, economics, social psychology,

---

[6] See F. J. Roethlisberger and W. J. Dickson, *Management and the Worker,* 1939, and *Management and Morale,* 1941, both published by Harvard University Press at Cambridge, Mass.; E. M. Hugh-Jones, *Human Relations and Modern Management,* Amsterdam: North-Holland Publishing Company, 1958; William G. Scott, "Modern Human Relations in Perspective," *Personnel Administration,* Vol. 22, No. 6, November-December 1959, p. 13; William Foote Whyte, *Man and Organization,* Homewood, Ill.: Richard D. Irwin, Inc., 1959; William N. Knowles, "Human Relations in Industry: Research and Concepts," *California Management Review,* Vol. 1, No. 1, Fall 1958, pp. 87–105; "Human Relations: Where Do We Stand Today?" *Management Record,* Vol. 21, No. 3, March 1959, pp. 78–84.

[7] Excellent examples of this approach are provided by leadership studies undertaken at Ohio State University. For a summary, see Carroll L. Shartle, *Executive Performance and Leadership,* Englewood Cliffs, N.J.: Prentice-Hall, Inc., 1956; also Carroll L. Shartle, "Top Management Organization and Related Areas," *Personnel Psychology,* Vol. 12, No. 1, Spring 1959, pp. 29–48. The group at Ohio State University has also developed scales for measuring the extent of assigned responsibility, authority, and delegation. (RAD scales.)

sociology, political science and allied social disciplines have contributed significant clues for interpreting working behavior. Today's analysis seeks to integrate, for example, modern political theories of bureaucracies with sociological and sociometric studies of status. It seeks explanations that cross-cut the social sciences and relate organizational effectiveness to such diverse variables as economic rewards and success, managerial policy and practice, in-plant communication, employee and manager attitudes, and informal as well as formal organization structures.[8]

3.3   Organization variables. The range and variety of approaches in recent years have tended to prevent emergence of any simple model of organization theory with universal acceptance. It is possible, however, to identify the principal types of factors or variables that are now widely believed to exert major influence on behavior in working organizations. A sort

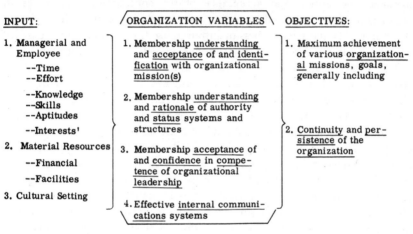

INPUT:

1. Managerial and
   Employee

   --Time
   --Effort

   --Knowledge
   --Skills
   --Aptitudes
   --Interests'

2. Material Resources

   --Financial

   --Facilities

3. Cultural Setting

ORGANIZATION VARIABLES

1. Membership understanding
   and acceptance of and identification with organizational
   mission(s)

2. Membership understanding
   and rationale of authority
   and status systems and
   structures

3. Membership acceptance of
   and confidence in competence of organizational
   leadership

4. Effective internal communications systems

OBJECTIVES:

1. Maximum achievement
   of various organizational missions, goals,
   generally including

2. Continuity and per-
   sistence of the
   organization

Figure 5.1   General Model for Organization Theory

of generalized model can be constructed, as shown in Figure 5.1. The dependent variables remain much the same: (1) the degree of success or effectiveness in attaining and carrying out the mission of the organization

[8] See Chris Argyris, *Personality and Organization,* New York: Harper & Brothers, 1957; also his "The Organization: What Makes it Healthy?" *Harvard Business Review,* November-December, 1958, Vol. 36, No. 6, pp. 107–116; W. C. Schutz, *FIRO: A Three-Dimensional Theory of Interpersonal Behavior.* New York: Holt, Rinehart & Winston, Inc., 1958; James G. March and Herbert A. Simon, *Organizations,* Pittsburgh: Graduate School of Industrial Administration Carnegie Institute of Technology, 1958; Talcott Parsons, "Suggestions for a Sociological Approach to the Theory of Organizations," *Administrative Science Quarterly,* Vol. 1, Nos. 1 and 2, June and September 1956, pp. 63–85 and 225–239; R. V. Presthus, "Toward a Theory of Organizational Behavior," *Administrative Science Quarterly,* Vol. 3, No. 1, June 1958, pp. 48–72; Daniel J. Levinson, "Role, Personality and Social Structure in the Organizational Setting," *Journal of Abnormal and Social Psychology,* Vol. 58, No. 2, March 1959, pp. 170–181; for a bibliography, see Paul Wasserman, *Measurement and Evaluation of Organizational Performance,* Ithaca, N.Y.: Cornell University, Graduate School of Business and Public Administration, 1959.

and (2) the ability of the organization to maintain and perpetuate itself.

It is important to bear in mind the normally complex nature of these goals.[9] Equally important is the cultural setting in which the working organization exists and operates. Political and social traditions must be recognized as influential with respect to the functioning of all organizations. Educational levels and sophistication of employees and managers, their economic aspirations, and their political ideals inevitably condition conceptions of missions and goals.

The list that follows identifies four major types of variables that influence organizational success. They are not mutually exclusive. Neither are they simple nor atomistic. Some of them may be readily subdivided, and some theorists place greater emphasis on particular sub-divisions than on others.

The four major types of influencing variables may be described as (1) members' perception and acceptance of the concept and mission of the organization; (2) their understanding and acceptance of authority and status structures; (3) the effectiveness of intraorganizational communications; and (4) the quality and competence (skill and knowledge) of leadership.

3.4 Concept and mission. Member understanding of the objectives and goals of an organization appears to influence member participation and effectiveness. Generally, these objectives must be socially acceptable and must impress workers as worthwhile and appropriate to gain employee enthusiasm and identification with the whole. They must be reasonably consistent with the personal goals of employees, so that the two can be integrated. Some hypotheses suggest that employees must make the mission of the organization their mission and that attitudes of loyalty to the organization are desirable if not essential. Many current practitioners in management also assume that attitudes indicating enthusiasm for supervisors, managers, and for related managerial policies and practices—widely described as "high morale"—are important correlates of high levels of production.

Evidence to support all these hypotheses is by no means conclusive. While a degree of acceptance of the organizational mission appears essential, the argument for "loyalty" is frequently questioned. Again, while several studies of employee morale find friendly identification with the smaller work group or crew to be positively correlated with relatively high output, no general rule appears to relate over-all synthetic morale as a significant variable.[10] At the same time, the mission of the organization must represent a reasonable reconciliation and combination of individual and group goals. The general position here—that team-members must view the successful attainment of their personal objectives as to some degree dependent on the success of organizational efforts—has wide acceptance. This is an important facet of

---

[9] See Philip Selznick, *Leadership in Administration; a Sociological Interpretation,* Evanston, Illinois: Row, Peterson and Company, 1957, p. 134.

[10] See Arthur Brayfield and Walter H. Crockett, "Employee Attitudes and Employee Performance," *Psychological Bulletin,* Vol. 52, No. 5, 1955, pp. 396-424; Frederick Herzberg, *et al., Job Attitudes: Review of Research and Opinion,* Pittsburgh: Psychological Service of Pittsburgh, 1957, esp. chaps. 3, 4.

identification. It is by no means limited to economic objectives. On the contrary, acceptance of organizational goals is positively related to the complex of personal objectives, including self-expression and continuing development. In some usage, this end is described as *self-actualization*.

Some critics conclude that demands for employee loyalty may seriously impair effective teamwork. Peter Drucker argues that employment should not be expected to develop a pervasive loyalty to the job and employer:[11]

> This attempt to gain total loyalty . . . is not only not compatible with the dignity of man, but it is not possible to believe that the dignity of man can or should be realized totally in a partial institution.

The concept of organizational goals is much broader than the earlier view that made profits the only significant objective. Advocates of what has sometimes been described as a "trusteeship" view have indicated that the mission of business organizations must include a high regard for the public interest. That view is opposed by critics who see no basic reason for any goal except profit.[12]

Modern organization theory recognizes that the purposes, goals, or missions of organization are not simple. A major contribution in understanding business organizations is this recognition of their multiple and varying goals. This view of the missions of business firms replaces the earlier concentration on the maximization of profits as the constant and perhaps sole objective in such organizations.

The earlier viewpoint still has wide acceptance. Many critics of modern theory argue that maximizing profits is always the basic objective and the source of all others. They conclude that other missions are actually steps toward maximizing profits. Moreover, they tend to ignore these other goals as explanations of decision-making and to assume that maximizing profits is the immediate clue to each day-to-day decision.

A considerable volume of recent research has evidenced the importance of these other objectives in managerial decisions. It appears that priorities in a business organization's objectives change from time to time. March notes that, at one time, a firm may give top priority to an increase in profits. At another, it may emphasize the goal of gaining a larger share of some particular market. At still another, it may place heavy emphasis on product research or consumer complaints. The firm makes and changes its commitments. Seybold reported a discussion of business objectives by a panel representing executives from several nations. They listed profit making, providing employment, performing services, fulfilling social obligations, promoting national interests and advancing an understanding of democracy as possible

[11] Peter F. Drucker, "Human Relations: How Far Do We Have to Go?" in "Human Relations: Where Do We Stand Today?", *Management Record,* National Industrial Conference Board, Vol. 21, No. 3, March 1959, pp. 80–82.

[12] See T. Levitt, "Dangers of Social Responsibility," *Harvard Business Review,* Vol. 36, No. 5, September-October 1958, pp. 41–50.

primary objectives of private business.[13] Changing commitments not only set the pattern or framework for decision making; they also set the bench marks or criteria by which success of business and of individual managers is evaluated.

3.5 Authority, responsibility and status. Modern theory places a high priority on the rationale of authority and status structures in an organization. Essential questions might be stated as follows: Do the allocations of authority and status make sense to members of the organization? Are authority and status distributed in a rational manner?

"Of course, it's just one man's opinion—but it's mine and I run this company! "

Figure 5.2 One Man's Opinion

Such questions evidence dissatisfaction with earlier thinking that related authority rather simply and directly to ownership and created status systems on the basis of delegated authority and earnings. In current analysis, the exercise of authority is regarded as a sensitive variable. Authoritarian managerial personalities, identified by attitudes that see all cooperators except top managers as order-takers, may be relatively ineffective leaders, as compared with those who exhibit a high sensitivity to others and an inclination to consult and discuss. Current theory also regards attitudes of managerial paternalism as generally objectionable. It suggests that the most appropriate viewpoint toward employees sees them as complete and whole people, generally equal to managers in basic elements of character and personality and in competence within their specialties. It proposes to relate responsibility to opportunity to participate, expecting employees to assume added responsibilities in the organization as they are granted opportunity.

Concern about the basis and nature of authority and the manner in which it is assigned is apparent. At the heart of current thinking is a questioning of the influence of *scalar authority*—that dictated simply by rank, position, and title. Modern theory concludes that such scalar authority has much less influence on the members of modern work groups than may have been typical in earlier periods. Other approaches offer greater promise.[14]

[13] James G. March, "Business Decision Making," *Industrial Research,* Reprint No. 47, Graduate School of Industrial Administration, Carnegie Institute of Technology, Spring 1959; Geneva Seybold, "Why Are We in Business?" *Management Record,* Vol. 23, No. 12, December 1961, pp. 2–7.

[14] For an interesting discussion, see F. Alexander Magoun, Chap. 5, "Misconceptions of Cooperation," in his *Cooperation and Conflict in Industry,* New York: Harper & Brothers, 1960.

Among common suggestions for constructive working relationships are those that propose a minimum of autocratic ordering and a maximum of freedom for thought and action by associates. Many students have noted that simple expressions of authority by managers tend to evoke resistance in employee reactions. Kline and Martin have provided an excellent summary of this viewpoint. They note that the simple delegation of authority creates a relationship in which subordinates must maintain the favor and support of bosses and are likely to do so by imitating their superiors. They conclude that[15]

> In these circumstances individual potentials for large numbers of people are gradually reduced to a low level. . . . Where creativity and innovation would be useful to both superior and subordinate, defensiveness and resistance are all too often the pattern of subordinate reaction. To meet resistance, superior authority brings more power to bear, which in turn causes more resistance—a well-known pattern. And so we have the cult of authority and control.
>
> To break out of this vicious circle, let us . . . talk not about delegating authority to act, but about granting freedom to act.

General Wood, former president of Sears Roebuck and Company, became concerned about this type of comparison many years ago. Emmet and Jeuck quote him as saying:[16]

> We complain about government in business; we stress the advantages of the free enterprise system, we complain about the totalitarian state, but in our industrial organization, in our striving for efficiency we have created more or less of a totalitarian system in industry. The problem of retaining our efficiency and discipline in these large organizations and yet allowing our people to express themselves, to exercise initiative and to have some voice in the affairs of the organization is the greatest problem for large industrial organizations to solve.[17]

At the same time, modern theory assumes that the basis for authority and status in working organizations must be consistent and compatible with the cultural setting. Workers may be quite uncooperative if they are first-class citizens in the community and second- or third-class in their jobs. An established status and authority system in business may become outdated and inappropriate. Many business organizations may have failed to adjust to changes in political institutions and traditions. The worker may find himself something of an alien in his job. Accustomed to freedom and democracy in politics, he finds himself closely restricted and required to conform where he works.

One sound basis for assignments of authority is specialized competence.

[15] Bennett E. Kline and Norman H. Martin, "Freedom, Authority and Decentralization," *Harvard Business Review*, Vol. 36, No. 3, May-June 1958, pp. 69–75. Quote from p. 71.

[16] General Robert E. Wood, quoted in Boris Emmet and John E. Jeuck, *Catalogues and Counters: A History of Sears Roebuck and Company,* Chicago: University of Chicago Press, 1950, p. 371.

[17] For journalistic impressions in this area, see Alan Harrington, *Life in the Crystal Palace,* New York: Alfred A. Knopf, Inc., 1959; Cameron Hawley, *Executive Suite,* Boston: Ballantine Books, 1953; William H. Whyte, Jr., *The Organization Man,* New York: Simon and Schuster, Inc., 1956.

This general rule applies to managers, for whom the emphasis is on specialized competence in management. It assumes that management is itself a distinctive and highly skilled occupation, not simply the representation and personification of ownership, a means by which the proprietor of a business tells employees what he wants and what to do.

Problems arise when members of an organization question the special competence of their managers. Employees may conclude that they are more competent for some managerial decisions than are their supervisors and leaders. (What are widely regarded by managers as union onslaughts in the area of management prerogatives may express employee questions about the competence of management. Continuing expansion in the range of subjects on which unions seek to bargain suggests a similar questioning.[18])

Status systems as well as authority systems appear as important considerations in modern theory. The rationale and logic of both are regarded as influencing member commitment and identification and, in turn, the effectiveness of the organization.

3.6   Internal communications. Organizational effectiveness may be influenced by communication facilities, channels and structures (see Chapter 24). Disgruntled, uncooperative employees often complain that they are left out and never get the word. Three principal dimensions of communication— downward, upward and horizontal—have received wide attention. Formal media, channels and processes may be less significant than informal patterns. Other variables include the quality of transmissions, barriers imposed by layers of supervision, and the listening attitudes of the parties—their receptivity to incoming transmissions.

The tradition that organizational information is a part of the private property of the employer may encourage managers to withhold information that employees want and need if they are to feel themselves a part of the organization. Those who make up each layer of management may hold back information as a means of gaining prestige and status. Employees may limit communications by attitudes that make them unreceptive. They may pay as little attention as possible to communications directed to them. They may discredit information released by managerial sources.

Modern organization theory places great emphasis on internal communications as the flux that binds the organization together and permits it to act as a unit. Internal communication may modify the information on which major decisions are made and thus shape all activities of the organization. The communication process may introduce bias and distortion in the information on which decisions are based. Those who gather and prepare and transmit information exercise what has been called "selective perception." A salesminded source of information may see every problem as a sales problem. Other information sources may see most problems as involving engineering,

[18] See Milton Derber, W. Ellison Chalmers, and Ross Stagner, "Collective Bargaining and Management Functions: An Empirical Study," *Journal of Business,* University of Chicago, Vol. 31, No. 2, April 1958, pp. 107–120.

or finance, or public relations. Additional bias or error may be introduced by the necessity to condense and interpret information before it is communicated.

3.7 Competence of leadership. Reference has been made to competence as a basis for authority and status systems. The quality of management and supervision is widely regarded as one of the most important variables in the success of working organizations. Much of the current interest in supervisory training and management or executive development is an expression of this concern.

Managerial skill and competence are not readily defined or measured. They are obviously a complex rather than a simple ingredient in the formula for successful organizations. Some early observers regarded profits as a criterion and measure of these qualities. In recent years, analysis has sought to identify and measure several elements in specialized managerial competence. Katz, Riegel, and others have developed lists of managerial skills.[19]

Mayo and his followers suggest that the crucial element in such competence is the human relations skill of managers.[20] Likert and others have reported findings that point to the employee-oriented manager as more effective than his production-centered counterpart. Studies have suggested that the ability to manage in a consultative manner, enlisting a high degree of employee participation, is an important clue to managerial competence.

Today's employees show a significant sensitivity to current symbols of specialized competence—degrees, diplomas, and certificates, for example. The older status symbols, including white collars and salary levels, appear to have lost much of their historic charm and impact. More sophisticated employees are much less impressed than were the workers of a generation past.[21]

Leadership requirements of working organizations differ: all organizations do not require the same types of leaders. Selznick, for example, concludes that "when choices and decisions can be made on the basis of known and objective technical criteria, the engineer rather than the leader is called for."[22]

Whatever the type of leader, however, he must be competent or he must create the *impression* of competence. Those who are to take directions from him cannot see their interests as adequately protected and advanced if they regard him as less than competent.[23]

---

[19] See Robert L. Katz, "Skills of an Effective Administrator," *Harvard Business Review*, Vol. 33, No. 1, January-February 1955, pp. 33–42; Roger M. Bellows, *Creative Leadership*, Englewood Cliffs, N.J.: Prentice-Hall, Inc., 1960, chap. 19.

[20] See Robert Tannenbaum, Irving R. Weschler, and Fred Massarik, *Leadership and Organization*, New York: McGraw-Hill Book Company, Inc., 1961.

[21] See Lyman W. Porter, "Differential Self-Perceptions of Management Personnel and Line Workers," *Journal of Applied Psychology*, Vol. 42, 1958, pp. 105–108.

[22] Philip Selznick, *Leadership in Administration: A Sociological Interpretation*, Evanston, Ill.: Row, Peterson and Company, 1957, p. 137.

[23] See Warren G. Bennis, "Revisionist Theory of Leadership," *Harvard Business Review*, Vol. 39, No. 1, January-February 1961, pp. 26ff.

Modern theory views leadership as a function that can be shared widely. The earlier idea of short-range delegation to a few is expanded so that leadership functions are shared by many. In this view, decisions should be influenced by all those who are competent and can be expected, on that account, to have worthwhile opinions on the question. The employee, by participating, develops a place in leadership and a responsibility for results.[24]

In his *New Patterns of Management,* Likert explains what he describes as the *newer theory* of management. Like McGregor's *Theory Y,* Likert's rationale emphasizes many of the considerations discussed in preceding pages. He notes that the newer theory recognizes a complex rather than a simple work theory, in which management appeals to workers' curiosity, creativity, and sense of personal worth and importance as well as desires for security and economic improvement. Managerial effectiveness is related to the subordinate's feeling that working experience is *supportive* rather than threatening to personal goals. It gains from thinking of each individual's perception of working relationships and from insuring that workers are participative members of one or more work groups. It relates the adequacy of supervision to the influence supervisors can exert on their superiors. It tries to insure that the organization's goals are harmonious with needs and desires of members. It maintains management practices and an organizational reward system that appeals to and motivates members.[25]

4.0 SUMMARY

Organization is a tool of management. It is a device through which people pool their skills and efforts to attain common objectives. Most workers today work in organizations, many of them very large. This chapter has considered theories about the effectiveness of working organizations.

Early theory was comparatively simple. Organizations were regarded essentially as means of delegating authority from owners and proprietors to assistants and rank and file workers. They were order-giving structures, with built-in powers of enforcement.

Modern theory is much more complicated. It recognizes the influence of social and political changes in world societies and the growing levels of worker knowledge and sophistication. Analysis identifies several types of factors that appear influential in today's working organizations. A generalized model can be pictured as in Figure 5.1.

This model suggests many of the problems with which modern management is concerned. It notes the importance of mission, of authority and status systems, and of intra-organizational communications and leadership.

[24] See, however, Erwin Schoenfeld, "Authoritarian Management: A Reviving Concept," *Personnel,* Vol. 36, No. 1, January-February 1959, pp. 21–24.
[25] Rensis Likert, *New Patterns of Management,* New York: McGraw-Hill Book Company, 1961, especially chap. 8.

Keeping abreast of changing theory is, in itself, a challenging responsibility for managers. Making applications and tests of new theory is a further responsibility. Tomorrow's managers must probably be specialists in management theory as well as management practice.

How are theories of organizational adequacy used in creating and administering effective working organizations? The next chapter provides part of the answer by noting the more common structural features of modern working organizations.

SELECTED SUPPLEMENTARY READINGS

Argyris, Chris, *Personality and Organization*. New York: Harper & Brothers, 1957; also "The Organization: What Makes it Healthy?" *Harvard Business Review*, Vol. 36, No. 6, pp. 107–116, November-December 1958.

Baritz, Loren, *The Servants of Power*. Middletown, Connecticut: Wesleyan University Press, 1960.

Comfrey, A. L., John M. Pfiffner, and Helen P. Beem, "Factors Affecting Organizational Effectiveness," *Personnel Psychology*, Vol. 6, No. 1, pp. 65–79, Spring 1953.

Griffiths, Daniel E., *Administrative Theory*. New York: Appleton-Century-Crofts, 1959.

Guest, Robert H., *Organization Change: The Effect of Successful Leadership*, Homewood, Ill.: The Dorsey Press, Inc., 1962.

Kline, Bennett E., and Norman H. Martin, "Freedom, Authority and Decentralization," *Harvard Business Review*, Vol. 36, No. 3, pp. 69–75, May-June 1958.

Likert, Rensis, *New Patterns of Management*, Chap. 8, New York: McGraw-Hill Book Company, Inc., 1961.

Presthus, R. V., "Toward a Theory of Organizational Behavior," *Administrative Science Quarterly*, Vol. 3, No. 1, pp. 48–72, June 1958.

Shartle, Carroll L., "Top Management Organization and Related Areas," *Personnel Psychology*, Vol. 12, No. 1, pp. 29–48, Spring 1959.

Swenson, Arthur L., "Development of Management Organization Theory," *Western Business Review*, Vol. 3, No. 2, pp. 26–29, May 1959.

Wilson, Charles Z., "Organization Theory: A Survey of Three Views," *Quarterly Review of Economics and Business*, Vol. 1, No. 3, pp. 53–65, August 1961.

SHORT CASE PROBLEM 5.1

Sears of Hexel

"Now here is some real honest advice for you young fellows. This is the kind of advice you don't usually get." Sam Sears, executive vice-president of Hexel, Inc. was speaking to the 24 new management and engineering recruits recently employed and gathered together for an orientation conference.

"No matter how you feel about such matters," Sears continued, "in this outfit, you will be known by the company you keep. If you want to keep moving to the top, you can never afford to live and play and associate with the wrong people. Hexel is not a bit different from other business in this respect, but most others won't be honest about it. They will give you a lot of guff about human relations and fraternizing and all being one big family, but they do exactly the same as we do. Here is an article in one of our leading magazines. It tells about a study they have made of this sort of thing. It says we all do it.

"Ten years from now, you'll tell me that this was the best advice you ever got. Here are a few specific pointers for you.

"First, don't try to be more than casually friendly with anybody you are supervising. And don't try to act friendly on the job or outside either. If you do, you can't crack down on them when they need it. You won't have the nerve to let the poor ones go when you should, either. You'll go soft, and a soft manager is as useless as a soft medic. You notice doctors learned a hundred years ago that they can't handle their own families.

"Second, whenever you get promoted, you and your wife move right in and find new friends at your new level. And tell friend wife to scratch out all the old ones if she wants to do her part. Remember, you'll be judged by the friends you keep.

"Third, watch out for invitations to the homes of men working for you. Don't accept them if you can possibly get out of it. You can always be going out of town or having guests or having another engagement. Be polite, but don't slip on this one. If you get caught, don't return the invitation. Have the folks in sometime when you are giving a big open house.

"Fourth, make a real effort to cultivate friends in the top brass. Believe me, a fellow in the front office appreciates it when one of you young men drop by to give him the scoop. The fellows in between are your stepping stones to the top. Remember that it's never what you know in business that counts; it's who you know. It's really, in my opinion, who you know and who you have forgotten that gets you places in our kind of system.

"Now look. I know this sounds hypocritical. It is. But that's the way human beings are. And business men are just as human as the next fellow."

Problem: After this session, there were very few questions from the new recruits. They seemed deeply impressed. In the corridor, one of them asked another: "Do you figure he gave last year's gang the same lecture?" Be prepared to discuss (1) the probable effect of this talk on the recruits and (2) the reliability of the statement.

SHORT CASE PROBLEM 5.2

Mediocrity of the Masses

In 1961, the Slippery Rock Petroleum Company was in what were regarded as final stages of negotiating the purchase of Piute Minerals Co. Piute had been successful in the petroleum industry and had a number of continuing contracts for supplying high octane fuel for military installations in the Rocky Mountain area. Slippery Rock considered Piute a valuable acquisition; stock holders of Piute were believed to favor the merger.

Slippery Rock has followed the pattern of numerous large corporate enterprises in maintaining a special Organization Planning Division, which has played an important part in the rapidly expanding firm and has recommended many of the arrangements instituted by Slippery Rock in its earlier acquisitions of smaller properties. Members of this staff division have enjoyed wide recognition in Slippery Rock, despite the fact that staff members generally describe it as the "reorganization" rather than the planning unit. Tod Mahoney is chief of the division.

Members of the Organization Planning Division had been working with the executive vice president, Steve Heneman, of Piute in discussing means of integrating the smaller firm. (Slippery Rock now includes approximately 7,000 employees; Piute is much smaller, with a total of about 1,800.) After a series of sessions at Slippery Rock's headquarters in Houston, Texas, three members of the staff division had been meeting with the officers of Piute in their central offices in Beaver River, Montana.

In the Montana discussions a serious controversy developed. The Piute officials, with Heneman as their spokesman, charged that Slippery Rock's organization planning was old fashioned and outdated. Arrangements should permit Piute to run its own show. Mahoney argued that such a position was silly, that Slippery Rock had always believed in extensive decentralization and proposed to impose a minimum of regimentation on the subsidiary. Mahoney did insist on the general supervision of the central or corporate staff divisions in Houston. He further proposed that Slippery Rock incorporate its established system of bonuses for line managers and time studies and incentive wage or premium pay for hourly rated employees in the refinery.

Heneman insisted that Piute's success had been in part attributable to the loose reins with which managers and employes were directed. He charged that Mahoney proposed "recentralization" instead of decentralization, with a general theory Heneman described as the "mediocrity of the masses." The conflict became somewhat personal; Heneman has been, since the early 1950's, a member of a national Committee on Organization Planning. He regards himself as rather expert on such matters. Mahoney has planned all the major organization changes in the rapid growth of Slippery Rock since 1951.

Slippery Rock executives took the straightforward position that, if and when the firm purchased Piute, the latter organization would have to accept whatever organizational arrangements were finally prescribed by the parent company. Piute executives said that, not only would most of their better managers look for other positions if the Mahoney program was followed, but rank and file employees would also be inclined to follow the lead of managers. Piute executives also called attention to the fact that rank and file Piute employees had formally declared their refusal to be represented by the same union as that of Slippery Rock workers.

Problem: Be prepared to analyze this controversy as an outside, neutral student of management. What, in your opinion, was the heart of the issue? How seriously do you regard it? Would you recommend that the parties plan to go ahead with the merger? If so, what are your recommendations for organizational relationships between the new acquisition and the parent company?

6. Organization Structures and Processes

Theories of organization are implemented and expressed in and through working organizations. In them, ideas and theories and philosophies of management take shape, somewhat as an architect's ideas and viewpoint are expressed in a home or business building.

It follows that working organizations vary according to the various viewpoints of their creators and maintainers. To the extent that those who build or use organizations conclude that the way to get things done is for managers to tell workers what to do and how to do it, they seek to develop an organization that facilitates this order-giving process. To the extent, on the other hand, that they place a high priority on cooperative thinking and planning and decision-making in working toward the mission of the firm or agency, they presumably try to develop a different type of structure.

Much of the responsibility for designing appropriate structures for working organizations can usually be traced to the personnel or industrial relations division. The creation, maintenance, and modification of such structures is a responsibility of top management, but specialized competence and advice are expected from the employee relations staff. Personnel departments generally develop and maintain *job descriptions* that indicate the contributions of each specialized working assignment. The same staff division may be charged with planning, reviewing, and continually improving internal communications. Personnel or industrial relations departments usually maintain the *personnel records* of all workers. They play an important role in employee and manager *training and development programs*. These and other employee rela-

98

tions functions are immediately useful if not essential in maintaining and modifying organization structures. It is not surprising, therefore, that *organization planning* usually involves and may be centered in the industrial relations division.

The working organization is one of the tools by which managers and workers seek to achieve their goals. Organization is a device for manipulating and controlling variables that influence and shape working behavior and effective cooperation in work.

1.0 PROCESS AND STRUCTURE

In popular usage, the term *organization* describes both an existing structure and the process by which such structures are created or established and modified. As a noun, "organization" may mean either the process of organizing or the resulting systematic combination, association, or whole. The basic nature of organization is best seen from the definition of the verb, "to organize," which means to arrange or create or constitute a group or association of interdependent parts, giving each a special contribution and relationship to the rest.

Henry LeChatelier, in his early *Methodology in the Experimental Sciences,* and Oliver Sheldon, in *The Philosophy of Management,* as well as others, were impressed with organizing processes rather than the structure of organizations. Sheldon defines organization as "the process of so combining the work" of individuals and groups with necessary facilities and materials as to "provide the best channels for the efficient, systematic, positive, and coordinated application of the available effort."

The result of the process of organizing is a structure that provides a systematic arrangement of functional assignments in which component parts have specialized duties, all presumably contributing to the over-all objective. As a structure, it is what the dictionary calls a "vitally or systematically organic whole; an association or society."[1] The key words in definitions of organization, both as a process and a structure, are "systematic" and "specialization." An organization is a systematic arrangement and combination. Equally important, an organization is based on the specialization and resulting interdependence of the parts which are combined.

1.1 Specialization. Working organizations vary widely in size and complexity. The simplest is frequently described as the *one-to-one organization,* in which each worker has his own supervisor. The classic illustration of this simple structure is the organization created and maintained by Robinson Crusoe with the essential cooperation of his man Friday. Current examples of this simple structure may be observed in thousands of small enterprises. Much more spectacular—and hence more likely to attract our attention—

---

[1] See Lyndall Urwick, *The Theory of Organization,* New York: American Management Association, 1953; Ordway Tead, *The Art of Administration,* New York: McGraw-Hill Book Co., Inc., 1951; Peter F. Drucker, *Concept of the Corporation,* New York: The John Day Co., 1946.

are the large-scale mass-employment firms, such as General Motors, Sears Roebuck, Montgomery Ward.

In the process of organizing, specialized assignments are identified. Robinson Crusoe, for example, assumed the major responsibility for decision-making. Friday's job consisted essentially of following instructions. This one-to-one relationship created what is now widely described as *vertical specialization,* which has a *scalar* authority structure. All who have enjoyed experience in military organizations are familiar with vertical specialization. It is prominent, also, in all large-scale business organizations.

Such vertical specialization in working organizations may also be described as specialization in and for decision making. Each scalar level is presumably experienced and expert in one type of decision. Specific authority is assigned to permit each level to make its decisions. The combination of these vertical, scalar specializations appears in most charts of organizations as the height or vertical dimension of the organization structure. It creates the pattern of *layering* that is widely recognized as having important implications for intra-organization communications.[2]

Specialization in the process of organizing and reorganization also involves *horizontal* distinctions in assignments. Horizontal specialization is based on differences in the tasks to be performed. Thus, a typical business organization distinguishes sales, production, finance, accounting, credit, and other such specialized tasks. Within the field of production, organization may recognize additional specialization, identifying such units as the foundry, machine shop, and paint shop.[3]

These two types of specialization are usually illustrated by the pyramid of organization outlined in Figure 6.1. Horizontal specialization gives the pyramid its width. At the base, where largest numbers of workers are employed, the range of jobs is very wide, with demands for a variety of skills. Higher, in the ranks of middle management, numbers are smaller and only the basic differentiations between major types of work—production, sales, design, for example—are evident. At the top, in the ranks of executives, specialization is by major function and in terms of leadership.

The height of the pyramid reflects the number of scalar levels it involves. Specialization on this axis distinguishes the rank and file at the base, first-line and second-line supervisors, the narrow or wide range of middle managers, and the top managers or executives of the organization at or near the apex.

1.2 Bases for specialization. In small organizations, both horizontal and vertical specialization are likely to be narrow and limited. The decision-making structure requires few layers. Along the base of the pyramid, the same employees may perform a variety of tasks in jobs that are more complex

---

[2] See the later discussion of communications in Chapter 7. For more on this type of specialization, see Herbert A. Simon, *Administrative Behavior,* New York: The Macmillan Company, 1949, pp. 9–11.

[3] See Luther Gulick and L. Urwick eds., *Papers on the Science of Administration,* New York: Institute of Public Administration, 1937.

than those in larger structures. In larger firms, additional specialization in both horizontal and vertical dimensions is necessary. The range of tasks to be performed is likely to be greater. Individual job assignments can be more specialized.

In larger organizations, horizontal specialization may be affected by (1) the location of shops and plants, (2) types of products, (3) the raw materials involved, (4) the necessary skills of employees, (5) production processes, (6) facilities, tools, and equipment, and (7) the time sequence of operations.

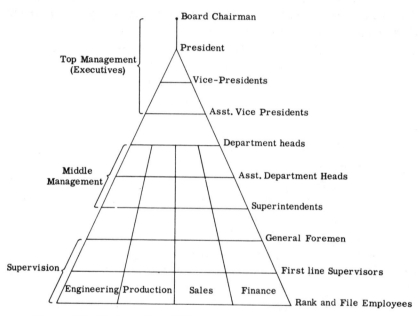

Figure 6.1 Horizontal and Vertical Specialization in the Working Organization: the Pyramid

These considerations are frequently described as the principal *bases for specialization*. Here is Ernest Dale's somewhat more detailed outline of these bases:[4]

1. Functions performed—such as finance, production, manufacture, engineering, and law.
2. Products, particularly those that are not only produced separately but also sold that way.
3. Location, frequently described as geographic or territorial organization, bringing together such activities as are carried on in a particular area.

[4] In *Planning and Developing the Company Organization,* New York: American Management Association, 1952, pp. 27–54.

4. Customers, wherein, as in radio or television, emphasis is placed on selling to individual clients.
5. Process or operational sequence.
6. Equipment and facilities.
7. Time or timing, with a common division stressing the three stages of planning, execution, and control.
8. Harmonious overlap, a principle similar to the singing of rounds, in which various stages, dependent on each other, are nevertheless carried on simultaneously. (Dale's illustration is production of the first atomic bombs.)
9. Co-ordination and balance, in which work is so divided as to provide checks and balances among divisions.

1.3   The Organizing Process. The process of organization, whether in the creation of a new structure or the continuing modification and development of an old one, may be conveniently viewed as including several sub-processes. They may be outlined as follows:

1. The organizing process divides the total mission of the organization into combinations of tasks to be performed by individual members and thus *defines jobs* throughout the structure.
2. Organizing creates structures, with a hierarchy of offices, with levels or echelons to which authority, responsibility, and status are attached.
3. Organizing creates structures of authority, status, and communications, associated with this hierarchy of offices.[5]
4. The organizing process inevitably introduces changes in individual roles and inter-personal relationships; it encounters and overcomes resistance to these changes.

1.4   Defining jobs. The process of organizing divides the work to be done in accomplishing the mission of the whole into jobs to be done by the members. This division of labor, already noted in Chapter 6, is perhaps the most obvious of the sub-processes. It includes more than the simple assignment of tasks, however, for each assignment also includes a measure of attached responsibility.

This preliminary step may be little or big, depending on the nature of the mission and the numbers of people and jobs to be considered. It may be a very simple step, in which an owner defines two jobs besides his own, with the three constituting the entire structure. It may, on the other hand, involve a high degree of what has been described as *horizontal* and *vertical specialization,* with numerous jobs and several levels of supervision and management. In an existing organization, this step may involve a reassignment of functions and responsibilities or the addition of new assignments. New goals, resulting from products or processes, may require new jobs or they may

[5] See Robert H. Roy, *The Administrative Process,* Baltimore: Johns Hopkins Press, 1958; Herbert A. Simon, *Administrative Behavior,* New York: The Macmillan Company, 1957; Robert S. Weiss, *Processes of Organization,* Ann Arbor: Survey Research Center, University of Michigan, 1956; Dale A. Henning and Preston P. LeBreton, *Planning Theory,* Englewood Cliffs, N.J.: Prentice-Hall, Inc., 1961; Henry A. Landsberger, "The Horizontal Dimension in Bureaucracy," *Administrative Quarterly,* Vol. 6, No. 3, December, 1961, pp. 299–332.

necessitate the assignment of new tasks in existing jobs. New processes may destroy old jobs at the same time that they create new jobs.

This preliminary step in a new organization is readily illustrated by the opening of a new plant to process taconite—low-grade iron ore. Mechanical processing to be followed was developed in years of experimentation in university and government laboratories and subsequently in small pilot plants. When it appeared both mechanically and economically feasible, several firms joined in the creation of a new working organization to undertake commercial production of the refined ore. The nature of the total job was known; machines had been developed; but no one had ever worked in an organization designed to produce and to sell the product. Organizers had to consider the total of tasks to be performed. They had to divide the total into jobs that could be performed by individuals. They had to provide for supervision, inspection, and management. They had to create an entirely new working organization.

In contrast to this situation—which is by no means uncommon in this period of invention and discovery in fissionable products, electronic devices, data processing, and computers—the canning industry has undergone a long process of changing jobs as tin cans and freezing have come to replace the home-canning activities of a generation past. Canning factories have had to reassign tasks as mechanical equipment replaced the hand operations that formerly prepared raw materials for cooking and canning. They have had to modify their organizations further as freezing replaced cooking in the preparation of many products. The industry has seen many mergers and consolidations that have further modified the tasks to be performed; especially those of managers.

In both the new organization and the changing established structure, the process has necessitated new definitions of jobs, new assignments of tasks, new allocations of authority and responsibility.

1.5 Hierarchy of offices. The definition of jobs, through its division of work and responsibility, creates a *hierarchy of offices*. This terminology is used to help rather than to hinder the understanding of what takes place, although it could be said that organization creates a hierarchy of jobs. The term *offices* carries a somewhat sharper distinction between work and responsibility—on the one hand—and the people who perform that work—on the other—than is common in the idea of the *job*. For the same reason, the term *office* is better than *position,* since the latter also emphasizes the personal assignment. The point is that the office is, in and of itself, an important element in the organization. It, rather than the person who holds the job, has a defined spot and defined relationships in the total structure and distinctive privileges and rights and responsibilities.

The idea of *office* thus adds to the usual concept of the job as a combination of tasks. The idea of *office* is frequently recognized in the common practice of describing top managers as *officials,* meaning office-holders. The conception of organizations as hierarchies of offices is helpful in maintaining perspective, for it suggests a degree of permanence and persistence that is less evident when an organization is regarded simply as a cooperating group of people. This bureaucracy is an obvious characteristic of structures and has been described as evidence of vertical specialization.

The fact that the office persists although incumbents change is important in the long-term operation of organizations. The place and function and responsibility of the office define the job and permit development of a job specification. Hence new job holders can be identified, not merely as identical with those who preceded them, but in terms of the requirements of the office.[6]

1.6 Authority, status, and communications. The organizing process creates a structure of authority as a part of its hierarchy of officers. In other words, it allocates power throughout the hierarchy.

The term "authority" has been frequently used in preceding pages. Common usage identifies it with *power,* and a common definition might suggest that it is the power to tell others what to do and to see that they do it. Much of our current thinking sees authority in political terms as flowing from some central reservoir or source. Social scientists, however, have long noted a more subtle quality of authority—the fact that it expresses the willingness of some to accept the dictation of others, who are thus endowed with authority. In other words, authority emerges when someone is willing to or does accept the decisions and instructions of another or when one or more people are willing to be subordinates to those who are accepted as superiors. Tannenbaum notes that individuals always have the opportunity to refuse to grant authority. The alternatives may not be acceptable, but the opportunity is real. As a result, the range of authority held by any individual is defined by the subordinates who have made such a grant.[7]

The manner in which individuals grant authority and organizers create hierarchies was carefully described early in the 1900's by the German sociologist, Max Weber (1864–1920). He identified the major factors in transfer of authority as legal and traditional as well as the personal leadership qualities of certain personalities. The latter he labeled *charisma.*[8]

Dubin has added to the definition of authority the notion of expectation. In the process of organizing, coordination is established and based in part on authority, which Dubin defines as "the expectation that direction will be followed."[9]

[6] See Robert Dubin, *Human Relations in Administration,* Englewood Cliffs, N.J.: Prentice-Hall, Inc., pp. 79–112; see also Alvin Gouldner, *Patterns of Industrial Bureaucracy,* Glencoe, Ill.: Free Press, 1954; also Philip Selznick, *Leadership in Administration: A Sociological Interpretation,* Evanston, Ill.: Row, Peterson & Company, 1957.

[7] See Robert Tannenbaum, "Managerial Decision-Making," *Journal of Business,* Vol. 23, No. 1, January 1950, pp. 22–39.

[8] For translations of the Weber analysis, see H. H. Gerth and C. Wright Mills, *From Max Weber: Essays in Sociology,* New York: Oxford University Press, 1946; see also, for a popular statement of the viewpoint, Peter Blau, *Bureaucracy in Modern Society,* New York: Random House, Inc., 1956.

[9] Robert Dubin, *Human Relations in Administration,* Englewood Cliffs, N.J.: Prentice-Hall, Inc., 1951, p. 229.

Authority is only one of the means by which leaders control those who follow. Influence may be effective in modifying behavior without the generally coercive pressure generated by grants of authority.

Why do individuals grant authority to others? They may do so in order to participate in attaining an objective they regard favorably. They may seek the approbation of fellow workers in an organization. They may receive rewards from those to whom the grant is made. They may feel compelled to grant authority because of traditions, including standards of morality, to which they subscribe. They may grant authority as a means of shifting responsibility. They may make such grants because of the persuasive influence of a leader.

Simon notes four types of motivations that explain individual grants of authority to leaders: rewards and sanctions, legitimacy, social approval, and confidence. In effect, grants based on legitimacy are similar to those attributes to moral compulsion; grantors feel that they should accept subordinate relationships. Confidence becomes a basis when the individual to whom the grant is made is regarded as having special skills, as, for example, in the common practice of subordinating oneself to one's physician or lawyer.[10]

Dubin follows Weber in distinguishing three kinds of organizational authority, the first based on *rational* grounds, the second based on *traditional* grounds, and the third based on *charismatic* grounds.[11]

The first type reflects the attitude of group members that leaders have the right to issue orders, a right prescribed by the rules of the organization to which they have in effect subscribed by their act of joining. The second type of authority is essentially that of legitimacy, in which group members believe in the traditional allocation of authority in leaders and accept that relationship. *Charismatic authority* is an aspect of devotion to an individual who, in Dubin's words, "is believed to have exceptional personal characteristics that set him above and beyond mere mortals."[12]

Throughout the continuing process of organizing and reorganizing and leading the organization, those who are to be its members must maintain a willingness to grant authority to their leader and to recognize that their action permits him to distribute that authority. This is, in many ways, the most important of the sub-processes in organization. Its implications for managers who assume the responsibility for organizing working groups are obviously important. To be effective, they must receive the grants of authority they require. They may try to buy these grants in terms of wages, salaries, and other compensation. They may—in loose labor markets—be able to compel such grants, because the alternatives in terms of unemployment and economic disaster are so serious. They may exhibit leadership qualities that members will regard as justifying such grants.

[10] See Herbert Simon, "Authority," in Conrad M. Arensberg *et al., eds. Research in Industrial Human Relations,* New York: Harper & Brothers, 1957, pp. 103–114.

[11] Dubin, *op. cit.,* p. 196.

[12] Dubin, *op. cit.,* p. 197.

Authority structures that are appropriate for working organizations have changed with industrialization, as have the individual grants of authority. In earlier periods, charismatic authority and authority based on tradition had wide acceptance. With increased education and sophistication of group members, the trend is presumably toward a more *rational* basis. For the future, it seems certain that participants can be expected to grant authority largely on the basis of their evaluation of a leader's specialized competence.

This likelihood is documented by a report by Marcson on authority systems for scientists in industry. He concludes that an effective structure in this situation must combine traditional bases with *colleague authority*. In the latter, the authority structure would be more like that of a university. It would permit a greater area of personal autonomy. It would associate authority more closely with professional competence.[13]

At the same time that the manager-organizer creates offices and a system of authority, he assigns roles to be played and creates a formal status system. Division of the total mission into jobs to be performed and development of a system of offices defines what role each office holder is to play.

Officeholders tend to play their roles as they see them, much as they would attempt to enact a role in a drama. Hence their perception of their role is a major factor in their employment behavior. If they feel that they have been assigned heavy responsibilities, they act accordingly. Similarly, if they see their job or office as one with little responsibility, their actions reflect this perception of their role.

Status means standing and implies rights, privileges, and, at the same time, restrictions on the action of the individual. Organization creates both functional and scalar status structures. The functional status structure is based on what the office contributes to the total organization. It reflects requirements in terms of skill, knowledge, and know-how. The accountant position is thus placed in a distinctly higher status than that of the common laborer. Scalar status, on the other hand, is based on power and authority. The general superintendent thus acquires a higher status than the line foreman.

Status is important to members of working organizations, in part because the twin processes of industrialization and democracy have destroyed older status structures based on family and caste. On-the-job status thus becomes more important. Again, the process of urbanization in which individuals may be lost in the large metropolitan community gives added importance to status in the workshop.

Status suggests "neededness" in the organization and thus contributes to each officeholder's sense of security. Status is associated with income and other rewards for performance, which provide another tie to security. The status structure as a whole presents a broad perception of the position or

[13] Simon Marcson, "The Scientist in American Industry," *Reports Series No. 99*, Princeton, N.J.: Industrial Relations Section, Princeton University, 1960.

standing of the office in the entire organization. It thus reinforces the office-holder's perception of where he stands.

Formal assignments of status to an office may not correspond with informal status granted to an individual. Just as individuals grant authority to others for a variety of reasons, their perceptions of status have several bases. Perhaps the most obvious of these is what the individual does. But status may also reflect perceptions of what individuals *can do.* Thus a medical doctor in a military organization may have higher informal status than is indicated by his rank. Status based on what the individual can do may be directly influenced by the organization, which may grant him authority that limits or extends what he can do. Informal status may be related to length of service, age, and seniority, although these particular factors may not influence the formal status of the job.

Status symbols are obvious in connection with formal status, where rank is evidenced by job titles, various privileges, priorities in work assignments, facilities, equipment, number of assistants, and many other symbols. Basic to many of the other symbols is the wage or salary.[14] It is possible that as the structure of wages and salaries continues to narrow, so that all employees are more nearly equal in what they can buy, status symbols get more attention. The importance of a college degree may be an example.

The organizing process, whether in establishing a new organization or remodeling an old one, assigns status, but it may also take away status. If it reassigns an office at a lower echelon, it thereby reduces status. This is one reason for resistance to change in reorganizations.

The organizing process also creates a formal network or structure for communications. It identifies responsibilities for communication, specifying by and to whom such transmissions shall be directed. It notes the necessity for upward and downward communication. It defines formal lines or channels through which communications are expected to flow.

In the same process, as has been noted, organizing creates the *layering* that may create serious barriers to communication and may become a major factor in the development of an extensive informal communications structure.

1.7 Resistance to change. Particularly in reorganization, the process may encounter strong resistance from group members. The organizing activity is not one in which inertia, friction, and opposition are unimportant. On the contrary, the initiation of changes that affect work assignments, authority, status and communication is likely to be regarded critically by many if not most members of an existing organization. Each individual has had to make personal adjustments to accommodate his own interests and viewpoints to

---

[14] See Daniel Seligman, "The New Masses, *Fortune,* May 1959, pp. 110ff; Cameron Hawley, *Executive Suite,* Boston: Houghton Mifflin Company, 1952; Alan Harrington, *Life in the Crystal Palace,* New York: Alfred A. Knopf, Inc., 1959; "The Rising Status of Status Symbols," *Wall Street Journal,* Oct. 29, 1957, pp. 1–2; Vance Packard, *The Status Seekers,* New York: David McKay Company, Inc., 1959.

the older structure. He has formed habits of thinking and acting based on these adjustments. The preliminary accommodation process may have been emotionally difficult with resulting painful memories. Under these circumstances, changes may appear to involve hazards. If change seems likely to limit present authority, to reduce formal status, or to remove some of the status symbols to which the individual has become accustomed, resistance is to be expected.

The thoughtful organizer, aware of the far-reaching impact of the organizing process, must take such reactions into account. Desirable reorganization may frequently be avoided or postponed for this reason. Organizers and those charged with responsibility for planning the future of organizations may be afraid to face the opposition to changes that seem essential.

The clue to effective organization planning and to the initiation of necessary changes is to be found in part in the nature of modern authority structures. Opposition is most serious when changes rely on traditional bases for authority; they thus ignore the rational bases that are prescribed by present levels of education and sophistication of today's workers. In so far as proposed changes will alter structures of authority and status, they can be expected to gain acceptance and support to the extent that they are communicaed and explained on a rational basis. It has been widely observed that employees accept change more readily if they have a hand in evaluating proposed changes before they are made.[15]

1.8 Organization charts. Most charts of organization detail assignments much more extensively than is indicated in the simple pyramid shown as Figure 6.1. Figures 6.2, 6.3, and 6.4 are examples of parts of organization charts in several types of business firms. Figure 6.2 represents a portion of an organization chart for a firm that maintains a number of regional divisions. Figure 6.3 shows the detail of top management and upper-middle management in an organization that emphasizes six major functions—manufacturing, sales, production, purchasing, defense contracts, and advertising. Figure 6.4 provides a somewhat more detailed chart of top management in a large manufacturing company. None of these charts, it should be noted, is complete; each is actually a "blow-up" of the top levels of the organizations they represent.[16]

[15] See Eli Ginsberg and Ewing W. Reilley, *Effecting Changes in Large Organizations,* New York: Columbia University Press, 1957; Marshall E. Dimock, *A Philosophy of Administration,* New York: Harper & Brothers, 1958; Frank J. Jasinski, "Adapting Organization to New Technology," *Harvard Business Review,* Vol. 37, No. 1, January-February 1959, pp. 79–86.

[16] For a broad sample of organization charts, see Louis A. Allen, "Charting the Company Organization Structure," *Studies in Personnel Policy, No. 168,* National Industrial Conference Board, 1959. For an intriguing analysis of the evolution of organization structures, see Mason Haire, "Size, Shape and Function in Industrial Organizations," *Human Organizations,* Vol. 14, No. 1, Spring 1955, pp. 17–22.

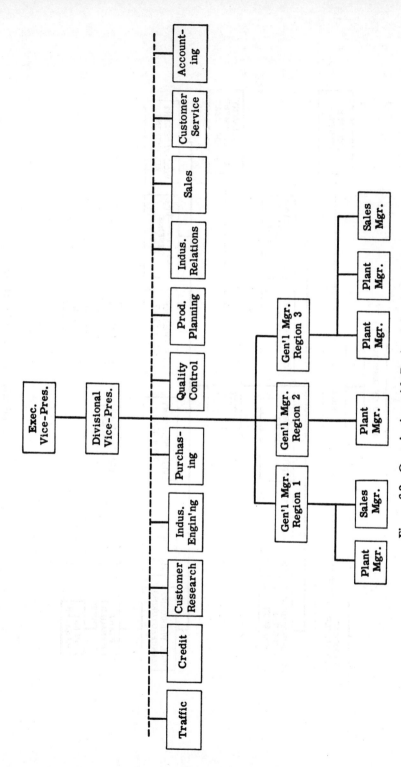

Figure 6.2 Organization with Regional Specialization

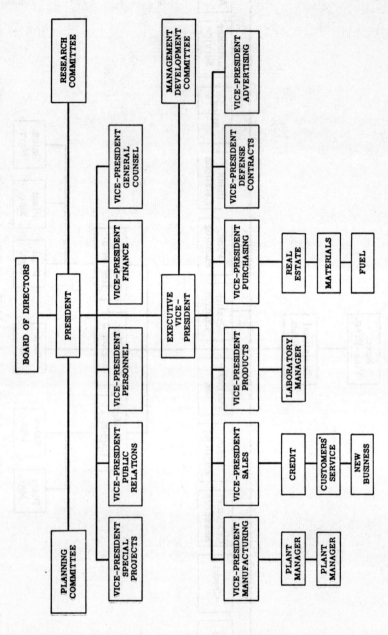

Figure 6.3 Organization by Major Functions

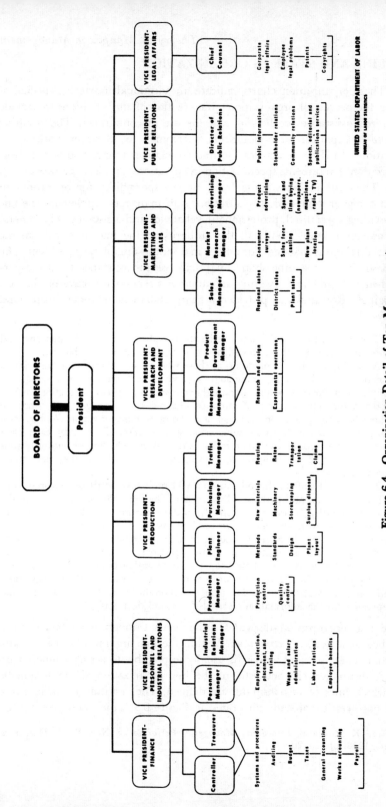

Figure 6.4 Organization Detail of Top Management

SOURCES: *Careers in Business Management*, Washington: Veterans Administration in cooperation with Bureau of Labor Statistics, Department of Labor, March 1960, p. 2.

2.0 LINE AND STAFF IN ORGANIZATION

These organization charts indicate an additional impact of specialization in the process of organization—the creation of *staff* divisions to provide specialized assistance to the *line* and the use of committees. The resulting *line-and-staff* pattern of organization is common in all larger working organizations. In these structures the *line* (sometimes referred to as the "line organization") represents specialization in operations, that is, in getting the job done. The *staff* includes those freed from responsibility for operations to permit a higher degree of specialization; staff managers supplement the line by providing specialized, professional-level advice and assistance. The general foreman, for example, with all the authority of the line, may call on the industrial relations manager for advice in a serious disciplinary problem. The supervisor in the machine shop (line) may ask for assistance from the personnel man (staff) in answering an employee's request for leave of absence.

Virgil K. Rowland has provided a sharp statement of these distinctions. He says: [17]

> The terms "line" and "staff" designate two distinct types of functions, and differences between them should never be allowed to become blurred.
>
> A line organization is made up of those who are concerned with the primary functions of a business: producing (a product or a service) and selling. In simple form, the line organization might consist of a group of production workers under a foreman, a group of salesmen under a sales manager, and a boss to whom both the production foreman and the sales manager report. As the company grows, other layers of supervision will be inserted. . . . In each case, however, the form of the organization is *line:* A straight line of authority runs from the head of the company to the worker at the bench and the salesman on the road.
>
> The original staff in this organization will probably consist of the president's private secretary, and perhaps a bookkeeper. These people have no place in the line of authority. They report directly to the company president, but they do not direct the work of those down the line. As the company grows, there may be an accounting department instead of a single bookkeeper and a variety of staff departments performing specialized functions. . . .
>
> And in theory, at least, these people have no authority over the line. If they do, a primary rule of modern management—that each person should have only one boss—is violated. . . . The staff's responsibility is to provide the line superior with the information he needs for sound decisions.

The line organization delegates assignments through what is generally described as a *chain of command*. Within the line organization, each manager and supervisor and worker is usually responsible to a single superior or boss. A distinctive characteristic of the line organization is the simplicity with which lines of responsibility are defined. The resulting *chain of command* has been graphically illustrated in Figure 6.5, which also provides an

[17] Virgil K. Rowland, *Improving Managerial Performance*, New York: Harper & Brothers, 1958, pp. 19–20.

illustration of the concept of scalar level and authority mentioned in preceding paragraphs.

2.1 Staff functions. Staff members, freed of direct responsibility for operations, are responsible for developing and maintaining high levels of expertness, keeping abreast of developments, and thus providing up-to-date,

THE CHAIN OF COMMAND

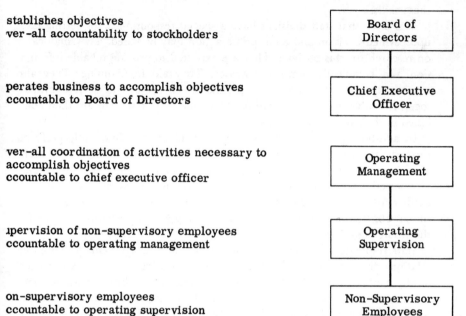

stablishes objectives
ver-all accountability to stockholders | Board of Directors

perates business to accomplish objectives
ccountable to Board of Directors | Chief Executive Officer

ver-all coordination of activities necessary to accomplish objectives
ccountable to chief executive officer | Operating Management

ıpervision of non-supervisory employees
ccountable to operating management | Operating Supervision

on-supervisory employees
ccountable to operating supervision | Non-Supervisory Employees

Figure 6.5   Chain of Command in the Line Organization
SOURCE: National Industrial Conference Board, *Studies in Personnel Policy, No. 153,* 1956, p. 13.

reliable information and advice and assistance to line managers. The growth and proliferation of staff in modern, large-scale organizations have been widely noted and generally explained as indicating the growing need for such expertness at management levels.[18]

Just how does the staff member or division assist the line manager? One school of thought—possibly they should be called "purists"—insists that staff personnel should confine their participation almost entirely to the provision of advice and counsel; they must not exercise authority excepting within their own staff division. An opposing, and perhaps more realistic, approach

[18] For more on this point, see R. H. Roy, *The Administrative Process,* Baltimore: Johns Hopkins Press, 1958, pp. 60–72; Ernest Dale and Lyndall F. Urwick, *Staff in Organization,* New York: McGraw-Hill Book Company, Inc., 1960.

insists that staff members should perform specialized services for line managers and should be given authority to do so.

The purist argument holds that staff members cannot maintain their expertness if they accept operating assignments, that their time and interest should not be diverted from the essentials of keeping informed and abreast of developments in their specialized field. Realists argue that staff members have expert skills beyond those of advising and that the organization needs these skills.

It is clear that staff divisions have a special responsibility for getting facts upon which decision and appropriate action may be based. They may carry on research for this purpose. They are expected to provide reliable information and technically competent advice. They aid in planning. They also continually audit and appraise operations. The results of such appraisal, together with the best information obtainable from research, are then combined in their recommendations.

In addition, in current practice, staff members may frequently perform, throughout an entire organization, certain functions requiring special technical competence. Thus, for example, the employee relations division may give selective tests and appraise the results even to the extent of screening all applicants and rejecting those who do not appear promising. This and other similar functions are performed by staff divisions as a specialized service for the whole organization.

Staff responsibilities are well illustrated by usual assignments to employee relations divisions. Although actual employee relations programs are carried out by managers at all levels, the personnel manager or labor relations director acts as an advisor and counselor to all managers. He or his assistants work with, for, and through these other managers. His staff may take the lead in planning employee relations policies and programs. They maintain a continuing appraisal of the whole program as it appears in day-to-day operations. They study the policies and programs of other organizations. They keep in touch with significant experiments, developments, and discoveries in the field and otherwise advance their professional competence and knowledge.

Saltonstall has helped to clarify the idea of staff in modern organizations by noting the wide range of roles it plays. Staff members are researchers and advisors. They are interpreters of company policy and of collective bargaining agreements. In addition, according to Saltonstall, they serve as coach, diagnostician, observer of needs, trainer and guide, coordinator, policy planner, creative thinker, catalyst, follow-up man, integrator of ideas, and strategist.[19]

In summary, the usual functions of staff in the modern line-and-staff organization may be said to include six major elements.

[19] See Robert Saltonstall, *Human Relations in Administration,* New York: McGraw-Hill Book Company, Inc., 1959, p. 117.

The staff division:

1. Provides a continuing review and appraisal of both policy and practice in the field of its specialization,
2. Makes special investigations and conducts research as a basis for improved policy and practice,
3. Provides specialized advice and counsel for all line managers,
4. Plans, recommends, and formulates plans for changing policy and practice,
5. Keeps informed of developments and reports in the field both inside and outside the organization, and
6. Maintains its own continuing development and specialized competence.

2.2 Staff and line relationships. How is staff expertness made available to and used by the total organization? Is it fed into the top of the organization and channeled to all levels through the chief executive? Do all "staff" divisions report directly to the president? How do they make their information, advice, and services available to those who have most need for them? Must the chief staff officer have high scalar status? The proper relationships of staff and line and the scalar status of staff have been favorite subjects for discussion. "Selling" top management on staff ideas has been a popular topic. Certainly the officers of an organization should have ready access to such competence and understanding as are provided by the staff. At the same time, however, most organizations provide for close, cooperative relationships with department heads, middle managers, and supervisors.

Must the "staff" member be purely advisory? Urwick has described insistence on the "advisory" status of staff as an "escape."[20] McGregor has provided a penetrating analysis of the realistic relationships of staff to line, which implies much more than mere counseling in the staff function.[21] He describes staff work as involving a process of "augmentation," in which the staff expert changes the attitudes, habits, and philosophy of line operators so that they want to carry out appropriate programs. In McGregor's language, the staff member must strive first to be "perceived as a source of help." Then, working "within the frame of reference of the line manager's perceptual field," he encourages managers to select and accept a course of action. He then provides "support" while the manager learns to follow the selected course, thus guiding the manager to a point where he assumes full responsibility for the program.

[20] *Op. cit.,* p. 17.
[21] Douglas McGregor, "The Staff Function in Human Relations," *Journal of Social Issues,* Vol. 4, No. 3, Summer 1948, pp. 6–23. See also R. C. Sampson, *The Staff Role in Management: Its Creative Uses,* New York: Harper & Brothers, 1955; "Line-Staff Relationships in Production," *Special Report No. 18,* New York: American Management Association, 1957.

Perhaps these relationships may be clearer if illustrated by the work and responsibility of the industrial relations staff division. The vice-president for industrial relations or personnel or the personnel director or employee relations director—whatever his title—usually reports directly to the president or an executive vice-president. He is a member of the executive committee and is present in all discussions of major policy. In them, he presents his interpretation of the employee relations viewpoint. He may, upon request, provide detailed information or an extensive review of relevant experience and expert opinion. He may, on instruction or on his own initiative or at the suggestion of his assistants, raise questions of policy or practice. He may propose changes in policy or program or appraise proposals advanced by other committee members.

At the same time, he and his assistants are constantly available to help at all levels in the organization. They may advise a foreman on an employee's request for leave of absence or counsel with a department head on priorities in a prospective layoff. By agreement, they may perform or supervise preliminary employment interviews or testing for all departments. They may act as spokesmen or chairmen of negotiating committees. They may represent the entire organization in union negotiations or in interpretations of a collective agreement or in handling grievances.

Staff managers may have great potential for influencing decisions. They are the experts; they speak with the authority of expertness. Scalar status is supplementary rather than central to the impact of the staff manager's counsel. One of the attributes of such expertness is the personal mobility of the staff manager. He can speak with candor because of that independence.

Dalton and others have noted the seeds of continuing conflict in staff and line relationships.[22] In part, it may be explained by distinctive personal characteristics of staff managers as contrasted with line managers. The staff group may be younger, have more formal education, and have more self-assurance than the line. Staff managers generally take an active part in professional associations. In these groups, and in the local communities in which they live, they may enjoy wider acquaintance among professionals in other fields, for example, law and medicine. As specialists, staff managers may achieve wider acceptance and status among the rank-and-file employees of the working organization.

Unspecialized line managers often feel that staff managers are continually reducing the range of line decisions and authority. They may resent the status accorded staff, the fact that staff managers may speak and write more effectively. The professional attitudes of staff managers mark them as somewhat unusual and perhaps "outside" the central organization. Perhaps the long-term solution for this conflict is development of a more nearly professional performance by line managers.

[22] Melville Dalton, "Conflicts Between Staff and Line Managerial Officers," *American Sociological Review,* Vol. 15, No. 2, June 1950, pp. 342–351.

3.0 FUNCTIONAL AND COMMITTEE STRUCTURES

As is apparent from the several figures in this chapter and the preceding discussion, all organizations of size tend to divide assignments according to the distinctive functions to be performed. Thus, for example, jobs that emphasize sales are likely to be grouped together in a sales department, and production jobs are combined in a production department. A "functional" department head provides leadership in each such division. Most large firms or agencies use such *functional organization.*

Additional complications may be introduced by an emphasis on *functional authority.* Frederick W. Taylor, the father of what became known as *scientific management,* proposed that technical specialists be given a relatively high scalar status in the line organization. They were made responsible and given authority, above the level of supervisors and foremen, for directing the performance of the particular functions in which they were expert. An employee in such an organization might be directed and supervised by several superiors. The functional specialist was authorized to direct supervisors as well as rank-and-file employees in the performance of tasks in the field of his expertness.

An example of this type of specialization may be seen in the provision of experts in machine set-up. Taylor suggested many others, including an order-of-work clerk, an instruction-card clerk, a time-and-cost clerk, an inspector, a repair specialist, and a disciplinarian, as well as the usual crew boss. In a large organization, each of these specialists was responsible to an over-all functional supervisor.[23]

Organizations may be divided into so many specialized parts that participants have difficulty in gaining perspective that includes the whole or even one of the larger segments of the total. To provide such perspective, many organizations lean heavily on committees. Three top-level committees have been shown in the organization chart in Figure 6.3.

As large-scale organizations have become prominent, dependence on committees has increased. Some observers have described a system of *committee management* in which the Board of Directors is regarded as the top committee. An executive or general management committee composed of the president, vice-presidents, and other top executives is not unusual. In addition, committees may be formed to maintain and improve communications, to advise on general policy, to analyze and advise on budgets, or to study and investigate a situation or problem of wide concern. One such committee may be concerned with disciplinary problems, another with employment stabilization through coordination of sales and production, another with interdepartmental transfers and promotions, another with employee suggestions, and still

---

[23] For a detailed description, see Henry H. Farquhar, "Functional Organization," in *Scientific Management in American Industry,* New York: Harper & Brothers, 1929, pp. 141–142.

another with materials, routing, and waste. Committees may be "standing"—continuing—or *ad hoc,* that is, for a particular assignment only. They may lean on staff divisions to provide them with assistants or they may have employees permanently assigned to them.

Committees may have responsibility and authority delegated to them by various officials. Members may be designated by the committee to exercise part or all of the committee's authority. On the other hand, committees may be advisory only, all authority and responsibility remaining in the usual officials.

Committees may supervise, review, evaluate, and forecast. They may be authorized to make final decisions or to limit their contributions to recommendations. They frequently have assignments in advance planning, research, and management development. They may be created at any level, from rank and file to board of directors or stockholders.

Committees have become an important part of many organizations. Some critics regard them as generally wasteful of time, occasioning unnecessary delays and frequently interfering with efficient management. Their value in advising managers is widely accepted, but critics present a strong argument against assignments of authority to committees. Values and problems of management committees have become the subject of frequent study.[24]

Studies of committee operation suggest that committees generally include two leaders, one a sort of foreman and driver and the other a catalyst who reduces irritation and friction and holds the group together. Committees can provide an important educational experience, especially for young, inexperienced managers. They can provide important channels for communication among specialized divisions and departments. They are effective in exchanging information and integrating experience as a basis for action. On the other hand, they are likely to be less effective in administration.

As in all management, the effectiveness of committees seems to be closely related to the leadership of chairmen or members. Some of the criticisms of committees—the time they take and their tendency to avoid or delay decisions, for example—can be met by such techniques as the preparation and circulation of agendas and the use of subcommittees or individual members to prepare draft statements in advance of committee sessions.

3.1 Multiple management. A special case of committee management, and one that has attracted wide attention is known as *multiple management.* It emphasizes the use of committees to increase the flow of ideas from less experienced managers and to train them for positions of greater responsibility. The program was developed at the main plant of McCormick and Co., food packers and distributors, in Baltimore, Maryland. The parent company reports that the plan has increased employee efficiency, reduced

---

[24] See Clarence B. Randall, "The Myth of Management Committee," *Dun's Review,* Vol. 76, No. 1, July 1960, pp. 37–39; Louis A. Allen, "Making Better Use of Committees," *Management Record,* Vol. 17, No. 12, December 1955, pp. 466ff. (The American Management Association sponsored a study of general management committees in 1960.)

labor turnover and absenteeism, and enabled the company to pay higher wages than those prevailing in the area and industry.

The plan provides for several "junior boards of directors." In the parent concern, there are three such boards, one representing white-collar executives and administrative employees, one representing factory supervisors and workers, and one representing the sales division. In each case, board members, varying from 15 to 20 in number, were originally appointed by the president and subsequently elected by the groups they represent. Board members rate each other at six-month intervals. The three with lowest ratings are replaced by election of three new members. These boards may study and review any phase of the company's operations. They may (but only by unanimous vote) make recommendations to the senior board of directors.[25]

4.0 INFORMAL STRUCTURES

To this point, attention has been directed to the formal organization structures with which specialization is implemented. Formal organization is that pictured on the usual organization charts. It is the structure formally established by managers, who define the tasks to be performed and assign responsibilities for their performance.

Experienced managers and students of organization recognize the presence of informal organizations that underlie or are superimposed upon these formal structures. These informal organizations create their own communication network and status structures and may redefine jobs so that both tasks and responsibilities are somewhat different from those shown in the formal structure. They involve relationships that confer influence, prestige, and status on a different basis, with lines of communication that may vary sharply from the lines of the formal structure.[26] The informal organzation reflects the special interests of participants—those, for example, that may draw the president more closely to the vice-president for sales than to other vice-presidents. Informal organization is also shaped by the special skill and competence, the length of service and reputation, and other personal characteristics of individual workers.

Sociometric studies of employment relationships provide numerous illustrations of these informal structures, one of which is pictured in Figure 6.6. In that figure, the solid lines show how formal authority and responsibility have been delegated and how functions have been identified and distinguished. Dotted lines, however, show the actual lines of day-to-day communication and collaboration. The individual numbered 51, for example, short-circuits number 5 in his relationships with number 1.

[25] See John R. Graf, *Junior Boards of Executives,* New York: Harper & Brothers, 1958.

[26] For further remarks on the informal structure, see Ernest Dale, *Planning and Developing the Company Organization Structure,* New York: American Management Association, 1952, p. 45.

The fact that such informal organization structures appear is important because they may reflect shortcomings of formal structures. Informal organization presumably develops to meet the needs of participants. The fact that informal organizations are so common suggests that formal structures are to some degree inadequate if not an actual barrier to effective collaboration.

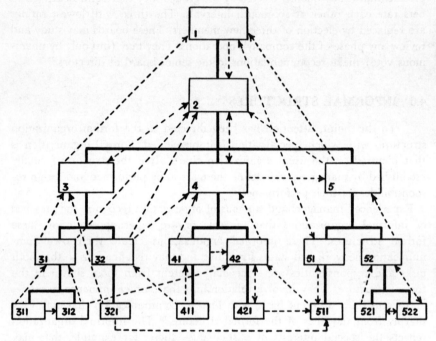

Figure 6.6   Contrasting Formal and Informal Structures
SOURCE: "Planning and Developing the Company Organization Structure," *Research Report No. 20,* New York: American Management Association, 1952, p. 46.

The organizing process creates structures and relationships. What appear to be necessary characteristics of the formal organization may, at the same time, neglect or conflict with the needs of individuals who fill positions in the structure. Apparent structural needs and personal needs of participants may not coincide. Workers may find themselves unsatisfied and perhaps frustrated by the relationships thus established. They may rebel against organizational constraints. They may create informal organizations to avoid them.[27]

[27] See Chris Argyris, *Personality and Organization,* New York: Harper & Brothers, 1957, pp. 229–243.

5.0 CHANGING STRUCTURES

Perhaps the most obvious characteristic of organization is the necessity for changes in structures. Present structures are quite different from the organization structures of a century ago or even of a generation past. Change continues; experiments with committees represent one tangible evidence of such change. Another obvious trend is that toward increasing ratios of managers and particularly of staff managers to the "productive" personnel. Among the major forces that may modify current structures is the development of electronic data-processing equipment and the application of mathematical solutions to management problems. As a result, the pyramids of the future may be more squat, with a broad base of skilled technical workers, relatively few levels of supervision and middle management, and a somewhat wider executive and top staff group.[28]

Some students of business organizations conclude that the ranks of middle management will be reduced, mainly by narrowing the structure. Electronic-data processing, together with improved communications facilities, may eliminate the need for much of the crew and supervisor type of middle management to which we are accustomed. In the Leavitt and Whisler view, the resulting structure might appear as a church steeple with a football on top.[29]

The further impact of automation may influence these changes. Preliminary investigations suggest that automation generally reduces number of members in work crews, at the same time that it increases the numbers and proportions of maintenance technicians. The result is that proportions of indirect workers, both foremen and maintenance men, are increased. At the same time, problems of coordination are increased, so that supervisors have broader responsibilities.

6.0 SUMMARY

This chapter has focused attention on process and structure in working organizations. The term organization refers to both (1) the structures created as a tool of management to implement its leadership and to satisfy the needs of team members and (2) the process of organizing. This chapter has described the bases for various structures, usual charts of these structures, the common differentiation of staff and line and the manner in which they cooperate, functional and committee structures (including multiple management), and the contrast of formal and informal organization in working groups.

Chapter 7 continues the examination of working organizations with special reference to the process of organizing and implications for *administration* of working organizations.

---

[28] See *Business Week,* October 22, 1960, p. 113.

[29] Harold J. Leavitt and Thomas L. Whisler, "Management in the 1980's," *Harvard Business Review,* Vol. 36, No. 6, November-December 1958, pp. 41–48.

SELECTED SUPPLEMENTARY READINGS

Allen, Louis A., "The Line-Staff Relationship," *Management Record,* Vol. 17, No. 9, pp. 346–376, September 1955.

Dalton, Melville, "Conflicts between Staff and Line Managerial Officers," *American Sociological Review,* Vol. 15, No. 2, pp. 342–351, June 1950.

Haire, Mason, "Size, Shape and Function in Industrial Organizations," *Human Organization,* Vol. 14, No. 1, pp. 17–22, Spring 1955.

Leavitt, Harold J., and Thomas L. Whisler, "Management in the 1980's" *Harvard Business Review,* Vol. 36, No. 6, pp. 41–48, November-December 1958.

Sampson, R. C., "Line-Staff Relationships in Production," *Special Report No. 18,* New York: American Management Association, 1957.

SHORT CASE PROBLEM 6.1

Status in Orbitronics

Orbitronics is one of the many small firms in the computer-control field. In 1960, the firm employed 260 engineers and scientists, following a period of very rapid growth. Business appeared to be promising, with a substantial backlog of orders. In 1959, the firm earned approximately $4 per share of stock and paid $2 per share. Salaries were approximately comparable to those of other similar firms. About ten per cent of the employees were stockholders.

Employees were not represented by any union as bargaining agent. An industrial relations department handled recruitment and selection, training and development, wage and salary administration, a broad program of benefits and services and, at the same time, conducted annual studies of employee attitudes, made salary surveys, and provided counseling for employees.

In June, 1960, four engineers asked for an appointment with the director of industrial relations. They described themselves as a committee representing most of the engineering employees. They expressed their strong and continuing interest in the firm's prospects and success and their general satisfaction with working conditions and employment relationships. They said, however, that the firm's practice of requiring all non-managerial workers to punch time-clocks was a subject of extensive and continued conversation among the engineers. They said that they assumed there were good reasons for this practice but that they and their colleagues would appreciate an explanation. The industrial relations director asked them directly about their attitude toward the practice. They said they didn't object if it was necessary; on the other hand, they did doubt the propriety of time-clocks for professional employees.

After twenty minutes of very friendly conversation, the leader of the group suggested that they had no desire to put the industrial relations director on the spot and that they would be happy if he would look into the matter and call them back for a subsequent discussion. They would, the engineers suggested, keep their colleagues informed of any developments.

The industrial relations director mentioned this experience at the weekly meeting of the executive council of company officers on the following Monday morning. Several members of the council were obviously disturbed by the request. Although the industrial relations director opposed any such action, the council as a whole decided to issue a statement to all employees, rather than to make an explanation to the committee of four. As one of the executives expressed it, "Dealing with that committee is too much like collective bargaining for my liking." The statement, printed and placed on bulletin boards and inserted in the following week's pay checks, explained that the time-clocks were for the protection of workers. They provided evidence that the men were actually at work when an accident should or did occur. They prevented arguments as to amounts of salary payments due and facilitated audits by representatives of the Wage and Hour Administration. At the same time, they tended to protect the interests of all employees against the unusual employee who was frequently late in coming to work.

The industrial relations director ran through the plant records. He found practically no tardiness; many men were checking in ahead of time.

Two weeks later, bulletin boards carried an invitation to all employees to attend a meeting to consider the possible advantages of a union. The invitation was signed by the same four men who had raised the question of the time-clocks.

Problem: Be prepared to discuss and evaluate the action of the industrial relations director and the executive council.

SHORT CASE PROBLEM 6.2

McMillan Company

In the McMillan Company, top management takes the position that any officer or executive should be well-rounded and capable of handling any executive position. As a result, the management insists upon frequent job rotation for all younger executives.

The concern has had serious manpower problems for many years. During and since World War II, they have suffered from a shortage of manpower and a heavy turnover in all divisions. Their recruiting is extensive and costly, but, as the president says, "Young men today don't seem to want an opportunity to work up; they want a soft spot right off." The firm pays what the executives insist are higher wages than their competitors pay. Yet they have been shut down by strikes three times since 1947. As the president says, "Nothing we can do seems to satisfy today's employees."

Four present executives have been vice-president of industrial relations in the last eight years. The third of these, now in charge of production, has said bluntly that he did a poor job in employee relations and thinks his successor is just as ineffective. He argues that a comprehensive reorganization is in order. He suggested an audit by outside consultants, but that idea has been, at least temporarily, rejected. A few stockholders, however, are outspoken in their criticism of the present management.

Problem: The president happens to be your father. He talks rather frankly with you and seems to value your advice. What will you tell him?

7. Working Organizations: Operation and Administration

Managers use their knowledge and skill both in organizing and in operating within the framework of organizations, and the employee relations staff is expected to have special expertness in both functions. Organization, it has been repeated, is a tool of managers. They create and develop and modify working organizations to facilitate attainment of organizational goals. They operate as managers within the structures and relationships thus established in their administration of managerial responsibilities. In one sense, existing organizations use managers—their special knowledge, skill, and competence.

The present chapter directs attention to this dual relationship—the manager's role in the organizing process and his role in administration. The preceding chapter has sketched the outline of organizational structures—the formal and informal patterns of interrelationships and interdependence organizations create and maintain. This chapter turns attention to the operation and management of working organizations. Only a short introduction to management or administration is included here, because Chapters 18 and 19 give much more detailed consideration to the jobs and responsibilities of supervisors and managers.

In studies of institutions, a distinction is made between those that are *enacted* or created and others that are *crescive* or growing. Working organizations illustrate this distinction. Some have only recently been established or are presently being formed. Others have a long history; the new manager steps into an ongoing organization, perhaps one with long traditions. In both types, the manager must organize, and he must operate or administer.

1.0 PRINCIPLES OF ADMINISTRATION

It should be clear that the organizer does much more than merely to endow a few coworkers with titles and draw formal charts that outline the functional and scalar divisions of the whole. He creates or modifies day-to-day working (and perhaps living) relationships. He assigns working responsibilities and defines limits of both responsibility and authority. He establishes patterns for delegation, identifying superiors and subordinates. In the process, he molds personal careers and facilitates or handicaps the attainment of personal goals.

Professor Edward Gross has provided an excellent overview of these managerial tasks in his "dimensions of leader behavior."[1] Gross notes that the leader defines goals and clarifies those established by the organization. He also defines and clarifies the means by which goals are to be achieved. He holds major responsibility for task assignment and coordination. He finds ways to link personal and organizational goals and to integrate personal support for the total mission. Finally, he has a "sparking function" in getting action at the correct time and place. These dimensions of leadership outline the management operation in the working organization as in other organizations.

Historic discussions of management and organization have generally described the top executives in working organizations as "generalists." They must, in this viewpoint, possess a wide range of knowledge and skills and expertness. The rapid growth of staff suggests that few individuals can attain and maintain such a wide range of expertness as is now required of top management. One way of meeting this limitation is the provision of expert advisors, the "staff."

It is worthy of note that this development has changed the job and the job requirements for executives. The captain of industry and the empire builder of a generation past—the executive who could do everything and decide every question—may not be well suited to positions of leadership in today's large organizations. Today's executive assignments may require special knowledge and skill in using staff advice and service and stimulating staff performance and translating expert counsel into appropriate action.

The most common staff specializations have been suggested by the organization charts in Figures 6.2 through 6.4. They include finance, personnel and labor relations (industrial relations), public relations, purchasing, traffic and the legal counsel. In most organizations of size, top management is provided with staff advisors who direct *staff divisions*. Within these divisions, these top advisors may maintain a line organization to produce the information and expert counsel and assistance required by the organization.

Numbers of staff workers have been increasing more rapidly than the numbers of rank and file employees, so that the proportion of staff in the

[1] "Dimensions of Leadership," *Personnel Journal,* Vol. 40, No. 5, October 1961, pp. 213–218.

total work force of working organizations has been growing. Put in a somewhat less attractive way, the growth of staff has contributed to a rising ratio
of non-productive to productive workers. There is evidence that this expansion has been greatest in firms whose growth and profits have also been
outstanding.[2]

1.1 Principles. Tradition developed in experience and modified by
limited research has provided several guiding rules or principles for manager-
organizers. Graicunas and Fayol provided the classic summaries of these
operating principles. Both were impressed, for example, with the principle
of *span of control,* which prescribes limits on the numbers of cooperating
subordinates who can be effectively directed by a superior or principal.[3]
Alvin Brown's *Organization: A Formulation of Principle,* first published in
1945, lists 96 of these principles.[4]

The American Management Association has an outline of "Ten Commandments of Good Organization."[5] According to these Ten Commandments, a good organization (1) defines responsibilities clearly, (2) makes
authority commensurate with responsibility, (3) informs all concerned about
changes in assignments, (4) sees to it that each member has only one boss,
(5) prevents superiors from giving orders to subordinates of another, (6)
restricts criticism of subordinates to private conversations, (7) insures prompt
decisions in disputes involving authority, (8) requires the participation of
immediate superiors in the promotion or discipline of their subordinates, (9)
does not ask subordinates to criticise their superiors, and (10) assists top
managers in self-evaluations.

One of the most useful outlines of such principles is that of S. Avery Raube,
who lists 12 of them, as follows:[6]

1. There must be clear lines of authority running from the top to the bottom
   of the organization. . . .
2. No one in the organization should report to more than one line supervisor.
   Everyone in the organization should know to whom he reports, and who
   reports to him. . . .
3. The responsibility and authority of each supervisor should be clearly
   defined in writing. . . .

[2] For studies of staff-work force ratios, see Alton W. Baker and Ralph C. Davis,
"Ratios of Staff to Line Employees and Stages of Differentiation of Staff Functions,"
Columbus, Ohio: *Research Monograph No. 72,* Ohio State University Bureau of
Business Research, 1954; "Organization to Staff Functions," *Studies in Personnel
Policy, No. 165,* National Industrial Conference Board, October 1958; Frederick
Harbison and Samuel E. Hill, *Manpower and Innovation in American Industry,*
Princeton University Industrial Relations Section, 1959.

[3] See V. A. Graicunas, "Relationships in Organization," in Luther Gulick and
Lyndall Urwick, *Papers on the Science of Administration,* New York: Columbia
University Institute of Public Administration, 1937, pp. 183–187; Henri Fayol, *In-
dustrial and General Administration,* London: Sir Isaac Pitman & Sons, Ltd., 1930.

[4] New York: Hibbert Printing Company, 1945. See pages 255–264 for summary
outline of these rules.

[5] For details see *Fortune,* July 1953, pp. 138ff.

[6] In "Company Organization Charts," *Studies in Personnel Policy, No. 139,* National Industrial Conference Board, 1953, pp. 6–11.

4. Responsibility should always be coupled with corresponding authority. . . .
5. The responsibility of higher authority for the acts of its subordinates is absolute. . . .
6. Authority should be delegated as far down the line as possible. . . .
7. The number of levels of authority should be kept at a minimum. . . .
8. The work of every person in the organization should be confined as far as possible to the performance of a single leading function. . . .
9. Whenever possible, line functions should be separated from staff functions, and adequate emphasis should be placed on important staff activities. . . .
10. There is a limit to the number of positions that can be co-ordinated by a single executive. . . .
11. The organization should be flexible, so that it can be adjusted to changing conditions. . . .
12. The organization should be kept as simple as possible.

1.2 Delegation. The general principle of delegation deserves special attention both because it is the very essence of administration—management· through organization—and because it is so frequently violated. Two sub-principles deserve note: *authority is delegated, responsibility is not;* authority should be delegated to the lower possible echelon at which it can be competently used.

Note that "delegation" means *letting go of.* It is a process in which a superior allocates a portion of his authority to his assistants, entrusting them with the assignment or job thus defined. Delegation creates a responsibility on the part of the subordinate; it does not, however, shift responsibility from the superior. The necessity for delegating has long been emphasized; one of the most severe criticisms of any manager is the common observation "He can't delegate." The elementary principle has been stated by Brown as a maxim: "Duties of less import should be delegated and those of greater import reserved."[7] Brown observes that delegation must be carried to the point where "reserved responsibility will not exceed the capacity of the delegant."[8]

When executives are reluctant or unable to delegate authority, sometimes it is because they cannot believe others can do the various jobs as well as they can. They may, of course, be right. The remedy, however, is to provide assistants who can accept responsibility and perform assignments. One reason why many executives and supervisors have difficulty in delegating is the fact that the delegator is not relieved of any of his responsibility. He is still responsible and becomes responsible for the action of· his assistant as well.

The principle of delegation is one of the most widely recognized and accepted and at the same time generally violated principles of organization. In part, violations reflect personal weakness and are matters of administration rather than of organizing; the officeholder rather than the structure of offices is at fault. The problem of delegation as it persistently appears to the

---

[7] Alvin Brown, *Organization Industry*, Englewood Cliffs, N.J.: Prentice-Hall, Inc., 1948, p. 76.
[8] Brown, *op. cit.*, p. 77.

administrator and organizer has been cynically outlined in the following
widely circulated but anonymous job description of the executive:

> As nearly everyone knows, an executive has practically nothing to do, except
> to decide what is to be done; to tell somebody to do it; to listen to reasons why
> it should not be done, why it should be done by someone else, or why it should
> be done in a different way; to follow up to see if the thing has been done; to
> discover that it has been done incorrectly; to point out how it should have been
> done; to conclude that as long as it has been done, it may as well be left where it
> is; to wonder if it is not time to get rid of a person who cannot do a thing right;
> to reflect that he probably has a wife and a large family, and that certainly any
> successor would be just as bad, and maybe worse; to consider how much simpler
> and better the thing would have been done if one had done it oneself in the
> first place; to reflect sadly that one could have done it in twenty minutes, and,
> as things turned out, one has to spend two days to find out why it has taken
> three weeks for someone else to do it wrong.

The principle of delegation cannot be sharply divorced from what is perhaps the most common simple declaration of organizational principle: that
authority must be equal to responsibility. The rule means that when responsibility is assigned to an office, a parallel delegation of authority is essential.
The individual to whom responsibility is given must also be granted authority
to take whatever action is necessary to carry out the assignment.

1.3   Decentralization. One form of delegation that has appeared prominently in recent years is that in which parent organizations have granted
increasing autonomy to separate plants and divisions. Such decentralization
is apparent in many large organizations and appears to be closely related to
both the simple "bigness" of some business and to more general understanding of the principles of delegation and participation. Central managements
have also recognized the need for place-to-place variations in their activities.
They have sought, at the same time, to utilize the decision-making abilities
of local and regional managers.

However, much formal decentralization is counterbalanced by the specification of central policy on all major and many minor issues. In many
arrangements, those in charge of individual divisions make tentative decisions, but action must be delayed pending approval by the central office.
Moreover, areas reserved for decision by top officials may include executive
and supervisory salary adjustments, public speaking by executives and supervisors, conference participation, grievance settlements involving money payments, capital expenditures of whatever size, and suggestion-system awards.[9]

1.4   The span of control. How broadly shall delegations be made? To
how many assistants shall the holder of responsibility delegate? How many
subordinates can be effectively directed by a superior? These are the questions to which the principle of "span of control" is directed.

Urwick's statement of the principle declares that "No superior can supervise directly the work of more than five or, at the most, six subordinates

[9] See Ernest Dale, *op. cit.,* p. 118.

whose work interlocks."[10] Urwick attributes the first modern evaluation of the principle to General Sir Ian Hamilton and to Mr. H. P. Kendall, both of whom wrote of it in the early 1920's.

The now classic statement by Graicunas appeared in the *Bulletin of the International Management Institute,* in 1933. This principle holds that the manager's or executive's span of control may exert great influence on the efficiency of management. The one-to-one, Robinson Crusoe-Friday, relationship represents the shortest span. As the span is broadened by including more subordinates whose jobs interlock, the number of interrelationships increases rapidly. Graicunas notes that:

> If A supervises two persons, B and C, he can deal with them individually or as a pair. The behavior of B in the presence of C and C in the presence of B will differ from their behavior when each is with A alone. Furthermore, what B thinks of C and what C thinks of B constitute two cross relationships which A must keep in mind when delegating work on which B and C must collaborate in A's absence. In other words, even in this extremely simple unit of organization, with two subordinates, a superior must keep up to six relationships constantly in mind.
>   Then, when a third subordinate, D, is added . . . he may have to reckon with . . . a total of 18.

Graicunas noted that addition of a fourth subordinate brings the total of interrelationships to 44, and a fifth subordinate brings that total to 100.

Criticisms of the span of control principle have been numerous. Some students have concluded that too rigid an application of the principle is responsible for the excessive layering characteristic of many large organizations and the attendant problems of communication. Others have noted that much depends on the nature of the work to be done and the level and detail of required supervision. On the basis of an empirical study, Suojanen concludes that "the span of control is no longer a valid principle of organization in view of the advances that have occurred in those social sciences that relate directly to administrative theory." He argues that, at the executive level in modern organizations, the development of primary relationships among members of the executive group has the effect of expanding the chief executive's area of supervision beyond what would be the limits prescribed by the span of control principle.[11]

Urwick notes that many criticisms of the principle are based on a misunderstanding which ignores the difference between supervision and communication. In Urwick's opinion, a superior may communicate with many or

[10] Lyndall F. Urwick, "The Manager's Span of Control," *Harvard Business Review,* Vol. 34, No. 3, May-June 1956, pp. 39–47. See also his "The Span of Control—Some Facts about the Fables," *Advanced Management,* Vol. 21, No. 11, November 1956, pp. 5–15; also Henri Fayol, *General and Industrial Management,* London: Sir Isaac Pitman & Sons, Ltd., 1949.
[11] Waino W. Suojanen, "The Span of Control—Fact or Fable," *Advanced Management,* Vol. 20, No. 11, November 1955, pp. 8ff. See also Louis A. Allen, *Management and Organization,* New York: McGraw-Hill Book Company, Inc., 1958, pp. 74, 142.

all of the individuals who are supervised by subordinates. He emphasizes the relationships of those who are supervised within the span of control—subordinates "whose work interlocks"—and concludes that the principle is sound since the span is closely related to efficient organization and administration.

2.0 TESTS OF ORGANIZATION AND ADMINISTRATION

"The new president is recognized as a great organizer and an expert in administration as well, and several members of the board of directors have forecast radical changes." When such a statement appears, what is the evidence on which it is based? What are the marks of a great organizer? How can a "good organization" be identified? What tests can and should be applied in appraising management within the working organization? What yardsticks can be used in an audit of management to measure the quality of organizing and organization?

Many managers "talk" a good organization. They say the right words in describing what they are doing and what they expect of the association they have created or reorganized. As Melville Dalton, author of *Men Who Manage,* has observed: "Moving from one staff to another did not change my impression that there was an awful gap between the boss's orientation talk and the way the job was done."[12] Former Dean J. Hugh Jackson is credited with a somewhat similar report on his study of top management. The chairman of the board of a large organization had just explained to him that every vice-president had been selected as a man who would always speak his own mind. He turned to the assembled executives and asked if he had accurately described the situation. The answer, echoed right around the table without hesitation, was "Yes, Mr. B.!"

2.1 Secondary criteria. For the most part, working organizations tend to be evaluated in terms of secondary rather than primary criteria of success. The answer to the question "How good is this management?" is usually given in terms of what the organization has or has not done. This is, of course, a natural and not unreasonable method of appraisal, since organizations are created to get things done. To the extent that they accomplish their missions, that accomplishment is an indicator of their effectiveness.

The most obvious dependence on such secondary criteria is the persistent tendency to evaluate private business organizations in terms of their profits. The usual annual and quarterly reports to stockholders provide excellent illustrations. Major attention is directed to comparisons of profits in current quarters and years with those of earlier periods and to forecasts of prospective earnings. In the usual private business, such measures of profit represent the real "payoff" and, in a sense, the acid test of the organization.

Measures of profit, useful as they are, have limitations. Like other sec-

---

[12] In the *Wiley Bulletin,* Vol. 4, No. 2, Fall 1960, p. 4. His book was published by John Wiley & Sons, Inc., in 1959.

ondary criteria, they may be influenced by many factors other than that which is being appraised. Moreover, since they are a measure of end results, they may be delayed indicators or symptoms of organizational health or illness. Profits may be high or low as a result of many conditions other than the quality of the organization. Cyclical swings in business, clearly beyond the control of any individual business management, may sharply restrict or expand current profits. High levels of profits may appear long after an organization has begun "coasting," i.e., benefiting from earlier but presently reduced effectiveness. Forecasts of profits suffer from the same limitation. What is needed is a set of yardsticks that can be applied to current organization, that can measure its present temperature, blood pressure and metabolism. The need is for direct, primary indicators of organizational and managerial quality.

2.2   Built-in bench-marks. A later chapter is devoted to periodic audits of the manpower management program as a whole, including organization. There, emphasis is placed on the desirability of building in bench-marks with each program. Evaluation and appraisal of management suffer because such yardsticks are not established when programs are undertaken.

Realistic audits of organization can be facilitated by building in measures of the purposes and immediate and long-term objectives in each organizational change. If, for example, a change is made to insure wider understanding of the organization's mission, a method of measuring such understanding can be established and observed from the time the change is made. If reorganization proposes to improve internal communications, methods of measuring results—frequent tests of information, for example—can be planned in advance. Continued observation can then measure accomplishments without waiting for ultimate effects on sales or profits or other secondary criteria.

2.3   Application of principles. Professional audits usually encounter a notable absence of such built-in yardsticks. They turn to the general principles of organization noted in Section 1.0 and attempt to measure the extent to which the organization has applied and is applying these principles. They look for evidence on such points as the following:

Are lines of authority clear? The answer must be found in practice and in the attitudes of participants, not simply in the formal lines shown in a published organization chart.

Does each participant actually report to one and only one direct superior, and does each clearly understand this relationship?

Are job descriptions explicit with respect to assignments of authority and responsibility?

Is each assignment of responsibility supported with adequate grants of authority?

Do superiors recognize their continuing responsibility for the actions of those to whom they have delegated?

Is delegation made to the lowest possible level, so that those who hold positions in higher echelons are performing no tasks that could be performed by their assistants?

Is layering held to a minimum or are there excessive ranks and echelons? What can be noted about the span of control principle? Are some managers expected to direct numerous closely interlocking jobs? On the other

---

SUMMARY

Organization is something small business operators are currently hearing a lot about. The term crops up constantly in the business and industrial press. To some plant owners it may sound like big business exclusively. But actually it isn't—or shouldn't be. The organizational setup deserves close attention in any concern made up of two or more people. Good or bad, it exists in all but the single-man firms. To rate your firm's organization, read the following statements. After each, check as objectively as you can the response which best fits conditions in your firm.

                                                                                NO   YES

1. The term "organization" has real meaning in your firm.   ☐   ☐
2. Basic company policies are clearly stated in writing.   ☐   ☐
3. Duties and responsibilities are spelled out in detail.   ☐   ☐
4. Personal characteristics have been taken into account.   ☐   ☐
5. Standard operating procedures have been established.   ☐   ☐
6. Each man has just one boss.   ☐   ☐
7. Organization relationships are charted on paper.   ☐   ☐
8. Actual company conditions are recognized and reflected in the organization chart.   ☐   ☐
9. The top man operates within the organization framework.   ☐   ☐
10. Organization structure is reviewed periodically.   ☐   ☐

Now give yourself 10 points for each "yes" box checked. A score of 80 and over is good, 70 to 40 is fair, and 30 or less shows a real need for improvement. Finally, after reading the whole Aid, re-check your answers and see if your rating would be the same.

Figure 7.1 Checklist for Rating Organization
SOURCE: "Rating Your Firm's Organization," *Management Aids for Small Manufacturers,* No. 93, April, 1959.

---

hand, is organization needlessly complicated by a thoughtless application that creates too many chiefs for the number of braves?

Is there evidence of adequate flexibility in the organization?

Such questions are applicable to working organizations of all but the smallest size. They can be helpful in firms with 15 or 20 or 50 employees, as well as in the industrial empires of big business. The Small Business Administration has recognized this in preparation of its "Rating Your Firm's

Organization." The checklist shown as Figure 7.1 is from that bulletin.[13]

Attempts to measure the extent to which these principles have been applied in the organizing process and are effective in the organization usually involve impressionistic, subjective evaluations. Somewhat more objective measures can be developed through appropriate research, as illustrated by the RAD scales developed at Ohio State University to measure the extent of assigned responsibility, authority and delegation.[14]

2.4 Appraisal of the organizing process. Existing organizations and their current organizers may be evaluated also from an approach that seeks evidence of their knowledge and understanding of the organizing process outlined in Section 1.0 of Chapter 6. It is possible, of course, that an excellent organization may have emerged largely by chance. As already noted, heavy reliance has been placed on managerial intuition. Management by intuition is now regarded, however, with serious misgivings. Hence a few questions about managers' understanding of the organizing process are in order.

Such questions will be concerned, to begin with, about how well the process of organizing has defined each of the jobs to be performed. The large number of arbitrations that arise out of conflicts over the meaning of such assignments testify to the frequency with which this part of the organizing process has been neglected.

Are levels of offices similarly clear? Does each office fit into one level in the bureaucracy, with responsibility and authority appropriate to that level? Are structures of authority and scalar status clearly and rationally defined? Does organization provide an effective communications structure?

Such questions can lead to a penetrating and valuable type of appraisal. They suggest evaluation in terms of the theories that are presumably implemented in the process of organizing and managing. At the same time, they suggest several useful measures of existing organizations. This type of appraisal deserves special attention, for it is likely to become much more common in the future.

Modern organization theory suggests, for example, that member understanding and acceptance of the mission of the organization is important to its success. One test of an organization may, therefore, seek to discover the extent to which its members have a clear understanding of its mission and the degree to which they have associated themselves with that mission. Evidence on their knowledge of the mission may be collected by interview or questionnaire. Employees who resign may be asked about the mission in their *exit interviews*. Employee suggestion systems may provide clues when they include requests for more information on what the firm is doing or intends to do. Studies of employee attitudes can provide measures of acceptance of

---

[13] *Management Aids for Small Manufacturers*, No. 93, April 1958.
[14] See Carroll L. Shartle, *Executive Performance and Leadership*, Englewood Cliffs, N.J.: Prentice-Hall, Inc., 1956, pp. 96, 190.

the mission as well as personal alliance and loyalty in seeking to accomplish the mission. Studies can discover the extent to which employees have accepted the goals of the organization as their personal goals. Measures of loyalty, so often a vague, undefined concept, may appraise this personalization of the mission.

Similar studies may note the extent to which departments, divisions and crews participate in the feeling of identification with the over-all mission of the organization.

Modern organization theory also places a high degree of importance on internal communications. An up-to-date appraisal of organizations can note the effectiveness of communications and the attitudes of participants toward communications. Measuring sticks include morale and attitude studies, scales for the measurement of transmitted information, and other similar instruments.

Member acceptance of formal authority and status systems deserves similar consideration. On what basis have managers sought to gain acceptance of these systems? Are employees expected to accept them because they are traditional? Are leaders in the organization expected to justify charismatic authority? (The answer to this last question appears generally affirmative.) How do participants regard these systems?

Such questions will also elicit an appraisal of *leadership*. They can discover how members of working groups regard the competence of supervision and management at various levels. Do employee and union demands for greater influence in managerial decisions indicate a lack of confidence in the competence of managers?

It is to be noted that instruments and devices by which these tests are made represent important tools of the industrial relations manager and his staff. The process of perfecting these and additional instruments represents a major challenge to industrial relations research.[15]

3.0 SUMMARY

This chapter, building on the outline of organization structures in Chapter 6, has been concerned with the administrative process, widely accepted principles of administration, and problems of appraising or evaluating working organizations. This chapter has only sketched a general outline of management or administration, because management jobs receive detailed attention in chapters on supervisory and management development (Chaps. 18 and 19). A summary of the major points, including brief reference to those made in Chapter 6, might be developed somewhat as follows:

1. Organization is a tool of management, used to create *a systematic union of people* in a *hierarchy of offices*.

[15] See Rensis Likert, "Measuring Organizational Performance," *Harvard Business Review*, Vol. 36, No. 2, March-April 1958, pp. 41–50; Rensis Likert, Chris Argyris, James March, and Herbert Shepard, "Management Implications of Recent Social Science Research," *Personnel Administration*, Vol. 21, No. 3, May-June 1958, pp. 4–14.

2. Formal organization is created by authority; informal organization is spontaneous.

. 3. Formal organizations include *concepts* or *missions* and *structures* of offices and positions.

4. Working organizations specialize horizontally for types of work and vertically for assignments of authority and responsibility.

5. Bases for horizontal specialization include skills, products, processes, tools, equipment, and customers; for vertical specialization the basis is presumably the specialized competence of supervision and management.

6. The organizing process (a) divides the work to be done, assigning duties and responsibilities; (b) creates a hierarchy of offices and roles with titles and symbols; (c) creates formal systems of authority and status; and (d) creates a structure for internal communications.

7. Accepted principles of management emphasize delegation, span of control, balance of authority and responsibility, clarity of lines, simplicity, and flexibility.

8. The most common check or evaluation of private working organizations is that which notes what are regarded as their results or evidence of their success.

9. The most useful test of organizers and managers is probably one that measures them against principles and up-to-date theory, evaluating the extent to which they have implemented these guides.

Organizations are created and maintained to accomplish missions or objectives. They have goals. To accomplish these goals, organizers and managers establish guiding policies. Some of the most important of these policies refer to their intentions in the management of the people who fill the offices of their organizations. Our attention turns, therefore, to the nature and significance of general policy in manpower management, which is the subject of the chapter that follows.

SELECTED SUPPLEMENTARY READINGS

Bendix, Reinhard, "The Cultural and Political Setting of Economic Rationality in Western Europe," *Reprint No. 149,* Berkeley, Calif.: University of California Institute of Industrial Relations, 1960.

Berle, A. A., "Economic Power and the Free Society," Santa Barbara, Calif.: Fund for the Republic, December 1957.

Dale, Ernest, *The Great Organizers.* New York: McGraw-Hill Book Company, Inc., 1960.

Dubin, Robert, *Human Relations in Administration,* pp. 79–112. Englewood Cliffs, N.J.: Prentice-Hall, Inc., 1951.

Jasinski, Frank K., "Adapting Organization to New Technology," *Harvard Business Review,* Vol. 37, No. 1, pp. 79–86, January-February 1959.

Lawrence, Paul R., *et al., Organizational Behavior and Administration,* Homewood, Illinois: Richard D. Irwin, Inc., 1961.

Simon, Herbert, "Authority," in Conrad M. Arensberg, *et al.,* eds. *Research in Industrial Human Relations,* pp. 103–114. New York: Harper & Brothers, 1957.

Erwin S. Stanton, "Which Approach to Management—Democratic, Authoritarian or . . . ," *Personnel Administration,* Volume 25, Number 2, March-April, 1962, pp. 44–47.

Urwick, Lyndall F., "The Manager's Span of Control," *Harvard Business Review,* Vol. 34, No. 3, pp. 39–47, May-June 1956.

Young, William D., "A Note on 'Syntality' in Small Work Groups," *Personnel Administration,* Vol. 24, No. 1, pp. 39ff. February 1961.

SHORT CASE PROBLEM 7.1

The University as an Organization

Our speaker on November 11th, Dr. X, gave us a great deal to think about. On the basis of his long experience as a faculty member, department head, and dean, he suggested that business could learn a lot about organization by studying the relationships within a first-class university. Both policies and practices, he concluded, could be readily transferred from the campus to the business district.

He began by pointing to the fact that the typical organization of our better universities has a long history and has been adopted all over the world in such educational institutions. Further, he noted, there have been very few "business failures" among the universities. Many of them have a long, successful record that extends back several hundred years. They have had very few internal conflicts sufficiently serious to handicap their operations or cause work stoppages. Yet they have traditionally been regarded as economically poor. Their relatively low salaries have always been a matter for public comment and concern. How, he asked, have they managed to keep going and to grow and expand in the face of these obvious difficulties? The answer, he concludes, lies in the general principles that guide the organization and administration of all great universities. He listed the following major principles:

1. Everyone, inside and out, knows why they exist and thinks they should continue their work.
2. Authority in these organizations is clearly defined and specifically allocated.
3. Administrative managers handle financial policies and practices without invasions of their managerial prerogatives.
4. Faculties handle educational policy and practice without interference from administrators.
5. Faculties are fully consulted in the selection of administrators.
6. All faculty members participate in decisions on educational policy and practice.
7. Relationships allow a maximum of freedom for individual ideas and action.
8. Personnel decisions are made by senior co-workers.
9. Status is defined by a traditional rank system.
10. Recruitment is based upon widely accepted evidences of competence—advanced degrees, experience, reported research.
11. Promotion is based on self-established criteria known to all—teaching, research, publication, public service, etc.
12. An annual review by colleagues is an established practice.
13. The salary classification system is related to rank.
14. Status symbols are widely known and accepted—standard job titles, degrees, membership in learned societies, gowns, hoods, etc.
15. Security is supported by a national organization of faculty members—A.A.U.P.

16. Members develop personal pride in both the organization and their position.

Problem: Evaluate the speaker's argument.

SHORT CASE PROBLEM 7.2

Pibson Canning Company

The Pibson Canning Company includes only about a hundred permanent employees. But the president, having read about multiple management, wants to secure the benefits of committee organization. Several years ago, he created a Junior Board of twelve members. He encouraged the Junior Board to look into all aspects of the business and consider both policy and practice.

Members of the Junior Board have, at least until recently, taken their responsibilities seriously. They have studied the past and present business experience of the firm. They have made a total of 22 major recommendations.

Early in their experience, they recommended a gift of $25,000 to a campaign which was raising funds for a community hospital. The city is small and has never had a hospital. The firm is the largest employer in the city. Yet the Board of Directors, most of whose members now live in Florida and California, turned this suggestion down with short consideration.

More recently, the Junior Board, after lengthy study and discussion, recommended that the firm contract for and farm a large portion of the land on which its raw material is grown. In this instance, again, the Board of Directors was abrupt in dismissing the suggestion.

Although many minor suggestions have been approved, these two major setbacks have seriously affected the morale and interest of Junior Board members. Several of them have asked to be replaced.

Problem: Should the Junior Board have made such recommendations? The Junior Board has scheduled a meeting to discuss its status and future. As a member, what would you say? Even without the benefit of greater detail, how would you suggest that this committee arrangement be improved?

8. General Policy on Manpower Management

The first major functional division of activities in the field of manpower management, according to the outline presented in Chapter 1, is concerned with organization and policy. Preceding chapters have sought to evidence the importance of organization and administration in setting the tone and climate for effective, satisfying work. Attention turns, in the present chapter, to the part played by general manpower policy and the importance of appropriate policy in managing manpower resources.

Policy-making represents one area of management in which an *A* for effort and intention is appropriate, for policy is a matter of *intentions*. Policies flow from goals or objectives or missions and represent *chosen courses* to be followed in seeking to attain such objectives. Managers develop, advance, and articulate the policies they regard as appropriate for this purpose. As suggested by Figure 4.1, proposed policies express their theories about how goals are achieved.

Policy on manpower management is only a part of the total policy of the working organization. It presumably should be consistent and compatible with other policy in which intentions are defined with respect to other resources. At the same time, manpower policy is not limited to the proposals of managers. It includes provisions, modifications and amendments proposed by employees, their unions, and public agencies. Some statements of manpower policy may represent the joint conclusions of managers and unions, expressed in collective bargaining agreements. Less obviously, shrewd managers may plan their policy proposals to incorporate informal suggestions from employees. Similarly, they may anticipate the policy preferences of public regulatory agencies.

General policy on industrial relations expresses the *broad intentions* of the parties with respect to relationships of people in the working organization. It thus prescribes the general guidelines for more specific policy in each of the other functional areas. This chapter is concerned with the formulation, determination, and communication of *general policy*. Later chapters note its implications for such activities as recruitment, selection, training and development, compensation, and the maintenance of morale.

1.0 POLICY: THE INTENTIONS IN MANAGEMENT

A cynical observation repeated in cartoons and comic postcards runs somewhat as follows: "Please don't ask us why; it's just our policy!" Similarly, the traffic officer who issues a ticket and the foreman who issues orders to his crew are frequently caricatured as saying: "I don't make the policy; I just enforce it." The "bible" of the timid or more constrained manager has become his handbook of SOP, standard operating policy. The concept of policy as an outline of guiding rules has attracted wide attention.

Meanwhile, policy is a subject that has come to occupy increasing prominence in all courses in management. Students may be urged to give more attention to policy and less to techniques. They are encouraged to aspire to become policy-makers rather than technicians who carry out the policies made by others. A cap-stone course in "Business Policy" is a common feature of college curricula in business or management.

What is this policy that has become so important to managers and embryo managers? Why is an understanding of policy more to be desired than proficiency in practice, programs, techniques, and procedures?

A policy is *a predetermined and accepted course of thought and action that is defined and established as a guide toward accepted goals and objectives.* Individuals have their personal policies which they have developed to keep them on the track toward their personal objectives. Organizations have managerial policies for the same reason. Some of the most important organizational policies outline selected intentions with respect to the management of people. They provide the guidelines for employment relationships in the organization, just as purchasing policy may require competitive bids or selling policy may seek to maintain a list price. To quote S. A. Raube of the National Industrial Conference Board, policies "provide the base for management by principle as contrasted with management by expediency."

These guide lines on relations with people are what is meant by *personnel, labor, manpower management, or industrial relations policy.*

Such policy seeks to keep management on the track toward the objectives it has set for itself in these relationships.¹ Policy—including policy on the management of and relationships with people—is a case of management talking to itself. In such policy, a management tells itself—and perhaps others to whom the policy is communicated—how it proposes to attain the goals it regards as most important. It marks a map with the routes it proposes to follow to get where it wants to go.

Labor policy is defined by the *Industrial Relations Glossary*² as "the principles or objectives established by a company for the guidance of the management in its relations with employees." The *Management Dictionary*³ defines *manpower policies* as "statements of the goals or aims and objectives which define the intentions of the organization with respect to manpower management. . . ."

Essentials in these definitions are apparent. Policies are recognized *intentions*. Labor or industrial relations policies are intentions or established *courses* with respect to the relationships with the people who make up the organization.

1.1 Policies, programs, practices, and procedures. Policy is, in a sense, the starting line for all managerial relationships with employees. The management of people begins with ideas, implicit or explicit, as to what are the purposes, goals, and intentions in such employment. On the basis of such objectives, we may declare our policies, which are descriptions of the course we intend to take. On the basis of such policies, managements develop *programs*—carefully planned campaigns or procedures—presumably designed to carry out established policies. Carrying out the programs results in certain activities or *practices* and *procedures*.

Policies declare what we intend to do; they describe the course we have set for ourselves. They describe *what* is intended; programs and practices and procedures describe *how* we propose to do what the policies outline. *Programs* represent simple or complex activities, presumably developed to implement policy. They may require appropriate action or practice at all levels throughout an organization. *Practices* and *procedures* are the specific actions that may be combined in a program. *Procedures* may be more formally detailed or specified than practices.

An illustration of these relationships may help to make the distinctions clear. Our firm may have adopted a *policy* of providing training for all employees as a means of preparing them for promotion. To implement this policy, we may have developed an extensive *training program*. That *program* may include specific job training for new employees, supervisory training for foremen and supervisors, and management development for members of the management group. In the supervisory training program, we may include *role playing* as one of many training practices. Again, it may be our practice to announce the availability of training courses in the spring and fall of each

¹ Edward Schleh, "Personnel Policy—A Track to Run On," *Personnel,* Vol. 30, No. 6, May 1954, pp. 445–453.
² *Bulletin, 6,* University of Minnesota Industrial Relations Center, 1948, p. 8.
³ A. E. Benn, New York: Exposition Press, Inc., 1952, p. 258.

year. As a further step in the implementation of the policy, we may maintain specific *procedures* for enrollment or for maintaining an appropriate record of individual training.

These distinctions are not complicated. Nevertheless, policy is frequently confused with practice and procedure. Perhaps this is because programs and procedures are obvious and tangible, while policy may or may not be explicitly stated. In such cases, observers may infer policy from practice. Such an inference may be in error. For example, the fact that a firm consistently pays the highest wages or salaries in an area may be regarded as expressing a definite policy to be leaders in this respect. This assumption may be incorrect; the practice may result from the firm's policy to pay the same wages and salaries in all of its several plants located throughout the country.[4]

1.2 Public policy. In a course or text that is concerned primarily with management in a firm or agency, major attention is given to policy in the individual organization. All such policy must be viewed, however, in a setting defined in part by public policy on employment relationships. In the United States, for example, public policy specifies such working conditions as minimum wages and normal hours for many workers, provides general rules for the relationships of employers and unions, and outlines a broad pattern of public benefits designed to maintain the economic security of workers. While nothing similar to a Declaration of Independence provides a succinct summary of such public policy, these ground rules are widely recognized. Some of them have been traditional since establishment of the nation. Some are outlined in the declarations of policy in national legislation. As a basic policy, we insist that each worker must be free to choose among jobs. Again, we propose a system of public employment offices to help individuals find the jobs they want and to assist employers in finding jobholders.

Other labor policies refer to specific employment conditions under which we want people to work. We insist that employment shall be postponed until young people have completed specified schooling. The 1935 Wagner Act declared the public policy that employees shall have the right to bargain collectively through unions of their own choosing. Federal and state minimum-wage laws declare as public policy that they disapprove working conditions detrimental to minimum standards of health, efficiency, and general well-being. The 1947 Amendments to the National Labor Relations Act declare that employers and unions must recognize each other's legitimate

---

[4] For excellent examples of these distinctions, see the many reports on industrial relations policy and industrial relations practice, such as Ernest C. Miller, "Personnel Policy in a Decentralized Organization," *Personnel Journal*, Vol. 38, No. 7, December 1959, pp. 257–260; R. R. Hopkins, "Industrial Change and Employment Policy," *Personnel Management*, Vol. 16, No. 349, September 1959, pp. 138–144; Carroll E. French, "What Basic Policies Should Govern Personnel Administration?" in *Addresses in Industrial Relations—1957 Series,* Ann Arbor, Mich.: Bureau of Industrial Relations, University of Michigan, 1957; David P. Mayer, "What is Policy?" *Personnel Administration,* Vol. 20, No. 1, January-February 1957, pp. 33–35; H. Ellsworth Steele, W. R. Myles, and C. McIntyre, "Personnel Practices in the South," *Industrial and Labor Relations Review,* Vol. 9, No. 2, January 1956, pp. 241–251.

rights. Federal legislation requires reporting of activities by unions and specifies guiding rules for certain benefit trust funds. State right-to-work laws
express public policy on requiring employees to be union members.

1.3 Formal and informal policy. What of the firm or agency that has
no labor policy? The answer is that such a firm probably doesn't exist. What
is meant in statements that a firm has no policy is that no formal statement
of policy has been circulated or communicated. That does not mean, however, that there is no policy. It may mean, moreover, that managers, supervisors, employees, and the public must infer policy from the actions of top
managers.

Many thoughtful managements have provided carefully formulated statements of general policy in manpower management. For example, the general
manager and chairman of the board of Stop and Shop, Inc., Mr. Sidney R.
Rabb, has outlined what he describes as their "ten commandments" as
follows:[5]

1. To deal with each employee fairly and with respect for his human
   dignity.
2. To treat each employee as an important person in the organization.
3. To recognize that each contributes to and that each depends on the
   accomplishment of the whole group.
4. To provide the best wages and working conditions and social benefits consistent with current business practice and company earnings.
5. To make every effort to insure security of employment and income
   for all employees.
6. To provide safe and pleasant work environments.
7. To employ people whose qualifications and experience fit the requirements of each position.
8. To develop employees in accordance with their natural capacities
   and to build a trained, efficient "team."
9. To afford opportunities for advancement based on merit.
10. To conduct fair and just relations with representatives chosen by
    employee groups.

Similarly, in a booklet entitled "The Principles of Aldens," that firm has
outlined specific policies on employer-employee relations. The statement proposes, for example, to maintain one rule of fairness, with no favoritism; to
avoid discrimination; to maintain wages, salaries, and benefits that compare
favorable with progressive companies; to give prompt and thoughtful attention to grievances; to encourage employee suggestions; and to promote from
within the organization whenever possible. An excellent illustration of such
a formal declaration is that of Thompson Products (now Thompson, Ramo,
Woolridge), shown as Figure 8.1. Many other carefully considered statements, some much more detailed, will be found in employee handbooks and
orientation materials.

[5] In "The Wonderful Power of People," published by Stop and Shop, Inc., undated.

"OUR PLEDGE"

We pledge, so long as the affairs of this company are in our hands, that the following principles will govern our relations with members of the organization:

1. We will pay wages which will always compare favorably with prevailing rates in the area for the occupation. Any employee or group of employees at any time may request a wage survey to verify the fairness of the rate.
2. With friendliness, we will meet with employees from any group or department, or their proper representatives, to discuss any requested improvements in conditions, hours, policies, or practices.
3. Any grievance will be fairly and promptly settled through steps provided in our posted Grievance Procedure.
4. Practices with respect to paid vacations, paid holidays, overtime premiums, recognition of length of service, retirement benefits, and general conditions such as safety, cleanliness, and employee accommodations will always compare favorably with good community practices.
5. We will devote our best efforts and thinking to the building of a growing business within which will prevail an atmosphere of friendship and harmony with steady jobs and opportunity for all.

(From "Human Relations Policy," Thompson Products, Inc., 1957)

Figure 8.1 Formal Policy Statement

1.4 Significance of policy. Reference has been made to the current emphasis on policy in educational preparation for management. Such an emphasis is justified; there are important reasons why all managers should understand the nature and impact of policy in working organizations.

Determination of policy requires decisions that transcend the immediate situation and thus set a course for continuing decisions. Policy decisions become the compelling precedent for numerous subsequent decisions in specific situations. Policy decisions therefore require a special level of thoughtfulness and competence. The derivation of the term policy suggests such consideration, for it implies sagacity, shrewdness, and wisdom.

As Peter Drucker has noted, basic policy decisions require the balancing of values and objectives, needs and goals. They require judgment and the ability to comprehend and give priorities to a variety of goals.[6] Personnel or manpower policies, for example, must be related to all the goals of the whole organization and its members. The pattern and interrelationship of these goals are seldom simple. Even for the small private firm, profitmaking is not usually the sole nor even the most important long-term goal. As Drucker, Joynt, Newman, Mee, and many others have noted, policies must also reflect the kind of reputation a firm seeks, its conception of broad social and local community responsibilities, its balancing of long-term and short-term objectives, and its philosophy of management-supervisor-employee relationships.[7]

[6] Peter F. Drucker, The Practice of Management, New York: Harper & Brothers, 1954.
[7] See William H. Newman, "Objectives That Shape the Character of a Company," *Journal of Business,* Vol. 26, No. 4, October 1953, pp. 211–223. John B. Joynt,

Policy is important, however, not only because it involves difficult decisions and expresses the basic philosophy of the organization but also because it sets the pattern for all the programs, practices, and procedures that are developed to translate policy into action. That is why policy on employment relationships is frequently described as the keystone in the arch of manpower management. That is why, also, trouble-shooters called in to improve current employee relations programs begin with a survey of labor policy. To summarize:

1. Since policy states the intentions of the program, its clear definition and broad, uniform understanding are essential to consistent action throughout the organization. In the absence of firm policy, individual divisions and departments are likely to develop and apply their own policies and interpretations. Chaotic programs are a frequent expression of this condition, with employees requesting transfers to divisions with more satisfactory policies, and with individual departments seeking to outdo each other in the liberality and generosity of their policies.

2. Sound policy is, of course, an essential basis for sound practice. If the stated course of action is not clear, or if policies are haphazard, conflicting, or ill-advised, programs for their accomplishment inevitably reflect these deficiencies.

3. Policy is the essential yardstick by which to measure accomplishment in the program. No one can tell whether a program is effective in the absence of an understanding of what it is designed to accomplish. Hence, appraisal of the entire manpower management program begins by evaluating policy and then turns to comparisons of practice and the results of practice with policy.

2.0 LEVELS OF POLICY

Some policy making in a firm or an agency is the usual responsibility of each scalar level or echelon throughout the organization. Thus, for example, in a state public employment service, individual offices may develop policies with respect to office hours or internal practice in taking registrations (although policy at this level comes close to practice or procedure), while general policy for the service may be developed by the state legislature and the federal congress. In the usual practice, lower levels of the structure are granted authority to establish policies in rather strictly limited areas with emphasis on selection of appropriate practices; inclusive, pervading policies may be developed only in upper levels of management.

In a related but somewhat different sense, two distinct levels of policy may be noted. One may be called the *general manpower or employment policy* of

"Management's Basic Function: Policy Formulation," *Advanced Management*, Vol. 19, No. 8, August 1954, pp. 11–15; John F. Mee, "Management Philosophy for Professional Executives," *Business Horizons*, December 1956, pp. 5–11.

the organization. The other level consists of *specific policies* with respect to major activities in manpower management.

2.1 General policy. As noted above, general policy emerges from the detailed, thoughtful balancing of numerous and perhaps conflicting goals and objectives of the total organization. It represents conclusions based on weighing and ranking and integrating these objectives. It can be regarded as the highest level of policy because it develops accepted courses defined by choices among numerous alternatives in the major goals of the organization and its members. In contrast, *specific* policy represents the application of predetermined general policy to particular employment activities and functions, such as staffing or collective bargaining.

Since policy is a declaration of intentions and a selection of set courses to be followed, general policy in managing people in an organization must carefully consider the ultimate ends or objectives to be sought. The formulation of general policy must, therefore, lean heavily on the philosophy of managers and their acceptance of various theories of work and organization. It must determine what weights are to be placed on conditions believed to influence performance in work and the success of working organizations. It must decide, for example, how much weight shall be given to insuring a wide understanding of the mission of the organization. How important is the economic security of employees? To what extent shall the organization seek to encourage wide participation in management? How seriously shall managers regard the extent to which employees identify themselves with the whole? How may these and other objectives be combined to chart the course to be followed in managing people?

Such questions of primary objectives and goals are complicated because these objectives are always plural. Few if any organizations can claim to have a single, simple objective. Despite the constant reiteration that *the objective* of the private firm is *profit,* the fact is that most firms seek many objectives, of which profit is but one. This plurality of goals carries over into each major phase of management, including the management of people. Although increased *worker productivity* is widely described as *the* goal, it also is only one of several. *General employment policy* represents the reconciliation of all these objectives in a general course to be followed throughout the organization.

Examples may be helpful. The firm that seeks to outdistance competitors may place a higher priority on developing managerial leadership for the future than on immediate increases in productivity. It may emphasize encouragement of creativity and originality among employees. It may seek, perhaps as most important, to encourage suggestions for improving products and creating new products. If it requires specially qualified technical talent, policy may propose maintenane of high levels of job satisfaction that will hold and retain qualified employees. In many American firms, a traditional high priority goal is the desire of a management to be favorably regarded by employees. To some extent, the policy of paternalism, not unusual for many older firms, is an expression of this objective.

Some managements give heavy weight to maintaining a reputation as a "leading" or "progressive" or "enlightened" management. Some feel heavy responsibilities, if not obligations, to the local communities in which employees live. In recent years, some firms have sought to demonstrate, by their relationships with employees, the superiority of the system of free enterprise over socialist economies.

General policy results from a process of noting, evaluating, weighing, balancing, and combining such goals and selecting general courses to be followed. It thus describes selected routes, intended patterns of managerial attitudes and actions.

Resulting patterns of policy must be subject to change, for a complex and balanced general policy that is appropriate at one time may become unacceptable at a later period. Changing philosophies, as well as new knowledge and changing theories, require changes in policy. Meanwhile, changes in the external environment of the firm, in its competition or in public regulation, also justify frequent review and revision of policy.

The development of general policy requires the knowledge and perspective and experience of the most competent members of management. For that reason, general policy in manpower management—as in finance, marketing, or research—is a matter of concern to the top executives of the working organization. As general policy, it affects and should reflect all activities throughout the whole structure, from automation to purchasing. Thus a decision to emphasize the development of employee identification with the goals of the organization will require understanding and appropriate action in sales as well as in production, marketing, and research and development. Again, a policy of maximizing employee security may affect labor costs in every department. Policy that proposes a maximum of employee participation has implications for the behavior of every foreman and supervisor.

2.2 Specific policy. Specific policy on employment and manpower management interprets and applies general policy to each major activity in managing people. Once general manpower policies have been defined, they must be translated into policies on staffing, on compensation, on employee and management development, and on collective bargaining.

Development of specific policy requires a weighing and balancing of general policies not unlike the determination of priorities in goals at the general policy level. Specific policy determination is complicated by the fact that applications of general policy to particular problems creates new questions. In staffing, for example, how are twin policies of finding the best man for each job and encouraging employee development for promotion to be reconciled?

Figure 8.2 may be helpful in understanding and recognizing these principal levels of industrial relations policy. It has been developed in conferences with managers to help them understand the relationships among the over-all, inclusive values to be sought (the top level), general manpower policy (level number II) and specific or functional policy (level number III). In Section I, managers who use the checklist try to develop the weights they would apply to each of the intentions at this "where we want to go" level. Then, in Section II, they consider the implications of these objectives for their decisions on general manpower policy.

Section III of the figure directs discussion of policy to the specific activity level, with prorities to be assigned to such items as provision of competent leaders, recruitment, selection, promotion from within, relationships with unions, and other similar operational activities.

3.0 POLICY DEVELOPMENT AND COMMUNICATION

Section 2 of this chapter suggests that development of general policy on industrial relations must have the attention of top executives and administrators. In public agencies, such policy may be declared by legislative bodies. Such a viewpoint is, however, somewhat misleading. As a matter of reality, rank-and-file employees may influence and modify general policy. First-line supervisors may also have a great deal of influence in shaping such policy. Staff members in an industrial relations or personnel department may be influential in determining both general and specific policy. The most significant word in the preceding sentences is "influence." With or without any formal assignment to create general policy, members of an organization may nevertheless influence that policy. They may have little or great influence. Employees may organize, forming unions to represent them and thus to consolidate their influence. Staff members have prestige and status based on their specialized competence, so that their recommendations on policy carry great influence. Policy making is thus much more than a simple, formal process; its formalities mask what may be a much more subtle, complex, participative process.

3.1 **Who makes policy?** What are the major sources of influence in policy making? Who determines what policies, general and specific, shall provide the road map for employment relationships? The question is not who states them but who determines them.

In our system, part of our labor policy is public; it is determined by our legislators and administrators. Congress, presumably expressing the will of our citizens, has established the principle that employees may bargain through unions. A state legislature, presumably expressing the will of its citizens and ultimate determiners of public policy, decides that no one shall work at wages below a specified minimum. A city council may establish the policy that picketing shall not interfere with traffic. Or a local mayor or police chief may rule that police will prevent certain activities of pickets.

Other labor policy is made by unions. They may determine that members

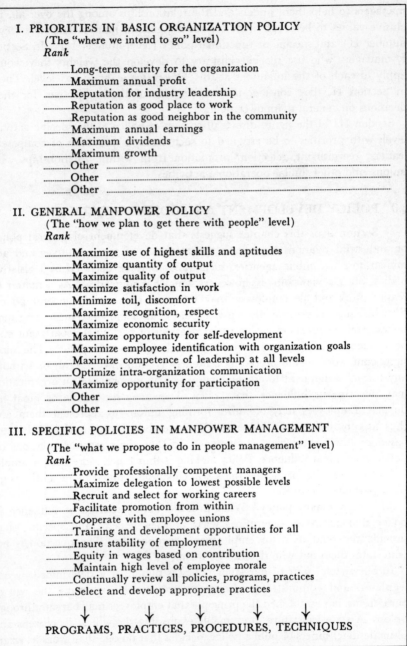

Figure 8.2   Checklist of Policies for Manpower Management

shall not cross picket lines, or that no member shall work on a job on which non-union craftsmen are employed, or that members will not work without a current contract.

The individual employee may have an extensive labor policy of his own. He may decide that he will work only on weekdays, or that he will only work at his trade, refusing any other kind of employment. He may have a policy of refusing to travel, working only on jobs he can reach from his present home. He may insist on wages representing the "scale" and determine not to work on a piecework or output basis. He may decide for or against joining a union.

The employer must establish numerous labor policies. In part he is a "joint determiner," for many labor policies are established in negotiation and in contract administration. In part he acts unilaterally, deciding what policies he will maintain in the employment he directs. Because the employer acts in a very broad area and managers have major responsibility for so many conditions of employment, they have been and are major determiners of employment policy.

Although prestige is associated with policy making, not all employees and managers show equal interest in participating in the policy-making process. Because it is widely recognized that the privilege of setting policy also carries responsibilities, some employees as well as managers are inclined to avoid policy making.

3.2   Staff and line responsibility. Personnel and industrial relations staff divisions do not determine general manpower policy, for such policy takes into account goals and objectives that lie beyond the area of specialized competence represented by any single staff division. On the other hand, they may exert great influence on general policy on employment relationships. If the chief personnel officer is a vice-president or member of the executive council of management, such an influence is facilitated. If the personnel division has specialized competence, if it keeps abreast of developments in the field, its advice may carry great weight.

Here is how one business organization describes this relationship:

> All policies with respect to personnel shall be formulated by, or cleared through the Executive Director of Personnel and reviewed by the President, or in his absence the Chairman of the Board, before decision is made to submit them to the Executive Committee for final approval.
>
> The Personnel Division shall guide and control the application of Personnel Policies throughout the company in collaboration with the responsible managers, but all Executives, Managers and Supervisors shall accept the responsibility for properly administering these policies within their respective areas.

What is the responsibility of employee relations staff members in labor-policy determination? They must try to guide policy-makers toward sound, appropriate policy. They should provide facts and specialized knowledge as a basis for decisions on policy. They are the principal counselors on labor policy. Their expertness should reflect a thorough understanding of what labor policy is legally acceptable, what policies have been effective in other firms, what policy is out of date, and where added policy is needed.

Policy is formulated when it is put together in a systematized statement or formula. Policy formulation is a continuing process, because new and modified policies are constantly being adopted and must be integrated with each other and with older policy.

Ideas for changes in or expansion of labor policy come from a variety of sources. They may originate with rank-and-file employees. Expressions of *employee dissatisfaction* or of the need for additional policy may be gained from reports of supervisors, suggestion systems, attitude surveys, publications, and other means of in-plant communication. Employee reactions to present or proposed policy may be solicited through interviews, including *exit-interviews,* or may be apparent in union publications or letters to the editor of the employee magazine.

Supervisors are an important source of suggestions on manpower policy. Foremen and supervisors hold major roles in the whole employee relations program. Deficiencies in current policy may become quickly apparent to them, as may an unfilled need for policy. Policy deficiencies often become apparent in supervisors' training courses, when these involve a free exchange of ideas and opinions.

Another major source of suggestions for changes is the *experience of other firms.* Staff representatives are responsible for keeping informed of these developments and noting their implications for policy. To some extent, this information is reported in the periodical literature of the field, the journals and the labor reporting services. Conferences arranged by local and national professional associations and university industrial relations centers often give major attention to policy questions. Both periodicals and conferences report on research that may suggest changes in current labor policy or necessary additional policies.

Grievances and arbitrations involving contract interpretation may disclose deficiencies in policy and suggest desirable changes. Records of similar developments in other organizations may be helpful in suggesting desirable modifications of policy.

One of the most common bases for revision of labor policy is the continual *review or audit* of employment relations, in which deficiencies in both policies and practice are disclosed.

All managers, in all divisions and at all levels in the organization, can make suggestions for needed new policy and for revisions in existing policy. In addition, however, if management is to implement a policy encouraging employee participation, it must provide ample opportunity for employees to express their preferences.[8]

3.3 Employee representation plans. The participation of rank-and-file employees in policy making need not be limited to collective bargaining. Even within organizations in which all or practically all employees are represented by unions, there is room for much wider employee participation. In several European nations, rank-and-file employees participate through

---

[8] See Ernest C. Miller, "Personnel Policy in a Decentralized Organization," *Personnel Journal,* Vol. 38, No. 7, December 1959, pp. 258–259.

works councils or *employee representation plans* in addition to their union representation. In the areas in which employees have specialized competence, management can gain valuable insights and ideas from such participation. Many managers in the United States may regard all representation plans as illegal. Others fear that such arrangements may become stepping stones toward formal unions of employees.

3.4 Communication and interpretation. If policies are to provide guides for practice, they must be widely known and understood. Policy must be translated into action. Such translation requires wide knowledge of the policies and common understanding of their meaning.

Recognition of the necessity for communicating policies throughout an organization is not new. Figure 8.3 provides evidence on this point in a historic combination of general and specific policy and shop work rules posted where all could see them. Some firms continue the practice of posting general and specific employment policies in prominent positions on bulletin boards throughout the plant. More common today is the practice of outlining employment policy in an *employee handbook*. In many organizations, general and specific policies are detailed in a *policy manual* which is placed in the hands of all managers and supervisors and may be available to all employees.

A first step in communicating and interpreting employment policy is to put it in writing. Many managers, however, are reluctant about committing themselves in writing. They argue that such statements may be misinterpreted and thus cause confusion. They regard some policies as confidential or secret.

The fact that policy is written tends to keep it in the forefront of attention and thus to encourage its constant recognition. Clarence Francis has stated this argument clearly:

> If you write it (policy) down, you have got to live up to it or die trying. If you set a high standard, you will fall far short of perfection. But your performance, simply because you have pledged yourself to the standard, will be better than it would be if you lacked a specific goal.[9]

Also important is the fact that written policies are more readily communicated to all members of the work team. The writing of the policy encourages both greater exactness and precision and more careful, critical attention. As a result, written policy may be assumed to be more carefully considered and certain.

Such a written statement may appear to employees, however, as a hollow shell and a glorified combination of big words that mean little. Statements of general policy have a tendency to sound somewhat like campaign speeches; they promise everything in general but nothing in particular. They are sub-

[9] In "The Causes of Industrial Peace," New York: National Association of Manufacturers, 1948.

Rules for Employees in 1880 by the owner of the Mt. Cory Iron Works

1. Office employees will daily sweep the floors, dust the furniture, shelves, and closets.
2. Each day fill the lamps, clean chimneys, and trim wicks.
3. Each man will bring in a bucket of water and scuttle of coal for the day's business.
4. Make your pens carefully—you may whittle nibs to your individual taste.
5. This office will open at 7 A.M. and close at 8 P.M. daily, except on the Sabbath, on which day it will remain closed.
6. Men employees will be given an evening off each week for courting purposes, or two evenings a week if they go regularly to church.
7. Every employee should lay aside from each pay a goodly sum of his earnings for his benefit during his declining years, so that he will not become a burden upon charity of his betters.
8. Any employee who smokes Spanish cigars, uses liquor in any form, gets shaved at a barber shop, or frequents pool and public halls, will give us good reason to suspect his worth, intentions, integrity, and honesty.
9. The employee who has performed his labors faithfully and without fault for a period of five years in our service, who has been thrifty and attentive to his religious duties, who is looked upon by his fellow men as a substantial and law-abiding citizen, will be given an increase of five cents a day in his pay—providing a just return in profits from the business permits.

Figure 8.3   Early Employment Policy

ject to wide and varying interpretations. For this reason, any summary statement of general policy should be explained, perhaps by illustration.

Employee relations staff members usually have the responsibility for preparing such materials and keeping them up to date. For example, assume a firm has adopted a general policy of non-discrimination, which has been stated as follows:

> *Non-Discrimination in Hiring*—No discrimination shall be made in either recruitment and selection or in promotion on the basis of nationality, race, sex, or political or religious affiliation.

As soon as the policy is approved, a more detailed statement of specific policy is prepared for the guidance of all supervisors and managers. A portion of this specific policy, that relating to recruitment and selection, is reproduced as Figure 8.4. A similar statement in another section of the policy manual outlines guide rules for action on promotion.[10] Note that the policy makes existing application forms obsolete. It has immediate implications for employment interviews. It may cause numerous problems in some departments if present employees object to newcomers selected under the new policy. Supervisors must be cautioned to make a record of reasons for rejection, lest they be charged with violations of the policy. A variety of procedural changes may be necessary in putting the new policy into effect.

Detailed interpretations of policy are especially important if the wording of policy statements is involved and complicated, as is commonly true of

---

[10] For more on procedures, see *Personnel Procedure Manuals,* New York: National Industrial Conference Board, June 1961.

negotiated policy. The language of most collective bargaining agreements is difficult, to say the least. Ample evidence on that point is provided by the number of arbitrations that are required to interpret these clauses. When a

---

3.21   Policy (Adopted 6/1/60, Minutes, Page 503) provides that there shall be no discrimination on the basis of nationality, race, sex or political or religious affiliation in hiring.

Observations:

(1) *Application form* will be revised immediately to eliminate present items 3, 4, and 5. All old forms are to be forwarded to Room 309 immediately.

(2) *Interviewers* in Employment Division will discontinue use of questions relating to race, religion, ancestry, or color.

(3) *Supervisors and foremen* will note in detail on referral form reasons for rejection of any applicant.

(4) *Supervisors and foremen* will advise this division of any problems arising out of applications of the new policy.

Fig. 8.4.   Standard Policy Statement

new contract clause is negotiated, both management and union may provide lengthy explanations. One management prepares a detailed analysis of the new agreement, with running comments and interpretations of all changes, as illustrated in Figure 8.5.

If employees are expected to regard policy as reasonable and sound, they need some background with respect to the need for the policy and the nature of the considerations that led to its acceptance. This requirement represents another of the prices that must be paid for effective participation by members of the organization. It does not mean that employees must vote on each policy to be adopted. It does not even mean that they must agree that it is wise policy. It does mean that they must be permitted to see the situation as it appears to those who have created the policy. With such conditions in mind, employee consideration and discussion of policies can provide valuable contributions. At the same time, the opportunity to participate within these limits can assure understanding and acceptance that are essential to maximum contribution and identification with the organizational objectives thus prescribed.[11]

4.0   TESTS OF LABOR POLICY

J. Howell Turner provides a succinct outline of tests to be applied in evaluating employment policy as these yardsticks appear to an experienced manager. He concludes:[12]

---

[11] See Rensis Likert and Samuel P. Hayes, Jr. eds. *Some Applications of Behavioral Research*, Geneva, Switzerland: UNESCO, 1957, pp. 48ff.

[12] J. Howell Turner, "Essentials in the Development of Personnel Policy," *Addresses on Industrial Relations*, Bulletin 25, Bureau of Industrial Relations, University of Michigan, 1957, p. 1.

63. Minutes shall be kept of all Labor Relations Committee meetings. These minutes shall be signed by representatives of the Local Union and the Company, and sufficient copies shall be furnished to all Committee members, an accredited representative of the Local Union, *and one each to the Union's International Office and the Industrial Relations Department of the Company. The foregoing shall be the responsibility of the Labor Relations Committee.*

Copies of minutes are also to be forwarded to the Union's International Office and to the Company's Industrial Relations Department. Responsibility for preparation and distribution of minutes has been made the joint responsibility of the Company and Union members of the Labor Relations Committee. From the practical standpoint, the Company will probably have to continue to do the work involved.

SECTION VII. *REVIEW BOARD*

64. *To assist in the attainment of the mutual objectives of the parties as set forth in this Agreement, promptly after the execution of this Agreement there shall be established a Review Board.*

New.

65. *Composition*

The Review Board shall be composed of ten (10) members, five (5) of whom shall be appointed by the Union and five (5) of whom shall be appointed by the Company. At least three (3) of the members appointed by the Union shall be chosen from the Executive Board of the International Union, and at least three (3) of the Company members shall be representatives of departments at its Minneapolis executive offices. Six (6) members shall constitute a quorum, but in the event of unequal representation, only an equal number of Company and Union representatives shall be entitled to vote on matters brought to a ballot. Each party shall designate a co-chairman, and such two co-chairmen shall jointly carry out any functions of the Board as may be delegated to them.

66. *Meetings*

The Review Board shall conduct regular meetings not less than once each quarter and special meetings upon written request of either party to consider any grievances referred to it by a plant Labor Relations Committee. All regular and special meetings of the Board shall be held at such place or places as may be jointly agreed to by the two co-chairmen.

This provision establishes a joint committee, comparable to the plant Labor Relations Committee, to deal with the company-wide aspects of the labor-management relationship under the Master Agreement. This approach is an experiment which the Union and the Company have agreed to try in the hope that with continuing machinery of this nature, we can more effectively deal with the areas of disagreement which continue to crop up during the contract year, in spite of the fact that to all intents and purposes, a satisfactory agreement was reached during contract negotiations. The new Board takes over the International Officer-Company executive discussions which previously operated at the Fourth Step of the grievance procedure and at the equal-committee phase of the arbitration procedure. In addition to this function in the formal grievance procedure, the Board may develop interpretations of Master Agreement provisions and deal with disagreements and problems which arise outside the provisions of the agreements. The composition of the Board has been made flexible so as to provide adequate local representation for the discussion of matters relating to a single plant.

Fig. 8.5. Commentary and Interpretation of Contract Clauses.
(Used by permission of General Mills, Inc.)

It seems to me that there can be five major guides set forth to serve as reference points in the development of personnel policies.

First of all, such policies should accurately represent management philosophy. A second essential is that the intent behind policies should be understood by all members of management; this will promote uniform application of policies. Third, personnel policies have to be realistic enough to stand up under crises. Fourth, they should be fair in the eyes of employees, share owners, customers and the public. Finally, they should be self-perpetuating.

In an audit of employment relationships, these checks are spelled out in somewhat more detail. They have been outlined as follows:

(1) Labor policy should be clearly stated, so that what it proposes is evident. This implies that it is explicit rather than implicit, that those responsible for policy have taken the time to think it through and weigh its meaning and implications.

(2) Policy within a firm should be *consistent with public policy.* Since public policy disapproves employer domination of a union, for example, firm policy should not seek to maintain such domination. Individual firm policy should be consistent with the *spirit* rather than the letter of the law, so that the intentions and settled course of the organization are appropriate in terms of public opinion in the society in which the firm operates.

(3) General labor policy should be *uniform throughout the organization.* Variations may be permitted in specific policies—on staffing, compensation, benefits, and services, for example—to take account of place-to-place variations. Although general policy—such as the willingness to negotiate with unions of employees or the intention to pay wages that reflect differences in job contributions—may be widely applicable, many details of policy may have to be tailor-made.

(4) Policies must be *communicated* to all who are responsible for seeing that they are implemented in the over-all program. To this end, specific means must be provided for informing all levels of management, as well as rank-and-file employees, of the detailed labor policy of the organization.

(5) An elementary test of policy involves its *accurate reflection of the actual intentions* of policy-makers. Here the question is whether policy is a matter of high-sounding general principles to which those who lead in policy making subscribe with unspoken reservations or, on the other hand, whether policy realistically describes carefully considered intentions.

(6) One of the most important questions to be asked about labor policy concerns what may be called its *quality.* In such an evaluation, current policy—both general and specific—must be compared with *ideal employment policy,* meaning policy that is suggested by the accumulated knowledge and best thinking—the tested theories—with respect to the nature of work and working relationships and organizations. At the same time, an assessment of policy must take into account the particular circumstances in which the organization is involved.

5.0 SUMMARY

The message of this chapter concerns the nature and the importance of general policy in the management of people. Policies define the courses to be followed in programs and practices throughout a working organization. Policies translate the philosophy of policy-makers into selected intentions and accepted courses. Policies provide guidelines for action throughout the whole management process.

Because policies must incorporate the theories and philosophies of numerous individuals and groups in the selection of general intentions, determination of both general and specific policy is a complex and difficult process. Policy on manpower management in a firm must integrate and combine the ideas and influence of individual managers and employees, and perhaps incorporate the viewpoints of unions, all within the framework of public policy on the management of people and in the setting of a particular firm.

Some policy is formally declared, stated, published, widely circulated and communicated. Other policy is informal and implicit rather than explicit. It must be inferred from program and practice.

Development of general employment policy is an assignment to top management in all working organizations. Managers may also decide on specific or implementing policy, but that responsibility can be delegated. Managers at all levels have a responsibility to contribute their ideas with respect to desirable policy and changes in policy. They have a responsibility, also, to know and understand and interpret policy. Industrial relations and personnel staff divisions are generally charged with responsibility for the formulation of policy to be recommended to top management, for facilitating the communication and interpretation of policy throughout the organization, and for continuing review and evaluation of all employment policy.

The significance of policy arises from the fact that it sets the pattern and thus prescribes the programs, practices, and procedures to be followed throughout the organization. Because it declares intentions, policy provides the measures and standards with which programs and practice may be evaluated. Hence any appraisal or audit of employee relations begins with an assessment of policy. Audits of policy consider the clarity of policy statements, their consistency with public policy, the uniform understanding of general policy throughout an organization, the effectiveness of communication and interpretation, the accurate translation of managerial philosophy into determined intentions and the basic quality of policy.

Consideration of policy in manpower management continues in the chapter that follows. In that chapter, particular attention is given to bilateral policy—that established by collective bargaining with unions of employees.

SELECTED SUPPLEMENTARY READINGS

Appley, Lawrence A., "Essentials of a Management Personnel Policy," *Personnel,* Vol. 23, No. 5, pp. 430–436, May 1947.
Bambrick, James J., "Guidelines for Developing Workable Personnel Policies," *Personnel,* Vol. 38, No. 5, pp. 69–75, September-October 1961.
Joynt, John B., "Management's Basic Function: Policy Formulation," *Advanced Management,* Vol. 19, No. 8, pp. 11–15, August 1954.
Mayer, David P., "What is Policy?" *Personnel Administration,* Vol. 20, No. 1, pp. 33–35, January-February 1957.
Mee, John F., "Management Philosophy for Professional Executives," *Business Horizons,* pp. 5–11, December 1956.
Miller, Ernest C., "Personnel Policy in Decentralized Organization," *Personnel Journal,* Vol. 38, No. 7, pp. 257–260, December 1959.
Selekman, B. M., "Varieties of Labor Relations," *Harvard Business Review,* Vol. 27, No. 3, pp. 175–199, March 1949.
Thompson, Stewart, "Selected Examples of Company Creeds," *Research Report No. 32,* American Management Association, 1958.

SHORT CASE PROBLEM 8.1

Astra Corporation

"The best test and the acid test of sound policy in industrial relations," said the Astra Corporation's general manager, "is our ability to make a union unnecessary in this organization. I say that," he continued, "not because of any personal objection to unions. If I were an employee of most organizations, I think I would belong to a union, even if I had to organize it. Unions never appear unless management is negligent. Employees join unions because management has somehow overlooked their interests and needs.

"If policies are carefully considered and kept up to date," he went on, "they should provide ideal working conditions. They should insure the selection of the right employees for each job. They should make the firm's objectives coincide with those of employees. They should insure the protection of employee interests in a manner superior to anything a union can possibly do. Under these circumstances, if unions gain membership among employees, one can only conclude that managers have been inadequate."

Six months after this statement to his associates, the general manager was presented with a demand for an election among employees of Astra. Shortly thereafter, a local of the International Association of Machinists was certified as their bargaining agent. The general manager immediately asked for the resignation of the industrial relations director and all members of his staff. He began an immediate search for replacements and told the first applicant that, in his opinion, the test of the new manager's success would lie in his ability to get rid of the union within twelve months.

Problem: (1) Summarize the points you would make in agreeing with or challenging the manager's viewpoint. (2) How would you regard the test to be applied to the new industrial relations director?

9. *Labor Movements*

Around the world, as the process of industrialization advances, organizations of employees have appeared and sought to influence working conditions, the policies and practices of management, and public policy on working conditions and relationships. These associations have developed varying forms and structures and proposed differing goals that range from revolution to cooperation with employers. They have been widely described as *labor movements* or parts of a world-wide labor movement. Many theories have sought to explain why they appear and why workers join and support them. Everywhere they exert an influence that shapes employment and working relationships. A series of international associations has sought to join members of national groups in cooperation toward common objectives. Employers have formed organizations to counteract and to confine the influence of these associations of employees.

In the United States, the influence of what is often described as *organized labor* is apparent in day-to-day relationships between managements and unions and in continuing pressures on legislatures and public officials. The power and influence of the labor movement in this country is by no means confined to the approximately 17 million union members, nor even to the additional millions of employees who work under conditions prescribed by union-management agreements. Negotiated conditions of employment create patterns of relationships that are widely copied by firms and agencies in which no formal collective bargaining takes place. In addition, union influence on the federal Congress, state legislatures, and county and municipal lawmakers and administrators helps to shape working conditions for all workers.

Unions have played a growing role in the economic and political life of our nation as well as in the determination of managerial policy and practice.

The present chapter provides a background of information and theory as perspective with which to view and understand the labor movement and union influence in management. It serves as an introduction to a discussion of the process of *bilateral policy making* through *collective bargaining* and *contract administration*. It directs attention to one of the most important elements in modern industrial relations systems (see Chapter 2) and to the management function generally described as *labor relations*.

1.0 UNIONS AND THE LABOR MOVEMENT

The term "labor movement" is generally applied to *all the various types of associations of workers that appear in industrialized or partially industrialized economies*. Thus the international labor movement has included the early associations of journeymen or day workers, which appeared as the guild system gave way to factories in England and the nations of western Europe. It has also included the socialist and syndicalist movements of the 19th century and the early craft unions that appeared in the American colonies. It includes the more mature and extensive structures of unions in today's highly industrialized economies as well as the newly formed associations of workers in recently industrialized economies of the less developed nations.

The *Encyclopedia of the Social Sciences* defines the term "labor movement" as "all of the organized activity of wage earners to better their own conditions either immediately or in the more or less distant future." The same source notes that the labor movement arises with the emergence of a wage earning group. The movement does not become formal, however, until the group develops some consciousness that its interests are distinctive and until it realizes that its group interests require protection and advancement.

Professor John R. Commons, who wrote the report on the Labor Movement in the *Encyclopedia,* provided an excellent summary of its breadth and complexity. He says:[1]

> The labor movement is thus seen to be amazingly complicated and diverse. . . . The movement in one country is not comparable with the movement in another country. . . .
> Within the movement itself there are many conflicting trends, which weaken its aggressiveness; these range all the way from communism, syndicalism and unionism to cooperation, and they are broken up again into many different forms and temporary combinations. . . .

Although the terms "union" and "organized labor" are frequently and popularly used as synonymous with the "labor movement," each carries a somewhat distinctive connotation. *A union is a continuing, long-term asso-*

---

[1] John R. Commons, "Labor Movement," *Encyclopedia of the Social Sciences,* New York: The Macmillan Company, 1933, Vol. 8, p. 695; see also pp. 682–696.

ciation of employees, formed and maintained for the specific purpose of advancing and protecting the interests of members in their working relationships. As will be noted, unions are of several types, in the sense that they propose a variety of courses with different policies and practices. They are also of various sizes, in the sense that they include small local associations as well as multi-million-member, nationwide and international structures. They vary also in the composition of their membership, from auto workers to zerographers.

"Organized labor" is a term used in the United States to distinguish members of American unions from unorganized employees. The term is sometimes used in a more restrictive sense to apply to members of unions affiliated with the nationwide American Federation of Labor-Congress of Industrial Organizations, the AFL-CIO, thus excluding the approximately three million members of unaffiliated unions.

1.1   Unions and industrialization. Kerr, Dunlop, Harbison, and Myers conclude: "Industrialization everywhere creates organizations of workers, but they differ widely in their functions, structure leadership and ideology."[2] Why do these movements appear? What are their roots and sources? Why do workers everywhere form and join and support labor movements? Is participation an expression of such basic human needs that it is everywhere and in all cases inevitable? If so, are these needs persistent, so that membership in and support of unions is to be anticipated as a permanent characteristic of industrial employment? Is existence of these movements a sign of inadequacies in management?

Students of industrial relations have long sought answers to these questions. Tentative conclusions about the nature of labor movements have been and are an important part of managerial philosophy. Theories as to why workers form and join labor movements exert a strong influence on managerial policy. Many managers of a generation past, for example, based their relationships with employees on the theory that unions were the products of agitators. They ignored the complaints and demands of union members and agents and concentrated on banishing agitators.

Studies of early labor movements have described them as *protests* of property-less employees against conditions of employment to which workers object. Commons notes, in his analysis of labor movements, that they are "always a reaction and a protest against capitalism."[3] Incipient or beginning labor movements spotlight the changes to which workers object. The unions that appear in early stages of industrialization protest what is happening to workers in this process. Kerr, Dunlop, Harbison, and Myers have detailed these objections as observed in the newly emerging labor movements of various less developed economies.[4]

[2] Clark Kerr, John Dunlop, Frederick Harbison, and Charles A. Myers, *Industrialism and Industrial Man,* Cambridge, Mass.: Harvard University Press, 1960, p. 215.

[3] Commons, *op. cit.,* p. 682.

[4] Kerr, *et al., op. cit.,* chaps. 7 and 8.

Agricultural economies avoid these movements. When industrialization begins, however, a new group of industrial workers with new skills and new attitudes must be committed to industrial employment. The group is generally recruited from the ranks of former agricultural labor by offering greater economic rewards. Industrial workers must be found and encouraged to commit themselves to careers as employees in the new factories. They must be trained to work under the changed conditions of industrialized employment. They must learn to live together in new towns and cities. They must be provided with new types of economic security—wages, insurance, benefits —to replace the security they have lost by leaving their earlier employment.

At the same time, these workers must accommodate themselves to new patterns of work rules, quite different from those to which they were accustomed in agriculture. Because of their lack of experience in working with more complex tools and equipment and perhaps in working as members of large teams, new systems of work rules must be enforced. As these rules impose discipline and set the pace of work, workers may find them objectionable and irritating.

Old habits and customs no longer suffice as guides in daily working behavior. In their absence, workers may find themselves uncomfortable. They may be critical of new rules imposed as replacements for traditional controls. Workers may become personally disorganized, unsatisfied, and frustrated. The most obvious objects of such reactions are the new working conditions, the new rules, and the managers who have taken the lead in imposing the new order.

Newly industrialized workers join new labor movements as protests against these conditions. Their behavior, long described as industrial unrest, takes many forms. Unrest may be inarticulate, involving extensive absenteeism, frequent job changes, thievery, picking fights, wandering from one plant or locality to another. It may erupt and become articulate in crowd or mob behavior, with strikes, demonstrations, and parades. It may, on the other hand, if effective leadership appears, take the form of long-term, enduring associations.

Changing objectives in continuing movements are shaped by the rapidity of industrialization and the extent to which industrialization changes working conditions and habits. Objectives are also shaped by the political structure of the society, the rule-makers, and their reactions to worker protests. Thus in an autocratic, family-dominated, dynastic society, new movements may stress class consciousness and worker solidarity. In competitive societies, the rallying point is more likely to be the control of jobs and such specific working conditions as wages and hours.

Largely because labor movements have proposed varying objectives, students of these movements have developed a variety of theories to explain their emergence and continued support. All theories seek to answer the questions: Why do workers form and join labor movements? Why do they support these associations? Will they continue to do so, or are there discernible points at which these movements will decline or disappear?

1.2   Revolution theory. Most spectacular of these theories is the Marxist or *revolutionary* explanation. The classic expression of this analysis is the *Communist Manifesto,* written by Karl Marx and Friedrich Engels in 1847 as a basis for formation of the Communist League in 1848. In their view, all history is the record of dynamic class struggles. The working classes created by industrialization will, as they saw it, reorganize society, overthrow capitalist rulers, and substitute common ownership of all capital and property with economic equality for all. Socialist and communist labor movements are therefore steps or devices to this end, means of preparing for "the revolution."

Revolutionary labor movements have appeared in all older industrialized nations. Following the early Communist League, a socialist International Workingmen's Association was formed in 1864. After a series of reorganizations, the third Communist International, with headquarters in Moscow, was formed in 1919. Today, revolutionary unionism remains a potent force in the world, although it is now overshadowed by the political movement led by Soviet Russia and the satellite nations. Communism still seeks control of labor movements, however, and Communists exert a controlling influence in the World Federation of Trade Unions.

Revolutionary unionism has not been popular in the United States, although the Trade Union Unity League, organized by William Z. Foster in 1920, claimed 100,000 members before its dissolution in 1935. Another revolutionary movement, the Industrial Workers of the World, was formed in 1905 and lasted until World War II.

Emphasis on revolutionary objectives appears as a reaction to arbitrary, restrictive controls imposed by the rule-makers on labor movements. If, in early stages, these movements are rigorously suppressed, they are more likely to advocate revolutionary objectives. If movements are accepted and members have time to adapt themselves to new and different working careers, movements are likely to become reformist rather than revolutionary. Revolutionary potential is at its height in the early stages.

1.3   Industrial democracy. A non-revolutionary theory that has achieved wide acceptance is the theory of *industrial democracy.* Its ablest spokesmen were Sidney and Beatrice Webb, English economists, who conducted extensive studies of English unions. From a detailed analysis of early unions, they noted that these associations exerted an influence on employment that paralleled the development of democracy in government. They concluded that unions represent a means by which workers can cope with the stronger political and economic power of employers and thus can introduce democracy into working relationships.

Sumner Slichter carried this viewpoint somewhat further in his analysis of the purposes and values of union membership. Slichter noted that through their unions, members developed a whole network of work rules and traditions, a "system of industrial jurisprudence." These rules became a means of protection to employees in their work, much as the system of public law protects citizens from arbitrary action by government.[5]

1.4 Business theory. The business theory of unions is distinctive principally in its emphasis on the economic rather than on the political power of worker associations. The American labor movement is widely cited as the best illustration of this viewpoint. This theory has been expressed by several early leaders of the American Federation of Labor and was the most evident theory in that organization until the Federation accepted political action as an important activity. In essence, the theory holds that members join unions to be represented in bargaining about working conditions and in the day-to-day control of work relationships. Members see their union as their business agent or representative.

Samuel Gompers, who was the first president of the A.F. of L., expressed his acceptance of this theory on many occasions. He firmly opposed alliances with reformist or revolutionary associations. The union, in this view, is a means of increasing members' wages and economic security, reducing hours of work, protecting health, and preventing tyrannical employer action.

Adolph Strasser and John Mitchell are other A.F. of L. leaders who expressed this idea of union goals. All opposed revolutionary unionism and stressed the day-by-day "bread and butter" benefits to be gained through union membership.

1.5 Socio-psychological theories. Unions have also been regarded as providing opportunities for members to satisfy a broad range of basic human wants and needs. Some observers have concluded that union political and economic action may be the most obvious reason for participation in a labor movement, but other satisfactions also play an important part. Membership gives a feeling of belonging, security, freedom, and strength that may be especially important to workers in large working organizations. Members may feel greater security in expressing their opinions. They can gain recognition and status by accepting responsibilities in union committees and as union officers. They find opportunities for social life within the union. Carleton H. Parker was an early spokesman for this view. In his view, union membership offers opportunities to satisfy what he regarded as the basic instincts of workers, opportunities denied them by the conditions of industrial employment.[6] Similar views have been expressed by Clinton Golden and Harold J. Ruttenberg,[7] and a classic statement is that of Robert F. Hoxie.[8]

---

[5] See Sumner H. Slichter, *The Challenge of Industrial Relations,* Ithaca, N.Y.: Cornell University Press, 1947; also Sumner H. Slichter, James J. Healy, and E. Robert Livernash, *The Impact of Collective Bargaining on Management,* Washington, D.C.: The Brookings Institution, 1960, chap. 31.

[6] Carleton H. Parker, *The Casual Laborer and Other Essays,* New York: Harcourt, Brace & World, Inc., 1920.

[7] In *The Dynamics of Industrial Democracy,* New York: Harper & Brothers, 1942.

[8] In *Trade Unionism in the United States,* New York: D. Appleton-Century Company, Inc., 1921. For more on these theories, see Richard A. Lester, *As Unions Mature,* Princeton, N.J.: Princeton University Press, 1958;

1.6 Changing theory. American attitudes toward unions have changed as unions have grown and modified their goals and policies. Modern theory recognizes that participation in the labor movement is probably not single-minded, with only one purpose. Workers join for several reasons. Movements change as work, working conditions, and societies change.[9]

In a much earlier analysis, Selig Perlman concluded that the objectives of labor movements change; so no simple theory can explain the varieties of movements that have appeared, nor can such a view account for time-to-time changes in these movements.[10] He explained that labor movements take forms dictated by (1) the resistance of capitalistic employers, (2) the degree of dominance by intellectuals over incipient labor movements, and (3) the maturity of what he calls the "trade union mentality." Employees, Perlman argued, recognize the scarcity of economic opportunity and see their interests as opposed to those of employers, who control that opportunity. Programs undertaken by groups of employees at one time may emphasize the control of jobs, and at another, political action, depending on the dominance exercised by intellectuals and the degree of resistance expressed by capitalist employers.

Many recent studies have sought to check these theories in terms of the stated reasons of union members for their participation. Such studies ask members why they have joined and why they support their unions. Rosen and Rosen asked union members what they thought their union should be doing in several areas; then they measured member satisfaction with what the union, in their opinion, was doing in these areas.[11] Father Purcell has reported on the "dual loyalty" he discovered among workers in the meat-packing industry.[12] Uphoff and Dunnette studied union member attitudes toward unionism in general, the local union, local officers and practices, the national union, and national officials and practices.[13]

The pattern of reasons for union membership probably changes with time, so that theories that appeared to explain the labor movements of the 18th and 19th centuries provide less plausible explanations for today's membership and support.

1.7 Types of unions. These theories of labor movements suggest that unions are of several types. Some of them are *revolutionary* in that they propose a comprehensive change involving the destruction or overthrow of present political and social controls and the substitution of a radically dif-

[9] See Mark Perlman, *Labor Union Theories in America*, Evanston, Ill.; Row, Peterson & Company, 1958.

[10] Selig Perlman, *A Theory of the Labor Movement*, New York: The Macmillan Company, 1937, and reissued by Augustus M. Kelley in 1949.

[11] Hjalmar Rosen and R. A. Hudson Rosen, *The Union Member Speaks*, Englewood Cliffs, N.J.: Prentice-Hall, Inc., 1955.

[12] Theodore Purcell, *The Worker Speaks His Mind on Company and Union*, Cambridge Mass.: Harvard University Press, 1953; also his *Blue-Collar Man*, Cambridge, Mass.: Harvard University Press, 1960.

[13] Walter H. Uphoff and Marvin D. Dunnette, "Understanding the Union Member," *Bulletin 18*, Minneapolis: University of Minnesota Industrial Relations Center, July 1956; also their "What Union Members Think of Unionism," *Personnel*, Vol. 33, No. 4, January 1957, pp. 347–352.

ferent social and political order. They propose a major shift in the source of power and authority, perhaps involving the use of force to effect this change.

Other unions are essentially *reformist*. They propose changes, but they regard them as consistent with the existing mores of society and possible within the framework of the societies in which they operate. When such unions become the advocates of extensive reforms extending well beyond the area of working conditions, they are practising *uplift unionism*. Many early American unions were interested in a wide variety of reforms, including the abolition of imprisonment for debt, free schools, changed systems of taxation, and elimination of property requirements for voting.

As noted, the most common type of American unions is *business unionism*. It stresses economic advantages to be gained through collective action, principally in dealing with employers but also by effective political representation of union members. Business unionism concentrates attention on improving working and living conditions of employees. Its viewpoint is typified in the description of the principal local union official as the *business agent* of the members.

Business unionism depends in large measure on the process of *collective bargaining* to achieve its objectives. Collective bargaining describes the process in which conditions of employment are determined by agreement between representatives of an organized group of employees, on the one hand, and one or more employers, on the other. It is called "collective" because employees form an association that they authorize to act as their agent in reaching an agreement and because employers may also act as a group rather than as individuals. It is described as "bargaining" in part because the method of reaching an agreement involves proposals and counterproposals, offers and counteroffers.

As indicated by Professor Slichter, however, collective bargaining does more than merely establish a few simple working conditions, of which wages and hours are recognized as most important. It also defines a broad area of civil rights in employment. It specifies both managerial and union action according to rules rather than to arbitrary and capricious decisions. It thus provides an objective declaration of policies governing specified areas of employment relationships. Within these areas, also, it establishes procedures and practices for implementing these policies. (The usual outcome of collective bargaining is the *collective agreement* or *labor contract*. This is the written statement of the terms and provisions arrived at by collective bargaining.)

Although collective bargaining is generally said to reflect the weakness of individual employees, employers may also feel the need for association with other employers. One theory of collective bargaining regards associations of both employers and employees as examples of "groupism," in which individuals having common interests band themselves together to enhance their power. In several European nations, the development of employer associations has closely paralleled the growth of unions. Unions deal with these associations rather than with individual employers. A similar practice is evident in many industries and localities in this country.

1.8   Membership: composition. Unions vary also in the types of workers that they include as members. In the American colonies, for example, each local union usually included members of a single craft. These *craft unions* were supplemented, after the middle of the 19th century, by *industrial unions,* which included workers with a variety of skills employed in a single industry, such as coal mining, steel, rubber, and automobiles. Industrial unions accepted semiskilled and unskilled workers as well as craftsmen. Many of the largest and most powerful unions in the United States today are industrial unions. Many of the older craft unions have relaxed their membership requirements to permit admission of non-craft members; consequently, there are few pure craft unions today.

The term *labor union* is popularly used to refer to both craft and industrial unions.

1.9   Affiliation. In the United States, the large majority of all union members belong to organizations affiliated with the AFL-CIO. They are described as *affiliated unions.* Approximately 3 million other employees belong to *unaffiliated* or *independent* unions. Some unaffiliated unions have been expelled from the Federation for allowing themselves to become Communist dominated or for violating the Federation's Codes of Ethical Conduct, for example, permitting undemocratic administration or the improper use of union funds. Other unaffiliated unions have remained outside for reasons of their own, as exemplified by several of the railroad brotherhoods. Some, like the United Mine Workers, have made frequent changes from affiliated to unaffiliated status.

Company unions are organizations whose membership is confined to the employees of a single firm. Although a few locals of affiliated unions have such a composition, the designation generally refers to unaffiliated unions. In the early years of this century, many employers sponsored and supported such associations, frequently as a means of preventing the organization of their employees by outside affiliated unions. Sponsored associations of employees were frequently called *dependent unions.*

2.0   THE AMERICAN LABOR MOVEMENT

The American labor movement can trace its beginnings to small craft unions in the colonies. Unlike their counterparts in Great Britain and on the continent, they included few associations of semi-skilled workers. In England, the Webbs report that the pioneers in the labor movement included semi-skilled woolen workers from the West and Midland framework knitters. In the colonies, factories were discouraged, so that large numbers of semi-skilled machine-tenders did not come together in single establishments.

2.1   Emergence and growth. The earliest union in the United States was probably that of the cordwainers in Philadelphia, formed in 1792. After half a century in which unions remained as isolated, local associations, national unions of typographers (1850), stonecutters (1853), hat-finishers (1854), and several other skilled trades were formed. By the end of the Civil War, at least 32 such organizations were in existence.

The Civil War encouraged cooperation among unionists at the same time that it forced a relaxation of employer opposition to unions. Immediately following the war, attempts were made to perfect nationwide associations of an intertrade nature. Earlier organizations on a national scale had included only members of a single trade; the newer organizations sought to cement the bonds among trades. The first of these associations was the National Labor Union, formed at Baltimore in 1866. It was an association of city central bodies, each composed of representatives from several local craft unions. Because of its dependence upon these city federations, and because many of them were weak, the organization as a whole was ineffective and short-lived.

Three years later, in Philadelphia, another attempt at amalgamation was made in the formation of the Knights of Labor. The Knights proposed to include not only the members of existing craft organizations, but also all other skilled and unskilled labor. Leadership in the movement was assumed by the garment-cutters. Local unions were subject to district councils, and the latter, in turn, were responsible to a central administrative body. The organization increased rapidly in size, reaching a maximum membership of 703,000 in 1886. Thereafter, as a result of several unsuccessful strikes and the diversity of interests of its members, the organization declined as rapidly as it had developed.

The American Federation of Labor was formed in 1886. Approximately fifty years later, the Congress of Industrial Organizations was organized. In 1955, these two associations of international unions developed a program for consolidation and integration within the framework of the AFL-CIO.

2.2 Craft vs. industrial unionism. In the 20-year period from 1935 to 1955, the American labor movement was sharply divided over the issue of expanding industrial unionism. The argument developed as employment in the large mass-production industries expanded rapidly after the turn of the century.

In 1933, a minority within the American Federation of Labor undertook a determined movement to organize unskilled and semiskilled workers in mass-production industries and to include the new unions in the Federation. Proponents pointed to the changing character of modern industry, in which craftsmen were becoming less important numerically, whereas semiskilled machine tenders were increasing in numbers. They concluded that any labor movement restricted to skilled workers must inevitably decline in power and value to its members. They also emphasized the necessity of more effective political action by organized labor. They argued that unskilled employees created serious competition for skilled tradesmen, and that the Federation should bring the unorganized into union ranks.

Opponents of this change contended that opening the doors to the unskilled would effect a leveling of wages. They held that effective organization of unskilled employees is, in the long run, impossible. For that reason, they insisted, such organization would dilute the bargaining power of skilled employees.

Following the Federation's convention in 1935, a group of the unions most insistent on an active campaign to organize semiskilled and unskilled employees formed the Committee for Industrial Organization. The Committee initiated an active organizational campaign in the mass-production industries. It attracted wide attention by the perfection of a powerful industrial union in rubber, a series of successes in the steel industry, and a sit-down strike against the General Motors Corporation in January and February, 1937. On November 14, 1938, the Committee held a constitutional convention and formed the Congress of Industrial Organizations.

The new Congress maintained its own organization throughout the next 17 years. It conducted organizing campaigns, frequently seeking to enlist workers who were also eligible for membership in the A.F. of L. unions. The C.I.O., at its peak of membership in 1945–47, included some 6 million members. The A.F. of L. was only a bit larger at that time, but its membership continued to grow in postwar years. Late in 1955, the two organizations agreed to merge in a new American Federation of Labor and Congress of Industrial Organizations, generally described as "AFL-CIO."[14]

2.3 Membership. Today's American labor movement includes some 17 million members. In 1900, total membership was less than one million.

During the present century, numbers of unionists in the United States have increased greatly, although the growth of the movement has been subject to periods of acceleration, deceleration, and declines as well as advances. Data on union membership for each year since 1897 are presented in Table 9.1.

Present union membership represents about one-tenth of the total population, about 25 per cent of all workers and 34 per cent of non-farm workers. Not all the labor force, by any means, can be considered as eligible for organization. Employers, self-employed, farmers, domestic workers, and many professional workers are not eligible for membership in organizations designed to bargain with employers. The total organizable group includes approximately 50 millions. The 17 million union members represent about one-third of this eligible group. Calculations of these percentages are complicated because membership reports by American unions frequently include foreign members, particularly those in Canada, Mexico, Puerto Rico, and the Canal Zone. More than a million Canadians are affiliated with American internationals.

All membership figures until 1960 were essentially estimates. Member unions in AFL-CIO reported membership to the parent federation for per

[14] See James O. Morris, *Conflict Within the AFL: A Study of Craft versus Industrial Unionism*, Ithaca, N.Y.: Cornell University Press, 1958; Walter Galenson, *The CIO Challenge to the AFL*, Cambridge, Mass.: Harvard University Press, 1960.

Table 9.1   Membership in American Labor Organizations, 1897–1960

Year	Total Membership	Year	Total Membership
1897	440,000	1926	3,592,000
1898	467,000	1927	3,600,000
1899	550,000	1928	3,567,000
1900	791,000	1929	3,625,000
		1930	3,632,000
1901	1,058,000	1931	3,526,000
1902	1,335,000	1932	3,226,000
1903	2,824,000	1933	2,857,000
1904	2,067,000	1934	3,249,000
1905	1,918,000	1935	3,728,000
1906	1,892,000	1936	4,164,000
1907	2,077,000	1937	7,218,000
1908	2,092,000	1938	8,265,000
1909	1,965,000	1939	8,980,000
1910	2,116,000	1940	8,944,000
1911	2,318,000	1941	10,489,000
1912	2,405,000	1942	10,762,000
1913	2,661,000	1943	13,642,000
1914	2,647,000	1944	14,621,000
1915	2,560,000	1945	14,796,000
1916	2,722,000	1946	14,974,000
1917	2,976,000	1947	15,414,000
1918	3,368,000	1948	15,600,000
1919	4,046,000	1949	15,800,000
1920	5,034,000	1950	15,800,000
1921	4,722,000	1951	16,750,000
1922	3,950,000	1952	16,750,000
1923	3,629,000	1953	16,948,000
1924	3,549,000	1954	17,022,000
1925	3,566,000	1955	16,802,000
		1956	17,490,000
		1957	17,369,000
		1958	17,029,000
		1959	17,117,000
		1960	17,049,000

SOURCES: John M. Brumm and Nelson M. Bortz, "Brief History of the American Labor Movement," *Release W-558,* Washington, D.C.: Bureau of Labor Statistics, October 1947; Leo Wolman, *Ebb and Flow in Trade Unions,* New York: National Bureau of Economic Research, 1936; subsequent directions of national and international unions and releases by the United States Department of Labor; Harry P. Cohany, "Membership of American Trade Unions, 1960," *Monthly Labor Review,* Vol. 84, No. 12, December 1961, pp. 1299–1308.

capita taxes and as a basis for their voting strength in conventions. Figures for 1960–61 have been prepared by the Department of Labor, which found some estimates necessary to supplement reported numbers. Department of Labor calculations do not include all small, intra-state, unaffiliated unions.

It is apparent, however, that membership expanded rapidly after the National Labor Relations Act was passed in 1935, with plateaus from 1944 to 1950 and from 1953 to 1960. As a proportion of non-agricultural employees, membership reached its peak in 1945.

2.4 Degree of penetration. Union membership is not spread evenly

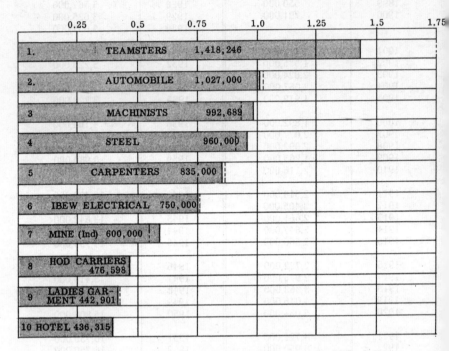

Figure 9.1 Membership of the Largest Unions in the United States
SOURCE: Data from the "Directory of National and International Unions in the United States," 1959, p. 10. The 1961 data are estimates. The 10 unions included 44 per cent of the total union membership.

over all occupations and industries. The most highly or thoroughly organized are railroads, construction, printing, maritime, trucking, musicians, steel, automobiles, rubber, electrical manufacturing, and aircraft. The largest unions are the teamsters, automobile workers, steel workers, machinists, carpenters, electrical workers, and mine workers, each with more than a half-million members. The first three unions have more than a million members each. Figure 9.1 compares the membership figures of the 10 largest unions in the nation in 1960.

Almost half of all union members (46.5 per cent) were in manufacturing, according to reported memberships in 1958. In non-manufacturing, transportation accounted for 15 per cent of the total; contract construction, 13 per cent; the service industries, 7 per cent; government, 5.8 per cent; trade, 4.7 per cent; mining and quarrying, 3.5 per cent; telephone and telegraph, 2.3 per cent; electric and gas utilities, 1.4 per cent; agriculture and fishing, 0.2 per cent; and finance and insurance, 0.6 per cent.[15]

The current industrial distribution of union members may be less significant than the impressive changes that are taking place. Proportions of union members in manufacturing industries, for example, are declining. Proportions in contract construction, government, mining and quarrying, and finance and insurance show increases in the 1957–1959 period. Decreases are reported in trade, telephone and telegraph, electric and gas ultilities, and agriculture and fishing.

Approximately 3.3 million union members are women, and the number has been growing. The 3.3 millions represent about one-sixth of all *union* members, whereas women represent approximately one-third of the entire *labor* force. Since the number of women in the labor force is increasing, future union membership, also, will probably include more women.

2.5   White-collar unionism. Growth in the labor movement in the United States has been impressive. Continued expansion in the years ahead, however, will require encounters with some formidable hurdles. If the labor movement is to grow, or if it is even to maintain its present degree of penetration in the labor force, it must find new members in new areas and occupations that may be less readily organized.

Present union membership shows a heavy concentration in the manufacturing industries and in the East, Middle West, and West. To expand union membership, it must probably be extended into the South. Approximately two-thirds of all manufacturing employees are union members. They, together with organizations of craftsmen, form the central core and substantial foundation for the entire labor movement. Among the unorganized employees, largest numbers are in small manufacturing plants, retail and wholesale trade, banking, finance, insurance, government, and the services of hotels, restaurants and laundries.

Of the approximately 20 million white-collar workers, employees in professional, technical, and clerical occupations—not including managers, officials, and proprietors—approximately 2.2 million are organized. Many of the 7 million technical and professional workers are probably not eligible for union membership in present organizations. The white-collar workers represent a major group into which organization must expand if it is to grow. The years since World War II have seen more rapid growth in these occupations than in the labor force as a whole. In 1959, the total of 28 million white-collar workers in all occupations made up 42 per cent of the civilian labor force. The increase in this group since 1947 was 38 per cent, as compared with an increase of 13.4 per cent for the labor force as a whole.

[15] *Directory of National and International Unions in the United States*, 1959, pp. 12–14.

Since 1956, numbers of white-collar workers in the labor force have exceeded those of blue-collar workers. Yet organization has achieved much less penetration in the white-collar group. Whereas approximately one-fourth of the entire labor force and about one-third of the eligibles in the labor force as a whole are members of unions, the proportions among white-collar workers are probably not greater than 10 per cent. Exactness in such calculations is difficult, for most white-collar unionists are members of unions that include both blue-collar and white-collar occupations. The Brotherhood of Railway Clerks includes the largest number of white-collar members. Other unions with considerable numbers of white-collar members include those of the auto workers, steel workers, retail clerks, teamsters, office employees, communications workers, the electrical workers, and public employees.

American unions report a total of about 17 million members. Of the total of 17 millions, about 14 millions are members of unions affiliated with the AFL-CIO. Figure 9.2 shows the long-term growth in that membership. The AFL-CIO proportion of total membership was decreased in 1955, when four of its national unions with 1.5 million members were expelled. The independent group was further increased by expulsion of the Teamsters, with another 1.4 million members in 1959.

2.6 Union structure. Members of the American labor movement are represented by a complex structure of local, state, national, and international unions. For the movement as a whole, there are approximately 184 national and international organizations. Of these, 134 are affiliated with the AFL-CIO. The total movement includes about 80,000 local unions, of which some 60,000 are included in the AFL-CIO. Independent or unaffiliated unions are not, for the most part, different in structure from those which are affiliated. Examination of the structure of the AFL-CIO and its affiliates should, therefore, provide an adequate view of this structure.

Figure 9.3 charts the structural organization of the AFL-CIO. The numbers referred to are as of January, 1960.

2.61 National convention. The legislative arm of the AFL-CIO is the national convention, held every two years. The convention is the supreme authority within the federation; its decisions are final. Special conventions may be called to supplement the regular, biennial meetings. Voting in the conventions is by delegates. The number of delegates from each union is in proportion to the paid-up membership of the various nationals and internationals; other affiliated groups are allowed one vote apiece.

2.62 Executive council. The executive arm of the Federation consists of its president and secretary-treasurer, supplemented by 27 vice-presidents to constitute the *Executive Council.* Vice-presidents are elected by vote of the convention. The Executive Council meets at least three times each year and carries out policies determined by the conventions. The federation's officers are advised by the six vice-presidents who constitute an *Executive Committee,* which meets every two months. In addition, a *General Board,* which includes the Executive Council plus an officer from each of the nationals and inter-

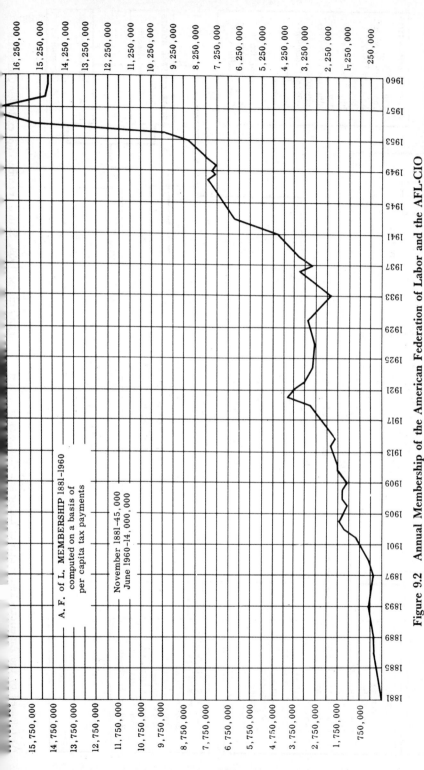

Figure 9.2 Annual Membership of the American Federation of Labor and the AFL-CIO

SOURCES: Membership figures based on reported payments of per capita taxes. Directly chartered locals are excluded from some annual reports, as are Canadian members. Data from *Proceedings* of annual conventions, *Directory of National and International Labor Unions in the United States, 1959*, Washington, D.C.: United States Department of Labor, (Bulletin No. 1267), 1959; "Union Membership, 1960," Washington, D.C.: United States Department of Labor, *Preliminary Release*, November, 1961.

A. F. of L. MEMBERSHIP 1881-1960
computed on a basis of
per capita tax payments

November 1881-45,000
June 1960-14,000,000

7

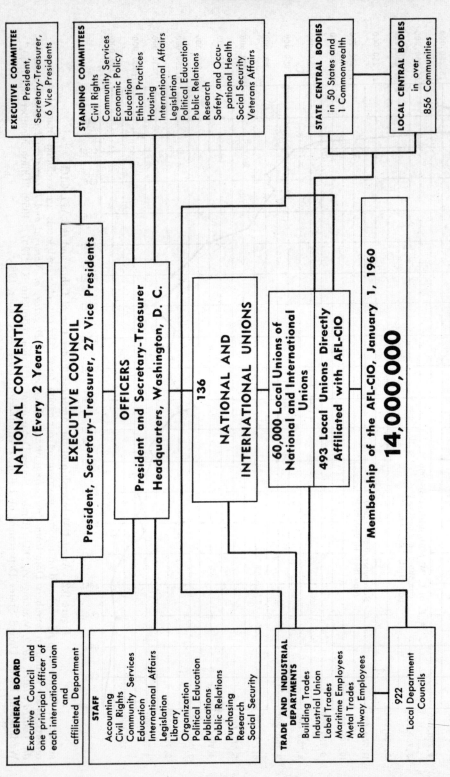

EXECUTIVE COMMITTEE
President, Secretary-Treasurer, 6 Vice Presidents

STANDING COMMITTEES
Civil Rights
Community Services
Economic Policy
Education
Ethical Practices
Housing
International Affairs
Legislation
Political Education
Public Relations
Research
Safety and Occupational Health
Social Security
Veterans Affairs

STATE CENTRAL BODIES
in 50 States and 1 Commonwealth

LOCAL CENTRAL BODIES
in over 856 Communities

NATIONAL CONVENTION
(Every 2 Years)

EXECUTIVE COUNCIL
President, Secretary-Treasurer, 27 Vice Presidents

OFFICERS
President and Secretary-Treasurer
Headquarters, Washington, D. C.

136 NATIONAL AND INTERNATIONAL UNIONS

60,000 Local Unions of National and International Unions

493 Local Unions Directly Affiliated with AFL-CIO

Membership of the AFL-CIO, January 1, 1960
14,000,000

GENERAL BOARD
Executive Council and one principal officer of each international union and affiliated Department

STAFF
Accounting
Civil Rights
Community Services
Education
International Affairs
Legislation
Library
Organization
Political Education
Publications
Public Relations
Purchasing
Research
Social Security

TRADE AND INDUSTRIAL DEPARTMENTS
Building Trades
Industrial Union
Label Trades
Maritime Employees
Metal Trades
Railway Employees

922 Local Department Councils

Figure 9.3 Structure of the AFL-CIO

As released by the American Federation of Labor and Congress of Industrial Organizations, 1959. Stated membership excludes Canadian

174

nationals and from the several departments, meets annually to consider policy questions raised by the Executive Council.

As the chart indicates, the officers of the AFL-CIO are assisted by an extensive technical and professional staff, shown in the left-hand section of the figure. Staff activities are listed alphabetically rather than in the order of importance. The central organization has a heavy responsibility for public relations and legislative representation at the federal level. It has its experts on social security, unemployment insurance, fair employment practices, and other matters of concern to union members. Organizing activities occupy much of the attention of staff and officers. Political activity in national campaigns has become more important since World War II. The federation also encourages special *worker-education* programs designed primarily to prepare union members for responsibilities of leadership in the movement.

2.63 Nationals and internationals. The 135 national and international organizations are the sovereign bodies of the American labor movement. Internationals are so called because they have local unions and members in Canada, Mexico, or Central American nations. Nationals and internationals affiliate with the AFL-CIO. They may leave the federation at will; their association is voluntary. They hold major voting strength in the federation and thus control its policies and practices. They may issue or withdraw charters to their locals. Their relationships with locals and with members are specified by their individual constitutions. Some national organizations have many locals, others relatively few. Seven of them, in 1959, had less than 10 locals. Five had more than 2,000 locals. While the federation or its officers may criticize the policies or actions of an affiliated national union, and while the convention of AFL-CIO can suspend or expel a member national union, the federation cannot effectively control its members except by exerting influence or taking drastic action.

The international unions are thus the residual holders of sovereign power in the American labor movement. Through their control of votes in AFL-CIO, they dictate its policy. Through their authority to create or destroy locals and to discipline them, they direct the members of their own organizations. Some of them have accumulated large financial reserves in benefit funds. Others own extensive property, so officials can exert a wide influence both within and outside the labor movement. It is for this reason that regulations designed to insure responsibility and integrity of union officers are directed principally at the national unions, as are the regulations concerning the handling of pension, welfare, and other benefit funds.

As already noted, national unions vary widely in size as measured by numbers of members. In 1960, the AFL-CIO included two unions with more than a million members, 3 with from 500,000 to 1,000,000 members, 34 with from 100,000 to 500,000 members, and 95 with less than 100,000 members. Six of the national organizations include less than 1,000 members, and 21 have less than 5,000.[16]

---

[16] "Collective Bargaining in America," *Labor's Economic Review*, Vol. 5, No. 1,

2.64   Local unions. The entire structure rests on the more than 60,000 local unions and their members. As the chart indicates, almost all of these are locals of the member nationals and internationals. Some 500 locals, however, are directly affiliated with the AFL-CIO. These directly affiliated unions are in part the result of the AFL-CIO organizing campaigns. In some cases, existing local organizations—often with a mixed membership not well-adapted to any national organization—have petitioned to maintain direct affiliation with the federation. Some affiliated locals represent the beginnings of new internationals to be admitted to the AFL-CIO when they have achieved sufficient membership.

Local unions are the grass roots of the labor movement. Under the charters granted them by the national organizations, they elect officers and business agents; admit members; negotiate agreements; undertake organizing campaigns (frequently with assistance from national organizations); maintain committees on membership, contract administration, political activity, worker education, recreation and other activities of interest to their members; collect dues; discipline members; own property; and conduct their business much as do the members of other societies.

2.65   Departments. At the left of the chart, six Trade and Industrial Departments are listed. They bring together the national organizations whose members are most likely to be working together. Thus, for example, the building-trades department includes nationals of carpenters, electricians, and other building-trade unions. The industrial union department includes many of the former members of the C.I.O.—automobile, steel, rubber, and other industrial unions. The Union Label and Service Trades Department combines the efforts of unions that seek to promote consumer and union member interest in goods and services marked with the union label.

Although participation is voluntary, many of the national unions have joined these departments. In them they can plan and execute joint organizing campaigns. The departments have a major responsibility for preventing and settling jurisdictional disputes that arise when the members of two unions claim the right to perform the same job.

2.66   Departmental councils. These councils represent local offices of the departments. They carry on the work of their departments in the major localities in which problems appear.

2.67   State and local central bodies. National and international members of the AFL-CIO may elect to join state and local *central* bodies as a means of exerting greater influence in state and local affairs. Membership in them is optional, but non-affiliated unions cannot become members. State and local bodies do not usually undertake collective bargaining. Rather, they provide specialized staff for public relations and for representation in legislative bodies, maintain committees on matters of regional or local interest, and express the union viewpoint in relationships with public administrators in

January 1960; "Union Membership, 1960," *Preliminary Release,* Washington: Department of Labor, November 1961.

such matters as unemployment insurance, fair employment practice, and minimum-wage administration.

Figure 9.4 is the organization chart of one such state central body. The figure suggests the major activities of the organization.

2.7 International cooperation. American labor organizations have played an active part in several associations formed to join members of the labor movement in various nations. Following World War I, American unions joined in planning the International Labor Organization, established

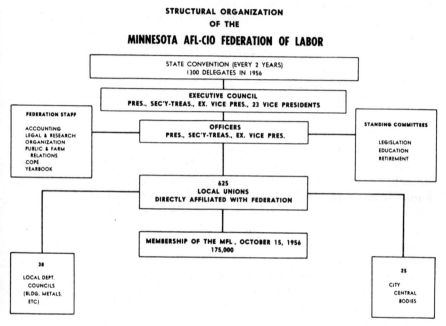

Figure 9.4 Organization of a State Central Body
The Minnesota AFL-CIO Federation of Labor.

by the Treaty of Versailles that ended World War I. The I.L.O. maintains a continuing program for the improvement of working conditions. It conducts studies and releases reports on working conditions throughout the world. It publishes the *International Labour Review,* which includes important statistical series on employment, unemployment, wages, earnings, and living costs as well as research reports. It holds annual conferences which discuss employment relationships and prepares draft conventions on such subjects as minimum wages and working hours for consideration by national legislatures. Since the formation of the United Nations, it has been associated with that organization as a "specialized agency."[17] Most of its activities are directed

[17] See John B. Tipton, *Participation of the United States in the International Labor Organization,* Urbana, Ill.: Institute of Labor and Industrial Relations, 1959.

from the central office in Geneva, Switzerland, but I.L.O. also provides smaller branch offices in several nations.

The American emphasis on business unionism, rather than on political action, has limited collaboration with the several international associations that have united labor movements in many nations. The American Federation of Labor joined the International Federation of Trade Unions in 1910. After World War I, however, I.F.T.U. became active politically, and the A.F. of L. left the association in 1923. The A.F. of L. rejoined I.F.T.U. in 1937. Meanwhile, the new Congress of Industrial Organizations in the United States became active in the World Federation of Trade Unions, W.F.T.U., established in 1945. The C.I.O. withdrew from W.F.T.U. in 1949, when it became apparent that the new organization was heavily influenced by Russian Communists. In 1949, both the A.F. of L. and the C.I.O. joined a new organization representing unionists in some 40 nations and known as the International Confederation of Free Trade Unions, I.C.T.F.U. The United Mine Workers, at that time an unaffiliated union, also joined the new organization.

During and after World War II, both the A.F. of L. and the C.I.O. became much concerned about the expansion of Communism and its tendency to restrict the freedom of unions. In 1945, the A.F. of L. opened an office in Brussels, and in 1948 the Federation appointed a special representative for Latin America and supported the new Inter-American Confederation of Labor. Meanwhile, the C.I.O. had established a Committee on Latin American Affairs in 1939.

Much of the American interest in international cooperation has been directed toward maintaining the freedom and independence of labor movements in other nations. American unions have been effective opponents of totalitarian domination of unions and of the "labor fronts" that forced the unions and employers to cooperate in the political programs of authoritarian governments.

Meanwhile, national unions in this country have affiliated with international associations of workers in their particular industries and occupations. Some fifty American unions, including those of the automobile and transportation workers, coal miners, and others, are affiliated with international secretariats.[18]

3.0 EMPLOYER ASSOCIATIONS

Collective bargaining may involve the discussion and negotiation of working conditions in a single establishment by organized employees of that plant and their employer. In other cases, it may involve employees of many

---

[18] See John P. Windmuller, "ICFTU after Ten Years: Problems and Prospects," *Industrial and Labor Relations Review*, Vol. 14, No. 2, January 1961, pp. 257–272; for a report on Soviet unions, see "The Trade Union Situation in the U.S.S.R." Geneva, Switzerland: International Labour Office, 1960.

firms. In some cases, employers may negotiate as individuals; in others they may form associations for dealing with a union or unions.

Powerful social and economic movements often create powerful reactions. Early labor movements encountered strong efforts on the part of employers and of governments to control worker participation and limit union activity and influence. The Kerr, Dunlop, Harbison, and Myers study[19] found that the objectives of early labor movements were shaped by the reactions of the public and owner "elites." Powerful dynastic rulers feel constrained to repress early industrial unrest, regarding it as a serious threat to their paternalistic leadership. (Public regulation of the labor movement may encourage its political activity.) On the other hand, in communities dominated by a rising middle class, employee organization may be regarded as normal and appropriate.

When unions first appear, some employers seek allies to strengthen their influence and power in controlling worker organizations. In England, many employers appealed to the government for assistance in restricting the demands of early unions. In the more recently industrialized nations, employers may unite to present a solid front for this purpose. In earlier-industrialized nations, some employers continue to operate as individual bargainers, while others join employer associations which represent them in negotiations and in legislative halls.

In several European nations, the employers of a majority of workers negotiate through employer associations. In the United States, approximately one-third of the workers covered by collective agreements work under conditions negotiated through such associations. About one-sixth of all collective agreements are negotiated by multi-employer groups. Multi-employer bargaining is an established practice in several large industries, such as the wood, coal, steel, apparel, construction, longshoring, trucking, railroading, and several service industries.

While most American employers still bargain as individuals, a tendency away from this practice is evident. As industry-wide bargaining has been advanced by stronger and more effective unions, associations of employers for bargaining purposes have become more common. The development of *master contracts* and industry-wide agreements to which all or most employers in an industry or area are parties is now widespread.

Best known and most influential of nationwide employer associations are the National Association of Manufacturers and the Chamber of Commerce of the United States. They do not engage in negotiations but speak for their members on major issues. In addition, some 5,000 state and local associations represent employers. The most numerous are in the construction industry.

Not all earlier employers' associations were interested in carrying on collective bargaining. Many of them, in years past, were active in preventing collective bargaining and sought to destroy or restrict labor organizations. These were the *belligerent employers' associations*. They were paralleled by

---

[19] *Industrialism and Industrial Man,* pp. 213ff.

another group of associations that sought to bargain for their members: the *bargaining* or *negotiatory associations.*

The activities of early belligerent associations deserve brief mention because they color the memories of older unionists and probably exert a continuing influence on bargaining attitudes and relationships. They did not confine their attacks on unions to the courts or to lobbying at federal and state levels. They sought to use the courts to limit union action; they tried to secure enforcement of contracts that made union membership illegal; they secured injunctions against union meetings and demonstrations; they lobbied for tighter controls on union boycotts. In addition, however, they maintained blacklists of union organizers and other troublemakers; some associations provided strikebreakers and armed guards. Others employed secret operatives who infiltrated unions and reported on their plans and deliberations. Some associations sought to control newspapers and flooded the public with pamphlets seeking to discredit union leaders.

Two levels of *association bargaining* are notable—industry-wide, and local. In industries producing pottery and glassware, wallpaper, automatic sprinklers, stove castings, and elevators, agreements on a national, industry-wide scale are well established. Pierson suggests that four conditions are favorable to mutually satisfactory industry-wide bargaining: a strong, industry-wide union; an inclusive employers' association; a long history of collective bargaining; and a national product market.[20]

Most master agreements are limited to local associations of employers. Localities may be as small as a single city, or they may cover an entire state or region. They may be restricted to a single industry. However, in many cities, employers' associations represent a broad cross section of the industries in the region. In many localities, employers' associations maintain a file of current agreements, conduct surveys of wages, hours, pensions, insurance, and other "fringe" practices, and advise and consult with employers on both negotiations and subsequent day-to-day contract administration.

Tendencies toward industry-wide bargaining have occasioned widespread discussion of its advantages and disadvantages. Many unions and managements feel that they achieve greater wage stability and fewer industrial disputes in multi-unit bargaining. Employers feel that they achieve a more even balance of power with the union. They can employ more skilled negotiators. They can unite in resisting "unreasonable" demands. On the other hand, uniform standards may not fit local conditions. Individual firms may try with some success to gain advantages. Many managements are reluctant to give up their rights to make individual decisions. When strikes occur under association bargaining, they are likely to be long and expensive. Unions frequently feel that they are less effective when they have to deal with an association of employers.

[20] Frank C. Pierson, "Multi-Employer Bargaining: Nature and Score," *Reprint No. 4,* Los Angeles: University of California, Institute of Industrial Relations, 1949.

Negotiating associations help employers prepare for and carry on contract negotiations. *Administrative associations* have the responsibility of handling day-by-day problems arising in the administration of the agreement, particularly grievances and contract interpretations.[21]

4.0 SUMMARY

In all industrialized nations, labor movements are among the most impressive products of the industrialization process. Everywhere, industrialization requires the recruitment and commitment of large numbers of property-less wage earners, a group Marx described as the "industrial proletariat." Everywhere, these workers have formed associations in protest against the new working conditions and work rules imposed as a part of large-scale industrial organization.

What do wage earners expect of their unions? Why do they join with others in these universal movements? Why do they continue to support their unions after the pattern of industrialization is well established and widely accepted? Many theories of labor movements have been advanced to answer these questions. Some observers have seen them as steps toward the ultimate revolution and classless society visualized by early spokesmen for socialism. Others consider labor movements as essentially political vehicles with wide social and economic reforms as their goals. Some students of early unions have described them as means of introducing industrial democracy in working relationships to parallel the development of political democracy in society.

Other theories explain the emergence and ongoing support of unions as a means of balancing the economic power of employers. Workers join unions to gain greater influence in labor markets. Many analysts have seen unions as offering opportunities for the satisfaction of a variety of basic human needs. Current studies of union member attitudes provide evidence that union members in this country generally approve of the programs their unions have undertaken and suggest no lessening of member interest in the movement.

It is reasonable to conclude that the reasons for joining and supporting these movements change as the process of industrialization continues. In early stages, as class consciousness develops among industrial workers, they may be strongly motivated toward radical action. What happens next appears to depend largely on the reactions and practices of the ruling groups, the rule-makers in each newly industrialized society. If their reaction is rigid and negative and oppressive, revolutionary unionism is encouraged. The potential for revolution is greatest in this early stage in the development of labor movements.

With the passage of time and mutual adjustments to the requirements of the new system, the values labor movements offer their members tend to

---

[21] See Jesse Thomas Carpenter, *Employers' Associations and Collective Bargaining in New York City,* Ithaca, N.Y.: Cornell University Press, 1952.

change. In the more mature industrialized society, they may become essentially reformist political movements. Or, in a political democracy, if economic gains have been shared with wage earners, they may become business unions, which are economic agents for their members.

This chapter should be regarded as background with which to interpret the present policies and practices of the American labor movement. They are the subject of the chapter that follows.

SELECTED SUPPLEMENTARY READINGS

Dunlop, John T., "The Development of Labor Organization: A Theoretical Framework," in Richard A. Lester and Joseph Shister, *Insight into Labor Issues.* New York: The Macmillan Company, 1958.
"Labor Movements," *Encyclopedia of the Social Sciences,* Vol. VIII, pp. 682–696.
Lester, Richard A., *As Unions Mature,* Chap. 9. Princeton: Princeton University Press, 1958.
Rezler, Julius, *Union Growth Reconsidered.* New York: Kossuth Foundation (207 East 37th St.), 1961.
Purcell, Theodore V., *Blue Collar Man,* Chaps. 4, 5, 7, 8, 9. Cambridge: Harvard University Press, 1960.
Rosen, Hjalmar, and Ruth Alice Hudson Rosen, *The Union Member Speaks,* Chaps. 5, 6, 7. Englewood Cliffs, N.J.: Prentice-Hall, Inc., 1955.
Uphoff, Walter H., and Marvin D. Dunnette, "Understanding the Union Member," *Bulletin 18,* University of Minnesota Industrial Relations Center, July 1956.
Ulman, Lloyd, "American Trade Unionism—Past and Present," Chaps. 13 and 14 of Seymour E. Harris, *American Economic History.* New York: McGraw-Hill Book Company, Inc., 1961.

SHORT CASE PROBLEM 9.1

Walcott Company

Mr. Elmer Walcott started the Walcott Company in 1914, when he hired three mechanics to join him in the production of welding equipment. He had been granted three patents that were important to the immediate success of his firm. After several difficult years, the business has gradually expanded. Mr. Walcott still owns about 70 per cent of the capital stock of the firm. It now employs 1,400 men and women who are engaged in coil winding, assembly, wiring, packaging, shipping, and research. The business has been profitable; consequently, Mr. Walcott is widely described as a millionaire who started with nothing but an idea.

Mr. Walcott has built no cathedral buildings as memorials to himself. Rather, the firm's four divisions are now scattered in four buildings that have been purchased at salvage prices.

Mr. Walcott has been widely described in the community as a generous employer. He has consistently paid wage rates a cut above those specified in local union contracts. He has, for several years, provided employee services and benefits that are more generous than the usual pattern in the community. He initiated an employee profit-sharing program in 1952.

No union has demanded recognition as the bargaining agent for Walcott employees until the present time. A week ago, the business agent for a local of the I.A.M. wrote the firm's personnel manager asking for a negotiating session. He said that the union represents a majority of workers in the assembly department of one plant. He has proposed what he describes as a "standard agreement." It includes, among other provisions, a cost of living clause, participation in the pension plan sponsored by the union, and a union shop with checkoff.

Mr. Walcott has reacted bitterly to this development. He assumes that the negotiator represents a majority of employees in the department and is legally within his rights. But Mr. Walcott feels that employee action in joining the union indicates an attitude that combines ingratitude and disloyalty. He says that he has no interest in being associated with such a crew. He has called his managerial associates together and announced that he proposes to sell the firm as soon as possible.

Problem: John Walcott, Jr., generally regarded as the "heir to the throne" has asked you to come in as a consultant. He wants to discover why employees have organized in the face of what are generally regarded as ideal working relationships and what this development means to the firm's managers. He has arranged for a preliminary meeting of top managers in which you are asked to discuss possible explanations and implications of these developments.

SHORT CASE PROBLEM 9.2

France Rivet Company

The France Rivet Company has no union. Many efforts have been made to organize employees, but no union has asked for recognition as bargaining agent. Whether any or a large proportion of employees may be union members is not known by the employer.

During the past two days, however, pickets representing an international industrial union have appeared before the plant. They carry banners describing the employer as "unfair." The industrial relations director has talked to a half-dozen employees. He asked them if they belonged to a union or if they knew why the plant is being picketed. All answers were negative.

To this time, the pickets have been rather ineffective. Few, if any, employees have been prevented from working. Trucks have continued deliveries. Some feeling of tension, however, is apparent; employees obviously dislike crossing the picket line. Customers also may object, although none is known to have avoided the plant on that account.

The industrial relations director, however, is under pressure to get rid of the pickets. Plant officials and managers are afraid they may shut off customers or interfere with both receiving and shipping of materials. Several managers have suggested that the whole procedure is a "shakedown," that some union official is getting set to ask for a payoff. Other members of the managerial group think legal action should be taken; they want the industrial relations director to get an injunction. The firm's business is nationwide.

Problem: What should the industrial relations director do, if anything? Has he already made mistakes in handling the matter?

10. Union Theory, Policy, and Practice

Management, and manpower management in particular, is different because of unions. Bilateral policy is likely to be quite different from that established by managers on a unilateral basis. The day-to-day practice of managing is modified by the influence of unions. That influence extends from philosophies to problems and affects both policy and practice.

The union contribution to bilateral employment policy begins with a different philosophy from that of most managers—a changed ordering of values and beliefs. Further, unions and their members rely on somewhat different theories to bridge the gaps between philosophy and policy and between policy and programs. Unions see the problems of management in a somewhat different perspective from that with which managers view the same problems.

Unions propose to aid their members in the achievement of personal goals through employment. However, unions may add organizational goals as well. They have developed carefully considered policies, roadmaps for their guidance, just as managerial policies guide spokesmen on the other side of the bargaining table. Unions have their standard operating practices, similar to and at the same time different from those of most managers.

The predominant pattern of values in the philosophies of American unions is much like that of many American managers. Most unions in the United States are strongly committed to ideals of personal freedom, democracy, and the enterprise system. They are outspoken in championing these ideals, both at home and abroad. However, their theories lead them to somewhat distinctive policies and to practices that many managers find objectionable.

In a nation committed to the encouragement of bilateral employment policy developed through collective bargaining, competence in management requires an understanding of union viewpoints and programs. Such an understanding can go far to reduce union-management conflict and to facilitate joint policy determination. Managers need to understand the practice of *labor relations,* the negotiation and administration of union-management collective agreements. At the same time, managers need to recognize the *pervasive influence* of the labor movement on all employment relationships, including those in which employees are not formally represented by unions.[1]

This chapter examines the theories, policies and practices of American unions. As a starting point, it may be helpful to note how one American union states its objectives. Here is the declaration of intentions of the International Brotherhood of Pulp, Sulphite and Paper Mill Workers:

> The Constitution of the International Brotherhood of Pulp, Sulphite and Paper Mill Workers lists the following as the objectives of the Union:
> 1. To secure and maintain a living wage and to lessen the hours of labor for its members.
> 2. To assist each other in obtaining employment in preference to persons not connected with this union.
> 3. To use every honorable method to elevate its membership in the economic, moral and social scale of life.
> 4. To help safeguard the principles of democracy.
> 5. To work for the establishment of political and social equality regardless of race, color or creed.
> 6. To promote friendly relations between labor and government and labor and industry.[2]

1.0 UNION THEORY

All unions assume that "in union there is strength"—that working together in their unions, members can exert a strength, influence, and power that far exceeds the potential of individuals. Most American unions propose to use their power in a business-like manner; they expect to exert their influence within the framework of the free enterprise system to secure concessions from employers and the managers who represent them. They have their theories about how their power can be most effectively applied; such theories dictate their policies and practices.

Business unionism has been described as the predominant American type of labor organization, but American unions have not always accepted a pure business theory of the labor movement and do not presently adhere to such a simple view. Some American unions have adopted *reformist* programs; a few have been *revolutionary.* Many unions have sought to provide services beyond those of immediate economic gains for their members and other em-

---

[1] See in this connection James K. Dent and Romeo de la Paz, "Union Security and Management Attitudes," *Personnel Psychology,* Vol. 14, No. 2, Summer 1961, pp. 167–181.

[2] Miles E. Hoffman, "A Contemporary Analysis of a Labor Union," *Labor Monograph No. 4,* Fort Edward, N.Y.: International Brotherhood of Pulp, Sulphite and Paper Mill Workers, p. 9.

ployees. In other words, while the business theory has dominated, other theories have influenced the policy and practice of the American labor movement.

1.1   General welfare. Most union members and leaders assume that what is good for the labor movement is good for the nation. They argue, for example, that the higher wages for which unions strive are the source of purchasing power that stimulates and forces the continuing growth of the economy and is the only adequate protection against economic stagnation. The theory holds that the source of drive and power in the free economy is the pressure of consumer demand. It notes that wage-earners are the "spenders" of the nation, that income directed to them goes immediately into channels of demands for finished products and services. Unions conclude that every advance in wages is a push toward expansion and growth.

This is only one phase of a sort of *general welfare* theory of unions. Another concludes that one major function of business is to provide employment—that creation of jobs is as important to all as production of goods and services. It identifies union goals in protecting members' jobs with economic progress, betterment of life for all. Union insistence on health and welfare plans for their members is regarded as setting a pattern that will benefit millions outside the labor movement.

Political activities of unions are assumed to be directed toward the welfare of the nation as a whole. The labor movement has undertaken extensive foreign organizing activities that are regarded by members as a public service to the cause of political democracy and freedom in the continuing conflict with Communist nations. Union labels, it is said, protect the health of those who watch for them, insuring that products are made or served under healthful, sanitary conditions. In short, unionists identify the labor movement with more of the good life for everyone, so that what benefits the movement helps toward that goal.

This general welfare theory has encountered many critics, of course. In recent years, for example, critics have charged unions with responsibility for *wage-push inflation*. Unions have found it difficult to argue that, although they have been successful in forcing higher wages for their members, these increases have not become the source of pressure for rising prices. Their answer notes the distinction between wages and labor costs; it is conceivable certainly that higher wages may be offset by greater productivity, so that labor costs are not increased.

The general welfare theory faces its most difficult tests in years immediately ahead, for industrialization all over the world has increased competition in international markets. Evidence indicates that labor costs in some major industries are pricing American products out of important markets. American unions may have to develop a new policy on wages to combat inflation in the years ahead.

1.2   Labor-marketing theory. Free unions everywhere assume that most of the conditions under which employees work are determined by employee influence and power in labor markets. They place great emphasis, therefore, on the effectiveness of employee representation in such markets. They see themselves as economic agents of their members in these markets. Further, they see great possibilities of influencing conditions in a wide range of markets through political action.

It is often said that American unions operate on a *lump-of-labor theory*, which assumes that demands for labor are inelastic. The theory gets its name from the conclusion that a fixed amount of work will be done, regardless of labor cost. While the theory had wide acceptance in the early days of unions, it has much less influence today. Most unionists recognize elasticity in demands for labor, whether or not they use the term, and their wage policy intends to avoid pricing that is likely to put members out of work.

On the other hand, a modern amended theory has had wide acceptance. It holds that elasticity of demand in many labor markets is not great, because buyers of labor will simply incorporate higher labor costs in higher prices. Since World War II, rising prices have been common and a large share of total demand has been generated by military and defense expenditures that are not highly sensitive to prices. In such markets, unions have assumed that rising wages would have little effect on employment.

1.3 Productivity theory. American unions have long supported a *productivity theory* of wages; in fact, the American Federation of Labor has officially endorsed it. In essence, this theory simply holds that *wages are determined by the productivity of workers, so higher productivity justifies higher wages.* The productivity in question may be described as "average" rather than "specific" or "marginal." This theory holds that the general level of wages should be determined by improving productivity; as the latter rises, wages should also rise. Labor's productivity theory suggests a policy that proposes to adjust wages at regular periods to changes in average productivity. It justifies a policy of *productivity increases* that assure from 2 to 4 per cent wage advances to absorb rising man-hour productivity as disclosed by industry-wide or nationwide indexes.

1.4 Bargaining theory. American unions have, as one reason for their advocacy of business unionism, generally accepted a *bargaining theory* of wages. In its simplest form, it holds that levels of wages in each labor market are set by the opposing economic strengths of employers and workers. If employees, by acting in concert through their union as bargaining agent, increase their economic strength, they can thereby raise wages. In effect, economic strength is measured by ability to withhold labor and thus force employers to forego employment or to find substitutes for labor.

The bargaining theory is something of a corollary to the lump-of-labor theory mentioned above. Even the 19th-century advocates of these theories recognized, however, that the bargaining power of unions could be influential only within limits. Even without formal curves of demands, it was clear that high-wage demands could force employers to cease operations or find substitutes for labor or enter other labor markets and employ other occupations.

Modern advocates of the bargaining theory see it as a modification of generally accepted wage theory. That modification suggests that neither employers nor employees enter labor markets with precise prices or narrow lines representing demands and supplies; rather, both include an element of flexibility that creates bands rather than lines. Within these bands, this theory holds, wage rates are established by the bargaining strength of the parties. Within such a band of possible wage rates, the individual worker, with little economic strength, must accept the lowest of several rates. The union, on the other hand, can exert its greater economic strength to secure higher rates.

1.5 Loyal opposition to management. Business unionism generally concludes that management's function is to manage, but that the union has a responsibility to challenge the quality of management and thus to force continually better management. This viewpoint applies with special emphasis to management's utilization of manpower. In the whole broad field of the application, utilization, and conservation of human resources, the union plays the part of critic. It will be aware of the best in policy and practice and insist that management measure up to such levels. This theory of the union's responsibility follows from the conception of the union as the employee's business agent. It also incorporates union productivity theory; only the best in policy and practice can make employees as productive as they should be.

The theory does not imply that unions should become managers or that unions should help employers manage. On the contrary, it implies that unions should refuse responsibility for management so that they can be constantly in the position of critic. However, the theory may justify demands for specific managerial policies and practices. Such demands are not considered union activity in management, but they may raise costs and thus force managers to do a better job of managing.

Many managements that deal regularly with unions argue that unions seldom confine their loyal opposition to policies and practices in the area of employment relationships. To many such managers, the union assault on management prerogatives implies a union theory of general participation in management.

2.0 GENERAL MANPOWER POLICY AND PRACTICE

Section 1 has outlined a few of the principal theories that have wide acceptance by American unions and that influence their philosophy of participation and help them define their role in employment. Reference has been made to some of the rather clear implications of these theories for policy, the general courses they prescribe. This section directs additional attention to the common policies of unions, the set courses they have accepted as guides for organizations and their members. The section also notes the most common practices by which unions try to follow and implement accepted policies.

In the earlier discussion of managerial policy, a distinction was made between general and specific policies. The same distinction may be helpful in understanding the activities of unions. They have adopted general policies that prescribe broad, inclusive practices. At the same time, they have established specific policies with respect to specific activities—hiring, promotion, wage and salary administration, and employee benefits and services, for example. This section of the chapter outlines several general policies that have wide acceptance among American unions and notes the practices unions follow in seeking to make these general policies effective.

2.1 Union authority and responsibility. Perhaps the most elementary policy of most American unions is the determination to create and maintain powerful, authoritative unions that can speak with assurance for their members and enforce the agreements they conclude. If the union is to be effective as the representative of employees, this policy assumes, it must be sure of itself. It must be able to say what members will and will not do, so far as agreements with employers are concerned. Policy proposes, therefore, to maintain the power of the union, to insure its permanence, and to give it strength and authority.

This basic policy of business unionism leads to a variety of practices designed to provide *union recognition* and *security*. The ultimate in conflict tactics, the *strike,* represents an expression of the power of the union in its ability to withhold the services of its members. Unions accumulate impressive *financial resources* to buttress their strength and to provide *strike aid* that holds members together in enforcing union strategy. Unions exercise *disciplinary power* to force reluctant members to conform to the union's strategy and to punish dissenters, whose defection is regarded as endangering the union's effectiveness as bargaining agent for all its members.

2.11 Union security. Union security refers to the right of the union to speak for its members and perhaps for other non-member employees in negotiating agreements and in enforcing the provisions of such contracts. It involves the assurance that an employer will recognize the union as the agent of employees.

In earlier periods, discussion of union security centered around this primary question of *recognition.* Unions demanded that employers recognize the union as the bargaining agent for its members or for all workers in the bargaining unit. Often, when several unions contended for the right to represent employees, each demanded recognition as sole bargaining representative.

Modern practice begins with a definition of the appropriate *bargaining unit* in terms of the jobs to be included. A bargaining unit may be defined by craft lines, further bounded by specified firms or localities. Again, a bargaining unit may include a wide range of occupations within a particular firm. Unions may find themselves in conflict over the boundaries of the bargaining units they seek to represent. Because of the frequency and severity of such conflicts, the federal government, in the National Labor Relations Act of 1935, gave the National Labor Relations Board authority to designate appropriate bargain units in interstate business. Many states provide *state labor relations boards* with similar authority in intrastate disputes.

For the bargaining unit thus defined, practice requires identification of the union that is to be *bargaining agent*. Since several unions may compete for this recognition, inter-union conflict may arise. Here again, federal and state legislation since 1935 have provided agencies with authority to *certify* bargaining agents. Federal and state labor relations boards may call for membership *authorization cards* or hold *elections* and designate one union as the *certified bargaining agent* for the unit.

The bargaining agent, whether voluntarily recognized by the employer or formally certified by a federal or state board, may be granted any one of several *types of union security*, which may be outlined as follows:

1. *Anti-union shop.* Before federal and state legislation protected all employees in their right to become union members, some firms maintained what was called the *closed anti-union shop*. They refused employment to union members. They enforced a sort of negative union security.

2. *Open shop.* The weakest form of union security is the *open shop* in which employers refuse to recognize any union as bargaining agent for employees or members and in which the employers insist on their right to deal with all employees individually. Employers hire members or non-members but negotiate individually with each worker. They recognize no unions and conclude no collective agreements.

3. *Exclusive bargaining agent.* Under the *sole or exclusive bargaining agent* type of security, the union is accepted as the agent for all employees in the unit. While no requirement of union membership is included, the union is responsible for negotiating with respect to working conditions for all employees, including those *not* members of the union.

4. *Preferential shop.* Under the *preferential shop,* additional recognition is granted the union by agreement that the management will give first chance for employment to union members.

5. *Maintenance of membership.* This is a type of recognition that first gained wide usage during World War II, when the War Labor Board ordered it as a compromise settlement of union demands for the closed shop. Under maintenance of membership, all employees who are or who become members of the union on or after a specified date must remain members in good standing for the full term of the agreement. The arrangement includes an "escape period" of 10 to 15 days after contract negotiations during which members may resign if they wish.

6. *Agency shop.* The *agency shop* requires that all employees in the bargaining unit pay dues to the union, although they do not have to join it. This arrangement is quite similar to the so-called "Rand formula," in Canada. It overcomes union criticism of "free riders" (who share the benefits gained by negotiation without contributing) and, to some degree, meets the objections of many employers to forced union membership.

7. Union shop. More common in current practice is the *union shop.* Under this arrangement, all employees in the bargaining unit must be or must become members of the union. Management is permitted to hire non-unionists, but they must join the union if they remain beyond the close of the probationary period.

8. Closed shop. The *closed shop* allows the greatest union control of labor supplies. Under this arrangement, only union members may be employed. Management agrees to seek all employees for the bargaining unit from the union, and the union agrees to supply such numbers as may be needed. Employees must maintain their union membership in good standing.

9. The checkoff. In about two-thirds of all agreements, union security provisions are supplemented by the checkoff. Under this arrangement, the employer deducts union dues (and sometimes initiation fees and assessments) from pay checks and remits these collections to the union. In earlier periods, unions frequently negotiated a compulsory and automatic checkoff, under which union members were compelled to allow these deductions. Present practice—the *voluntary checkoff*—requires that individual members must have personally authorized such deductions.

At the present time, about three-fourths of all employees covered by collective agreements in the United States work under union shop provisions. Other forms of union security include maintenance of membership, 7 per cent; sole bargaining agent, 19 per cent; and the agency shop, less than one per cent.

Unions have encountered something of a dilemma in policy arising from demands for union security by organizations of their own employees. As early as 1951, employees of the Air Line Pilots Association found it necessary to seek National Labor Relations Board support for their demands for recognition. In 1957, AFL-CIO organizers encountered strong opposition when they sought to bargain through the Field Representatives Association. In 1961, the Federation of Union Representatives (F.O.U.R.), composed of organizers from several unions, encountered a refusal to bargain when they sought recognition.

2.12 Strikes, picketing, and boycotts. The strike is widely regarded as the union's most powerful weapon. As a matter of policy, American unions have consistently opposed any infringement on their right to strike. At the same time, they recognize that strikes can be disastrous to unions and their members. For this reason, many international unions restrict the right of locals to call strikes, requiring the approval of international officers before resort to such stoppages.[3]

Several types of strikes may be identified. Most common is the *economic strike,* in which union members cease work in order to enforce their demands

---

[3] See "Strike Control Provisions in Union Constitutions," *Monthly Labor Review,* Vol. 77, No. 5, May 1954, pp. 497–500.

for additional pay or related employee priviieges or benefits. In an *unfair labor practice strike,* members cease work to protest an alleged unfair labor practice (to be described in Chapter 11) on the part of an employer.[4] In a *sympathetic strike,* union members cease work, not in protest against employment conditions in their own firm, but as a means of supporting other union members who are on strike in other firms. A *general strike* represents the extension of the sympathetic strike to include all or most union members in a community or region. It is a generalized protest of organized labor against conditions affecting some members. An *outlaw strike* is one undertaken without proper authorization from union officials in accordance with the rules of the union. In a *flash strike* or *quickie,* certain members of the union cease work, perhaps without warning. Most flash strikes are also outlaw strikes. In a *sitdown strike,* strikers cease work but do not leave their place of work, remaining in the plant and in control of production facilities. A *slowdown strike* is not really a strike in the usual sense. Employees do not leave their work. They limit output while remaining on the job.

Picketing, in which union representatives parade with banners, is used to inform the public that a labor dispute is in progress and to enlist popular support for the union. Picketing may also advise the public that an organizing campaign is in process. It may reflect disputed union jurisdictions. Picketing may be designed to interfere with business and thus to force an employer to comply with union demands.

The effectiveness of picketing is enhanced by rules governing the members of associated unions. They will "respect" and will not cross a picket line. Hence, transportation services may be stopped, so that supplies cannot be delivered or products distributed. Picketing by one group of employees generally stops other employees from working at the same location.

The *boycott* is designed to prevent an employer from selling his products or services. American labor has long used it—it was among the favorite devices employed by the Knights of Labor. In earlier practice, unions effected boycotts by publishing "unfair" or "we don't patronize" lists in their papers and magazines. More recently, the practice has taken the form of refusing to work on or to install materials produced by employers who have not come to terms with the union, or of refusing to use the products of other, competing labor organizations.

A distinction is made between "primary" and "secondary" boycotts. The first is directed only against an offending individual or firm. It consists merely of withholding patronage. The secondary boycott, on the other hand, involves efforts to induce or coerce third parties, not directly concerned in the dispute, to refrain from patronizing the offending party. The third party may be a contractor who uses certain materials or products, or it may be the public at large.

2.13 Internal control and discipline. Union constitutions grant their

[4] For more on this important distinction, see Walter L. Daykin, "The Distinction between Economic and Unfair Labor Practice Strikes," *Labor Law Journal,* Vol. 12, No. 3, March 1961, pp. 189–97.

officers powerful controls that may be applied to members who criticize the actions of officers or refuse to follow the terms of negotiated agreements. Unions enter into "contracts" with employers and their associations. A minority of members may not approve the terms of agreements negotiated by their representatives. Yet, if the union is to be responsible, it must insist that all members observe the terms of the contract. Many unions have written into their constitutions procedures designed to require members to accept majority decisions. They provide for fines and other penalties, including expulsion from the union.

Some unions have taken steps to modify this procedure. The Upholsterers' International Union, for example, has written a "bill of rights" for members into its constitution. The union permits appeals by members to an outside, neutral appeals board. The United Automobile Workers has also created an independent appeals board to hear complaints from members.[5]

2.14 Financial strength. It is frequently observed that unionism in the United States is big business. Many of the internationals and some local unions have accumulated impressive financial resources. They own valuable headquarters buildings like those of the AFL-CIO, the Machinists, and the Teamsters in Washington, D.C. They have invested in real estate and own shares in banks and other business. The growth of union welfare and benefit programs has tended to increase such investments.

Annual income from dues is in excess of 600 million dollars. About 250 millions of this total goes to the internationals. The Labor-Management Reporting and Disclosure Act of 1959 has provided details on the financial aspects of American unions. Monthly dues average about $3. Some 71 per cent of the reporting unions charge less than $5 per month. Initiation fees range from no fee to more than $100, with one-fourth of all unions charging $5 or less. Approximately 10 per cent charge initiation fees of more than $100. A few unions charge transfer fees; more than half amount to less than $3; about 5 per cent charge more than $100. Work permit fees for non-members are issued by less than 10 per cent of reporting unions. Two-thirds of the monthly permit fees are less than $5. Table 10.1 summarizes the distribution of unions according to levels of dues and Table 10.2 provides more detail on union initiation fees.

International unions and the AFL-CIO are supported by per capita taxes paid by locals in behalf of their members. For AFL-CIO, locals pay a per capita tax of 4 cents per month. Internationals receive per capita taxes of 50 cents or more per month, depending largely on the range of benefits and services provided for their members.[6]

---

[5] For details of these provisions, see Jack Stieber, Walter E. Oberer and Michael Harrington, "Democracy and Public Review," Santa Barbara, Calif.: Center for the Study of Democratic Institutions, 1960; "A More Perfect Union," Detroit 14, Mich.: The UAW House, 1960; "I.S.O. Forum: Union Appeals Board," *Social Order,* Vol. 4, No. 1, January 1954, pp. 13–19; Clyde W. Summers, "Disciplinary Powers of Unions," *Industrial and Labor Relations Review,* Vol. 3, No. 4, July 1950, pp. 15–32.

[6] For details on union finances, see the annual reports of the Bureau of Labor-Management Reports, Department of Labor, Washington, D.C.

Table 10.1   Union Dues

[See accompanying text for explanation]

Amount of dues (per month)	Number of local unions with a—	
	Prevailing fee[1]	Maximum fee
Total	39,650	8,997
No dues required	847	....
Less than $1	891	1,266
$1.00 to $1.99	1,940	2,019
$2.00 to $2.99	4,277	1,713
$3.00 to $3.99	11,004	1,941
$4.00 to $4.99	9,157	972
$5.00 to $5.99	5,705	335
$6.00 to $9.99	2,547	483
$10.00 to $24.99	444	63
$25.00 to $35.00	5	4
Amount not determinable[2]	2,185	201
Amount not reported	648	....

[1] Local unions which reported a prevailing figure for dues and a range of dues were tabulated only by the prevailing figure for dues.

[2] Amount of dues has not been established or is based upon some variable, such as earnings, and no average or prevailing amount was reported.

SOURCE: *Report of the Bureau of Labor-Management Reports, Fiscal Year, 1960,* September 14, 1960, U. S. Government Printing Office, p. 26.

The Bureau of Labor Statistics has outlined a neat summary of the services provided by unions for their members. It is shown in Figure 10.1. The flow of local dues and per capita taxes is compared with the services provided by locals, internationals, and the top-level federation. The chart omits reference to city and state centrals and councils: their activities are similar to those listed for the federation.

2.15   Organizing the unorganized. American union spokesmen have long assumed that strong unions are growing unions and a powerful labor movement is one that keeps expanding. On the other hand, unorganized workers appear as serious competition to union members and hazards to the wages and working conditions unions have negotiated. Hence the general policy of strength and power prescribes a continuing program of organization. The AFL-CIO has a staff of organizers, as do most member nationals and internationals. Special organizing campaigns are planned and directed at particular regions and occupations—the South, for example, or white-collar workers in financial institutions or in public offices. These white-collar workers represent an area of special concern to many unions today, for it is apparent that if the movement is to grow, it must organize white-collar, technical, and perhaps professional workers.

Continuing shifts of power within the labor movement result from the policy of organizing the unorganized. Thus, the building trades and construction workers, long-term powers in AFL-CIO, have been losing to the industrial unions. In the future, machinists, teamsters (outside the Federation)

Table 10.2 Initiation Fees of American Unions

[See accompanying text for explanation]

Amount of initiation fee	Number of local unions with a—	
	Prevailing fee[1]	Maximum fee
Total	38,823	9,824
No initiation fee required	1,905	....
Less than $1	179	14
$1	1,291	152
$1.01 to $1.99	68	101
$2	1,956	285
$2.01 to $2.99	185	66
$3 to $3.99	1,365	435
$4 to $4.99	388	84
$5	9,625	1,464
$5.01 to $9.99	1,858	408
$10	5,372	1,974
$10.01 to $14.99	381	716
$15	1,861	870
$15.01 to $24.99	939	657
$25	2,047	802
$25.01 to $49.99	808	495
$50	2,648	451
$50.01 to $99.99	1,319	298
$100	1,340	158
$100.01 to $149.99	593	75
$150	610	37
$150.01 to $199.99	164	14
$200.00	472	9
$200.01 to $249.99	86	7
$250.00	177	14
$250.01 to $500.00	225	58
$500.01 to $1,400.00	17	11
Amount not determinable[2]	442	169
Amount not reported	402	....

[1] Local unions which reported both a prevailing fee and range of fees were tabulated only by prevailing fee.

[2] Amount of fee has not been established or is based upon some variable, such as earnings, and no average or prevailing fee was reported.

SOURCE: *Report of the Bureau of Labor-Management Reports, Fiscal Year, 1960,* U.S. Government Printing Office, September 14, 1960, p. 27.

and electrical workers may dominate because of their greater success in expanding organization.

2.2 Democratic control and leadership. The labor movement intends to be essentially a democratic movement. American unions have stressed democratic policy making and administration. They have promoted leaders from the rank-and-file membership. They have provided special educational programs to assist members in preparing themselves for positions as officers at local and national levels. They have struggled, sometimes without success, to prevent gangsterism and racketeering in their unions. With some notable

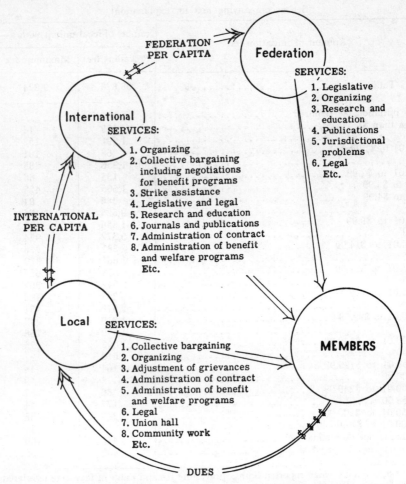

Figure 10.1   Flow of Union Revenues and Services
SOURCES: "Directory of Labor Unions in the United States," Bulletin
No. 1127, United States Department of Labor, 1953, p. 3.

—and notorious—exceptions, they have sought to maintain democratic controls.

Members have faced the complex problem of granting adequate organizational authority to union officers and at the same time preserving freedom for discussion and criticism by their members. Member determination to assure the power of their unions has sometimes encouraged compromises with internal democracy. Zealous members and leaders often believe that ends justify the means that force members into conformity. Pressures to conform are as notable in unions as in other forms of organizational cooperation. Nevertheless the persistent policy of the labor movement has sought democratic control and leadership. Indeed, that policy has been so dominant that it has been difficult to establish and maintain powerful central federations.

2.21 Rank-and-file leadership. American unions have generally encouraged the election of rank-and-file members to union offices. They have not sought the leadership of intellectuals as did some early English unions. Most of the international officers are men who have moved to these positions from memberships in local unions.

Significant changes and trends in union leadership are apparent. Early leaders were—and perhaps had to be—men of immediate action, frequently arbitrary in their decisions, convinced that they knew best what was good for their members. In many ways, these older leaders—some of whom continue to control large unions—matched their counterparts across the bargaining table, the captains of industry and empire builders.

As unions have become more secure, leadership has tended to pass to more negotiatory types and to men with special competence in managing large organizations whose members demand additional participation in policy-determination. In the most recent phase of this continuing change, an apparent trend toward greater managerial competence and toward what may be called trusteeship is evident. The emerging type of leadership has been described as *fiduciary.* The newer leader is much more aware of his responsibility to represent members and to consider their opinions. At the same time, he recognizes the potential dangers of conflicts of interest as outlined by AFL-CIO ethical codes and the Federal Pension and Welfare Disclosure Act.[7]

2.22 Workers' education. American unions have supported a variety of special educational programs for their members and officers. In earlier periods, the Federation supported worker colleges, including The Brookwood Labor College, established in 1921 at Katonah, New York, and Commonwealth College at Mena, Arkansas. Support has been given, also, to summer schools for workers, some of them held on university campuses. Various short courses and conferences are provided to focus attention on such subjects as the public relations of the labor movement, international labor problems, benefit and welfare programs. In metropolitan areas, night classes offered by the city central, frequently in cooperation with high schools and colleges, give special attention to the needs of rank-and-file members who aspire to leadership in the labor movement. Several of the internationals maintain staff departments to plan and direct such educational programs.[8]

2.23 Individual freedom. The problem of balancing the freedom of union members to express their opinions and to criticize the policies of their unions and officers against the protection and strengthening of the union

[7] See Jack Barbash, *Unions and Union Leadership.* New York: Harper & Brothers, 1959, especially Section 2, Chaps. 8–14.

[8] For details of these cooperative programs, see Caroline F. Ware, *Labor Education in Universities,* New York: American Labor Education Service, 1946; Jack Barbash, *Universities and Workers Education,* New York: Harper & Brothers, 1955.

has been persistent. "Troublemakers" within the ranks are a continuing source of annoyance if not of hazard. Officers and members as well face continuing temptation to discipline these critics or to force them out. To do so, under the common provisions of union-shop agreements, means that they must also lose their jobs. This type of problem has been so persistent and troublesome that it has occasioned public intervention (see Chapter 11).[9]

Individual unions, as noted, have taken several types of action to insure democratic controls and the protection of individual members. Immediately after the union of the A.F. of L. and the C.I.O. in 1955, the new federation established a Committee on Ethical Practices. That committee drafted its Codes of Ethical Practices, which were adopted by the Annual Convention in 1957.

Six codes are included in the formal Codes of Ethical Practices adopted by the AFL-CIO. The first deals with the issuance of local union charters. The second specifies standards of behavior in the handling of health and welfare funds. Code III is designed to force member unions to purge their organizations of racketeers, crooks, communists, and fascists. Code IV outlines principles to guide union officials in avoiding conflicts of interest arising out of their investments and business interests. Code V requires appropriate accounting and auditing practices to insure that union funds and property are used as intended for the benefit of members. Code VI deals specifically with democratic processes within unions and requires elections at specified intervals. It also requires that conventions be open to the public and that safeguards be provided for the protection of individual members in expressing their views.[10]

2.3 Political action. Although it is evident that the American labor movement has not taken the form of a formal labor party, American unions have long sought political influence. Acceptance of business unionism has not precluded a general policy of using the pressure of political action to gain advantages for members and for other employees.

Policy on political action has changed from time to time and has varied among unions and groups of unions. In colonial times, workers joined with farmers and others in forming what was known as the "caucus." In the late 1730's and early 1740's, the Caucus forced the establishment of a public bank which issued paper currency as a means of relieving hard-pressed debtors. Later in the same century, unions played a part in forming the Sons of Liberty, which was active in demonstrating against British economic controls. In 1828, members of the labor movement formed the Workingmen's

[9] For excellent analyses, see Archibald Cox, "The Role of Law in Preserving Union Democracy" and David L. Cole, "Union Self-Discipline and the Freedom of Individual Workers," in Michael Harrington and Paul Jacobs, eds., *Labor in a Free Society,* Berkeley, Calif.: University of California Press, 1959; also Leo Bromwich, "Union Constitutions," New York (60 East 42nd St.): The Fund for the Republic, 1959.

[10] Copies of the Codes are available from the AFL-CIO headquarters in Washington, D.C. See also "Codes of Ethical Practices of the Labor Movement," *Monthly Labor Reveiw,* Vol. 80, No. 3, March 1957, pp. 350–53.

Labor Party of Philadelphia, with a platform plank demanding a 10-hour working day. A similar Workingmen's Party was formed in New York the following year. In the 1830's, employees joined with farmers in New England in forming a political association to work for shorter hours and for public education.

In the latter half of the 19th century, numerous efforts were made to gain union objectives through political action. The National Labor Union, formed in 1866, undertook a campaign for the 8-hour day. A Greenback Labor Party gained more than a million votes in 1878 in a campaign that proposed currency reforms, shorter hours, and the restriction of prison labor and immigration. Meanwhile, the Knights of Labor, an association of several hundred local organizations formed in 1878, was widely regarded as exerting powerful political influence.

The American Federation of Labor, established in 1886, declared a non-partisan political policy. It proposed to endorse no political parties, but to examine the platforms of all candidates and to reward labor's friends and punish its enemies. Lobbying activities were, however, among its most important responsibilities. The Federation approved numerous political planks, including the 8-hour day, public factory and mine inspection, employer liability for accidental injuries to workers, the abolition of sweatshops. Federation representatives appeared before Congressional committees to protest the use of injunctions in labor disputes and to demand legislation limiting the use of the anti-trust law against unions.

Current union political policy was greatly influenced by the great depression of the 1930's and the New Deal period. The A.F. of L. and the newly organized C.I.O. were encouraged to "get out the vote" and to enforce the earlier policy with respect to labor's friends and enemies. Committees raised funds for the support of approved candidates. The C.I.O. established its Political Action Committee to report on senators and representatives and to canvass voters for friends of organized labor. After the enactment of the Taft-Hartley Act in 1947, the A.F. of L. created a new Labor's League for Political Education which cooperated with the CIO-PAC in the election of 1948. In the 1952 election, both the A.F. of L. and C.I.O., for the first time, formally endorsed the democratic candidate for the presidency. At the constitutional convention of 1955 which brought the A.F. of L. and the C.I.O. together, a new Committee on Political Education, generally called COPE, was established as a combination of the earlier LLPE and CIO-PAC. COPE is assigned responsibility for insuring that employees register, vote and take an active part in the political activities of communities, states, and the nation. It reports on the voting records of officials.

3.0 SPECIFIC POLICY AND PRACTICE

The general policy of American Unions, described in the preceding section, has clear implications for specific policy in day-to-day, on-the-job working relationships. Most obvious is the policy on collective bargaining in which unions propose to establish and maintain collective agreements. Through these negotiated "labor contracts," they seek to facilitate employee participation in decisions affecting working conditions and employer-employee relationships.[11]

3.1 Collective agreements. The natural outcome of collective bargaining is the *collective agreement*. It is a written summary of the policy and practice to which the parties have agreed in their negotiations. It may begin with a statement of policy in which they indicate the general attitude with which they have worked out the terms of their agreement and with which it is to be interpreted in day-to-day administration. For example, here are two such introductory statements:

> 1. The purpose of this agreement is to provide orderly collective bargaining relations between the Company and the Union, to secure a prompt and fair disposition of grievances and to eliminate interruptions of work and interference with the efficient operation of the Company's business. (Steel industry)
> 2. It is the intent and purpose of the parties to this agreement to promote harmony between the Company, its employees, and the Union, and to increase the efficiency of the plants of the Company to the end that the employees and the Company may mutually benefit and to provide procedure for the prompt, peaceful and equitable adjustment of differences which may arise from time to time between the Company and the Union or between the Company and any employee covered by this agreement, to the end that there shall be no interference with the production of the plants during the life of this agreement. (Diecasting)[12]

Following such an introductory statement, the agreement includes a series of clauses, each relating to particular working conditions. One classification of these clauses includes the major divisions shown in Table 10.3.

The collective agreement is in essence a contract, although it cannot fully qualify for that designation because it involves an agreement to deliver personal services.[13] Like a contract, it outlines the conditions on which the parties have agreed and the *term* or *duration* of their agreement. The most common term is one year; however, a notable trend toward longer agreements can be noted. Almost as many contracts run for two years as for one, and about one-fifth of all recent agreements have a 3-year term. A few 5-year agreements have been negotiated. Many of the longer-term agreements include a *reopening clause,* which allows the union to reopen discussions on limited issues, usually wages, once or more during the term of the agreement.

3.11 Negotiation. Development of collective agreements is accomplished

---

[11] For details, see Harold W. Davey, *Contemporary Collective Bargaining* (Second Edition), Englewood Cliffs, N.J.: Prentice-Hall, Inc., 1959, Chap. 1; also Edwin F. Beal and Edward D. Wickersham, *The Practice of Collective Bargaining,* Homewood, Ill.: Richard D. Irwin, Inc., 1959, Part I.

[12] Many additional examples of these clauses are shown in the source from which these have been selected: "Union Contracts and Collective Bargaining Practice," *Labor Equipment,* Vol. 4, Englewood Cliffs, N.J.: Prentice-Hall, Inc., par. 53022.

[13] Free men cannot by contract enslave themselves. The rule of *specific performance* cannot apply.

through the practice of *negotiation,* which represents one of the major activities of business unionism. *Negotiation* refers to the process of making proposals—often described as "demands"—discussing such proposals, advancing counterproposals, bargaining, and, if possible, arriving at an agreement. Negotiation may involve radical demands advanced as a basis for later concessions and "horsetrading." It may include threats of strikes that become news and attract public attention. Less obviously, it may require long preparation by both parties, with the collection and analysis of data and the citing of cases and provisions of agreements in other firms and localities. These practices are so important to modern labor relations that they are discussed in some detail in Chapter 12.

Table 10.3   Scope of Contract Clauses

Preamble and Purpose
Union Recognition and Scope-of-unit
Parties to the Contract
Union Security
Union Representation
Grievance Procedure
Arbitration
Union Activities in the Plant
Management Prerogatives
Labor Management Cooperation
Strikes and Lockouts
Wages
Working Time and Leave
Employment Relationships
Working Conditions
Insurance and Benefit Plans
Special Employees
Formal Provisions

SOURCE: *Labor Equipment,* Vol. 4, "Union Contracts and Collective Bargaining Practice," Englewood Cliffs, N.J.: Prentice-Hall, Inc., 1953 to date, current.

3.12   Contract administration. Collective bargaining normally results in a collective agreement or labor contract. That document must be interpreted and applied. Questions and arguments may arise over the meaning of its provisions. Important issues may have been overlooked. Representatives of management and of the union may have conflicting opinions as to the meaning and application of the agreement. In short, gaining a written statement of the results of negotiation is but the first step; numerous additional practices must implement and apply it. Such interpretation and application of the collective agreement is described as *contract administration.*

3.13   Shop stewards and business agents. Negotiations and administration may be undertaken by the members of unions, or by committees representing them, or by their local or national officers. In many industrial unions, the *shop steward* is the principal representative of members in day-to-day contract administration. He is an unpaid, elected union officer and fellow employee. Although he can give only part-time attention to union matters, he is the local expert on the terms of agreements and their interpretation. He maintains close relationships with foremen and usually presents employee grievances to the appropriate foreman or to a grievance committee.

Some unions provide a *business agent* to represent them in negotiations and contract administration. The business agent is a paid, usually full-time union official. He may be responsible for the collection of dues and for checking on members who are delinquent. He may act as treasurer for a local union. He is the counselor for union members on all sorts of personal problems. He may represent several locals.[14]

3.2 Wages and hours. Almost everyone in the United States has heard the oft-repeated observation that the only wage policy of unions is their demand for *more*. Of course, unions do seek more for their members, and wage increases are unquestionably the most common goal in negotiations. Nevertheless, such a generalization can be misleading; union wage policy is much more complex.

As a part of the general policy to improve the living conditions of members and workers, the whole labor movement has held to a policy proposing rising real wages and living scales. Unions propose to raise real wages and hence to see to it that wage rates and earnings rise more rapidly than costs of living. As noted, they propose to relate wages to productivity and hence to insure employee participation in the growing output of employment. They seek to protect labor's share of income, to see that rents and interest and proprietary and managerial shares are not increased at the expense of workers. They may even propose that a larger over-all share of income be distributed to workers, on the ground that such a changed distribution is necessary to maintain purchasing power, prevent stagnation, and assure continued growth in the economy.

In some cases, union policy has been concerned with an employer's ability to pay. In others, policy has proposed to ignore this consideration. Union policy has sometimes argued—as, for example, in the requirement of minimum wages—that the economy will be better off without employers who "are so inefficient" that they cannot afford to pay.

Most union officials and probably a majority of members are keenly aware of the realities of competitive business and favor a policy that protects "the goose that lays the golden egg." They seek to avoid wage rates that are likely to have adverse effects on members' employment. They understand the economic facts of life and recognize elasticities in demands for labor. Their wage policy is reasonably sophisticated and carefully considered in terms of the best available facts. They may not, of course, have reliable facts with respect to the profit position of individual employers. In many firms, however, unions have purchased small amounts of stock in order to receive

[14] See Hjalmar Rosen and R. A. Hudson Rosen, "The Union Business Agent's Perspective of His Job," *Reprint Series No. 64,* University of Illinois, Institute of Labor and Industrial Relations, August 1958.

the regular reports given stockholders.

Union wage policy frequently reflects union competition for members. Each union may seek to get more for its members than its rivals or than other unions with which comparisons will be made.

Policy on wages and hours is related. Many unionists subscribe to the historic union couplet: "Whether you work by the hour or the day, reducing the hours increases the pay." Union campaigns for shorter hours are as old as the labor movement in this country. To some degree, these goals actually seek higher wage rates; by specifying maximum hours at regular pay, they gain premium rates for overtime. In part, campaigns for shorter hours have justified such reductions on health grounds. In part, they have proposed more time for family and community responsibilities. Demands for continued reductions persist and are likely to do so in the future.

3.21 Standardization. To implement their wage policies, unions propose a *standardization* of wages and the provision of *union scales.* These are the rates that have been negotiated for various jobs in one or more firms. The scale tends to prevent "deals" with individual employees. On the other hand, the scale is described as a minimum rate; the implication is that an employer can pay as much more as he wishes. Actually, the scale becomes both minimum and maximum for covered employees. Indeed, some agreements have incorporated specific provisions against *snowballing,* the practice in which an employer offers rates above the scale.

In some industries, unions insist on piece rates or incentive wages that provide added earnings for superior performance. In such situations, standardization is applied only to the base rate or minimum.

Unions may also seek to preserve *historic differentials.* They propose to maintain the relative positions of various occupations in the scales they negotiate. Efforts to raise wages, however, may create hazards to these historic relationships. Differentials in the wage structures of individual industries and of the economy as a whole have narrowed. Some occupations have gained a good deal more than others. In many industries, wage increases for highly skilled union members have not kept pace with advances in jobs requiring less skill.[15]

3.22 Benefits and services. In current practice, earnings include a growing range of employee benefits and services. Union policy may propose improved pensions, hospitalization, medical, or other benefits. For wages as a

---

[15] This type of change is well illustrated by the shrinking differentials in the building trades. In 1907, when the journeyman rate averaged 43.5 cents, the rate for helpers was 23.5 cents. The differential of 20 cents represented 85 per cent of the helper rate or 46 per cent of the journeyman rate. By 1958, the rates were $2.83 and $3.68, and the 85 cent differential represented only 30 per cent of the helper rate and 23 per cent of the journeyman rate. See *The American Worker's Fact Book 1960,* Washington: United States Department of Labor, 1960, pp. 108–109. See also Simler, Norman J., "The Impact of Unionism on Wage-Income Ratios in the Manufacturing Sector of the Economy," *University of Minnesota Studies in Economics and Business,* No. 22, 1961.

whole, these benefits now represent a supplement of more than twenty per cent, and the trend has been upward.

Union policies with respect to such benefits have undergone significant changes. Early unions sought to provide benefits for their members. Some unions, notably those in railroading, have long emphasized this policy. Not all unions, however, supported early campaigns for public old age pensions and unemployment insurance. Some unions feared that public provisions might reduce member interest in union programs. Later, in part as a result of the aging of the labor force, unions became powerful advocates of public benefits and, at the same time, negotiated additional fringes.

3.3 Protection of job rights. Self-preservation of the union has required a policy of protection for the rights of members. The whole strength and future of the organization are jeopardized if members find their jobs eliminated, either by members of another union or by employer action. Hence most unions seek to insure that jobs held by their members are reserved for members of their union and that employers will not eliminate members' jobs without offering other satisfactory employment.

To implement this policy, both the A.F. of L. and the C.I.O.—and the present AFL-CIO—have sought to prevent *dualism* within their organizations. *Dualism* is the situation in which two member nationals claim the right to represent the same groups of workers. One reason for the reluctance of the A.F. of L. to encourage industrial unionism in the early years of the present century was the fear that new industrial unions would seek to organize or represent workers who were members of or eligible for older craft unions.

3.31 Jurisdictions. Efforts to prevent dualism represent one form of the general practice of establishing and maintaining *jurisdictions*. A union's jurisdiction is the range of jobs for which it has the exclusive right to represent employees. It may be defined by the charter of the national union or by the charter granted by the national to a local. Jurisdictions may be based on (1) trade or industry, or (2) locality, or (3) a combination of the two. They thus insure that all work of a certain type in a specified locality will be regarded as the private preserve of the members of one union—the carpenters or the electrical workers, for example. Such rules are enforced by agreement with other unions affiliated with the same central organization.

Sometimes unions fail to agree among themselves as to their jurisdictions. Both trade and territorial jurisdictions may become a matter of dispute. In such cases, picketing by one or both of the conflicting organizations is not unusual.

Both the earlier A.F. of L. and the present AFL-CIO recognize these jurisdictional disputes as a serious threat to the unity of the labor movement. The policy of anti-dualism is based largely on this recognition. Departments within the AFL-CIO were established in part as agencies for the settlement of jurisdictional disputes. The problem remains a persistent source of friction within the movement, because opportunities for challenging jurisdictions are created by continuing technological and other changes and because inter-union rivalries are by no means eliminated by confederation. In recent years, jurisdictional strife has frequently arisen out of struggles between expelled unions and others within the Federation. *Raiding*—a campaign to get members of one union to leave it and join another—is by no means a discarded practice in the American labor movement.

3.32 Membership restriction. Determination to protect the jobs of members has also encouraged unions to restrict membership by refusing to admit new members who might compete for the jobs of those already in the union. To limit available supplies of workers, membership requirements of varying severity may be established. Generally speaking, in industrial unions, anyone who is acceptable to the employer is allowed to join the union, so that the only limitations are those of the hiring office. In crafts unions, requirements may specify licensing, apprenticeship, or the passing of a test of knowledge or proficiency, or both.

Both craft and industrial unions have sometimes maintained what is known as a *closed union*. This control has been accomplished by admitting only specified numbers of members or by limiting eligibility for membership to relatives of present members, or by setting initiation fees at figures beyond the reach of many candidates. Less frequently, unions may impose limitations based on race, sex, or nationality. The *closed union* is widely regarded as inappropriate for democratic societies. Today's unions, however, find it difficult to discard policies developed when many of them were small, fraternal groups, and practices associated with such policies tend to persist.

3.33 Work restriction. Featherbedding, a policy that proposes to save jobs for members by limiting labor supplies, may be translated into practices that limit the output of workers. When labor supplies appear likely to be in excess of needs, job protection may take the form of *restriction of output*. The theory of the lump-of-labor may suggest that work must be spread to maintain employment. Restriction of output under such circumstances may appear as a means of maintaining earnings as well as protecting jobs.

Restriction of output is one of the oldest forms of protest and one of the most common forms of industrial unrest. Both organized and unorganized industrial workers have practiced restriction. Among union members, the most common practices involve the informal creation of bogeys, pars, or quotas for the work-day. Another practice requires inefficient work practices —such as those in which local printers insist on setting type although mats make such work unnecessary (the "bogus type" requirement). Another prevents foremen or supervisors from performing any part of the jobs they supervise. Still another requires minimum crews in numbers larger than are needed. Unemployment insurance, the public policy of full employment, the economic pressure of international competition, and the growing economic understanding of employees have encouraged many unions to reduce or eliminate such practices. They are less attractive in markets in which labor is in short supply. Many of them have been eliminated by negotiation.[16]

3.34 Protection against discrimination. One of the strongest appeals of all unions is their ability to protect the individual employee against arbitrary and capricious discharge and to prevent discriminatory treatment in work assignments, layoff, promotion, and transfer. Much of the work of the steward involves settling arguments that arise over wage rates, work assignments, promotions, and other day-to-day employer actions that may be regarded as unfair to some union members.

3.35 Grievance procedures. Unions have proposed and negotiated formal *grievance procedures* to insure each member a full hearing of his complaints or grievances. Almost all—more than 90 per cent—of all current agreements include such provisions. They provide that when employees feel that they have been unfairly treated or that their treatment is not consistent with the collective agreement, they may challenge the action and file a grievance. Usually, as a first step, the issue is discussed with the foreman or supervisor. The grieving employee may plead his own case or he may be represented by the shop steward or have the latter accompany him. If the matter is not settled in this conference, it is written up and becomes a formal grievance.

In some provisions, the next step involves consideration of the grievance by a special committee. Members may all be representatives of the union or they may include equal numbers of management representatives. If their decision is not satisfactory to the grieving employee, it may be submitted to the plant's industrial relations director, or it may go to a two-man committee including a local union officer and the firm's personnel or labor relations director. Some plans provide for a step in which an international union officer may take the issue to the president or general manager of the firm. Most procedures now provide for *terminal arbitration;* the last step is submission of the issue to a neutral third party. This arbitrator may be an individual or a panel of three. His decision is final and binding on both parties, as provided in their collective agreement.

4.0 SUMMARY

This chapter provides a broad outline for understanding the philosophy, theories, policies, and practices of American unions. The labor movement has emerged as a protest movement in the process of industrialization. Its traditions and philosophy are as old and probably as complex as those of industrial proprietorship. Understanding and appreciation of these views are

---

[16] An excellent example is provided in longshoring. See Max A. Kossoris, "Working Rules in West Coast Longshoring," *Monthly Labor Review,* Vol. 1, No. 84, January 1961; see also Paul A. Weinstein, "Featherbedding: A Theoretical Analysis," *The Journal of Political Economy,* Vol. 68, No. 4, August 1960, pp. 370–387.

essential in the knowledge and perspective of managers who maintain day-to-day relationships with unions and, indeed, of all managers.

Unions have their theories about employment and the relationships it creates. While union members and officials accept much the same viewpoint with which managers build their philosophy of industrial relations, organized labor also has its own pattern of values and its own theories, many of them unacceptable—and perhaps unknown as well—to many managers. For example, unions identify themselves as champions of the common people and hence of the public welfare.

Unions have frequently advanced a lump-of-labor theory. Unions have given their own twist to productivity theories of wages. They have advanced a bargaining theory of wages. Union theory holds that they have a responsibility to challenge management decisions and force higher wages as means of insuring better management.

Several general policies of unions—seeking strength and authority, developing democratic leadership, and using the political strength of labor organizations to further the interests of unionists—help to explain much of the day-to-day practice of labor relations. In the same way, union policy on collective bargaining, wages, and the protection of job rights of members gives meaning to such practices as "no contract, no work," the union scale, jurisdictions, and featherbedding.

A summary of the prime policies of American unions would note their stated and well-recognized intentions to:

1. Represent their members in free labor markets, helping them to recognize the greatest opportunities for employing their maximum skills and aptitudes and gaining a maximum of financial and other compensation for these services.
2. Represent all employees, both in labor markets and in the power struggles of politics—within the general framework of a free, democratic society.
3. Make the objectives of unions the goals of all citizens and hence represent the public interest in contests with representatives of property and wealth.
4. Provide constant checks on the efficiency and fairness of management, acting as a sort of loyal opposition to insure that managers know and use the best practices of up-to-date leadership in the organizations they direct.
5. Protect the long-term strength and growth of free economies by maximizing the share of national income accruing to workers.
6. Encourage the spread of free collective bargaining throughout the world, assisting less powerful labor movements in gaining strength and influence and combatting tendencies toward subordination and government control.

Managers find themselves in agreement with many of these policies and with the practices they prescribe. They may strongly oppose others in the list, however. Differences in philosophies, theories, policies, and programs generate conflict. To protect themselves, societies find it necessary to develop public policy on employment relationships and particularly on the relationships of managers and unions. Such public policy on labor relations is the subject of the chapter that follows.

SELECTED SUPPLEMENTARY READINGS

Bromwich, Leo, *Union Constitutions.* New York: The Fund for the Republic, 1959.
"Codes of Ethical Practices for the Labor Movement," Washington, D.C.: AFL-CIO Department of Publications, 1956.
Fromm, Erich, *et al., Labor in a Free Society,* 186 pp. Berkeley: University of California Press, 1959.
Hutchinson, John, "Captain of a Mighty Host," *Yale Review,* Vol. 50, No. 1, pp. 42–52, Autumn 1960. Available as Reprint No. 154, University of California Institute of Industrial Relations (Berkeley), 1960.
"A More Perfect Union: The UAW Public Review Board: Why, What, How?" Detroit 14: UAW Publications Department, 1960.
"Problems of Changing Power Relationships in Collective Bargaining," in *Proceedings of the Sixth Annual Industrial Relations Conference,* pp. 3–35, Institute of Labor and Industrial Relations, University of Michigan-Wayne State University, 1961.
Stieber, Jack, Walter E. Oberer, and Michael Harrington, "Democracy and Public Review," Santa Barbara, Calif.: Center for the Study of Democratic Institutions, 1960.
Uphoff, Walter H., and Marvin D. Dunette, "What Union Members Think of Unionism," *Personnel,* Vol. 33, No. 4, pp. 347–352, January 1957.

SHORT CASE PROBLEM 10.1

The AMAC Company

AMAC has negotiated a union shop agreement for ten years. Union proposals this year include a request for work-spreading and guaranteed wages. The union asks for a clause that will reduce weekly hours from 40 to 32 whenever it becomes necessary to lay off more than 20 per cent of the regular work force. During the period in which the 32-hour week is maintained, employees would be paid for 36 hours, thus splitting the wage loss. Only employees who are retained in such periods would receive this wage, but those laid off would receive unemployment insurance plus the negotiated supplemental unemployment benefits already provided in the industry.

Relationships between management and union have been friendly. Negotiations in the past have always resulted in compromises. But this demand appears likely to result in an impasse. Union spokesmen insist that the matter has been thoroughly discussed with members who are willing to strike if necessary. Managers say that the demand is unrealistic and economically impossible. Both parties have calculated what it would have cost to implement the provision during the past ten years. The union says it would have added little or nothing to unit labor costs; the firm insists that it would have increased costs as much as 5 per cent in three of the ten years.

Problem: (1) Where do union members get the ideas for such proposals? Can you trace this one back to some bit of philosophy or theory? Try your hand at preparing a brief for each of the parties to be used in negotiations during the next class period.

(2) The union later proposed, as an alternative, that all workers with one year of service be put on salaries, with no increases in rates. Summarize your reaction to and arguments on this proposal.

SHORT CASE PROBLEM 10.2

Attendance at Union Meetings

Local 1135 can't get members to attend its regular meetings. Union officers feel that attendance is important; they insist that members need to know about matters discussed in such meetings. Members frequently criticize union officials unjustly because the members are uninformed with respect to essential facts.

Examination of the records indicates that average attendance over the past three years amounts to only 18 per cent of the eligible membership. Frequent discussions of this problem in regular meetings resulted, two months past, in a local rule that provides a fine for any unexcused absence. The fine is small, and many members have apparently decided to pay it rather than to attend.

Two members of the local, however, have offered no excuse for their failure to have paid or tendered payment of their regular dues. The secretary-treasurer of the local has refused to accept the usual payment without the additional charge. He has recommended to the executive committee of the local that the two members be regarded as delinquent in the payment of their dues. Under the existing union shop provisions, the local could ask for their discharge by the employer if they are held delinquent.

Problem: Assume you are consulted, on a confidential basis, by members of the local. What advice would you give them?

SHORT CASE PROBLEM 10.3

A Union of Engineers

The Bell Company has a large engineering department. Two years ago, a majority of the engineers formed a union. They have not affiliated with any international and have no association with other similar organizations. Their membership has increased and now includes about 90 per cent of the group.

In planning for negotiations, several members of the planning committee have suggested that the union should demand a union shop. The company has union shop clauses in several agreements with production employees. Other members of the committee feel that the union shop provision would create a lot of resentment among the 10 per cent who are not now members. Maintenance of membership and the Rand agency shop formula have also been proposed.

Members of the union have sought outside advice on what type of union security may be appropriate. Most of their advisers who are union members have advised a union shop.

Problem 1: Assume that you have been asked for an opinion. What would you advise?

Problem 2: The union has been advised by several unions representing hourly rated employees that it should join a national organization and come into the Central Labor Union. If they do not do so, they have been warned, they will get no assistance in a strike. Members of other unions may not observe their picket lines. What would you advise?

SHORT CASE PROBLEM 10.4

Leave of Absence for Union Duty*

The background: An employee was granted a leave of absence to serve as union representative. Leaves for personal reasons, as well as for the express purpose of holding union office, were provided in the contract. In its request, the union did not mention the length of the leave. The company was similarly silent in granting permission. The clause on leave of absence had two sections. The first, on general leave, limited such absence to one year. The second (on union business) made no mention of duration.

While the employee was on leave, the company notified the union several times that the employee would lose his seniority if he did not return to his job at the conclusion of his leave. After the employee had served a year as union representative, he was notified by the company that his name was being removed from the seniority list for not returning to work within the year. The union charged the company had acted unfairly in taking away his seniority and job benefits.

The issue: Did the company violate the contract by canceling the employee's seniority rights when his leave of absence for union business exceeded one year?

The Union argues: The section of the contract that restricts leaves of absence to one year applies to personal needs of individual employees, not to leave for union business, which is treated separately in the contract. Moreover, it has been customary in the industry to grant union leaves of *indefinite* duration. The union does not question the company's right to grant or withhold such leaves but feels the company cannot change its mind once its discretion has been exercised. Otherwise, employees on union leave could be harassed by the company and subject to a constant "beck-and-call."

The Company Argues: The contract limits all leaves of absence to one year. It does not make exceptions for union business. Union leaves were treated separately because of the special provision that no more than two employees could be on such leave at the same time. Besides, the provision for union leave is discretionary rather than mandatory with the employer. If it wishes, it can withhold such leave entirely. If it grants it, it can establish conditions or limitations. The contract provides that employees failing to report at the conclusion of a leave of absence lose their seniority. And in bargaining for a new contract (prior to the expiration of the employee's union leave), the union did not try to have this provision changed.

Problem: Use the actual arbitration case summarized here to check your knowledge and understanding of bilateral employment policy and to decide on a reasonable, non-technical resolution of the issue.

SHORT CASE PROBLEM 10.5

Supervisor Doing Bargaining Unit Work**

The Background: A sump pump was used to keep water out of the pit below a machine. Whenever the pump failed to function, the machine was stopped and the

* *Employee Relations and Arbitration Report,* Vol. 21, No. 22, Page 6, May 1, 1961.

** *Employee Relations and Arbitration Report,* Vol. 21, No. 12, *Pages 5 and 6,* December 12, 1960.

water shut off to prevent electrical damage and injury to employees. A midnight shift foreman came on duty and found the sump pump was not working properly. He had the machine shut down and ordered the operator to get a lift truck to remove the pump for repairs. Together they took the pump from the pit, cleaned it, and replaced it. The pump still did not operate properly. They repeated the removal, dismantling, cleaning and replacing twice more before the pump functioned normally. The entire process took about two hours. The union filed a grievance claiming the foreman had violated the agreement by performing bargaining unit work. The contract prohibited supervisory employees from doing work which would cause any employee to suffer layoff or loss of pay, except in emergencies, for instruction or familiarization, or because of temporary unscheduled absences of key employees.

The Issue: Was the agreement violated?

The Union Argues: The pump repair was bargaining unit work that took two hours to perform. It was work that should have been done by a bargaining unit employee, since it was within the duties of the mechanic's classification. It was not work of an emergency nature; nor was it done for the purpose of instructing or familiarizing a unit employee with it. There was no absence of a key employee. The work belonged to the mechanic classification. The machine operator should have been upgraded to this classification and assigned to do the job at the mechanic's rate.

The Company Argues: The repair job was not work within the mechanic's classification. Operators had always done these repairs in the past without receiving a higher rate. No employee was laid off or lost pay as a result of the foreman's assistance on the repair job. The union had agreed that supervisory employees could do bargaining unit work when the work required only one hour or less. In this case, the foreman was unfamiliar with the pump. For this reason, the repairs took longer than usual. In addition, the foreman was performing his supervisory duties during this two hour period. This was one of the contingencies under which a foreman can do work normally performed by bargaining unit employees.

Problem: Use the actual arbitration case summarized here to check your understanding of bilateral employment policy and to decide on a reasonable, non-technical resolution of the issue.

11. *Public Policy on Labor Relations*

Policy on manpower management in modern industry is a composite that includes the policies of owners and managers, of employees and their unions, and of public policy. Chapter 10 has outlined the most important policies of American unions and the major practices through which unions seek to implement these policies. The present chapter shifts attention to *public policy* with particular reference to policy on the relationships of employers and unions—labor relations policy.

Most managers find their management influenced by developments in labor relations and by public policy on employer-union relationships. They need to understand how public policy regards unions and union participation in management and how public policy has changed and developed. They need to recognize that modern policy on the management of people is trilateral and tripartite.

As has been indicated in Chapter 10, unions complicate the problems of management by proposing policies that are in part consistent and in part conflicting with the general manpower policy of many firms. Unions argue from different philosophies and interpret with different theories. As a result, while many of the goals sought by managers and unions are compatible if not identical, there are significant differences. Unions and managements give different priorities to various goals, as illustrated by economic security, the maintenance and increase of wages, protection against discriminatory treatment of employees, protection of job rights and many others. Also, they hold different theories, and thus prefer different routes toward common goals.

Such differences are matters of public concern. The public interest and welfare are involved. Citizens and their representatives in government have opinions about what are to be regarded as top priorities in management policy. Public opinion creates its own hierarchy of goals for employment relationships and translates these values into public policy.

Governments intervene in management-union relationships to encourage or enforce the acceptance of public policy. As noted in Chapter 2, the role of government is a major variable in all industrial relations systems. Public intervention exerts a significant influence on employment relationships in all industrialized societies.

Both managers and unions frequently insist that they could play their roles more effectively and serve the public better if governments left them to their own resources. Managers have frequently argued that, without public intervention, they could avoid such prescribed working conditions as premium pay for overtime and minimum wages and thus reduce costs and prices. They could deal with employees as individuals, refusing to bargain collectively, with additional economies.

Union leaders have expressed similar irritation about public regulation. Without it, they feel, they could exert the full economic power of the labor movement. They could enlist the cooperation of employees in all industries to enforce their demands and secure much greater concessions from employers. They could, they insist, improve the lot of employees and raise living scales throughout the nation.

In modern democratic societies, the basic rule-makers, the citizens, have insisted on public intervention to restrict the behavior and modify the policies of both employer-managers and unions. Governments have established ground rules that require some policies and prohibit others. They have insisted that the goals of the whole society take precedence over those of either of the parties and that public policy be implemented through the practices of both.

Such public policy, requiring extensive governmental intervention, accords government a role paralleling those of managers and unions and creates what has been described as tripartite employment policy.

This chapter is concerned with the development of public policy on union-management relations. It is essentially historical. After a preliminary section on major issues in public policy, it traces the rising trend of public intervention in labor relations. The role of government in this area has become so important that an additional chapter outlines in some detail the major guidelines of current public policy.

1.0 PHILOSOPHY AND THEORY IN PUBLIC POLICY

Public policy sets the general course which citizens as rule-makers propose to follow and declares their intentions, just as the policies of managers and unions outline their intentions and proposed courses. Public policy on labor relations specifies intentions with respect to the activities of the parties—

managements and unions—and the process of collective bargaining. Public policy develops from social goals—the ends to be attained through union-management relationships. It relies on theories to relate goals to appropriate policies. It specifies practices, imposing rules and regulations, to implement its policy. It creates agencies with authority to enforce approved practice. Through this process, government takes a hand in the modern tripartite policy and practice of labor relations and manpower management.

1.1   Philosophy and theory. Just as managerial and union policies can be traced to respective philosophies and theories, public policy has its roots in social philosophy and theory. Citizens and public agencies prescribe policies for unions and managements and union-management relationships that appear consistent with society's social and political philosophy and theories.

During much of the history of the United States, public policy has sought to implement a laissez-faire philosophy that tends to restrict public intervention. The essence of that view is that the best government is one that rules or regulates the least, and that public intervention should therefore be held to a minimum. The laissez-faire view is epitomized in Adam Smith's classic reference to the invisible hand that leads individuals in seeking their own interests to maximize the economic welfare of their society.

This philosophical position is sometimes expressed in terms of the *superiority of self regulation*. It holds that preferable to public regulation is the situation in which individuals and groups are encouraged to develop and maintain their own controls. Social acceptance of laissez faire and self-regulation appeared to justify a policy of non-intervention that dominated labor relations throughout most of the 19th century in this country.

Laissez faire dignifies the individual at the same time that it restricts intervention in his behalf. A goal of individual, personal freedom that thus appeared entirely consistent with the laissez-faire philosophy plays an influential part in much of this nation's historic policy on labor relations. It has occupied a high priority in the hierarchy of national values since colonial times. Citizens have faced difficult choices in attempting to reconcile this goal of individual freedom with another—that of social welfare. The struggle to determine the ranking of these objectives is evident in our changing public policy.

To develop appropriate policies, society has had to depend on theories that relate accepted goals to the behavior of managers and unions. One such explanation may be described as a *balance of power* theory. It holds that the security and welfare of a society require a balancing of power among influential special-interest groups. Governments protect themselves and their publics against domination by encouraging the development of *countervailing power* in rival organizations.

A corollary to this theory holds that the most effective governmental action is one that *restricts* or *limits* rather than *eliminates* conflict and competition among such rivals as employers and unions. Public policy, in this view, need not seek to substitute cooperation for competition in collective bargaining. It will not try to develop complete accommodation and agreement between the parties. Indeed, public policy will propose to prevent such comprehensive cooperation as might involve collusion in a new and more influential power center.

Democratic societies usually accept the theory that powerful organizations to which they grant broad areas of discretionary power must be expected to maintain a high level of *internal democracy* as a measure of security for the democratic system. Autocratic organizations, to put the theory another way, are something of a threat to accepted social goals. In labor relations, both unions and employer associations—and perhaps large business organizations—must be closely regarded on this account. When unions were small, fraternal groups, their internal government was of little public interest. When they opened their ranks to millions and availed themselves of public protection and support, this development justified public concern.

1.2 Major questions. Societies develop and revise public policy by reference to their changing philosophies—the range and ranking of values that make up their accepted beliefs—and to theories that seem most likely to advance socially accepted goals. Some questions to be answered in public policy arise out of manager or union practices. For example: How shall employer blacklisting or union picketing be regarded? Shall public policy permit employers to use deputized guards in strikes or allow unions to engage in sit-down strikes or secondary boycotts? Public policy weighs these practices in terms of their probable influence on the balance of power between unions and employers and the likelihood that the parties will impose adequate self-regulation.

Other difficult questions are raised by the policies of the parties. To what extent, for example, shall unions or employer associations be permitted to regulate the behavior of their members? How much required conformity to either a union or employer *party line* is appropriate in a democratic society? What limitation, if any, shall be applied to the political use of union or employer financial resources? To what extent shall unions be permitted to make political contributions to parties or candidates their members may not personally favor? Shall associations of employers be permitted to insure their members against strike losses by strike-aid agreements (see Chapter 13, Section 2.4) or shifting work and contracts to non-struck members?

A persistent question concerns the weight to be given to ownership and proprietary rights. How shall the public appraise the determination of an employer to continue operations in the face of a strike? What area of managerial decisions shall be reserved as exclusive for owners? Or are all such decisions to be regarded as appropriate for bargaining on request of a representative union?

Shall the investment by employees of their time, energy, and skill be regarded as an investment comparable to owners' investment of financial resources? Does an affirmative answer justify a public policy of recognizing something in the nature of job rights for workers?

Other questions concern the waste of human resources occasioned by strikes and lockouts. Such waste may be increased by permitting the parties to work out their own solutions. It might be reduced by intervention. How much intervention is justified in the public interest on this account?[1]

These and many other related questions require answers in public policy on labor relations. Public policy has provided answers. There is, however, no national manual of public policy. Some of the answers are not national in scope; the federal-state system permits different answers in cities, counties, states, and at the federal level. Some public policy is explicitly stated; some legislation includes a preliminary section for that purpose. Other public policy has been stated by courts in their interpretations of the rules of the game. To an increasing degree, public policy is declared by such administrative agencies as the National Labor Relations Board and similar state agencies.

The section that follows traces the development of public policy from the colonial period to the present time.

2.0 HISTORIC CHANGE IN PUBLIC HISTORY

Questions about the relationships between employers or managers and unions attracted little attention in colonial times because few workers belonged to unions. The colonies were not industrialized, in part because colonizing nations sought to maintain them as sources of raw materials to be processed abroad. Attitudes toward employers and unions were largely shaped by traditional viewpoints in parent nations. After the colonies secured their independence, industrialization was speeded. Unions became more common; their proposals and policies attracted greater attention. Public policy, for a century, was expressed by the courts and based on their interpretation of the common law. Late in the 19th century, the first legislation provided statutory expression for public policy. Since enactment of the Sherman Act in 1890, a series of federal laws has highlighted changing public intentions with respect to the relationships of employers and unions. Supplementary state and local legislation and a growing volume of relevant court decisions and administrative rulings trace the evolution of American public policy in the area of union-management relations.

One of the most interesting attempts to trace these changes has been provided by Elias Lieberman, in his *Unions Before the Bar*.[2] Lieberman describes five stages in the development of public policy on unions in the United States. The first stage, characteristic of the colonial period and most of the first half of the 19th century, was dominated by a policy of what he calls "open suppression." Attitudes toward worker organizations were heavily

[1] See Maxwell S. Stewart, "Labor and the Public," *Public Affairs Pamphlet No. 301*, Public Affairs Committee, Inc., August, 1960; *Goals for Americans*, Englewood Cliffs, N.J.: Spectrum Books, Prentice-Hall, Inc., 1960, pp. 151ff.
[2] New York: Oxford Book Company, Inc., 2d ed., 1960.

influenced by the presence of slave labor. Unions that sought to combine workers in demands for higher wages were judged to be illegal conspiracies. The classic expression of this view is found in the *Philadelphia Cordwainers* case (1805).

Lieberman's second stage, which he describes as "reluctant tolerance," was ushered in by the case of *Commonwealth v. Hunt,* in 1842. The major change in this court decision recognized a distinction between ends sought by unions and the means they used to achieve these ends. Either ends or means could be illegal; if a court regarded either as illegal, it could properly restrict union action. A third stage, "judicial prejudice," appeared with the enactment of the Sherman Act in 1890. The fourth, "social recognition," was marked by the National Labor Relations Act in 1935. The fifth, a stage of "social responsibility," is just ahead.

2.1 Combination Acts and conspiracies. When unions first made their appearance—emerging from journeyman guilds—public policy in older nations opposed them and their demands for collective bargaining. In England, members were prosecuted and punished for joining. A series of laws known as *Combination Acts* made illegal any cooperative association formed for the purpose of changing wages or prices. The last of these laws, passed in 1800, forbade any association of employees to seek to raise wages, prevent employees from working, interfere with employers in hiring employees, hold meetings to organize employees for these purposes, or collect funds for any such organization.

When the Combination Acts were repealed in 1824, common law rules of *civil* and *criminal conspiracy* were frequently used to achieve somewhat the same general policy. However, in a long series of laws—in 1859, 1871, 1875, 1906, and 1913—public policy in England was gradually modified to free unions and their members from these hazards and restrictions and thus to encourage collective bargaining.

In the United States, no legislation comparable to the Combination Acts was enacted. Moreover, the rules of criminal and civil conspiracy, effectively used to restrict unionists and their activities in Great Britain, were invoked less frequently in this country. Public policy gradually came to accept unions and to allow them greater freedom. No federal restrictive legislation appeared until the Sherman Anti-trust Act was passed in 1890.

Throughout this long period, public policy was expressed in court decisions. As noted, some of these decisions created rules that outlawed organizations by holding that member action in combining created an illegal conspiracy. Other, later decisions accepted the propriety of organization but found either the purpose or certain actions illegal. The courts became the spokesmen for the rule-makers; from the union viewpoint, the judges became the rule-makers. Even after enactment of the *Sherman Act* in 1890, judges continued, by their interpretation of the law, to make the rules as they applied to unions.

2.2 Labor injunctions and yellow-dog contracts. The court's opinions were implemented in their orders, principally injunctions, and in their interpretation of contracts, especially those in which employers sought to limit union membership. When courts held unions illegal as conspiracies or combinations for an illegal purpose, they could order penalties for participation. More often, however, they ordered unions simply not to perform certain actions—making demands, holding meetings, forming parades, picketing —under penalty of punishment for contempt of court. They issued *labor injunctions,* a term that came to epitomize what union members and leaders regarded as persecution.[3]

Meanwhile, courts also upheld what unionists described as *yellow-dog contracts* or *ironclads.* These are agreements in which employers included a provision that required, as a condition of employment, the employee's promise not to be or to become a member of any labor organization. From the time of the first appearance of these contracts in the 1880's, unions sought to have them declared illegal. State legislation to this effect was enacted in several states, and a similar provision was made a part of the *Erdman Act* of 1898, which regulated employment on interstate railways. In two cases decided by the Supreme Court, both federal and state legislation of this type was held to be unconstitutional. In *Adair v. the United States,*[4] the Erdman Act provision was voided, on the ground that it violated the fifth amendment to the federal Constitution. In the *Coppage case,*[5] the Court applied a similar rule to state legislation aimed in this direction. It held that the action of the Kansas state legislature in making it illegal for an employer to require such an agreement as a condition of employment was in violation of the fourteenth amendment to the Constitution.

In general, public policy supported the right of an employer to accept or refuse collective bargaining until after World War I. Public policy as declared by the Supreme Court was clearly stated in 1917 in the *Hitchman case.*[6] The Court held that the right of an employer to enforce a yellow-dog contract would be protected by the federal courts.

2.3   The Sherman Act (1890). The "anti-trust act" of 1890 was designed to force the dissolution and prevent the development of business combinations whose operations involved restraint of interstate trade. Although some question exists as to whether Congress recognized the possibilities of the Act's application to labor organizations, it was immediately used to attack unions. In a series of cases, culminating in the *Danbury Hatters' case* (Loewe v. Lawlor, 208 U.S., 274, 1908), the courts held that it could be applied to unions and their individual members and that certain union activities, notably the boycott, were punishable under its provisions. In the Hatters' case, the union was found guilty of combination in restraint of trade, and penalties amounting to some $250,000 were assessed against the union and its mem-

[3] See Donald L. McMurry, "The Legal Ancestry of the Pullman Strike Injunctions," *Industrial and Labor Relations Review,* Vol. 14, No. 2, January, 1961, pp. 235–56.
[4] 208 U. S. 161 (1908).
[5] *Coppage v. Kansas,* 236 U. S. 1 (1915).
[6] *Hitchman Coal and Coke Company v. Mitchell,* 245 U. S. 249 (1917).

bers. The American Federation of Labor assisted in meeting the assessment and immediately undertook a campaign to have the law repealed or revised.

2.4   The Clayton Act (1914). The Clayton Act is a modified attempt to regulate monopoly and restraints of trade. In it, labor organizations secured the insertion of provisions to protect unions from such attacks as had been possible under the earlier Sherman Act. Section 6 of the Act declares "That the labor of human beings is not a commodity or an article of commerce." The section then goes on to specify that:

> Nothing contained in the anti-trust laws shall be construed to forbid the existence and operation of labor, agricultural, or horticultural organizations instituted for the purpose of mutual help and not having capital stock or conducted for profit or to forbid or restrain members of such organizations from lawfully carrying out the legitimate objects thereof, nor shall such organizations or the members thereof be held or construed to be illegal combinations or conspiracies in restraint of trade under the anti-trust laws.

This statement was regarded by unionists as clearly excluding labor organizations from anti-trust regulation. In addition, Section 20 of the Act provides that no injunction shall be issued by the federal courts in a labor dispute "unless necessary to prevent irreparable injury to property or to a property right of the party making the application, for which injury there is no adequate remedy at law." The section also asserts the right to strike by providing that no such injunction "shall prohibit any person or persons, whether singly or in concert, from terminating any relation of employment or from ceasing to perform any work or labor, or from recommending or advising or persuading others by peaceable means to do so."

The Act was widely described as a new *magna carta* for labor. But this description became less common as the courts developed their interpretations of the new legislation. The law also included, in its Section 16, a provision that allowed private suits in equity to restrain a violation of anti-trust regulations. This was a new feature, not included in the Sherman Act. It became widely used as firms entered such suits to prevent boycotts and related activities of labor organizations.

In a series of decisions, the Supreme Court indicated that there were distinct limitations on the immunity granted unions by the Act. Thus, in one of the first cases, that involving the *Duplex Printing Press Company*,[7] a union boycott which extended beyond the locality in which the dispute occurred was held to be illegal. Four years later, the Supreme Court ruling in the *Coronado Coal Co. case*[8] further limited labor's gains from the Clayton Act. In the Coronado case, the Court indicated that unions could be sued, even though they were not incorporated, and that funds collected by unions to be expended during strikes are subject to execution. Although the basic issue as to whether the action of the union was in restraint of trade did not finally

---

[7] *Duplex Printing Press Co. v. Deering*, 245 U. S. 443; 41 S. Ct. 172 (1921).
[8] *Coronado Coal Co. v. United Mine Workers of America*, 268 U. S. 295; 45 S. Ct. 551 (1925).

come to the Court, the union paid some $27,500 to the plaintiff companies to settle the matter out of court.

In 1927, the Supreme Court decided the *Bedford Cut Stone Co. case.*[9] As a result of a dispute with the company, the union ordered its members throughout the country not to work on the stone produced and processed in quarries of the employer. The Supreme Court authorized issuance of an injunction to prevent the boycott and held that the union's action constituted an illegal interference and restraint of trade.

2.5 Railway Labor Acts. Meanwhile, employment relationships on the railroads had become the subject for extensive federal legislation, some of which established a pattern for other intervention by both federal and state governments. As early as 1888, the federal Arbitration Act had provided special machinery to insure the peaceful settlement of disputes. The Erdman Act of 1898, the Newlands Act of 1913, the Adamson Act of 1916, and the Transportation Act of 1920 sought to provide special conciliation procedures and thus to guarantee peace in transportation.

The later Railway Labor Act of 1926 provides the earliest clear-cut statement in federal law of a national public policy favoring collective bargaining. It declares that employees shall have the right to bargain collectively through representatives of their own choice. It specifically outlaws interference by employers either in the formation of labor organizations or the choice of representatives. It outlaws the yellow-dog contract. At the same time, it outlaws the closed shop but (since 1951) permits the union shop and the checkoff. The law provides for elections to determine bargaining representatives.

While the Act originally applied to owners and employees of steam railroads operating across state boundaries, 1936 amendments expanded its coverage to include air carriers and their employees. Coverage extends to subsidiary activities of the railroads, including express, Pullman, bridge, terminal, refrigeration, storage, and deliveries. Independent electric railways are excluded.

2.6 The Norris-LaGuardia Act (1932). Both before and after enactment of the Sherman Act, employers frequently applied for injunctions to prevent what they regarded as improper actions of unions and their members. After the turn of the century, the device was widely used, principally because it was much more effective and immediate than the relief that might be obtained by subsequent suits for damages.

As use of the injunction for this purpose became more general, the scope of these orders was expanded. Injunctions prohibited picketing, mass meetings, boycotts, parades, and other demonstrations, as well as violence, property damage, and personal injury. Organized labor became alarmed lest these orders might undermine the effectiveness of unions. A campaign was organized to limit the rights of courts to issue such orders.

As has been noted, Section 20 of the Clayton Act included provisions

---

[9] *Bedford Cut Stone Co. v. Journeymen Stone Cutters' Association of North America,* 274 U. S. 37 (1927).

limiting the action of federal courts in this respect. It provided that injunctions could be issued only to prevent irreparable injury to property or a property right for which there was no adequate remedy at law. Court decisions convinced unionists that Clayton Act provisions had made little if any change in the status of the labor injunction. Most labor disputes could be found to involve the possibility of irreparable damage to property or property rights. Violators of these injunctions were still liable to be held in contempt of court. They were not entitled to jury trial. Evidence might be presented in the form of affidavits, with no opportunity to cross-examine witnesses. Violators of the injunction might be punished by fine or imprisonment in a degree determined entirely by the discretion of the court. Injunctions might be issued in "omnibus" form, covering the actions of a wide range of persons, some of whom were only remotely connected with the dispute, and prohibiting a similarly broad area of action.

The Norris-LaGuardia Act of 1932 sought to restrict the use of injunctions in labor disputes. It provides that federal courts may issue injunctions in labor disputes only under specified conditions. Five conditions must prevail if an injunction is to be issued. Unlawful acts must have been threatened or must be in process and likely to be continued. Substantial and irreparable damage to property must be anticipated. There must be no adequate remedy for damages. The local police must be unable or unwilling to provide adequate protection against the threatened damage.

The Act rules out certain provisions frequently included in earlier injunctions. Injunctions must not prohibit or restrain employees from ceasing or refusing to work or from being members of unions. They cannot forbid contributious to persons involved in a labor dispute or being prosecuted in court for participation in a labor dispute. They cannot prohibit publicizing, without fraud or violence, the facts in a labor dispute or assembling in connection with a labor dispute.

The Act further requires that the party seeking relief must have made reasonable efforts to settle the dispute by negotiation. The court order must be limited to the specific complaints considered by the court. Members and officers of organizations involved in labor disputes may not be held accountable unless it is shown that they participated in the action or authorized or ratified or had full knowledge of it. In contempt cases, if the objectionable action occurs in the presence of the court or interferes directly with the administration of justice, the offender may be punished by the court with no jury trial for the offender. In *indirect contempt,* in which the action falls outside these limits, those charged are entitled to jury trial. They may also secure a hearing before a judge other than the one who issued the injunction. The Act also outlaws use of the yellow-dog contract.

2.7 The National Industrial Recovery Act (1933). As a part of the National Recovery program initiated in the depth of the depression in 1933, the National Industrial Recovery Act was passed. It is notable as having laid a foundation for the National Labor Relations Act of 1935. Section 7a of the 1933 law specifically provided that employees should have the right to bargain collectively through representatives of their own choosing. At the same time, the experience of the National Labor Board (established as a temporary agency to deal with labor disputes arising in the recovery program and to enforce the provisions of Section 7a), together with the experience of the various industry labor boards created in automobile, steel, textile, petroleum, newspapers, and other industries, laid the foundation for the provisions of the National Labor Relations Act. The National Industrial Recovery Act was held unconstitutional in May, 1935.

2.8   The National Labor Relations Act (1935). The Railway Labor Act and the Norris-LaGuardia Act evidenced the beginning of a sharp change in popular attitudes toward collective bargaining. Sentiment turned toward a position holding that public welfare would be advanced by encouraging strong, independent unions to bargain with employers. Labor organizations were also regarded as desirable to insure enthusiastic participation of employees in employment and to effect an equitable distribution of income. This point of view gained increasing acceptance in the early years of the 1929 depression. With the advent of the Franklin D. Roosevelt administration in 1933, this position became politically dominant.

Since 1935 major national public policy on labor relations has been expressed in the National Labor Relations Act of 1935. In the recognition that it gave to unions and the power and authority it allowed them, it was a sharp turn from earlier stages.

Principal features of the National Labor Relations Act include:

1. It declared the public policy of the United States to be to encourage and facilitate collective bargaining through unions in which employees select representatives of their own choice.

2. It defined the rights of employees to participate in self-organization, to join, form, and assist labor organizations, to bargain collectively through representatives of their own choosing, and to engage in concerted activity for the purposes of collective bargaining and other mutual aid.

3. It prohibited certain employer actions that are defined as "unfair labor practices," including interference with employees in the exercise of the rights mentioned above, domination of a labor organization, discrimination in employment on the basis of union membership, discrimination against an employee for filing charges under the Act, and refusal to bargain collectively.

4. It created the National Labor Relations Board as the chief administrative agency under the Act, and gave the Board three principal functions, as follows:

(a) The determination of appropriate bargaining units.

(b) The certification of unions as bargaining agents on petition from employees.

(c) The prevention of unfair labor practices.

Constitutionality of the National Labor Relations Act was established by the Jones and Laughlin Case in 1937.[10]

For 12 years, the National Labor Relations Act remained the principal evidence of a national policy on collective bargaining. During this period,

[10] *NLRB v. Jones and Laughlin Steel Corporation,* 301 U. S. 1; 57 S. C. 615.

unions increased their membership from four millions to almost 15 millions. The new law unquestionably aided their growth. It firmly established the right of employees to bargain through representatives of their own choice. Enforcement of the unfair labor practices provisions eliminated many of the practices of employers and their associations by which they had prevented organization and dominated local unions.

Action of the National Labor Relations Board in defining bargaining units and certifying bargaining agents settled many controversies over recognition and union security. They facilitated organization and further restricted employers who sought to maintain an open shop, avoiding collective bargaining.

Rulings of the National Labor Relations Board created rules on determining bargaining units, on elections, on free speech for employers, on captive audiences (employees required to listen to an employer's representatives on company time), on employer financial aid to favored unions, on required subjects for compulsory collective bargaining, and on many other details of both contract negotiation and administration. They brought the federal government into the bargaining process to a far greater extent than ever before.

Courts sensed the changing attitudes toward unions and their activities and moved to apply the new rules. In 1940, the decision in the *Apex Hosiery Co. case*[11] held that activities of the union intended to keep the company's product from reaching the market did not constitute a restraint of trade. These actions, the court found, could not be regarded as exerting a significant influence on competition and the price of the product. The Court said that, in the earlier *Danbury Hatters' case,* the activities to which objection was raised were so widespread as to affect the whole market. Further, the Court held, local violence does not constitute restraint of interstate trade but was a matter to be handled by the local police and other law enforcement officials. In *United States v. Hutcheson,*[12] the Court was asked by the federal Department of Justice to forbid a strike and secondary boycott undertaken by the carpenters' union, which was engaged in a jurisdictional dispute at the Anheuser-Busch plant in St. Louis. On the basis of the definition of a labor dispute provided by the Norris-LaGuardia Act, the Court held that these activities were expressly legalized by the Clayton Act and that the union was therefore within its rights.

2.9 Taft-Hartley Act (1947). Rapid growth of unions following passage of the National Labor Relations Act, increasing political activity of unions led by the newly formed C.I.O., and a sharp increase in strikes immediately following World War II were important factors in encouraging additional federal legislation. Employers made much of complaints that some of the rules of the National Labor Relations Board encouraged strife and conflict. Employer associations charged that the 1935 law gave an unfair advantage to unions and was thus one-sided. It was clear that the power of unions had grown dramatically since public policy formally endorsed

---

[11] *Apex Hosiery Company v. Leader,* 310 U. S. 469; 60 S. Ct. 982 (1940).
[12] 312 U. S. 219; 61 S. Ct. 463 (1941).

union membership and collective bargaining. Unions were no longer the small, weak associations of earlier years. Public policy sought to reestablish a balance between powerful employers and powerful unions.

Revised policy took the form of the Labor Management Relations Act of 1947, more widely described as the Taft-Hartley Act. It was framed in terms of amendments to the National Labor Relations Act. The general intent is suggested by its statement of policy:

> Industrial strife which interferes with the normal flow of commerce and with the full production of articles and commodities for commerce, can be avoided or substantially minimized if employers, employees, and labor organizations each recognize under law one another's legitimate rights in their relations with each other, and above all recognize under law that neither party has any right in its relations with any other to engage in acts or practices which jeopardize the public health, safety, or interest.
>
> Experience has further demonstrated that certain practices by some labor organizations, their officers and members have the intent or the necessary effect of burdening or obstructing commerce by preventing the free flow of goods in such commerce through strikes and other forms of industrial unrest or through concerted activities which impair the interest of the public in the free flow of such commerce. The elimination of such practices is a necessary condition to the assurance of the rights herein guaranteed.

The 1947 law proposed added restraints on both employers and employees in collective bargaining. Organization and procedure of the National Labor Relations Board were changed. The number of Board members was increased from three to five. A new General Counsel was given final authority for investigation of charges and prosecution of complaints. The law provided for judicial review of Board actions. It required that Board hearings be conducted, so far as practicable, according to rules of civil procedure for district courts. The Board was authorized to ask federal Courts of Appeals to enforce its orders. Employer or union refusal to comply became punishable by the court as contempt.

To achieve a balance of power, the law changed Board procedure to permit employer petitions in representation cases, to assure freedom of expression on the part of both employers and unions, to prevent secondary boycotts and jurisdictional strikes, to limit union controls on employment through closed-shop and checkoff provisions, and to permit employer contributions to health and welfare funds only under specified conditions. The Taft-Hartley Act also outlined "unfair practices" of labor organizations, paralleling those formerly defined for employers. It also made the Federal Mediation and Conciliation Service an independent agency, outside the Department of Labor.

Other Taft-Hartley changes were designed to force unions to remove Communists from positions of influence; to file financial statements showing receipts, expenditures, and the salaries of officers; to accept financial responsibility under collective agreements; to delay nationwide strikes pending an extensive procedure of investigation; to abandon strikes against the federal government; to give up practices involving "exactions" from employers for work not performed; and to limit the political activities of unions. Also, the law established a six-month statute of limitations on unfair labor practices, created a joint committee to study labor relations, and outlined regulations designed to protect union members against excessive initiation fees and other arbitrary union action.

It is evident, especially with the advantage of several years' perspective, that both the National Labor Relations Act (1935) and the Taft-Hartley, Labor Management Relations Act (1947) represented impressive extensions of public intervention into manager-union relationships and into their collective bargaining and contract administration. Public policy, in a 25-year period, had substituted a myriad of rules and regulations for the light lacework or filigree of earlier controls. Some employer and union spokesmen charged that it had substituted a wholly new system of rigorously prescribed and controlled relationships for the former "free" collective bargaining. It had effectively denied the theories of both unions and employers that their interests are consistently the interests of the public. It had reemphasized the theory that public policy should strive to develop and maintain a balance of power between employers and unions and should so define the rules of the game as to prevent unfair advantage for either and to protect the public against objectionable or dangerous practices of both.

Employers and their associations expressed satisfaction with the changes introduced by LMRA. Union spokesmen described it as the "slave labor act." Some weaknesses were almost immediately apparent; the NLRB, for example, was overwhelmed by its new responsibility to conduct elections as a basis for union-shop clauses. The requirement that union officials provide affidavits declaring that they were not Communists created bitterness among officers and members, who charged it was a slanderous and discriminative attack on the whole labor movement.

In 1951, the Labor Management Relations Act was amended to permit union-shop agreements without the necessity of elections supervised by NLRB. At the same time, the rules were changed to exempt officers of the American Federation of Labor and the Congress of Industrial Organizations from the requirement to file non-Communist affidavits. In 1954, the Communist Control Act, while not an amendment to the LMRA, specified that unions dominated by Communists could not use the services of the NLRB to secure certification or to prevent unfair labor practices of employers. The act created a federal Subversive Activities Control Board to determine the reality of Communist control.

2.10   The Landrum-Griffin Act (1959). The most recent in this series of federal laws involved additional intervention, so far as regulation of unions is concerned. The Labor-Management Reporting and Disclosure Act of 1959, widely described as the Landrum-Griffin Act, covers much more than reporting and disclosure. The complexities of some of the new rules will not be clarified for several years, for court decisions will have to interpret the wording of many sections.

Greatest immediate pressure for this legislation came from hearings begun in 1957 under the auspices of the Senate Select Committee on Improper Activities in the Labor or Management Field, widely known as the McClellan Committee. These hearings produced spectacular testimony, widely reported in the press as well as by radio and television. Under questioning, consultants to employers described their gifts to union leaders and their campaigns to undermine the leadership of other union officials. Numerous union officers, when questioned about their relationships with employers and their use of union funds, "took the fifth" (refusing to answer questions on the ground that replies might incriminate them). Their defiance of the committee was probably as damaging to public confidence in union leadership as the facts developed in the investigation.[13]

Congressional action as expressed in the Act appears to reflect a general dissatisfaction with the behavior of both employers and unions, but particularly with unions. Both had frequently seemed to show little concern for the public interest. Attention had been attracted by numerous complaints from union members, calling attention to the lack of democratic safeguards in union procedures and to penalties arbitrarily imposed on dissenting members. The merger of the AFL and CIO in 1955 may have generated fear that unions were moving into a dominant position.

Against this background, the Landrum-Griffin Act appears as a demonstration of public determination to maintain control, to restrict both employers and unions, and to insist on greater public accountability from each of them. The act revises public policy on a wide range of activities. It includes a bill of rights for union members, an extensive list of required reports from both unions and employers, a rule-book on the exercise of union trusteeships and the conduct of union elections, and numerous revisions of older rules on such issues as the voting rights of economic strikers, secondary boycotts, picketing, and hot cargoes.[14]

[13] See Senate Committee on Improper Activities in the Labor or Management Field, *First Interim Report,* 85th Cong., 2nd sess., Washington, D.C.: U.S. Government Printing Office, 1958; Senate Committee on Improper Activities in the Labor or Management Field. *Second Interim Report,* 86th Cong., 1st sess., Washington, D.C.: U.S. Government Printing Office, August 5, 1959; see also Simon Rottenberg, "A Theory of Corruption in Labor Unions," Washington, D.C.: National Institute of Social and Behavioral Science, June, 1960; Sylvester Petro, *Power Unlimited,* New York, Ronald Press, 1959; Robert F. Kennedy, *The Enemy Within,* New York: Harper and Brothers, 1960; Edward H. Chamberlain and others, *Labor Unions and Public Policy,* Washington, D.C.: American Enterprise Association, 1958; David J. Saposs, "Labor Racketeering: Evolution and Solutions," *Social Research,* Vol. 25, No. 3, Autumn, 1958, pp. 253–70.

[14] For advance interpretations of Landrum-Griffin provisions, see Russell A. Smith, "The Labor-Management Reporting and Disclosure Act of 1959," *Virginia Law Review,* Vol. 46, No. 2, March, 1960, pp. 195–251; Benjamin Aaron, "The Labor-Management Reporting and Disclosure Act of 1959," *Harvard Law Review,* Vol. 73, No. 5, No. 6, March and April, 1960.

The declaration of policy with which the act begins is reproduced as Figure 11.1. Major provisions can be outlined as involving: A. Taft-Hartley Amendments; B. Reporting Requirements; and C. Safeguards for Democracy.

2.11 Taft-Hartley Amendments. Both unions and employers sought amendments of the rules prescribed by the Taft-Hartley Act. Major changes of this type are outlined below:

(1) *Legislative no-man's land.* Because of the doctrine of *federal supercession,* states had been prevented from enacting and enforcing local rules in firms and unions that were within the jurisdiction of the National Labor Relations Board, even though the Board had declined to take jurisdiction (because, for example, it regarded the firm involved as too small to justify federal attention). The 1959 law allows states to act in such situations. At the same time, to lighten the Board's duties in cases of unfair labor practices over which it must accept jurisdiction, the Board was authorized to delegate the supervision of elections to its regional directors.

(2) *Economic strikers.* Where economic strikers had formerly been barred from participation in elections, the new law permits them to vote under such regulations as the NLRB may prescribe in elections held within 12 months after the beginning of a strike.

(3) *Secondary boycotts.* Here the 1959 legislation sought to close what employers regarded as loopholes in the earlier rules. Unions may not coerce a secondary employer as a means of controlling his employees in a boycott. They may not seek to coerce employees of railroads or of government to further such a boycott.

(4) *Picketing.* Retail stores selling a product of a manufacturer with whom a union has a dispute may not be picketed on this account; the new rule does permit use of handbills and advertising as well as union rules that forbid crossing picket lines.

"Recognition" or "blackmail" picketing is ruled out if an employer has recognized another union as prescribed by law and a valid election has been held during the preceding 12 months, or if no petition for an election has been filed after 30 days of picketing. If the purpose of the picketing is to give public notice that the firm is not organized, it must not interfere with normal delivery and other services.

(5) *Hot-cargo agreements.* The rule against such agreements is restated to make it clear that no secondary person or group may be forced to agree not to handle the products of a struck employer.

(6) *Special industry exemptions.* The new law relaxed the rule on the closed shop in the construction industry, exempting it from the general prohibition and allowing agreements requiring union membership within seven days after hiring. It also noted a special case in the garment industry, where it permits agreements that forbid farming out work to non-union jobbers.

2.12 Reporting and Disclosure Requirements. Perhaps the greatest

LABOR-MANAGEMENT REPORTING AND DISCLOSURE ACT OF 1959

(LABOR REFORM ACT)

Act of September 14, 1959. P.L. 86-257, 86th Congress, 1st Session, 73 Stat. 519.

AN ACT

To provide for the reporting and disclosure of certain financial transactions and administrative practices of labor organizations and employers, to prevent abuses in the administration of trusteeships by labor organizations, to provide standards with respect to the election of officers of labor organizations and for other purposes.

Be it enacted by the Senate and House of Representatives of the United States of America in Congress assembled,

[¶ 31] **Short title. Section 1.**—This Act may be cited as the "Labor-Management Reporting and Disclosure Act of 1959".

[¶ 32] **Declaration of findings, purposes and policy. Sec. 2.**—(a) The Congress finds that, in the public interest, it continues to be the responsibility of the Federal Government to protect employees' rights to organize, choose their own representatives, bargain collectively, and otherwise engage in concerted activities for their mutual aid or protection; that the relations between employers and labor organizations and the millions of workers they represent have a substantial impact on the commerce of the Nation; and that in order to accomplish the objective of a free flow of commerce it is essential that labor organizations, employers, and their officials adhere to the highest standards of responsibility and ethical conduct in administering the affairs of their organizations, particularly as they affect labor-management relations.

(b) The Congress further finds, from recent investigations in the labor and management fields, that there have been a number of instances of breach of trust, corruption, disregard of the rights of individual employees, and other failures to observe high standards of responsibility and ethical conduct which require further and supplementary legislation that will afford necessary protection of the rights and interests of employees and the public generally as they relate to the activities of labor organizations, employers, labor relations consultants, and their officers and representatives.

(c) The Congress, therefore, further finds and declares that the enactment of this Act is necessary to eliminate or prevent improper practices on the part of labor organizations, employers, labor relations consultants, and their officers and representatives which distort and defeat the policies of the Labor Management Relations Act, 1947, as amended, and the Railway Labor Act, as amended, and have the tendency or necessary effect of burdening or obstructing commerce by (1) impairing the efficiency, safety, or operation of the instrumentalities of commerce; (2) occurring in the current of commerce; (3) materially affecting, restraining, or controlling the flow of raw materials or manufactured or processed goods into or from the channels of commerce, or the prices of such materials or goods in commerce; or (4) causing diminution of employment and wages in such volume as substantially to impair or disrupt the market for goods flowing into or from the channels of commerce.

Figure 11.1 Declaration of Policy—Landrum-Griffin Act

change introduced by the new law is the clear intention to make union administration and employer-union relationships matters of public information. To that end, the law provides for a wide range of periodic reports from employers, labor relations consultants, unions, union officials and employees, and union trusteeships. The nature of these reports in terms of what they must cover may be outlined as shown in Table 11.1.

One result of this legislation is quickly apparent; we shall know much more about the detailed financial and other activities of the parties and their agents than ever before.[15]

2.13 Democratic Administration of Unions. The reporting requirements of the act encourage more democratic control of unions. In addition, the law includes a series of provisions designed to protect the individual rights of union members, to insure equal opportunities for all members to participate in honest elections, and to safeguard members and unions against improper use of union funds.

Title I of the Landrum-Griffin Act is a Bill of Rights for Members of Labor Organizations. All members are assured equal rights in nominating candidates for union office, voting in elections, attending and participating in meetings, and expressing their views and opinions. Procedures are specified for increasing dues and fees and for making assessments. Union members are assured the right to sue and to appear as witnesses and communicate with legislators. Rules limit the disciplinary power of unions with respect to their members. Members and all employees affected by a collective agreement are entitled to copies of the agreement. Unions are required to inform their members of these provisions.

Special rules are defined for union elections. They require the use of secret ballots, opportunity for members to make nominations, advance notice to all members, the right of any candidate to have an observer at polls and at the counting of ballots, publication of voting results, conduct of elections according to the union constitution, preservation of election results for at least one year, prohibition of the use of union funds to support a candidate, and elections at no more than five-year intervals for national and international unions, four-year intervals for intermediate bodies, and three-year intervals for locals.

Further, the act protects members against trusteeships by permitting unions to place locals under the control of trustees only to correct corruption or financial malpractice, to assure performance of agreements, to restore democratic procedures or to carry out other legitimate objectives of the union.[16] Union officials who have financial responsibilities must be bonded and must

---

[15] For details of these reports, see the annual report of the Bureau of Labor-Management Reports, U.S. Department of Labor; the detailed instructional booklets from that bureau for employers, unions, union officials, labor relations consultants, all available without cost from the BLMR area or Washington, D.C. office.

[16] Arnold R. Weber, "Local Union Trusteeship and Public Policy," *Industrial and Labor Relations Review*, Vol. 14, No. 2, January, 1961, pp. 185–205.

Table 11.1

Reports Required by the Labor Management Reporting and Disclosure Act of 1959

From Employers:

    Payment or loans to any union, union official or representative

    Payments to employees designed to persuade other employees not to organize or join a union or bargain collectively

    Payments designed to get information about employees or unions in a labor dispute with the employer

    Agreements with a labor relations consultant designed to persuade employees not to bargain collectively or to get information about a union in dispute with the employer

    Payments to labor relations consultants for these purposes.

From Labor Relations Consultants:

    Name and address

    Terms and conditions of agreements with an employer by which the consultant will (1) persuade employees to follow a particular course with respect to their action in collective bargaining or refraining from bargaining collectively; (2) supply information on employee or union activities in connection with a labor dispute with the employer.

From Unions:

    Union Constitution and by-laws

    Name, address, names and titles of officers

    Initiation fees, transfer fees, work permit fees

    Dues

    Qualifications for and restrictions on membership

    Method of making assessments

    Procedures for member participation in benefits

    Procedures for disbursement of funds, including authorization

    Provisions for audits of finances

    Method of calling meetings

    Method of selecting all officers and delegates

    Method of disciplining officers or agents for breach of trust

    Procedures and ground for fines, suspensions, expulsion

    Hearings provided for disciplinary cases

    Determination of bargaining demands

    Method of ratifying contract terms

    Method of authorizing strikes

    Procedures in issuing work permits

    Financial report—assets, liabilities, receipts by source, salaries, allowances and other payments to officers and any others who received more than $10,000 loans to officers or members of more than $250, loans to business, any other disbursements.

From Union Officials and Employees*:

    Holdings of securities or receipt of income or other benefit from an employer

    Business transactions or relationships with an employer

    Buying, selling, leasing or otherwise dealing with an employer.

    Payments from an employer or a labor relations consultant acting for the employer

    Membership participation in election of officers of parent union

From Unions on Trusteeships:

    Name and addresses of trusted organization

    Date trusteeship established

    Reasons for trusteeship

   * Required only if the official or employee or his wife or minor child benefited from a possible conflict of interest.

Table 11.1 (Cont.)

Membership participation in selecting delegates
Membership participation in election of officers of parent union
Financial details of trusted organization when trusteed.
Annual financial report
All receipts by source, salaries, allowances, loans and other disbursements as in
  reports from all unions.

---

refrain from personal activities that could involve a conflict of interest with the organization they represent. They must account to their organization for any profits arising out of union business.

The act provides a penalty either of imprisonment up to five years or of a fine up to $10,000, or both, for violation of trusteeship provisions and for theft of union assets. It further protects unions from domination by gangsters, hoodlums and racketeers by barring such persons from union office. Unions may not employ—except for clerical and custodial duties—anyone who in the preceding five years has been a Communist or has been convicted of robbery, bribery, extortion, embezzlement, grand larceny, burglary, arson, violation of narcotics laws, murder, rape, assault with intent to kill, assault which inflicts grievous bodily injury, violations of Title II or III of the present act, or conspiracy to commit any of' these. The same requirements apply to employment as a labor relations consultant or by an employer association dealing with unions.

3.0 SUMMARY

This chapter has sought to provide perspective and background with respect to public policy on labor relations in the United States. The chapter begins with a brief analysis of the overall objectives in public policy and the questions for which policy seeks answers. The remainder of the chapter provides an overview of historic changes in American public policy.

For all managers, public policy prescribes the broad dimensions of managerial policy on labor relations. It dictates a philosophy and a hierarchy of goals to which the firm's philosophy and goals must conform. To the extent that managers regard public policy as unreasonable, uninformed, or misguided, they may seek to reshape it. They can do so only by challenging the philosophy it declares or the theories by which it translates its goals and objectives into policies.

Perspective from such a review facilitates an understanding and appreciation of current policy. At the same time, the historic trends noted in preceding pages justify the conclusion that modern managerial policy on employment relationships is truly tripartite. Employees and their unions and government all exert a powerful influence on managerial policy in this area.

Current policy on labor relations is so extensive and pervasive, affecting so much of modern managerial policy and practice, that an additional chapter considers in some detail the present rules of the game with respect to union-management relationships in manpower management.

SELECTED SUPPLEMENTARY READINGS

Aaron, Benjamin, "The Labor Management Reporting and Disclosure Act of 1959," *Harvard Law Review,* Vol. 73, Nos. 5 and 6, March-April, 1960. (Available as *Reprint No. 94,* Institute of Industrial Relations, University of California at Los Angeles, 1960.)

Chamberlain, Edward H., et al., *Labor Unions and Public Policy.* Washington, D.C.: American Enterprise Association, 1958.

Fleming, R. W., "Emergency Strikes and National Policy," *Labor Law Journal,* Vol. 11, No. 4, pp. 267–336, April, 1960. (Available as *Reprint Series No. 84,* University of Illinois Institute of Labor and Industrial Relations, June, 1960.)

Hearings of the Senate Committee on Improper Activities in the Labor or Management Field, *First Interim Report,* 1958, and *Second Interim Report.* Washington, D.C.: Government Printing Office, August, 1959.

Kennedy, Robert F., *The Enemy Within.* New York: Harper & Brothers, 1960.

Petro, Sylvester, *Power Unlimited.* New York: The Ronald Press Company, 1959.

The Public Interest in National Labor Policy, New York: Committee for Economic Development, 1962.

Rottenberg, Simon, "A Theory of Corruption in Labor Unions," Washington, D.C.: National Institute of Social and Behavioral Science, June, 1960.

Shister, Joseph, "The Role of the State in Collective Bargaining," *Proceedings, Twelfth Annual Industrial Relations Conference,* McGill University, September, 1960. (Available as a Reprint from the Department of Industrial Relations, School of Business Administration, University of Buffalo.)

Stewart, Maxwell S., "Labor and the Public," *Public Affairs Pamphlet No. 301,* Public Affairs Committee, Inc., August, 1960.

SHORT CASE PROBLEM 11.1

Federal Wage Controls

Consider the following excerpt from a 1960 editorial:

"No current domestic problem in the United States deserves more public attention than that of inflation. The continuing rise in costs of living offers a greater threat to the well-being of our citizens than any other this editor can call to mind. Inflation makes a mockery of our American ideals of saving and thrift. It imperils the welfare of all our senior citizens who have sacrificed to put something away to take care of themselves in their declining years. It is a constant hazard to the wages and salaries of public employees who, for the most part, are always behind the parade of those who earn more as prices rise. It thus reduces the attractiveness of public service, forcing many able citizens to leave employment in our schools and public agencies in order to meet the higher costs of raising their families.

"It is ironic indeed that those who are likely to suffer most from inflation in the years ahead are also those who have the largest part in causing the ceaseless upward spiral of prices. They are the wage earners, the members of unions whose spokesmen maintain a steady pressure for more. In all the years since World War II, wages have increased an average of almost 5.5 per cent per year. Meanwhile, workers have seldom increased their output per manhour in the same measure; the average for the same years is no more than 3 per cent per year.

"Inflation under these circumstances is inevitable. It is as simple as two and two. Prices are cost determined; wages are inevitable costs.

"In some other nations, unions have seen the light. They have joined with employers and held the line on wages. They have stopped the creeping misery of inflation. Their members and their officers have accepted their responsibilities as citizens. They deserve great credit and appreciation for this courageous action.

"In the United States, no such action appears likely. Not a single prominent union official has yet admitted the basic responsibility of union members for what has taken place and is taking place.

"We conclude that nothing short of federal legislation can meet this persistent emergency. We propose a law that will prohibit any wage increase in excess of the preceding year's productivity gain. We think that courageous statesmen in the Congress must face and control this hazard. Nothing short of detailed regulation can protect all of us from the selfishness of the few."

Problem: Take a position on this issue and prepare arguments to support your stand.

SHORT CASE PROBLEM 11.2

Leaves for Public Service

Joe Mahoney is an assembler in the Wadsworth Manufacturing Company plant, where he has been employed for 11 years. He has always had an active interest in politics, having been a candidate for several part-time offices. He has been successful in several elections and has served as a member of the school board and an alderman in the city council.

In 1954, Joe decided to run for the state legislature. He was elected after a very active and sometimes bitter three-month campaign.

From time to time, when he was an alderman, he had asked for a few days off to attend all-day hearings or to join other aldermen in trips to conferences or meetings. Most of his work, both as a member of the school board and as an alderman, was performed outside working hours. When he began his active campaign for state representative, he asked for and was granted a leave of absence. Now that he is elected, he has asked for an additional leave of absence for the three months during which the legislature is in session. He has requested, also, that his group insurance and other benefits be continued during his absence.

His employer is undecided as to what action to take on this request. Repeated absences of two or three months make it necessary to employ a replacement. The employer is somewhat concerned also because Joe, in his campaign, has advocated a tax program that would be expensive to the firm. He has also favored labor legislation with which the employer is not sympathetic. The employer has suggested that Mahoney might find it embarrassing to be on leave from the firm, that his objectivity and fairness might be questioned. Mahoney takes an opposite view. He argues that the employer should encourage active participation in politics by employees. He points to the fact that state representatives have no group insurance or other benefits and suggests that, if an employee has to give up such benefits, employees as a group will find it impossible to accept public office.

Problem: You have been asked to prepare a statement for the advice of company officials in this situation. Should a leave of absence be granted?

12. *Labor Relations: Current Rules*

What attitudes and behavior are appropriate for the manager who seeks to comply with both the letter and spirit of current public policy on labor relations? What may he reasonably expect in terms of attitude and action from the union representatives with whom he may be working? How has changing public policy, as outlined in the preceding chapter, defined the rules of the game in modern labor relations?

This chapter undertakes a systematic review of the more important of these rules of the game. It deals with only the more important general rules; detailed procedures are spelled out in thousands of pages of law, court decisions and interpretations, administrative rulings, and the precedent established by hundreds of arbitration awards. For details, the manager must depend on his legal advisors, the several labor reporting services, and other similar sources of professional counsel.

Understanding of current public policy may easily be obscured by a tendency to label it. Professor Slichter, a keen analyst of developing public policy, suggested that public policy tends to encourage a "laboristic" type of society. Some employers and employer associations have asserted that modern policy has made us a socialistic society. More enthusiastic commentators have described our public policy as leading toward more "humanistic" relationships.

One complication deserves special mention. In this country, as has been noted, no single agency and indeed no level of government has the sole right to state public policy on labor relations. Attention in the preceding chapter has focused largely on federal legislation, in part because it affects largest numbers of employers and workers and in part because it tends to set patterns to be followed in other jurisdictions. States, counties, and municipalities, however, may develop distinctive policies. Their jurisdictions tend to overlap. In general, federal rules apply to industries whose operations cross state lines. Federal legislation is based on the "Commerce clause" of the Constitution, which grants the federal government authority in the regulation of conditions affecting interstate commerce. State and local governments may not maintain policy that conflicts with federal regulation within the area of interstate commerce.

For some employers and employees, however, policy has been confused because the National Labor Relations Board holds jurisdiction but may not care to exercise control. Because a federal agency has preempted the area, state regulations can be ruled invalid. The general principle involved is described as "supersession." It holds that if Congress has enacted legislation covering a particular area, state legislation in the same area will not be enforced. Even if the federal legislation is of such a broad and inclusive nature that it can not be or is not applied to a particular case, state legislation will not be permitted.

In a series of cases, beginning in 1947, the Supreme Court defined a very broad jurisdiction for the federal government in matters of labor relations.[1] It further held that within this area, state labor relations boards could not exercise jurisdiction. Meanwhile, for administrative and other reasons, the National Labor Relations Board had declined to exercise its jurisdiction with respect to certain types of cases, notably those involving small firms and local problems of law and order.

To reduce or eliminate the resulting no-man's land,[2] the Labor-Management Reporting and Disclosure Act of 1959 includes the following statement [Title 7, (c) in Section 701 a]:

> (c) 1. The Board, in its discretion, may . . . decline to assert jurisdiction over any labor dispute involving any class or category of employers, where, in the opinion of the Board, the effect of such labor dispute on commerce is not sufficiently substantial to warrant the exercise of its jurisdiction. . . .
> 2. Nothing in this act shall be deemed to prevent or bar any agency or the courts of any state . . . from assuming and asserting jurisdiction over labor disputes over which the Board declines . . . to assert jurisdiction.

While this provision clarifies state and federal relationships so far as NLRB jurisdiction is concerned, many other overlaps remain, as illustrated by the varying public policy on union security clauses to be noted in a later section.

Discussion of current rules in this chapter relates them to three major questions. Section 1 describes policy with respect to what may be described

---

[1] The principal cases are *Bethlehem Steel Company v. New York State Labor Relations Board*, 330 U.S. 767 (1947); *LaCrosse Telephone Corporation v. Wisconsin Employment Relations Board*, 336 U.S. 18 (1949); *Garner v. Teamsters Union*, 346 U.S. 486 (1953); *Weber v. Anheuser-Busch*, 348 U.S. 468, 1955.

[2] See, in this connection, Jonathan Matthew Purver, "The Supreme Court and the Federal-State 'No-Mans' Land,' " *Labor Law Journal*, Vol. 11, No. 11, November, 1960, pp. 1031–37.

as good faith in collective bargaining. Section 2 considers approved and proscribed practices or tactics of employers and unions in their continuing competition and conflict. Section 3 is concerned with the rules on union democracy and union political activity.

1.0   RIGHT AND OBLIGATION TO BARGAIN

Current public policy in the United States leaves no room for question about its intention to permit and indeed to encourage collective bargaining. The right of employees to form and join unions of their own choosing is clearly declared in the National Labor Relations Act and similar state legislation.

More than a dozen states and Puerto Rico have state labor relations acts modeled after federal legislation.[3] They declare the intention to protect rights of employees to join unions of their own choice and to bargain collectively through their unions. These state laws provide administrative agencies to settle questions of bargaining units and bargaining agents, following the NLRB pattern. Usually the union thus selected is recognized as the exclusive bargaining agent for employees in the unit. All of the acts specify *unfair labor practices* on the part of employers; in most laws unfair labor practices of unions are also identified. Prohibited actions of employers include the use of spies, yellow-dog contracts, blacklisting employees, refusal to accept the decision of a suitable tribunal in arbitration, entering into agreements with minority groups of employees, and the unfair practices defined in the original National Labor Relations Act at the federal level.

Unfair labor practices of unions include sit-down strikes; use of force, coercion, or violence; refusal to accept the decision of an appropriate tribunal; secondary boycotts; and mass picketing.[4]

Public policy quite evidently intends that individual workers shall be protected in the exercise of the right to bargain collectively, as is indicated by the unfair labor practices of employers identified in these laws. Public policy further proposes to restrict employers in tactics designed to limit membership or to dominate the bargaining organizations of employees. At the same time, it proposes to require employers to meet with such organizations to provide necessary wage data and to bargain in good faith with them.[5]

Public policy expects unions that represent employees to be chosen by their members. To facilitate such choice, both federal and state legislation provides public assistance in settling controversies over appropriate bargaining units and certified bargaining agents.

1.1   Good faith. Public policy requires that employers and unions bar-

[3] The number continues to grow slowly. For details, consult one of the labor reporting services.
[4] For details, see *The American Workers' Fact Book*, Washington: United States Department of Labor, 1960, pp. 301ff; "Labor Relations" Volume, section on State Labor Relations Acts, *Labor Equipment*, Englewood Cliffs, N.J.: Prentice-Hall, Inc.
[5] See Walter L. Daykin, "The Legal Status of Collective Bargaining," *Labor Law Journal*, Vol. 10, No. 1, January, 1959, pp. 11–17ff.

gain *in good faith* with respect to matters of wages, hours, or other working conditions. This requirement has occasioned extensive intervention by public regulatory agencies. Does this mean that both parties must agree, at least to some extent, to each other's proposals, as an evidence of good faith in bargaining? Bargaining in good faith requires that the parties communicate and negotiate, that proposals be matched with counter-proposals, and that both make every reasonable effort to arrive at agreement. If a party simply refuses to discuss a proposal or to meet for that purpose, or repeatedly fails to attend scheduled meetings, or fails to provide authorized negotiators to discuss a proposal, such actions have been held to violate this requirement.

On the other hand, the requirement of bargaining in good faith does not require concessions or partial agreement. Neither an employer nor a union needs to agree with any proposal as an evidence of his good faith in the matter. What is necessary is that each party undertake discussion of a proposal with an open mind and a sincere intent to find a basis for agreement.[6]

1.2 Scope of compulsory bargaining. By law, the area of "wages, hours, and other conditions of employment" is subject to compulsory bargaining; both parties must bargain if requested to do so. Other questions are permissive; parties may agree to bargain about them.[7] In the viewpoint of many managers, this question as to what must be bargained raises one of the most critical issues in current public policy. Employers have sought to contain the scope of bargaining. Unions have sought to enlarge it. National Labor Relations Board and court decisions have made it clear that scope is not limited to wages and hours. New subjects become proposals for bargaining each year.

Public policy clearly intends to permit collective bargaining over a wide range of issues and collective agreement up to but not including the extent in which it destroys the effectiveness of either of the power centers or creates a state of collusion.

1.3 Industry-wide bargaining. To maintain balance between the power centers of unions and employers, public policy has recognized the growing tendency toward bigness in both business and unions. It has sought to balance power at the national rather than the local level. It has thus provided an incentive for wide affiliation on the part of both employers and unions.

The decision to seek a balance of power principally at the national level is evidenced by the acceptance of *industry-wide bargaining.* In earlier periods, suggestions proposed numerous restrictions on this practice, including a rule that bargaining be limited to employers and employees within a hundred-mile radius. The only major concession to such proposals in present policy is the rule designed to settle emergency strikes by requiring that employees *of each employer* be polled on their employer's most recent offer.

1.4 Public employees. The right to organize and be represented in

---

[6] See *Globe Cotton Mills v. NLRB,* IRC, Par, 18,327.
[7] See Wallace B. Nelson, "Management Prerogatives and the Work Rules Controversy," *Labor Law Journal,* Vol. 11, No. 11, November, 1960, pp. 987–1004.

bargaining by a union of the employee's choice extends to public as well as private employees, but with important boundaries and restrictions. In some areas, policemen and firemen may organize, but they may not join "outside" unions that include other employees or unions that are affiliated with state and national federations. In many cases, also, public employees may join unions and, through their unions, present bargaining demands, but they cannot conclude collective agreements with the agencies in which they are employed. On this point, some public policy apparently regards it as illegal for public officials to make such agreements, on the ground that they cannot delegate the administrative responsibilities assigned them by law. Further, in many jurisdictions, including that of the federal government, public employees may not strike to enforce their demands.

The propriety of such limitations is the subject of continuing discussion. Union spokesmen insist that present policy makes public employees second-class citizens. On the other hand, complete relaxation of the present rules could create hazards to essential public services—fire-fighting and maintenance of law and order, for example. Perhaps an arrangement that provides special grievance procedures for all public employees could justify some restrictions on their organizational activities.

1.5 **Union security and responsibility.** The measure of union security presently contemplated in public policy varies with the nature of the industry and the region or locality. Federal jurisdiction permits the union shop, the agency shop, and, for the building trades and the garment industries, closed shop provisions. Some 19 state laws are more restrictive; they prohibit union shop provisions. Popularly described as *right-to-work laws,* union spokesmen have dubbed them "Wreck" laws. They provide that the right to work shall not be denied to anyone because of failure to maintain union membership. They prohibit both closed and union shop provisions and maintenance of membership as well. Agency shop provisions appeared questionable under federal rules. However, in September, 1961, the National Labor Relations Board ruled that they are acceptable. Eleven states specifically outlaw the agency shop. Eight states have no legislative rule on the agency shop, but administrative rulings make it improper in five of them. Constitutionality of such legislation has been upheld by the United States Supreme Court.

Unions have undertaken strenuous campaigns to prevent the spread of right-to-work laws and to have existing laws repealed; employer associations have hailed them as desirable if not essential in all jurisdictions. Much of the union opposition to the Taft-Hartley Act centered on a permissive provision that allows states to legislate rules that supplement federal provisions. Before enactment of this provision, the general rule of federal pre-emption was regarded as having excluded state control of union security.

Public policy on the question of union security is handicapped by the absence of impressive evidence on the effects of such security on union strength and bargaining relationships. Unions insist that their responsibility and effectiveness require such security as is assured by the union shop.

Critics, on the other hand, insist that such security encourages union leaders to neglect or to ignore the wishes of members; that it gives the organization too much authority and impresses an undesirable degree of conformity on members; that it introduces imbalance rather than balance in the relationships of unions and employers; that it is un-American in requiring workers to join a union in order to get and to hold a job. Careful appraisals of these claims and counterclaims are handicapped by the limited evidence on what effects actually follow in the presence of compulsory union membership.[8]

Security may be strengthened by the *checkoff* of union dues. Here again, practice is not uniform. Federal rules permit the use of the checkoff but only on a voluntary basis, authorized in writing, and revocable from year to year.

Unions may sue and be sued for damages arising out of failure to perform as agreed. Taft-Hartley amendments to the National Labor Relations Act specifically provide that unions may be sued in the United States district courts for violation of contract provisions and for injuries resulting from secondary boycotts. Moreover, they may be held liable for back pay in reinstatements of employees improperly released at the insistence of the union. Damages may be assessed against the union and its assets, but not against individual members.

Long before enactment of the Labor Management Relations Act, unions and their members had been held accountable. The Supreme Court expressly stated that a union may be sued, even though it is not incorporated, in the *Coronado Coal Company* decision. The Danbury Hatters' case and other less prominent cases have shown the possibilities in such suits.

On the other hand, most employers hesitate, even when faced with damages resulting from failure on the part of the union to fulfill the terms of an agreement, to undertake such suits. The employment relationship is not satisfactory if the parties are engaged in continual legal struggles—if the union of employees regards the employer as threatening the treasury of their organization and possibly their own savings through legal action. That is why employers who have sued unions and recovered damages have frequently returned them or refused to accept them.

Unions may incorporate under the laws of several states. Federal incor-

[8] A mass of controversial literature and a few careful studies are available on this issue. See, for example, "Trouble, U.S.A.," a documentary film available from the National Association of Manufacturers; Philip D. Bradley, "Involuntary Participation in Unionism," Washington, D.C.: American Enterprise Association, 1956; "Personal Freedom and Labor Policy," New York: Institute of Economic Affairs, New York University, 1958; "Twenty Questions about the Right to Work," National Association of Manufacturers, 1956; Jerome L. Toner, "Right-to-work Laws and the Common Good," *Reprint* by the United Steelworkers of America (1500 Commonwealth Building, Pittsburgh, Pa.), 1959. See also, Earl F. Cheit, "Union Security and the Right to Work," *Labor Law Journal*, Vol. 6, No. 6, June, 1955, pp. 357ff.; Maurice C. Benewitz, "Nature and Effect of State Right-to-Work Laws," *Wayne Law Review*, Vol. 1, No. 3, Summer, 1955, pp. 165–92; Frederick Meyers, "Effects of Right-to-Work Laws: A Study of the Texas Act," *Industrial and Labor Relations Review*, Vol. 9, No. 1, October, 1955, pp. 77–84; Arthur Lenhoff, "The Right to Work: Here and Abroad," *Illinois Law Review*, Vol. 46, No. 5, November-December, 1951, pp. 669–718.

poration was authorized by law from 1886 to 1932. Unions generally do not wish to incorporate, on the ground that incorporation might make them more vulnerable to nuisance suits designed to harass them and deplete their treasuries. Also, neither the usual form of incorporation for profit nor that of the non-profit corporation is well-suited to union organizations and activities.

1.6 Management security. To what extent does current public policy propose to define an area of management prerogatives and to assure managers freedom to act on a unilateral basis within such an area? Public policy appears to assume: (1) that employers and managers can by negotiation define such exclusive areas as they will, and (2) that managerial efficiency may be of secondary importance as a criterion of the proper scope for unilateral action.

Despite the continuing protests of managers, current public policy gives little weight to the theory that property rights insure an area of exclusive decision-making for managers as the representatives of owners. On the other hand, any area of exclusive jurisdiction on which the parties agree is acceptable. On that principle, three-fourths of current collective agreements now include management clauses that outline such an area. They have become increasingly common.

Two principal types of such clauses have appeared: one simply reserves to management the right to make decisions in all areas not covered by the other clauses in the agreement; the other specifies in some detail the subjects within the exclusive jurisdiction or management. Among the subjects most frequently mentioned in the second type of provision are policies on finances, interest rates, loans; sales and organization policies, market areas; materials, processes, and products; plant location; work assignments; production schedules. Even within these areas, however, many agreements permit grievances if employees feel that they have been adversely and unfairly treated. Here are examples of such clauses:

> (.3) Subject to the provisions of this agreement and the collective bargaining rights of the union, it is recognized and agreed that the management of the mills and the direction of the working forces is vested in the employer; among the rights and responsibilities which shall continue to be vested in the employer, but not intended as a wholly inclusive list of them, shall be: the rights to increase or decrease operation; to remove or install machinery, and to increase or change production equipment; to introduce new and improved productive methods and facilities; to regulate the quality and quantity of production; to relieve employees from duty because of lack of work; to employ, lay-off, re-employ, and transfer employees; to demote or discharge employees for cause as the efficient operation of the plant shall, in the opinion of the management, require, provided that none of such rights shall be exercised in violation, of any provision of this contract.
>
> (.1) Except as otherwise in this agreement expressly provided, nothing in this agreement contained shall be deemed to limit the company in any way in the exercises of the regular and customary functions of management, including the making in connection there with of such rules relating to operations as it shall deem advisable. (*Leather Industry*)
>
> (.3) "Any of the rights, powers or authority the company had prior to the

signing of this agreement are retained by the company, except those specifically abridged, delegated, granted or modified by this agreement, and any supplementary agreements that may hereafter be made."

With respect to frequent assertions by managers and owners that current policy interferes with the efficiency of management, present policy appears to answer that if efficiency must suffer, it is of less consequence than the limitations that would otherwise have to be imposed on employee organization and representation. Policy may be interpreted to imply that the pressure of union demands may actually force greater managerial efficiency and that the participation of intelligent union representatives can improve managerial decisions.

Perhaps it should be noted that public policy in this country does not propose an extent of participation like the system of *codetermination* established in Germany in 1951. In the coal and steel industries of West Germany, law requires that 5 of the 11 directors of major firms be selected by employee labor organizations. Some precedent for such provisions exists; both in France and Germany, employee representatives had participated in the deliberations of boards of directors.[9]

2.0 CONFLICT AND COMPETITION

Public policy seeks to maintain independence as well as balance in the relationships of employers and unions. It seeks to avoid detailed public intervention and regulation by encouraging the self-determination of working conditions. It recognizes the necessity for keeping employers and unions independent. It also proposes to limit the practices they may properly use in their competitive struggles. Public policy imposes limitations on their conflict tactics, in part to preserve a balance of power and in part to avoid injury to neutrals.

2.1 The Strike. Public policy is clear in its intention to preserve the right to strike, although it recognizes some limitations. Federal civil service employees who strike are barred from reemployment for three years. In states and localities, similar limitations are imposed on public employees. In some jurisdictions, employees in hospitals and public utilities are denied the right to strike. Further, the type of strike may be significant. Thus *sitdown strikes* are regarded as illegal. *Sympathetic strikes* and *general strikes* may be regarded as essentially secondary boycotts and improper on that account. In the federal jurisdiction and in that of several states, special provisions apply to strikes that are regarded as *emergency stoppages,* in that they threaten or hazard public health and welfare. In such disputes, provisions impose

---

[9] See Paul Fisher, "Works Councils in Germany," Office of the United States High Commissioner for Germany, Frankfurt, Germany, March, 1951, especially pp. 39–42. Clark Kerr, "Collective Bargaining in Post-war Germany," *Industrial and Labor Relations Review,* Vol. 5, No. 3, April, 1952, pp. 323–42; Oscar Weigert "Co-Determination in Western Germany," *Monthly Labor Review,* Vol. 73, No. 6, December, 1951, pp. 649–56.

compulsory delay or *cooling off periods* and forbid strikes during these delays.

Federal rules regard jurisdictional strikes as improper, instructing the National Labor Relations Board to give priority to petitions in such disputes and to use injunctions to stop strikes. Further, employers are given the right to sue for damages occasioned by jurisdictional strikes.

From the standpoint of unions and their members, the "employment status" of strikers is important, for it determines their right to vote in elections to select a bargaining agent. In an *unfair labor practice strike*, employees maintain their status and can vote. If an employer is found to have committed an unfair labor practice, employees must be reinstated. In an *economic strike*, employees may be replaced, but they retain their voting rights for one year.

Court decisions on the legality of strikes have long emphasized the purpose of the strike as one major consideration and the method or conduct of the strike as another. They have held that a strike may be legal or illegal in either respect. If the purpose of the strike is primarily to inflict injury on an employer or others, it is illegal. If, on the other hand, the primary purpose is to advance the economic status of strikers, the strike is regarded as legal. For that reason, in part, union leaders see to it that strikes involve an issue of wages or hours. As to methods or means, the question is one of the peaceful or violent conduct of the strike.[10]

Public policy has encouraged employers and unions to establish their own rules with respect to strikes within the general framework of public rules. Many agreements now provide that, if the parties fail to negotiate a new agreement by the time of termination provided in an existing agreement, the latter is extended until negotiation is successful. They may specify that conditions thus determined shall be retroactive to the termination date of the present agreement. They may agree to arbitrate issues unsettled by negotiations. They may include a *no-strike clause* to accompany a satisfactory grievance procedure, thus reducing the likelihood of stoppages during the term of the agreement. Many unions, however, are reluctant about agreeing to such restrictions lest their agreement make them liable for damages in the event of *quickie, outlaw* strikes. In 1962, in the Lucas Flour Company Case, the U.S. Supreme Court ruled that when parties negotiate a broad arbitration clause covering differences in contract interpretation, the union thereby gives up its right to strike on such issues.

Public policy has faced something of a dilemma with respect to what are generally described as *national emergency strikes,* believed to endanger public health and safety. They most frequently involve transportation.

Within the federal jurisdiction, the principle of *compulsory delay* may be imposed to insure a cooling-off period in which issues can be thoroughly discussed with the help of neutral conciliators. If a strike appears imminent and the President regards it as threatening public health or safety, he may

[10] Walter L. Daykin, "The Right to Strike," *Labor Law Journal*, Vol. 6, No. 6, June, 1955, pp. 361–74.

require a delay while he appoints a board of inquiry to investigate the issues and report its findings. When the board reports its finding of facts (recommendations for settlement are prohibited), if the dispute remains unresolved, the President may seek an injunction against either a strike or a lockout for a period not to exceed 80 days. During this period, if the dispute has not been settled, the National Labor Relations Board is instructed to have employees ballot on whether to accept each employer's "final offer." If the dispute is not settled in the course of this procedure, the President may present the matter to Congress for special action. Seizure of the plant, firm, or business by the President, frequently undertaken in the past, has been held by the Supreme Court to be improper because of the specific procedure provided by the Act.[11]

Serious questions have been raised about the equities in all such procedures. Where public agencies intervene to prevent a strike, the effect is to weaken the economic power of the union. In the absence of seizure—or even when the government takes over—interests of owners are protected. Earnings continue, while employees are forced to work under conditions they regard as unsatisfactory. The union is presented to the public as the trouble-maker.

Current proposals for changes in these rules generally seek to protect public and union interests and make strikes more costly to employers. Some proposals would confiscate profits during the period of public operation. Others would give the President a choice of actions including early investigation and mediation, seizure and operation, injunction to end the work stoppage, appointment of investigating boards, release of such board findings, and release of recommendations for settlement advanced by investigating boards.

Question may be raised, also, as to the reality of public hazard in some of these stoppages.[12]

2.2 Picketing. Picketing is regarded as legal as long as it involves no coercion, intimidation, or violence. In 1921, the Supreme Court ruled mass picketing illegal in the Truax case.[13] Later in the same year, in the American Steel Foundries or Tri-City case,[14] the Court upheld the legality of peaceful picketing but specified that the number of pickets should not exceed one at each entrance to the plant. Thereafter, the courts tended to distinguish peaceful picketing, in which no violence or intimidation occurred and in

---

[11] *Youngstown Sheet and Tube Co. v. Sawyer*, S. Ct. 52, ALC 616 (1952). See also Bernard Yabroff and Daniel P. Willis, Jr., "Federal Seizures in Labor Management Disputes, 1917–1952," *Monthly Labor Review*, Vol. 76, No. 6, June, 1953, pp. 611–16.

[12] See, in this connection, Irving Bernstein *et al.* eds, *Emergency Disputes and National Policy.* New York: Harper and Brothers, 1955, especially George H. Hildebrand, "An Economic Definition of the National Emergency Dispute," and Frank C. Pierson, "An Evaluation of the National Emergency Provisions," Chapter VIII, pp. 129–46; "Collective Bargaining in the Basic Steel Industry," U.S. Department of Labor, January, 1961.

[13] *Truax v. Corrigan*, 257 U.S. 312; 42 S. Ct. 124.

[14] *American Steel Foundries v. Tri-City Central Trades Council*, 257 U.S. 184; 42 S. Ct. 72.

which the number of pickets was limited (thus indicating the intention merely to persuade, rather than to threaten), from mass picketing, which was generally regarded as illegal and involving coercion and intimidation.

In several cases decided in 1940 and 1941,[15] the Court re-emphasized the right to picket as an expression of the freedom of speech guaranteed by the Constitution, but suggested that the right was conditioned by freedom from violence. If the picketing was "blended with violence," the constitutional immunity might be neutralized. On that basis, "chain picketing," in which pickets link arms or stay so close together that contact with a picket cannot be avoided by anyone crossing the picket line, is not peaceful.

On several types of picketing, current rules are somewhat fluid. They include *stranger picketing,* in which pickets are not employees of the employer being picketed, and organizational or *recognition picketing,* and that which may appear in jurisdictional disputes. Current interpretations forbid organizational picketing when a rival union has been lawfully recognized, when an election has been conducted within the preceding 12 months, or when the union has not filed petition for an election within 30 days. On the other hand, what is called *extortionate picketing,* in which an employer is called upon to pay for having the picketing cease, is banned.

·2.3   **The boycott.** The boycott has long been a highly controversial practice. Unions regard it as a natural means of extending their power and influence. Employers insist that it leads inevitably to the use of coercion.

The boycott is a combination to restrict patronage. If it combines only those directly involved in a dispute, it is *primary.* It becomes *secondary* when it enlists the cooperation of others, not parties to the dispute. Coercion may be used to get such cooperation.

The traditional statement on the legal status of the boycott holds that primary boycotts are legal and that secondary boycotts are usually illegal. Enforcement of this rule is complicated, however. While it is clear that federal rules forbid secondary boycotts to facilitate organization or to gain an advantage in inter-union competition or to force concessions from employers, prevention of such practices requires convincing evidence not always easily obtained. The National Labor Relations Board's General Counsel is charged with responsibility for prompt action on petitions alleging illegal boycotts.

2.4   Restriction of output. What about practices in which unions require employers to hire more employees than they need? Such featherbedding practices take many forms. They may set quotas or bogeys for their members. They may require *full crews* that employ more workers than are needed.

Public policy that has been expressed in legislation is confined to the federal level. In 1946, the Federal *Lea Act* sought to prevent the American Federation of Musicians from requiring broadcasting stations to employ extra, unneeded workers.

The act forbids demands for employment in excess of the numbers actually

---

[15] *American Federation of Labor v. Swing,* 312 U.S. 321; 61 S. Ct. 568 (1941); *Milk Wagon Drivers Union of Chicago, Local 753 v. Meadowmoor Dairies,* 312 U.S. 287; 61 S. Ct. 552 (1941); *Thornhill v. Alabama,* 310 U.S. 88; S. Ct. 736 (1940).

needed; it outlaws payment of funds to the union or its members in lieu of excess employment; it forbids more than one payment for such services as performed; and it prohibits payment for services that are not to be performed. It outlaws compulsion designed to force stations to refrain from broadcasting non-commercial, educational, and cultural programs or programs originating outside the United States. It prohibits compulsion to force stations to pay an *exaction* for the privilege of producing or using transcriptions and other reproductions. Fines and imprisonment are provided for violations.

The Taft-Hartley Act introduced a broader prohibition of exactions, defined as charges for work not performed or to be performed. Except for the most obvious and extreme demands of this type, however, public support for regulation is not evident. Many featherbedding rules are rather obviously intended to spread or make work and thus to protect the economic security of workers. Unorganized as well as organized employees vary their work pace to "make the job last." This is an area in which public policy appears to expect the parties to develop their own rules. A national commission reported in 1962, suggesting steps to be taken in reducing such restrictive practices in railway transportation. These proposals may suggest the outlines of broader public policy.

2.5 Employer practices. Public policy imposes numerous limitations on employer practices in dealing with unions. Most obvious are the prohibitions, already detailed, with respect to unfair labor practices introduced by the National Labor Relations Act and incorporated in similar state legislation. These rules preclude most of the activities that characterized early belligerent associations and their members, including blacklisting "troublemakers," discriminating among employees on the basis of union membership, using spies to undermine the unity of unions and the influence of their leaders, and giving support to friendly or dominated unions. Employers may not seek to influence employee and union action by threats or promises; they must not, for example, threaten to close the plant or move away if employees insist on collective bargaining. Similarly, they cannot promise to raise wages if employees vote against union representation.

Employers must not import strike-breakers across state lines (*Byrnes Act*, 1936). They may not move their plant to another location to "wrest bargaining concessions" from a union (*Sidele Fashions Inc.*, 133, NLRB 49, 1961). So far as freedom of speech is concerned, present rules permit an employer to discuss unions and organizing campaigns freely with employees, so long as such communications contain no threats or promises. The mere expression of employer opposition to such activity is not *per se* evidence of an unfair labor practice. Board rulings permit employers confronted with a demand for recognition to question employees about their union affiliations. Employees may be called together for a talk by an employer without granting similar time for a union meeting.

Under present rules, also, employers may petition for representation elections when faced with a demand for union recognition. Also, they can expect union consideration of their bargaining proposals. It is an unfair labor practice for unions to refuse to consider such proposals. Employers are assured of a considerable degree of responsibility on the part of unions as a result of the rule that unions may be sued for damages.

Employers may resort to the *lockout,* in which an employer or association of employers refuses employment to workers with whom they are in dispute. When unions developed the practice of striking individual firms in an association, employer association members sometimes retaliated by locking out employees in other member firms. This practice has, however, become less acceptable to employers, because unemployment benefits have been made available to locked out employees.

Employers must use the lockout with care, lest it be ruled an unfair labor practice. It is appropriate only in the face of a serious and immediate threat of a strike and when it cannot have, as a major impact, a disruptive effect on the collective action of employees.

Employer associations may provide *strike aid* for members as well as insurance against losses occasioned by strikes (see section 2.4, Chapter 13).

Many employers interpret the National Labor Relations Act, as amended, to bar any formal advisory association of employees. Employers have largely discontinued the earlier practice of encouraging such *shop committees.* This may well be a misinterpretation of public policy, for such committees and *representation plans* could be helpful as a supplement to union-management agreements. Such practice is widely used and favorably regarded by both employers and unions in several European nations.

2.6 Use of conciliation. Public policy proposes to minimize time lost on account of work stoppages, in part by preventing many of them, in part by reducing the duration of those that occur. Special provisions for national emergency disputes have been enacted. In addition, federal and state governments provide mediation and conciliation services. They are available to assist the parties in resolving differences. The two terms, *mediation* and *conciliation,* are used as though they were synonymous; some states describe their agencies as one, some prefer the other; at the federal level, the two are combined in the Federal Conciliation and Mediation Service. Conciliation is the process of reconciling differences. Mediation adds the possibility of somewhat more positive action, with the mediator advancing his own proposals for settlement. In practice, public representatives meet with the parties, help them obtain a clear view of their differences and communicate with each other, suggest ways in which the same issues have been resolved by others, and provide a neutral, helpful viewpoint.[16]

Conciliation facilities are available at the request of either or both parties. They may be asked to intervene by the President, a governor, or other public official.

---

[16] See Arthur S. Meyer, "Functions of the Mediator in Collective Bargaining," *Industrial and Labor Relations Review,* Vol. 13, No. 2, January, 1960, pp. 159–65.

Arbitration is another means of settling differences that is encouraged by current public policy. Conciliation services will suggest possible arbitrators. In some states, *compulsory arbitration* is required for disputes in public utilities and hospitals. Under such provisions, the parties have no choice in the matter. They must submit their unresolved differences to the decision of a neutral arbitrator.

In more common practice, employers and unions negotiate an arbitration clause. In such *voluntary arbitration,* the clause may provide that issues unsettled by negotiation will be submitted to arbitration. More frequently, it provides that arbitration will be used to settle issues arising out of day-to-day administration of their agreement. In such disputes, the decision of the arbitrator will be accepted as final and binding by both parties. Approximately ninety per cent of all agreements now include such a clause. In most of them it is limited to grievances that have been processed through several preliminary steps in a formal grievance procedure.

Arbitration tribunals may be individuals or panels. In panel arrangements, common practice provides that each party shall name one arbitrator and the two shall select a third, neutral chairman. In some industries, *permanent umpires* or *chairmen* have been selected by the parties to hear all their disputes. The more common practice selects an arbitrator for each dispute on an *ad hoc* basis.[17]

3.0 UNION DEMOCRACY

Public policy leaves no question about its intention to accept unions. It regards unions as here to stay. It recognizes their need for union security to an extent that may require union membership of individual employees if a majority of co-workers so desire. It proposes to prevent employer interference in the organization and administration of unions.

At the same time, however, public policy proposes that unions shall maintain a high level of accountability for their actions. Public policy no longer regards them as private fraternal societies; they are to be at least semipublic in character. Both federal and state legislation express these intentions. The federal Disclosure and Reporting Act of 1959 has been outlined. (See Chapter 11, Section 2.10.) One-third of the states—those with greatest industrial activity—have somewhat similar regulations.

3.1 Democratic control. Public policy proposes that unions shall be democratically controlled and responsive to the wishes of their members. They shall not be allowed to become the tools of gangster or racketeering or Communist elements. They shall not, on the other hand, act in an arbitrary and unreasonable manner in dealing with critics and dissidents among their

---

[17] See Clarence M. Updegraff and Whitley P. McCoy, *Arbitration of Labor Disputes,* 2nd ed., Washington, D.C.: Bureau of National Affairs, 1961; Maurice C. Trotta, *Labor Arbitration,* New York: Simmons-Boardman Publishing Corporation, 1961.

members.[18] Rules on trusteeships, elections, and penalties imposed in disciplinary actions evidence the intention to assure full freedom of members to express their opinions. State *union democracy* laws, although they vary in the details of rules, express the same general intention.[19]

Individual members as well as minority groups gain some protection, also, from common provisions for *decertification*. In the Federal jurisdiction and that of many states, union certification is available as evidence that the union has been selected as the choice of a majority of its membership. This process works both ways; the same agencies will accept petitions for decertification. If investigation discloses that a majority of employees in a bargaining unit no longer wishes to be represented by the bargaining agent, the union may not be recognized by the employer.

3.2   Political action. Public policy recognizes that both employers and employees are citizens. As such they have rights to express their opinions, to vote and to campaign for candidates of their choice. No public policy forbids an employer or a union party. Several attempts have been made to organize national labor parties.

On the other hand, public policy does oppose the use of organized business or union financial resources to influence elections. Both employer and union contributions to political parties or candidates are restricted. The Federal Corrupt Practices Act, as amended, makes contributions illegal in elections involving federal officials and members of Congress. Four states have similar legislation covering state elections.

4.0   SUMMARY

This is a chapter on current ground rules of public policy on labor relations. It outlines the general guiding principles to be observed by managers and unions in their relationships. Three major areas of policy have been identified, including the right and obligation to bargain collectively, approved practice in union-management competition and conflict, and assurance of union democracy.

A few general principles may be recognized from these rules and regulations. They can be outlined as follows:

1. Collective bargaining is to be encouraged as a means of self-regulation, in lieu of detailed public intervention and determination of the conditions of employment.

[18] See David J. Saposs, "Labor Racketeering: Evolution and Solutions," *Social Research*, Vol. 25, No. 3, Autumn, 1958, pp. 253–70.
[19] See Henry Mayer, "Public Regulation of Internal Union Affairs," *Labor Law Journal*, Vol. 10, No. 2, February, 1959, pp. 87–99; Chester A. Morgan, "State Regulation of Internal Union Affairs," *ibid.*, Vol. 6, No. 4, April, 1955, pp. 226–33; "State Laws on Rights of Members in Internal Union Affairs," *Monthly Labor Review*, Vol. 81, No. 8, August, 1958, pp. 871–77; George Strauss, "Control by the Membership in Building Trade Unions," *American Journal of Sociology*, Vol. 61, No. 4, May, 1956, pp. 527–35.

2. As organizations protected against employer attack by public intervention, unions are to maintain a high level of internal democracy.
3. In all collective bargaining relationships, public policy will insist that both parties act in a manner consistent with the usual rules of law and order.
4. Public intervention will be used to insure the strength of both parties and their ability to compete with each other in an approximate balance of power.
5. Public intervention will be used to restrict and reduce conflict that involves hazards to public health and safety and that occasions a heavy waste of human or other resources.
6. Even though a broad area of self-determination may encourage some inefficiencies, they are preferable to more extensive regulation. Values other than efficiency and profit and productivity deserve high priorities in the public policy of democracies.[20]

Chapter 13 turns to the day-to-day practice of management through collective bargaining. It directs attention to usual means of negotiating and administering collective agreements.

SELECTED SUPPLEMENTARY READINGS

"Almost Unbelievable," New York (99 University Place): Textile Workers Union of America, 1961.

Bradley, Philip D., ed., *The Public Stake in Union Power.* Charlottesville, Va.: University of Virginia Press, 1959.

"The Case for the Union Shop," Industrial Union Department, AFL-CIO, *Publication No. 11,* about 1959.

Goldberg, Arthur J. and Lambert H. Miller, "Unions and the Anti-trust Laws," *Labor Law Journal,* Vol. 7, No. 3, pp. 178–92, March, 1956.

Hildebrand, George H., "Collective Bargaining and the Post-War Inflation," *Reprint No. 93,* Los Angeles: University of California Institute of Industrial Relations, 1960.

Kerr, Clark, "Unions and Union Leaders of Their Own Choosing," *Reprint No. 109,* Los Angeles: University of California Institute of Industrial Relations, 1958.

Mason, Edward S., "Labor Monopoly and All That," *Proceedings,* New York: Industrial Relations Research Association, December 28–30, 1955, pp. 188ff. (Note also the discussion of the paper.)

Meyers, Frederic, "Price Theory and Union Monopoly," *Industrial and Labor Relations Review,* Vol. 12, No. 3, pp. 434–45, April, 1959.

Nelson, Wallace B., "Management Prerogatives and the Work Rules Controversy," *Labor Law Journal,* Vol. 11, No. 11, pp. 987–1104, November, 1960.

"Requirements for Electing Union Officers," Washington, D.C.: Bureau of Labor-Management Relations, United States Department of Labor, 1960.

Selekman, B. M., "Trade Unions—Romance and Reality," *Harvard Business Review,* Vol. 36, No. 3, pp. 76–90, May-June 1958.

[20] See in this connection, Clark Kerr, "An Effective and Democratic Organization of the Economy," Chapter 6, in *Goals for Americans,* Englewood Cliffs, N.J.: Prentice-Hall, Inc., 1960, pp. 149–62.

"A Taft-Hartley Case Study," Industrial Union Department, AFL-CIO, undated but about 1959.

Tyler, Gus, "A New Philosophy for Labor," *Occasional Paper,* New York (60 East 42nd St.): Fund for the Republic, 1959.

SHORT CASE PROBLEM 12.1

The Troublemaker

Your firm has concluded agreements with a plant-wide local of a national union for more than ten years. Although negotiations have been strenuous and sharp, the organization has done an excellent job of contract administration among its members. Once an agreement was signed, union officials saw to it that members lived up to its terms. The agreement includes a union-shop clause.

Recently, a committee of local union officials called on you for cooperation. One employee has given them a great deal of trouble. He pays his dues, but he refuses to join in supporting any other union activities. He consistently refuses to contribute when the union "passes the hat" for any purpose. He attends union meetings, where he argues at length against every proposal advanced by union officers. He is a troublemaker, and appears to enjoy creating friction, jealousy, and discontent. He constantly criticizes the employer as well as union officers. He has frequently charged that the union did not get a good "deal" in negotiations and suggested that union officers "sold out" to the employer.

The union committee wants your help in getting rid of this troublemaker. They have heard that he can't be discharged for his actions, but they suggest that you arrange his work assignments in such a way that he will quit. They say something is almost sure to happen to him if he doesn't get out.

Problem: What's your answer to the committee?

SHORT CASE PROBLEM 12.2

Organization of Organizers

Business Week (January 14, 1961) reported on the expanding organization of union organizers in part as follows:

> Businessmen were treated this week to the sight of a union president trying to decide whether to recognize a union. The president was David Dubinsky, head of the 450,000-member International Ladies' Garment Workers' Union, a vice-president of AFL-CIO, and a veteran fighter for labor and liberal causes. The union was formed by his ILGWU organizers.
>
> *Growing Trend*—Dubinsky's dilemma is one that all international union presidents are afraid they may have to face. As unions become institutionalized, organizers see themselves more and more as employees as well as crusaders. They see union higher-ups as management. And they believe what they preach to unorganized workers: employees need a union to represent them in dealing with management.
>
> Dubinsky ignored an offer by the organizers' union to submit to a check of its membership cards and attempted—unsuccessfully—to delay a National Labor Relations Board hearing scheduled for next week. His apparent reluctance to recognize the union is based, at least in part, on typical management reactions.
>
> For company and union management alike, union pressure for higher wages restricts the amount of money that can be spent on other things. In the union's case, this might be a leaflet campaign or a strike fund. Also, grievance procedures and work rules limit both company and union officials in their freedom to run their own show.

Special Problems—These familiar motives underlie much of the historic opposition to organizers' unions. Other objections, however, stem from labor's special nature.

In the traditional labor view, an organizer is not just a hired hand; he is a participant in a missionary cause whose relation to the cause would be destroyed if he were placed too firmly in an employee's slot. Usually he is a member of the union he serves, with a vote in its decisions and the opportunity to rise politically in its ranks. His influence on other members makes him a valuable ally—or dangerous opponent—of the union administration.

Problem: 1. Do you conclude that such organization and collective bargaining as is here proposed is consistent with current rules designed to implement public policy? What are your reasons for this conclusion?

2. In your opinion would an international union of union organizers, combining the locals (made up of organizers within each national or international union) be consistent with public policy? Your reasons?

SHORT CASE PROBLEM 12.3

Collective Bargaining for Public Employees

Public officials, including personnel managers in federal, state, and local agencies, have become increasingly involved in discussions of union membership and collective bargaining for public employees. In 1959, a national committee studied the special problems involved in such employer-union relationships in an attempt to develop an acceptable policy for public agencies. The subject has featured the programs of numerous conferences in which representatives of such agencies reported on growing pressures, compared experience, and exchanged opinions. The advance program announcement for one such conference in 1961 provided the following short description of the issue:

> Current public policy generally prevents public employees from "full" collective bargaining. While some may belong to unions and negotiate with respect to their working conditions, they generally have no formal collective agreements and cannot strike to enforce their demands. Often they can belong only to unaffiliated unions.
>
> Many union spokesmen regard this limitation as imposing second-class citizenship on public employees. They argue that all employees must have the right to strike. They also insist that there is no good reason why public employees should not negotiate collective agreements just as private employees do. Firemen and policemen, as well as most other civil service employees, in this viewpoint, are presently the objects of undeserved discrimination.

Problem: Take a position on this question: Should public employees be permitted to negotiate collective agreements and have the right to strike to enforce their demands? Prepare the argument you will make if called upon to defend your position, indicating clearly the assumptions and theory that guide you in resolving the issue.

13. Negotiation and Administration

Not every manager is directly and actively engaged in collective bargaining, but every manager's responsibilities are influenced by such bilateral policy-making. What the manager says and does and many of the problems that confront him show the impact and imprint of union policy and practice as well as related public policy, discussed in immediately preceding chapters.

The practice of labor relations develops patterns of manager and employee behavior that are influential in firms that have no unions of employees and that do not engage in collective bargaining. Similarly, collective bargaining attitudes and behavior developed in relationships with production workers are simulated in the management of white-collar, clerical, and other indirect workers. The practice of collective bargaining results in points of view and attitudes on the part of managers, supervisors, and employees that extend all through the relationships of employment. At the same time, the political influence of both managers and unions helps in developing public policy that affects all managers.

The collective bargaining process represents an activity with impressive dimensions. On the average, almost 400 collective bargaining agreements are signed, sealed, and delivered each working day—more than 100,000 of them each year. Negotiation is somewhat seasonal, with heavy concentrations in the spring and fall. Each of the resulting agreements outlines a balancing of promises which one or more employers and the unions of their employees accept as defining a satisfactory basis for their collaboration.

This well-established practice of negotiating employment conditions and relationships is one of the most impressive creations of the whole process of industrialization. Its misfires and flameouts, evidenced in the average of some 3,000 strikes per year, seem somewhat less impressive or discouraging in this perspective.

This chapter turns attention to the usual, day-to-day practice of managing with and through collective bargaining. It notes the impact of union and public policy on the general manpower policy of firms and agencies and on their practice of management. The chapter emphasizes three phases of collective bargaining. Section 1 outlines practice and trends in negotiation. Section 2 turns to practices and trends in contract administration. A third section gives brief attention to an extension of collective bargaining in what may be regarded as experiments with union-management cooperation.

1.0 NEGOTIATION

The *collective agreement* or *labor contract* is the charter on which employers and unions agree. It is a written statement of terms mutually accepted as defining the relationships and working conditions to be maintained in the bargaining unit. It usually consists of a preamble, a series of clauses, and perhaps one or more appendices that list job classifications, wage rates, and other relevant details. Development of a satisfactory and workable agreement is a complicated and delicate assignment for the representatives of both employers and employees. Staff representatives and negotiators may have to study past relationships, look into the experience of other firms, agencies, or industries, and forecast probable developments in the national or international economy to prepare themselves for negotiations.

1.1 Form and substance. *Negotiation* is the process which creates the *collective agreement*. Negotiation may be brief if there are few differences to be reconciled. It may, on the other hand, extend over a period of weeks or months. The negotiating process is essentially one of advancing proposals, discussing them, receiving counterproposals, and resolving differences. The process may involve elements of trading as concessions are granted by each of the parties.

Negotiations may begin by an exchange of letters between the parties. Or one party may announce the intention to seek certain changes, allowing the announcement to become news. Negotiations continue until differences are resolved or until the parties find that they cannot arrive at a satisfactory agreement without assistance. Conciliation and mediation services may help in settling their differences. Certain unsettled issues may be submitted to arbitration. If agreement is not achieved in negotiations, employees may strike, in which case settlement of the strike involves further negotiation. They may, on the other hand, continue working without an agreement while negotiation goes on.

In essence, the negotiating process indicates that managers and union representatives who negotiate in good faith accept the necessity for compromise with respect to attainment of their personal and organizational goals. They appreciate the advantages of accommodation and recognize the necessity for finding a basis for working together. They identify some mutual goals that justify a higher priority than some of their individual objectives. Managers have adopted what Selznick describes as a process of *cooptation,* which he defines as "absorbing new elements into the leadership or policy-determining structure of an organization as a means of averting threats to its stability or existence."[1] To some degree, union members may be said to have accepted a similar principle as representatives of employers influence the programs of their unions.

Negotiators include designated representatives of management and union officials representing the bargaining agent of employees. If question has been raised as to the appropriate bargaining unit, federal or state agencies may have made a determination on this point. If question has been raised about the right of the union to represent employees, it may have been *certified* as the bargaining agent by the same agencies. Management may be represented by its *labor relations director* or, if the firm bargains through an employer association, by specialists from that organization. The union may be represented by its *business agent,* or by a *bargaining committee* of members, perhaps assisted or led by one or more representatives of the international union.

Either or both of the parties may also be represented by attorneys. Such practice appears to be most common when company or union expects the resulting agreement to be rigidly interpreted. Some representatives of both employers and unions are critical of this practice, insisting that attorneys tend to introduce undesirable formality and confusing legal expressions. If attorneys have little experience in labor relations, this result is to be expected. On the other hand, many labor relations directors hold law degrees, and attorneys experienced in labor relations may act as catalysts, absorbing some of the heat and facilitating calm consideration of difficult issues.

Some bargaining is industry wide. In such practice, employers may be represented by a *bargaining committee,* selected by individual firms and authorized to conclude an agreement for them. When bargaining is restricted to a single locality, employers may be represented by an employer association, such as a General Contractors' Association. For the union, uniformity in local or regional agreements may be achieved by including representatives of the national organization or by requiring that a national officer countersign each local agreement.

Agreements are constantly changing. Walter Reuther, president of the Automobile Workers, has, for this reason, described collective agreements as *living documents.* They change as ideas, ideals, goals, and policies are modified. Thus there cannot be a permanently perfect agreement—a model that

[1] Philip Selznick, "Foundations of the Theory of Organization," *American Sociological Review,* Vol. 13, February, 1948, pp. 34ff.

will remain exemplary. Moreover, change requires some flexibility, some give in day-to-day application.

Practice in negotiations varies widely and is heavily influenced by the attitudes with which the parties approach bargaining. Most of the negotiating sessions that attract wide public attention evidence inflexible positions taken by one or both parties, with threats of strikes and lockouts, night-long sessions, and the intervention of federal and state conciliation officers. Many negotiating sessions, however, are short and unspectacular. When both parties actively seek agreement, and especially when they have enjoyed reasonably satisfactory contractual arrangements for some time, modifications may be minor and quickly accepted. In a few negotiations, it appears clearly that one party does not actually seek agreement, that for political or other reasons agreement is avoided. Such an objective has been charged against unions that have allowed Communists to gain control.

Much depends on the experience of the parties in contract administration. In one pattern, firms follow a policy of "arms-length" negotiation and administration. They resist concessions and insist on the letter of the agreement in subsequent day-to-day applications. Such an attitude tends to prolong negotiations, since union representatives conclude that they must negotiate minute details.

Today's contracts are much longer and more detailed than those of ten or twenty years ago. In part, their expansion reflects the wider range of subjects presently negotiated. In part, it results from a tendency to be much more specific and detailed in each provision. Although both managers and union representatives frequently deplore this trend, it persists and becomes increasingly evident.

1.2   Usual clauses. So far as public policy is concerned, the parties may negotiate agreement on whatever subjects or issues seem to them to be important, except that they may not agree to cooperate in some unlawful act. The subjects covered in individual agreements vary; some firms or unions are not concerned about issues that others emphasize.

Many agreements begin with a general policy statement to indicate the spirit in which the parties undertake their cooperation and to guide them and others in the interpretation of specific clauses. They may provide a harmony clause specifying the responsibilities of each party in carrying out the terms of the agreement.

In terms of broad subject areas, the most common clauses in current agreements are of nine types, as follows:

1.21   Wages and salaries. Clauses describe methods of payment, hourly rates, monthly or annual salaries, incentive pay based on production, bonuses, commissions, and other special variations of compensation. Where provisions cover large numbers of occupations or wage classes, the printed or mimeographed agreement usually includes a detailed list of rates or ranges of rates. The clause may specify automatic increases at periodic intervals. It may provide for a system of *job evaluation* to determine relationships among job rates, or *escalator* provisions that increase wages with advances in living costs, or *improvement factor* or productivity increases. Questions about *portal-to-portal pay, down time* (when equipment fails or materials are not available), *call-in time* (when employees are called in for only a few hours), *call-back time* (when they are called back after their shift ends), *learner rates,* and other such details are usually covered in this section of the agreement.

1.22 Hours of work. Clauses outline regular working hours, various shift arrangements, time off for meals, and provisions for *overtime pay.* They indicate how many and what *holidays* are to be observed, under what circumstances employees may be asked to work on holidays, what is to be done when holidays fall on Saturdays or Sundays, and distinctions, if any, as to the holiday privileges of various occupational groups. They specify *vacations* and may outline approved bases for *leaves of absence.*

1.23 Employee benefits and services. These are the so-called *fringes* and may include a wide range of benefits, services, and welfare programs, such as pensions, health insurance and welfare plans, hospitalization, sickness and disability benefits, and many others (See Chapter 22).

1.24 Union security. Clauses stipulate the type of recognition to be accorded the union. As already noted, the most common provision is the *union shop. Maintenance of membership* or the *agency shop* are other common provisions. The *check-off* may be authorized. The contract may permit or require use of the *union label* on products or the wearing of union buttons. It may outline the practice in providing *union stewards* and the freedom with which union officials will be permitted access to the plant.

1.25 Management security. Clauses define the area within which managers have exclusive jurisdiction. As noted in Chapter 12, they are of two principal types, one reserving for management all subjects not specifically covered in the contract, the other naming aspects in which management's rights are not contested.

1.26 Discipline. From the individual employee's standpoint, clauses that protect him from arbitrary disciplinary action may be among the most important in the entire agreement. Such clauses usually provide that management shall establish shop rules and have the right to discipline employees for *just cause.* They may actually list the recognized causes for disciplinary action, mentioning insubordination, intoxication, dishonesty, violation of shop or company rules, fighting, horseplay, and others. They may specify the nature of punishment, providing for fines, enforced layoff, loss of seniority, transfer, and discharge.

1.27 Grievances. The usual grievance clause begins with a definition, indicating what may be regarded as grievances. A grievance is commonly defined as a written complaint filed by an employee and claiming unfair treatment. Most grievances arise out of the interpretation or application of the contract. Clauses prescribe the procedure to be followed in disposing of such grievances. (See section 3.36, Chapter 10.)

No-strike clauses may be incorporated as an exchange for the formal grievance procedure and terminal arbitration. Their usual provisions are illustrated by the following example:

> *No-strike agreement.* At no time, during the full term of this Agreement, shall the Union or any of its members authorize or engage in any strike, walk-out or other type of work stoppage. At no time, during such terms, shall the Employer lockout any of its Employees.

1.28 Promotion, layoff, recall, transfer. The usual clause defines the bases for actions of this type. This section may include a detailed outline of the *seniority system.* It may describe preferences in the assignment of jobs, the selection of vacation periods, the choice of shifts, and other similar privileges. These clauses establish, also, the machinery to be used in day-to-day application of the seniority principle, as, for example, in *posting* and *bidding* on job openings, or in some other appropriate technique. Provision may be made to grant *superseniority* to union officers, stewards, and members of grievance committees or to permit *synthetic* seniority, in which employees on leave continue to accumulate seniority to be used after their return.

1.29 Contract term or duration. Most agreements in this country are for one year. Recent practice, however, has tended to lengthen the term. Clauses may permit one or more *reopenings* on wages only, thus allowing the parties to negotiate changes in wages without disturbing other contract provisions.

Many agreements require advance notice of intentions to propose changes, so that both parties may have an opportunity to study and plan for discussions. Some agreements provide that issues not settled through negotiation by the time of the termination date shall be submitted to arbitration. Others permit extensions of the current agreement while negotiations are in process.

Both the range of subjects covered by these clauses and the detail with which each subject is presented have tended to increase. Spokesmen for employers and managers have frequently deplored the inclusion of areas in which they feel managers should have a free hand. Daykin found eight principal areas in which modern grievance clauses, for example, have substituted bilateral decision-making for traditional management determination. He lists provisions defining the rights reserved to management, assigning the working force, allocating overtime, making production changes, determining rates of pay, selecting and discharging, making shop rules, and determining relative skills.[2] Derber and others analyzed the range of negotiation in 51 firms to note what managerial functions were subject to the negotiating process. Their conclusions on this question are summarized in Table 13.1.

Despite managerial pessimism, it is possible that the scope of bargaining may narrow in the years ahead. If managers improve their specialized expertness, if they achieve something approximating professional competence, unions and their members may be willing to grant a larger sphere for exclusive,

[2] Walter L. Daykin, "Arbitrators' Determination of Management's Right to Manage," *Research Series No. 6,* Bureau of Labor and Management, University of Iowa, 1954.

**Table 13.1 Number of Establishments in Which Selected Managerial Functions
Were Subject to Negotiations with the Union.†**

(*N* = 51)

Item	No. of Estab-lishments	Per Cent
1. Promotion to non-supervisory position	42	82.4
2. Promotion to supervisory position	1	1.9
3. Distribution of overtime	47	92.2
4. Number of employees on a job or machine	23	45.1
5. Contracting work out	9	17.6
6. Scheduling of operations	5	9.8
7. Layout of equipment	0	0.0
8. Plant location or relocation	1	1.9
9. Transfer of employees within plant	47	92.2
10. Customer relations and/or services	0	0.0
11. Job content	36	70.5
12. Level of work performance	30	58.8
13. Selection of new employees	4	7.8
14. Job-evaluation program	12	23.5
15. Source of materials used	0	0.0
16. Assignment of new employees	23	45.1
17. Product prices	0	0.0
18. Physical examinations	4	7.8
19. Accounting practices	1	1.9
20. Number of shifts	10	19.6

† From Milton Derber, W. Ellison Chalmers, and Ross Stagner, "Collective Bargaining and Management Functions, An Empirical Study," *Journal of Business,* Vol. 31, No. 2, April, 1958, pp. 107–20.

unilateral decision-making by management. Management can, as Steele has noted, gain greater freedom of action if it can justify such a grant of authority.[3]

1.3 Preparation for negotiations. In some earlier practice, representatives of the parties entered the bargaining process with little advance preparation. Union spokesmen were the moving party; they made their proposals for change. Employer representatives regarded their function as essentially one of resistance and opposition. They made few plans because they did not know what the union would propose. This type of employer negotiation has been described as "negative" or "No! No!" bargaining.

Although the extent of advance preparation by both managers and unions differs, many of them spend months getting ready for negotiations. Unions study experience with existing agreements in the industry, noting points on which they desire changes. They may investigate the financial condition of firms in the industry as well as their economic prospects. They note established practices in related industries that might be brought into their agreement. They may poll their membership to discover what changes are desired.

[3] H. E. Steele, "Earned Freedom for Management," *Advanced Management,* Vol. 22, No. 11, November, 1957, pp. 13–18.

Many managements undertake a similar preparation for the negotiating process. They seek information on the nature of settlements made by other employers in the same or related industries. They study the operation of the present agreement to discover sections in which they desire changes. They forecast business prospects and secure information on the labor markets in which they must shop. They try to anticipate union demands and have at hand the arguments they may use in opposition to demands they regard as unreasonable.

General Foods Corporation provides an example. "Preparation for negotiations," their brochure explains, "is a continuous, year-round process." The General Foods program begins in the first month of an annual agreement. Reports from operating divisions suggest "bugs" in the new agreement and interpretations that appear necessary for its application. Each month, experience is reviewed to provide a basis for future negotiations. In the months just preceding negotiations, management's proposals are organized and supporting information is prepared.[4]

Both management and union need facts as well as philosophy and policy to guide them in actual negotiations. Representatives know the basic policies of the organization they represent. They should be well informed on current practice in the industry and locality and on recent changes in practice. Pertinent legislative action and administrative rulings by such agencies as the National Labor Relations Board, the Wage and Hour Administration, and related state and local agencies may be relevant. Both parties may require extensive statistical and other information with respect to their experience and that of other firms and unions. Research units in private firms, governmental agencies, and unions may undertake studies to secure such information and to arrange for its presentation in convenient form.

As experience in collective bargaining has accumulated, both employers and unions have recognized the need for dependable data. The National Labor Relations Board has ruled that employers must furnish detailed facts on wages and earnings if the union asks for such data.[5] Barkin has outlined the union's needs for financial information as including facts on profits before and after taxes; the distribution of firm income; prospective business, prices, and profits; and present and future break-even points.[6]

Bargaining is facilitated when the parties have clearly in mind the limits within which they can make concessions. On the basis of preparatory discussions in both firms and unions, representatives are informed on the priorities to be given various proposals and the ranges within which concessions may be made. They know what their principals want them to do and the extent to which they can go in accepting the other party's proposals. In some

---

[4] See also "How One Company Prepares for Collective Bargaining: A Step-by-Step Guide," *Personnel*, Vol. 33, No. 1, July, 1956, pp. 58–71.

[5] See Walter L. Daykin, "Furnishing Wage Data for Bargaining," *Labor Law Journal*, Vol. 4, No. 6, June, 1953, pp. 417–22.

[6] Solomon Barkin, "Financial Statements in Collective Bargaining," *New York Certified Public Accountant*, July, 1953, pp. 439–46.

negotiations, firms prepare *bargaining books* as documented manuals for the use of negotiations.[7]

1.4 Positive bargaining. Most managers have now concluded that collective bargaining is here to stay and have modified their attitudes and participation to correspond with this conclusion. Many managers no longer wait to hear the union's proposals before deciding what to discuss. They have taken a cue from union tactics and announced their own positive objectives well in advance of negotiations. They have followed such announcements with explanatory and educational campaigns designed to encourage an understanding of management's views and goals by rank and file employees and by the public.

Some employer attempts at such *positive* bargaining have consisted of demands designed for trading. They have asked for concessions they did not expect to get but hoped could be traded for the most objectionable union proposals. Others have been quite serious in their demands.

General Electric and Westinghouse have received wide publicity for announcing in advance their proposals and concessions and insisting that they would take a strike rather than accept less or give more. In actual negotiations, some flexibility has appeared, but the basic management position has been maintained.

This general trend toward positive bargaining is in itself an evidence of maturity. Negotiation is a two-sided process. Management should use the process to encourage changes it sees as necessary. If its position is sound, there is no reason why it should not take as much initiative as unions.

1.5 Work rules issues. Employer positive bargaining has frequently demanded relaxation of work rules that, in management's opinion, involve restriction of output. As a result, although negotiation of work rules is not at all new, it has attained a new prominence in recent years. Some discussions appear to suggest that unions have only recently sought to participate in defining the amount of work to be done in a job. It should be clear that unions have negotiated work rules on the railroads, in printing, and in other industries for a much longer period.

Rapid technological change—automation—has occasioned great concern about job security among the members of many unions. They regard some negotiated rules that limit work as highly important in protecting their jobs. To employers, these same provisions may appear as *featherbedding* and major interferences with efficiency and productivity.

Some unions have sought to extend such protection by contract clauses that limit the right of management to contract out work that could be done within the firm. At the same time, many firms and industries have felt a growing challenge from both foreign and domestic competition. The steel industry has made much of the fact that European as well as Japanese steel is available at prices that make it attractive. Railroads have lost much of their business to trucking.

[7] See Zoe Campbell, "The Use of Bargaining Books in Negotiations," *Management Record,* Vol. 19, No. 4, April, 1957, pp. 118ff.

Alert managers have found ways to negotiate changes in work rules. They have been successful when they approached these issues with understanding. Fears about job security can be reduced by appropriate *retraining programs* and agreements that give displaced workers first chance at new jobs created in the process of technological change. More adequate and extensive unemployment insurance benefits can assist workers in finding suitable jobs. In longshoring, meatpacking, and other difficult and controversial situations, negotiation has developed acceptable change. Formation of a national committee to study such problems on the railroads was a step in this direction. In 1961, American Motors and the United Auto Workers developed a formula for *profit-sharing* as a justification for relaxed work rules. Numerous examples of what Barkin describes as constructive bargaining relationships suggest that work rules issues can be solved by negotiation.[8]

1.6 Public representation. The Kaiser Steel Corporation and the United Steel Workers initiated a modification in bargaining that may achieve wider acceptance and influence collective bargaining in the future. In January, 1961, they announced an agreement to include three public representatives in their bargaining sessions. The innovation followed a pattern established in 1959 as part of the settlement in a three-month strike. The parties had agreed at that time to create a nine-member committee to work out long-range plans for sharing the results of company operations equitably with stockholders, employees, and the public.

The new plan provides that the parties, including public members, will meet regularly to discuss such problems as arise. They will not confine their participation to bargaining sessions. On the other hand, in the bargaining process, when management and union fail to agree, public members may study their differences, make reports and recommendations to the parties, and subsequently release such reports to the public.

1.7 Hazards in winning. Whether the final agreement emerges from negotiating sessions or involves a work stoppage, the side that gets most of its proposals assumes that it has won. Some victories may be hazardous. In so far as they result from misrepresentation, manipulation, or crude economic force, they may generate a process of retaliation that effectively prevents efficient collaboration. The union or management that has lost under such circumstances may begin immediately to strengthen its forces to prepare for future negotiations and to use every opportunity to undermine its opponent. Winning on any such basis may be an effective means of losing in the longer run. This retaliatory process is frequently evident. A firm or a union puts across a big deal and wins a widely publicized struggle. At the same time, it creates a continuing resistance to effective cooperation and a forceful incentive for the other party to prepare for an even more bitter struggle in the not-too-distant future.

[8] See Solomon Barkin, "Work Rules: A Phase of Collective Bargaining," *Labor Law Journal*, Vol. 12, No. 5, May, 1961, pp. 375–79; Walter L. Daykin, "Work Rules in Industry," *Ibid.*, pp. 380–86; Max Kossoris, "Working Rules in West Coast Longshoring," *Monthly Labor Review*, Vol. 84, No. 1, January, 1961, pp. 1–10.

2.0 CONTRACT ADMINISTRATION

Collective agreements must be administered. As in the case of legislation, their administration—the manner in which they are applied and
interpreted—may have more far-reaching effects on employment relationships than the detailed wording of the agreements. No agreement can reflect
perfect foresight with respect to the problems to be encountered. Questions
of meaning and intent will almost certainly arise. Contract administration
must answer these questions and thus supply essential interpretations.

Making an agreement work is less spectacular than negotiating such an
agreement. The process is, however, difficult and complicated. Numerous
sharp differences of opinion may appear, and some may become matters of
dispute.

Contract administration involves the application, interpretation, and enforcement of the terms to which the parties have agreed. Initiative must
be taken, in the administrative process, by both managers and union officials.
The union may assign responsibilities for administration to shop stewards,
local presidents or business agents, and officials of its national union. Management may delegate such responsibilities to foremen and supervisors, plant
managers, and its labor relations division.

After even the most careful negotiation, a contract requires thoughtful,
understanding administration. In-plant *communications* play an important
part. *Interpretation* is a continuing process. Oral and written interpretation
may be supplemented by a formal grievance process, in which terminal,
voluntary arbitration provides final interpretations. Meanwhile, those who
administer agreements may have to agree on amendments and revisions.

2.1 Communication and interpretation. Evidence of the importance of
communication and interpretation is provided by the study of contract administration by Derber, Chalmers, and Stagner. They analyzed contracts and
practices in 48 firms and found marked deviations in actual practice from the
terms of applicable agreements. Reported practice was consistent on union
security in 83 per cent, on grievance time limits in 81 per cent, on use of
the grievance steps in 68 per cent, on arbitration and writing up grievances
in 64 per cent, and on time study in 56 per cent. On the other hand, practice
was consistent on the scope of grievance procedure in only 48 per cent, on
safety and rule-setting in only 45 per cent, on technological change in only
35 per cent; on the use of seniority in layoffs in only 32 per cent, and on
discharge for inefficiency in only 12 per cent.[9]

Administration is facilitated by continuing communications that inform
all representatives of management as well as employees and union agents
of developments in both negotiating and administrative processes. In some
practice, negotiation is conducted by or in the presence of committees representing both management and the union. Committee members can and do
spread the word as to the nature of issues and the meaning of solutions

[9] Milton Derber, W. E. Chalmers, and Ross Stagner, "The Labor Contract: Provision and Practice," *Personnel,* Vol. 34, No. 4, January-February, 1958, pp. 19–30.

developed in negotiations. Negotiations in the West Coast pulp and paper industry, for example, provide a "goldfish bowl" procedure, in which 17 employer and 17 union representatives negotiate in a theater that permits as many as 200 management and union representatives to watch the process.

Following negotiations, oral and written communications can provide information on interpretations of various clauses of the agreement. Company and union may have agreed that a provision on vacation pay has a specific meaning. Settlement of a grievance may have given additional meaning to the disciplinary clause. All foremen and shop stewards can be informed of such interpretations.

The process of interpretation assumes added importance because the language of collective agreements is notoriously difficult. Studies of the reading ease of collective agreements have found them to be written at difficult or very difficult levels, far above the usual reading habits of those who must interpret them in day-to-day practice.[10]

2.2 Grievances. The grievance procedure provides much of the interpretation in current practice. Parties may agree to clauses which they recognize as having obscure meaning. They may conclude that specific interpretation can best be accomplished when and if the problem appears and in terms of the situation in which it arises. Grievance clauses provide a means for securing interpretations. Management may then go ahead, applying its interpretation of the contract, subject to the protest and grievance of employees who regard this application as unreasonable. An arbitrator may give meaning to the contract in his decision and award, as the final stage in the grievance procedure.

Numbers of such arbitration awards are not known. In 1959, the American Arbitration Association docketed 2,816 cases, some of which involved several grievances. In fiscal 1959, the Federal Mediation and Conciliation Service received 2,294 requests for appointment of panels or arbitrators. One estimate places the total number of cases decided in this manner at 20,000 per year.[11] Several types of issues arise frequently, of which the most important are those involving disciplinary action, the application of seniority provisions, the application of job and pay classfications, setting production standards and work rules.

The importance of arbitration in interpreting agreements is likely to increase as a result of court decisions in 1960. The United States Supreme Court held that where contracts include a general arbitration clause, disputes must be arbitrated unless their subject is specifically excluded from coverage.[12] Further, the usual arbitrator's decision must be accepted as final and

---

[10] See Jeanne Lauer and Donald G. Paterson, "Readability of Union Contracts," *Personnel*, Vol. 28, No. 1, July, 1951, pp. 3–6; Joseph Tiffin and Francis X. Walsh, "Readability of Union-Management Agreements," *Personnel Psychology*, Vol. 4, No. 4, Winter, 1951, pp. 327–37.

[11] Paul M. Herzog and Morris Stone, "Voluntary Labour Arbitration in the United States," *International Labour Review*, Vol. 82, No. 4, October, 1960, pp. 302ff.

[12] *Steelworkers v. American Manufacturing Company*, 363 U.S. 564; 80 S. Ct. 1343 (1960); *Steelworkers v. Warrior and Gulf Navigation Company*, 363 U.S. 569; 80 S.

binding, and courts may not overrule it simply because they differ in their interpretation of the agreement. These decisions may encourage management to file its grievances as a means of requiring an outside review of contract interpretations, especially in work-rule cases. In the past, management has not generally filed grievances, preferring to act and then allow employees to protest if they regard the action as unreasonable.

2.3 Amendment and revision. Changes may be made in the agreement during its stated term. Some agreements plan for these changes by providing a *reopening clause* which allows either party to seek specified changes—most frequently in wages—one or more times during the term of the agreement. In any case, since the agreement involves only the two parties, they can change any provision any time by mutual agreement.

Both parties may note such changes as they wish to propose when a new agreement is negotiated. Suggestions for such changes arise from several sources. Revisions found necessary to make the present agreement satisfactory are one such source. Arbitration awards are another. Unsettled issues— questions on which the parties remain sharply divided—represent a further indication of desirable change. Grievances may have been adjusted on a temporary basis by a grievance committee or by joint action of the management and a union or by an outside arbitrator. All such experience builds a record that is useful in future negotiation. Thus, the agreement grows as the parties work together. This close relationship of contract administration to changes argues strongly for practice in which those who administer agreements shall play an important part in negotiations.

2.4 Administrative associations. In some employer associations, their representatives play the major role in contract administration. Each member may be entitled to the services of specialized staff in interpreting the agreement and settling disputes that arise. All members may agree, for their mutual protection, that disputed provisions will be interpreted only by association staff or by arbitration in which the association presents the employer case.

Such administrative associations may also provide assistance in strikes and lockouts. They may encourage employer *strike-aid plans* which have appeared in several industries, including airlines (since 1958), newspapers (since 1950), railroads (since 1959), and Hawaiian sugar production (since 1956). It may be noted that these plans have appeared in industries that cannot recover strike losses and in which a strike causes great public concern and strong pressures to find a settlement quickly.

Railroad and newspaper plans are of one type; they insure member firms against losses occasioned by strikes. The airlines agreement, initiated by six major carriers, provides mutual assistance rather than insurance.

Effects of strike-aid ventures are not yet clear. They could occasion more thoughtful, carefully considered negotiation and administration. They could,

---

Ct. 1347 (1960); *Steelworkers v. Enterprise Wheel and Car Corporation*, 363 **U.S.** 569; S. Ct. 1358 (1960).

on the other hand, simply raise the level of strife—with bigger and better strikes and lockouts—if employers regard these mutual aid plans as justifying inflexible positions.[13]

3.0 UNION-MANAGEMENT COOPERATION

Union-management cooperation represents an extension of negotiation and administration. It is not new. Several programs have been in operation almost half a century. The best-known programs are those developed on several railroads, but plans have also been established in clothing, electrical manufacturing, ladies' garments, carpet weaving, glass, street railways, and the cloth hat and cap industry. The Baltimore & Ohio program, one of the earliest, was initiated in 1923.

Ernest Dale[14] described four degrees of cooperation in these plans. In the first, *informational cooperation,* the parties merely cooperate in gathering information. In a second degree, which he calls *advisory cooperation,* each side consults with the other. In a third stage, *constructive cooperation,* each party makes suggestions for improvements. The fourth level involves *joint determination,* in which the union and the employer make decisions jointly.

Dale concludes that cooperation is likely to be most successful when subjects have a high degree of interest for both parties and when standards of professional competence can be easily checked. He found accident prevention the subject most likely to succeed. Waste reduction is another subject in which cooperation is widely effective. Control of apprenticeship is another.

Joint responsibility in time study and joint control of discipline are among the areas in which failure is most frequent.

Cooperative relationships are arranged and maintained through one or more committees. Committees may employ consultants in safety, time study, job evaluation, and similar specialties. They facilitate the participation of employees in solving problems of mutual interest. In all plans, unions are not only accepted and recognized but welcomed as representatives of cooperating employees.

Individual employees share in financial accomplishments. Some plans include profit-sharing; in others, financial rewards take the form of bonuses for superior output.

Favorable results have been credited to these provisions. Productivity and profits have been increased; waste and accidents have been reduced. Em-

[13] See Anthony P. Alfino, "The Airlines Pact for Mutual Strike Aid," *Management Record,* Vol. 22, No. 10, October, 1960, pp. 9ff; "New Focus," *Business Week,* September, 24, 1960, pp. 280ff.
[14] See Ernest Dale, "Increasing Productivity through Labor-Management Cooperation," *Industrial and Labor Review,* Vol. 3, No. 1, October, 1949, pp. 33–34; for details of one program, see W. R. Dymond, "Union-Management Cooperation at the Toronto Factory of Lever Brothers Limited," *Canadian Journal of Economics and Political Science,* Vol. 13, No. 1, February, 1947, pp. 1–42. See also, Robert Dubin, "Union-Management Cooperation and Productivity," *Industrial and Labor Relations Review,* Vol. 2, No. 2, January, 1949, pp. 195–209.

ployee earnings have increased. Attitudes of the parties have changed. Employees have less suspicion that the employer is out to get rid of the union. Management problems, both internal and external, are more widely understood and appreciated.

Union-management cooperation is still distinctly experimental. Skepticism and cynicism represent a major hazard to all such plans. Both among employers' representatives and within unions, numerous participants refuse to believe that the other party will consistently cooperate. They feel sure that the program is a subterfuge that obscures other objectives.

Both managements and unions may become dissatisfied with plans because results of cooperation develop slowly. Programs may have been oversold, so that participants expect too much. A frequent difficulty arises from the limits imposed on the area of cooperation, including both subjects and degrees of cooperation. Employers or unions may try to maintain lists of tabooed subjects.

One of the most widely discussed types of union-management cooperation is what is known as the *Scanlon Plan*. It is discussed in some detail in section 3.2, Chapter 21.[15]

In both world wars, somewhat similar union-management committees in Great Britain, Canada, and the United States made valuable contributions in finding solutions for such problems as absenteeism, tardiness, inadequate housing, and transportation and accidents. Almost all of them were dissolved, however, when war-time pressures for cooperation were relaxed.

Experience in the older industrialized nations of Europe indicates that some type of employee representation plan, supplementing collective bargaining, is entirely possible and offers important advantages. A system of representative committees, selected by employees and meeting regularly with employers, can do much to improve communication within the organization, to provide an opportunity for effective employee participation, and to relieve collective bargaining of many issues that now clutter and retard negotiation. Discussion with such groups can keep employees and management informed on matters of mutual interest.

Some managers fear that such programs will be regarded as attempts to undermine the union. As one result, union demands might become more difficult. This is not, however, a necessary or inevitable result. Both parties would have to join in planning such a program. Both management and union may be expected to recognize the multiple nature of loyalties in employment and hence cease the struggle for exclusive loyalty to company or union.

4.0 SUMMARY

Practice in collective bargaining involves two distinctive steps or stages

---

[15] See Frederick G. Lesieur, *The Scanlon Plan,* New York: John Wiley and Sons, Inc., 1958; Gilbert K. Krulee, "The Scanlon Plan: Cooperation through Participation," *Journal of Business,* Vol. 28, No. 2, April, 1955, pp. 100–13. (See also Chapter 21, section 3.3.)

—negotiation and administration. Each is and has been undergoing continued change. Both managers and unions have learned that negotiation and contract administration are multi-purpose practices that require thoughtful advance preparation and expert direction. They see the negotiation process as an educational opportunity, a chance both to learn and to teach. The same opportunity is available in contract administration.

One result is that both give greater attention to preparation for negotiations. Another is a trend toward much more positive bargaining by employers. That, in turn, has directed increasing attention to the negotiation of revised work rules. One interesting innovation has brought public representatives into bargaining sessions. Both parties show awareness of hazards in all-out efforts to win at any cost.

Modern practice gives increasing attention to communicating and interpreting contract provisions. In addition to such procedures as "goldfish bowl" bargaining sessions and interpretive bulletins, grievances and arbitration are recognized as influential guides to the meaning of clauses. So also are proposals for amendments and revisions.

Some employers shift responsibilities for administration largely to their administrative associations.

The final section of the chapter notes continuing experiments in union-management cooperation, in which the parties build broad programs of mutual aid on the foundation provided by bargaining relationships.

Attention turns, in the next section, to the function of staffing the working organization. Problems in that area require that general manpower policy, as developed under the influence of public policy and collective bargaining, be implemented through staffing policy and related practice.

SELECTED SUPPLEMENTARY READINGS

Barkin, Solomon, "A New Agenda for Labor," *Fortune,* pp. 249ff., November, 1960.

Carpenter, Walter H. and Edward Handler, "Small Business and Pattern Bargaining," *Management Research Summary* (Small Business Administration), June, 1961.

Dubin, Robert, "A Theory of Conflict and Power in Union-Management Relations," Industrial and Labor Relations Review, Vol. 13, No. 5, pp. 501–18, July, 1960.

Form, William H., "Organized Labor's Place in the Community Power Structure," Industrial and Labor Relations Review, Vol. 12, No. 4, pp. 526–39, July, 1959. (Available as a reprint from the Labor and Industrial Relations Center, Michican State University, October, 1959.)

Friesen, E. P., "The Human Elements in Labor Relations," *Canadian Personnel and Industrial Relations Journal,* Vol. 6, No. 4, pp. 32–37, October, 1959.

Kennedy, Van Dusen, "Grievance Negotiation," *Reprint No. 70.* Berkeley, Calif.: Institute of Industrial Relations, University of California, 1955; also Chapter 21 in Arthur Kornhauser et al., *Industrial Conflict,* Society for the Psychological Study of Social Issues, New York: McGraw-Hill Book Company, Inc., 1954.

McDermott, Thomas J., "Use of Factfinding Boards in Labor Disputes," *Labor Law Journal,* Vol. 11, No. 4, pp. 285–304, April, 1960. (Available as *Business Re-*

search Reprint 6, School of Business Administration, Duquesne University, 1960.)

"Management Rights and the Arbitration Process," Washington, D.C.; Bureau of National Affairs, Inc., August, 1956.

"New Style Runaway Shop," *Industrial Union Digest,* Vol. 5, No. 3, pp. 147–52, Fall, 1960.

Ruttenberg, Harold J., *Self-Developing America.* New York: Harper & Brothers, 1960.

Steele, H. E., "Earned Freedom for Management," *Advanced Management,* Vol. 22, No. 11, pp. 13–18, November, 1957.

Stieber, Jack, "Company Cooperation in Collective Bargaining in the Basic Steel Industry," *Reprint Series No. 30,* Michigan State University Labor and Industrial Relations Center, 1960.

SHORT CASE PROBLEM 13.1

*Layoff for Disobeying Supervisor**

An employee working at his regular assignment was told by his foreman to discontinue his work and "take care of a hot job." The employee told the foreman that he would do the emergency job after he finished his regular task. The foreman walked away without replying. The employee was delayed in completing his job because of the faulty functioning of an indicator he was using. When the foreman returned about an hour later, and saw him still at work on his regular job, he dismissed him for the day. The company's "General Working Rules," prohibited an employee from refusing to perform properly assigned work and from refusing to obey a reasonable order. Layoff was the penalty for the first infraction. The employee charged the company with violating the agreement in suspending him without sufficient cause.

The union argued that the contract required advance notice before *any* layoff could be effected. He was not given this notice. In addition, because the agreement contained no management rights clause reserving discipline to the company, the company had no right to discipline the employee. The union also alleged that the employee was unfairly dismissed because the foreman sought to make an example of him for the other employees.

The company contended that the grievant's layoff did not breach the contract. As a long-time employee, and ex-foreman, the grievant should have known of the urgency attending a reassignment to a "hot job." Such reassignments were of frequent occurrence occasioned by business pressures. Because the grievant did not complete his job, four employees could not continue their jobs. The company also maintained that the requirement of advance notice before any layoff did not pertain to disciplinary layoffs, but only for layoffs in the event of a reduction in their work force. Disciplinary rules and layoffs for their infractions were provided in the "General Working Rules." These rules had always been observed by the union.

Problem: Did the disciplinary layoff violate the contract? The relevant clause is as follows:

"In the event any layoff is necessary, the Company will notify each employee to be laid off at least twenty-four hours in advance of layoff."

* From *Union Contracts and Collective Bargaining Report,* Par. 13.3, No. 13–5, Englewood Cliffs, N.J.: Prentice-Hall, Inc.

SHORT CASE PROBLEM 13.2

Harmony Clause

Here is the text of two clauses proposed by the management of a firm in the wood-products industry: *'

Article 2—Purpose of Agreement—Section 1. The Employer and the Union enter into this Agreement for the following purposes:

(a) To set forth the established rates of pay, hours of work, and other working conditions;

(b) To express definitely on the part of the Employees of the Employer that they will, in consideration of the rates of pay, hours of work, and other working conditions set forth in this Agreement, render responsible and efficient service;

(c) To improve, through workmanship and cooperation, the economy of operation, quality and quantity of product, cleanliness of the plant, and protection of property;

(d) To insure and advance between the Employer, the Union, and the Employees, good will, mutual respect, stable and harmonious relations, mutual cooperation, and a better and closer understanding;

(e) To provide for the safety and welfare of the Employees to the fullest extent reasonably possible;

(f) To provide for an adequate procedure, in the interest of industrial peace, for the adjustment of complaints and grievances;

(g) To pledge to each other, fair, considerate and courteous treatment;

(h) To commit the Employer not to engage in any lockout and the Union not to authorize or engage in any strike, walkout, or other type of work stoppage, as described in Article 28, Section 1, of this Agreement.

Section 2. It is the duty of the Employer and its representatives, the Union and its representatives, and the Employees to cooperate fully, individually and as a group, in the fulfillment of the purposes expressed in Section 1 of this Article.

Article 3—Responsibilities—Section 1. Each of the parties to this Agreement acknowledges the rights and responsibilities of the other party and agrees to discharge its responsibilities under this Agreement.

Section 2. The Employer (its officers and representatives, at all levels) is bound by this Agreement responsibly to observe the provisions of this Agreement.

Section 3. The Union (its officers and representatives, at all levels) is bound by this Agreement responsibly to observe the provisions of this Agreement.

Section 4. In the interest of harmonious relations and genuine collective bargaining, neither the Employer nor the Union shall issue or distribute any derogratory statements or make any false accusations, concerning each other.

Problem: Assume that you were representing the union in these negotiations. How would you regard these clauses? Do you see any provisions to which you would object? If so, why?

SHORT CASE PROBLEM 13.3

Lawyers in Negotiations

According to his job description, the labor relations director of the Spingle Company negotiates and administers their labor agreements. In practice, however, he is a member of a negotiating team composed of the production manager, the firm's legal counsel, and himself.

---

* From *Union Contracts and Collective Bargaining Report*, Par. 56,311, No. 12— 17, Englewood Cliffs, N.J.: Prentice-Hall Inc.

For several years, union representatives have suggested that the legal counsel be excluded from negotiations. They argue that he prevents agreement by his quibbling over words, that he doesn't keep up with bargaining in other firms, and that he is "old-fashioned." They insist that the whole atmosphere of negotiation is handicapped by his participation.

The employee relations director, informed of this situation by his labor relations associate, has reported these suggestions to the firm's executive committee, of which the legal counsel is a member. The counsel defends his participation and insists that he is needed, that he protects the firm from mistakes in language that might cost thousands of dollars during the term of an agreement.

The union has recently announced that if the counsel is to remain a member of the bargaining committee, they, too, will have a lawyer. No one is happy at this prospect—except possibly the two lawyers.

Problem: You are the employee relations director. The labor relations director reports to you. The president has indicated that he regards the problem as yours. What will you do?

SHORT CASE PROBLEM 13.4

Voting on a Final Offer

Members of Local 101 of the United Aircraft Workers' Union are negotiating a new contract with an airframe manufacturer in the Midwest. The present contract expires on May 31, which is five days ahead. Company and union have been negotiating since March 15th.

The union has demanded continuation of the terms of the present contract with respect to its escalator clause, an annual productivity increase amounting to 2½ per cent or 5 cents per hour—whichever is greater—a non-contributory health and pension plan (insurance, hospitalization, and pensions), current seniority rules, and other provisions. In addition, the union asks for a new "guaranteed annual wage" plan. Under terms of this proposal, employer and employees would contribute equally to a reserve fund, sharing a total contribution of 7½ cents per hour. The amount of this reserve would be available to pay regular, straight-time weekly wages for all employees having two or more years of service who are discharged (not for cause) or laid off during each year. Wages would thus be guaranteed for each calendar year.

The employer and the union have come to an agreement on all issues except that of the guaranteed annual wage. The employer insists that such a guarantee is impossible and that the label is misleading. He also argues that such a guarantee is undesirable, since it tends to "freeze" employees in the locality and prevent their acceptance of more promising jobs. The employer has offered what he describes as his final counterproposal. In it, he indicates his willingness to provide generous severance pay—scaled according to average weekly earnings and length of service—for all employees who are discharged (not for cause) or are laid off for more than two weeks. In addition, he offers a "personal security" plan, in which employees would be permitted to buy stock in the firm at half its current market price. Both employer and union negotiators have agreed that estimated costs of the proposals are approximately equal.

Union officials insist that a strike will be called if the contract is not signed before the end of the present agreement. Union members have already authorized such a strike. Union negotiators also insist that they cannot and will not accept the employer's proposal in lieu of their demand. The employer, however, regards his offer as better for employees than what the union has proposed. He argues that members of the union would recognize its superiority and would accept it if given the opportunity.

Problem: You have been called in by the employer at this point to advise and assist him in his negotiations. His first question to you is: will members actually strike in the face of his offer? What is your advice on this point, and how do you arrive at this conclusion?

The employer indicates that he is contemplating a further step. He is considering a proposition to the union in which, if they will agree to poll their members before striking, he will offer to grant either his plan or the union's guaranteed annual wage proposal, whichever employees prefer. What would you advise on this point? Do you conclude that such an offer on his part would result in the selection of his plan? What is your forecast and why?

IV. STAFFING THE WORKING ORGANIZATION

14. *Staffing Policy and Process*

Staffing, or *manning,* has long been regarded as a sort of basic, never-ending function in industrial relations. It is the continuing process of determining manpower requirements, discovering workers, interesting them in joining the working organization, selecting those regarded as best fitted for membership, preparing them for effective participation, and holding them throughout the long or short period in which their continued collaboration is mutually advantageous. It is thus the oldest of specialized activities in manpower management. It is also the most universal; every working organization faces and must solve its staffing or manning problems.

The staffing process includes a number of steps or stages. A preliminary step involves the determination and identification of present needs and the forecasting of future manpower requirements. Next, adequate numbers and types of manpower must be discovered and *recruited.* For those available, the right numbers and types must be *selected.* Those chosen must be employed or *hired* and placed in the positions for which they are qualified. They must be informed or *oriented* with respect to the part they are to play in the total operation of the working organization. Thereafter, they may be *promoted, transferred,* and, in the case of employees who find working relationships unsatisfactory or who are no longer needed, they must be terminated. Under some circumstances, they may be demoted. The staffing process generally includes these seven activities, or *personnel actions*—the determination of personnel requirements, recruitment, selection, placement, orientation, promotion, and transfer. Demotions and terminations are also generally regarded as essential parts of the staffing process.

All managers have a direct interest in the staffing process; their success depends largely on its success. Workers have an obvious interest; it is a major factor in shaping and directing their careers. Personnel and industrial relations staff members have special concern and responsibilities; they are expected to develop sound staffing policy and practice and to assist all other managers in maintaining appropriate programs.

Industrial societies have a direct and clear interest in this staffing process. The manner in which it is performed affects not only the efficient application of human resources but the very goodness of life for most citizens. The staffing process inevitably exerts a major influence on material living scales as well as the satisfaction of other, non-material needs of workers and their families. The kind of job each worker holds determines in large measure the goods and services, the necessities and luxuries, his or her family can enjoy.

At the same time, the attitudes of workers toward their work carry over into family and community relationships. Social status and prestige are associated with occupation and position in the working organization. Where the breadwinner has a job determines, also, where his family will live—not only with respect to which side of the railroad track, but also whether in New York City or Chicago or on a western ranch. The hours to which the worker is committed influence his availability for community service and community life. Staffing is thus a many-sided process and one that concerns not only the firm or agency and the individual worker but also his family, the community, and the whole society of which he and his family are a part.

One gross dimension of the volume of staffing may be seen in the size of the national labor force. In the United States, some 75 million adult citizens are presently working or seeking work. The number grows each year; by 1970, the total will be about 87 million.

A second and perhaps more meaningful dimension is that which measures changes in jobs. Nation-wide sampling studies of the mobility of American workers indicate that, on the average, each member of the labor force changes jobs once every four years. Put another way, an average of about one-fourth of the labor force changes jobs each year.

Job changes solve some staffing problems. Most of them also create new problems. For example, to maintain average manufacturing employment of 218,000 in the state of Minnesota in 1958, employers recorded 238,000 job changes—117,000 hirings, and 121,000 separations. If *selection ratios* were high—if each firm were able to hire one of every two applicants—firms examined more applicants than the total of employment.

Finding jobs for 75 million would be a major assignment in the most dictatorial type of society, where individual workers could be told where to work and required to accept these assignments. In our system, where each individual worker must make his own decisions on when and where to work and what kind of work to do, the problem is much more complicated. And, however difficult it may have been in the past, it must unquestionably become more involved in the future. The total size of the labor force, as has been noted, will increase. Numbers of jobs are growing; the *Dictionary of Occupational Titles* already lists some 30,000.

Meanwhile, proportions of younger, threshold workers are increasing. Older workers, established in their working careers, require less attention, for many of them will follow the pattern they have undertaken. Young workers must find initial jobs. They make more job changes in their early working years. Younger workers will enter the labor force during the 1960's at a rate approximately twice that of the preceding 20 years. Figure 14.1 spells out these changes in some detail.

**HERE IS THE LABOR FORCE BALANCE SHEET
FOR THE 1960s**

(MILLIONS)

NUMBER OF WORKERS IN 1960 . . . . **73.6**
  SUBTRACT:
      Withdrawals—
      death, retirement,
      marriage,
      childbearing, etc. . . . . **−15.5**
1960 WORKERS STILL IN LABOR FORCE IN 1970 . . . . **58.1**
  ADD:
      Young entrants . . . . **+26.0**
      Adult women
      returning to work . . . . **+ 3.0**
NUMBER OF WORKERS IN 1970 . . . . **87.1**

Figure 14.1   Labor Force Balance Sheet for the 1960's

From "The Challenge of the 1960's," Washington, D.C.: United States Department of Labor, 1960, p. 13

The process of staffing is further complicated by technological change. If automation is indeed introducing a second industrial revolution—if it means that the process of technological change will be speeded—the staffing process in turn will be complicated. Firms and managers will not only have to staff for current jobs; they will have to forecast a changing job-mix in the near future and plan on staffing for such a different pattern. They must recognize and plan for the changing occupational structure of the labor force. This change is well illustrated by experience in the steel industry, where white-collar employment has grown about 185 per cent in the past 25 years, while blue-collar jobs have increased only 21 per cent.

Plants and firms as well as people are mobile. Whole industries spring up in new locations and older industries move or establish new plants in areas that have been predominantly agricultural. Southern states have subsidized the construction of factories, and areas in New England have undertaken redevelopment of older industrial cities. All require new or different manning.

1.0 STAFFING POLICY

Development and maintenance of sound policies on staffing require difficult decisions. The basic guide is what has been described in Chapter 6 as *general manpower policy* or *general policy on manpower management*. Decisions on the over-all intentions and courses for an organization have clear implications with respect to its employee relations. They set the broad pattern to which staffing policies must conform. All general policy requires continual modification and development, which necessitates appropriate changes in staffing policy.

Staffing policy must take account, also, of changes in public policy on the employment and application of human resources. Nowhere is this more evident than in the recently industrialized economies of the world. Within our own society, also, and that of other highly industrialized economies, public attitudes and opinion have changed and are changing.

1.1 Implications of general policy. General manpower policy outlines a broad framework of intentions. It defines broad courses of action the firm or agency has selected to define proposed relationships with members of its working team. The manner in which these choices in general manpower policy sketch or outline a pattern for staffing policy may be shown by a somewhat oversimplified example. Suppose the Atlas Missile Company has decided to emphasize the following intentions in its general manpower policy:

1. To maintain strict conformity to both the letter and spirit of relevant public policy.
2. To attempt to use highest skills and aptitudes of all workers.
3. To assure opportunity for personal development.
4. To facilitate individual satisfaction in work.
5. To encourage individual participation in decisions.
6. To encourage personal identification with organizational goals.
7. To maximize quality of individual contributions.
8. To assure the competence of leadership.
9. To provide a high level of economic security.
10. To maintain employment stability.

It will be evident that each of these general policies has implications for staffing policy. Each of them prescribes a somewhat narrower road or course for the satisfaction of manpower requirements—for recruiting, for selection, and for placement. Even the tenth of the general policies, the maintenance of stability in employment, requires that staffing be held to a minimum that can be continually employed, that individuals selected may have to be somewhat versatile and that they must be regarded as long-term team members rather than temporary fill-ins. Some of the same implications are evident in general policy 9, on economic security. Item 4, which proposes to facilitate satisfaction in work, requires a specific policy of discovering what personal qualities are characteristic of people who can be satisfied by available and future jobs. It thus introduces an additional consideration in the development of job specifications.

As will be noted in subsequent chapters, each element in this 10-point general manpower policy also prescribes policies for other major activities or functions—for training and development, for work motivation or incentivation, for maintaining a continuing audit of manpower management, and for industrial relations research.

General policy prescribes only the broad outlines of staffing policy. Specific policy on staffing seeks to achieve the best possible balance among planks in the general platform. Some staffing policies that appear appropriate for one or another of these items may interfere with achievement of others. To maximize the quality of individual contributions, for example, may suggest the employment of individuals who have learned a trade and are already skilled and experienced. Such individuals, however, may have minimal qualifications for continued development and versatility. They may know one job well but not be qualified to prepare for new jobs.

1.2 Changing theory. Managers translate general manpower policy into staffing policy by use of the theory bridges discussed in Chapter 4. They depend on theory to suggest how general policies can best be implemented in staffing policy.

Primary theory in all staffing programs is the theory of *individual differences*. The theory is concisely expressed in the statement usually credited to William James. "There is very little difference between one man and another," he said, "but what little there is is very important."

Theories of personality have undergone and are undergoing great change. Earlier theory tended to assume greater simplicity of personality. It listed basic *instincts* or *needs* that were regarded as mainsprings of behavior. It frequently proposed a comparatively simple classification of personality types. Character analysis, phrenology, and handwriting were accepted as indicators of these types, and applicants were hired on the basis of such marks. Modern theory presents a much more complex view of personality, with emphasis on aptitudes, interests, mood, and temperament.

1.3 Public policy. Some of the boundaries of staffing policy are established by public policy. The Report of the President's Commission on National Goals provides an excellent summary of public policy.[1] It notes the necessity for equality of opportunity in employment, the efficient utilization of manpower resources, maximum choice in jobs, collective bargaining, limi-

---

[1] The American Assembly, *Goals for Americans: Report of the President's Commission on National Goals*, ed. H. M. Wriston, Englewood Cliffs, N.J.: Prentice-Hall, Inc., 1960, pp. 1–24.

tations on manager and union influence on individual lives, increasing economic security, low levels of unemployment, growing research, and broader in-firm educational opportunities. Each of these goals has implications for staffing policy.

Staffing policy must give careful attention to growing public concern about middle-aged and older workers, working women, members of minority groups, those who are available on only a part-time basis, and the handicapped. Public policy may prescribe detailed rules, as illustrated in fair employment practice legislation. The federal government, some 20 states, and more than 40 cities now have such rules. Although laws vary in specific provisions, they are similar in forbidding discrimination in hiring by employers, unions, and employment agencies. Some laws go further and prescribe discrimination in subsequent employment—in promotions, work assignments, and transfers, for example. Thirteen states have now prohibited discrimination based on age. The first of these laws was enacted in New York in 1945. They generally exempt agriculture, domestic service, and religious and educational institutions.

To implement this legislation, various jurisdictions have developed rules that prohibit inquiries about changed names, birthplaces, homes of parents, birth certificates, baptismal records, religious affiliations, church attendance, complexion or color, citizenship, date of arrival in the United States, maiden names, use of foreign languages, names and addresses of relatives, and membership in organizations or clubs. Objection may be raised to photographs required as a part of application forms. F.E.P. agencies have also required staffing schedules that can be examined to note evidence of discrimination.[2]

In at least one state, Connecticut, the Civil Rights Commission has banned the use of such terms as "young" or "under 40" in advertising for help unless age is a bona fide occupational requirement.

Popular discussions of staffing policy with respect to older workers have been stimulated by the aging of our labor force in the United States. Largely because of low birth rates in the 1930's, the labor force has included increasing proportions of middle-aged and older workers. This trend will be slowed throughout the decade of the 1960's, as large numbers of young workers enter employment. Popular concern may be somewhat reduced by this change.

1.4 Modern staffing policy. Modern staffing begins with the long look ahead, *hiring for careers* rather than for jobs. It recognizes the complexity of personalities and the problem of defining manpower requirements in terms that facilitate identification of the best candidates. It proposes *selective placement* for handicapped members of the labor force. It recognizes dangers of stagnation in conformity when recruitment seeks newcomers who are like those already in the organization. It relates staffing to organization planning,

---

[2] See John Hope, Jr., *Equality of Opportunity*, Washington, D.C.: Public Affairs Press, 1956.

10*

to training and development, and to programs designed to maintain the morale of employees.

Current restrictions on management's rights to hire and fire are a factor. Policy recognizes that hiring is much more "for keeps" than it was in the days when workers were employed on short-term basis and released whenever work was slack. *Merit-rating* in unemployment insurance has also contributed to the long look by charging benefits to employers' accounts. Collective bargaining has influenced staffing by protecting employees against arbitrary discharge.

Perhaps most important, however, is the fact that managers have faced and anticipate a continuing shortage of technically trained workers. Expanding organizations can rarely find enough qualified recruits to meet requirements of new jobs. They must develop workers—and perhaps redevelop them—to meet changing manpower requirements. Meanwhile, recruits are given the promise of an opportunity to continue personal development—to experience *personal appreciation*—as a means of encouraging identification with the goals of the organization. Hiring for careers rather than for jobs is thus a major distinction of modern policy.

Modern policy thus relates recruitment and selection to *promotion* and *transfer*. It links selection for working careers with a considered policy of promotion from within. It seeks to attain a balance between two objectives—finding the best possible man for each vacancy and providing maximum opportunities for advancement for all members of the organization. It combines transfers, or *horizontal promotions,* with *vertical promotions* to create added opportunities for personal development.

Within the organization, staffing policy recognizes the wide acceptance of the principle of seniority but seeks to temper it with recognition of varying competence and promise. It proposes a complex rather than a simple application of the seniority principle. It intends to assure every employee fair, impartial consideration whenever opportunities for advancement appear and, above all, seeks to avoid favoritism or nepotism. Policy proposes that all employees shall be fully familiar with both policy and practice in filling jobs.

Modern policy recognizes that managers and team members face difficult problems in trying to avoid too great conformity on the part of all members. In part, the tendency toward conformity—with hazards to individual initiative and creativity—results from the pressures of the organization on its members. Team members on the way up are likely to conclude that the easiest path is that which follows rather precisely the pattern of those already at the top. Pressures to dress alike, talk alike, and think alike are very great. In addition, the process of staffing—particularly in recruiting and selection, —may tend to favor those who most resemble present members of the organization. Interviewers compare applicants with successful performers already on the job. Tests are checked by giving them to present jobholders. Norms are established by reference to employee scores (see Figure 14.2).

Managers are aware of this hazard. A recent cartoon has the manager advising an applicant, "It isn't because of your lack of aptitude, or previous experience, or your unproven adaptability. It's just that I don't like you!"[3]

2.0 DEFINING AND FORECASTING MANPOWER REQUIREMENTS

Staffing policy generally proposes that the organization's current and future manpower needs shall be defined in terms of both quality and quan-

"I like your looks, Gillis... you're hired!"

Figure 14.2 Hazards of Inadequate Job Specifications.
SOURCE: *Commerce,* Chicago Association of Commerce and Industry, 30 West Monroe, Chicago 3, Illinois.

tity. Needs shall, so far as possible, be forecast, so that manpower is available when needed. Modern practice provides a variety of techniques and procedures for this purpose. Personal qualifications or specifications are defined by *job analysis* and recorded in *job descriptions* and *job specifications*. Quantitative requirements are developed through various methods of *time study* and *work measurement*. Forecasts of future requirements depend on *organization planning* and on careful calculations of changing job specifications.

2.1 Job analysis. The first step in the definition of manpower requirements is job analysis. A *job* is a collection of tasks, duties, and responsibilities

[3] See Joseph R. Gusfield, "Equalitarianism and Bureaucratic Recruitment," *Administrative Science Quarterly,* Vol. 2, No. 4, March, 1958, pp. 521–41 for additional discussion of this problem.

which, as a whole, is regarded as the established assignment to individual employees. A *job* may include many positions, for a *position* is a job performed by and hence related to a particular employee. Thus, an employee has his *position,* but many positions may involve the same assignment of duties and constitute a single job. For this reason, Otis and Leukart define a job as "a group of positions involving substantially the same duties, skills, knowledges, and responsibilities." The *job* is impersonal; the *position* is personal.

Job analysis is the procedure by which the facts with respect to each job are systematically discovered and noted. It is sometimes called *job study,* suggesting the care with which tasks, processes, responsibilities, and personnel requirements are investigated. Job analysis should be distinguished from a related term, *worker analysis,* although the distinction is essentially one of emphasis and differing procedures.

Worker analysis focuses attention on appraisal of the characteristics of employees, using physical examinations, tests, interviews, and other procedures for this purpose. Worker analysis is a technique used principally by the public employment service as a basis for placement.

A *job description* is a systematic outline of information gained from notes taken and recorded in the job analysis *report.* It describes the work performed, the responsibilities involved, the skill or training required, the conditions under which the job is done, relationships with other jobs, and personal requirements of the job.

The *job specification* is also a product of job analysis. The term has been popularized by the United States Employment Service, which uses it to refer to a summary of the personal characteristics required for a job. The job specification describes the type of employee required (in terms of skill, experience, special aptitudes, and perhaps tests scores of various types) and outlines the particular working conditions which are encountered on the job.

An *occupation* is a job that is common in many firms and areas; it is a generalized job. Thus, the job of Tool and Die Maker is found so generally throughout metal-working industries that it may be described as an occupation. Generalized job descriptions for tool and die makers may be called *occupational descriptions.* A nationwide compilation of job titles and briefs of job descriptions is known as the *Dictionary of Occupational Titles* (or D.O.T., in personnel jargon).

Job families or *occupational families* are groups of jobs or occupations having similar personnel requirements.

Reference is also frequently made to jobs in terms of *levels of skill* required. Thus, a job may be said to require skilled, semiskilled, or unskilled or common labor. *Skilled labor* is that performed by craftsmen who have had long periods of formal training (often in an apprenticeship program), possess a thorough knowledge of the processes involved, are capable of exercising independent judgment, and have a high degree of manual skill in the operations performed. *Semiskilled labor* generally exhibits a high level of manipulative ability which is, however, limited to a well-defined work routine. Such labor is not expected to exercise much independent judgment. Training is generally short and limited in scope. *Unskilled* or *common labor* is that which performs simple manual operations that are readily learned in a short time and that require exercise of little or no independent judgment. In addition, reference is sometimes made to *threshold workers,* who are those who have no employment experience.

Job analysis is often described as fundamental to the manpower management program because results of job analysis are so widely used. Job information provided by job analysis is used in:

1. Organization and integration of the whole work force and in organization planning.
2. Recruitment, selection, and placement.
3. Transfers and promotions.
4. Training programs.
5. Wage and salary administration.
6. Settlement of grievances.
7. Improvement of working conditions.
8. Setting production standards.
9. Improvement of employee productivity through work simplification and methods improvement.

The purposes and uses to be made of job analysis determine the procedure to be followed in the job analysis program. With respect to each job, job analysis seeks to discover:

(1) *What the worker in the job is expected to do.* Questions here concern the specific operations and tasks that make up the work assignment, including whatever thinking, knowledge, and skill are required for these tasks. For example, the job may require employees to carry or transport materials, bend them, cut them and grind, polish, or assemble. It may require employees to measure, compute, calculate, or plan.

(2) *How the job is performed.* Here the focus is on methods, including the use of particular tools or equipment and the sequence of steps involved.

(3) *Skills required for effective performance.* Concern on this point is directed to the identification of required skills and some measure of their level. Does the worker need the skills of a journeyman machinist or those of a tool and die maker? Does the job require bookkeeping skill or that of a professional accountant?

(4) *Job relationships.* In its simplest form, such information indicates experience required and opportunities for advancement. It notes that satisfactory workers ordinarily come to this job from one or a sequence of lesser assignments. It also notes the usual patterns of promotion from the job. With increasing interest in long-term worker careers, attention may be directed to aptitudes that will be required in subsequent assignments.

2.2 Measured requirements. For use in staffing, what has sometimes been described as the *ideal job analysis* seeks to describe personal requirements of each job in measurable terms and to indicate appropriate measures or levels. For example, if job analysis identifies an acceptable range of intelligence or of mechanical aptitude, this measured requirement can be used in identifying appropriate candidates for the job.[4]

Much of the research by modern industrial relations and personnel departments has been undertaken to approximate these ideal job descriptions and thus facilitate improved staffing. One approach analyzes jobs to discover *job attributes* and *worker attributes*. Both may be quantified. Attributes of the job and its environment include the duties performed, responsibilities, motions involved, equipment and materials used, and working conditions. Attributes of workers include aptitudes, interest, personality variables, physical characteristics, knowledge, training required, and others. Factor analysis is used to reveal the most significant factors and clusters of factors in the jobs and individuals under observation.[5]

Studies seek to discover levels of test performance that are correlated with high-level job performance. Dunnette and Kirchner, for example, identified test differences between industrial salesmen and retail salesmen. Dunnette has measured interest differences among engineers in different types of jobs. Guerin has repeated earlier studies of typical occupational levels of intelligence. Studies of this relationship, as evidenced by the Army General Classification Test, are illustrated in Figure 14.3.[6]

2.3 Sources of job information. Information about jobs may be secured from three principal sources: (1) employees on these jobs; (2) other employees, including supervisors, who know these jobs; and (3) independent observers who watch employees performing their jobs.

To tap these sources, several methods of securing job information are currently used. In one of the most common, a job questionnaire is submitted to each employee. An illustration of such a questionnaire is given in Figure 14.4. When employees have returned the completed forms, they may be submitted to supervisors for their comments.

[4] See Henry C. Link, *Employment Psychology,* New York: The Macmillan Company, 1921, p. 279.

[5] See Ernest J. McCormick and associates, "A Study of Job Interrelationships," Occupational Research Center, Purdue University, August, 1954.

[6] See Marvin D. Dunnette and Wayne K. Kirchner, "Psychological Test Differences between Industrial Salesmen and Retail Salesmen," *Journal of Applied Psychology,* Vol. 44, No. 2, April, 1960, pp. 121–25; also their "Identifying the Critical Factors in Successful Salesmanship," *Personnel,* Vol. 34, No. 2, September-October, 1957, pp. 54–59; also their "A Check List for Differentiating Different Kinds of Sales Jobs," *Personnel Psychology,* Vol. 12, No. 3, Autumn, 1959, pp. 421–30; R. B. Cattell, M. Day, and T. Meeland, "Occupational Profiles on the 16 Personality Factor Questionnaire," *Occupational Psychology,* Vol. 30, No. 1, January, pp. 10–19; Sidney A. Fine, "Temperament and Interest Requirements of Jobs," *Personnel Administration,* Vol. 20, No. 2, March-April, 1957, pp. 21–27; James W. Guerin, "Occupations and General Intelligence," *Public Personnel Review,* Vol. 15, No. 2, April, 1954, pp. 82ff.

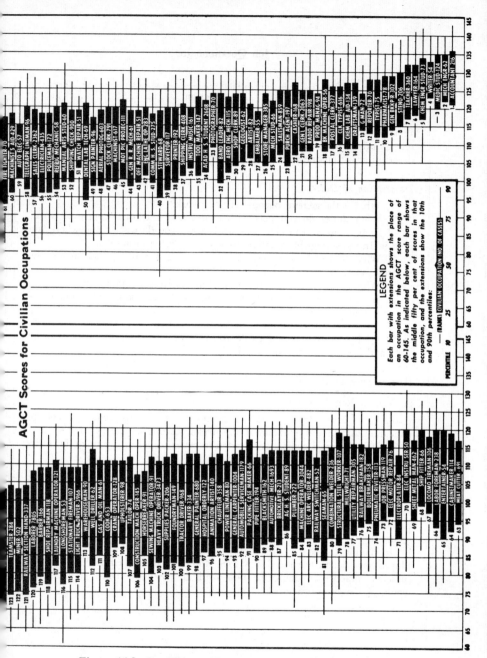

Figure 14.3 Intelligence Test Scores by Occupations.
SOURCE: *Technical Report for the First Civilian Edition of the AGCT,*
Science Research Associates, Inc., 1960, p. 13.

Job Questionnaire

Title of Position ....

Department ....Section ....

Division ....Date ....

Please read all of the questions before making any entries; then answer each one as briefly as possible, consistent with complete information. Return this description within one week to the Job Analyst, Personnel Department.

Description of Duties

1. What is the general purpose of your work?

2. What *duties* do you personally perform in the usual course of work? (Tell from where you receive your work, what you do with it and where you send it. In answering this question discuss your daily routine.)

3. What duties do you perform only at stated periods, such as weekly, monthly, etc.?

4. What occasional duties do you perform at irregular intervals?

5. How many employees do you supervise? (List job names and number of people in each job.)

6. To whom are you directly responsible?

7. What, if any, instructions do you receive as to how the work is to be done and from whom are they received?

Performance of Duties

A. Mental Requirements

8. What is the lowest grade of grammar school, high school or college education that should be required of a person starting in your position?

9. If any special courses are needed in order to perform your duties satisfactorily, name them.

B. Skill

10. What past experience is it necessary for a new employee to have in order to learn to perform the duties of your position? Name the kind of experience, where and how it could be obtained and the time required to secure it.

11. Having the above education and experience, what would a new employee have yet to learn and how long would it take the employee to obtain sufficient practice in doing the new work to reach the point at which he would be barely satisfactory?

Fig. 14.4 Job Questionnaire.

12. In what lower positions could an employee receive training for your position?

13. For what higher positions in the company does your present work train you?

14. What, in your opinion, is the most difficult part of your work and why is it difficult?

C. Physical Effort

15. Roughly, what proportions of your time are spent in: Standing ....%, Sitting ....%, Moving about ....%, Other ....%?

16. What machines or other equipment do you personally operate; regularly or only occasionally?

17. Roughly, what proportion of your time is spent in operating each machine you use? State also what degree of speed is required on each machine.

18. What, if any, are the physical requirements for the proper performance of your duties? (Strength, height, dexterity, etc.)

19. Please list any other requirements not covered above and any personal qualifications and characteristics which you believe a candidate for your position should have.

Responsibility

20. What is your responsibility for money, securities or other valuables?

21. What is the nature and extent of your responsibility for the employees under your supervision?

22. Give the nature and extent of any responsibility you may have other than for men or money?

23. What personal dealings with customers do you have in performing the duties of your position? State the nature of your business with the customers.

24. Roughly, what proportion of your time is spent in dealing with customers?

Working Conditions

25. What are your usual working hours?

26. What are the disagreeable features of your work?

Use this space and additional sheets of paper, if necessary, for any special features of your work not covered above, and for answers to questions for which more space is needed.

Your name ....

Years in this position ....

Fig. 14.4 Job Questionnaire (*Cont.*).

In another approach, supervisors and foremen are given special training and asked to analyze the jobs under their supervision. In still another, special job-reviewing committees are established. Those who have had most experience prefer trained job analysts. Frequently, however, staff members can be trained as analysts. Shartle concludes that counselors and interviewers can be trained to become satisfactory analysts.[7]

The technically competent job analyst knows what to look for in the job. He asks questions of employees on the job as well as of other employees and supervisors. He studies records of performance and output. He is familiar with analyses of similar jobs, in the same and other firms or agencies. He avoids introducing his own ideas—for example, those of monotony or of ideal working conditions—into the job description. He carefully avoids describing the employee rather than the job, for he is fully aware that many of the employee's personal traits may have no relevance. He is on the alert to discover the *crucial task* in the job, the likely source of job failure.

With respect to the nature of the job, usual items include:

1. The job title.
2. The classification title and number, if any. (May use the D.O.T. identification.)
3. Numbers of employees holding this job.
4. A job summary which, in one to three paragraphs, outlines the major functions and the tools, machinery, and special equipment involved in the work.
5. A job breakdown, listing the sequence of operations that constitute the job and noting the level of difficulty and the *crucial task*. These operations are appraised as to the proportion of total time allocated to each.
6. A description of material used.
7. A statement as to the relationship of the job to those jobs with which it is most closely associated.
8. A notation as to jobs from which workers are promoted and others to which the operators may be promoted from this job.
9. Training required and usual methods of providing such training.
10. Amounts and types of compensation.
11. Usual working hours.
12. Peculiar conditions of employment, including unusual circumstances of heat or cold, humidity, light, ventilation, or any others.

With respect to the employee, the data generally available from the job description include:

1. Notations as to preferred sex and ages.
2. Special physical characteristics, such as size or weight, strength required in back, arms, or legs (types to avoid may also be noted).

[7] Carroll L. Shartle, *Occupational Information*, 3d ed., Englewood Cliffs, N.J.: Prentice-Hall, Inc., 1959, pp. 96–110.

I. IDENTIFICATION DATA

    JOB TITLE: CODE NUMBER:
    ALTERNATE TITLE: DEPARTMENT:
    DATE OF ANALYSIS: DIVISION:

II. JOB SUMMARY

    Under the direct supervision of the GENERAL OFFICE MANAGER, performs such secretarial and clerical duties as typing, takes dictation, interviews, handles confidential data, handles mail, answers telephone, and performs other similar and related duties while relieving the GENERAL OFFICE MANAGER

III. WORK PERFORMED (JOB CONTENT)

Routine or daily duties:
1. Performs general office work in relieving company officers of minor executive and clerical duties. (3 hrs)
2. Takes dictation, transcribes from notes and uses Ediphone. (1 hr)
3. Interviews persons seeking GENERAL OFFICE MANAGER, determines importance of their calls, makes decisions on those warranting time of the GENERAL OFFICE MANAGER. (1 hr)
4. Makes appointments and reminds GENERAL OFFICE MANAGER of them and of other meetings. (1/2 hr)
5. Types routine correspondence on own initiative; prepares confidential correspondence as directed. (1 hr)
6. Answers telephone as relief for TELEPHONE OPERATOR.
7. Sorts and distributes personal mail in the general office.

Periodic duties:
1. Reminds GENERAL OFFICE MANAGER of weekly staff meetings, organizational reports, records and statistics that are prepared on a scheduled basis.
2. Accompanies GENERAL OFFICE MANAGER To weekly staff meetings, takes and transcribes notes for his files.

Occasional duties:
1. Files confidential materials.
2. Performs other similar and related duties as may be prescribed by the GENERAL OFFICE MANAGER.

IV. MINIMUM JOB REQUIREMENTS (JOB SPECIFICATIONS)

    EDUCATION: SEX   AGE
    EXPERIENCE:
    ABILITIES:

    RESPONSIBILITIES:

    KNOWLEDGE:

                                        JOB ANALYST EGW

Figure 14.5 Job Description
SOURCE: Edgar G. Williams, "Planning for Job Evaluation," Business Information Bulletin No. 19, Indiana University Bureau of Business Research, February, 1954, p. 10.

3. Special physical dexterities required, such as finger dexterity and ambidexterity.
4. Special emotional qualifications.
5. Special mental abilities required, such as intelligence, initiative, learning speed, and sensory abilities, including sight, smell, hearing, and touch.
6. Special cultural requirements, such as education, familiarity with languages, sciences, or arts.
7. Required experience and skill.
8. Usual sources.

These items are illustrated in Figure 14.5. Excellent illustrations and helpful suggestions may be found in the published generalized job descriptions prepared by the Occupational Research Program of the United States Employment Service. The Employment Service has developed occupational descriptions to parallel its labor-market information on each job and has combined the two in its *Occupational Guide Series.*

The most extensive summary of brief occupational descriptions is, that provided by the *Dictionary of Occupational Titles.*[8] These brief occupational descriptions for some 30,000 jobs facilitate the use of common or standard job titles. Their classification system provides leads to job families. A page of these occupational titles and summaries is illustrated in Figure 14.6.

The *job specification* is a derivation from the job description. It places major emphasis on the personal characteristics required by the job. It is essentially a set of specifications for people, somewhat comparable to materials specifications.

In the usual form, the job specification (after identifying the job by title and number) includes a brief job summary, designed to give the recruits a "feel" of the job and to set the stage for greater detail. Following this summary, the *job spec* outlines personnel requirements. In a preferable procedure, it specifies in detail the definitive qualities required of jobholders. It may stipulate a specified period of experience in a particular job or jobs. It state physical requirements, such as height, weight, special strength, and others. It may identify tests to be taken and state required scores. It may specify general and special educational requirements. Figure 14.7 illustrates such a job specification.

In so far as is possible, modern job specifications seek to describe measurable qualifications: education and experience in terms of years, for example; intelligence levels in terms of scores; and trade knowledge in terms of performance on a standard trade test. Specifications may suggest the relative importance of such qualifications as memory, solving arithmetic problems, understanding mechanical devices, greeting and meeting visitors, speaking and writing, planning and making decisions rapidly. Some special purpose job specifications, developed as an aid in selection and placement of handi-

[8] Published by and available from the United States Government Printing Office.

shop for processing. May engrave lettering and designs into dies, using a pantograph engraving machine [ENGRAVER I (print. & pub.)].

FORCE MAKER (jewelry). Makes the upper (forcer) die used in shaping jewelry: Cuts steel block to size, using an automatic hacksaw. Impresses the previously carved, raised design of the lower die into the steel block, using a drop hammer [DROP HAND]. Removes excess metal from imprint made by the lower die on the upper die, using a milling machine [MILLING-MACHINE OPERATOR I]. Shapes the upper die, carefully following the impression made by the lower die, using various hand tools, such as chisels and files. Hardens and tempers the die. Polishes the die so that a mirrorlike finish will be imparted to the metal to be shaped.

DIE MAKER (mach. shop) 4-76.010. die cutter; form-block maker. Specializes in the construction, repair, and maintenance of dies for forging, punching, stamping, or other metal-forming work [MACHINIST, TOOL MAKER].

DIE FINISHER (mach. shop) clearing-hammer operator; die barber; die fitter; die scraper; die trimmer; draw-die finisher. Smoothes and finishes the surface of dies after they have been cast, heat treated, or machined, filing, scraping, and grinding the dies, and fitting multiple-part dies together.

DIE GRINDER (mach. shop). Grinds the internal surfaces of dies to accurate dimensions on a precision grinding machine.

DIE MAKER, FORGE (mach. shop). Finishes forge dies by hand, scraping, grinding, and filing machined dies to exact dimensions.

DIE MAKER, TRIM (mach. shop) trimmer maker. Makes dies for trimming flash (excess metal) from edges of forgings.

DIE POLISHER (wire). Reconditions worn wire-drawing dies: Laps, turns, grinds, files, and cleans dies, using lapping machines, bench lathes, power grinders, and hand tools. Inspects dies for smoothness by touch. Verifies diameters of dies by manually forcing a piece of wire through reconditioned dies and gaging wire for size, using micrometer calipers.

DIE REPAIRMAN (mach. shop) die calker. Repairs worn dies by filling worn sections with molten metal and grinding and filing surfaces to their original dimensions.

DIE SINKER (mach. shop). May make or finish dies, but usually performs a particular operation on sets of dies, such as cutting designs or lettering called for in the finished product, or cutting, by routing and profiling operations, deep cavities in forge dies.

DIE-TRY-OUT MAN (mach. shop) die fitter; dei-lead-off man; die setter; die troubleman. Performs the original set-up, try-out, and final adjustment of new dies, and repairs worn dies used in a sheet-metal press. Bolts upper die in ram and lower die in bed of press. Paints upper die one color and lower die another. Operates machine through its cycle by running driving motor a few revolutions at a time until upper die descends into lower die. Examines dies for mixing of two colors of paint as an indication of high spots. Files, grinds, and chisels high spots, indicated by mixing of two paint colors, using hand and power tools, until dies fit. Paints template (accurate pattern of finished stamping) and inserts it in machine. Brings dies together slowing with template between them, removes template from dies, notes further high spots (recorded by paint rubbed from template to dies), and further grinds, files, chisels, scrapes, and polishes dies.

EDGERMAN (mach. shop). Operates various types of metal working machinery, such as planer, shaper, or milling machine, to reduce the edges and other surfaces of dies to accurate dimensions.

DIE MAKER (paper goods) 4-42.301. Makes dies for scoring or cutting out paper or fiber box and carton blanks. Draws design on plywood sheets according to blueprints and cuts along the lines with a jigsaw, or measures, saws, and fits together wooden blocks to make specified design. Inserts strips of steel in the saw cuts in plywood sheet or in wooden block design, using a rule to make certain the die edges protrude at specified heights. Fastens die in a rectangular iron frame (chase), using wedges (quoins) and a hammer.

Fig. 14.6 D.O.T. Occupational Descriptions.

JOB SPECIFICATION
John Doe Shipbuilding Company

PAYROLL TITLE _Hand Burner_ CLASSIFICATION TITLE_____

_____Hand Burner_____ Acetylene Burner Operator___

DEPARTMENT_____ OCCUPATIONAL CODE_____

_____Plate Shop_____ _____6-85.219_____

FOREMAN_ John Jones _____ TELEPHONE__ 158 _____

JOB SUMMARY: Cuts mild steel plates into various shapes
with an oxyacetylene cutting torch guided by layout markings
on the material. With an oxyacetylene cutting torch, cuts
steel plates and shapes to various dimensions and sizes as
marked and laid out by LAYOUT MAN, manually moving the cutting torch along prescribed lines so that flame will cut the
squarely or with a specified bevel, as indicated by layout
symbols; occasionally heats metal to dry surface, or pre-
heats metal for cutting, bending or shaping, or to burn off
paint, rust or scale, preparatory to Arc Welding.
        Works under supervision of LEADERMAN (BURNING).

EDUCATIONAL STATUS__ Speak, read, write English ____

EXPERIENCE REQUIRED_3 Months as hand burner helper___

KNOWLEDGE AND SKILLS: Must know oxyacetylene cutting
and heating procedure and how to adjust fuel pressure; must
be able to select proper burning tips, to clean and adjust
torch and torch tips.

PHYSICAL REQUIREMENTS____ Standard Physical Examination

PERSONAL REQUIREMENTS_None_ MARITAL STATUS_ Open _

SEX__Male___ AGE RANGE_18 and overCITIZENSHIP._ Open _

REFERENCES REQUIRED: WORK_Yes__ CHARACTER_None__

WORKER MUST FURNISH_8" pliers; 10" crescent wrench;___

WAGE CODE_3 a_____   gloves; helmet.

HOURS____8___ DAYS____6___ SHIFT_Day; swing; graveyard

TESTS: APTITUDE_ None._ TRADE_Performance burning test

Figure 14.7 Job Specification

SOURCE: Carroll L. Shartle, _Occupational Information_, New York:
Prentice-Hall, Inc., 1959, p. 171.

capped workers, go into much greater detail. They indicate levels of strength and such abilities as vision and hearing. They describe proportions of time spent in standing, walking, stooping, climbing, pushing, pulling, lifting, and using right and left hands, for example.

Lead time—the length of time required to find a satisfactory new employee from outside the organization—is an item that may be added to many of the job specifications in current use. For some jobs, it may be very short. If their requirements are not highly specialized, candidates may be immediately available in the locality. For many of the technical and professional positions that have now become so important in newer industries, lead time may run into months. For one such job—obviously an extreme illustration—recruiters concluded after rather careful investigation that not more than six qualified candidates could be found in the United States. For many of these positions, time must be allowed for those recruited to give several months' notice to their employers.

2.4 Job standards, time study. Job analysis describes the qualities required of workers and the conditions under which the work is performed. Standards of performance help to indicate the numbers of employees required. Various systems of *time study* and *work-load analysis* are used to define the quantity of work expected in each job and thus to specify quantities of manpower required for staffing. The same studies may also facilitate *work simplification,* in which methods of job performance are improved.

Quantitative needs for production jobs are usually measured by one of several systems of *time study* and *motion analysis.* All begin by establishing standard conditions under which the job is performed. Then, through a process of *job breakdown,* each job is outlined as a sequence of *tasks* or *job elements.* In some procedures, *standard times* have been established for these elements, so that the over-all timing for the job may be estimated by combining these operations.

In the more common practice, workers are timed in their performance of the job. Time study engineers or analysts observe their performance and, using one or more stop watches, record the time it takes to complete the job cycle. In some practice, motion-picture cameras are used, with a clock in the pictures, to permit micromotion study. Recorded times are averaged. They are then *leveled* or *adjusted* for the *pace* of the employee. If the analysis concludes, for example, that the worker has been performing at an unusually high speed—say 120 per cent of normal—average times must be adjusted upward for this condition.

Adjusted time is then further modified to provide allowances that supplement the time actually expended in completing the work. The amount of such supplementary allowances depends on a variety of characteristics of the working situation but usually includes time for personal needs and for untimed and irregular occurrences, such as cleaning the machine.

After averages of observed time have been adjusted for pace and supplemented by allowances, they are regarded as *standard* or *task times.* Such standards are used in calculating quantitative manpower requirements, in rating employee performance, and in various systems of incentive wages.

Time study may be applied to routine clerical and other white-collar positions. For supervisors and managers, however, *work-load measurement* and *time-budgeting studies* are usually more useful. Both are less formal and are less widely used than time study. Work-load analysis records the output of office employees and calculates an approximation of standard times for repetitive operations such as transcribing letters, posting accounts, or preparing vouchers. Time budgeting provides special calendars in which working hours are divided into 10- or 15-minute periods. Employees keep detailed records of what they are doing in each such period for sample days or weeks. Records are analyzed to discover how time is spent and to suggest more efficient utilization as well as to estimate personnel requirements in expansions, decentralization, and other similar changes. *Work-sampling* procedures may be used, in which observers note what work is being performed at random times throughout the work day.

Activities designed to provide measures of standard performance in terms of output have frequently encountered employee suspicion and opposition. In the minds of many production workers, time study and work simplification are closely related to the *speedup,* in which employees are given heavier assignments without proportionate increases in earnings. Typical employee reactions hold that management uses time study to get more out of workers. If such studies are made, employees argue, managers must think employees are being paid too much or are not working hard enough. Further, in these opinions, if employees work hard and earn more, time studies will be used to cut incentive rates. Many of these conclusions are buttressed by experience. Efforts of unions to set performance standards for their members and to restrict output to pars and bogeys are to some degree a reaction and resistance to time studies and standard setting.

Employee criticisms frequently focus on the nature of the time-study procedure. The leveling process is challenged; workers argue that those who time them cannot be objective in their estimates of pace. Experienced time-study engineers insist, on the other hand, that they have developed procedures to insure reasonable accuracy. It may be noted, in this connection, that even small errors can exert an influence on earnings as great or greater than annual negotiations. More subtle, perhaps, is the feeling that all such quantitative analysis implies that management feels that employees are shirking, or that they are dishonest.

Because the setting of standards is important to employees, many unions have expressed a desire to participate in the process. In a number of instances, firms have arranged training courses in time and motion study for union members or have agreed that union technicians will check on the analysis made by the employer's time-study men. In other cases, unions have employed such technicians to make time studies. Some unions provide special courses in time study for their members.[9]

[9] See George S. Odiorne, "Joint Training in Time Study," *Personnel,* Vol. 30, No.

Employees can gain from job and methods study. Their cooperation and participation in the process are entirely justified. Work may be simplified; hazards, discomfort, and fatigue may be reduced by methods analysis and improvement. Job satisfaction may be increased. Sound standards of performance tend to reduce unfairness that may exist in situations where no standards have been established and where some employees are not doing their fair share. For these reasons, many unions have accepted joint responsibility for job study programs.[10]

2.5 Staffing schedules. From the data of job analysis and time studies, a *staffing schedule* or *manning table* can be constructed which summarizes numbers of employees for each job title. The manning table (a portion of one is illustrated in Figure 14.8) lists all jobs by title and number and indicates the number of employees employed in each job. It may also include a notation as to required training time and may classify employees as to sex, age, marital status, handicaps, and such other characteristics as may be significant and useful.

Formal manning tables with such detailed data are probably the exception rather than the rule in current practice. Usually, authority to hire specified numbers is granted when departmental budgets are approved. Manning tables can, however, suggest opportunities for improved efficiency as well as better employee relations. Analysis, from time to time, of the numbers employed as related to levels of current operations may disclose significant labor-hoarding and underutilization. It may also find objectionable overloading and overutilization in some situations. Similar comparisons of staffing in particular departments and jobs from one firm to another may disclose extensive underutilization and waste of manpower.

Manning tables are frequently accompanied by *replacement schedules* that forecast future requirements. Such schedules, prepared and maintained by each department, identify present jobholders by name and age. They then name the person regarded as immediately available as a replacement for the first. The schedule may name a second candidate and specify a date when he is likely to be ready for the position.

The manning table is also supplemented by the *personnel* or *skills inventory*. In the inventory, each employee may be indexed by both primary and secondary skills. For this purpose, the individual employee's record is consulted to discover what jobs he has performed, either before or since joining the organization.[11]

Data-processing equipment has been found useful in keeping the skills inventory up to date and making its information quickly available. It can provide current lists of employees for any skill category. It can indicate, also, the sources that have been found most helpful for whatever skills are in short supply.

3, November, 1953, pp. 203–5; also Phil Carrol, *Timestudy Fundamentals for Foremen,* New York: McGraw-Hill Book Company, Inc., 1952.

[10] See, however, William Gomberg, *A Trade Union Analysis of Time Study,* Englewood Cliffs, N.J.: Prentice-Hall, Inc., 1955.

[11] See *Personnel Policies and Practices Report,* Par. 5703, No. 11–111.

PERSONNEL INVENTORY

PLANT JOB NUMBER	OCCUPATIONAL IDENTIFICATION DATA			MINIMUM TRAINING (Months)	NUMBER NOW EMPLOYED		MINIMUM EXPERIENCE or TRAINING REQUIRED OF NEW WORKERS in MONTHS				UPGRADED	
	PLANT JOB TITLE	U.S.E.S. OCCUPATIONAL DICTIONARY JOB TITLE	U.S.E.S. D.O.T. CODE		TOTAL	Female	SAME JOB	RELATED EXPERIENCE	VOCATIONAL TRAINING	TECHNICAL TRAINING	FROM	TO
	(1)	(2)	(3)	(4)	(5)	(6)	(7)	(8)	(9)	(10)	(11)	(12)
	PRODUCTION LATHE DEPARTMENT (6)											
1	Foreman	FOREMAN (mach. shop)	5-92.768	60	3	0	6	12	0	0	2	-
2	Lathe Hand First Class	ENGINE LATHE OPERATOR I	4-78.011	24	22	0	6	12	0	0	3	1
3	Lathe Hand Second Class	ENGINE LATHE OPERATOR II	6-78.011	4	66	6	0	6	6	0	4	2
4	Drill Press Opr.	*DEEP-HOLE DRILLER (mach. shop)	6-78.011	1	3	1	0	6	6	0	5	2
5	Saw Operator	*BAND-SAWING-MACHINE OPERATOR	6-78.611	2	2	1	0	0	0	0	6	4 or 3
6	Helper	*MACHINIST HELPER	8-78.10	0	9	0	0	0	0	0	-	4 or 5
	GRINDING DEPARTMENT (6) (105) (8)											
11	Foreman	FOREMAN (mach. shop)	5-92.768	60	2	0	6	12	0	0	13	-
12	External Grinder	CYLINDRICAL GRINDER OPERATOR II	6-78.521	4	9	2	0	6	6	0	15 or 16	11
13	Internal Grinder	INTERNAL GRINDER OPERATOR I	4-78.512	20	2	0	6	12	0	0	12 or 14	11
14	Centerless Grinder	CENTERLESS GRINDER OPERATOR	6-78.511	10	9	2	6	6	6	0	15 or 16	13
15	Burrer	*BURRER, HAND	6-77.510	2	2	2	0	0	0	0	-	13
16	Trucker	*TRUCKER, HAND	8-78.10	0	2	0	0	0	0	0	-	15

* Entry Jobs

Minnesota Division of Employment and Security

Figure 14.8 The Manning Table or Staffing Schedule

2.6 Organization planning. Staffing should be closely coordinated with organization planning, since every change in the organization affects manpower requirements. When an organization is to be expanded, with new products and processes, then job descriptions, specifications, and manning tables may be prepared in advance. Plans are made with respect to reassignments of present employees as well as the recruitment of others. Some employees may be given the opportunity to undertake special training.

Similar problems arise in internal reorganizations.

3.0 SUMMARY

Staffing is the oldest and most common assignment to personnel and industrial relations divisions. Most of the early personnel departments were essentially employment offices. Determining and forecasting manpower requirements, recruiting, selecting, placing, and orienting are still major responsibilities in modern industrial relations staff divisions. Expenditures for these purposes represent one of the more important items in the budgets of today's staff departments.

Policy on staffing should be consistent with the complex of general manpower policy. In some earlier practice, manpower was hired as needed, for the jobs to be done. It was released whenever the need ceased, whenever the particular job ran out. Comparatively little consideration was given to long-run staffing requirements at rank-and-file levels, and not too much thought concerned future requirements for supervision and management.

Modern practice has required much greater attention to general policy and to the development of appropriate staffing policy. Human resources have become both more costly and in shorter supply. Public policy proposes to continue this condition by maintaining *full employment*. Public policy is reinforced by the growing educational and technical requirements of jobs. Few jobs can be filled by *raw labor*. Staffing policy must think in terms of more stringent immediate requirements plus the personal versatility to learn and develop as the pace of technological change modifies job specifications.

Changing theories of work and organization have had a powerful impact on staffing policy. If efficient performance cannot be assured simply by varying financial rewards, more attention must be given to the aptitudes and interests of employees. If employees cannot be expected to respect supervisors merely because they represent owners, far more attention must be given to the quality of leadership at supervisory and management levels. If the organization is to benefit from increased participation in its decisions, it must recruit and develop team members who will be qualified to accept these added responsibilities.

Staffing policy must carefully regard the growing tendency to employ for careers rather than simply for jobs. The trend to restrict arbitrary dismissals of employees is unmistakable. In several foreign nations, employees with specified length of service cannot be dismissed except for serious cause. Hiring is for keeps.

The process of staffing begins with decisions on job requirements. For this purpose, standard practice uses job analysis. In that procedure, a major goal is the determination of measurable requirements that can be matched with measured personal qualifications. From the job analysis, job descriptions are prepared and job specifications focus attention on the personal requirements of the job.

Qualitative job specifications may be supplemented by time studies or work-load analyses that permit decision on the necessary complements of divisions and units.

Manning tables summarize manpower requirements for the organization. They may be accompanied by replacement tables, which indicate when positions are likely to become vacant and what resources within the organization are available to fill these vacancies. In organization planning, these manning and replacement tables provide a crude measure with which to forecast requirements. For all such changes, firms and agencies may maintain inventories of skills, which facilitate transfers and promotions from within.

The next step in the process of staffing is that of recruitment. It discovers sources and encourages candidates to apply for employment. Thereafter, a variety of selection procedures identifies those who are to be offered membership in the organization. Recruitment and selection programs receive attention in the chapters that follow.

SELECTED SUPPLEMENTARY READINGS

Bellows, Roger M., *Psychology of Personnel in Business and Industry*, 2nd ed., chap. 9, "Job Analysis," Englewood Cliffs, N.J.: Prentice-Hall, Inc., 1960.

Dunnette, Marvin D. and Wayne K. Kirchner, "Identifying Critical Factors in Successful Salesmanship," *Personnel*, Vol. 34, No. 2, September-October, 1957, pp. 54–59.

Gomberg, William, *A Trade Union Analysis of Time Study*, chaps. 16 and 17, Englewood Cliffs, N.J.: Prentice-Hall, Inc., 1955.

Gusfield, Joseph R., "Equalitarianism and Bureaucratic Recruitment," *Administrative Science Quarterly*, Vol. 2, No. 4, pp. 521–41, March, 1958.

Handbook of Personnel Management and Labor Relations, sec. 5, pp. 1–43. New York: McGraw-Hill Book Company, Inc., 1958.

Heneman, Herbert G., Jr., and John G. Turnbull, *Personnel Administration and Labor Relations*, chap. 5. Englewood Cliffs, N.J.: Prentice-Hall, Inc., 1952.

Hope, John Jr., *Equality of Opportunity*, Washington, D.C.: Public Affairs Press, 1956.

"Manpower Challenge of the 1960's," Washington, D.C.: United States Department of Labor, 1960.

Mark, Jerome A., "Comparative Job Performance by Age," *Monthly Labor Review*, Vol. 80, No. 12, December, 1957, pp. 1467–71.

Rowland, Virgil K., *Managerial Performance Standards*, chap. 8, New York: American Management Association, 1960.

Shartle, Carroll L., *Occupational Information,* 2nd ed., chap 6, Englewood Cliffs, N.J.: Prentice-Hall, Inc., 1959.

SHORT CASE PROBLEM 14.1

Objections to a Time Budget

Miss Lenore Wicklund has worked as a principal clerk for the Browder Printing Co. for eight years. She is conscientious and, at the same time, almost proprietary in her attitude toward the firm, which she has seen grow from 10 to 98 employees.

Her supervisor has told Miss Wicklund that he thinks she is not making full use of her talents, because she insists on handling all details of every job she undertakes. He has suggested that she delegate much of the routine in her assignments to newer clerical employees. Miss Wicklund insists that she can't trust them.

Recently, her supervisor has asked Miss Wicklund to maintain a time budget and send it to him each week. She has flatly refused. She says that it is insulting, that it takes too much time, and that it would be meaningless.

Problem: Your job is to advise the supervisor. What should he do?

SHORT CASE PROBLEM 14.2

The Pierce Manufacturing Company

The Arkansas (Little Rock) division of the Pierce Manufacturing Co. has encountered difficulty in its job analysis program. A new industrial relations director, taking over less than a year ago, began the program by asking employees to fill out a job questionnaire. When answers came in, he asked supervisors to comment. In many cases, employees indicated that they were performing tasks which supervisors questioned. Some supervisors insisted that employees were not actually doing all they claimed. In some cases, supervisors admitted that employees were doing what they claimed but said that they should not be doing some of the tasks.

The new industrial relations director now finds himself faced with a difficult problem. He sought only to find out what each job involved. Now he is being asked to settle arguments as to what should be expected of jobholders and, even more difficult, what to do about employees who insist they have long been expected to do more than their supervisors think they are doing.

Problem: Should the industrial relations director ignore these controversies? If so, whose word should he take as to job content? If not, how should he move to resolve the differences?

SHORT CASE PROBLEM 14.3

The Best Man Policy

South-West Plastics is a relatively young firm, established in 1951. It has expanded rapidly; it now employs 700 hourly rated workers. Management is young and energetic and is generally regarded as superior, both in the industry and in the community in which the firm operates.

South-West has given wide circulation to its basic manpower policy, both within the firm and throughout the state. Employees are organized. Management is said to have encouraged their collective bargaining. The current contract includes a grievance provision, with terminal arbitration. Under the grievance procedure, two employees have carried their complaint to arbitration. The submission to the arbitrator is as follows:

"Did the company err in refusing Jack Smith and Jim Jones promotion to the pin-punch job on March 6th?" The parties agreed in the arbitration hearing that the arbitrator should make whatever recommendations seemed appropriate to his decision.

The finding of facts outlined the issue as follows: Two vacancies developed as a result of expansion. Smith and Jones applied for them. The foreman in charge of the vacancies refused to accept either Smith or Jones. Instead, he selected two others with less experience and less seniority. The foreman explains that his action expresses his conclusion that the two junior employees were qualified for the jobs. They were the best men. In his opinion, neither Smith nor Jones was as well qualified as they.

Policy on staffing declares that:

> It is our policy to secure the best man available for each position in the organization. When it appears that two men of equal ability are available, one from outside and the other a present employee, the employee shall have first chance at the job. Within this framework of policy, seniority and qualifications shall govern in promotions.

In its presentation of the case before the arbitrator, the union declared that it had no complaint about the policy. The union favors the "best man" rule. Union spokesmen said, however, that the decision made by the foreman was arbitrary, that the senior men should have been given a chance to try out on the new job. They pointed to a contract provision that outlines a procedure in which the departmental foreman and the departmental shop steward review the qualifications of bidders and decide which if any should be promoted.

Problem: If called on to arbitrate this dispute on the facts as summarized, how would you decide the issue? What suggestion or order would you include in your award? (For a decision in a somewhat comparable case, see Reynolds Metal Award, 10 ALAA, #71,241.)

15. Sources and Recruitment

Job analysis, supplemented by time studies, manning tables, and staffing schedules, states the problem for staffing. Management uses these devices and techniques to define its manpower requirements and to forecast future needs. They thus provide an essential guide for the continuing process of recruitment.

Recruitment, including the identification and appraisal of sources, is thus a second step in the total staffing process. That process begins with the determination of manpower needs for the organization. It continues with recruitment, selection, placement, and orientation. The staffing process cannot be entirely divorced from the process of development and training, but the latter activities may be so extensive in themselves that they are reserved for treatment later in this book.

Recruitment may be relatively simple, as when the small store or filling station identifies someone to help out in busy periods or to accept long-term employment as a clerk or attendant. It may, on the other hand, be a complex and expensive activity, involving promotions from within the larger organization as well as advertising, placing orders with an employment office, visiting known sources such as schools and colleges, and perhaps sending recruiters into foreign nations to discover needed scientists or engineers.

This chapter is concerned with the problems managers face in recruiting the manpower they need. The chapter suggests the choices open to managers —the range of possible sources and of recruitment practices and techniques. Some managers may overlook or ignore important possibilities; they may have fallen into the habit of following a simple pattern, not recognizing important alternatives. Others may have done little to check the value and usefulness of sources and practices. They may continue to recruit from high schools, even though their experience with employees from these sources has been unsatisfactory. They may employ practices in college recruitment that are ineffective. They may ignore possibilities of recruitment from within their organizations.

Such haphazard practice is usually symptomatic, however, of much more serious problems involving choices among recruitment policies. Their satisfactory solution requires careful consideration of the goals of recruitment in terms of general manpower policy. A preliminary question, for example, concerns the emphasis to be placed on quantity as compared with quality. Does recruitment emphasize the numbers of candidates who can be interested in possible employment with the organization? Or does it concentrate on discovery of smaller numbers of more likely prospects? Other problems are concerned with the attitudes with which recruitment is conducted. Shall every candidate with minimum qualifications be hired? What consideration shall be given to career guidance? How important are the opinions and preferences of supervisors? What public policy must be considered? What about providing employment for the handicapped? Should every large organization recruit a fixed proportion of its employees from those on parole, as a contribution to their rehabilitation?

1.0 RECRUITMENT POLICY

Chapter 13 has emphasized the necessity for developing policy on staffing that is consistent with the general manpower policy of the organization. Before steps can be taken to identify and recruit appropriate human resources for the new organization or to develop an effective recruitment and selection program, additional policy is necessary as a guide to practice in these staffing functions. The range of choice with respect to such practice is very broad. Some policy and practice may be appropriate for a public utilities firm that services northern Montana; the same policy and practice may be quite inappropriate for a construction firm in San Francisco or an oil refinery in Houston, Texas.

Sound policy is essential as a guide in making choices among what may be regarded as *standard operating practices.* As has been frequently noted, decisions on sound policy will require careful evaluation of both general policy and management theory. These requirements may perhaps be made more tangible by outlining some of the questions that deserve careful answers as a basis for *recruitment policy* in a firm or agency. It will be helpful, in noting these questions, to consider how different answers would be appropriate for the northern utility, the western construction company, the oil refinery in Texas, and a large retail store in Atlanta.

1. What is the general nature of *present* and *prospective manpower requirements?* To what extent must they be professional, technical, skilled, semi-skilled, or unskilled? Here, as in all policy and practice in recruitment, the job descriptions and job specifications resulting from job analyses provide

the natural starting point. The information they provide is essential if recruitment is to be at all systematic.

2. How important—in terms of costs—is manpower for the firm or agency? Labor costs as a proportion of total costs may be much less in the refinery than in the retail store, for example.

3. What are the long-term *career plans* for managers and employees? Does the firm offer careers for all or part of the recruits? How does it forecast future requirements?

4. What recruitment and selection facilities are available to the firm? Does it have, within the organization, a staff division that is prepared to provide these services? Must it depend largely on public and private *employment services?*

5. What limitations on recruitment and selection are imposed by public policy? Is the situation one that precludes the employment of women, for example? Must serious consideration be given to employment of minorities, or are there no problems on this score? Will the firm be expected to provide employment for some, perhaps many, part-time workers?

Some answers to these questions will depend on experience. Other questions can only be answered in terms of attitudes, assumptions, and theories. For example, we may conclude that we can train inexperienced employees for most of our jobs in a short period. We may assume that our jobs will provide the challenge and opportunity that will hold employees, so it may be worthwhile to undertake expensive recruitment. We may, on the other hand, conclude that we can get and hold employees with specialized training by offering slightly higher wages than our competitors; we will therefore recruit from their employees.

We may assume that none but specially talented and trained workers will fit our requirements, or, on the other hand, we may conclude that mine-run workers can be adapted to most or all of our needs.

These and other opinions deserve critical examination. What does our experience and that of others indicate as to their reliability? Is there relevant evidence from research?

Managers generally take for granted that potential candidates for employment will, in their own self-interest, give their time to recruitment and selection procedure without compensation. Attitudes of applicants may change; especially in the case of technical and professional workers, managers may face resistance to this viewpoint.

For all recruitment, a preliminary question of policy considers the extent to which it will emphasize inside and outside sources. Will the organization depend largely on present employees as likely candidates for such employment opportunities as appear in the future? Or will it generally look at other sources, outside the organization? For most larger organizations, the question is not one of "either-or" but one of relative use. The question is: under what circumstances and to what extent shall we seek to find the manpower we require within our own ranks? When will we go outside?

To the extent that new recruits are to be drawn into the organization, additional policy questions must be considered. How will the organization define its intentions with respect to these recruits? What shall it seek in them —polished skills, experienced performance, or aptitude and potential for development? How can superior sources be identified? What recruitment policy is essential to conform to public policy? How shall recruitment regard minority groups, women workers, older workers, the handicapped, and those available only on a part-time basis? Shall policy favor the employment of friends and relatives of present employees?

If answers to all these questions are to be dependable, policy will carefully regard the evidence of effectiveness in recruiting as provided by experience within and without the individual firm. Studies can be made to discover experience with promotions from within. Employee attitude studies can discover the reactions of present employees to both internal and external recruiting. Records of employment by source permit calculations of the relative success of those employed. A crude measure of recruitment calculates a *recruitment ratio* as the number of actual persons hired per hundred applicants. Research can measure the results of recruitment interviews, advertising, and other techniques. Studies in other firms can provide evidence to support or question the assumptions and theory on which practice relies. Sound policy in recruitment, as in all manpower management, requires such tests and audits and research.

2.0 RECRUITMENT FROM WITHIN

Many current statements of general manpower policy declare the intention to give present employees first chance at all employment opportunities in the organization. *Promotion from within* is a widely accepted and long-established policy in many organizations, large and small. Even when no such policy has been formally stated, practice often indicates its general acceptance. In some organizations, such a policy is stated in collective bargaining agreements with one or more unions. As such, it is a continuing guide to practice within these bargaining units.

Observation suggests that the policy is at least as generally accepted in clerical, supervisory, and even managerial ranks in many organizations. Public agencies generally follow a similar pattern in which, however, civil service examinations may be required as evidence of competence for promotion.

Managements consider several variables in deciding on the extent to which they will depend on inside and outside sources. Among the most important are the following:

(1) *The effect of this policy on the attitudes and actions of all employees.* This is perhaps the most frequently noted; it is often cited as the major reason for a policy of promotion from within. Most employees are likely to feel more secure and to identify their own long-term interests with those of

the firm when they can anticipate first chance at job opportunities. On the other hand, it is reasonable to expect somewhat less concern about high-level performance under these circumstances. General application of the promotion from within policy may encourage mediocre performance.

(2) *The level of specialization required of employees.* In many organizations the principal source for qualified workers may be the ranks of present employees who have received specialized training. In new industries—electronics is an example—no other source may be as satisfactory.

(3) *The emphasis in general manpower policy on participation by employees at all levels.* New employees from outside, inexperienced in the firm, may not know enough about its products or processes to participate effectively.

(4) *The need for originality and initiative.* If managament feels that it is training for these qualities, it may prefer its own people. If, on the other hand, it feels no such assurance, that fact may argue for the importation of new people with different ideas.

(5) *Acceptance of the seniority principle.* In most organizations, if emphasis is to be placed on promotion from within, seniority will play an important part. It is the simplest basis on which to decide who merits advancement. Few organizations have developed methods of appraisal that have general acceptance and can be used in lieu of seniority.

(6) *The mobility of managers.* In many organizations, promotion from within is a reward for joining the organization. Many managers may not develop and maintain a professional level of competence; as a result, they cannot move to other organizations without great sacrifice. As managers become more professional, this consideration carries less weight.

Personnel Policies and Practices Report concludes, "Companies are drifting away from promotions from within."[1] Two causes are cited: (1) the movement away from paternalism that has accompanied growing unionization and (2) the tendency to decentralize large organizations.

2.1 Terminology of internal recruitment. *Internal recruitment* is implemented through promotions and transfers. In less frequent *personnel actions,* employees may be *demoted.* Some may eliminate themselves from the ranks of inside sources by resigning. A few may be *terminated* or *dischaiged.* *Promotion* is defined as a movement to a position in which responsibilities are increased. Conversely, *demotion* is a shift to a position in which responsibilities are decreased. Promotion involves an increase in rank, and demotion is a decrease in rank. Ordinarily, promotion is regarded as a change that results in higher earnings, but increased earnings are not essential in a promotion. Presumably, promotion places employees in positions that carry greater prestige as well as increased responsibilities. Promotions may be unaccompanied by salary or wage increases. Indeed, such *dry promotions* are sometimes given in lieu of increases in compensation.

[1] Par. 165, No. 15—43, 1961.

That promotions cannot be too closely linked to wage and salary adjustments is apparent when all compensation is adjusted upward to keep pace with the cost of living. Such across-the-board raises are not regarded as including any element of promotion.

Many organizations maintain *systematic promotion plans.* The essential characteristic of all of them is their provision of previously outlined channels in terms of which promotions are planned. Most systems make use of some sort of graphic portrayal of promotional lines and opportunities associated with each position. Such "promotional charts," "opportunity charts," or "fortune sheets," as they are variously described, clearly distinguish each job and, by lines and arrows connecting various jobs, show the lines of advancement up to and away from them.

Most current plans for systematic promotions represent adaptations of two older, well-established arrangements. One of these, usually credited to the Gilbreths, is called the "three-position plan." Each position is related to two other positions—one from which employees are promoted and another to which promotions are made. There are three levels of attainment for each position: that of the student, that of the actual operator in the position, and that of the instructor.

Another widely known system involves what is known as the "multiple chain promotion plan." It provides for a systematic linking of each position to several others from which promotions are made, and to still others to which incumbents may be promoted. It permits multiple promotional opportunities through clearly defined avenues of approach to and exit from each position in the organization. Each of these avenues is prearranged, and all are clearly indicated in the general chart of the whole systematic promotional plan.

A *transfer* involves the shifting of an employee from one job to another without special reference to changing responsibilities or compensation. Transfers may and generally do occasion changes in responsibilities and duties. They may also involve changes in pay.

Two principal types of transfers may be distinguished. The most frequent type of transfer appears when the need for manpower in one job or department is reduced or increased. Employees may then be transferred to or from other jobs or departments to meet the changing demand. Such shifts are *production* transfers. A second type, generally described as *personnel* transfers, involves shifts made to meet the requests or needs of employees. Although many of them may have their roots in faulty selection and placement, others arise because individuals find their interests changing, or family considerations suggest a change in residence, or employees find themselves unhappy with co-workers or believe they would be happier in another crew. Health may also be a consideration; injuries or illness may have changed employee qualifications or attitudes.

Generally, a sharp distinction is made between *temporary* and *permanent transfers,* because practice in wage and salary administration regards the two differently. Some collective agreements provide specific limits on the length of temporary transfers.

Releases and *terminations* represent a severing of the employment relationship. The most common form of release is the *layoff*. In it, the employee is temporarily separated from the employer on the initiative of the employer *without prejudice to the employee*. Layoffs are occasioned by lack of work. Both employer and employee understand that the employee will be recalled whenever work is available. The worker may continue to describe himself as an employee, although temporarily out of work. In some cases, layoff is for a definite period; in others, the employer may not be able to estimate when he can recall the employee. A few layoffs are disciplinary. Layoff is then a sort of *suspension* imposed as a penalty.

Quits, resignations, and *discharges* or *terminations* represent conclusive and final separations. Quits and resignations sever the employment relationship on the initiative of the employee. Discharges and terminations are releases initiated by the employer with or without prejudice to the employee. Some releases are occasioned by the elimination of jobs and involve no prejudice.

2.2 Seniority. The policy of promotion from within is most commonly implemented through the practice of *seniority*. That practice may have a variety of applications. Most common is its use in layoffs and rehires. Seniority may also be influential in transfers, promotions, and demotions. Other applications relate seniority to job assignments, the selection of shifts and vacations and eligibility for overtime work.

For promotions and sometimes for favored work assignments, practice implements seniority by a *posting and bidding* process, which requires that notice of each opportunity be advertised and that interested employees bid for it by advising managers that they wish to be considered.

Seniority means *length of service*. It may be calculated as the time elapsed since the employee's name first appeared on the payroll, or it may be measured as the number of days of service since that date. Frequently, absence from the payroll for extended periods causes *loss of seniority,* or an employee laid off who fails to respond or is not available for employment when he is called loses his seniority.[2] New employees, placed on *probation* for a period of 30 to 90 days, acquire no seniority during probation. If they are retained beyond this period, their seniority is calculated from the date on which they were hired. Employees continue the accrual of seniority during absence occasioned by illness, accident, or approved leaves of absence (for jury duty, voting, military service, maternity, and special assignments for a union). Suspensions generally stop the accumulation of seniority for the period of absence.

Employees may lose seniority rights. The most common causes are quitting; being discharged for cause; violation of leave-of-absence provisions, especially

[2] See Philomena M. Mullady, "Seniority—A Changing Concept," *Personnel,* Vol. 33, No. 1, July, 1956, pp. 78–81.

failure to return promptly; unexplained absence; and failure to report within a specified period after notification of recall to work.

Trainees and *apprentices* are usually granted seniority only within their own groups. If the work force is reduced, numbers of trainees and apprentices may also be restricted to maintain a specified ratio.

Most arrangements also provide for the *exemption* of a small group of "exceptional" employees. They include persons being specifically trained for managerial positions. Sometimes it is agreed that a fixed percentage of all employees shall be so regarded, commonly ten per cent.

2.3 Super-seniority or top seniority. Simple seniority arrangements may be modified by special provisions granting preference and special rights to union stewards or members of a grievance committee. Foremen and supervisors, like union stewards, are usually granted top seniority. Practice is not uniform, however, with respect to foremen who may be relieved of supervisory responsibility when the work force is reduced. In some situations employees have hesitated to accept promotion to supervisory positions lest they lose their seniority status and rights.

2.4 Range of seniority rights. A basic consideration in provisions establishing seniority is that which determines the range of seniority rights. Calculation of length of service may be made on either a *departmental* or a *plant-wide* basis. It may be limited to a single plant, or it may extend to several plants operated by the same employer, in which case it is described as *company-wide.* In some cases, it may be limited to a single craft in a system of *occupational* seniority.

Some practice goes so far as to provide *rate-bracket seniority,* in which senior employees in each rate range or salary classification enjoy seniority rights with respect to work assignments, layoff and recall, and promotion.

Bumping is the procedure in which an employee with seniority, finding his own job no longer available, demands the job of someone having less seniority. The displaced employee may repeat the process on someone with still less seniority, and *bumping* may continue down to the level of probationary employees. A single layoff may thus occasion many changes. In plant-wide seniority, bumping, especially in times when many employees are laid off, may create serious disorganization and disruption throughout the plant. In one example, ten to twelve changes were made before a single employee left the payroll. Because each employee was entitled to a three-day notice, a single release took from two to three weeks.

2.5 Policy on seniority. Employers and managers have generally criticized seniority rights and have struggled to limit their influence. They have argued that the seniority system encourages half hearted performance and inefficiency, that it affects morale adversely, that it handicaps managerial action. They insist that it pays employees simply for "sticking around" rather than for their contribution to the work of the organization.

Most unions, on the other hand, have favored seniority for their members and insisted that it play an important part in promotions, work assignments, layoff and recall. They argue that it is essential to prevent favoritism and arbitrary action by foremen and supervisors. They insist that no other, better measure of competence or ability has been developed. They resist the frequent attempts of management to give personnel ratings or appraisals greater influence than seniority.

Unions face problems of their own in the application of seniority. Members may prefer some form of job spreading, which protects the jobs of long-service workers, to a layoff. In some employee benefits—for example, supplementary unemployment benefits—seniority may mean that long-term workers continue working to provide larger unemployment benefits for those with less seniority. When employees are represented by several unions, each may seek its own seniority list and insist that members of rival unions may not bump its members.

Seniority has important implications for the public interest. It may be regarded with public favor because it encourages the retention of older employees, who, if released, generally have greater difficulty in finding new employment. On the other hand, seniority has some tendency to demobilize human resources. It may encourage workers to remain in jobs in which they are not making their maximum contribution.

Despite general employer opposition, the formal and informal influence of seniority is heavy, both in blue-collar and white-collar positions. Top managers frequently declare that it plays a larger part in promotions among supervisors and managers than among lower ranks. The major explanation for this influence is to be found in the absence of objective measures of superiority and in the general conclusion that length of service should be rewarded.

The heavy weight given seniority is evident in current practice. Healy found that in two unionized firms more than 80 per cent of those promoted were the senior bidders. He found that in the third firm included in his study—a firm without unionized employees—83 per cent of those promoted were also senior employees.[3]

Seniority can add significant complications to problems in mergers. How shall seniority in the components of the combination be related to seniority in the total? This question can be expected to gain increasing attention from unions, for many of their members may lose important rights in the process of combination.[4]

2.6 Tests for promotion. Seniority is widely recognized as far from perfect as a basis for promotion. Some current practice has sought to sup-

---

[3] James Healy, "The Factor of Ability in Labor Relations," *Proceedings,* Eighth Annual Meeting of the National Academy of Arbitrators, Washington, D.C.: Bureau of National Affairs, 1955, pp. 45–54. See also Clifford M. Baumback, "Merit and Seniority as Factors in Promotion and In-Grade Progression," *Research Series No. 11,* University of Iowa Bureau of Labor and Management, 1956; Dale D. McConkey, "Ability v. Seniority in Promotion and Layoff," *Personnel,* Vol. 37, No. 3, May-June, 1960, pp. 51–57.

[4] See Mark L. Kahn, "Seniority Problems in Business Mergers," *Industrial and Labor Relations Review,* Vol. 8, No. 3, April, 1935, pp. 361–78.

plement it with various types of tests and examinations. To be eligible for promotion, each candidate may have to pass a special test designed to measure knowledge and skill required in the vacant job. Such tests have long been used in the civil service. They have, however, achieved no wide acceptance in private employment. Their construction and maintenance are expensive. Few firms employ enough workers in each job to justify the expense of developing such devices. They are generally confined to identification of only a part of the total personal qualifications for the job, usually to technical knowledge or special skills. Broader questions of personality and leadership are not answered. In spite of these limitations, both managers and union leaders have encouraged their use and appear likely to experiment with them in a wider range of occupations and industries.[5]

2.7 Demotion. Some employers insist that they do not need a policy on demotion because they will not demote. Whenever circumstances make it necessary to reduce an employee's responsibilities, he will be released. It is argued that demotion inevitably creates frictions and destroys the self-assurance and value of the demoted employee. Demotions may become almost imperative when certain activities are restricted or eliminated. Government agencies face this problem in "RIFS"—reductions in force. Without demotions, business organizations may find themselves with a number of department heads for nonexistent departments. Sometimes these managers can be transferred or promoted. In other situations, they must either be demoted or released. Policy should probably permit individuals to choose between demotion and release.

Demotions may become necessary as a result of errors in promotion. Policy may provide for demotions in such cases by creating a six-month or one-year probationary period in all promotions. In some practice, personnel ratings are used as the index of satisfactory performance. An unsatisfactory rating automatically requires demotion. Under the provisions of many collective agreements, demotions may be protested through the grievance procedure.

3.0 TRANSFERS, LAYOFFS, AND TERMINATIONS

Staffing from within the organization is by no means simply a matter of promotions and demotions. To fill some requirements, employees may be moved horizontally in transfers. Others may be laid off for varying periods. Some members of the organization's work force—frequently those on whom management is counting most—may decide to leave. Others may fail to measure up to requirements for continued membership; they may have to be released.

3.1 Transfers. Major questions of policy on transfers concern the condi-

[5] See "Building Better Promotion Programs," *Pamphlet No. 2,* Washington, D.C.: U. S. Civil Service Commission, July, 1952.

tions under which transfers will be made and the basis for compensating employees in transfers.

As in policy on demotion, some employers prefer an informal policy on *personnel transfers*. They argue that such changes "take care of themselves" and that policy should let them do so. If an employee wants to transfer, let him ask. If a supervisor thinks an employee should move, let him make necessary arrangements for the shift. But difficulties may develop out of such a policy and the informal procedure it encourages. Requests for a transfer by an employee may irritate his supervisor. Such requests may be avoided because employees are afraid of this reaction. Some departments get the reputation of being easy to transfer from, whereas others are regarded as exactly the opposite. Some foremen and department heads suggest and recommend transfers, sometimes merely to get rid of employees they dislike. Other supervisors never make such suggestions, lest the suggestions be regarded as admissions that supervisors have done a poor job of selection or that they cannot get along with those they supervise. As a result, some divisions are cluttered with misfits who should have been transferred.

To avoid these effects, more specific policy indicates when and under what circumstances transfers will be made.

Production transfers are initiated by the employer to meet his needs. They raise a number of difficult questions. To what jobs may the employer reasonably ask an employee to shift? How about transfers to other divisions or to distant plants? Is the employee required to accept such a transfer? If he doesn't accept the proposed transfer, does that mean he will be laid off, so that the choice is to change or to go without work? If only a part of the work group is to be transferred, who is to make the change? If the rate on the new job is lower, is the employee's rate reduced? If the new job pays a higher rate, shall he get this increase? Does the transferred employee have first chance at his earlier job when employment expands? What happens to his seniority in such transfers?

Current policy provides few standard answers to these questions. Many firms prefer to make transfers as simple and easy as possible, so that the work force may be shifted to such jobs as are under most pressure. Some unions favor somewhat the same viewpoint as a means of stabilizing employment for their members. Other unions, however, regard a relatively inflexible policy as superior, for somewhat the same reasons. The latter unions hope thereby to protect the *job rights* of employees by requiring or insisting on the employees' presence if the job is to be performed.

In permanent personnel transfers, the employee normally receives the rate of pay on the job to which he is transferred. In production transfers, common practice pays the rate of the regular job or that of the new job, whichever is higher, although there are exceptions when a shortage of work reduces employment and such transfers are necessary to provide work. On temporary transfers, employees may continue at their usual rate.

When transfers require an employee to move to another locality, current practice frequently provides financial assistance for this purpose. The extent of such assistance often varies with the rank of the employee or manager; rank-and-file employees may receive minimal assistance, whereas managers are aided in moving, in buying homes, and in compensating for losses they may have taken in selling their homes.

3.2 Layoffs. In general, managements seek to avoid layoffs, in part because they may easily cause the loss of valued employees. A laid-off employee is a likely candidate for recruitment by another employer. At the same time, layoffs tend to reduce the employer's credit in unemployment compensation accounts and thus to make him liable for higher tax rates in many states. Policy frequently requires that employees subject to layoff shall be given priority in filling any jobs in other departments for which they may be qualified.

Seniority usually plays an important role. In earlier periods, those laid off first and for longest periods of time were employees who were regarded as least valuable. In other practice, the employee's need was regarded as the most important consideration. Employees with heavy family responsibilities were retained as long as possible. Favorites of the foreman frequently received preferential treatment.

Current policy on layoff is closely related to ideas of work sharing. In work-sharing plans, layoffs are limited and hours are reduced. These arrangements tend to hold the work force together. They keep employees from collecting unemployment compensation. But they may require that employees be assigned to jobs for which they are not well qualified. They may keep employees from accepting jobs in which they could earn more.

3.3 Quits. From the point of view of an employer, a quit or resignation may be a matter either of relief or concern. Some quits may be regarded as solving problems—situations in which employee performance was only partially satisfactory and prospective relationships were not promising. On the other hand, the resignation of satisfactory and promising employees represents a considerable loss and may be symptomatic of serious shortcomings in the whole employment relationship. Those who quit may have received extensive and expensive training. The employer may have an investment in them.

Most employer policy seeks to prevent such separations. Several questions must, however, be answered. How far will the employer go in trying to hold valuable employees? What added compensation, if any, shall be offered to those who indicate an intention to resign? Will the employer adopt the general principle that "you're worth as much to us as to anyone else"? Will outside offers be matched?

Some employers make no promotions or individual salary or wage adjustments in such circumstances, holding that wage and salary policy allows no deviations from job rates. Others allow personal adjustments to the top of a salary grade to meet competitive offers.

Policy frequently requires that all quits shall be carefully investigated and explained by supervisors. *Exit interviews* may be required. Resulting explanations may disclose a pattern in these losses and thus suggest a review of both policy and practice in training, supervision, compensation, promotion, or other conditions of employment.

3.4 Discharges. Early policy generally regarded discharge as the unquestioned prerogative of the employer or his representatives. He offered employment; he could terminate that offer at will. No such policy has any wide acceptance in industry today.

Most current policy limits involuntary separations to those resulting from (1) discontinuing the job, department, or plant operation and (2) serious violation of work rules or demonstrated inability to perform available work.

In the first of these two situations, an employee may be encouraged to transfer into other jobs for which he is, or may become, qualified. In disciplinary cases, current policy generally requires that discharge must be for specified cause. Such action requires one or more warnings, except in the most serious offenses. In most current policy, discharged employees may seek redress for any unfairness through the grievance procedure.

Current policy on terminations recognizes the heavy costs of such releases. Some proportion of all those terminated may soon have to be replaced. Their replacements have to be recruited, selected, and perhaps given expensive training. Meanwhile, terminations may influence the attitudes and contribution of other employees. They may influence recruitment far into the future.

A policy of *vertical reduction*—in which all budgets are slashed by a fixed percentage or all employment is reduced from bottom to top of the organization—may be very costly for these reasons.

4.0 RECRUITMENT FROM OUTSIDE

Few firms or agencies can fill all their manpower requirements from within. Over a period of years, such internal staffing is possible only for an organization that requires less and less manpower. Separations create vacancies that must be filled, and new jobs have specifications that cannot be met from the inventory of present skills. Staffing policy must, therefore, assume that some recruitment will look to sources outside the organization. This section describes the most common of these sources and policy and practice in recruitment from them.

4.1 Personal applications. In periods of normal business activity, many managements find that the source from which they draw the largest number of new employees is that generally described as "applicants at the gate." In depression, dependence upon this source is encouraged by the fact that the number making application is greatly increased, while needs are reduced.

Applications may also be received through the mail. Although it is generally impossible to promise employment without a personal interview, mail applications frequently provide an introduction to desirable sources. Applicants who write may be invited to appear personally at their convenience.

4.2 Nominations by present employees. Some firms encourage present employees to suggest candidates for employment and to assist them in filing applications. In situations of acute shortage, firms have offered special financial rewards to employees for this assistance.

Policy on this type of recruitment is divided. In that which is most common, however, managers favor such employee action and regard the policy in itself as a valuable asset, both in finding satisfactory candidates and in maintaining good will among present employees. There are some hazards in the practice, since recruitment based on employee nominations may encourage family cliques and inner circles of close friends. Also, nominations by present employees may result in types of discrimination that are outlawed by fair employment practice rules. This procedure has been cited as evidence of discriminatory practice by New York's Anti-Discrimination Commission. On the other hand, there are real gains, for employees react favorably to the opportunity to help select their colleagues and fellow workers.

4.3 Labor organizations. Unions may be an important source of employees. In closed shop relationships, all recruits must be union members, and employers often call on unions to supply whatever additional employees may be needed.

The value of unions as a source depends largely on the amount of attention local officers give to job finding. Some locals act as employment services and use their union office facilities for this purpose. Others provide little or no assistance of this kind.

4.4 Advertising. Perhaps the most common recruitment practice is advertising. Many kinds of advertising are used for this purpose, including billboards, handbills, newspaper display and classified ads, help-wanted cards in streetcars, buses, and private automobiles, radio and television announcements, and even sound trucks. The range of media used reflects the immediacy of the need and the tightness or looseness of local labor markets. Public agencies as well as private firms advertise their needs and seek to encourage applications.

Advertising is a powerful technique. It may, in slack periods, have more effect than is intended, with undesirable side effects. For this reason, thoughtful managers use this means of recruitment with care.

When advertising brings in large numbers, costs of screening may be heavy. Advertising throughout a wide area may encourage the migration of more candidates than are required, so that idle applicants become a burden on the locality to which they move. Signed advertisements may tend to irritate present employees, who may feel that they should be promoted into the positions described. Unsigned, "blind" ads may not be effective, for employees often fear they may find that the advertiser is their present employer.

In a variation of the usual advertising practice, some firms hold an "open house" to which potential employees are invited. They have an opportunity to tour the plant and to meet managers and employees. Brochures describe the firm and its products and explain its policies in employee relations. Short movies and slides may relate local activities to those in other divisions. In some programs, newspaper advertisements invite potential employees to visit with a firm's personnel staff on a confidential basis with a promise of something like vocational counseling.

4.5 Scouting in schools and colleges. Recruitment from educational institutions is the well-established practice of thousands of firms and public agencies. Firms that require large numbers of clerical workers or that seek applicants for a continuing apprenticeship program usually recruit from local high schools or those of the surrounding region. In other cases, vocational high schools or private vocational schools supply the normal needs for semi-skilled and skilled additions to the labor force. Scouting for college and university graduates, including those with advanced degrees, is well established and has gained growing acceptance with increasing demands for technical and professional workers.

Scouting is by no means limited to recruitment from schools. Many firms arrange for their scouts to visit local public employment offices to meet with possible recruits attracted in advance by local publicity. Scouting may include foreign sources; in its early use, it was employed to encourage immigrant workers from the skilled and unskilled of various European nations.

Scouting is expensive, perhaps the most expensive recruitment practice. It has frequently been criticized, in part because some scouts have misrepresented jobs and opportunities.

As markets for several types of college graduates become tighter, many firms have felt that they must be generous in their offers to meet competitive opportunities. They have encouraged likely candidates to visit the firm. They have developed attractive publications that describe opportunities in glowing terms. They have used a variety of sometimes questionable practices to develop allies among influential faculty members. Educational institutions have become critical of these and related recruitment practices. Scouting for college graduates has become one of the most widely discussed problem areas for industrial relations staff members and top managers. Studies and reports of experience have appeared in growing numbers.[6]

4.6 Employment agencies. For many organizations, public and private employment services offer a means of shifting some recruitment responsibility and securing a degree of specialized expertness without maintaining a staff group for that purpose. Some firms have joined with others in local communities to provide such services on a cooperative basis. For the most part, however, use of outside services is confined to two types, the private employment agency and the federal-state public employment service.

The *private employment agency* charges fees for its services. It is a business in itself, big business in a way, for there are some 5,000 private agencies

[6] See "Campus Scramble," *Wall Street Journal*, February 15, 1961, p. 1; "A Guide to College Recruitment," Washington 15, D.C.: Society for Personnel Administration 1956.

with about 25,000 employees. Usual charges for their services amount to about 50 per cent of the first month's earnings for salaried workers. Fees are usually paid by applicants.

Some private services are well staffed with competent specialists. Some maintain high standards of ethical practice and give careful attention to the qualities and needs of clients. Others are less expert or ethical. In earlier years, private agencies were frequently criticized for practices in which they made careless recommendations, misrepresented jobs, and collaborated with unscrupulous employers and supervisors to increase turnover and placement fees. Competition with free, public services has played a part in eliminating these earlier objectionable practices. Legislation, including provisions for public inspection and licensing of private agencies, has also encouraged improved practice.

Private agencies are now regulated in 44 states, Puerto Rico, and the District of Columbia. Usual regulations require each agency to obtain a license and to post a surety bond. Laws limit fees, prohibit undesirable practices identified from past experience, prescribe certain records and reports, and authorize a public agency to issue additional rules and regulations.[7]

Public employment offices are available in all larger cities and all counties throughout the nation. There are 1800 full-time offices (with others that operate for one or two days each week or are opened during particular seasons of the year). They employ some 10,000 staff members. Local offices are operated by state divisions of employment in cooperation with the Bureau of Employment Security of the Federal Department of Labor. Detailed administration is specified by the states; general policy is developed on a cooperative basis with the federal Bureau of Employment Security. Funds for the support of these offices are provided by federal appropriation and allocated to the states on the basis of services performed. Applicants are not charged for these services.

Public employment offices are responsible for the administration of unemployment insurance benefits; in some localities this function attracts so much attention that they have come to be regarded as "unemployment offices." Their activities, however, are by no means confined to assisting the unskilled, semiskilled, and unemployed. On the contrary, they register and place thousands of skilled technical and professional workers. They have undertaken an extensive program of job studies to define realistic job specifications and provide essential information for vocational guidance. They have thus provided the information presently published in the *Dictionary of Occupational Titles*, the *D.O.T.* They are the principal source of labor market information and employment trends in industries and occupations, all essential in vocational counseling. They have developed aptitude test batteries that are now used in assisting clients and in providing guidance information for senior students in about one-third of the high schools in this

---

[7] For details, see "State Laws Regulating Private Employment Agencies," *Bulletin 209*, U.S. Department of Labor, January, 1960.

country. Local and regional offices undertake area employment surveys to forecast employment opportunities and future manpower requirements. Staff members have formed the International Association of Public Employment Services (IAPES) to encourage the professional development of employees and the maintenance of opportunities for professional careers in the public service.[8]

Some employers recruit all production workers through the public employment service. Others combine this source with others, including private agencies. Some employers regard the service as a source for production workers only, assuming that skilled technical and professional employees are not available from this source. Other employers avoid the public service on the assumption that it can supply only those who have registered to receive unemployment benefits.

Several important policy questions involving the public service are attracting increasing attention. To what extent shall employers regard use of the public service as an obligation? Is there a responsibility to give public notice of existing employment opportunities so that unemployed may be able to find work without resort to fee-charging agencies? Does the public interest require some central reporting of such opportunities? Must the public employment service become a national manpower agency as a basis for rapid mobilization of human resources for defense? Is the provision of public offices an unwarranted interference with private business, particularly that of the fee-charging agencies? Should public offices be restricted to finding jobs for the insured unemployed? Should they be barred from assisting employed workers who are looking for better jobs?

Current answers to these questions depend on the viewpoint toward such emotionally charged variables as government intervention, the weight to be given to preparation for international hostilities, and the social interest in manpower mobility and in optimal uses of manpower resources. A strong case can be made, however, for encouraging the development of a professionally competent public service, both as a means of improving the disposition of resources in peacetime and mobilizing them for war or defense. There is great and evident public interest in finding the best possible job for every worker, employed or unemployed.

4.7 Executive recruitment. What are the outside sources for managers and executives? What is the common policy and practice in their recruitment?

Executive search has become a big business in the United States. Special private employment services have been formed to assist firms in their recruitment at this level. They are generally not listed in directories as employment agencies; they are consultants to management. They hunt for

---

[8] See "How the Public Employment Service Helps Small Businesses," Washington, D.C.: Small Business Administration, rev., January, 1959. The U. S. Department of Labor also publishes the *Occupational Outlook Handbook,* the most inclusive forecast of employment opportunities (Bulletin 1300, Bureau of Labor Statistics, 1961).

candidates who meet job specifications, looking generally to men already employed in similar positions. For this reason, they are frequently charged with *pirating*, raiding the firms in which they find qualified candidates. They are paid by the firm for whom they conduct the search. Their charges for each position may amount to one-fourth of the annual salary involved. No estimates of the total number of such agencies is available. They appear, however, to be increasing in numbers. That this type of recruiting is becoming more popular is suggested by the report from one agency that its business has doubled in recent years.[9]

4.8 Other sources. In some localities, fraternal organizations, lodges, and churches may serve as effective employment agencies. For certain types of employees, inquiries may be addressed to other business organizations or to former employers. Sometimes it is desired, as a matter of policy, to take a certain proportion of all employees from penal institutions.

5.0 SUMMARY

Recruitment, in any large organization, is a continuing, complex, and expensive procedure. No standard manner of calculating recruitment costs has achieved wide acceptance. Estimates of average costs in individual firms range from less than a hundred dollars per employee ultimately hired to more than a thousand dollars on the same basis. Some employees may be recruited from applicants who come to the firm on their own initiative; others may have to be sought in distant localities, perhaps in foreign nations. Management has a wide choice of potential sources as well as recruitment techniques. At the same time, managements face difficult choices in deciding on recruitment policies, a step that should precede decisions on where to search for applicants or on what methods to use in the recruitment process.

Policy on recruitment begins with an assessment of the implications of general manpower policy. As noted in Chapter 13, these intentions shape all the policy on staffing, from job analysis to final placement and continuing follow-up. What are the firm's intentions with respect to its members? With what attitude shall managers approach the problem of finding people to fill jobs? Such questions immediately raise the issue of internal versus external recruiting. How shall the two be combined? In effect, this question cannot be divorced from the whole policy on employee development.

In most current practice, recruitment begins with a *personnel requisition,* in essence a statement of the intention to hire, combined with a reference to the *job specification.* Recruitment may then turn either to internal or to external sources. It may promote or transfer present employees, in which case it may occasion a whole chain of changes, with the ultimate requirement of additions from outside.

In every such personnel action, the question of whether employees are

---

[9] For an interesting account of usual practice, see "When a Company Wants Brass, Executive Searchers Go to Work," *Business Week,* December 5, 1959, pp. 142ff.

selected for jobs or for careers cannot be ignored. In promotions from within, a whole complicated seniority system may be involved. If its limitations are to be overcome, generally acceptable indicators of potential ability must be developed.

Recruitment from without requires careful consideration of a wide range of sources and a number of common practices. Choices are by no means simple; decisions must take into account the attitudes of present employees as well as public concern about the long-term employment, development, and effective utilization of manpower resources.

One crude measure of recruiting effectiveness is the *time lag* between requisition and placement. Another is the *recruitment ratio*—the number of candidates that must be found to fill each job. Such measures can be somewhat refined by calculating them for each major type of placement—semi-skilled, skilled, technical, engineering, professional.

Experience with various sources deserves careful analysis. Individual schools and colleges, for example, can be compared with respect to the numbers of candidates found, the number sufficiently interested to apply, and the employment experience of recruits hired from each. For criteria of success on the job, reference may be made to subsequent promotions, supervisors' ratings, unusual or critical incidents, or combinations of these and other indicators.

Such studies must be repeated frequently at the same time that new comparisons are made. Sources cannot be assumed to have a standard product; a source that has been outstanding may not continue in that relative position. One of the problems to be expected arises from the fact that if relatively unsatisfactory sources are eliminated, earlier comparative studies cannot be replicated.

Recruitment provides the supplies of candidates from which those to be employed or appointed to new positions must be selected. The chapter that follows describes the screening and selecting process and the additional questions of policy that must be faced in this aspect of staffing.

SELECTED SUPPLEMENTARY READINGS

Barton, Lewis D., "How the Public Employment Service Helps Small Business," *Personnel Management,* chaps. 8 and 12, Homewood, Ill.: Richard D. Irwin, Inc., 1959.

Baumback, Clifford M., "Merit and Seniority as Factors in Promotion and In-grade Progression," *Research Series No. 11,* State University of Iowa, Bureau of Labor and Management, April, 1956.

Bellows, Roger M., *Psychology of Personnel in Business and Industry,* 3rd ed., chap. 10, Englewood Cliffs, N.J.: Prentice-Hall, Inc., 1961.

Handbook of Personnel Management and Labor Relations, secs. 7 and 9, New York: McGraw-Hill Book Company, Inc., 1958.

Kahn, Mark L., "Seniority Problems in Business Mergers," *Industrial and Labor Relations Review,* Vol. 8, No. 3, pp. 361–78, April, 1955.

Slichter, Sumner H., James J. Healy, and E. Robert Livernash, *The Impact of*

Collective Bargaining on Management, chap. 3, Washington, D.C.: The Brookings Institution, 1960.

Society for Personnel Administration, "A Guide to College Recruitment," *Pamphlet No. 12,* Washington 15, D.C., 1956.

"State Laws Regulating Private Employment Agencies," *Bulletin 209,* United States Department of Labor, January 1960.

SHORT CASE PROBLEM 15.1

Decisions on Promotions

Until December, 1959, the Phoenix Controls Company had a manager of sales, Mr. Uphoff, and four assistant managers, Messrs. Walton, Wilson, Williams, and Whitehead. On December the 8th, Mr. Alcorn, the executive vice-president, announced that Mr. Uphoff had accepted a position with one of the firm's competitors. He would be replaced immediately by Mr. Walton, who had been promoted to sales manager.

On December 12th, Messrs. Wilson, Williams, and Whitehead asked for and were granted an appointment with Mr. Alcorn. In his office, they protested his action in promoting Mr. Walton. They said that they liked him and had enjoyed working with him, but they could not understand why he was selected for the promotion. All of the three, they pointed out, had longer records of service with Phoenix than Mr. Walton. In terms of performance, they knew that the records indicated that each of the three of them had accomplished more than Walton had. They felt that he was the least qualified of the four to assume over-all direction of the program. They would have been entirely satisfied if any of the three had been selected for the assignment.

They expressed their reactions with some feeling but seemed on the whole to be entirely sincere and deeply concerned. Indeed, in answer to a question from Mr. Alcorn, all agreed that they simply could not work effectively under Mr. Walton's direction. They regretted, they said, having to be so positive about the matter, but they would have made their position quite clear had they been asked for an opinion before the appointment was made.

Mr. Alcorn heard them out, asking few questions. He then set up an appointment for the afternoon of the 14th, saying that he would give the whole matter some serious thought and would perhaps discuss it with other officers.

At 4:00 P.M. on the 13th, Mr. Whitehead presented his resignation to Mr. Alcorn's secretary, explaining that he had accepted a similar position in the firm to which Mr. Uphoff had gone.

Problems: (1) How do you forecast the outcome of this situation? Why? (2) Do you feel that the matter was mishandled? Why? (3) If asked to advise Mr. Alcorn, what principles would guide you in your counsel?

SHORT CASE PROBLEM 15.2

The Critical Recruit

As an engineer in Section C of the Merco Missile Division, George DeLong had little desire to become a supervisor. He was somewhat flattered but not enthusiastic when the opportunity came to him. He liked his job. He had serious questions about his abilities as a group leader. He asked for and received permission to discuss the matter with his colleagues in Section C. They encouraged him to accept the promotion; several of them said that they had recommended that he be appointed. On the basis of that vote of confidence, he accepted the appointment.

For the first six months after he became supervisor, everyone seemed anxious to help him succeed. He enjoyed the friendly loyalty and support of his colleagues as well as the increased responsibility of the job. He was complimented by the general manager on the work of his crew and on their attitude toward both his own leadership and toward the firm. He seemed to be effective in representing the interests and viewpoints of the crew members; their suggestions were well received by division managers.

In October, one of the men found it necessary to resign; he felt impelled to return to the East, with his family, to take over a family business there. George was faced with the problem of recruiting a replacement. The personnel office helped him in locating several men in other firms who seemed to have the necessary qualifications. After a number of them had been interviewed and introduced to members of George's section, he called a meeting of the entire crew to discuss the several candidates.

In the discussion, although several of the possible replacements appeared as satisfactory, attention centered on one younger man, Fred Peters. Peters had graduated from the University of Washington during the preceding year. He was an outstanding student, as indicated by his grades. He had expressed himself well and freely in the interviews with crew members. He was critical of his present employer and especially of his supervisor, but he seemed to have reasons for these attitudes. George sensed the general agreement that he was first choice among the recruits.

Fred Peters joined the group a month later. From the start, he was what one of the men quickly described as obstreperous. He was full of ideas, generally good ones. He spoke up promptly in expressing them. He was frankly critical of the group's approaches to several problems. He didn't hesitate to criticize George on occasion and to express his criticisms in group meetings. He often referred to opinions of other group members as old-fashioned and outmoded; usually when he did so he referred to some recent research that appeared to substantiate his point. On several occasions, when George summarized what he thought was the majority opinion of the group, Fred challenged the accuracy of George's evaluation and the soundness of his opinion.

Other members of the group came to George with expressions of dislike for Fred and sympathy for George. Some members made a formal request that George terminate Fred before the expiration of his probationary period. George, for the first time, wished he had not become a supervisor. He thought of asking the manager to let him return to the ranks. He discussed the situation at home: his wife agreed with crew members that Fred just didn't fit.

Problem: What is the next step with respect to Fred Peters?

SHORT CASE PROBLEM 15.3

Bonus for New Employees

The Southern Foundry and Machine Shop has military contracts and expects an even larger volume of such contracts after the fall elections. The local labor market for employees of the type required by the firm is tight. To meet its present and prospective manpower needs, the industrial relations division has developed a several-sided recruitment program. It offers a $10 bonus to any employee who secures an application for employment for a person hired within the following six months. It advertises in local papers, describing hourly rates about 12 to 15 cents above the union scale in the locality. It also advertises generous vacations, opportunities for overtime and Sunday work, and a choice of shifts, with shift differentials for night work. Management is frank in declaring its intention to hire good men away from other local employers.

Other managements are bitter about this procedure. They have discussed the situation in the local employers' association (of which the firm is a member). A local committee has called on the president of SFMS to ask that recruitment efforts be directed toward other localities. No change can be observed. Efforts to bring political pressure on the offending firm have been unsuccessful.

Problem: Assume that you are president of the local Industrial Relations and Personnel Managers' Association. Several members want the association to do something about this situation. Outline the steps you wold take or the position you would assume.

SHORT CASE PROBLEM 15.4

Discharge for Refusal to Bump? *

The Background: A laid-off employee was recalled to fill temporarily a sick employee's job. On the sick worker's return, the foreman told the substitute to exercise his seniority and continue his employment by bumping a junior man or taking another job. Instead he chose to return to layoff status. The company notified him he was still considered as employed and that he should report for work or explain why not. When he did not answer, the company sent him a notice that he was considered to have quit and that his name had been removed from the seniority list. The employee failed to respond to either notice, but filed a grievance protesting the removal of his name.

The Issue: Was the company justified in removing his name from the seniority list?

The Union Argues: The contract makes it mandatory for the company to notify a laid-off employee and the union *by registered mail* that the employee's name is to be removed from the seniority list. This the company failed to do. The employee was told to bump a junior man or take another job. But no other job was available, and his regular job was not open. It has been company policy to allow employees to bump or not as they saw fit. The employee exercised this option by returning to layoff. If this policy has been changed, the company has changed it without consent of, or notice to, the union. Under these circumstances, the employee's name was removed improperly from the seniority list.

The Company Argues: It is incumbent on a senior employee to exercise his seniority when his own job is not open, or have an acceptable reason for not doing so. The registered mail requirement applies only when an employee is laid off for lack of work of any kind. When work of some kind is available, an employee cannot arbitrarily decide whether he wants it or not. Work was offered to the employee. He refused it. While there have been instances in which bumping was not made mandatory, the practice has been almost universal in its application. This entire matter should be considered moot, since the employee disregarded the notices and failed to contact management to explain his failure to report for work. For this reason, the company was justified in denying his grievance.

Problem: Use the actual arbitration case here summarized to check your theories and philosophy with respect to this common practice and to decide on a reasonable resolution of this issue.

SHORT CASE PROBLEM 15.5

Shift Preference†

The Background: A third-shift employee applied for transfer to the second shift. The employer denied his request because there was no opening. The union said

* *Employee Relations and Arbitration Report,* Vol. 21, No. 20, Page 5, April 3, 1961.

† *Employee Relations and Arbitration Report,* Vol. 21, No. 18, Pages 5 and 6, March 6, 1961.

there didn't have to be an opening: All that was necessary was that he have more seniority than a second-shift employee.

The Issue: Did there have to be an opening on a shift before a worker could exercise his seniority rights on shift preference?

The Union Argues: The parties definitely recognized the existence of a shift preference by the clause distinguishing the method of computing seniority for purposes of layoff and for *purposes of shift preference.* Past practice (far from substantiating the company position) indicates that the present employee is the only one who was ever denied the right to exercise his seniority in shift preference. The Company is trying to improve its efficiency in plant procedures because it is unhappy with the present arrangement that lets employee exercise his seniority rights in moving from one shift to another. It should take this up in future negotiations rather than expect an arbitrator to rule in its favor.

The Company Argues: The shift preference based on seniority applies only when there is a shift opening. Sometimes, too, workers mutually agree to change shifts with company approval. But a worker cannot move from one shift to another merely because he has more seniority than an employee on the preferred shift. The employee's claim that he has always changed shifts solely on the basis of seniority is not borne out by the records that show his only shift change was on the basis of a job opening. Not only has it been the company's past practice to allow the exercise of seniority only when an opening presented itself but its contracts with other craft unions back up this contention. The employee's seniority rights were not denied. He could not apply them unless there was an opening on the shift.

Problem: Use the actual arbitration case summarized here to identify what you regard as basic questions raised by such an issue. Then be prepared to decide the issue and justify your award.

SHORT CASE PROBLEM 15.6

Comparison of Sources

You are given the following performance records of two groups of workers, one made up of employees secured from the public employment service (Source 1) and the other secured from private agencies (Source 2).

Employees from Source 1		Employees from Source 2	
Performance Scores in Units	Numbers	Performance Scores in Units	Numbers
80 to 90[a]	5	75 to 85[a]	3
90 to 100	10	85 to 95	7
100 to 110	15	95 to 105	10
110 to 120	20	105 to 115	15
120 to 130	30	115 to 125	25
130 to 140	10	125 to 135	25
140 to 150	10	135 to 145	20
		145 to 155	15

[a] Upper class limit means up to but not including the given figure.

To discover:
(a) The mean of scores for Source 1.
(b) The mean of scores for Source 2.
(c) Standard deviation of each series.
(d) Median of each series.
(e) P_{90} for each series.
(f) Whether the two sources are significantly different.

16. *Selection and Placement*

Nowhere in the entire manpower management program is there greater opportunity and necessity for careful implementing of general manpower policy than in selection. Nowhere is current management theory more influential, more exposed, and more questionable.

Selection is the process in which candidates for employment are divided into two classes—those who are to be offered employment and those who are not. The process might be called *rejection,* since more candidates may be turned away than hired. For this reason, selection is frequently described as a *negative process,* in contrast with the positive program of recruitment.

Selection is generally negative, for several reasons. Many managers who readily admit that they cannot feel at all sure about spotting potentially satisfactory employees nevertheless conclude that they can recognize those likely to be unsatisfactory. Such a viewpoint is somewhat justified; it should be easier to notice the absence of what is regarded as an essential qualification than to identify the whole combination of personnel characteristics outlined in job specifications.

Meanwhile, most selection procedures and techniques—interviews, tests, references, and others—may be more reliable in noting shortcomings than in identifying applicants likely to be successful. Job specifications, an essential basis for selection, may be broad, lacking in sharp definition of job requirements. Specified qualifications are likely to be stated in non-quantitative terms, avoiding objective standards. The discriminative power of most selection procedures is low. Measured correlations between the results of interviews or tests, for example, and criteria of success rarely account for more than a small fraction of the total variance. The extent to which the typical employer can choose is quite constrained; he can rarely exclude as freely as he wishes. All these limitations create errors in selection.

Selection is, from the manager's viewpoint, a critical process. The average job involves a heavy investment of capital to supplement the efforts of job-holders. Induction and training costs are impressive. As a sort of law, every addition to the payroll creates additional potential for management problems. The hazards are impressive, and the probabilities of excellent selection relatively small. Hence, many managers would rather miss large numbers of good candidates than accept one likely failure. This view is reinforced by difficulties in releasing those who are hired.

Current extensive attention to and concern about selection is entirely appropriate. Lengthy selection procedures, with combinations of critical tasks defined in job descriptions, sharp job specifications, careful comparisons of sources, interviews, tests, references, and physical examinations are designed to reduce errors and restrict the chances that must be taken. Even the multi-stage process leaves a wide margin for chance, because the various stages and indicators overlap. Tests check on many of the same qualities that are evaluated in school performance and employment interviews, for example. On the other hand, each little bit of improvement introduced by one segment of the selective process is worthwhile.

The negative nature of the usual selection process is suggested by its frequent designation as a *succession of hurdles*. Figure 16.1 provides a graphic representation of this procedure. Individual applicants may be rejected at each of the hurdles; the successful candidate must clear all of them.

Not all selection processes include all these hurdles. Some procedure is simple. The complexity of the process usually increases with the level and responsibility of positions to be filled.[1]

1.0 POLICY ON SELECTION

Several of the most common planks in the platform of general man-power policy point directly at the process of selection. They can only be implemented through appropriate selection policy and practice. The intention to assure competent supervision and leadership, for example, requires selection of appropriate potential. Encouragement of employee participation implies the selection of candidates who want to and can make a contribution. If employees are to develop and appreciate in value, they must have the aptitudes for development.

Selection policy tends, therefore, to vary with general policy. Several selection policies, however, have wide acceptance and explain most current practice in selection procedure.

1.1 Differential selection. Many larger organizations maintain different

[1] See, "The Value of Five Screening Techniques," *Management Record*, Vol. 21, Nos. 7–8, July-August, 1959, pp. 229ff.; William R. Spriegel and Virgil A. James, "Trends in Recruitment and Selection Practices," *Personnel*, Vol. 35, No. 3, November-December, 1958, pp. 46–48; Lewis B. Ward, "Putting Executives to the Test," *Harvard Business Review*, Vol. 38, No. 4, July-August, 1960, pp. 6–15.

selection policies for individual departments, divisions, and jobs. In what is called *differential selection,* they recognize that selective policy for construction workers, for example, must be quite different from policy on selecting members of the supervisory and managerial group. In part, this difference arises out of the manner in which many craftsmen are recruited, with their unions playing an important role in that process. In part, the differential approach is specified by the fact that while the firm holds managerial and supervisory forces intact over long periods of time, it hires building craftsmen for specific contracts. Managers may have to find and select several thousand craftsmen to build a large dam or power plant. They, and the workmen involved, know that work will continue for only a year or

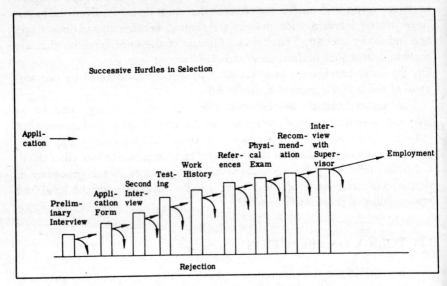

Figure 16.1   Successive Hurdles in the Selection Process

so. For such employees, recruitment and selection are "for the job." In contrast, when the firm recruits and hires young engineers or managers, it intends to hire for careers.

1.2   Selection and development. Policy on selection cannot be divorced from that with respect to employee development. When general policy emphasizes workers' careers, it usually contemplates a great deal of promotion from within. The combination adds to the complexity of problems in selection, for the potentially most efficient machine operator or craftsmen may have little potential for supervisory or managerial tasks. Further, even if such potential exists, it may have little opportunity to express itself if the firm provides inadequate opportunities for continuing development.

1.3   Centralized hiring. One phase of selection policy that has achieved general acceptance is provision for centralized hiring in large firms. In earlier practice, individual divisions and departments frequently hired without reference to what action others might be taking at the same time. As a result, employees might be released by a department at the time that applicants with similar abilities were being sought and hired by another. Present practice, influenced in part by unemployment compensation legislation and in part by short supplies of skilled workers, has emphasized the need for a central employment office. Such an arrangement helps to stabilize employment.

1.4 Public policy. As in recruitment, policy on selection must take full account of the implications of public policy, for example, the prohibitions against hiring women and children for specified types of work and during prescribed hours. The federal Fair Labor Standards Act prohibits "oppressive child labor," and state laws also limit employment of children below stated ages. They also require approved work certificates for older children. State laws prohibit employment of women in specified industries and limit the hours during which women may work in others. Prohibition of the closed shop by both federal and state legislation means that union membership must not be a requirement for hiring except for exempt groups. Some states prohibit discrimination among applicants on the basis of age.[2]

Fair-employment practice legislation, forbidding discrimination on the basis of race, religion, and nationality, has been outlined in the preceding chapter. Such laws are becoming more common, both at state and local levels. They set patterns for selection as well as for recruiting.

The Atlas Company, it may be recalled, proposed to observe the spirit as well as the letter of public policy. That intention creates several additional requirements for policy on selection. Social interests require that firms give special attention to the problems of *threshold workers,* since the numbers of such new entrants will be much greater in the decade of the 1960's than in any preceding period. Similarly, the proportion of females, especially in middle-age groups, is increasing. Their effective employment is a matter of social concern.

Part-time employment is also becoming more common. Public policy proposes that opportunities be provided for growing numbers of these part-time workers.

Meanwhile, effective placement of the handicapped continues to be an important plank in the platform of public policy.

1.5 Vocational guidance. Public policy seeks the most satisfying and productive careers possible, for all citizens. Whether or not firms and managers recognize the fact, both recruitment and selection exert a powerful influence on long-term careers. Frequently, when workers are asked how they selected their careers, the answer is that a job was available in some local firm.

---

[2] The number of such state laws is growing. See Chapter 14, section 1.3.

Selection practice in individual firms and agencies plays an important role in determining levels of utilization for the nation's human resources. It has obvious influence on the extent of both unemployment and *underemployment*—unemployment within employment—in which workers cannot maximize contributions. Employment of young workers may aid or preclude the full development of their potential skills and aptitudes.

Managers may recognize an obligation for assistance in *career guidance* and *vocational counseling.* Professional staff managers, competent in vocational counseling, may recognize an obligation to discuss long-term employment opportunities with young, threshold candidates. They may feel it necessary to advise that they look elsewhere for more appropriate opportunities. In smaller firms with only a few professional staff members, this service probably cannot be provided. In such cases, perhaps policy will dictate that applicants be advised to secure counseling assistance in local employment offices before deciding on a choice among employment opportunities.

1.6 Pirating. The problem of pirating extends beyond recruitment and creates policy questions for selection as well. What shall be the attitude of the firm when it finds applicants who are employees in the plant across the street? Policy varies. Some firms regard such applicants with special favor, on the theory that their availability is a compliment to the firm. Other managers object to such candidates, on the ground that they are "job shoppers," willing to change employers frequently in order to gain slight increases in wages or salaries. Such managers frequently propose tacit agreements that a group of local, competitive firms will not hire away from each other.

The rationale behind such agreements is clear. To some, it may be persuasive. (Similar agreements not to raid each other have been described among universities and colleges.) When such changes are common and involve movements in several directions, this "job hopping" is a way of raising wages and salaries. It may unstabilize employment in the local market. It may be costly for employers, who have to process large numbers of applicants to keep the same number of jobs filled. It may encourage relatively short service, with little identification by employees with the interests of any single employer. On the other hand, the right of any employee to look for an opportunity he regards as better cannot be questioned. Employer agreements to rig the local labor market represent a highly questionable type of monopsony.

1.7 Career employment. Current selection policy seems to place increasing emphasis on career aspects of employment. Trends toward more required training, higher recruitment costs, the prevention of arbitrary discharges, and growing interest in employee loyalty and morale have encouraged a long view in selection. Such a long view increases the complexities in the problem of identifying satisfactory candidates.

These and other selection policies are implemented in a wide range of selection procedures, described in the sections that follow.

2.0 PRELIMINARY STEPS IN SELECTION

Selection begins by close reference to job specifications, preferably those that outline not only immediate job requirements but other qualities regarded as desirable for long-term employment in the organization. The common personal qualities that become bases for selection may be outlined as follows:

(1) *Skill.* This quality, which involves the ability to co-ordinate mind and body in the performance of more or less complicated operations, is probably the most universally considered quality. For some positions, for example that of a tool and die maker, certain high levels of specific skills are essential. There are no substitutes. Other positions require varying degrees of many types of skills—manual, mental, reading, reasoning, and others—and specific jobs require distinctive combinations.

(2) *Experience.* The value of experience has had wide acceptance. Various types of experience may be specified.

(3) *Age.* Experience may be closely related to age, and age may be regarded as a crude measure of experience.

(4) *Sex.* Sex is an obviously important consideration for many types of positions, although some hiring policy is based on beliefs and prejudices that have little or no relationship to job specifications. Some policy holds that certain positions should be restricted to men because the latter are breadwinners and women's place is in the home. Where so-called protective legislation makes the cost of employing women greater, or prevents them from meeting schedules of working hours, this fact must be taken into account.

(5) *Education and training.* These qualifications are regarded both as marks of the abilities of the individual and, in many cases, as definite specifications for certain jobs. Frequently, special types of education and training are required by the job.

(6) *Physical characteristics.* Job specifications may provide detailed guides to required physical qualities. Measurable physical qualities, such as various types of strength, vision, and hearing may require close attention. Reference to physical qualifications is particularly important in the placement of handicapped workers.

(7) *Appearance.* Appearance is probably the most misused of all criteria in selection. It may be highly important, in and of itself, if an employee's appearance affects his performance of the job. If a secretarial position to be filled actually requires a blonde with 38-24-36 specifications, these are essential facts and should be recognized. If, in another case, neatness and conservative dress and demeanor are requisite, there is no reason why these qualities should not be specified. But mistakes are encouraged by assuming that appearance can be interpreted to indicate skill, attitude, character, and ability.

(8) *Intelligence, initiative, and ingenuity.* These qualities are frequently noted in job specifications and evaluations and are among the personal qualities most difficult to identify and measure.

(9) *Aptitudes*. These are inherent capacities to learn and develop. Intelligence and initiative, already listed, are types of aptitudes.

(10) *Maturity and emotional stability*. These qualities may be regarded as essential to the acceptance of responsibilities. They refer to the candidate's personal adjustment, his emotional control, his ability to maintain a rational viewpoint under pressure and strain. Sometimes they are regarded as including judgment, the ability to weight alternatives and arrive at sound decisions.

(11) *Attitude toward work*. Here, the selection process usually seeks information on the applicant's reasons for applying, his objectives in work, his goals and ambitions and anticipations.

(12) *Personality*. For many types of jobs, this rather vague composite—the sum and organization of numerous traits and thus the general impression—is probably the most important item in the list. Current practice frequently tries to get away from its generality and looseness by breaking it into numerous components, as is illustrated by the personality tests to be described later in this chapter.

2.1 Screening. The order of selection hurdles is by no means uniform. Even within a single firm, the sequence and number of steps or stages in selection may vary with different types of positions and candidates. Something of a common pattern can be described, however. The first steps in almost all programs involve *screening,* meaning a coarse, crude sifting of applicants to avoid further concern about those who are obviously unsuitable. In screening, almost all selection uses one or more types of *application blanks* and some sort of *preliminary* interview. Sometimes applicants who are successful with these hurdles are then tested, and steps are taken to check their references. In alternative practice, they may be given their physical examinations before they go through a testing procedure.

2.2 Application blanks. The application form is a universal device for selection except in the most casual employment. The question most frequently asked, "What items should be included?" is best answered by reference to job specifications. A single blank may be useful for many jobs, since the qualifications for such jobs vary mainly in the combinations of characteristics and the degree to which each is present. However, current practice frequently provides several types of application forms. Somewhat different information is sought for white-collar positions, as compared with shop or production jobs.

Fair employment practice rules have required changes in many application forms. Under these rules, questions on nationality, race, religion, and place of birth may be regarded as evidence of discriminatory attitudes. For the same reason, requiring photographs may be objectionable.

Some current practice uses two steps in taking applications. In the preliminary stage, applicants fill out a small card which records the name, address, telephone number, age, previous jobs, and claimed skills. When openings appear, likely applicants are called in for more information and are then asked to fill out a much more detailed form.

2.3 Crucial indicators. If large numbers of applicants are to be examined, decisions on crucial indicators can save much of the time of both applicants and employment staff members. Such items may be listed in a prominent position on the usual blank or they may be summarized on a small preliminary application. Thus, for example, in employment in some defense plants, citizenship is an essential. For many jobs, both distinctive skill and experience may be minimal requirements. In some selection, where the value of new employees depends entirely on their prospective long service in the organization, an arbitrary age limit may be appropriate. Sex may be another crucial indicator for some positions. Research may identify other crucial indicators. Some employers have found that the distance between living quarters and the plant is such an item.

2.4 Weighted application blanks. Application blanks may be developed to serve as highly effective preliminary screening devices. By careful study, such items as age, years of education, number of dependents, earnings, memberships in organizations, and years on previous jobs may be found to be closely correlated with success in the jobs for which candidates are applying. For example, a sales organization may find that each of these characteristics or factors has been notably significant in distinguishing its good salesmen from those who are poor. On the basis of past experience, a scoring system may be provided for all such items, and a *cutting score* may be established for the total. Such a weighted form may speed both recruitment and selection.[3]

Several studies have reported on the usefulness of these devices. Dunnette and Maetzold developed such a form for selection of large numbers of seasonal workers for the canning industry. They found such items as distance between home and plant, availability of a home telephone, marital status, number of dependents, veteran status, and other items useful indicators.[4]

In a somewhat similar procedure, six biographical items have been identified as "knock-out factors" in a preliminary screening program for salesmen. They include instability of residence, failure in business within two years, divorce or separation within two years, excessive personal indebtedness, too high standard of living, and unexplained gaps in the employment record.

---

[3] For details on weighted forms, see J. Welch, C. Harold Stone, and Donald G. Paterson, "How to Develop a Weighted Application Blank," *Research and Technical Report 11*, University of Minnesota Industrial Relations Center, 1952.

[4] Marvin D. Dunnette and James Maetzold, "Use of a Weighted Application Blank in Hiring Seasonal Employees," *Journal of Applied Psychology*, Vol. 39, No. 5, May, 1955, pp. 308–10; also Wayne K. Kirchner and Marvin D. Dunnette, "Applying the Weighted Application Blank Technique to a Variety of Office Jobs," *ibid.*, Vol. 41, No. 4, August, 1957, pp. 206–8; Joseph F. Hughes, Joseph F. Dunn, and Brent Baxter, "The Validity of Selection Instruments under Operating Conditions," *Personnel Psychology*, Vol. 9, No. 3, Autumn, 1956, pp. 321–24.

Harrell checked their application in a food company selection program and reported inconclusive evidence of their usefulness.[5]

2.5 **Item analysis for applications.** Many of the application blanks in current use raise questions about the thoughtfulness with which firms and agencies undertake recruitment and selection. They may justify questions about the general policy with which managers view employment and employee relations. They include items of doubtful significance. They include others that unreasonably invade the privacy of personal affairs. Requests for information for which no relationships to success are even suspected complicate the use of the form and make unreasonable demands on applicants. Insistence that an applicant fill out the form in his own handwriting is offensive unless handwriting is important to the work to be done. It suggests that the firm may be resorting to graphology—the inference of character from writing. It also results in blanks that are frequently unintelligible.[6]

3.0 EMPLOYMENT INTERVIEWS

The interview is unquestionably the most widely accepted practice in selection. Every selection program includes one or more interviews. In spite of the publicity given the use of tests and the frequently expressed concern about allowing test scores to become definitive in the selection process, tests are usually supplementary to interviews.

3.1 **Preliminary interview.** Some sort of interview is usually included in the preliminary stages of selection. Such an introductory interview may take place across the counter in the firm's employment office. It may consist essentially of a short exchange of information with respect to the firm's interest in hiring and the candidate's reason for inquiring. It may serve primarily to determine whether it is worthwhile for the applicant to fill out an application blank. Receptionists and secretaries frequently conduct such short preliminary interviews.

Applicants who pass this crude screening are usually asked to answer questions in the application form and then visit with an employment interviewer. In this more extended session, the interviewer assumes initiative. He seeks answers to specific questions and looks for significant reactions and expressions on the part of the applicant. The interview is generally quite directive, in that the interviewer, by his questions, leads the discussion to a series of points or items which he considers important. A portion of the visit may be non-directive in encouraging the applicant to discuss whatever subjects he regards as relevant and interesting. Employment interviews also give the applicant information on employment in the organization and on the firm's policies, practices, purpose, structure, and products.

[5] Thomas W. Harrell, "The Validity of Biographical Data Items for Food Company Salesmen," *Journal of Applied Psychology*, Vol. 44, No. 1, 1960, pp. 31–33.

[6] See Gilmore J. Spencer, "The Application Form Revisited," *Personnel*, Vol. 36, No. 5, September-October, 1959, pp. 20–30.

ROBERT N. McMURRY & CO.
332 S. Michigan Avenue
Chicago 4, Illinois

PATTERNED INTERVIEW FORM

Date_____19____

SUMMARY

Rating: 1 2 3 4 Comments:_____
IN MAKING FINAL RATING, BE SURE TO CONSIDER APPLICANT'S STABILITY, INDUSTRY, PERSEVERANCE, LOYALTY, ABILITY TO
GET ALONG WITH OTHERS, SELF-RELIANCE, LEADERSHIP, MATURITY, MOTIVATION; ALSO, DOMESTIC SITUATION AND HEALTH.

Interviewer:_____ Job considered for:_____

Name_____ Sex: M____ F____ Telephone No._____
IS THIS HIS OWN PHONE OR SOMEONE ELSE'S?

Present address_____ City_____ State_____
IS THIS A DESIRABLE NEIGHBORHOOD? TOO HIGH CLASS? TOO CHEAP?

Date of birth_____ Soc. Sec. No._____

Do you own a car? Yes____ No____ Make____ Age____ Condition of car_____
WILL HE BE ABLE TO USE HIS CAR IF NECESSARY?

Military Service Status:_____
IS THERE ANYTHING UNDESIRABLE HERE?

Why are you applying for work in this Company?_____
IS HIS UNDERLYING REASON A DESIRE FOR PRESTIGE, SECURITY OR EARNINGS?

WORK EXPERIENCE. Cover all positions. This information is very important. Interviewer should record last position first. Every month since leaving school should be accounted for. Note military service in work record in continuity with jobs held since that time. Experience in Armed Forces should be covered on supplemental form.

LAST OR PRESENT POSITION

Company_____ City_____ From____19____ To____19____
DO THESE DATES CHECK WITH HIS APPLICATION?

How was job obtained?_____ Superior_____ Title_____
HAS HE SHOWN SELF-RELIANCE IN GETTING HIS JOBS?

Nature of work at start_____ Starting salary_____
WILL HIS PREVIOUS EXPERIENCE BE HELPFUL ON THIS JOB?

Were promotions obtained or raises in pay received?_____
HAS HE MADE GOOD WORK PROGRESS?

Nature of work at leaving_____ Salary at leaving_____
ANY SUPERVISORY POSITIONS? ANY INDICATION OF AMBITION?

Was there anything you specially liked about the job?_____
HAS HE BEEN HAPPY AND CONTENT IN HIS WORK?

Was there anything you specially disliked?_____
WERE HIS DISLIKES JUSTIFIED?

How much time have you lost from work?_____ Reasons_____
IS HE RELATIVELY HEALTHY?

Reasons for leaving_____
ARE HIS REASONS FOR LEAVING REASONABLE AND CONSISTENT?

Part-time jobs_____
WILL THIS INTERFERE WITH THE JOB UNDER CONSIDERATION?

NEXT TO LAST POSITION

Company_____ City_____ From____19____ To____19____
DO THESE DATES CHECK WITH HIS APPLICATION?

Copyright 1949 Robert N. McMurry & Co.

Figure 16.2 Excerpt from McMurry Patterned Interview Form

The first stage of interviewing usually takes place in the firm's personnel office. Candidates who surmount preliminary hurdles may be tested, given physical examinations, or escorted to supervisors and managers for further interviewing. The applicant may be interviewed in greater detail and depth by another member of the personnel staff, or he may be asked to meet and visit with several supervisors and managers, either individually or in an interviewing panel.

DIAGNOSTIC INTERVIEWER'S GUIDE

NAME_____ DATE_____

ADDRESS_____ INTERVIEWER_____

The interviewer should begin each interview with this statement to himself, "This applicant will impress me according to my past experience with persons who remind me of him. Consequently I must be on my guard against such prejudices which may naturally arise on account of this. I must keep a record of the fact and judge the applicant on the basis of the facts only. The applicant is a blank to me now." (Interviewer should write out information received as answers to the questions in the space left for that purpose.) If extra space is needed use separate sheets of paper. All of this material should be included with the blank itself when returned to the personnel department. The questions which are listed below for the interviewer to ask the applicant are suggestive. Other queries pertinent to the applicant's history will naturally suggest themselves to the interviewer as he contacts the applicant.

Please read special instructions on last page before interviewing.

WORK HISTORY:

Interviewer says—

1. "Give me the names of your past employers. Begin with the last or present employer and go backward. Tell me:
   (a) How you got the job,
   (b) What you did, and,
   (c) Why you left.

2. How did your previous employers treat you?

3. What experience of value did you get from each job?

4. Did you do work of such quality that your employer would be glad to recommend you?

5. Were you ever criticized for the kind of work you did? Give me some examples of mistakes or failures.

6. Can you give me any example of success in your experience, particularly in handling people?

7. What kind of work did you enjoy the most and seem to progress the best in?—
   (a) Mechanical work?
   (b) Clerical and detail work?
   (c) Contact work?
   or (d) Do you know?

When the interviewer has secured as much information as it is possible for him to get concerning every phase of the applicant's work history, he should ask himself the following questions:

1. What kind of work history does the applicant have?
   (—) Poor — Fair ‖ Good — Excellent (+)
2. Has it been the type of work which has required meeting and handling different types of people? (+) Yes ‖ No (—).
3. Has the applicant indicated ability to work consistently? (+) Yes ‖ No (—).
4. Has the applicant indicated a serious and sincere attitude toward the work he has been doing? (+) Yes ‖ No (—).
5. Has the work been such as to necessitate the development of habits of persistence and aggressiveness? (+) Yes ‖ No (—).
6. Has the work history indicated a capacity for growth? (+) Yes ‖ No (—).
7. Does the work history reveal habits or attitudes which would make it easy for the applicant to adjust himself to the policies and procedures of this company? (+) Yes ‖ No (—).
8. Is this man a good soldier as evidenced by good team-work? (+) Yes ‖ No (—).

Published by E. F. Wonderlic, Glencoe, Illinois. The reproduction of any part of this test by mimeograph, hectograph, or in any other way, whether the reproductions are sold or are furnished free for use, is a violation of the copyright law.

Printed in U.S.A.

Figure 16.3 Excerpt from the Diagnostic Interviewer's Guide

3.2 Patterned interviews. In these secondary interviews, the most careful practice uses planned, structured procedures to assure comprehensive coverage of subjects regarded as significant for success in the organization. Patterned interview forms and diagnostic guides, illustrated in Figures 16.2 and 16.3, are frequently employed. Interviewing procedures may assume that the best guide to future performance is what the applicant has done in the past. Some patterned interviews make other assumptions, for example that childhood, educational, business and financial experience, as well as health and work experience can be interpreted to predict future promise and performance.

3.3 Panel interviews. Panel or board interviewing for supervisory and managerial positions has gained acceptance in recent years. In this procedure, the applicant meets with a group of interviewers. The panel interview seeks to facilitate (a) the pooling of judgments with respect to the candidate, and (b) acquainting the applicant with prominent members of the working organization.

In one variant of the board interview, the candidate is asked to go from one interviewer to another in a fairly lengthy sequence. He may be scheduled to meet from three to six staff and line representatives at half-hour intervals. These interviewers meet later to compare their appraisals. Little evidence is available on which to judge the values of panel interviews.[7]

3.4 Limitations of interviewing. Sophisticated managers have become increasingly aware of the inherent hazards of employment interviewing and their limitations as bases for predicting success in the working organization. This recognition has led to the studies that developed patterned interviews. Proportions of correct forecasts are still discouraging.[8]

Aside from the public relations aspects of interviewing—in which the procedure is recognized as creating a favorable or unfavorable public image of the employer—the major hazard in the process is that of *erroneous inference*. The danger is that interviews may be interpreted as having greater meaning and validity than is justified.

Mandell found that line managers often regarded their employment interviewers as prejudiced, with tendencies to favor candidates whose attitudes and viewpoints were similar to theirs. Other criticisms of interviewers suggested that they lack effective interviewing techniques, do not know enough about job requirements, and show no genuine interest in people.[9]

The fact that interviews are expensive cannot be overlooked. Some experience suggests that the average candidate is interviewed at least five times before he is hired. Even a brief interview involves significant costs to the employer. It may be wasteful, also, in terms of the applicant's time.

Hazards are increased because so many managers take for granted their own ability to read the subtleties of character and personality from con-

---

[7] See, however, Margaret Chandler, "An Evaluation of the Group Interview," University of Illinois Institute of Labor and Industrial Relations, Vol. 52, No. 60, April, 1955, pp. 26–28.

[8] See for example, K. A. Yonge, "The Value of the Interview; An Orientation and a Pilot Study," *Journal of Applied Psychology*, Vol. 40, No. 1, February, 1956, pp. 25–31; Robert L. Kahn and Charles F. Cannell, *The Dynamics of Interviewing*, New York: John Wiley & Sons, Inc., 1957; David J. Weiss, and Rene V. Dawis, "An Objective Validation of Factual Interview Data," *Journal of Applied Psychology*, Vol. 44, No. 6, 1960. pp. 381–83.

[9] Milton M. Mandell, "The Employment Interview," American Management Association, 1961.

versation with a candidate. All too many managers are quite sure that they can tell the honest from the dishonest, the creative from the routine, the mature from the immature—all on the basis of a half-hour interview.

One of the most common types of interviewing errors has been widely described as *halo* or the *halo effect*. It is the tendency to allow one prominent characteristic of the candidate to dominate appraisal of the entire personality, to color the interviewer's judgment on other traits. If the individual being interviewed has a pleasant voice and speaks well, that quality may make all his other qualifications look better. Any one of many individual characteristics may create the halo—dress, physical appearance, small mannerisms.

Closely related is what has been called *stereotyping*. The interviewer's experience may have created a close association between some particular trait and a distinctive type of personality. Whenever the interviewer discovers that the trait is present, he tends to ascribe to the interviewee all the other characteristics of the type. The interviewer may, for example, associate red hair with a fiery temperament. He may relate a single physical characteristic with racial types. He may stereotype all applicants from Oklahoma as Okies, all those from Minnesota as Scandinavians, all those from Stanford as "eggheads," or all graduates of your alma mater as playboys.

3.5 Character analysis. The simple fact is that many of us, including many managers and employment interviewers, are amateur *character analysts*. We may assure ourselves that we are too sophisticated to believe in character analysis, but we continue to practice it on a personal and private basis. Employment interviewing provides an excellent opportunity for the practice and, indeed, involves strong pressures on interviewers to resort to it.

In much earlier practice, answers were sought in *graphology*—the interpretation of handwriting—and in *phrenology*—similar inference from the shape and irregularities, the bumps, on the head. Both of these devices have been repeatedly exposed as unreliable. The most persistent form of character analysis, however, involves the inference of a wide range of personal traits from physical features. Classic examples refer to the "weak chin," the "clammy hand," the "receding forehead," the failure of a person to "look you in the eye," or his "shifty eyes," thin lips, prominent veins, and many others. A noted columnist, Dick Nolan, has commented on one system of character analysis as follows:[10]

> Today I will deal with the problem of Professor de Beaumont. He has been examining thousands of ears. To conclude that the phrenologists are all wrong. You don't read character by feeling bumps on the head. You read character by studying ears. . . .
> Professor de Beaumont's 1958 discoveries, if valid, would have saved the swains of 1835 a lot of trouble. No groping about. Just a straight-forward inspection of the ears which might be done, so to speak, in the ordinary course of business.

[10] From the San Francisco Examiner, October 21, 1958, reproduced by permission.

If the tops of the ears are on a level with the eyes, says the Professor, it means a lively disposition and much intuition. If the ear tops are on a level with the eyebrows, though, it indicates a pre-occupation with material things.

Ears that are flat to the head mean that their owner is calm and capable. But ears that stick out (Ah, there, Bing!) indicate a lack of common sense and an unstable, violent, brutal and quarrelsome disposition.

Small ears? You're a dimwit. Big ears? You have power and strength. Very big ears? You have force and pride.

The Professor says that just any old kind of big ears will not do, either. For instance, if the outer shells of your big ears are flaring it means that you're a fault finder. A well developed inner shell means a leaning toward sentiment and emotion. Well rounded ear lobes show that you're sensitive.

Several "systems" of character analysis have enjoyed extensive support from business as aids in selection.[11] The most careful study of such relationships is probably that of Dr. W. H. Sheldon. He has identified some 76 types of body structure, which he finds are reflected in or associated with differences in temperament and personality. Distinctions are based on ratings applied to three primary types: endomorph, mesomorph, and ectomorph. Sheldon does not suggest that these types commonly appear in "pure" form. He concludes that personalities can be classified by appraisals of the relative strength of these three "primary components of morphology." According to Sheldon, the endomorph—with a large stomach, weak and undeveloped muscles and bones, and a low specific gravity—is characterized by a slow and relaxed appearance and manner and a social and convivial temperament. The mesomorphic type—with prominent muscles and bones and thick skin—he says, is bold and forward, has apparent drive, and is dominating and combative. The ectomorphic type—fragile, delicate, with long, slender extremities —is retiring, inhibited, and seeks to avoid sociability, according to this analysis.

The three temperamental types alleged to be associated with these physical types have been described as viscerotonia (the deliberative type, dependent on people); somatotonia (lots of vigor, drive, and action); and cerebrotonia (fast reactions, curious, experimental, quiet).[12]

Such *observational methods* of selection deserve mention because they are by no means entirely discarded, even though their reliability has been repeatedly challenged. They have just enough *face validity* (no pun intended) to keep them selling. Their use persists because most users do not recognize the probabilities of chance association. Human character and personality are far too complex to be critically evaluated by reference only to external features.

---

[11] See, for example, Perrin Stryker's "Is There an Executive Face?" in *Fortune* for November, 1953, pp. 145ff., which quotes several top managers in endorsements of the Merton System.

[12] This is necessarily an inadequate description of the Sheldon analysis. For full details, see W. H. Sheldon and S. S. Stevens, *The Varieties of Human Physique,* New York: Harper & Brothers, 1940, and *The Varieties of Temperament,* New York: Harper & Brothers, 1942.

4.0 TESTING IN SELECTION

Testing represents an additional tool in the kit of the employment office. It supplements direct personal contacts in interviews of various types with a wide range of tests. All operate on the general theory that human behavior can best be forecast by sampling it. The test creates a situation in which the applicant reacts; reactions are regarded as useful samples of his behavior in the work for which he is applying.

Formal testing programs have become increasingly common in modern selection. A major reason is their convenience. Another is their relatively low cost. Perhaps unfortunately, test results appeal to many managers because they provide quantitative measures of something. They are, for this reason, more easily compared. They seem to bring the personalities of applicants down to a common denominator. Another reason for the growing use of tests is the fact that they have been and are the subject of extensive research.

Part of the popularity of testing in selection is attributable to wartime experience. In both World Wars I and II, tests were used by the military services in sorting and classifying the large numbers of draftees who had to be assigned to various duties.[13] Many who observed their usefulness in the military services welcomed their adaptation to similar problems in civilian industry.

4.1 Types of employment tests. A simple classification of the tests used in selection would distinguish five principal types, including *achievement, aptitude, interest, personality,* and *combination* tests. *Achievement tests* sample and measure the applicant's accomplishments and developed abilities. They are performance tests; they ask the applicant to demonstrate certain knowledge and skills. *Aptitude tests* measure an applicant's capacity, his potential. Their simplest form is the intelligence test, which is intended to measure the ability to learn, to remember, and to reason. *Interest tests* use selected questions or items to identify patterns of interests—areas in which the individual shows special concern, fascination, and involvement. *Personality tests* probe for the dominant qualities of the personality as a whole, the combination of aptitudes, interests, and usual mood and temperament.[14]

4.11 Achievement tests. These are probably the most familiar type, for special forms of such tests are used to determine class standing in the schoolroom as well as admission to many colleges and universities. They measure what the applicant can do, what tasks he can perform right now. Thus, a typing test provides material to be typed, and notes the time taken and the errors made. Similar tests are available for proficiency in shorthand and in

---

[13] In this country, World War I produced the Army Alpha and Beta Intelligence tests. In World War II, the general classification test developed by the army (AGCT) became the most widely used psychological test. In addition, tests were developed for mechanical, clerical, radio code, night vision, weather observer, and aircraft warning aptitudes.

[14] For detailed lists of tests and a more complicated classification, see *The Fourth Mental Measurements Yearbook,* New York: Gryphon Press, 1953.

operating calculators, adding machines, dictating and transcribing apparatus, and simple mechanical equipment.

4.12 Trade tests, measuring the applicant's trade knowledge and, perhaps his skill in the trade, are a type of achievement tests. They may actually involve the performance of simple operations requiring specialized skill. Principal emphasis in this country, however, has been given to oral types of trade tests. Such tests consist of a series of questions which, it is believed, can be satisfactorily answered only by those who know and thoroughly understand the trade or occupation. The oral form of trade test may be supplemented by written, picture, or performance types. The written type substitutes a series of questions to which candidates are to write appropriate answers. Picture tests provide for graphic answers to questions and are particularly appropriate in examining such workers as electricians and draftsmen.

Trade tests are convenient in identifying what are sometimes called "trade bluffers"—people who claim knowledge and job experience they do not have.

4.13 Intelligence tests. These, providing a measure of the applicant's *intelligence quotient* or percentile rank in a specified population and appraising one or more of several types of mental ability, including memory, reasoning, vocabulary, and social perceptions, are the best known and most widely used aptitude tests.

Instruments are variously described as tests of intelligence, mental ability, or mental alertness, or simply as "personnel" tests. They were originally planned to measure the ability to learn—a definition of intelligence which reflects the early history of these tests.

When intelligence tests are used to measure the abilities of children, results are frequently stated in the form of *intelligence quotients.* The intelligence quotient is the ratio of the mental age, as defined by test performance, to chronological age. These intelligence quotients may be translated into percentile ranks by reference to a distribution of large numbers in a specified population—those entering military service or college freshmen, for example. With adults, intelligence quotients are not meaningful, and dependence is placed on percentile ranks based on extensive experience with the tests.

4.14 Aptitude tests. Other tests measure such potential abilities and capacities as mechanical aptitudes or musical aptitude. The range of such abilities is suggested by Professor Truman L. Kelley's classification of nine classes of group factors, including abstract verbalization, spatial relations, numerical ability, motor abilities, musical abilities, social intelligence, mechanical intelligence, interests, and strength. Special tests designed to measure potential abilities in these and related areas may be found to be appropriate in selection for various positions.

Earliest tests of this type are those that appraise clerical aptitude, spatial relations, mechanical aptitude, and various types of dexterity. A number of standardized tests of these aptitudes are available, together with norms based on large numbers of scores.

One popular reaction to aptitude tests is illustrated by Figure 16.4.

Tests of aptitude are widely used in the selection programs of modern industry and in vocational guidance. The federal Bureau of Employment Security has developed a General Aptitude Test Battery, GATBY, which it has administered to hundreds of thousands of students and applicants for jobs.

"I took our aptitude test at the plant this morning. Thank heaven, I own the company. "

WALL STREET JOURNAL

Figure 16.4   One Reaction to Aptitude Tests
SOURCE: The Wall Street Journal, October 6, 1960. Reproduced by permission of Cartoon Features Syndicate.

4.15   Interest tests. These are designed to discover patterns of individual interests and thus to suggest what types of work may be satisfying to employees. For selective purposes, interest analysis begins by discovery of patterns of interests that appear to be associated with success in various types of jobs. Thereafter, applicants are given an interest inventory which identifies their interest patterns and thus permits comparisons with the occupational keys. Most widely used of the interest scales are "Strong's Vocational Interest Blank" for men and women, and the "Kuder Preference Record."

4.16 Tests of *emotional stability, adjustment,* or *personality* indicate the basic temperament of the candidate and what may be described as his characteristic mood. Such an assessment is admittedly complex and difficult. It seeks to indicate what the candidate will do, to evaluate his motivation and drive. Many complex qualities are reflections of what may be regarded as the emotional adjustment and maturity of the individual. Several attempts have been made to appraise that adjustment. The Minnesota Multiphasic Personality Inventory, for example, distinguishes nine diagnostic categories and is based on twelve scales.[15]

Several projective tests—including adaptations of the Rorschach technique and the Thematic Apperception Test—are also used as possible indicators of personality. In these testing procedures, the candidate projects his personality by interpreting what he sees in ink blots or pictures. He writes short stories suggested by similar stimuli. Experienced analysts then seek to read into his test behavior an estimate of attitudes and emotional patterns.[16]

Personality tests have had wider use in industry in recent years both because several of them have become available for that purpose and because managers have come to emphasize the importance of emotional characteristics. Especially at supervisory and managerial levels, the mood of the employee and his ability to get along with others may be highly important. Emotional maturity may influence the ability to withstand stresses and strains, to maintain objectivity, to gain the respect and cooperation of subordinates. Their use may prevent personal tragedies. The terms in which personality tests describe applicants suggest the possible usefulness of these devices. One study reported the usual adjectives as impulsive, dominant, stable, sociable, objective, firm, content, happy, sympathetic, controlled.[17]

4.2 Tailor-made tests. Some tests have wide application and are used by firms, agencies, and educational institutions. Most of these tests have been *standardized;* they have been widely administered, and norms have been developed from their wide application. The usefulness of special norms is apparent. They make the tests more valuable and give test results added meaning in an organization for which no special studies are possible.

In contrast to these standardized tests, some firms and agencies develop their own *tailor-made tests.* Generally, this procedure is undertaken only when there is a continuing demand for large numbers of new employees in a single job. For example, a firm may have to employ several hundred salesmen each year, or equally large numbers of demonstrators or agents. In such cases, the work and expense involved in developing one or more special tests may be justified. The procedure in creating special tests is first to identify

[15] Hypochondriasis (H_s), Depression (d), Hysteria (H_y), Psychopathic Deviate (P_a), Masculinity-Femininity (M_f), Paranoia (P_a), Psychasthenia (P_t), Schizophrenia (S_c), and Hypomania (M_a). For a description of the Humm-Wadsworth procedure, see Personnel Evaluation Method, Los Angeles, Doncaster G. Humm, 1945. For a more recent development, see the California Psychological Inventory.

[16] See M. R. Harrower and M. E. Steiner, *A Manual for the Group Rorschach and Multiple Choice Tests,* Springfield, Ill.: Charles C. Thomas, Publisher, 1951.

[17] See Ingo Ingehohl, "Personality Tests—Just what are they Talking About? *Advanced Management,* Vol. 22, No. 8, August, 1957, pp. 16–24.

levels of success—to distinguish those who succeed on the job from those who are not successful. A criterion of success is defined. A test is then devised to measure traits that appear to be related to success as defined by this criterion.

4.3 Cutting scores and profiles. Practice usually prescribes *critical* or *cutting scores,* representing the point at which applicants will be regarded as having passed the hurdle. Such scores may be established by reference to reported experience, when standard tests are used. For other tests, special analysis of the firm's own experience becomes the basis for this decision. Such scores recognize the limitations of the test; they balance the advantages of excluding all who appear likely to be failures (and thus losing some who may be satisfactory) against the desirability of getting all who have a fair chance of success (and thus including some who are likely to fail).

Only in the simplest of testing programs—where, for example, the only test given is one of typing and shorthand proficiency—is heavy reliance placed on a single test. Generally, applicants take a combination of tests, a *test battery.* Test scores are recorded on a *test profile.* The test profile reports individual test scores in a form that permits ready comparison with what is regarded as the desirable pattern. Figure 16.5 is an illustration of one such profile.

4.4 Test construction and administration. The construction of tests, including such tailor-made devices as the weighted application blank, requires special technical knowledge and skill. Items must be developed, tried, evaluated, weighted, and combined. Without such treatment, a test may appear to be appropriate or useful but may in fact be misleading and worthless. For the most part, individual firms must leave test construction to university and consulting staff members; few firms can afford to provide specialists for this purpose.[18]

For standard, widely used tests, test manuals describe the conditions under which they are to be administered. Failure to observe these conditions may destroy the value of the test. Scores may be influenced by variations from standard administration. Taking a test in the middle of a noisy corridor may be quite different from a similar experience in a secluded private office. The manner in which instructions are given, the steps taken to put the applicant at ease and give him confidence, the emphasis placed on success in the particular test, attempts to explain just what the test measures—these and other possible variables may exert significant influence on the test score.

4.5 Test scoring and interpretation. For standard tests, manuals include instructions for scoring. Electronic scoring services have become available. Scoring methods may be simple—for example, adding scores for individual items—or they may be quite complex. Some tests penalize what are regarded as wrong or negative answers; some result in wide ranges of scores; others emphasize patterns rather than absolutes.

[18] See C. Harold Stone and William Kendall, *Effective Personnel Selection Procedures,* Englewood Cliffs, N.J.: Prentice-Hall, Inc., 1956, pp. 163–73; Lee J. Cronbach, *Essentials of Psychological Testing,* New York: Harper & Brothers, 1960; Dorothy Adkins Wood, *Test Construction,* Columbus, Ohio: Charles E. Merrill Company, 1960.

ABILITIES AND KNOWLEDGE		Low	Below Avg.	Avg.	Above Avg.	High
GENERAL ABILITY	Ability to solve problems, to think, reason, and learn. W			O X		
	Ability to learn rapidly, to adapt quickly to changing situations, complex processes and new relationships; flexibility; general learning ability. T				O X	
	Ability to think with words and symbols; facility in reading and expression; ability to follow instructions easily. L				O X	
	Ability to adjust quickly and accurately in situations involving numbers; ability to understand and solve quantitative problems easily. Q			X	O	
	Ability to reason through observation; ability to see differences between objects. N-V				X	O
FLUENCY	Ability to express one's self; ability to get ideas across when under pressure of time. 40			O X		
ARITHMETIC	Skill in shop arithmetic; ability to handle routine arithmetic problems. 300				O X	
MECHANICAL	Understanding of mechanical relationships; knowledge of mechanical principles; ability to grasp principles underlying mechanical actions. B				O X	
	Ability to visualize the size and shape of objects and how they look when they are fitted together. M				O X	
HUMAN RELATIONS KNOWLEDGE AND SUPERVISORY PRACTICES	Recognition of desirable human relations principles, practices, and policies in supervision. HS				O X	
	Appreciation of the thinking, attitudes, and opinions of persons faced with supervisory actions involving people; understanding of supervisor's ability to function effectively. SP			O X		

Figure 16.5   Excerpt from Test Profile
SOURCE: Courtesy Orlo L. Crissey and General Motors Institute.

Raw or absolute test scores may not be meaningful. To give test scores greater meaning, crude scores are usually translated into measures of position in large and clearly identified populations. For example, the range of scores on a test of mechanical aptitude might extend from 20 to 200 in a group of 5,000 semiskilled machine tenders. These raw scores could be arrayed from lowest to highest and divided into fourths, noting the median or central score and the quartiles. Or they could be divided into hundredths and percentiles noted. Thereafter, any raw score could be translated into a position in this distribution by reference to these percentiles. Scores may be refined to provide various indicators of relative position and may be described as *standard scores, z-scores, stanines,* and by several other similar designations as shown in Figure 16.6.

For all but the simplest of tests, interpretation of test scores requires special knowledge and skill. For all tests in the selection procedure, an essential question is their relationship to the jobs to be filled. In selection, the fundamental test of every test is what it contributes to identification and measurement of qualities specified by an adequate job or *career specification.* For many jobs, what appear as low scores may be preferable to high scores, as when applicants are being selected for routine, dead-end jobs. For other

12*

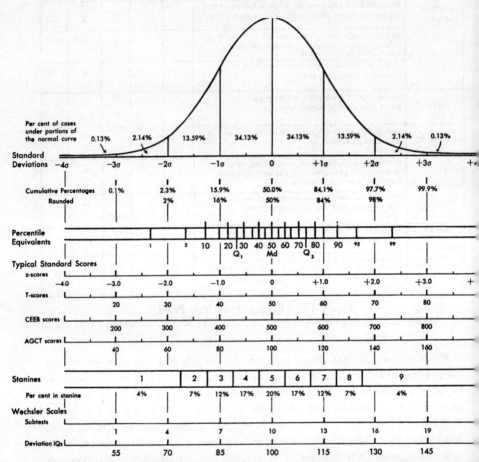

NOTE: This chart cannot be used to equate scores on one test to scores on another test. For example, both 600 on the CEEB and 120 on the AGCT are one standard deviation above their respective means, but they do not represent "equal" standings because the scores were obtained from different groups.

Figure 16.6   Indicators of Position in Test Scores
SOURCE: *Test Service Bulletin No. 48,* January, 1955, p. 2, by permission of the Psychological Corporation.

tests, relationships between test scores and criteria of success may be curvilinear.

4.6 Appraisal of test results. The acid test of every test used in selection is what it contributes to improvement in the selective process. Sound policy on testing, therefore, proposes that all tests—as well as other selective practices—must be tested and retested at frequent intervals. The value and reliability of tests cannot be taken for granted.

Many tests are complicated instruments. They seek to measure characteristics that are difficult to evaluate in other ways. They are, in many cases, short cuts to answers that would otherwise be available only after a considerable period of time and a lengthy evaluation of behavior. Frequent checks, in which test results are compared with a criterion—usually a measure of success on the job—are essential for most tests.

The fundamental consideration in any testing program is that tests shall be of demonstrated *validity* and *reliability* in appraising the qualities noted in the job specification. *Validity* means the ability of a test actually to measure the quality it is assumed to appraise, as evidenced by some acceptable criterion. In other words, if the test is assumed to measure an individual's ability to sell certain goods and is used for that purpose, it is "valid" only to the extent that it measures that ability. *Reliability,* in this usage, refers to the test's consistency, the tendency to give the same appraisal each time it is applied.

Practice frequently seeks to *validate* tests by (1) a *follow-up* procedure in which test scores are compared with job performance, and (2) analysis of test scores for present employees, together with ratings or other appraisals of their performance.

Measurement of validity is facilitated if both test results and the accepted criterion of successful performance are expressed in quantitative terms. Test results are usually directly available in this form, but measures of successful performance may be less readily accessible. The ranking for each employee may be plotted against his test score in a *bi-variate chart,* or *scatter diagram,* illustrated in Figure 16.7. Test scores are measured on the *X*-axis, or *abscissa,* and successful performance is measured on the *Y*-axis, or *ordinate.*

Validation involves comparing test scores with a selected criterion. In test construction, reference is frequently made to *cross-validation,* a process in which the device is rechecked against a group regarded as assuring an independent evaluation of test effectiveness.[19]

Test *reliability* is frequently checked by administering the same test twice to the same group, noting the extent to which it orders the results in a similar pattern each time. (The procedure assumes that there has been no opportunity for individuals to study the test or to practice between administra-

[19] See, for an example, James J. Kirkpatrick, "Validation of a Test Battery for the Selection and Placement of Engineers," *Personnel Psychology,* Vol. 9, Summer, 1956, pp. 211–27.

tions.) In training programs, tests used as examinations may be tested for reliability by a split-test method. (See Chapter 18, Section 4.3)

4.7 General principles. Tests can be of great assistance in many selection programs. On the other hand, because many of them are complicated instruments designed to evaluate complex human characteristics, they can easily be misused and misinterpreted. Under these circumstances, several general rules deserve mention.

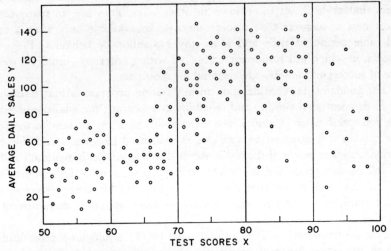

Figure 16.7 Graphic Comparison of Sales and Test Scores
SOURCE: Sales and test scores of 154 retail salesmen.

1. Tests should be regarded as a supplement to rather than a substitute for other selection techniques and devices.

2. Except for simple tests of achievement and performance, the validity of tests must always be checked. If validity has been repeatedly demonstrated in the experience of others, that fact gives some assurance. In the absence of such standard practice, tests should be tested in the situation in which they are used.

3. Most of the tests available for selection emphasize what the applicant does or can do rather than what he will do. The significance of variation in motivation is largely ignored. Yet it is possible, as demonstrated experimentally, to modify the level of group performance on a test of intelligence by providing unusual motivation.[20]

4. Tests are more useful in spotting potential failures than in identifying those who will be a success on the job. They can discover the absence of required qualities more readily than the presence of other characteristics important in success.

[20] See Albert Porter, "Predictors of Organizational Leadership," Unpublished Thesis, Stanford University, January, 1961, p. 137.

5. Test administration can never be ignored; careless administration may easily render test results worthless.

6. The amount of improvement which tests can contribute to a selection program depends on several circumstances. If the rest of the selection procedure is not carefully considered, testing may, for that reason, add a major increment to the total. In any case, the information provided by testing is likely to overlap similar information available from experience, references interviews, and other sources.

4.8 Special policy questions. Testing raises special problems for selection policy. Some of them are to some extent applicable to interviewing and to the use of references.

A preliminary question concerns the security with which testing materials are regarded. For some tests, practice permits extensive improvement. If some applicants are given access to tests, they may gain an important advantage. For this reason, the suppliers of test materials have an obligation to exercise rigorous controls over their distribution, and those who administer tests have a similar responsibility.

Since many of the tests are complicated, their administration and interpretation cannot be carelessly regarded. Test administrators, in such cases, should have special training and experience.[21]

The ethics of testing deserve consideration. Should applicants or employees, including managers, be required to take tests of emotional maturity and personality? Or are such tests invasions of personal privacy? Should such test results be incorporated in personnel records and made available to those responsible for promotion? Answers should recognize that those tested generally do not even know what they are disclosing about themselves.[22]

Some concern has been expressed lest the use of tests may enforce an undesirable degree of conformity in employee, supervisory, and managerial ranks. If tests are checked and validated against present jobholders, will their subsequent use as selective devices eliminate non-conformists?[23] There is, certainly, a pressure toward conformity. If personality tests result in barring applicants with various questionable or "red flag" patterns, the range of personality variation should—within the limits of test reliability—be constrained.

---

[21] One of the largest distributors of testing materials, the Psychological Corporation, distinguishes three levels of tests, for purposes of distribution. Tests regarded as making up level "A" are available to any reputable firm; those in level "B" can be secured by any organization having on its staff at least one person who has taken an advanced-level course in testing or its equivalent; tests in level "C" are available only to "persons with a Master's degree in psychology or equivalent training in the field of testing as applied to personnel."

[22] See Saul W. Gellerman, "The Ethics of Personality Testing," *Personnel*, Vol. 35, No. 3, November-December, 1958, pp. 30–35.

[23] For a strong positive argument, see William H. Whyte, Jr., *The Organization Man*, New York: Simon and Schuster, Inc., 1956.

On the other hand, the influence of tests in this direction is limited; tests are only one of many screening factors. Recruiting from a few selected colleges, judging personality by appearance in interviews, and leaning heavily on supervisor's ratings are at least as likely sources of undesirable conformity.

The security of personal test scores is a matter of heavy responsibility. Policy may provide that only the professional members of the industrial relations staff have access to test scores and that information on test results will be made available to supervisors and managers through only such professionals. The latter may indicate only that the test results suggest satisfactory or unsatisfactory performance in the organization.

Such questions have been widely recognized and discussed because some unions have sought to negotiate against testing and have been successful in banning aptitude tests. Also, disclosure of personal information from interviews and testing may become the basis for suits for damages. Policy may require, for this reason, that no letters of reference or recommendation contain such information.

Applicants are frequently concerned about what has been widely described as *faking* test performance. In general, the idea holds that shrewd candidates can make a test show what they want it to show. Possibilities of faking unquestionably exist, especially in tests designed to identify interests, attitudes, moods, cultural preferences, and similar characteristics. On the other hand, the possibilities of gaining advantage on many of the tests used in selection are slight. Achievement tests could unquestionably be faked to show that the individual could not do as much as he actually can. Intelligence tests might be faked to make the applicant appear less intelligent. The hazards in such faking appear small.

Specialists in test construction have a number of techniques designed to discover manipulation and faking, and applicants rarely recognize these traps or have time to counteract them. Several of the tests include a measure of misrepresentation—a *lie scale*. Others include repetitive items that check on the consistency of answers by varying the approach.

Managers and test administrators have an obligation to watch for any kind of faking, including misrepresentation in the employment interview. There, faking is a well-established art. Every alert and experienced interviewer knows that he must be watching for the special interview behavior of applicants.

5.0 REFERENCES AND PHYSICAL EXAMINATIONS

A majority of the application forms in current use include a request for the names of references, and many selection procedures ask candidates to provide letters of recommendation. Some practice checks all such references; in other practice, they are generally ignored unless some special question is raised.

Two types of references may be distinguished. One is the *character refer-*

ence, listed as a potential source of information with respect to the general character and reputation of the applicant. The other is the *former employer reference,* which names someone who is presumably willing and able to speak about the applicant's earlier work.

Letters of recommendation may also be classified as (1) special letters directed to a specific employer with respect to the particular applicant and (2) general "to whom it may concern" letters, usually carried by the applicant and offered as evidence of his character and experience.

5.1 Limitations of references. Several limitations on the value of references and letters of recommendation are apparent. Character references are likely to be selected by the applicant to include only those who will speak well of him. Employment references may also be selected in that they may name a supervisor or foreman known by the applicant to be friendly. Some favorable replies from references and letters of recommendation must be recognized as efforts to get rid of unsatisfactory employees.

References may be reluctant about providing critical information, lest the comments become known to the applicant. Phone calls as checks on references get away from some of these difficulties, particularly if the parties in these conversations are well known to each other. The confidential nature of inquiries and responses, always stressed in the check of references, may be carelessly regarded. Letters and notes recording telephone checks get into personnel files, where they may become available to the person involved.

Further weaknesses in the use of references arise out of failure to relate them directly to requirements. Some firms have developed special forms for letters of inquiry, prescribing qualities identified in job specifications.[24]

The value and usefulness of recommendations have been reduced by the common tendency to ask for them but make no use of them. Some firms justify this practice on the ground that the request impresses candidates with the carefulness of selection.

Some current practice supplements a check of references and letters of recommendation with a *field investigation* in which a credit agency or other independent investigator makes a special study of the applicant. Such practice adds to the expense of selection, but it may provide important information, particularly if the employee is to be placed in a position with heavy responsibilities. Question is sometimes raised about the ethics of such an investigation.[25]

5.2 Physical examinations. A selective device used almost universally is the physical examination. Most firms and public agencies require that an applicant have a physical examination before he can be accepted for employment.

[24] See Robert B. Sleight and G. D. Dell, "Desirable Content of Letters of Recommendation," *Personnel Journal,* Vol. 32, No. 11, April, 1954, pp. 421–22; Milton Mandell, "Checking References: How to Get the Facts," *Supervisory Management,* Vol. 3, No. 3, March, 1958, pp. 10–16.

[25] See B. J. Speroff, "Saved from Hiring an Arsonist," *Personnel Journal,* Vol. 38, No. 7, December, 1959, pp. 263ff.

In earlier practice, the applicant had to "pass" his physical. This meant, in general, that he must be certified as in good health. That point of view in giving such examinations has been criticized.

The purpose should not be to eliminate applicants, but to discover what jobs they are qualified to fill. The examination should disclose the physical characteristics of the individual that are significant from the standpoint of his efficient performance of the job he may enter or of those jobs to which he may reasonably expect to be transferred or promoted. It should note deficiencies, not as a basis for rejection, but as indicating restrictions on his transfer to various positions.

Current practice facilitates such a matching of physical requirements and physical qualifications by a special phase of job analysis that describes *physical demands* of the job. At the same time, the physical examination of candidates identifies *physical capacities*.

6.0 PLACEMENT AND ORIENTATION

The applicant who clears all the hurdles is presumably offered a job. Final acceptance, for production workers, usually depends on the approval of the supervisor with whom he will work. In some practice, that approval is secured early in the selection process as one of the crucial steps, thus preventing the needless testing and interviewing and reference-questioning of applicants who may ultimately be rejected at the point of hiring.

Practice in placement has become somewhat more formal as general policy has come to place more importance on the attitudes of all employees. Recognition of the frequently high turnover in early months has exerted a similar influence. Effort is made to gain the favorable reaction of fellow workers, so that the new recruit is welcomed to the work group. Increasing attention is given to the orientation and induction of new employees. Special programs assist him in adjusting to work in the organization and in feeling at home with his associates.

Some larger firms provide a formal orientation training program. Others assign responsibility for orientation to the supervisor. Some practice includes a *buddy system* or *sponsor system,* in which an older member of the work group accepts special responsibility for the new member. A wide variety of printed material, employee handbooks, information sheets, pamphlets on fringe benefits, and picture stories of the firm's plants and products may be distributed to recruits to help them visualize the entire operation and its objectives.[26]

7.0 SUMMARY

Selection is the process in which managers decide on the acceptance or rejection of recruits and other applicants. It may be a simple or a complex

[26] See *Personnel Policies and Practices Report,* Par. 155, No. 15–27, 1961.

process, depending on the nature of the positions to be filled, conditions in labor markets from which applicants must be drawn, and the manpower policy of the firm or agency. In the most common programs, it involves a succession of hurdles to be cleared by successful candidates.

The managerial problem is that of identifying adequate numbers of applicants who can be expected to become satisfactory and successful employees. The problem is frequently made more difficult by vagueness in job descriptions and specifications, the limited range of choice open to managers, and the lack of assurance in the processes used to identify and measure required personal qualifications. The process is simplified if general manpower policy proposes only to hire to meet immediate needs, with little concern about

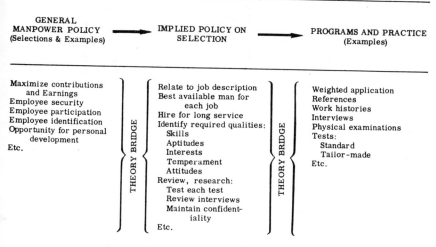

GENERAL MANPOWER POLICY (Selections & Examples)		IMPLIED POLICY ON SELECTION		PROGRAMS AND PRACTICE (Examples)

Maximize contributions and Earnings
Employee security
Employee participation
Employee identification
Opportunity for personal development
Etc.

THEORY BRIDGE

Relate to job description
Best available man for each job
Hire for long service
Identify required qualities:
  Skills
  Aptitudes
  Interests
  Temperament
  Attitudes
Review, research:
  Test each test
  Review interviews
  Maintain confidentiality
Etc.

THEORY BRIDGE

Weighted application
References
Work histories
Interviews
Physical examinations
Tests:
  Standard
  Tailor-made
Etc.

Figure 16.8 Selection Policy and Practice

long-term employment relationships. It is simplified, also, if little employee participation is expected.

The basic relationship, in which general manpower policy implies selection policy and the latter suggests specific selection programs, is illustrated in Figure 16.8. Managers move from left to right in the pictured relationship largely on the basis of their theories and assumptions.

Selection programs normally include a series of selection techniques, of which interviewing, testing, checking references and letters of recommendation, and physical examinations are typical. These procedures are used to compare applicants with job and career specifications. Required qualifications range from age and physical characteristics to emotional maturity. Some are readily checked. Others are more obscure and make the problem of identifying likely candidates—and even the simpler problem of spotting unlikely prospects—a complex assignment. The goal is to improve the percentage of success and to reduce the proportion of errors in selection.

Figure 16.9 was developed by Meyer and Bertotti to suggest usual difficulties in identifying potential for management. It may be useful, however,
in showing how difficulty varies with the various types of personal characteristics described in job specifications.

Sound policy on selection seeks to implement the general manpower policy
of the organization. To that end, it must propose continual checks on the
effectiveness of selection procedures. Each practice should be closely related
to job specifications that define the goals in selection. Each practice can be
checked by follow-ups that compare evaluations made during the selection

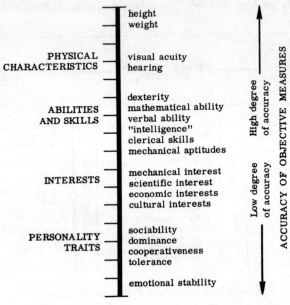

Figure 16.9 Measuring Human Characteristics
SOURCE: Herbert H. Meyer and J. M. Bertotti, "Uses and Misuses of
Tests in Selecting Key Personnel," Personnel, Vol. 33, No. 3, p. 280,
published by the American Management Association, Inc.

process with performance in employment. Improvements in individual hurdles make only small contributions to success in the entire process because
of overlap in which interviewing, for example, appraises the same qualities
as testing.

Sophisticated management recognizes the necessity for such validation of
selection procedures. It is also aware of their impressive limitations.

The most careful administration of a selection program may be ineffective
in staffing if new recruits fail to make personal adjustments to their work
and decide to quit. The selection process frequently includes a carefully
planned placement and orientation program to assist in this adjustment
process.

Employees hired for long-term contributions will, in most cases, require opportunities for further training and personal development. The next section of this book turns attention to this developmental process, with special reference to management responsibilities in appraising employee needs and potential for development.

SELECTED SUPPLEMENTARY READINGS

Bellows, Roger M., *Psychology of Personnel in Business and Industry,* 3rd ed., chaps. 11, 12, and 13, Englewood Cliffs, N.J.: Prentice-Hall, Inc., 1961.

Dunnette, Marvin D. and Wayne K. Kirchner, "Validation of Psychological Tests in Industry," *Personnel Administration,* Vol. 21, No. 3, pp. 20–27, May-June, 1958.

Gellerman, Saul W., "The Ethics of Personality Testing," *Personnel,* Vol. 35, No. 3, pp. 30–35, November-December, 1958.

Handbook of Personnel Management and Labor Relations, sec. 8, New York: McGraw-Hill Book Company, Inc., 1958.

Harrell, Thomas W., "The Validity of Biographical Data Items for Food Company Salesmen," *Journal of Applied Psychology,* Vol. 44, No. 1, pp. 31–33, February, 1960.

Stark, Stanley, "A Note on the Use of Evidence in *The Organization Man,*" *Current Economic Comment,* University of Illinois. (Available as *Reprint Series No. 71,* University of Illinois Institute of Labor and Industrial Relations, November, 1958).

Stone, C. Harold and William E. Kendall, *Effective Personnel Selection Procedures,* chaps. 5–12, Englewood Cliffs, N.J.: Prentice-Hall, Inc., 1956.

Stryker, Perrin, "Is There an Executive Face?" *Fortune,* November, 1953, pp. 145ff.

Ward, Lewis B., "Problems in Review: Putting Executives to the Test," *Harvard Business Review,* Vol. 38, No. 4, pp. 6–16, July-August, 1960.

SHORT CASE PROBLEM 16.1

The Ona Mower Company

Mr. Robinson is industrial relations director for the Ona Mower Company. The firm employs some 1,200 hourly rated production workers, most of them as semi-skilled machine tenders. It has experienced a rapid increase in the demand for power motors and, as a result, the employee relations staff has been asked to recruit up to 500 additional employees.

Labor markets in the locality are tight. Most of the applicants, as a result, are recent high-school graduates, without experience. Most of them have enough mechanical aptitude to meet production job requirements. The industrial relations staff is impressed with the evidence, however, that a large proportion of these threshold employees should, on the basis of their interests and aptitudes, probably seek careers in other occupations.

Under pressure to secure new employees rapidly and in large numbers, the staff is disturbed by the influence this first job may have on the careers of these youngsters. Staff members have asked Mr. Robinson what to do. Should they tell such applicants that they do not belong in semiskilled production jobs? Or should they send them along to foremen for possible hiring without advising them further?

Problem: Write a memorandum for Mr. Robinson to staff members in which you answer their questions on this point.

SHORT CASE PROBLEM 16.2

Use of References

The X-Press Company requires that all applicants for employment give the names of three former employers as references. In practice, in the selection procedure, one of the three is queried about the facts of earlier employment described on the application form.

Recently, the staff has speculated about the soundness of this practice. Some staff members have raised questions about the implications of this "sampling" procedure. They suggest that inquiries directed to one or the other of the two remaining names might produce quite different evidence. They argue that all three should be questioned if heavy reliance is to be placed on references as a basis for acceptance or rejection.

Another staff member has suggested that the entire procedure should be discarded. He argues that, in the first place, the statements made in reply to such inquiries are not reliable, that references do not disclose the most important facts. Second, he insists that staff members can and do place a wide range of interpretations on these statements.

The personnel manager has been concerned by these criticisms. He is particularly worried because of a recent experiment. In that test, all his staff members were asked to examine references for 50 recent applicants and to rank each for acceptance or rejection. Names of applicants were deleted. Staff members disagreed on more than 30 of the 50 references.

Problem: What recommendation would you make in this situation?

SHORT CASE PROBLEM 16.3

A Vice-President for Discouragement

Selection procedure in a medium-sized manufacturing firm has, for several years, maintained a panel-type interviewing procedure, one interview following another, for all applicants who are believed likely to move into supervisory and managerial positions. Candidates, after a preliminary screening interview by a recruiter, meet with each of six company officers, including one representative of the Industrial Relations Department.

One vice-president is insistent that he be included on all such panels. He is impressed with what he regards as a tendency of modern business to "coddle" and "baby" new recruits. He says they should know the basic "economic facts of life." He thinks they should be told to expect to work long hours and to encounter many frustrations and discouragements. Accordingly, in his visits with candidates, he "gets rough" and "gives them the works."

The effects of his interviewing are readily apparent. Several candidates regarded by other interviewers as most promising have decided against joining the firm. Some of them have said bluntly that they don't want to work with an outfit that has such a vice-president. One candidate advised two panel members that they ought to leave the firm on this account.

Problem: What should be done about this person someone has dubbed the "vice-president for discouragement"? He has several years to serve before retirement. Would it be fair, if it is possible, to keep him off the panels? Could he be encouraged to change his tactics? What approach would you suggest?

SHORT CASE PROBLEM 16.4

Test Scores and Ratings

Management wishes to evaluate the possible covariation of admission-test scores and ratings secured by the same individuals after they have been employed for a considerable period of time. Data are summarized below.

Estimate a rating for an applicant who scores 80 on the test. How much dependence can be placed on such an estimate?

Admission-Test Score	Rating	Admission-Test Score	Rating
67	80	87	89
76	70	88	92
66	74	91	90
99	83	78	94
94	79	75	82
85	75	92	66
80	91	99	98
92	82	78	78
79	77	58	78
71	86	88	94
83	89	80	73
94	94	82	75
100	100	98	81
75	77	70	56
98	93	88	94
85	86	98	97
82	81	79	82
89	93	82	86
93	88	79	81
75	83	81	77
91	95	74	72
77	79	74	81
100	81	97	93
89	92	75	74
72	75	95	97
84	87	62	65
93	89	81	70
86	93	97	91
79	89	79	76
94	92	60	65
81	68	90	88
71	77	79	76
71	84	82	84
75	78	91	93
79	78	65	74
77	79	91	82
86	82	82	73
94	85	99	90
81	67	80	78
77	76	81	81
84	77	77	79
91	83	74	74
93	87	95	93
83	96	80	82
87	83	65	68

SHORT CASE PROBLEM 16.5

Selection of Engineers

In two years, the Stickeegoo Company hired 114 non-experienced technical persons with bachelors degrees. For 72 of them, full data are available with respect to entrance-test scores, employment-interview ratings, and subsequent supervisors' ratings. Entrance-test scores include the Minnesota Engineering Analogies Test and the Strong Vocational Interest Blank. For the latter, special keys have been developed for (1) interest in ideas and concepts, (2) interest in the solution of practical problems, (3) interest in materials and processes, and (4) interest in people.

Information from supervisors includes (1) a careful job description for the positions held by each employee; (2) a series of five-step ratings on such broad areas as technical competence, human relations ability, creative ability, initiative and perseverance, and over-all job performance; and (3) answers to a series of 62 statements about job behavior, each answered in terms of "yes" or "true," "not true at present," or "?".

These employees have been assigned to jobs in various departments throughout the organization. As a means of checking on the effectiveness of selection procedure, the Employee Relations Research Division has compared data recorded at the time of employment with subsequent supervisors' ratings. First, however, on the basis of job descriptions, the new employees have been classified as working in (1) research and development, (2) applied research and process engineering, (3) production and technical service. Six of the men held jobs so broad that they could not be fitted into any of these classifications.

The following tables 1, 2, and 3 summarize the results of these comparisons. For each of the three groups, tables relate predictor information to supervisory evaluations.

Problem: Prepare a statement indicating rather precisely what conclusions or tentative conclusions are justified by this analysis. Then prepare a recommendation with respect to future practice in the use of these predictors in selection.

Table 1

Correlations* between Test Scores, Interviewer Ratings,
and Supervisory Ratings of Effectiveness for
Research and Development Engineers
$N = 29$

		Supervisory Ratings				
		Technical Competence	*Human Relations*	*Creative Ability*	*Perse- verance*	*Over-all Effectiveness*
	Interviewer Rating	*.33*	.25	−.07	.14	.20
	MEAT Score	*.35*	.07	.10	.07	.06
	Interest in Ideas	*.32*	−.19	−.15	−.28	−.27
Predictor Information	Interest in Practical Prob.	.15	−.11	.03	−.01	−.08

* Correlations significant at the 10% level or better are italic.

	Technical Competence	Human Relations	Creative Ability	Perseverance	Over-all Effectiveness
Interest in Materials and Processes	*−.39*	.12	−.25	−.05	.01
Interest in People	*−.33*	.02	−.21	−.07	−.01

Table 2

Correlations* between Test Scores, Interviewer Ratings, and Supervisory Ratings of Effectiveness for Applied Research and Process Engineers
$N = 18$

		Supervisory Ratings				
		Technical Competence	Human Relations	Creative Ability	Perseverance	Over-all Effectiveness
	Interviewer Rating	.11	.30	−.01	*.39*	.28
	MEAT Score	*.54*	−.13	*.54*	−.10	−.25
	Interest in Ideas	.06	.20	.33	.25	.10
Predictor Information	Interest in Practical Prob.	−.11	.30	.04	*.46*	.34
	Interest in Materials and Processes	−.31	−.20	−.27	.13	−.11
	Interest in People	.03	.18	.00	−.01	.03

* Correlations significant at the 10% level or better are italic.

Table 3

Correlations* between Test Scores, Interviewer Ratings, and Supervisory Ratings of Effectiveness for Production and Technical Service Engineers
$N = 19$

		Supervisory Ratings				
		Technical Competence	Human Relations	Creative Ability	Perseverance	Over-all Effectiveness
	Interviewer Rating	.23	−.03	.32	.10	.31
	MEAT Score	.20	−.26	−.29	−.25	−.12
	Interest in Ideas	−.14	*−.48*	−.15	−.23	*−.45*

* Correlations significant at the 10% level or better are italic.

Predictor Information	Interest in Practical Prob.	−.11	−.57	−.17	−.24	−.43
	Interest in Materials and Processes	−.31	−.44	−.42	−.26	−.31
	Interest in People	−.01	.11	.04	.13	.36

V. MANPOWER TRAINING
AND DEVELOPMENT

17. *Personnel Appraisals*

This is the first of four chapters that form a section on employee and management development. This chapter is concerned with the manager's problems in evaluating the people who make up working organizations. The chapter is included in the section on employee development—or what has also been described as *personal appreciation*—because some appraisal of individual needs and qualifications for development is an important step in all development programs.

The broad process of evaluating one's associates in working organizations is probably universal. Employment usually begins with an appraisal, and evaluations continue throughout the working life. Everyone makes some evaluation of supervisors, fellow-workers, and subordinates. Everyone is to some extent appraised by his colleagues. Very few working days go by without some discussion of the value and capability of crew-members, foremen, and managers, by crew-members, foremen, and managers.

The problem area for consideration in this chapter is not concerned with the presence or absence of personnel appraisals; its persistence must be taken for granted. Problems arise out of the degree of accuracy to be expected of and read into these appraisals: their dependability and their usefulness. The basic process of personnel appraisal is an unescapable responsibility of management. Attention is directed to differences in purposes, in policy, and in practice.

For the purposes of this discussion, the term *personnel appraisals* refers to all the formal procedures used in working organizations to evaluate the personalities and contributions and potential of group members.

Although appraisals are widely described as *ratings*, rating represents only one form of personnel *evaluation*. The term *rating* refers to various formal systems of appraisal, in which the individual is compared with others and ranked or rated. He is rated in the sense that he is measured or compared and classified. Those who rate him assign a relative position to him or to certain of his qualities or characteristics. Thus, Arbuckle may be rated second as compared with Pederson, who is thus rated one notch higher. Or Arbuckle may be rated first on initiative, as compared with Pederson, who is rated second. More frequently Arbuckle may be rated *excellent* on initiative, as compared with what the rater regards as *normal* or *average*. In many formal systems, both Arbuckle and Pederson may be given scores representing an aggregate value developed by combining scores on each of a series of qualities.

Modern management makes somewhat less use of the term *rating* than was common in earlier periods, for several reasons. Most important, many managers now realize that rating is only one part or phase of a broader, continuing process of personal appraisal. Also, many managers have become somewhat skeptical of the meaning and of the usefulness of formal ratings and have become convinced that they must be supplemented by broader appraisals. One reason for the change has been the extension of formal evaluations to managers at various levels. When they found themselves being rated on these formal scales, managers took a more critical look at this procedure. They questioned whether formal ratings, limited to a few designated qualities, were appropriate for managers. Terminology has changed, substituting *appraisal* for *rating*. Practice has also changed to broaden the evaluation process and combine formal ratings with supplementary observations, records, and evaluations.

Appraisal or evaluation of employees, including supervisors and managers, is undertaken for several purposes. Such evaluations—perhaps best known as *personnel* or *merit* or *efficiency ratings*—may be used in salary or wage adjustments. They are often used in determining eligibility for promotions. In some working organizations, including public agencies, low ratings may become the basis for demotion. The rating process is widely used as a device to require supervisors to become well acquainted with their crew members. Sometimes ratings determine who will be laid off. Ratings are probably the most widely used criterion of successful performance in studies of selection procedures and training programs. Several surveys have reported on these common uses of employee appraisals.[1]

Today's practice still makes extensive use of formal ratings—assignments of ranks and scores on personal qualities. In addition, however, today's practice supplements these measured and ranked evaluations with descriptions, anecdotes, incidents, and other opinion and evidence.

[1] For example, see Roland Benjamin, "A Survey of 130 Merit Rating Plans," *Personnel*, Vol. 29, No. 3, November, 1952, pp. 289–94; "Merit Rating of Rank and File Employees," *Survey No. 41*, Bureau of National Affairs Personnel Policies Forum, February, 1957; William B. Wolf, "Merit Rating as a Managerial Tool," *Management Series No. 1*, University of Washington Bureau of Business Research, 1958; *Personnel Appraisal and Review*, Ann Arbor: Foundation for Research on Human Behavior, 1958.

The narrower *rating* process has had wide acceptance in part because it creates what appear to be *measures* of personal qualities. Workers and managers can not be measured with respect to such characteristics as initiative, persistence, self-control, perspective, judgment, honesty, dependability, determination, and many more like them, as they can for height or weight or age or experience. Rating, however, may produce a numerical value for each quality. Employee Miles, for example, may emerge from the rating procedure with a score of 6 out of a possible ten on honesty or originality. The total of his scores may be 76 out of a possible hundred. He can be readily —if not very meaningfully—compared with employee Hook, who scores 60 on the same rating scale. Many managers have felt that such comparisons are sufficiently dependable to be helpful. They give an appearance of objectivity. They permit an over-all, composite valuation. They encourage raters to think in terms of specific qualities.

More sophisticated managers who continue to use formal rating procedures now insist that they take them "with a grain of salt." They recognize that the numerical values thus developed are approximations. They search for supplementary indicators at the same time that they try to improve the rating procedure.

1.0 POLICY ON PERSONNEL APPRAISALS

What general manpower policy and theory explain the practice of personnel appraisals? What intentions are to be implemented through this practice?[2]

Current general manpower policy frequently proposes to maintain incentives for superior performance. It intends to reward employees in proportion to their contribution. Having established scales that approximate the comparative values of jobs, managers propose to relate individual compensation to personal performance and contribution on the job. In the absence of objective measures, personnel appraisals provide an essential substitute.

Again, current policy frequently proposes *promotion from within*. At the same time, it intends to maintain and improve the quality of leadership and management. Personnel appraisals are widely used to identify those who should be promoted. Such evaluations are generally the most important considerations in promotions, with the possible exception of seniority.

Current policy often proposes to maximize employee participation in the areas of decision making in which each employee has competence. Appraisals may provide a means of assessing the extent of individual participation as

---

[2] It may be worth noting that the practice—and presumably the underlying policy— has a long tradition. Somewhat formal appraisals were used, even before the Industrial Revolution, to stimulate improved on-the-job performance. Reformer-cooperator Robert Owen used a system of *character books* and *character blocks* in his New Lanark cotton mills in Scotland. Each employee had such a book, in which daily reports and comments by supervisors were recorded. The block was a colored symbol, each side marking a level of performance, displayed on the employee's work bench.

Why an Appraisal and Development Plan?

The Company's most valuable asset is its employees. One of the most important qualifications of a supervisor, regardless of level, is the ability to train, develop, and treat people in a manner that wins confidence and gets results. A good supervisor knows his employees as individuals. He considers each employee's performance, his interests, his make-up and his environment in developing his work force.

Toward this end, the Company established a number of years ago an Appraisal and Development Plan for use on a uniform basis in all departments. It is a very helpful guide to a highly important aspect of good supervision.

Primary Purpose of Plan

To aid the employee in his growth and development by appraising all phases of his performance and then by following through with constructive discussion and guidance.

Additional Benefits

When this is done thoughtfully and skillfully, the Plan will accomplish several addtional and highly important purposes. It will:

Promote the employee's job satisfaction and morale by letting him know that his supervisor is interested in his progress and development.

Serve as a systematic guide to the supervisor in planning the employee's further training.

Assure considered opinion of employee's performance rather than snap judgment.

Assist in planning personnel moves and placements that will best utilize each employee's capabilities.

Assist in locating and recording special talents and capabilities that might otherwise not be noticed or recognized.

Provide employee an opportunity to talk to supervisor about job problems, interest, future, etc.

Figure 17.1 Policy Statement on Employee Appraisals

From Performance "Appraisal and Employee Development Guide," San Francisco: Standard Oil Company of California, Revised December, 1959.

well as the level of competence. At the same time, policy may seek a maximum of employee identification with the organization and its objectives. Appraisal may be used to secure evidence of success in attaining this end.

For large numbers of employees, supervisors, and managers, a policy of great personal importance is that which proposes to maximize the opportunity for personal development and *personal appreciation*. This means that each member of the organization is to be given a chance to develop his highest talents. To some degree, these capacities are identified in the selection process. Even more dependence, however, is usually placed on qualities the team member can demonstrate in various jobs. Personnel appraisals are used to provide evidence on this latter point, to suggest what potential exists for further development. In this usage, appraisals may guide the organization in its relationships with the individual worker and, at the same time, assist the individual in planning his personal growth throughout his career (see Fig. 17.1).

Several other common intentions in general manpower policy underlie the practice of personnel appraisal. For example, measures of employees, supervisors, and managers supplied through appraisal may appear essential for the continuing *review and audit* of personnel management. Ratings may be extensively used as criteria in continuing research. The process of appraisal may be regarded as an important educational device in the development of managers.

Whatever general policy may be most influential in encouraging personnel appraisals, it raises additional policy questions with respect to the administration of the appraisal program.

1.1 Use of appraisals. A preliminary question concerns the uses to be made of appraisals, the purposes they are to serve. As noted, there are many possibilities; appraisal represents a multi-purpose practice. Most of the other questions of policy can be answered only in terms of decisions with respect to these applications.

Personnel Policies and Practices Report describes the most common application of appraisals as a device to improve performance on the job. In a sample of firms, other applications and the percentages of firms reporting each usage are as follows:

Basis for promotions and transfers	66.0 per cent
Determining wage increases	63.2 per cent
Establishing training needs	61.3 per cent
Improving morale (indication of interest)	61.3 per cent
Discovery of supervisory potential	52.8 per cent

Reporting firms believe that the system helps supervisors to improve their judgment of workers, makes supervisors feel that they are participating in management, and provides important data for evaluating selection procedures, especially tests.[3]

1.2 Qualities. What qualities and characteristics are to be rated? A sharp distinction between two types of appraisal may be noted on this point. One type evaluates *performance,* what the worker has done and is doing. For hourly rated workers, it emphasizes quality and quantity of output. A second type of appraisal focuses attention on *potential,* the capacity for development. Some appraisal systems combine the two; many do not. Some collective agreements specifically restrict the appraisal of hourly rated workers to performance.

Frequent surveys have sought to discover how organizations answer this question of qualities to be rated. One of the most extensive has provided the

[3] *Personnel Policies and Practices Report,* Par. 5302, No. 11—50, 1960.

summary shown in Table 17.1. There it will be noted that "quantity of work"
is the most common item, with "cooperativeness" the next most frequent.

Table 17.1   Items in Personnel Appraisals

Item Rated	Number of Times Found in 50 Merit-Rating Forms†
Group 1: The Old Standbys	
Quantity of work	44
Quality of work	31
Group 2: Job Knowledge and Performance	
Knowledge of job	25
Attendance	14
Punctuality	12
Safety habits	7
Good housekeeping	3
Group 3: Characteristics of the Individual	
Cooperativeness	36
Dependability	35
Initiative	27
Intelligence	17
Accuracy	14
Industry	14
Adaptability	14
Attitude	13
Personality	13
Judgment	12
Application	10
Leadership	6
Conduct	6
Resourcefulness	6
Health	5
Neatness	5
Appearance	4
Enthusiasm	4
Potential	4

SOURCE: "Marks of the Good Worker," *National Industrial Conference Board Management Record*, Vol. 18, No. 5, May, 1956, pp. 168–170.
† Integrity, loyalty, speech, tact and thoroughness were rated by three or fewer companies.

1.3   Standard practice. Shall all employees be evaluated by the same set of standards? Or, at the other extreme, shall a different instrument and procedure be developed for each job in the organization? Can a firm or agency depend on a *standard* rating *scale* or form and a standard procedure? Many organizations follow this latter practice. Is such practice consistent with the policy for which appraisals are undertaken? A number of firms have concluded, in recent years, that it is not. Some of them have a number of rating forms and procedures. They follow different practices in appraising hourly rated workers, supervisors, middle managers. Others give those who make appraisals a preliminary questionnaire that asks what qualities are important in the jobs involved. Appraisers are then instructed to report on these particular qualities.

1.4 Coverage of appraisals. Who shall be appraised? Shall the practice be applied to all members of the organization? Older policy regarded "rating" as appropriate only for beginners, probationary workers, hourly-rated employees, and clerical workers. Later, the practice was extended to supervisors and foremen. With the growing emphasis on management development programs, appraisals of managers became common. The survey by *Personnel Policies and Practices Report,* mentioned in earlier paragraphs, found that 72.1 per cent of all firms report that they maintain formal rating programs. In 34 per cent, these programs cover all employees. Some 16.3 per cent exclude hourly rated workers, 10.2 per cent exclude administrative and executive groups, 4.8 per cent leave out exempt employees, and 2 per cent do not cover office employees.[4]

Policy on coverage may be based on a number of preliminary decisions. The use to be made of appraisals has an important bearing; if they are to become a basis for promotions, that fact suggests that they cover those regarded as eligible for such actions. If they are to be part of the employee development program, very wide coverage is thereby prescribed. If they have direct bearing on wage and salary increases, that use may require inclusion of all affected employees. In general, as managers have come to realize that everyone in the working organization is appraised, formal plans have been extended, on the theory that they can improve on the otherwise unavoidable informal appraisal process.

1.5 Who makes appraisals? Presumably, the answer to this question requires consideration of who—in the employment relationship—is best prepared to make appraisals. Policy makers face a range of possible choices. The most common answer is that appraisals will be made by one or more superiors. This means that the rank-and-file employee will be rated by his foreman and perhaps by the general foreman; the foreman by the general foreman and perhaps the next in line above him. Managers, if this answer is accepted, are rated by those to whom they report.

A good argument can be made, however, for the conclusion that the men working for a supervisor or manager are in the best position to appraise him. They may be closer to him and more easily observe his day-to-day actions and decisions. Appraisals by subordinates have received serious consideration for this reason.

A third possibility would have each individual evaluated by his *peers,* those at the same level and with whom he must maintain close cooperative working relationships. A fourth possibility would combine two or more of these three. A fifth choice could provide what is sometimes described as *field review,* with specialized appraisers, either from the industrial relations

[4] Par. 5315, No. 11–61.

staff of the organization or from outside. Finally, some firms have experimented with *self-appraisal,* in which each employee evaluates his own performance and potential.

As noted, by far the most common answer provides for appraisal by direct supervisors. At least three-fourths of reported practice follows this pattern. A much smaller proportion, probably not more than 10 per cent, provides rating committees, and lesser proportions use *peer* or *mutual* appraisals or evaluations by subordinates or by special appraisers.

1.6 Timing. When shall evaluations take place? How often shall employees be appraised? Current practice indicates that answers to these questions follow a fairly simple pattern. Most firms and agencies make appraisals either annually or semiannually; no clear preference for one or the other is evident in surveys. In addition, many organizations provide for a special appraisal just before the end of the probationary period, and some rate new employees more frequently during their first year.

1.7 Degree of formality. To what extent shall the appraisals be stereotyped, with a set form and procedure? Firms show wide variation in their answers to this question. Some adhere rigidly to a *rating* that requires quantitative values for a list of qualities, with little supplementary comment. Others go to the other extreme and prescribe a letter from the appraiser to be placed in the employee's personnel file. The letter may or may not be structured. Some practice simply asks the appraiser to record what he thinks is a fair appraisal.

Some organizations answer this question with a variety of degrees of formality. For hourly rated employees they prescribe a specific appraisal form in which performance is rated without comment. At the other extreme, these same firms may ask for a nonstructured annual appraisal from each manager's superior. In middle levels, they may include use of a formal rating scale, supplemented by extensive comments. When specialist appraisers are used, they may and usually do provide rather formal summaries, but these appraisals are not restricted by any simple scoring or scales.

1.8 Availability of appraisal information. Who is to be the custodian of the information reported from appraisals? To whom is such information to be available? Where and for how long shall it be kept? To some extent, answers are dictated by the purposes of appraisal. Thus, if it is to influence promotions, it must be available to those who make decisions on promotions. If it is to serve as a basis for training, some or all of the appraisal data must be available to those who determine eligibility for training programs. If it is to be used in counseling employees, it must be available to counselors and perhaps to each counselee.

The most common practice makes appraisal results available to the employee's supervisor. Frequently, the person appraised may be asked to look over his appraisal and make any comments he thinks appropriate. Often, also, the individual may be shown his appraisal in a counseling interview. Policy will weigh the obligation to advise those appraised against the hazards of injuring working relationships as a result of these disclosures.

Similar consideration may be given the question of filing appraisal reports and holding them. In the individual's personnel file, they may be available to supervisors and managers at all levels in the organization. They may be made the basis for letters of recommendation. Adverse criticism at one rating period may constitute a "black mark" on the employee's record for many years. As a matter of policy, some firms maintain a special file of these records, available only through the personnel staff. They remove older appraisals after a two- or three-year period.

1.9 Improving appraisals. What steps will be taken to maintain and improve the quality of appraisals? What will be done to discover and recognize their limitations and deficiencies and to overcome these shortcomings? Answers to these questions range from a simple "nothing" to elaborate programs of analysis, special research, and almost constant revision. One common answer proposes to train all appraisers to do a better job. Some policy proposes to define special qualifications for appraisers and to restrict the practice to those who meet these qualifications. Research has suggested that the quality of appraisals is heavily influenced by the intelligence of appraisers. Other studies have demonstrated that training in the appraisal process can improve resulting appraisals.

2.0 CURRENT PRACTICE

Broad outlines of current practice have been noted in the first section of the chapter. Special appraisal practices and techniques have been developed as means of formalizing practice and improving it. Current practice makes specific assignments of appraisal responsibilities and uses a variety of semi-formal and formal *rating forms* and *scales*. In the most common practice, appraisals are made by one or more direct superiors or supervisors. They may cover the area of actual *performance* on the job, or *potential* for more difficult assignments, or both. The appraisal process may include a *counseling procedure* in which the worker is informed of the opinions expressed in the appraisal.

2.1 Rating scales. Common practice provides some type of rating *form* or *scale,* designed to direct the appraiser's attention to specific characteristics of the worker and his work. It seeks to overcome the tendency to generalize and, at the same time, to provide a common basis for comparing the appraisals of several team members. In effect, it seeks to reduce these personal evaluations to ratios with a common denominator.

For this purpose, the usual appraisal instrument or rating scale lists from five to thirty qualities, characteristics, or attributes and records the appraiser's opinion of the degree to which each of these items applies to the individual *ratee.* Some scales are simple in the sense that they ask questions to be answered "yes" or "no." For example, the form may ask: "Has the ratee demonstrated initiative or originality?" or "Does he get along well with fellow workers?" More common practice allows the *rater* to check varying degrees with respect to each of several items. In some scales, qualities are defined, in an attempt to insure common understanding of their meanings. Some scales ask raters to relate the degree of each quality to what they regard as average. Scales may include items such as the "quantity of work," even when objective records show how much the ratee has done. This practice is sometimes defended on the ground that it permits a check on the reliability of the rater. Some scales are more complicated; they ask raters to select from a group of statements those that apply to the ratee. They seek to hide or obscure the measurement process, on the theory that raters may try to manipulate scales to provide favorable ratings for favorites.

A useful classification of the most widely used scales might note three principal types, including (1) *ranking* (including paired comparisons), (2) *graphic*, and (3) *checklist* scales. They are described in the paragraphs that follow. In the next section, attention is directed to various modifications in these basic types of rating scales and in their administration and application.

2.2 Ranking systems. Perhaps the simplest systems are those in which ratees are simply ranked in order on each quality. For example, in the *Order-of-Merit*[5] or *Man-to-Man* scale, each rater merely ranks his ratees for each quality. Thus, for leadership, he may rank them: (1) Jones, (2) Smith, (3) Brown, and so on; while for judgment he may rank them: (1) Smith, (2) Jones, (3) Brown, and on through the list.

A useful variant of this type of scale involves what is called *alternation ranking*. Ratings may be made on individual qualities or on over-all fitness for a particular position. From a complete list of all ratees, the rater is instructed first to cross out the names of any persons he does not know well enough to rank. His attention is then directed to two numbered columns (see Figure 17.2). He is asked to place the name of the person having most of the attribute at the top of the first column and that of the person having least at the bottom of the second. Both names are then struck out of the total list. The rater follows this same procedure for all remaining names on the list. The procedure has some advantages. It facilitates discrimination by comparing extremes in each choice. It also reduces the difficult problem of maintaining a standard for each quality.

The method of *paired comparisons* is not unlike this alternation-ranking procedure. Paired names of all those to be rated are typed on cards. Each ratee is compared with each of the others to be rated. Raters check the name of the superior person on each card. The system provides a total score or rank for each ratee. These totals may be translated into standard scores, which are calculated by relating the actual scores to the standard deviation and average of all scores (see Figure 16.6).

A somewhat similar procedure is followed in *sociometric* appraisals in which group members rank those they regard as the most satisfactory fellow

---

[5] See A. G. P. Elliot, "What Does Merit Rating Measure?" *Personnel Management*, Vol. 35, No. 325, September, 1953, pp. 135–40.

RATING-RANKING SCALE

Consider all those on your list in terms of their (quality). Cross out the names of any you cannot rate on this quality. Then select the one you would regard as having most of the quality. Put his name in Column I, below, on the first line, numbered 1. Cross out his name on your list. Consult the list again and pick out the person having least of this quality. Put his name at the bottom of Column II, on the line numbered 20. Cross out his name. Now, from the remaining names on your list, select the one having most of the quality. Put his name in the first column on line 2. Keep up this process until all names have been placed in the scale.

COLUMN I (MOST)	COLUMN II (LEAST)
1.	11.
2.	12.
3.	13.
4.	14.
5.	15.
6.	16.
7.	17.
8.	18.
9.	19.
10.	20.

Fig. 17.2   Alternation Ranking Form.

workers. Within individual work crews, members are asked to identify those among their associates with whom they communicate most frequently and those they prefer to work with. Such *mutual* or *peer* or *buddy ratings* have been used in a variety of situations, including the military services.

Ranking procedures are usually restricted to relatively small groups, for rather obvious reasons. The number of comparisons in a group of 30 is 435, which is probably about the maximum for ranking methods.

2.3   Graphic scales. Most of the scales in current use are *graphic*. They provide a chart or graph, with a list of qualities and range of degrees for each quality. Sometimes, instead of numbers, letter grades are listed, and raters are asked to grade each quality as A, B, C, and so on. Such a scale, using numbers, is illustrated in Figure 17.3. Often the lines are supplemented by simple descriptive words or phrases. Thus, under the line for health, the words "excellent," "average," and "poor" are placed at equally spaced intervals, or *judgment* may be described as "exceptional," "very good," "ordinary," "poor," or "rash." While the varying degrees thus identified are usually given numerical weights, in other practice no such quantitative values are printed on the form. They may, however, be applied to the rating by subsequent use of a transparent rule or stencil. Sometimes lines are drawn in the finished rating to create a profile of the ratee.

Several methods are used to help raters apply uniform standards with respect to each of the several qualities or attributes. As noted, each quality may be defined in detail. Sometimes the name of the attribute is not em-

Name		Position			Location				Rating as of	19
Check rating figure for each quality:		5 Excellent		4 Good	3 Average	2 Fair	1 Poor			
QUALIFICATION	5	4	3 RATER 2	1		5	4	3 REVIEWER 2	1	
IS	Ambition									
	Character									
	Education									
	Health									
	Loyalty									
	Outside Interests									
	Personality									
KNOWS	Present Activity									
	Other Activities									
	Procedure & Policy									
DOES	Accepts Responsibility									
	Application									
	Attendance									
	Care & Exactness									
	Cooperation									
	Expression									
	Follows Instructions									
	Housekeeping								-		
	Initiative									
	Intelligence									
	Judgment									
	Rate of Work									
	Sense of Economy									

Figure 17.3 Simple Graphic Rating Scale

phasized. For example, the "efficiency rating" long used in Federal agencies lists 15 "elements." Element number 5 is described in this instruction as follows:

> Consider industry: diligence; attentiveness; energy and application to duties; the degree to which the employee really concentrates on the work at hand.

The scale which follows describes degrees as ranging from "greatest possible diligence" to "lazy." In other practice, uniformity of standards is sought by detailed description of each of several degrees for each quality. This practice is illustrated in Figure 17.4.

Several scales seek to check the judgment of raters by requiring them to justify each rating in terms of an incident or anecdote involving the ratee.

The graphic scales already noted illustrate the tendency to seek ratings on both *performance* and *potential* in the same scale. A rating confined strictly to *performance* on the job is shown in Figure 17.5. That form also illustrates the careful definition of degrees as well as specific provision for discussion with the ratee.

2.4 Check list of phrases. There are, of course, many variations from these common rating devices. One such variation is illustrated by the scale, widely used in the public service, developed by J. B. Probst. It seeks to reduce interpretation by raters, by asking that the latter check brief phrases if they

EMPLOYEE'S SIGNATURE	Exceptional (100 85)	Good (80 75)	Marginal (70 65)	Unsatisf'ry (60 55 50)	Reading	Factor	Extn.	Var.	TOTAL
1. QUALITY OF WORK: Consider accuracy, thoroughness, and facility with which his work can be followed by others.	Accurate and Capable	Few Errors Good Quality	Work Spotty, Rather Careless	Frequent Errors					
2. QUANTITY OF WORK: Consider the amount of work and the promptness with which completed.	Unusually High Results	Turns Out Good Volume	Fair Results	Very Slow Worker					
3. DEPENDABILITY: Consider how reliable and trustworthy when given an assignment.	Absolutely Dependable	Trustworthy	Usually Reliable	Uncertain, Unreliable					
4. KNOWLEDGE: Consider acquaintance with requirements of job gained through experience and education.	Outstanding	More Than Adequate	Requires Coaching	Inadequate					
5. INTEREST AND INITIATIVE: Consider the amount of interest in position and ability to think and put it into action.	Keenly Interested	Frequent New Ideas	Requires Considerable Directing	Constant Directing					
6. COOPERATIVENESS: Consider ability to get along with associates and ability to carry out instructions.	Favorable Influence on Associates	Gets Along Well With Associates	Indifferent	Disagreeable			*		
7. VERSATILITY: Consider ability to perform job other than own; ability to learn new methods.	Very Good Knowledge of Other Operations	Good Ability and Knowledge	Learns Slowly	Inadequate Slow to Absorb					
8. PUBLIC RELATIONS: Consider general conduct on and off job; how it reflects upon the public relations of the department.	A Model Example to Associates and Public	Good Conduct and Attitude on and off Job	Conduct, Attitude Questionable	Unsatis. Conduct and Attitude					

COMMENTS AND SUGGESTIONS:_____ TOTAL SCORE_____

RECOMMENDED:_____   ☐ APPROVED
         DIVISION HEAD OR DISTRICT ENGINEER   ☐ DISAPPROVED _____
                                        PERSONNEL OFFICER - DIRECTOR OF HWYS.

Figure 17.4 Rating Scale with Descriptive Phrases

describe the ratee. Interpretations are then made by those in charge of the rating program. Raters are instructed to express opinions only if they feel qualified to do so. More complicated checklists give appraisers a choice of short sentences from which to choose, as in the *forced choice* scales described in the next section.

2.5 Measured job performance. In both the public service and private firms, many managers have concluded that no list of six to twelve qualities can adequately outline the responsibilities of employees, especially when the appraisal system is expected to include supervisors and middle managers. At the same time, more thoughtful managers have recognized the uncertainties in appraising potential for higher levels of responsibility. They have noted

PERFORMANCE ANALYSIS

For period ending_____

Name_____ Dept._____ Clock_____ Job Title_____ Job No._____

Describe briefly the SPECIFIC WORK this employee performs _____

FACTORS	QUANTITY — Consider output of satisfactory work during a given period of time.	QUALITY — Extent to which work produced meets quality requirements of accuracy, thoroughness, and effectiveness.	KNOWLEDGE OF JOB — Extent of job information and understanding possessed by employee. Consider knowledge required to fulfill job description.
UNSATISFACTORY — Performance with respect to factor is deficient enough to justify release from present job unless improved.	☐ Output inadequate to retain in job without improvement.	☐ Quality too poor to retain in job without improvement.	☐ Knowledge inadequate to retain in job without improvement.
FAIR — Performance with respect to factor is below the requirements for the job and must improve to be satisfactory.	☐ Output below job requirements.	☐ Work below standard quality requirements.	☐ Lacks required knowledge for job title
GOOD — Performance with respect to factor meets the job requirements. THIS IS THE BASIC STANDARD FOR RATING EACH FACTOR.	☐ Output satisfies job requirements.	☐ Work satisfies quality requirements.	☐ Knowledge satisfies ordinary requirements of job title.
VERY GOOD — Performance with respect to factor is beyond the ordinary requirements for good performance for the job title.	☐ Output exceeds job requirements	☐ Quality high. Work very well done.	☐ Very well informed on all phases of work in job title.
EXCEPTIONAL — Performance with respect to factor is excellent, approaching the best possible for the job.	☐ Unusual speed and volume of output.	☐ Unusual accuracy, thoroughness and effectiveness.	☐ Exceptionally well informed. Has knowledge to handle work of most complex nature in the job title.

Does he:

YES NO

1. Work well with others ? ☐☐
2. Work without an excessive amount of supervision ? ☐☐
3. Properly use machinery, equipment or materials to avoid damage ? ☐☐
4. Have required physical characteristics for all work in job title. ☐☐

YES NO

5. Avoid wasting supplies ? ☐☐
6. Work carefully, and use equipment and safty devices in order to avoid injury to self and others, and maintain a neat ordery work area in accordance with good-housekeeping principles. ☐☐
7. Maintain satisfactory attendance ? ☐☐

COMMENTS_____

This analysis has been discussed with me _____

Employee's Signature   Supervisor's Signature   CI. No.   GROUP

ROUTING : WHITE - Originating Dept.   CANARY - Personnel Dept. Records Section

Figure 17.5   Job Performance Scale

SOURCE: By permission of Boeing Airplane Company.

the common differences of opinion on such qualities as "capacity for development," "ability to manage," and "leadership." In some current practice, therefore, an attempt is made to establish standards of performance for each job and then to compare the performance of incumbents with this standard.

Appraisal begins with a study of each job and the definition of numerous —sometimes as many as a hundred—specific duties or responsibilities for which standards of performance are established. Thus one such scale lists 36 common duties of middle managers and allows the addition of as many more for individual jobs. Not infrequently, ratees are asked to join in the identification of these responsibilities and in the setting of acceptable standards. Further, each ratee may be asked to rate himself on performance as compared with these standards at the same time that he is rated on the same scale by his supervisor. In some practice, the individual's appraisal is accomplished in a conference in which he and his supervisor go over each of these items and tentatively agree on the ratee's measure of performance.[6]

Unless there are large numbers in each job, the procedure requires a tailor-made scale for each individual employee. On the other hand, the practice does force raters and ratees to give careful thought to what is expected in each of the jobs for which they are responsible. It has the advantage of getting both rater and ratee to consider the other's opinion as to what the job involves and what standards of performance appear reasonable. It lets ratees know more precisely what is expected of them.

2.6 Weighting and scoring. Completed scales may be used in "raw" form to provide a picture or profile of each rater's opinion of each ratee. In other practice, appraisals are *scored* to provide a composite figure representing the total rating. In the simplest procedure, numerical values are attached to the degrees of each quality, and their total is regarded as the rating of the individual. Where several raters appraise each ratee, a composite rating may be prepared, and the average or median numerical score may be accepted as representative.

Any attachment of numerical values to ratings results in some weighting of the qualities. All qualities may be judged on the same range of values; equally weighted. On the other hand, one quality may be given a greater range than others, or its high degrees may be given larger values.

In many situations, those in charge of the program wish to avoid equal weighting. They argue that no amount of *health*, for example, should be allowed to offset a deficiency in judgment or dependability. Accordingly, they give some qualities greater and others less than average weight.

3.0 LIMITATIONS AND MODIFICATIONS

Few managers or firms have found a way to get along without appraisals, but a great deal of attention has been given to the common de-

---

[6] For an excellent report of this practice as applied to managers, see Stephen Habbe, "Rating Managers in Terms of Job Duties," *Management Record,* Vol. 23, No. 10, October, 1961, pp. 23–29.

ficiencies in appraisal procedures. Sophisticated managers, both staff and line, have become increasingly critical of the simpler practices described in the preceding section. These managers have given a great deal of attention to policy on appraisals and to both rating scales and the administration of the rating program. They note possible hazards to employee morale if those who receive high ratings are not promptly rewarded in pay and promotions. They provide training for those who are to make appraisals. They recognize the more common deficiencies in rating as a method of formal appraisal. They may have developed more complicated scales. In a few cases, they have discarded these formal instruments and substituted less formal, less structured, and less quantitative evaluations.

3.1   The "rating game." Fundamental to many of the limitations of personnel ratings is the fact that rating procedure becomes something of a game or contest. Raters, confronted with a more or less formidable list of characteristics to be scored, may regard the assignment as not only an unpleasant chore but something of an insult, a challenge to their ability to judge the workers they are to rate.

Not infrequently, the rater does not have adequate information to answer all of the questions in the formal scale nor does he know all of those he is asked to appraise. The procedure takes time which he could be devoting to other assignments he prefers. He may, from his own experience, have serious doubts about the meaning of resulting summaries or scores. He may be critical of the weighting of qualities. These attitudes may, in themselves, adversely affect the value and usefulness of the program.[7]

Attitudes of suspicion may be encouraged by frequent changes in scales and procedures. Raters may feel that the process is something of a contest between their evaluations and opinions and those of the staff managers responsible for the rating program. In effect, the rater's reaction is to ask: "Why don't they simply ask me whether Jones is a good worker or a promising candidate for advancement? Why do they try to complicate the question and confuse me with all these details?" He may answer his own questions somewhat as follows: "They don't trust my judgment. They think I can't appraise my associates. They think I'll play favorites. They are trying to trap me." His reaction may well be one of trying to "beat the game."

3.2   Central tendency; leniency. Critical rater attitudes become evident in the deficiencies generally described as *central tendency* and *leniency*. Central tendency is the inclination to rate all or most qualities and ratees close to the average or middle of the range. It may result from the fact that raters do not know ratees well enough to express a discriminating opinion. To some degree, it probably reflects a common desire to avoid extremes. Raters may check "average" on the ground that it will not injure

   [7] Mahoney and Woods have suggested that a program developed by managers themselves may improve these attitudes. See Thomas A. Mahoney and Richard G. Woods, "Developing an Appraisal Program through Action Research," *Personnel*, Vol. 38, No. 1, January-February, 1961, pp. 25–31.

the ratee and, at the same time, that it will not expose their lack of more definitive information.

The related limitation of *leniency* reflects a desire to err on the generous side, to avoid controversy by giving each ratee the "benefit of the doubt." To rate Jones "below average" on initiative may provoke a discussion, perhaps with those who review the rating, perhaps also with Jones. "Average," however, may be acceptable to both.[8]

Perhaps the most common practice designed to overcome these deficiencies is that of training raters. In rater training programs, raters are assisted in developing common definitions for each of the qualities to be scored as well as common standards for scoring. A second attack uses ranking or ordering techniques to force some spread or dispersion in evaluations. Other, more complicated variations include the use of *forced distributions* and *forced choice*. (Both are described later in this section.)

3.3 Halo. Another common deficiency of ratings tends to allow one quality to color the entire appraisal or to make all qualities fit a sort of "general impression." This *halo effect*, noted as a hazard in interviewing, destroys the value of ratings on individual qualities and reduces the total rating to a sort of over-all, bird's-eye impression.

The "halo" tendency has been clearly identified and widely reported. A ratee who makes a good appearance, for example, may be rated high on such presumably unrelated qualities as dependability and cooperation. On the other hand, an outstanding weakness may occasion lower ratings on several or all other qualities. In some cases, the halo is encouraged by the fact that listed qualities are not mutually exclusive.

3.4 Varying standards. Another common problem in rating arises out of the application of differing standards by raters. Thus, one rater may consistently rate higher than his colleagues, while another rates lower. This creates obvious problems in combining or in comparing the ratings of several raters. Combined with central tendency, it may also give rise to a situation in which one or two raters make the major decisions for a panel of four or five. Only the ratings of the two may show enough spread to push individual ratees above or below the average.

A *systematic error* or constant error is a consistent tendency to overvalue or undervalue ratees on a given characteristic. It indicates the application, by the rater under consideration, of a standard lower or higher than that used by other raters. *Total errors* are measures of variation above and below the scores given the same ratees by other raters. They may reflect a lack of consistency on the part of a rater in applying standards. Thus, a high total error may be occasioned by a continuing tendency to score too high or too low, but it may also show a tendency to score too high in one case and too low in another. Ratings may be adjusted for a consistent or systematic error.

---

[8] In this connection, see the interesting proposal to introduce discriminate binary scoring as a means of distributing ratings in Bernard M. Bass, "Reducing Leniency in Merit Rating," *Personnel Psychology*, Vol. 9, No. 3, Autumn, 1956, pp. 359–69.

Adjustment is impossible where the tendency of the rater shifts from over-valuing in one case to undervaluing in another.

The usual practice in measuring these errors is not complicated. Measurements of total and systematic errors are usually applied to individual traits rather than to the rating as a whole. To measure the total error for each trait, it is necessary first to discover the mean or average rating on that characteristic for all raters. This average may be designated as M. Then the individual rater's rating on this trait for each ratee is noted, and may be designated as R. The total error for each rater on the given trait is, then,

$$\text{T.E.} = \frac{\Sigma |R - M|}{N}$$

where differences $(R - M)$ are added without regard to sign, and N is the number of persons rated.

The systematic error on each trait is found as

$$\text{S.E.} = \frac{\Sigma (R - M)}{N}$$

where the differences are added algebraically, and N is again the number of persons rated.

The method of measuring total and systematic errors of ratings is illustrated by reference to some simplified data in Example 17.1.

3.5 Interdepartmental differences. These represent a special case of different standards. If ratings prepared in different departments are to be combined, variations in the standards applied in the several units may create serious problems. In the federal government, for example, the level of ratings in certain bureaus and divisions has appeared higher than that in others, although no reason for a distinctive quality of personnel was evident. This same situation is frequently encountered in large business organizations. In such situations, ratings may have to be adjusted if they are to be meaningful throughout the whole organization. One means of adjustment translates numerical scores in each division into a percentile rank or a standard score (the latter based on the standard deviation of the ratings in the unit). In some practice, translation into percentile ranks is regularly made as a convenience in explaining ratings to employees.

3.6 Validity and reliability. The importance of checking on the validity and reliability of interviews and tests has been described. Ratings or broader personnel appraisals, like tests, may not provide useful indicators of what they are supposed to appraise. They may not be consistent in their evaluations.

Checking the validity of ratings is complicated by *criterion* problems. Personnel appraisal is undertaken precisely because no objective measure is available. *Performance ratings* have an advantage in that they can sometimes be compared with actual records of output. *Potential ratings* or appraisals can be analyzed and compared with the career experience of those

EXAMPLE 17.1

Total and Systematic Errors of Three Raters

Data: Ratings (assumed for illustration) accorded ten rates on a single trait by three raters.

Ratees	Rater A	Rater B	Rater C	Total	Mean M_r	Rater A	Rater B	Rater C
	Ratings					Errors		
A	7	7	4	18	6	1	1	−2
B	6	5	7	18	6	0	−1	1
C	8	7	6	21	7	1	0	−1
D	8	8	5	21	7	1	1	−2
E	9	8	10	27	9	0	−1	1
F	4	5	3	12	4	0	1	−1
G	6	6	3	15	5	1	1	−2
H	3	4	2	9	3	0	1	−1
I	9	9	6	24	8	1	1	−2
J	5	4	3	12	4	1	0	−1

Total Errors: $$\text{T.E.} = \frac{\Sigma|R - M_r|}{N}$$

Rater A: T.E. = 6/10 = 0.60
Rater B: T.E. = 8/10 = 0.80
Rater C: T.E. = 14/10 = 1.40

Systematic Errors: $$\text{S.E.} = \frac{\Sigma(R - M_r)}{N}$$

Rater A: S.E. =   6/10 =   .60
Rater B: S.E. =   4/10 =   .40
Rater C: S.E. = — 10/10 =   1.00

appraised, in terms of promotions, salary advances, and other such evidence. Such comparisons are of dubious value, however, if ratings have been used as a basis for the same promotions and salary increases. Sometimes meaningful checks compare ratings with measured intelligence and other scores or tests of qualities similar to those rated in the appraisal process.

A measure of the reliability of ratings is available from the analysis of total and systematic errors. The usual methods of checking test reliability are not readily applicable to appraisals; it is not generally feasible to require repetitive appraisals at short intervals or to undertake the common odd-even, split test type of analysis (See Chapter 18, section 4.3).

Measurement of validity and reliability is complicated. Kallejian, Brown, and Weschler found that personality characteristics of the superior—his own attitudes and personal needs—have a significant influence on his ratings. They noted further that most supervisors are not aware of the factors that reduce the validity of their ratings.[9] Sorenson and Gross found that raters

[9] Verne Kallejian, Paula Brown, and Irving R. Weschler, "The Impact of Inter-

were, however, aware that they felt some bias and that their ratings showed unreliability.[10]

3.7 Modifications; critical incidents. A wide variety of modifications in appraisal practice has appeared in efforts to overcome these common deficiencies of rating. Reference has been made to the practice of asking appraisers to note examples of the ratee's behavior that justify their evaluations. The objective is clear; the practice seeks to force careful consideration and to insure that the appraiser has information to justify his conclusions. A formal application of this approach is represented by the *critical-incident* technique. It asks raters to consider each of their conclusions in terms of specific incidents that provide sharply significant or definitive evidence to support the appraisal.

The critical-incident procedure may provide the appraiser with a list of suggested or illustrative incidents. For example, one firm illustrates the rating for "dependability" with a list that includes: left work without leave, late to work, stopped before quitting time, took excessive relief, failed to report for overtime, loafed at or between jobs, did personal work on the job, neglected assigned task, did extra work during idle period, notified foreman in advance that he would be out of work.

3.8 Forced distributions. Some current practice approaches the problems of central tendency and leniency the hardhanded way. It simply instructs appraisers that only a specific proportion of the total number they appraise can have scores in the higher and middle levels. It forces them to distribute their ratings. It may, for example, require raters to conform to a system that places 10 per cent in the lowest category, 20 per cent in the next, 40 per cent in the middle, 20 per cent in the next, and 10 per cent in the top group. Thus raters are in effect required to normalize the distribution of their ratings. The procedure may be applied to over-all ratings or to individual traits.

3.9 Forced choice. *Forced choice* (also called *preference check list*) rating is a further variant from the simple graphic scales. It is designed to require sharp discrimination among raters and particularly to reduce the tendency of many raters to give average, lenient, or "easy" ratings.

In its most common form, the forced-choice procedure provides a check list of specific descriptive phrases, so arranged that their selection permits scoring but does not specify their scoring effect. The rater, required to choose from among these statements, cannot be sure what effect his decision will have on composite ratings. In the usual procedure, the rater selects from within each group of four or five statements the one that is most appropriate and that which is least appropriate for the ratee under consideration.

In the practice of the United Parcel Service, employees who are being

personal Relations on Ratings of Performance," *Public Personnel Review,* Vol. 14, No. 4, October, 1953, pp. 166–70.

[10] A. G. Sorenson and G. F. Gross, "Inter-Rater Reliability from the Viewpoint of the Rater," *Personnel and Guidance Journal,* Vol. 35, No. 6, February, 1957, pp. 365–68.

prepared for added executive responsibilities are rated by two superiors. The forced-choice scale includes ten blocks, each composed of five statements. The five include two that are favorable, two unfavorable, and one that is essentially neutral. Raters begin by numbering the most appropriate 1, the next 2, and so on to the least appropriate, which is numbered 5. As noted, other procedure frequently selects the most appropriate and the least appropriate in each block.

Some of the scales in current use include as many as 50 such blocks. One typical format creates each block in the following form.

Most Appropriate	*Least Appropriate*	*Observation*
1	1	Easy to get acquainted with.
2	2	Places great emphasis on people.
3	3	Refuses to accept criticism.
4	4	Thinks generally in terms of money.
5	5	Makes decisions quickly.

Raters are instructed to check the most appropriate and the least appropriate phrases in each block, even if they feel that none is exactly fitting.

3.10 Less formal appraisals: the field review. Some firms have been so impressed with the limitations of formal rating that they have tried less structured procedures. In the least formal, supervisors and managers are requested once each year to formulate a summary letter with respect to each of their subordinates. The letter or memorandum may be quite informal, with no set list of qualities to be considered and no requirement of comparisons with a standard or with other employees. Some experiments with this practice bring all appraisers together to explain uses to be made of these records and to suggest the questions to be considered in preparing these statements.

In another experiment—*the field review*—specialists in appraisals observe and visit with workers, supervisors, and managers and develop evaluations on the basis of these observations.

Sessions and Taylor, reporting on studies by the Air Force, conclude that rating by members of the operating line is likely to be less successful than that undertaken by neutrals who are thoroughly familiar with the jobs and men.[11]

In the practice described by Machaver and Erickson, appraisals are based on interviews conducted by a "personnel specialist." The specialist discusses his evaluations with each superior. The latter makes final decisions on the evaluation, with the help of the specialist. Appraisals are in narrative style

[11] Frank Q. Sessions and Calvin W. Taylor, "In-Service Versus Out-of-Service Administration of Tests and Criteria," *Personnel Psychology*, Vol. 14, No. 1, Spring, 1961, pp. 67–72; William V. Machaver and Willard E. Erickson, "A New Approach to Executive Appraisal," *Personnel*, Vol. 35, No. 1, July-August, 1958, pp. 8–14; Wallace H. Best, "Some New Directions in Personnel Appraisals," *Personnel*, Vol. 34, No. 2, September-October, 1957, pp. 45–50; Theodore L. Sharp and Larry C. White, "An Approach to Employee Evaluation: the Field Review," *Public Personnel Review*, Vol. 17, No. 1, January, 1956, pp. 13–16

and related to specific actions and performance. The superior subsequently counsels the ratee. The superior is trained for the counseling interview.

4.0 COUNSELING ON APPRAISALS

Current practice is far from uniform with respect to counseling those who are appraised on the basis of their ratings or appraisals. Surveys of current practice report that from one-third to nine-tenths of the responding firms say that they discuss appraisals with those appraised.[12]

For the most part, such discussions are personal and private, although a few firms have brought ratees together for a discussion of their ratings. In some, the discussion and counseling responsibility is assigned to members of the industrial relations or personnel staff.

Although a major policy in most appraisal programs is the assistance of individual employees in their improvement and development, and although it is difficult to see how such assistance can be provided without these discussions, many organizations have expressed doubt about appraisal counseling and some have discontinued the practice. Thoughtful managers have become dubious about much of the theory on which these interviews are based.

Much of the current practice in discussing appraisals with those rated is based on theory that may have limited rather than general applicability. It holds that we learn more rapidly if we have frequent reports on our progress and that we like to have frequent evaluations by competent evaluators. It assumes that we like to know how we are doing in our continuing efforts to improve. Indeed, some of the counseling programs are described as "How am I doing?" sessions.

Questions are appropriate, however, about whether these theories are equally applicable to grade-school students, college students, rank-and-file employees, and managers. Are they appropriate in describing the reactions of production workers as well as white-collar clerical groups? Are they generally true, or are there wide individual differences? Are the supervisors and superiors in management who normally do the counseling qualified in the same sense as teachers in schools and universities? Do they have the same kind of evidence on which to base their recommendations? Will their criticisms and evaluations and suggestions for change be accepted by those counseled in the same spirit as the suggestions of teachers? Is it not possible that the setting for counseling—in which the counselor may well have a great deal to say about the salary or wage as well as the whole future career of the counselee—may influence the degree to which these theories are appropriate and useful?

Thoughtful managers have become increasingly doubtful about the useful-

---

[12] National Industrial Conference Board reports indicate that such discussions are more frequent with salaried than with hourly rated workers. *Personnel Policies and Practice Report* (Par. 5311, No. 11—57, 1960) indicates that nine out of ten firms report such counseling.

ness of counseling based on personnel appraisals. They are concerned about the possible adverse effects on day-to-day working relationships that may follow such counseling. Likert has reported on the experience of a group of personnel men who undertook an experiment in appraisal and counseling. They developed what appeared to be a satisfactory performance-rating system. They agreed that ratees should be informed of resulting ratings. They further agreed that the review of each appraisal should motivate the ratee to overcome his weaknesses. Yet none of them could play the role of counselor in a manner satisfactory to the group. In each attempt, the ratee developed reactions indicating his fear, resentment, and hostility.[13]

Numerous modifications of practice have been suggested to conserve the values of counseling on appraisals and, at the same time, to avoid the hazards of this procedure. Most of them contemplate special preparation for counseling. Supervisors and managers as well as those who are rated may be given a special training course for this purpose. They may be tutored and given experience in role-playing sessions. Soik emphasizes the "climate" of the interview, concluding that it should be directed to job performance rather than "man-centered."[14]

Hapcock and Mayfield conclude that special training and advance preparation are essential if counselors are to be effective. Hapcock questions whether, when the employee recognizes his weaknesses, he will always take steps to correct them and whether telling employees how they stand will relieve their uncertainty and insecurity.[15] Mayfield regards the appraisal interview as a responsibility of management but he concludes that both the rater and ratee should prepare in advance for this session.[16]

Maier describes three types of appraisal interviews, "Tell and Sell," "Tell and Listen," and "Problem Solving." He concludes that the ideal appraisal interview is of the third type.[17] His comparison of these types is outlined in Table 17.2.

Another suggestion proposes that the interviewer be freed of the responsibility for direct criticism by asking the interviewee to open the discussion by outlining what he regards as his weaknesses. Some programs use a system of *self-rating* as a preparation for these sessions. The ratee thus

---

[13] See Rensis Likert, "Motivational Approach to Management Development," *Harvard Business Review*, Vol. 37, No. 4, July-August, 1959, pp. 75ff; see also Thomas L. Whisler, "Performance Appraisal and the Organization Man," *Journal of Business*, Vol. 31, No. 1, January, 1958, pp. 19–27; Allen R. Solem, "Some Supervisory Problems in Appraisal Interviewing," *Personnel Administration*, Vol. 23, No. 3, May-June, 1960, pp. 27–35; Douglas McGregor, "An Uneasy Look at Performance Appraisal," *Harvard Business Review*, Vol. 35, No. 3, May-June, 1957, pp. 89–94.

[14] Nile Soik, "The Employee Performance Review," *Journal of The American Society of Training Directors*, Vol. 12, No. 11, November, 1958, pp. 36–45.

[15] Robert Hapcock, "Don't Go by the Book in Appraisal Interview," *Office Management and American Business*, Vol. 21, No. 11, November, 1960, pp. 60–61.

[16] Harold Mayfield, "In Defense of Performance Appraisal," *Harvard Business Review*, Vol. 38, No. 2, March-April, 1960, pp. 81–87.

[17] Norman R. F. Maier, "Three Types of Appraisal Interview," *Personnel*, Vol. 34, No. 5, March-April, 1958, pp. 27–40.

takes the initiative in bringing up the question of his needs and opportunities for improvement.[18]

Most of these suggestions seem to overlook the possibility that much of the counseling presently associated with appraisals should probably be done on a day-to-day basis, as a part of the job of supervision. If the superior is discussing the employee's actions when they occur, an annual rating will have little to add in terms of how the subordinate is doing. Carried to its logical conclusion, this approach to the problem may imply that there is little place for formal appraisals as a basis for counseling sessions if supervision and leadership are adequate. Certainly, it suggests that many of the deficiencies of appraisals can be reduced by effective supervision. Appraisals and subsequent counseling can never take the place of good supervision and direction.

At the same time, experience and research point clearly to the need for checking on the side effects of and reactions to both appraisal and any subsequent procedure.

5.0 SUMMARY

General policy on manpower management usually proposes that recruitment and selection shall provide adequate quantities of the right types of manpower. It also intends that most employees, from rank-and-file production jobs to high levels of management, shall have an opportunity to continue their development and to prepare for jobs involving higher skills and greater responsibility. In this sense, the *development* function follows and supplements the *staffing* function.

A preliminary step in development involves personnel rating or appraisal. It provides more or less formal procedures for making and recording opinions on the value—as indicated by performance on the job and by opinions about potential skills and capacities—of those who are to be given opportunity for further advancement. Usually such appraisals are repeated at stated intervals, thus providing a basis for comparing an employee's current rating with those of earlier periods.

These appraisals may be used for many purposes other than to assist in individual development. They are frequently the basis for wage and salary adjustments and promotions or demotions. They may be a means of insuring that supervisors become well acquainted with those they are directing. Resulting "ratings" are widely used as criteria in studies of sources, selection practices, supervisory actions, promotions from within, and a variety of training and development programs.

Although personnel rating has become standard practice in a large share of all employment, it deserves very critical study. The rating practice raises difficult, complex policy questions with respect to the uses of these alleged

---

[18] See, for example, Robert R. Blake, "Re-examination of Performance Appraisal," *Advanced Management*, Vol. 23, No. 7, July, 1958, pp. 19–20.

Cause and Effect Relations in Three Types of Appraisal Interviews

Method	TELL AND SELL	TELL AND LISTEN	PROBLEM SOLVING
Role of Interviewer	Judge	Judge	Helper
Objective	To communicate evaluation To persuade employee to improve	To communicate evaluation To release defensive feelings	To stimulate growth and development in employee
Assumptions	Employee desires to correct weaknesses if he knows them Any person can improve if he so chooses A superior in qualified to evaluate a subordinate	People will change if defensive feelings are removed	Growth can occur without correcting faults Discussing job problems leads to improved performance
Reactions	Defensive behavior suppressed Attempts to cover hostility	Defensive behavior expressed Employee feels accepted	Problem solving behavior
Skills	Salesmanship Patience	Listening and reflecting feelings Summarizing	Listening and reflecting feelings Reflecting ideas Using exploratory questions Summarizing
Attitude	People profit from criticism and appreciate help	One can respect the feelings of others if one understands them	Discussion develops new ideas and mutual interests
Motivation	Use of positive or negative incentives or both (Extrinsic in that motivation is added to the job itself)	Resistance to change reduced Positive incentive (Extrinsic and some intrinsic motivation)	Increased freedom Increased responsibility (Intrinsic motivation in that interest is inherent in the task)
Gains	Success most probable when employee respects interviewer	Develops favorable attitude to superior which increases probability of success	Almost assured of improvement in some respect
Risks	Loss of loyalty Inhibition of independent judgment Face-saving problems created	Need for change may not be developed	Employee may lack ideas Change may be other than what superior had in mind
Values	Perpetuates existing practices and values	Permits interviewer to change his views in the light of employee's responses Some upward communication	Both learn since experience and views are pooled Change is facilitated

SOURCE: Reproduced by permission from Normal R. F. Maier, "Three Types of Appraisal Interviews," *The Appraisal Interview*, New York: John Wiley & Sons, Inc., 1958.

measures, the qualities they attempt to assess, the coverage of the appraisal program, the competence of appraisers, the degree of formality with which appraisals are conducted, and the dependability with which results can be accepted.

Simpler and more common practice uses a variety of ranking, graphic and check-list types of scales. As managers have become more sophisticated with respect to limitations of appraisals, they have developed more complicated instruments and procedures. The whole practice has taken on some aspects of a rating game, in which raters pit their skill and originality against staff managers, who seek to insure penetrating, considered evaluations.

Individual firms as well as public agencies and services have recognized numerous limitations in the simple procedure. They have noted the halo effect, difficulties in applying common standards, the tendency to score at the average, systematic errors of appraisers, and resulting questionable validity and reliability of appraisals. They have developed numerous modifications of simple procedures to overcome or limit these deficiencies. The use of critical incidents, forced distributions of scores, forced-choice systems, and field reviews are among the more prominent of these developments.[19]

In recent years, questions have also been raised about the usual practice of counseling on appraisals. Alert managers have become concerned about the hazards in such appraisals. Some have instituted training programs in both appraising and counseling. Others have discontinued counseling sessions. A few have sought to retain their value but restrict their hazards by asking those appraised to assess themselves as a basis for discussion of their strong and weak points and their need for improvement. A few managers have concluded that effective supervision can reduce or eliminate the need for such counseling.

Formal or informal appraisals set the stage for a variety of employee and management training and development programs. In the chapters that follow, attention is directed to these programs.

SELECTED SUPPLEMENTARY READINGS

Balinsky, Benjamin and Ruth Burger, "The Art of Constructive Criticism," *The Executive Interview,* chap. 9. New York: Harper & Brothers, 1959.
Handbook of Personnel Management and Labor Relations, sec. 15. New York: McGraw-Hill Book Company, Inc., 1958.
Kallejian, Verne, Paula Brown, and Irving R. Weschler, "The Impact of Interpersonal Relations on Ratings of Performance," *Public Personnel Review,* Vol. 14, No. 4, October, 1953, pp. 166–70. (Available as *Reprint No. 33,* Los Angeles: University of California Institute of Industrial Relations, 1953.)
Likert, Rensis, "Motivational Approach to Management Development," *Harvard Business Review,* Vol. 37, No. 4, pp. 75ff, July-August, 1959.

[19] See, for example, Paul C. Buchanan, "Testing the Validity of an Evaluation Program," *Personnel,* Vol. 34, No. 3, November-December, 1957, pp. 75–81; Robert H. Finn, "Is Your Appraisal Program Really Necessary?" *ibid.,* Vol. 37, No. 1, January-February, 1960, pp. 16–25; A. C. MacKinney, "What Should Ratings Rate?" *ibid.,* Vol. 37, No. 3, May-June, 1960, pp. 75–78.

Mayfield, Harold, "In Defense of Performance Appraisal," *Harvard Business Review*, Vol. 35, No. 3, pp. 89–94, May-June, 1957.

Performance Appraisal and Review, Ann Arbor, Mich.: Foundation for Research on Human Behavior, 1958.

Whisler, Thomas L., "Performance Appraisal and the Organization Man," *Journal of Business*, Chicago: Vol. 31, No. 1, pp. 19–27. January, 1958.

SHORT CASE PROBLEM 17.1

Arrow Division Appraisals

Following established procedure in the Arrow Division, the assistant manager, Mr. Blue, called in each foreman for a discussion of the individual's semiannual personnel rating. For most of those who rated well up in the scale for all qualities, these visits were—in Mr. Blue's opinion—worthwhile from both the firm's and the individual's point of view. In the case of Mr. Ford, one of the supervisors, the results have been less encouraging.

Ford, like all the others, had been rated on a graphic or profile type of scale. The original rating was made by Mr. Blue, who then passed his completed ratings to the manager for the latter's review and comment. The manager had made no changes whatever. He had countersigned the forms. "Counseling" sessions then required the assistant manager to discuss his personal evaluations with each of the supervisors.

In the counseling session, Ford disagreed with several of the "average" scores in his rating. He felt that he deserved better. In the course of the session, he repeatedly asked for illustrations of his alleged shortcomings. When he was given what Mr. Blue considered excellent examples, he either questioned the accuracy of the facts or countered with the question: "Why didn't anyone speak to me about the matter at the time?"

Since the counseling session, Ford's behavior and apparent attitude have given Mr. Blue continuing concern. Almost every day, he asks the assistant manager whether he is doing all right. When he corrected one of the men in his crew, he immediately reported the matter to the assistant manager and asked whether what he had done and the way he had done it appeared appropriate. Meanwhile, the grapevine has carried the rumor that he says he's looking for another job with an outfit that "treats foremen like human beings."

Getting and holding good supervisors has been a persistent problem for the firm. Ford's crew has been, on the whole, one of the best in the local organization in terms of getting out the work. The assistant manager doesn't want to lose Ford. He is even more concerned lest other foremen may have developed similar attitudes as a result of the counseling experience. He would like to discontinue the counseling procedure, but both the rating and the subsequent discussion with ratees are required procedure in the organization.

Problem: How would you advise Mr. Blue? Be prepared to take the role of a consultant in a counseling session with him on his problem.

SHORT CASE PROBLEM 17.2

Savers' Services Personnel Ratings

"Savers' Service" is an investment firm. More than 200 employees in the home office have been regularly rated at six-month intervals, by means of a graphic scale on which two supervisors or superiors rate each employee. The qualities are responsibility, dependability, initiative, interest in work, potential leadership, and community activity. Resulting ratings have been used to counsel employees, to influence promotions and salary adjustments, and as criteria for evaluating sources, methods of selection, and training.

At this time, it appears likely that the entire program will be discontinued. An experience with three employees appears to have convinced the top officers of the firm that ratings may represent a serious hazard to satisfactory relationship with employees. The three employees called on the president to express their dissatisfaction with ratings they had received. Their scores and composite ratings had been discussed with them. Because their ratings were comparatively low, they were not given a step increase in salary at mid-year. Approximately two-thirds of all employees received such increases.

The aggrieved employees argued that their ratings did not accurately represent their qualifications or performance. They insisted that "community activity" was not properly a part of their job, and that what they do off the job is none of the employer's business. They expressed their opinion that employees should organize a union and insist that salary increases be automatic.

The threat of a union has caused officers great concern. They have concluded that rating is a dangerous source of friction and that its hazards outweigh its values.

Problem: Assume that, as a member of the employee relations staff, you agree with other staff members that ratings are important and that hazards can be reduced. You have been assigned the task of preparing a memorandum outlining the staff position for possible submission to the president.

SHORT CASE PROBLEM 17.3

Errors of Raters

Three raters have accorded the following ratings on "initiative" to the 26 ratees listed below. Compare these ratees to discover their total and systematic errors.

Ratee	Rater A	Rater B	Rater C
A	7	9	5
B	8	9	3
C	8	8	6
D	7	8	5
E	6	8	5
F	7	9	5
G	8	9	7
H	5	7	7
I	7	7	6
J	6	7	6
K	4	6	6
L	7	8	7
M	8	9	8
N	9	9	9
O	6	7	7
P	7	7	6
Q	5	7	6
R	4	6	5
S	8	9	9
T	7	9	8
U	7	8	7
V	6	8	7
W	6	7	7
X	5	7	5
Y	5	6	6
Z	4	6	5

18. *Employee and Supervisor Development*

Few managers can escape a heavy responsibility for employee training and development. General manpower policy frequently proposes to give every employee an opportunity to continue his personal education and development while working. Even in the absence of such policy, many employees—from operatives on the machines to operators in the front office—require special educational preparation if they are to perform the jobs assigned to them. Management thus faces educational responsibilities at all levels in the organization. These responsibilities are persistent; new employees require preliminary training, and employees with longer service need additional training if they are to be advanced to more responsible jobs. Even the employee who stays on the same job is likely to require added training as his job changes.

Few of the positions for which managers must find and hold workers can be filled with raw, untrained labor. Jobs for what was long described as *common labor* are no longer common. Almost everyone who is to work must have some special knowledge and skill. Those without such minimum qualifications make up a disproportionate share of the unemployed and create difficult social problems.

Almost all of the training required for non-technical, non-managerial positions must be provided in employment. Although free public education is available to and required of all children in this country, it is focused on preparation for citizenship rather than for work. It is not work-oriented, occupational training. Only a small minority of all high school students is enrolled in vocational institutions. Vocational training at that level is widely regarded as inconsistent with an open-class social system. Of the more than a million new, threshold workers who enter the labor force each year, the large majority must have additional instruction for whatever jobs they are to fill.

After they have been trained for an initial job, the same workers will require frequent continuation training as they move through their working careers. Some of them, advanced to supervisory and management positions, must learn the new skills required in such assignments. Others, whose jobs are eliminated by changing demands or technology, will have to be retrained for the new jobs that emerge to meet the same types of changes.

Preliminary *work training, continuation training, supervisory* and *management programs,* and *retraining* are all important responsibilities of modern managers. These responsibilities are generally less impressive in very small firms, which may provide little more than the opportunity to learn that comes with working experience. Medium-sized organizations may not have extensive development programs; they may merely offer job training for new recruits, expecting to hire skilled, technical, and managerial personnel from larger organizations. Big firms may have to offer comprehensive programs for occupations from the semi-skilled to the technical and professional level, including several ranks of supervisors and managers.

This chapter first directs attention to the current pattern of managerial policy on training and development. It notes usual programs for rank and file employees and supervisors. The chapter closes with an outline of the most important principles of training to be observed in maintaining these programs.

1.0 POLICY ON TRAINING AND DEVELOPMENT

Training has always been an important responsibility of management. Today, this function has gained additional recognition because of growing acceptance of education and training as an investment in human capital. In earlier economic analysis, while the concept of personal growth and appreciation was recognized, its economic significance was largely ignored. In contrast, the current view emphasizes the importance of investments in human skills and knowledge.[1]

Training means to *educate somewhat narrowly, mainly by instruction, drill, and discipline.* It is regarded as applying principally to the improvement of skills and hence to learning how to perform specific tasks. Thus one might be trained to record sales or to operate a particular machine or to throw the discus or to weave a rug. In contrast, *development* emphasizes an unfolding process and carries an implication of growth and maturization.

Employment must provide opportunities for both training and development. New employees at all levels in an organization may require training for the tasks that make up their job assignments. Many rank and file employees who remain will also require training for new or changed jobs. Some

---

[1] For an excellent statement, see Theodore Schultz, "Investment in Human Capital," *American Economic Review,* Vol. 51, No. 1, March, 1961, pp. 1–17.

of them will need to be trained in the special skills required of supervisors. All will have to be assisted in personal development—in finding their long-term places in work and adjusting themselves to these careers. Additional attention must be given to the continuing development of leadership knowledge and skills for those who seek and are selected for managerial jobs.

Carefully considered policy defines rather specific intentions with respect to training and development, intentions that grow directly from general manpower policy. Development policy generally emphasizes management's responsibility for training and development and proposes to give all managers whatever specialized assistance is necessary to aid them in meeting this responsibility. Policy intends to relate training programs to defined needs of the organization and its members. It regards training and development as means of assuring all employees of greater security and of encouraging them to identify themselves with the organization and to participate in its activities. Perhaps the most obvious policy in many programs is that which intends to help employees in their personal improvement and appreciation.

1.1 Management responsibility. Training activities rest on a policy that recognizes training as a responsibility of every manager and supervisor. Managers will be given whatever specialized assistance they require to meet that responsibility. To implement the policy, staff trainers and *specialized training divisions* may be provided.

Such staff training units vary in terms of the size of the firm and the range of training programs. Several sections may be identified in terms of the types or levels of training to be provided. In large programs, a special *training standards division* may be responsible for defining objectives in measurable terms. An overall *co-ordinating division* may be responsible for appropriate arrangements with trainees, department heads, supervisors, and trainers. In many large programs, a *research division* maintains continuing studies of training activities to discover better ways of attaining established objectives.[2]

Although some types of training and development require the personal participation of supervisors and managers and all programs require their active, intelligent support, large-scale programs usually benefit from professional experience and competence. Policy often proposes that overall planning and direction of development programs will be provided by training specialists. They aid in the selection of employees to be trained, in the perfection of training plans, and in the development of appropriate training practice. They keep records of trainees in these programs. They explain training policies and programs to employees.

The job of the specialized *training director* or *administrator* is outlined in Figure 18.1, and the job of *training specialists,* who are non-administrative staff members in the training division, is described in Figure 18.2.[3]

[2] See Douglas Williams and Stanley Peterfreund, "The Education of Employees—A Status Report," New York: American Management Association, 1954.

[3] Staff specialists in training maintain a national professional organization, the National Association of Training Directors, which publishes a bi-monthly *Journal.*

TRAINING

(principal responsibility for planning, organizing, and directing training activities in a company)

JOB PROFILE

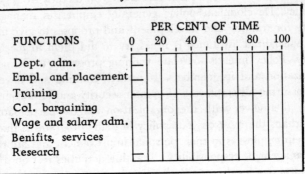

Reported Titles

Director of training; education and training director; manager, personnel training and development; training coordinator; personnel supervisor.

JOB DUTIES

Principal Duties

TRAINING	
Time	45%

Coordinates the training activities of the company, supervising one or more training specialists and maintaining programs which may include the following types of training: on-the-job, apprentice, supervisory, sales, and management. Consults with other managers to determine training needs. Prepares manuals and other materials for use in training sessions. Arranges training schedules. Conducts training sessions. Counsels employees concerning training opportunities.

ADMINISTRATION AND PLANNING	
Time	24%

In consultation with top management and members of the employee relations staff, sets training policies and organizes training activities to carry out these policies. Advises other managers, including those on the employee

Figure 18.1 The Training Administrator Job

(From "Jobs in Employee Relations," *Research Study No. 38,* New York: American Management Association, 1959, pp. 26–27.)

relations staff, concerning revisions of the organizational structure of the company. Responsible for maintaining records and preparing periodic reports and summaries of training activities. May supervise a staff of several training specialists.

Allied Duties

All Others	
Time	31%

Conducts studies, or participates in studies conducted by the employee relations research staff or independent research groups, to analyze and evaluate present and proposed training methods. May advise other employee relations staff members in establishing personnel specifications for use in selection and placement. May advise other managers and members of the employee relations staff on development and use of employee appraisal programs. May prepare and distribute handbooks and manuals. May consult with staff members who counsel employees on vocational or personal problems.

QUALIFICATIONS FOR EMPLOYMENT

Reported Education

Highest Degree Received	Per Cent	Most Frequently Reported Areas of Specialization
No degree	9	
Bachelor's	36	Industrial relations, psychology, economics, engineering
Master's	55	Psychology, personnel psychology, education
Ph.D.	—	
Total	*100*	

Reported Experience

An average of five years' experience in employee relations jobs prior to present position.

Recommended Preparation

The fact that more than half of those who now hold this position have a master's degree suggests that it represents minimal educational preparation. Courses regarded as most valuable fall in the field of psychology, industrial relations, engineering, and education. Preparation should also include experience in other industrial relations staff jobs.

Figure 18.1 (Cont.)

TRAINING

(member of a training staff, usually in medium-size and large companies)

JOB PROFILE

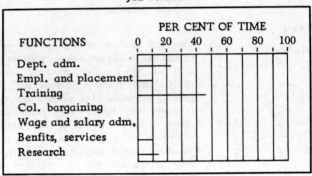

Reported Titles

Assistant director of training; assistant to the training director; assistant training consultant; training director; management development and training director.

JOB DUTIES

Principal Duties

TRAINING	
Time	84%

Devotes major portion of time to training activities which may include on-the-job, apprentice, sales, supervisory, or management training. Consults with other managers to determine training needs. Prepares manuals and other materials for use in training sessions. Schedules and conducts training sessions. Counsels employees concerning training opportunities.

Allied Duties

ALL OTHERS	
Time	16%

Participates in planning and organizing training activities. Keeps records and prepares periodic reports and summaries of training. May maintain a library of pertinent training

Figure 18.2   The Training Specialist Job
(From "Jobs in Employee Relations," *op. cit.,* pp. 37–38)

materials. May advise other managers, including members of the employee relations staff, on problems of recruiting and on the development and use of employee appraisal procedures.

QUALIFICATIONS FOR EMPLOYMENT

Reported Education

Highest Degree Received	Per Cent	Most Frequently Reported Areas of Specialization
No degree	8	
Bachelor's	69	Business administration, economics, sociology, psychology, education
Master's	23	Psychology, education, engineering
Ph.D.	—	
Total	*100*	

Reported Experience

An average of five years' experience in employee relations jobs prior to present position. However, this is frequently an entrance job; 30 per cent of the incumbents report no previous experience in employee relations.

Recommended Preparation

Educational preparation for these positions should include at least the bachelor's degree. There is distinct preference for graduate work and the master's. Appropriate major and minor fields include psychology, education, business administration, economics, engineering, and sociology. For many positions, a minimum of one or two years of experience in other employee relations staff jobs is required.

Figure 18.2 (Cont.)

Some firms provide impressive training facilities and equipment. Classroom aids include blackboards, projectors, charts, graphs, movies, stills and slides, talkies, flannel boards, flash cards, pamphlets, and numerous special adaptations of these devices. Larger organizations use tape recordings and teaching machines. Some courses combine teaching machines with closed circuit television to permit lectures that may be interrupted for student questions.[4]

1.2 Programs based on needs. Training needs may be discovered in employee counseling, or in selection, or in exit interviews. Other needs may be reported by supervisors and managers. Still others are evident when products and processes change. Employee attitude and morale surveys may call attention to such needs, as may suggestion systems and studies of in-plant communications. Policy may propose annual or other periodic surveys of training needs to insure that new needs are recognized and that existing programs are focused on current rather than past needs for training.[5]

1.3 Cooperation with schools. Some needs can be met by cooperative arrangements with high schools and colleges. Policy frequently proposes to enlist the cooperation of public schools, universities, colleges, and trade schools. Faculty members may be helpful in some in-plant training courses. Employees, including supervisors, may be enrolled in day or evening classes offered at the request of the employer. For other training—including apprenticeship and shop-steward training—union cooperation may be desirable. Many firms offer tuition reimbursement plans in which partial or total tuition costs are repaid. Some companies and unions sponsor off-hour college courses given especially for employees or union members. Other firms make educational loans to employees. Still others offer scholarships for employees or for their children.[6]

1.4 Security, identification, participation. Training and development policy frequently proposes to help employees in gaining added security, to develop personal identification with the organization, and to participate more extensively and effectively in the decisions that must be made. In many organizations, one way of stating this policy would describe it as *training for increased contribution and productivity.* Training is expected to develop more efficient workers, who will gain added security because of their proficiency. Most training programs are expected to give employees added understanding and skill that (1) will increase their value and earnings and (2) will improve their opportunity for steady work.

Training is also expected to help each employee to see a high level of

[4] Among the teaching machines used for this purpose are the Hughes Videosonic, the Rheem Didak, and the Auto Tutor and Scrambled Text. Sources of such equipment include the Eastman Kodak Company, General Dynamics Corporation, Thompson-Ramo-Woldridge and International Business Machines. See, for a brief summary, *Industrial Relations News,* Vol. 11, No. 41, October 14, 1961.

[5] See B. B. Jackson and A. C. MacKinney, "Methods of Determining Training Needs," *Personnel,* Vol. 35, No. 5, September-October, 1959, pp. 60–68.

[6] For details of such plans, see *Personnel Policies and Practices Report,* Pars. 3011 to 3908, 1961.

mutuality in personal and organizational goals. On that basis, he can confidently identify his personal interests with those of the total organization. The first employee contact with training is usually in an orientation course in which the new employee learns about the mission and purpose of the organization. *Orientation training* provides an overview of the whole organization and relates each division, department, job, and individual employee to the ongoing activities of the whole.

Some training programs emphasize the *economic problems* of the firm and industry. Others explain the system with which responsibilities are assigned and authority allocated throughout the organization. They are expected thereby to provide a basis for employee acceptance and participation, on the theory that, if employees understand, they will accept, approve, and support managerial policy and practice. Managers may overlook the possibility that the rationale may not be convincing.

1.5 Self-improvement. Policy underlying most training and development programs stresses the intention to help employees help themselves to become more skillful, useful, and valuable. Management proposes to offer opportunities for continuing self-improvement and to assist each worker to make the most of his talents and capacities.

Training for promotion to greater responsibilities is widely accepted as sound policy. Expressions of this policy appear in the recognition given those who complete various training programs and are awarded certificates and diplomas. Graduates of apprenticeship courses frequently enjoy a formal commencement ceremonial not unlike that for college graduation. Employees who conclude banking courses or those in insurance may receive certificates for framing and the right to append special titles to their signatures.[7]

As an aid in training, policy may propose individual counseling and guidance, in which employees are offered professional assistance in canvassing their personal assets and limitations and planning their working careers.

Most expressions of development policy assume that individual employees will take the initiative. Development is voluntary. Policy proposes to offer opportunities to employees. Practice, it may be noted, frequently makes the offer a requirement, for the offer of training is coupled with a specified or implied penalty for failure to accept. When jobs are being discontinued, for example, retraining may be essential to continued employment.

2.0 RANK-AND-FILE TRAINING

Some training programs are available to employees in all occupations and at all levels of responsibility and rank. Others are designed for individual occupations, or for rank and file, or for supervisors, middle managers, or

---

[7] Some of these self-improvement courses get pretty fancy and inviting. Grumman Aircraft Engineering Corporation, for example, offers a beauty course as an aid to efficiency and morale. Employees may study "figure analysis, walking, sitting and standing" and other essentials for the breadwinner. (*Personnel Policies and Practices Report,* Par. 245, No. 18—15, 1961.)

others. For convenience in description, it is convenient to classify programs as those for rank and file, for supervision, and for management, although some overlap is inevitable. This section is concerned with programs designed principally for rank-and-file employees.

2.1 Induction and Orientation. These programs are designed to familiarize new employees with their jobs, to introduce fellow-workers, and to relate the work of the recruit to that of the total organization. They may be available only to production or hourly rated workers, although others, including new managers, could benefit from similar provisions. They may be short, consisting of a single day of lectures, a plant tour, and the presentation of pamphlets explaining employment policies and the products, history and prospects of the organization. They may, on the other hand, involve an extended series of sessions plus continuing *sponsorship* arrangements.

2.2 Job Training. The most common of formal in-plant training programs is training for a job. Two methods are widely used. *Shop training or training on the job* places the employee in the workroom and provides supervision while he learns to master the operations involved. Often, such training includes some sort of *sponsorship* arrangement whereby an older employee or supervisor is charged with responsibility for instructing the newcomer and assisting him in mastering the job. Sometimes training on the job is supplemented by instruction in a classroom.

Large business organizations frequently provide what are described as *vestibule schools* as a preliminary to actual shop experience. In them, shop conditions are, as far as possible, duplicated, but output is not a major objective. Rather, the major purpose is instruction. Special instructors are provided. Smaller firms or agencies generally cannot afford to provide either the facilities or the instruction required for vestibule schools.

Current practice in job training (and to a lesser extent in programs for supervisors) has been strongly influenced by the war-time *Training within Industry program* (T.W.I.). The T.W.I. program was first designed to improve job performance through *Job Instruction Training* (J.I.T.), a procedure which emphasized four steps described as preparation, presentation, performance, and follow-up. T.W.I. noted that job training is improved by the discovery and designation of *key points* in the job—critical parts of the work which determine whether or not the entire job is done properly.

T.W.I. programs for supervisors included a course in *Job Methods Training* (J.M.T.), designed to help supervisors improve job performance, and *Job Relations Training* (J.R.T.), which emphasized improving relationships among co-workers and related departments.

2.3 Crafts training. Training for craftsmanship involves preparation, not for a single job, but for the many types of related jobs that may be given to a competent tradesman or craftsman. The extent and intensity of training vary among the crafts, but programs usually emphasize knowledge of past practice and develop a thorough familiarity with and skill in the use of all the tools of the craft.

Some fifty crafts have well-established *apprenticeship* requirements. They require training on the job as assistants to journeymen, in which the novice is expected to master the tradition and practice of the crafts. Some trades have what are known as *indentured apprenticeships,* which specify training periods extending from two to five years and designate those responsible for each training activity. A contract provides for wage advances at regular intervals throughout the period. About 250,000 apprentices are presently being trained in these programs.

Apprenticeship training can be traced back into medieval and ancient times. In earlier periods, apprenticeship was not restricted to artisans, but was used in training for the professions, including medicine, law, dentistry, and teaching. Some unions have found the system an effective means of restricting entrance to the trade. In other cases, apprenticeship has been used by employers to secure workers at less than standard rates of pay. Since 1937, a federal Apprenticeship-Training Service in the Department of Labor has acted as a clearing-house for information on apprenticeship programs.

Most states now have apprenticeship laws, with supervised plans for such training. Arrangements usually provide a mixed program of classroom and job experience and a gradual increase in wage rates, from 50 per cent of journeyman rates at the start to 90 per cent in the last year of apprenticeship.

Question is frequently raised about the efficiency of even the best of these programs. Requirements in terms of knowledge and skill in many crafts have been reduced by technological changes. Other training techniques may be superior to that of working as a journeyman's helper. In many crafts, ratios of apprentices are so low that they cannot replace more than one-fourth to one-half of the craftsmen who leave the craft each year. Most crafts training is now being provided by firms outside these formal programs.

Some training programs for managers resemble apprenticeship. For staff managers, a system of *internships,* in which inexperienced staff members supplement college courses with close association in an experienced staff group, may be useful. In management development programs, provision may be made for *understudy* relationships, which make the trainee an assistant to the current job-holder. The recruit learns by experience, observation, and imitation. If decisions are discussed with the understudy, he can become informed on the policies and theories involved. On the other hand, the method tends to perpetuate mistakes and other deficiencies characteristic of existing managerial practice. Some experience indicates that understudies are frequently neglected by those they assist.

2.4 Retraining. Large numbers of production workers are displaced by changing product demands and technological change, the latter popularly described as *automation.* They must be retrained for new and different jobs. A major question of policy concerns the responsibility for retraining. Shall each individual firm accept or be held responsible for employees thus displaced? Or shall retraining be regarded as partly or entirely a public responsibility?

Public financial support for retraining programs has been provided by European nations for several years.[8] In this country, a beginning was made in the Federal Area Redevelopment Act of 1961. The law provides some 4.5 million dollars of federal funds to aid state and local retraining programs in areas of substantial and *persistent unemployment*. Such grants are further bolstered by an additional 10 million dollars per year available to provide subsistence payments to trainees.

Meanwhile, in several firms, managers and unions have negotiated retraining benefits (see Chapter 22), and some states have liberalized unemployment insurance to permit benefit payments during retraining. Many questions of both policy and practice are presently unanswered, as, for example, how may displaced workers know what training to undertake? How can they relate their aptitudes and capacities to future opportunities to work?

2.5 Special-purpose courses. Many firms offer special courses to meet unusual educational problems. Courses have been designed to help foreign-born employees prepare for American citizenship, to teach civics, economics, time study, standard-setting, safety, basic English, reading, dietetics, public speaking, and public relations.

3.0 SUPERVISOR TRAINING

The need for special training for foremen and supervisors is widely recognized. Their jobs have become increasingly complex as the educational level of employees has risen and full-employment policy has encouraged tight labor markets. Public support for collective bargaining and the growth of unions have also created problems for supervisors. Managers at higher levels have noted these changes. They have become concerned, not only about the inadequacies of many supervisors but also about their alienation from management. As firms have grown, the long line of communication from the front office to the supervisor has been stretched.

Top management concern was heightened when, after passage of the National Labor Relations Act in 1935, many foremen became members of employee unions. They apparently saw their interests as more closely identified with those of rank-and-file employees than with management. Shortly thereafter, studies of employee attitudes and morale attracted wide attention. Many managers took for granted the close correlation of levels of morale with those of output or productivity. Managers gave increased attention to employee criticisms and complaints. Many criticisms pointed directly at the shortcomings of supervisors. Employees frequently questioned supervisory competence.

At the same time, many foremen were not happy with their jobs. Their freedom to act had been narrowed. New staff managers had been authorized to assume some of the foreman's authority. Personnel divisions frequently

---

[8] See Phyllis P. Groom, "Retraining the Unemployed," *Monthly Labor Review*, Vol. 84, No. 8, August, 1961, pp. 823–28; also No. 9, September, 1961, pp. 939–43.

screened all applicants for jobs and restricted the foreman's choice in hiring. Labor relations staff members negotiated labor agreements that imposed further restrictions. Staff members also told the foreman how to interpret these agreements. The supervisor's right to discharge employees was rigorously curtailed. In some organizations, functional specialists directed men on details of their jobs. The foreman's job had grown at the same time that his authority had been reduced.

The foreman's frustration may be increased by union rules that prevent him from returning to a non-supervisory job. Even when work is slack, it may be impossible to return to rank-and-file jobs because of inadequate seniority in such positions or because supervisors are barred from performing bargaining unit jobs.[9]

In larger organizations, employees see the foreman as the personification of management. He is their major link in communication with the rest of the firm. As actions speak louder than words, what he does appears as an expression of firm policy. The foreman is management's spokesman, in both word and action.

Managers have recognized, also, that the foreman is the potential middle or top manager of the future. Foremanship is the first step up the management ladder. Supervisory experience is the seed-bed for managers. Many firms, emphasizing a policy of promotion from within, must largely limit selection of future middle managers to choices among foremen and supervisors.

3.1 The supervisor job. The terms "supervisor" and "foreman" are often used interchangeably, although the supervisor is somewhat more frequently associated with office employment and the foreman with hourly-rated production employees. Some practice identifies supervisors with "exempt" employees, as defined by the Fair Labor Standards Act. The Taft-Hartley Act of 1947 defines supervisors as those who have authority to exercise independent judgment in hiring, rewarding, discipline, discharging, and taking other similar actions in the interests of employers. "Leadermen" or "leadmen" are frequently included as supervisors, as are "working foremen." On the average and throughout industry as a whole, from 5 to 8 per-cent of all employees are regarded as supervisors and foremen.[10]

Job descriptions in current use suggest the variety of responsibilities and the complexity of supervisory assignments. The most frequently mentioned tasks include care of equipment and stock, assigning work, maintaining standards of quantity and quality in production, getting material, accident prevention, recruiting, training crew members, enforcing shop rules and discipline, building and supporting morale, settling grievances, arranging transfers, evaluating workers, granting wage adjustments, and maintaining

[9] See *Notat Tire Award*, 10 ALAA, Par. 71,355, 1961; also *American Products Award*, 10 ALAA, Par. 71,364, 1961.
[10] Robert D. Loken and W. C. J. Thake, "How Many Managers?" *Management Review*, Vol. 42, No. 2, February, 1953, pp. 64–65.

effective communication with higher levels of management.[11]

As a manager, the foreman must be concerned with the application of the personal and material resources with which he is provided. On the one hand, he must requisition, stock, and distribute raw materials for the shop and conserve its equipment and facilities. On the other, he must provide leadership and direction for a group of assistants or associates. He must become expert in two areas: (1) his handling of materials and machines and (2) his leadership and management of people.

Perhaps the most obvious special knowledge and skill needed by the supervisor grows out of his responsibilities as a manager of production. Planning, scheduling, and routing are processes in which the rank-and-file worker has little concern. The foreman must be cost-conscious. He holds responsibility for both cost and quality control. As a production manager, the supervisor must understand the parts played by other parts of the organization.

An important part of what supervisors need to learn is technical; another and perhaps more difficult part has to do with the supervisor's attitudes and viewpoints. He must see problems from the point of view of the whole organization. He must see them as they appear to owners and managers and to members of his crew. As a foreman, he must recognize responsibilities both to higher echelons of management and to those he supervises.

He must interpret the firm's policies and practices to crew members. He is the channel for formal communication to and from the rest of the organization. He is expected to enforce safety and other work rules. He must act as counselor in discussions of employee problems. Most important, he is expected to perform all these functions in a way that will insure acceptance of his decisions by his men. In short, he must transform his position as an appointed leader into one in which he is accepted as the chosen leader of the group.

Recent suggestions by Likert,[12] based on extensive research at the University of Michigan, add to these complications. Likert notes that effective supervisors must have the capacity to exert an upward influence on their superiors. At the same time, he concludes that "subordinates react favorably to experiences which they feel are supportive and contribute to their sense of importance and personal worth." The foreman should be able to create such an impression on those he supervises.

In summary, the foreman may face responsibilities greater than his authority, while limits on his authority usually parallel limits on his competence. Solutions will necessarily either increase his competence and thus justify greater authority or further reduce responsibilities.

3.2 Policy on supervisor training. Policy on supervisory training programs proposes (1) to help present supervisors improve their performance

[11] For a careful summary, see John M. Pfiffner, *Supervision of Personnel,* 2nd Edition, Englewood Cliffs, N.J.: Prentice-Hall, Inc., 1958, Chaps. 12 and 15.

[12] Rensis Likert, *New Patterns of Management,* New York: McGraw-Hill Book Company, Inc., 1961, pp. 102 and 114.

in the jobs they hold and (2) to help them to prepare for greater responsibilities in higher levels of management in the future. It proposes to select candidates who have the capacity to develop. In many organizations, however, a major factor in such decisions is seniority. In other common practice, opinion and impression—if not outright favoritism—play a major part. Some organizations propose to promote "on merit," defining merit in terms of productivity on the job. Unfortunately, none of these bases for selection gives assurance that those selected will be successful as supervisors. The senior employee or the favorite may have little aptitude as a leader. The superior performer may be similarly limited.

Policy in many programs proposes to build up the security and status of foremen. In part, the objective proposes a rebuilding, designed to repair damage occasioned by earlier neglect and distribution of supervisory authority. Foremen are to achieve greater security by earning it. They are to be helped to develop specialized competence that will command recognition, acceptance, and respect.

This policy is supplemented by salary objectives that seek to insure stability in supervisory salaries at levels above the earnings of crew members. On the average, compensation for supervisors ranges from 20 to 30 per cent above that of those supervised. Most—approximately 90 per cent—of supervisors are paid on a salary basis. As fringe benefits have been negotiated for hourly-rated employees, employers have had to move rapidly to be sure that benefits for supervisors keep pace with those of rank and file.

The intention to assure technical competence proposes that the supervisor shall be helped to know and understand all about the processes in which his crew participates. Most policy also recognizes the importance of leadership skills. Policy proposes to help supervisors develop their (1) technical competence, (2) ability to delegate, (3) skill in communications, (4) use of consultation in supervision, and (5) personal interest in members of their crews.

3.3 Technical training. Current programs of foreman training include a heavy concentration on the products and processes involved. They describe the firm's operations: its policy and practice in purchasing, requisition, inventories, cost control, overtime, shop rules, and other standard operating procedures. They may instruct in planning, scheduling, and record keeping. They may offer special training in mathematics, science, bookkeeping, time study, job evaluation, legal regulations, and other technical fields. They often provide a mass of information, with published and mimeographed instructions and corrections. Training may include weekly meetings of foremen, with latest information on prospective developments in products and markets.

Programs recognize that the foreman must know his personnel procedures. He must interpret personnel and labor relations policy on a day-by-day basis. Training programs give special attention to the labor policies of the employer, the reasoning behind those policies, and the best methods of informing and explaining policies to employees. Programs, practices, and procedures are explained. Supervisors learn how employees are selected, transferred, promoted, trained, and paid, why job evaluation and morale surveys are used, and what services and benefits are available to employees. They are informed of common problems—*absenteeism* or *tardiness* or *discipline,* for example. They are shown how to *rate* or appraise employees and how to maintain day-to-day *personnel records.* They study practices in controlling absenteeism, tardiness, overtime, work-scheduling, and promotions and transfers.

If employees are unionized, training also explains the day-to-day procedures of *contract administration* and *grievance handling.* Supervisors learn how they can contribute to preparations for negotiating new agreements. They give special attention to the basic policies which guide the employer in contract negotiation and administration. They learn of their responsibilities in advising top management of the attitudes and reactions of crew members toward current contract provisions. They study the place of the supervisor in suggesting changes to be incorporated in future agreements.

3.4 Leadership training. In addition, today's foreman training is likely to include a heavy emphasis on the development of leadership. To that end, foremen are urged to become *effective communicators* and to develop a participative, consultative attitude toward, and a personal interest in, their crew members.

To improve communications abilities, these programs may provide courses in public speaking and writing. Most managerial theory concludes that communications skills must be reinforced by a *constructive attitude* toward communication. It recognizes that foremen may have concluded that they gain more by not communicating than by becoming an effective link in the infirm network. They may try to gain prestige and status by withholding information, thus suggesting that they are "on the inside." They may assume that they communicate only when they speak or write. Programs may seek to develop *effective listeners* as well as transmitters and to stress the importance of actions in communications.

Many programs aim at what is widely described as *consultative supervision.* In consultative supervision, the foreman cultivates suggestions from members of his crew. He advises them of assignments and problems. He asks their advice. He receives, considers, and discusses their suggestions. He may delegate authority to make many decisions. At the same time, he recognizes his ultimate responsibility. He sees that group members realize that he cannot avoid such responsibility.

Especially for the new supervisor, consultation may be difficult. He may fear its effects upon his acceptance as leader. Indeed, if the process is mishandled, employees may accuse him of "passing the buck" to them. Again, the supervisor may hesitate to give employees credit for their ideas. He may fear that employee suggestions will be regarded as indicating his own inadequacy.[13]

---

[13] See "Consultative Management," N.I.C.B. *Management Record,* Vol. 17, No. 11, November, 1955, pp. 438–39.

Most modern supervisory training programs stress the importance of personal relationships with employees and the supervisor's interest in crew members' ideas, thoughts, and welfare. Programs seek to develop an *employee-centered* rather than a *production-centered* supervisor. The employee-centered supervisor gives special attention to his responsibilities as a trainer, to the personal ambitions of group members, and to their problems. He is an interested counselor and adviser. He is *sensitive* to employee reactions. He is not unaware of production requirements, but they occupy less of his attention than these personal considerations.

Studies frequently indicate that the production-centered foreman is less effective than the supervisor whose major attention is focused on the people who make up his crew. Likert, Seashore, and others have reported the advantages of employee-centered supervision. Seashore, for example, notes that both employee productivity and morale are likely to be adversely affected by "close" supervision, that higher productivity is to be expected with employee-centered supervision than with that which is production-centered, and that employee interest and performance correlate positively with employee membership in a work-group with high group-pride, cohesion, and solidarity.[14]

To improve leadership, many programs now include what is widely described as *human relations* training. It is concerned with small group behavior in work, and traces much of its viewpoint to the followers of Elton Mayo and Kurt Lewin. It frequently refers to the classic experiment in the Hawthorne plant of Western Electric. Tannenbaum has noted four current viewpoints in which human relations is regarded as (1) a description of interpersonal behaviour, (2) a kit of tools for practitioners, (3) an ethical viewpoint or orientation, and (4) a scientific discipline.[15]

Most programs emphasize the importance of *communications,* especially *listening;* they stress *participation* as a factor in incentivation and identification, and try to develop *empathy* and *sensitivity.* They consider methods of overcoming *resistance to change,* the influence of informal organization, and the advantages of non-authoritarian leadership.[16]

3.5 Training Methods. Current programs use a variety of training methods. They may provide extensive *reading material.* They lean heavily on

[14] Stanley E. Seashore, in Rensis Likert and Samuel P. Hayes, Eds., *Some Applications of Behavioral Research,* Paris: United Nations Educational, Scientific, and Cultural Organizations, 1957, pp. 62–63; see also Rensis Likert, *New Patterns of Management,* New York: McGraw-Hill Book Company, Inc., 1961, Chap. 2.

[15] Robert Tannenbaum, "Some Basic Issues in Human Relations," *The Executive,* Vol. 3, 1950, pp. 15ff.

[16] The literature of human relations is, growing rapidly, so that choice of the most useful references is difficult. See, however, Robert Tannenbaum and W. H. Schmidt, "How to Choose a Leadership Pattern," *Harvard Business Review,* Vol. 36, No. 2, March-April, 1958, pp. 95–101; Robert N. McMurry, "The Case for Benevolent Autocracy," *Harvard Business Review,* Vol. 36, No. 1, January-February, 1958, pp. 82–90; Robert Tannenbaum, Irving R. Weschler, and Fred Massarik, *Leadership and Organization,* New York: McGraw-Hill Book Company, Inc., 1960; Clement J. Berwitz, "Beyond Motivation," *Harvard Business Review,* Vol. 38, No. 3, May-June, 1960, pp. 123–25; Robert Henry Guest, *Organizational Change,* Homewood, Illinois: Richard D. Irwin, Inc., 1962; Chris Argyris, *Interpersonal Competence and Organizational Effectiveness,* Homewood, Illinois: Richard D. Irwin, Inc., 1962.

conferences, projects, and cases. In the conference, mutual problems form the subject of discussion, and participants pool their ideas and experience in attempting to arrive at improved methods of dealing with these problems. The attitude is one of joint exploration. Members of the group come together to teach each other and to learn together. Conferences may include *buzz sessions* that divide conferees into small groups of four or five for intensive discussion. These small groups then report back to the whole conference with their conclusions or questions.

Many variations of the conference method have developed. In *brainstorming*, for example, conferees are given a problem and asked to be creative in suggesting solutions. They are encouraged to think broadly and to advance new and different answers. Criticism of proposals is restricted. Participants "hook on" to the ideas of others. Later, these ideas are critically examined.

The role-playing technique is widely used as one variant from the formal conference. In essence, it trains by engaging in a game of "let's pretend," and by carefully evaluating the performance of actors in the game. In the usual procedure, a "case" is outlined and the principal roles are described. Members of the study group are selected to act out each of these roles. Sometimes several casts of characters enact the scene, one after another. The rest make notes on these presentations. The group then discusses and criticizes the attitudes and actions of the players.

Conference groups or sub-groups may undertake *projects,* in which they try to improve conference leadership, the readability of written communications, or the reporting of accidents, for example. They may discuss *cases,* with attention focused on an illustrative situation. They try to develop principles from such cases.

Job rotation may assign assistant supervisors to a series of jobs in which they gain broad experience and meet a wide variety of problems. Although this device is more common in management training, supervisors are sometimes trained in *flying squadrons,* proficient in a wide range of supervisory jobs.

3.6 Programmed training. Experiments with teaching machines, which adapt the versatile computers to teaching processes, have influenced training programs for rank-and-file employees and for supervisors. Current experiments are evaluating their usefulness for the development of managers. Additional research in this area seeks greater understanding of the learning process. Meanwhile *programmed training* has already demonstrated impressive potential contributions. Programmed, tape-recorded job instructions, for example, can save time and improve the accuracy with which operations are learned.

Programmed training includes two essential components: one a step-by-step series of bits of knowledge, each building on what has gone before, and the second a mechanism for presenting this series and checking on the student's knowledge. The machine can ask the questions in proper sequence and indicate promptly whether answers are correct. The American Management Association has developed such a program for supervisors which is known as PRIME, meaning Programmed Instruction for Management Education.

4.0 TRAINING THEORY AND PRINCIPLES

The heart of training theory is *learning theory.* Training programs represent applications of learning theory—action believed to be effective in assisting employees in learning. Several of the theories that explain these programs should be made explicit, together with their implications with respect to the direction and evaluation of supervisory training programs.

One generalization affects all employment training programs. They are presumably *designed for adults.* Whatever theory is used to translate policy into training programs, therefore, should be appropriate for adults.

4.1 Principles of Learning. Basic to all training and development is learning on the part of those who are included in the various programs. Several explanations of the processes in which adults learn most readily, accurately, and swiftly can be briefly noted.

(1) Learning is *an adjustment* on the part of the individual. Whatever the part played by various groups in teaching and in aiding in the learning process, actual learning represents a change in the student. For this reason, *individual differences* play a large part in the effectiveness of the learning process. One person may learn something quite different from that learned by another as a result of similar training or experience. What can be learned easily by some individuals may be—because of differences in basic abilities or cultural attainments—very difficult for others.

(2) Studies of learning processes clearly evidence the importance of *motivation* in the learning process. Learning is facilitated when the student learns *because he wants to,* when he feels a need for learning and has a goal which he associates with the necessity for making such adjustment. Effectiveness of employees as learners, therefore, can be expected to reflect the clarity with which they visualize personal gains to be attained or enhanced or protected through training. The purpose and usefulness of each course may well be clearly indicated and frequently repeated. Employee election of a course or suggestions as to courses to be offered may be significant factors in their performance in the course.

(3) Learning is a *cumulative process.* Individual adjustment involves changes that reflect and are based on earlier changes. The individual's reaction in any lesson is conditioned and modified by what has been learned in earlier lessons and experience. For this reason, the backgrounds of trainees and minimal educational and experiential requirements for each course may well be recognized. At the same time, it is important that each step of the training program lay a proper *foundation* for the steps that are to follow.

(4) Learning is aided by the provision of (1) *standards* or *bench-marks* by which the individual may judge his progress toward goals and (2)

prompt *rewards* for success. Training programs should provide such yard-sticks so that individual trainees can know the extent to which they are actually learning. Frequent tests, carefully graded and returned, can help in this connection, as may diplomas, certificates, or other evidences of successful completion of a course.

(5) For some types of training, it may prove more efficient to teach only a *part* of a given sequence of operations at a time; later, these parts may be combined. In other operations, however, teaching the *whole* may prove distinctly superior. Frequently the most satisfactory arrangement is one in which the whole can first be studied, then the parts, and finally the whole again.

(6) *Accuracy* generally deserves more emphasis than *speed* during the learning process, for speed can be improved, but inaccuracy is more difficult to control.

(7) The so-called *law of exercise* points to the fact that a particular response to a stimulus becomes more certain the more often it occurs. In other words, *repetition* tends to fix the response or adjustment. This effect is emphasized if the repetition is frequent and rapid, without long intervening periods.

(8) Learning is closely related to *attention,* so that the learning process is more effective if distractions are avoided. On the other hand, the ability to concentrate attention is also limited, so that frequent pauses and rest periods may be desirable. Learning is facilitated when the learning situation encourages concentration.

(9) Learning involves long-term *retention* as well as immediate *acquisition* of knowledge. Such retention is encouraged by understanding in which the learner discovers the *why* of knowledge, the reasons and the application, and by *over-learning,* i.e., emphasizing and repeating. On the other hand, it appears doubtful that any adult learning can be justified simply as mental exercise or discipline.

(10) In the curve of learning, there are upward spurts of *understanding* followed by *plateaus* in which nothing seems to be added. These plateaus may indicate the need for a new "shot" of motivation.

Several other generalizations, frequently encountered in discussions of educational processes, could be added to this list. It appears, however, that what is most important is that the emphasis be placed—for adults—on *learning* rather than on *teaching.* In adult learning, *self-instruction* is likely to play an important part. Although an occasional well-done lecture may interest or perhaps inspire, the most effective teacher for adults may be more of a *questioner* than a lecturer. Teaching machines have been effective in employee development because they are effective questioners.[17]

---

[17] For additional discussion of these points, see D. H. Fryer, M. R. Feinberg, and S. S. Salkind, *Developing People in Industry,* New York: Harper & Brothers, 1956, especially Chaps. 4 and 5; William McGehee, "Are We Using What We Know About Training?" *Personnel Psychology,* Vol. 11, No. 1, Spring, 1958, pp. 1–12; Leona E.

4.2 Selection of trainers. In many programs, the selection of trainers is taken casually, frequently on the assumption that anyone who knows how to do what is to be done can teach it. Experience indicates that managers, executives, and supervisors, even though they may be highly efficient in their regular jobs, may not be satisfactory instructors. If formal lecturing or conference leadership is expected, it may be essential to secure professional instructors or else to provide special training for those selected as leaders. In general, all trainers selected from the operating line should be given instruction in how to train. For some of the more complicated programs, *training specialists* are essential.

4.3 Examinations and grades. As a general principle, trainees should be kept informed of their progress in learning. In part, this may be done on the job or in the classroom. In part, it may be done through tests and examinations. Teaching machines provide immediate marks and corrections. Tests usually delay such evidence.

If a test or examination is to have the desired effect, however, it must be dependable, consistent, and meaningful. In technical terms it must be *reliable* and *valid*. Participants must be convinced that the grade they receive is a just one. Because success in many courses is recognized as a basis for promotion, grades may be taken more seriously than in most public school or college classes. Questions should be clear and relevant, with clear-cut answers. They should be sufficiently difficult so that all trainees do not achieve equal scores.[18]

Participants should understand the *purpose* of the test. Among appropriate purposes are: to stimulate preparation, to inform both students and instructors of the trainee's progress, to provide a reasonable basis for a grade or score, to encourage student participation in class discussions. Tests may investigate *memory* as well as the *ability to analyze*. The type of test—objective, essay, case, problem, or other—depends on the purposes of the course and of the test.

Trainees should understand the inherent sampling process in every examination. Test scores should probably be regarded as *confidential information,* available only to the participant and the instructor. The range and

---

Tyler, *The Psychology of Human Differences,* New York: Appleton, Century, Crofts, Inc., 1956, especially Chap. 19; Billy E. Goetz and Warren G. Bennis, "What We Know About Learning and Training," *Personnel Administration,* Vol. 25, No. 2, March-April, 1962, pp. 20–29.

[18] The *reliability* of an examination, its *consistency* in distinguishing those who do well, can be checked in several ways. One *split-test* or *odd-even procedure* compares scores on two halves of the same test. Another repeats the test with the same trainees. *Item analysis* may be used to check the effectiveness of each item. In that process, total scores are arrayed, top and bottom thirds or quarters are identified, and each item is checked to note its ability to identify students whose scores fall in these extremes:

Validity may be measured by correlating test scores with an acceptable criterion. Measures of actual job performance or personnel ratings are the most common criteria.

14*

distribution of scores may be publicized, so that each participant knows his relative standing.

Counseling adult employees on test performance deserves thoughtful attention comparable to that given counseling on personnel ratings (see Chapter 17, section 4.0). Emphasis on wrong or inadequate answers tends to deflate and irritate most participants. The test as a whole is only a sample, and sub-samples have obviously limited significance. Hypercritical comments on test performance may create barriers that prejudice further learning. Scores on tests given during a course should be accepted as tentative, partial evaluations of performance, subject to revision as the student continues.

Shall grades be reported to supervisors of trainees and recorded in personnel files? Or shall records simply show *pass* or *fail* in each course? University executive development programs rarely report on the performance of participants. Some collective bargaining agreements bar reports of detailed grades of trainees.

4.4 Evaluation of training. A desirable if not essential characteristic of all training programs is a built-in provision for evaluation. All new training programs and methods—and preferably the old ones as well—should be regarded as *experimental* or on trial. Plans should be made, when courses are developed, for frequent checks on their effectiveness.

Training is a costly function, involving not only the expense of instruction but extensive amounts of worker time. Education may be regarded as a social investment; on-the-job training represents a sizeable investment for many employers. Evaluation may well check on costs, with comparisons of the costs of various methods of training.[19]

5.0 SUMMARY

Opportunity for development is an important consideration to many employees and managers. They see training and development programs as means of maintaining and increasing their personal contributions and rewards. Small firms provide little formal training, leaning heavily on the programs of larger business and government agencies. Most large firms, however, maintain a wide range of training and development programs designed to help employees increase their knowledge and skills and qualify themselves for continued employment and advancement. Policy seeks to assure employees every opportunity to improve themselves. Policy generally assumes that employees who are constantly improving themselves will be more satisfied, enthusiastic, and effective workers. They will become qualified, through these educational programs, for wider participation in thinking as well as doing.

The chapter sketches an overall view of training and development programs. It describes training and development policy, the principal types of

[19] See, for example, R. A. Bolda and C. H. Lawshe, "Evaluation of Role Playing," *Personnel Administration*, Vol. 25, Number 2, March-April, 1962, pp. 40–43.

training provided for rank-and-file workers and supervisors, the most common training arrangements and practices, and several general training principles that have achieved wide acceptance.

Development programs are by no means limited to rank-and-file and supervisory workers. Middle and top management development is the subject in Chapter 19.

SELECTED SUPPLEMENTARY READINGS

Barbash, Jack, *Universities and Unions in Workers Education.* New York: Harper & Brothers, 1955.

Belman, Harry S. and H. H. Remmers, "Evaluating the Results of Training," *Journal of the American Society of Training Directors,* Vol. 12, No. 5, pp. 28–32, May, 1958.

"Consultative Management," *Management Record,* National Industrial Conference Board, Vol. 17, No. 11, pp. 438–539, November, 1955.

DePhillips, Frank A., William M. Berliner, and James J. Cribbin, *Management of Training Programs,* chap. 4. Homewood, Ill.: Richard D. Irwin, Inc., 1960.

Evans, Chester E., "Supervisory Responsibility and Authority," *Research Report No. 30,* American Management Association, 1957.

Laws, Robert H., "A Survey of Economic Education Surveys," *Advanced Management,* Vol. 19, No. 2, pp. 30ff, February, 1954.

Whyte, William Foote, "Leadership and Group Participation," *Bulletin 24,* Ithaca, N.Y.: Cornell University, New York State School of Labor and Industrial Relations, May, 1953.

Wilkinson, Bryan and J. H. Myers, "What Good are Role-Playing Techniques?" *Advanced Management,* Vol. 19, No. 5, pp. 23ff, May, 1954.

SHORT CASE PROBLEM 18.1

Halsey McIntosh Development Program

Bernard England had been working for Halsey McIntosh for the three years following his graduation from one of the leading graduate schools of management. His employer is a large investment and underwriting organization. England had recently been made an assistant manager, with 20 recent business school graduates under his direction. All of these assistants were enrolled in a course in corporation finance offered by the Training Division of the firm.

After six weeks of the course, the group was given an examination. A week later, the training director called England to ask what he wanted done with the resulting examinations. England was somewhat surprised by the question. He asked what had been done with such tests in the past and was advised that, as a matter of established practice, test scores are made a part of the personnel record of each participant. Any other use of the scores is a matter for decision by the supervisor. Most supervisors, the training director suggested, kept the examinations in their offices for possible reference in the future. Some supervisors went over the tests with their men. The training director said that scores have already been incorporated in the personnel records. He proposes to send the tests to England for his use.

England recalls that when he took this same course his supervisor called him in and discussed each question in detail. He remembers that they had some spirited arguments about some of his answers. He still feels some sting from the arbitrary manner in which his supervisor dismissed his arguments. He remembers also that he felt his supervisor had not kept informed of recent developments and was somewhat outdated in his thinking. He concludes that he had better think carefully about what he should do with the tests.

Problem: Be prepared to offer advice to England on the decision he must make. For that purpose, consider the objectives in the course and in this mid-term test. What action on England's part will help to accomplish these objectives? What policy on training and development is involved? Try to be sure that the action you recommend is consistent with sound policy.

SHORT CASE PROBLEM 18.2

Beseler Electronics Training Program

Negotiation of a collective bargaining contract is conducted in the spring of each year. The union proposal in 1959 included one clause that occasioned wide discussion among managers. It involved the reporting of grades in company-sponsored training courses.

The firm conducts a number of training courses, some of them offered through the cooperation of two local colleges. Participation in these courses is optional for employees. Employees volunteer for or request permission to take these courses, most of which are given on company time. Actually, however, employees are in effect sent into these courses by their supervisors. The latter tell employees that they need the courses and that they will be excused from work during their attendance at classes. In addition, the Personnel Department exerts continuing pressure on managers, urging that they send employees into these courses to prepare them for changing products and production processes.

The new union proposal would limit the recorded grades in such courses to "pass" or "fail." It would specifically prevent the Training Division or the instructor from giving out any other information about performance in the course to anyone except the trainee.

Many managers feel outraged by the proposal. They insist that since the employee attends courses on company time—his absence is charged to the department budget—the supervisor has a perfect right to know what the employee is doing every hour of the course. They argue, also, that the provision would interfere with the educational process by limiting the counseling function in which supervisors could help maintain employee interest and activity in the course. They conclude that it is unreasonable to expect supervisors to send men into these courses if full information on each "student" is not continually available to the supervisor.

Union spokesmen insist that managers have already accepted the principle they are proposing. They point to procedure in the firm's management development program. Several managers have been sent to Stanford, Harvard, and the University of Michigan for university supplements to the in-firm program. While in these on-campus classes, they receive no grades, and no report of classroom performance, attitudes, or progress is made to the firm.

Problem: Prepare an advisory statement you could give the firm's negotiators. What policy would you recommend? How would you justify that policy in terms of general policy on training and development?

SHORT CASE PROBLEM 18.3

Selection of Foremen at Helex

Discussions in the Monday morning meetings of the executive committee at Helex are supposed to be strictly confidential. No one is permitted to discuss them outside the conference room. One item on the agenda for August 21st, however, has leaked. Almost everyone in the organization has had something to say about it.

Helex has a new president, Mr. George Rachter. He has had extensive management experience and has most recently spent two years in Europe as a part of the technical assistance mission furnished by the United States. He was formerly vice-president of a leading competitor in the industry.

On the 21st, Mr. Rachter raised a question about the adequacy of the supervisory training program in the firm. He had been studying the report on a Triple Audit survey of employee morale undertaken for the firm by the Industrial Relations Center of the University of Minnesota. The report indicated a wide difference in employee attitudes toward the supervision of different departments. Discussion developed the fact that, in general, employee attitudes toward supervisors were most favorable in those departments that followed a consistent practice of selecting foremen from among men who had experience as union shop stewards. Mr. Rachter was rather obviously startled and discomfited by this disclosure. He wanted to know how long the practice had been followed and why. He expressed his opinion that such an established practice could "get back to the union" and could easily influence men to seek steward jobs as steps toward the foreman position. He felt, too, that men who had been union stewards were likely to be prejudiced against the firm and its policies, so they could not develop the proper loyalty toward the firm.

The industrial relations vice-president tried to reassure him on these points. He pointed to the fact that he had himself been a union steward in the firm before becoming a member of management. He felt that the experience as a steward tended to develop many qualities that were helpful if not essential in a good foreman. He was supported in these arguments by the manufacturiig vice-president, who noted that two of his assistants had come up by the same route.

Mr. Rachter then took the position that if steward experience provided superior training for these jobs, something must be wrong with the supervisory training program. He proposed to look into the matter, for he felt that part of the difficulties in American management stemmed from the lack of status given foremen by the men who worked with them. The practice of selecting union stewards, he felt, worked in the wrong direction. He cited with enthusiasm the European practice he had observed, noting that however friendly a man might have been as a fellow-worker, when he was promoted to foreman, he became "Mister" to every man in the crew. He announced that he was going to enlist the aid of a consulting firm to audit the training program.

Some additional fire was added to the controversy when the president of the local union wrote a letter to Mr. Rachter, congratulating him on his stand. The union, he said, was disgusted with the firm's continued hiring of stewards for foremen. Members were contributing a part of their dues every month, he pointed out, to provide training that was subsequently used to the advantage of management. Further, he added, the former stewards were much more hard-boiled in their interpretations of the union agreement than other foremen.

Problem: Be prepared to take sides in this controversy. Also, consider whether steward training and experience are good in the preparation of foremen and why.

SHORT CASE PROBLEM 18.4

Training in Employment

Evaluate the training program of the X company by comparing means of the performance records of training and control groups. Are the differences significant?

Performance Records

	Control Group At End of Week:				Training Group At End of Week:		
Employee	1	2	3	Employee	1	2	3
A	10	15	12	A	12	15	14
B	8	7	8	B	16	16	17
C	16	14	13	C	15	14	18
D	15	16	19	D	12	14	16
E	15	20	25	E	10	10	11
F	9	10	8	F	13	14	12
G	12	7	5	G	10	9	12
H	13	15	14	H	9	9	9
				I	12	14	16
				J	11	15	19

SHORT CASE PROBLEM 18.5

Test of a Test

Compare the following odd-even scores on the final examination of the *I* company's sales training program, and calculate a coefficient of reliability for the examination.

Individual	Total Score	Total of Odd Scores	Total of Even Scores
A	98	48	50
B	97	40	57
C	97	47	50
D	95	46	49
E	93	45	48
F	94	50	44
G	92	42	50
H	90	45	45
I	85	40	45
J	84	44	40
K	83	40	43
L	81	41	40
M	80	38	42
N	80	39	41
O	74	36	38
P	74	34	40
Q	70	39	31
R	68	34	34
S	65	33	32
T	60	29	31

How much must the test be lengthened to give reasonable assurance of a reliability coefficient of 90?

SHORT CASE PROBLEM 18.6

Transfer Back into Bargaining Unit*

The Background: An employee with almost 14 years' seniority was promoted to supervisor. About six months later, because of a decrease in the supervisory force, he was demoted into the bargaining unit where he bumped a worker with less service.

* *Employee Relations and Arbitration Report*, Vol. 21, No. 24, Page 5, May 29, 1961.

The contract was silent on the seniority or job rights of supervisors promoted out of the bargaining unit into supervisory jobs. The Union filed a grievance, charging that the employer had breached the contract by replacing a regular employee with a supervisor.

The Issue: Did the demoted supervisor retain the seniority he had acquired in the bargaining unit before his promotion?

The Union Argues: The promotion to supervisor broke the employee's continuity of service, thereby depriving him of all seniority rights. Without union approval, he could not recover these rights and return to the bargaining unit. The company violated the contract by letting a supervisor displace a bargaining unit employee.

The Company Argues: The supervisor did not lose his bargaining-unit seniority when he was promoted. Seniority exists only by virtue of a contract. Once seniority is acquired by contract, it can be taken away only by contract. Nothing in this contract deprived an employee of his seniority when he was promoted to supervisor. Therefore, a supervisor returned to the bargaining unit retains all the seniority he has when he left it. And because the supervisor had more seniority than the employee he bumped, the company did not violate the contract by transferring him to a job in the bargaining unit.

Problem: Use the actual arbitration case summarized here to compare the viewpoints of managers and union representatives and to decide what is a reasonable solution for the issue thus presented.

19. Management Development

Current interest in training and development is by no means restricted to programs for rank and file employees and for supervisors. Although middle managers and executives seemed to be forgotten men in these programs for many years, that is no longer true. Management and executive development programs have now achieved wide acceptance. Almost half of all firms participating in several nation-wide surveys report that they maintain formal or informal arrangements to assist managers in their continuing development.

Many executives have concluded that adequate managerial competence cannot be provided without these programs. Some programs may be regarded as a reaction to public and union criticism of managers. Employees, with continually rising levels of educational attainment, have become more outspoken in their criticisms of manager decisions and actions. In part, management development programs are also a reaction to the rapid expansion of numbers and proportions of staff managers. Many staff managers have special academic preparation for the positions they fill: they are professionally educated. They have achieved wide recognition, acceptance and status in working organizations. The need for similar professionalism in line management is widely discussed.

Executives have noted the charge that the majority of business failures is attributable to executive and manager deficiencies.[1] According to Gaudet and Carle, who base conclusions on reports from 177 executives, executive failures are, in part, traceable to inadequate knowledge of labor management and not enough breadth of knowledge and skill. Many of those who fail are technicians rather than broadly oriented, professional managers.

[1] See Frederick J. Gaudet and A. Ralph Carle, "Why Executives Fail," *Personnel Psychology*, Vol. 10, No. 1, Spring, 1957, pp. 7–21.

Many alert executives recognize their personal need for specialized development programs, concluding that they are inadequately prepared to meet the wide range of problems with which they are faced. They propose to see that their successors are better prepared for the roles they are to play. Executive development or management development programs represent arrangements designed to meet these needs. On the one hand, they seek to identify individuals regarded as promising candidates for high-level managerial positions and to assist them in preparing for such responsibilities. On the other, they are designed to help present executives increase their managerial competence.

In part as a result of more common retirement provisions, needs for replacements in executive ranks are heavier than in the past and will be still heavier in the future.[2]

Many firms and agencies have concluded that the only way to secure satisfactory executives for the present and future is to establish formal development plans. This trend is international; similar programs for experienced managers have been developed in several European nations, including France, Switzerland, Holland, Italy and Russia.[3]

1.0 POLICY ON MANAGEMENT DEVELOPMENT

Over-all goals and objectives in these plans follow a common pattern. In general, policy proposes (1) to improve the qualifications of present managers and (2) to provide an adequate supply of well-qualified future managers.[4] More specific policy is not unlike that already explained as underlying

[2] See "The Growing Problem of Executive Turnover," New York: Booz, Allen and Hamilton, 1953.

[3] See Lyndall F. Urwick, Joseph M. Trickett, Robert G. Simpson, Douglas Williams, and Stanley Peterfreund, *Management Education for Itself and Its Employees*, New York: American Management Association, 1954; George C. Houston, *Management Development: Principles and Perspectives*, Homewood, Illinois: Richard D. Irwin, Inc., 1960; "The Soviet Executive," *Business Week*, January 30, 1960, pp. 100–101; David Granick, *The Red Executive*, New York: Doubleday & Company, Inc., 1960; Jane Dustan and Barbara Makanowitsky, *Training Managers Abroad*, New York: Council for International Progress in Management, 1960; Norman R. F. Maier, Allen R. Solem, and Ayesha A. Maier, *Supervisory and Executive Development*, New York: John Wiley & Sons, Inc., 1957; John W. Riegel, *Executive Development*, Ann Arbor, Mich.: University of Michigan Press, 1952; Thomas A. Mahoney, *Building the Executive Team*, Englewood Cliffs, N.J.: Prentice-Hall, Inc., 1961; Lyndall F. Urwick, *Management Education in American Business*, New York: American Management Association, 1954; "Current Practice in the Development of Management Personnel," *Research Report No. 26*, New York: American Management Association, 1955; *Executive Development in Small Business*, Washington, D.C.: Small Business Administration, February, 1954; James M. Jenks, "The Development of Middle Management Executives," *Advanced Management*, Vol. 25, No. 3, March, 1960, pp. 23–25; Willard E. Bennett, *Manager Selection, Education and Training*, New York: McGraw-Hill Book Company, Inc., 1958; "Management Development," *Journal of the American Society of Training Directors*, Vol. 11, No. 6, November-December, 1957.

[4] A survey by the National Industrial Conference Board in 1961 found that some 200 firms report that the improvement of performance on the part of present managers is regarded as the most important objective in their management development pro-

programs of supervisory training. Programs are intended primarily for line managers. Their heaviest impact is on middle management, from second level supervisors to vice-presidents.

1.1 Self-development. Most policy assumes that development must be a personal process in which the developing manager takes the initiative. Programs are intended to facilitate self-development. Some references to the function of the manager as including the development of his assistants suggest that leaders are the developers and that assistants are developed.[5] In such an atmosphere, assistants may wait for their leaders to get busy developing them.

Some current policy may overestimate the degree to which any one person can develop another. The manager may *suggest* continuing development to his assistants. He may *encourage* and *facilitate* such personal growth. He may *offer rewards* for development or impose penalties for failure to develop. Most policy, however, assumes the desirability of high levels of self-motivation.

1.2 Areas of development. Policy generally identifies areas or fields in which managers are expected to develop, but no single list or pattern has achieved universal acceptance. In broad terms, development means *improved and more competent leadership*. Frequently mentioned as a major area is breadth of *vision* and *understanding*, with fuller comprehension of social, economic, and political values and processes.[6]

Development of depth in *economic understanding* is another widely accepted objective. Improvement in *communications* skills is another. Some policy places special emphasis on encouragement of *originality* and creative thinking. Some proposes thoughtful consideration of management philosophy, ethics, and public responsibility. Policy often mentions improved management skills, with specific reference to analysis and reasoning, planning, organizing, evaluating, reading, writing, speaking and public relations.

Many of the most carefully considered programs recognize the presently limited understanding as to what special competence is required for successful management. They may propose to undertake, on their own or in cooperation with others, studies of job requirements for managers.

1.3 Responsibility for assistants. Policy usually places heavy responsibility on all managers, who are expected not only to maintain their own personal development program but to provide a suitable climate for the development of assistants. Some policy proposes to evaluate managers partly on the basis of the personal development of their subordinates.

---

grams. Helping selected managers prepare for advancement and preparing all managers to adapt to changing conditions are the second and third most common objectives of these programs. See Walter S. Wikstrom, "Why Companies Develop Their Managers," *Management Record,* Vol. 23, No. 11, November, 1961, pp. 6–8.

[5] See Chris Argyris, "Puzzle and Perplexity in Executive Development," *Personnel Journal,* Vol. 39, No. 11, April, 1961, pp. 463ff.

[6] See Morris S. Viteles, "Human Relations and the Humanities in the Education of Business Leaders," *Personnel Psychology,* Vol. 12, No. 1, Spring, 1959, pp. 1–28.

1.4 Equality of opportunity. Policy usually intends that all managers have equal opportunity to participate in the program. No one is to be excluded; there are to be no favorites. All managers will be encouraged to continue their self-development. All divisions and departments will participate in the developmental program. Those selected for participation in supplementary university or other classes will earn that added opportunity by demonstrating their capacity for, and interest in, continued advancement. Not all policy is so broad; some programs are available only to managers above specified levels and to those regarded as in line for top positions.

1.5 High-level sponsorship. Policy usually proposes top management sponsorship of and participation in these programs. Industrial relations, personnel, and training divisions may be charged with responsibility for detailed administration, but over-all direction is assigned to a committee of top executives or an executive vice president or other officer.

2.0 DEFINING DEVELOPMENT NEEDS

Policy can and does specify the general intentions of management development programs. It runs into difficulties, however, when it tries to be more specific in defining the types of development expected. What qualities are to be cultivated? What knowledge and skills are to be perfected in these programs?

For other training and development programs, as noted in Chapter 18, the answer is usually sought in job descriptions and job specifications. Few firms, however, have subjected high-level management positions to incisive job analysis. Usual procedures may not provide an effective or useful job specification. Activities and duties are more varied and diverse in higher echelons where policy making and leadership are major responsibilities. Job specifications are less certain and precise for the general management class of jobs.

The role of the modern manager must be defined in some detail if firms are to provide and maintain adequate opportunities for development. Appropriate relationships of managers and those who are managed, as well as the roles each must play, must be recognized and understood. Firms cannot develop adequate development programs without an up-to-date, penetrating analysis of manager jobs, duties, and responsibilities.

2.1 Occupational job descriptions. One of the most pressing prerequisites for effective management development, therefore, is the creation of realistic job specifications for managers. Some generalized job descriptions of top manager jobs are available. The *Dictionary of Occupational Titles* (DOT) recognizes a class of "managerial and official occupations" (with code numbers 0-70.00 through 0-99.99) which is described as follows:[7]

---

[7] "Occupational Classification and Industry Index," *Dictionary of Occupational Titles,* 2d ed., Vol. 2, Washington, D.C.: Government Printing Office, 1949, page 24.

This group includes occupations that are involved primarily with responsible policy-making, planning, supervising, coordinating, or guiding the work-activity of others, usually through intermediate supervisors. Typical of these occupations are managers or presidents of business enterprises, superintendents of construction projects, and purchasing and advertising agents. Executive secretaries and treasurers, although not usually involved in extensive administrative or managerial duties, are nevertheless included because of their official capacities.

Occupations that embrace supervisory functions of the character of foremen, but that involve limited aspects of policy-making and management, are not included. These occupations are coded with the Skilled Occupations.

The same source provides a description of the general manager job, as follows:[8]

> MANAGER, INDUSTRIAL ORGANIZATION (any Ind.) 0–97 41. general manager, industrial organization; manager, general; manager, plant; superintendent, industrial organization. Is responsible for the efficient management of an industrial corporation: Coordinates the operation of production, distribution, and selling departments. Determines administrative policies, and executes them through subordinate managers.

The *International Standard Classification of Occupations* provides a similar but somewhat longer specification.[9]

2.2 Managers vs. proprietors. Occupational descriptions for managerial jobs usually fail to make a sharp distinction between *managers* and *working proprietors*. The fact that some owners are their own managers tends to confuse managerial and ownership functions. Most managers in industrialized economies are not owners. The process of industrialization creates a demand for specialized managers who are employed by public or private proprietors.

Much of the current uncertainty about what special knowledge and skills are needed by managers can be traced to this confusion of *management and ownership*. The owner in modern large-scale industry is primarily an investor. He may assume little responsibility for what the industrial organization does or how it does it. He may not have and does not need any special competence in organizational leadership. The manager's responsibilities and requirements are distinctly different. He must organize, lead, and direct a working team. He may think of himself as the personal representative of owners. In modern societies, however, employees will also expect him to represent them in relationships with owners, and the public will hold him responsible for what the organization does.

Failure to recognize this distinction between *managers* and *proprietors* makes the needs in management development somewhat obscure, both in individual firm programs and in university education for management. Many collegiate business schools illustrate this confusion; they are not clear as to whether they are educating for management or for private ownership and proprietorship. Educational programs are complicated by the fact that man-

[8] "Definitions of Titles," *ibid.*, Vol. No. 1, page 816.
[9] *International Standard Classification of Occupations*, Geneva: International Labour Office, 1958, page 56.

agerial jobs are presumably changing, so that they will not be the same when students are ready for these assignments.[10]

Industrialization has created a large occupational class of *nonproprietor managers.* Their assignments and responsibilities presumably set the specifications for management development programs. These non-owner managers have become one of the most important occupational groups in modern societies, not only in numbers but even more in the responsibilities they hold and the power and influence they wield. As Berle has suggested, they hold positions of enormous power, without sharply defined responsibility. Society may, for this reason, demand something very close to professional competence and ethics from today's managers.[11]

The job of the manager-specialist, created in and by the process of industrialization, has become more complicated as firms have grown in size, as employees have become more sophisticated, and as public policy has demanded increasing consideration of individual and social welfare. Adequacy and competence in the assignment are assumed to require special aptitudes, knowledge, and skill. *Limited managerial resources* may be a major factor in restricting the pace of industrial development. Shortages of managerial skill and competence are prominent characteristics of all underdeveloped economies.[12]

2.3 Management science. Programs designed to develop effective managers are handicapped by confusion about the nature of management and related job requirements. In some viewpoints, management is essentially an *art,* and the effective manager an artist. In sharp contrast, another view describes a *science of management.* In current terminology, many of those who visualize operations research as effecting great changes in management describe such applications as *management science.*

Such divergent notions of management imply sharply different programs of management development. If management is an art, then special *artistic aptitudes* are the key to success. While education may help to develop them, a fundamental requirement of the successful manager, like that of the musician or painter, must be *inborn talent.* If, on the other hand, management

[10] See Aaron Gordon and James Howell, *Higher Education for Business,* New York: Columbia University Press, 1959; Frank C. Pierson (Editor), *The Educatoin of American Businessmen,* New York: McGraw-Hill Book Co., Inc., 1959; Heinz Hartmann, "Managers and Entrepreneurs: A Useful Distinction," *Administrative Science Quarterly,* Vol. 3, No. 4, March, 1959, pp. 429–451; Alfred Bornemann, "The Development of the Teaching of Management in Schools of Business," *Journal of the Academy of Management,* Vol. 4, No. 2, August, 1961, pp. 129–136; Norman Fisher, "The Making of a Manager," *Personnel,* Vol. 38, No. 5, September-October 1961, pp. 8–15; Dalton E. McFarland, "The Emerging Revolution in Management Education," *Journal of the Academy of Management,* Vol. 3, No. 1, April, 1960, pp. 15ff.; Dan H. Fenn, Jr. (Ed.) *Business Responsibility in Action,* New York: McGraw-Hill Book Company, Inc., 1961.

[11] See Adolf Berle, *Power Without Property,* New York: Harcourt Brace and Company, Inc., 1959.

[12] See Frederick Harbison and Charles A. Myers, *Management in the Industrial World,* New York: McGraw-Hill Book Co., Inc., 1959, Chapter 2.

is a science, the manager will require different aptitudes and preparation must emphasize *knowledge, analysis* and *research,* as well as skills.

Modern theories of management, such as those discussed in Chapters 4 and 5, imply that management is what is usually described as an *applied science.* Applied scientists use what is described as the *scientific method* in attacking their problems. They develop their *theories* to explain the behavior with which they deal. They turn to various basic or pure sciences for much of their theory and understanding.

Management, as an applied science, uses the method of science and develops and tests theories about the processes in which it works. The manager is the *specialist* who knows and understands *management theory* and its applications. At the same time, he has the skills necessary to make such applications in working organizations. As in other applied sciences—for example, medicine, engineering, or education—the applied scientist is a specialist in knowledge and skill. Managers acquire and use specialized knowledge and special management skills. Just as an engineer, for example, may have to translate the knowledge and theory of physics into the design of bridges, managers need their own special skills to fit the knowledge of behavioral sciences to problems of organization and leadership of work groups.[13]

2.4 **Professional management.** The notion that management is to be an applied science establishes the educational need for special knowledge and skills. It suggests, also, that just as practitioners in several other applied sciences have become professionals—doctors, educators, and engineers, for example—managers will move toward *professional qualifications.* As professionals in modern society they will be expected to meet several widely recognized requirements, which may be outlined as follows:

1. Mastery of an organized and growing body of *specialized knowledge,* including an understanding of both *theory* and *practice,* usually evidenced in part by completion of a *distinctive educational program;*
2. *Distinctive skills,* representing special aptitude plus training and experience;
3. A *professional attitude,* marked by determination to keep abreast of *new developments* in *theory, research* and *practice* in the field of specialization;
4. Recognition of special *public responsibility,* usually marked by appropriate *professional ethical codes.*

Several indications of a trend toward professional management can be noted. One of the most obvious is the development of *collegiate schools of*

13 See Delbert C. Miller, "How Behavioral Scientists Can Help Business," *Business Horizons,* Vol. 3, No. 2, Summer, 1960, pp. 32–37; Peter F. Drucker, "Thinking Ahead: Potentials of Management Science," *Harvard Business Review,* Vol. 37, No. 1, January-February, 1959, pp. 25–30ff; Ralph J. Cordiner, *New Frontiers for Professional Managers,* New York: McGraw-Hill Book Company, Inc., 1956; Herbert E. Krugman and Harold A. Edgerton, "Profile of a Scientist Manager," *Personnel,* Vol. 36, No. 5, September-October, 1959, pp. 38–49.

management and business administration. Another is the growing tendency on the part of many managers to look to behavioral sciences for assistance in solving their problems. The emergence and wide discussion of *theories of management* point in the same direction, as does the increased interest in research and in special educational programs for experienced managers.

One of the most impressive of these developments is the heightened interest in the *public responsibility* and *ethical practice* of managers.[14] Special *codes of ethics* for managers and wide provision of courses in managerial ethics for students of management have been proposed. Problems of *conflicts of interest* have been widely discussed, as have possibly unethical practices in the recruitment and management of employees and managers.

On the other hand, managers were apparently not regarded as professionals by the Selective Service Administration, which, until 1962, did not recommend deferment for graduate students in business administration.

Modern societies expect professionals to recognize their complex responsibilities and to develop and maintain appropriate ethical principles as guides for meeting these responsibilities. Professional managers may be expected to recognize that, at one and the same time, they have concurrent responsibilities to owners, co-workers, employees, and the public. As professionals, they may be expected to give top priority to their public responsibilities. Their position can be compared to that of the physician who must give adequate attention to the needs of his patient but must impose quarantine if that is necessary to protect the public interest. Again, the position of the professional manager is similar to that of the professional faculty member who recognizes responsibilities to his university paralleled by even greater responsibility to insure freedom in research and teaching.

Carried to its logical ultimate, professionalization might include licensing or certification of managers. Some local management associations have considered the preparation of examinations and the creation of examining boards. Such a movement is already underway in England.[15]

2.5 Manager careers and jobs. Forecasts of the future of management, such as those outlined in preceding paragraphs, have had a heavy influence in shaping both collegiate and business programs for management develop-

[14] See Louis William Norris, "Moral Hazards of an Executive," *Harvard Business Review*, Vol. 38, No. 5, September-October, 1960, pp. 72–79; Leon C. Megginson, "The Pressure for Principles: A Challenge to Management Professors," *Journal of the Academy of Management*, Vol. 1, No. 2, August, 1958, pp. 7–12; Benjamin M. Selekman, *A Moral Philosophy for Management*, New York: McGraw-Hill Book Company, Inc., 1959; "Keeping a High Shine on Ethics," *Business Week*, March 25, 1961, pp. 81ff; Robert W. Austin, "Code of Conduct for Executives," *Harvard Business Review*, Vol. 39, No. 5, September-October, 1961, pp. 53–61.

[15] See *National Scheme for Certificates and Diplomas in Management Studies*, London: British Institute of Management, 1951 (A handbook of courses and examinations). Caplow describes steps in the emergence of professions as (1) establishment of an association with specified requirements for membership, (2) wide recognition of a name or title for the occupation, (3) creation of a code of ethics, and (4) political agitation to maintain barriers to admission. See Theodore Caplow, *The Sociology of Work*, Minneapolis: University of Minnesota Press, 1957, pp. 139–140.

ment. For additional clues as to what these programs should try to do, their planners and directors have looked to the past and present of management jobs. They have examined the working careers of managers and studied the present responsibilities of manager jobs.

In one reported study, the editors of *Fortune* magazine noted the backgrounds and managerial experience of 1,700 top executives.[16] Most of them were born in the Middle West and Northeastern sections of the United States. Fathers, in the majority of cases, were in the same occupational category. Two-thirds of them were college graduates. Some 85 per cent had majored in law, business, economics, engineering, or science. Compared with a similar study undertaken in 1952, a trend toward liberal arts backgrounds was noted. Collegiate grades were distinctly above average. About one-third of the men had remained with the firms with which they started.

Most beginning jobs are in specialized management functions rather than general management. Some careers show an early rotation among various assignments with a sort of informal commitment to careers in general management. Others evidence a commitment to leadership in staff divisons and avoid rotation during early experience. They move into general management at high levels in their organizations. Several studies have sought to describe these managerial career patterns.[17]

Somewhat similar patterns are evident in the careers of top career officials in the federal government. Recruitment seeks candidates for specialist jobs, and subsequent career guidance encourages employees to maintain their specialization. With experience, however, those who demonstrate interest in management are given assignments that develop a broader view of the total operation of an agency. Opportunities for management training are provided.[18]

Analysis of management jobs seeks to discover common tasks and responsibilities, on the assumption that management should try to develop knowledge and skill appropriate to these assignments. One English study reports negative findings, concluding that managers have little common knowledge or experience and that management jobs involve capricious decisions.[19] Virgil Rowland expresses a contrasting viewpoint in his *Improving Managerial Performance.*[20]

[16] *Fortune,* November, 1959, pp. 138ff.

[17] See Melville Dalton, *Men Who Manage,* New York: John Wiley & Sons, Inc., 1959; Seymour Martin Lipset and Reinhard Bendix, *Social Mobility in Industrial Society,* Berkeley: University of California Press, 1959; W. Lloyd Warner and James C. Abegglen, *Big Business Leaders in America,* New York: Harper & Brothers, 1955; W. Lloyd Warner, Paul P. Van Riper, Norman H. Martin and Orvis F. Collins, "Profiles of Government Executives," *Business Topics,* Michigan State University, Vol. 9, No. 4, Autumn, 1961, pp. 13–24.

[18] See Marvin K. Bernstein, *The Job of the Federal Executive,* Washington: The Brookings Institution, 1958.

[19] R. V. Clements, *Managers: A Study of Their Careers in Industry,* London: George Allen & Unwin, Ltd., 1958.

[20] Virgil K. Rowland, *Improving Managerial Performance,* New York, Harper & Brothers, 1958, p. 11.

Studies at Indiana University have identified four primary management functions: planning, organizing, motivating, and controlling.[21] The *Fortune* survey, already noted, identified more than a hundred "executive actions" which were classified to provide a pattern of the executive job.[22] Ohio State University studies have developed a series of job descriptions for executive positions.[23] The Educational Testing Service describes executive jobs in terms of ten basic dimensions.[24]

Thomas A. Mahoney and others in the Management Development Laboratory of the University of Minnesota Industrial Relations Center distinguish a group of managerial *functions* or responsibilities from a second category of managerial *activities* representing the areas in which the functions are performed. The functions include planning, investigating, coordinating, evaluating, supervising, staffing, negotiating, and representing. Areas of activity include personnel, finance, materials, markets, methods, and equipment.[25]

2.6 Executive traits. Several studies have sought to identify the special characteristics that identify successful managers. The Small Business Administration attempted a summary which describes the good executive as intelligent, emotionally stable, skillful with people, instinctively accepting responsibility, dynamic, and able to express himself clearly. In addition, the summary lists "administrative traits," which include being a planner, an organizer, an assembler of resources, a director, and a controller.[26] Lee Stock-

---

[21] William G. Scott, "Modern Human Relations in Perspective," *Personnel Administration,* Vol. 22, No. 6, November-December, 1959, pp. 17ff.

[22] See also "The Executive," *Personnel Policies Forum,* Survey No. 37, Washington, D.C.: Bureau of National Affairs, July, 1956; Earl Brooks, "What Successful Executives Do," *Personnel,* Vol. 32, No. 3, November, 1955, pp. 210–25; Robert Teviot Livingston, *The Manager's Job,* New York: Columbia University Press, 1960.

[23] See Carroll L. Shartle, *Executive Performance and Leadership,* Englewood Cliffs, N.J.: Prentice-Hall, Inc., 1956; Ralph M. Stogdill, Carroll L. Shartle, and Associates, "Patterns of Administrative Performance," *Research Monograph No. 81,* Ohio State University Bureau of Business Research, 1956.

[24] See John K. Hemphill and Lewis B. Ward, "The Executive Study," *Personnel Administration,* Vol. 21, No. 1, January-February, 1958, pp. 49–55; John K. Hemphill, "Job Descriptions for Executives," *Harvard Business Review,* Vol. 37, No. 5, September-October 1959, pp. 55–68.

[25] See Thomas A. Mahoney, *op. cit.;* also his "New Way to Look at Manager's Jobs," *Factory Management and Maintenance,* December, 1957, pp. 110–12; also C. L. Bennett, "Defining the Manager's Job: The AMA Manual of Position Descriptions," *Research Study No. 33,* New York: American Management Association, 1958; Marshall E. Dimock, "Direction, The Heart of Administration," in *A Philosophy of Administration,* New York: Harper & Brothers, 1958, chap. 12; James G. March, "Business Decision Making," *Reprint No. 47,* Carnegie Institute of Technology Graduate School of Industrial Administration, 1959.

[26] "Executive Development in Small Firms," *op. cit.,* pp. 9–11. See also Joseph A. Litterer, "What Do Companies Look for in Their Executives?" *Personnel Administration,* Vol. 20, No. 6, November-December 1957, pp. 16–19; John B. Miner and John E. Culver, "Some Aspects of the Executive Personality," *Journal of Applied Psychology,* Vol. 39, No. 6, December, 1955, pp. 348–53; Perrin Stryker, "Who Is an Executive?" *Fortune,* Vol. 52, No. 6, December, 1955, pp. 107–9; Robert M. Wald and Roy A. Doty, "The Top Executive: A First-hand Profile," *Harvard Business Review,* Vol. 32, No. 4, July-August, 1954, pp. 45–54; Ephraim Rosen, "The Executive Personality," *Personnel,* Vol. 36, No. 1, January-February, 1959, pp. 8–20; L. S. Huttner et al.,

ford has suggested that general and specific traits of executives be distinguished. He includes as *general* traits: vitality or endurance, decisiveness, persuasiveness, responsibility, intelligence, development, and motivation. Among *specific* qualities, he includes resistance to frustration, resistance to involuntary thinking, social control, and emotional control.[27] Dooher and Marquis, who undertook a study of executives for the American Management Association, conclude that seven qualities are essential: understanding of the basic principles governing the industry, ability to evaluate data, a sense of social as well as of economic responsibility, a talent for developing both the business and its employees, courage to carry out plans, continuing insistence on research, and ability to judge personal value by comparison with past, present, and future objectives.[28] Others who have sought to identify qualities that make for successful executive performance include Argyris, Hook, and Gardner.[29] Gaudet, reporting on studies at Stevens Institute, concludes that analyses of executive failures identify personality defects ten times as frequently as lack of knowledge.[30]

In this connection, it should be recalled that current leadership theory includes two prominent camps or schools, the *structuralists* and the *situationists*. The former tend to explain successful leadership in terms of personality and personal traits. They are sometimes called the *correlationists*. Situationists are more impressed with the setting or environment. They argue that personal traits of executives must vary to fit the characteristics of associates and the time and place. Most management development programs combine these viewpoints; they seek to develop the qualities that appear to be generally required and, at the same time, to stress the quality of flexibility and adaptability.

2.7 Executive skills. Several reports on qualifications of managers describe what are called executive skills. One classification identifies three types of skills: technical, human, and conceptual. *Technical skills* are those that involve "specialized knowledge, analytical ability within that specialty, and facility in the use of tools and techniques of the specific discipline."[31] Human skills are those that provide facility and effectiveness in working with, moti-

---

"Further Light on the Executive Personality," *ibid.*, Vol. 36, No. 2, March-April, 1959, pp. 45–50.

[27] In his "Outline of Executive Development," *op. cit.*, pp. 22–24.

[28] M. Joseph Dooher and Vivienne Marquis, *The Development of Executive Talent*, New York: American Management Association, 1952.

[29] Chris Argyris, "Some Characteristics of Successful Executives," *Personnel Journal*, Vol. 32, No. 2, June, 1953, pp. 50–55; C. R. Hook, "For Executives Only: A Look at the Man Himself," *Management Record*, Vol. 14, No. 5, May, 1952, pp. 170–72; Burleigh B. Gardner, "Executives: Their Personality and Its Appraisal," *Advanced Management*, Vol. 18, No. 1, January, 1953, pp. 13–15.

[30] Frederick J. Gaudet, "Reasons for Executive Failure Point Way to Success," *Iron Age*, September 8, 15, and 22, 1960.

[31] See Robert L. Katz, "Skills of an Effective Administrator," *Harvard Business Review*, Vol. 33, No. 1, January-February, 1955, pp. 33–42; Theodore O. Yntema, "The Transferrable Skills of a Manager," *Journal of the Academy of Management*, Vol. 3, No. 2, August, 1960, pp. 79–86.

vating, and gaining the enthusiastic cooperation of people. *Conceptual skill is a combination of vision, imagination, and intelligence that assures perspective in viewing an organization and its future.*

Riegel identifies five classes of basic skills: executive skills to perform lesser jobs, to plan, to select subordinates, and to stimulate them; skills in negotiating; skills in investing and risk-bearing; skills in visualizing, devising, and bringing about improvements; and skills in co-operating with other managers and technicians.[32]

"Didn't they teach you to make decisions
at business school, Hobart?"

Figure 19.1   Inadequacy in Management Education
SOURCE: Joseph Serrano in *The Management Review*. Reprinted by permission of the American Management Association.

Perhaps the most frequently mentioned skill is that of making sound decisions. Management development programs, especially those involving collegiate studies, have made much of their training in *decision-making*. (See Figure 19.1.) Discussion of this phase of manager training seems to imply that managers have quite special and distinctive decision-making responsibilities. Analysis of decision-making processes in management, on the other hand, suggests that they are likely to be decentralized in most large working organizations. Managers rely on others to get the facts and to organize and present them. Each supplier of facts exercises some *selective perception* and discrimination in his choices and emphases. Communicators may add their own further interpretation and bias.

[32] John W. Riegel, *Executive Development, op. cit.,* pp. 197–198.

Also, it should be clear that managers need specialized knowledge and understanding as a basis for sound decisions, in addition to whatever skill may be involved. Just as lawyers and medical practitioners need specialized knowledge for the decisions they must make,. the manager needs a similar foundation for his decisions.

3.0 MANAGEMENT DEVELOPMENT PROGRAMS

Current management development programs seek to identify those who have the required basic abilities and to provide opportunities for the development of these aptitudes. To this end, current practice uses many of the training methods and techniques described in the preceding chapter. In-plant programs include lectures, conferences, role playing, case discussions, job rotation, understudy arrangements, projects, and combinations of these devices and procedures. Many firms provide scholarships that pay the cost of relevant courses available from colleges and universities. Some firms allow paid leaves of absence for attendance in residence in a university graduate school. Managers may be allowed to spend as long as a full year on campus in the Sloan programs at M.I.T. and Stanford. Thousands of managers attend management seminars conducted by the American Management Association in New York, at Colgate University, and at Saranac Lake. Others attend the special Advanced Management courses offered by local Chapters of the Society for Advancement of Management.[33] Several hundred managers enroll each year in the numerous university short courses and executive development programs.

No precise, standard pattern of management development courses has appeared. None would be appropriate, for programs have varying objectives and include managers with varying backgrounds and experience. Several common steps or stages in these programs can, however, be identified. They have been graphically outlined in Figure 19.2.

The first four steps in that process require little elaboration here. Policy decisions, assignments of program responsibility, and development of job specifications have been discussed. The need for advance planning of organizational change is widely recognized.

3.1 Identification of potential. Who is to be admitted to the program? The answer involves the identification of potential for higher management responsibilities. This is especially difficult, because qualities associated with executive success are not sharply defined, as has been noted in Section 2.

Current practice looks to many possible indicators: college grades and extracurricular activities (for those who are hired directly from academic sources); tests of intelligence, interests, and emotional stability; personnel ratings; experience; health; marital and community status; formal education; age; and others. Employment histories are examined for patterns that

---

[33] See "Local Courses in Management Training Offered for High Level Executives," *Business Week,* June 25, 1960, p. 173.

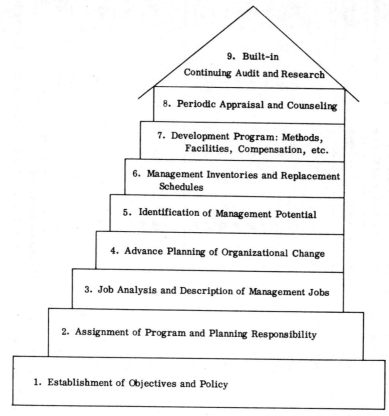

9. Built-in
Continuing Audit and Research

8. Periodic Appraisal and Counseling

7. Development Program: Methods,
Facilities, Compensation, etc.

6. Management Inventories and Replacement
Schedules

5. Identification of Management Potential

4. Advance Planning of Organizational Change

3. Job Analysis and Description of Management Jobs

2. Assignment of Program and Planning Responsibility

1. Establishment of Objectives and Policy

Figure 19.2   The Management Development Process

may be indicative. The most common practice asks senior managers to nominate candidates. Selections are then made by members of the committee in charge of the program.

C. Wilson Randle has developed lists of characteristics that have been associated with promotability. His summary list of these characteristics is shown in Figure 19.3.[34]

Mahoney, Jerdee, and Nash report a study designed to test predictors of management potential, including some 98 specific measures of personal characteristics, test scores, and biographical data. Nineteen of the measures showed significant correlation with criteria of managerial effectiveness. The combination of predictors successfully identified 71 per cent of the managers

[34] See also Stephen Habbe, "Finding Tomorrow's Executives," *NICB Management Record*, Vol. 17, No. 2, December 29, 1955, pages 474–77; Milton M. Mandell, "Selecting Trainees for Management," *Personnel Administration*, Vol. 19, No. 3, May-June, 1956, pp. 44–46; Erwin K. Taylor and Edwin C. Nevis, "The Use of Projective Techniques in Management Selection," *Personnel*, Vol. 33, No. 5, March, 1957, pp. 462–74; Thomas A. Mahoney, Thomas H. Jerdee, and Allan N. Nash, "Predicting Managerial Effectiveness," *Personnel Psychology*, Vol. 13, No. 2, Summer, 1960, pp. 147–63; Lyndall Urwick, *16 Questions about the Selection and Training of Managers*, London: Urwick, Orr, and Partners, Ltd., September, 1958.

Characteristic	Sales		Manufacturing		Engineering and Research		Finance and Accounting	
	Promotable executives	Inadequate executives	Promotable executives	Inadequate executives	Promotable executives	Inadequate executives	Promotable executives	Inadequate executives
For all categories								
DISCRIMINATING								
Position performance	50%	18%	48%	3%	47%	3%	49%	7%
Drive	47	27	52	10	36	4	48	20
Intellectual ability	44	23	41	3	47	4	46	13
Leadership	43	14	47	4	38	2	34	7
Administration	34	3	49	3	34	4	44	7
Initiative	36	23	49	6	30	1	37	13
Motivation	—	—	31	1	34	8	33	7
Creativeness	34	18	31	3	39	4	—	—
For this category only								
Acceptance	52	27	52	20	48	12	—	—
Planning	—	—	45	7	29	8	—	—
Flexibility	—	—	37	7	—	—	—	—
Analysis and judgment	—	—	50	7	—	—	—	—
Technical knowledge	—	—	—	—	73	46	72	33
Accomplishment	—	—	—	—	28	4	—	—
Socialness	—	—	—	—	43	19	—	—
Quality	—	—	—	—	—	—	30	0

Percentage presence as an outstanding quality

Fig. 19.3 Distinguishing Characteristics of the Composite Executive

C. Wilson Randle, "How to Identify Promotable Executives," by permission from *Harvard Business Review*, Vol. 34, No. 3, May–June, 1956, pp. 122–34).

Percentage presence as an outstanding quality

Characteristic	Sales		Manufacturing		Engineering and Research		Finance and Accounting	
	Promotable executives	Inadequate executives	Promotable executives	Inadequate executives	Promotable executives	Inadequate executives	Promotable executives	Inadequate executives
For all categories								
NONDISCRIMINATING								
Dependability	22%	14%	28%	20%	25%	8%	25%	27%
Self-control	21	9	28	13	20	12	19	7
Verbal facility	18	14	16	3	20	8	33	20
Self-confidence	13	14	13	1	11	4	15	13
Sensitivity	9	9	11	1	9	1	17	13
Objectivity	5	18	6	0	7	1	5	0
For this category only								
Accomplishment	26	5	23	3	—	—	—	—
Quality	18	1	—	—	—	—	—	—
Breadth of knowledge	34	23	—	—	—	—	—	—
Vision	11	18	7	0	14	1	11	7
Attitude	54	50	—	—	32	31	—	—
Planning	28	18	—	—	—	—	20	20
Acuteness	31	36	20	3	—	—	39	33
Capacity	—	—	—	—	—	—	47	33
Motivation	41	32	—	—	—	—	—	—
Creativeness	—	—	—	—	—	—	13	7

Fig. 19.3 (Cont.)

in the research sample and 66 per cent in a validation sample. The more effective manager appears to be somewhat more intelligent than the less effective manager; his vocational interests are similar to the interests of sales managers, purchasing agents, and manufacturing company presidents and less similar to interests of biologists, dentists, and technical craftsmen. The successful manager tends to be more aggressive, persuasive, and self-reliant. He has had more education and was more active in sports and hobbies. His wife also has had more education, and she has worked less after marriage.[35]

All such studies, including those cited in Section 2, face considerable uncertainty as to what constitutes *success in management*. What present managers regard as success and superiority may not be as readily accepted as management moves toward professionalization. Studies of past experience cannot provide assurance that the type of manager who is successful in today's firms will be the successful type for the decade ahead. Perhaps other studies can suggest *criteria of success* for the manager of 1970 or 1980. Studies of trends in manager jobs and careers might be helpful.

3.2   Inventories of Managers. Management development programs generally provide an *inventory of present managers,* which is combined with forecasts of future needs to create *replacement tables.* Forecasts of future organizational change and growth allow estimates of prospective needs for managers. Calculations of probable losses from death, illness, retirements, and resignations are elements in the continuing inventory. Alternate lines of promotion are marked and key positions for training and development are identified.

Personnel records are of obvious importance in this process. The composite *manager inventory* may be graphically shown, with colored tabs indicating the current level of individual qualifications. This *replacement* or *progress chart* is generally regarded as highly confidential. It is important to managers that they know they are included. But care is taken to prevent the impression that they are being manipulated and will have little opportunity to make choices about their own futures.

3.3   Development techniques. Development programs include special courses offered by training divisions, individual study, personal counseling and guidance by senior managers, job rotation, supplementary university

---

[35] Thomas A. Mahoney, *et al.,* "Predicting Managerial Effectiveness," *Personnel Psychology,* Vol. 13, No. 2, Summer, 1960, p. 161; see also C. W. Randle, W. H. Monroe and others, "Better Ways to Measure Executive Performance," *Management Methods,* Vol. 19, No. 4, January, 1961, pp. 64–76; E. K. Taylor, "The Unsolved Riddle of Executive Success," *Personnel,* Vol. 37, No. 2, March-April, 1960, pp. 8–18; Stanley Stark, "Research Criteria of Executive Success," *Journal of Business,* University of Chicago, Vol. 32, No. 1, January, 1959, pp. 1–14.

One attempt to identify future management potential has used what is called the "in-basket" test. The candidate is placed at a desk with a loaded in-basket and told

courses, conferences, lectures, and other specialized experience.

Many programs arrange for *job rotation,* seeking thus to familiarize the trainee with several major departments and functions. Also common are *understudy arrangements* in which the principal is charged with major responsibility for the progress of his understudy. Some programs make extensive use of *conferences* and *role-playing sessions.* They may also include variations of *multiple management* arrangements, which have sometimes been described as "seedbeds" for executives. (See Chapter 6, section 3.1.) Special training in rapid reading and courses designed to broaden the viewpoints of participants have been widely used. Candidates may become members of *T-groups* for special *sensitivity training.*

3.4   Periodic appraisals. Most programs review the progress of candidates at frequent intervals. Evaluators of candidates are generally their superiors. Some practice uses rating scales with appraisals secured from two or more superiors, much like the practice already discussed in Chapter 17. Use of periodic appraisals is generally accepted, with emphasis on specific *goals for performance* and evaluation against these goals.[36]

Rating procedures vary. Some ratings are annual; others are semi-annual. Some are quite formal, with qualities defined and measured on a five or ten-point scale. Others are informal, with superiors simply writing a report in which a few specified qualities are mentioned. Some rating procedures seek the opinions of peers, that is, other managers at the same level. Most practice, however, involves rating by the manager's superior, frequently supported by the approval of a manager at the next higher level.

Some practice uses *critical incidents* to justify and support these evaluations. Mahoney and others have studied the principal qualities on which managers are evaluated. They distinguish sixteen *personal characteristics* and twelve *performance measures,* as shown in Figure 19.4.[37]

3.5   Counseling and coaching. Programs generally contemplate counseling, either by senior managers or by special counselors. Planty and Efferson have outlined the purposes of such counseling as: getting the participant to do a better job, showing him how he is doing, discussing plans for future improvement, strengthening personal relationships between superior and subordinate and eliminating anxiety and tension. Hill and Hann describe coun-

---

to imagine that he is running his firm's local office. He is to act on each of the items in the basket within a specified time. Scoring is based on his disposition of the items.
[36] See Walter R. Mahler and Guyot Frazier, "Appraisal of Executive Performance: The Achilles Heel of Management Development," *Personnel,* Vol. 31, No. 5, March, 1955, pp. 429–441; William V. Mchaver and Willard E. Erickson, "A New Approach to Executive Appraisal," *Personnel,* Vol. 35, No. 1, July-August, 1958, pp. 8–14. For an excellent report of this practice as applied to managers, see Stephen Habbe, "Rating Managers in Terms of Job Duties," *Management Record,* Vol. 23, No. 10, October, 1961, pp. 23–29.
[37] Thomas A. Mahoney, Wallace Dohman and Thomas Jerdee, "Applying Yardsticks to Management," *Personnel,* Vol. 33, No. 6, May, 1957, pp. 556–62.

Personal and Performance Factors Most Frequently Appraised

PERSONAL CHARACTERISTICS	FREQUENCY OF MENTION	PERFORMANCE MEASURES	FREQUENCY OF MENTION
Personality	14	*General Performance*	11
Social acceptance	9	Quality of output	8
Motivation	5	Over-all performance	5
General personality	4	Quantity of output	5
Responsibility	3	Attendance	4
Character	2	Cost Control	1
Dependability	2	Safety	1
Self-control	2		
Confidence	1	*Supervision*	10
		General supervision	5
Mental	13	Training	5
Ability to learn	7	Motivating	3
Initiative	7	Directing	1
Judgment	4		
Analytical ability	2	*Organizing and planning*	8
Intelligence	1		
		Coordination	6
Leadership	3		
		Total	35
Skills	10		
Job knowledge	8		
Verbal facility	2		
Physical condition	3		
	—		
Total	43		

Fig. 19.4   Rating Yardsticks Applied to Managers

(From Thomas A. Mahoney et al., *op. cit.*, p. 560.)

seling interviews as largely non-directive, encouraging the trainee to "think out loud about his problems and progress."[38]

Counseling is expected to provide the personal touch in the educational process. In practice, much of the counseling has been based on periodic ratings. Senior managers discuss the ratings, suggesting means of improvement. In some plans, *gap sheets* have been used, showing the present evaluation on various qualifications and the necessary improvement to qualify for the next steps in the process. These gaps are the subject of specific planning for future development. Some rating scales for managers include a section in which steps to be taken are listed, together with a time-table for these actions.

As noted in the earlier discussion of counseling on ratings, that practice involves serious hazards. Many senior managers are not expert in counseling.

[38] See Earl G. Planty and Carlos A. Efferson, *Counseling Executives After Merit Rating or Evaluation*, New York: American Management Association, March, 1951; L. Clayton Hill and Arthur S. Hann, "Counseling Executives," in John W. Riegel, *Executive Development, op. cit.*, pp. 335ff.

They may dwell so heavily on short-comings that they discourage younger managers. The process of criticism may create feelings of resentment that hinder collaboration. Some firms have offered *training in counseling* for senior managers to prevent these adverse reactions. Others have developed *manager self-ratings* to be used in counseling. Some firms have discontinued formal discussion of the appraisals.[39]

3.6 University supplementary courses. Many programs supplement in-plant experience with participation in one or more university management development programs. Current programs vary in length, curricula, the level of management they are designed to help, and in the type of faculty they provide. Most of the shorter courses—two to four weeks—emphasize a non-technical approach to leadership training, somewhat similar to that provided for supervisors. Longer sessions—some continuing for three months—present capsule courses in the principal functional areas of management—finance, production, marketing, industrial relations, and accounting.

Most programs are designed for middle managers. A few have been restricted to high-middle and top management groups. Most of the programs are offered by resident faculty members.[40]

Several distinctive values are claimed for on-campus programs. Perhaps most important are the opportunity to think without the usual interruptions occasioned by office problems and the chance to exchange ideas and view-points with others of comparable interests and experience. Opportunities to become acquainted with the independent views and research findings presented by faculty members are also cited as valuable contributions. Challenging discussions involving broad economic and social perspectives are encouraged in the campus atmosphere. The concept of life-long learning for professional groups is well implemented in these programs.

3.7 Compensation and side effects. All these programs involve hazards as well as advantages. The selection of certain individuals may create serious jealousies and discontent among unsuccessful aspirants. The only answer is, of course, a careful explanation of the basis for selection and an honest willingness to consider any qualified person who may have been overlooked.

Another somewhat similar problem arises when the number of vacancies to be filled is smaller than the number of candidates who are ready for these responsibilities. This situation can be avoided by more careful forecasts.

[39] See John J. Grela and Frank B. Martin, Jr., "The Counseling Interview: Crux of a Man's Development," *Personnel Journal*, Vol. 37, No. 6, November, 1958, pp. 209–12; W. R. Spriegel and V. A. James, "Trends in Training and Development, 1940–1957," *Personnel*, Vol. 36, No. 1, January-February, 1959, pp. 60ff.

[40] For more detail on these programs, see George W. Bricker, Jr. and William A. Hertan, "Executive Development Programs," *Personnel Policies and Practices Report*, Par. 27,251, November 21, 1960, Englewood Cliffs, N.J.: Prentice-Hall, Inc.; American Management Association, "Annual Guide to Intensive Courses and Seminars for Executives"; Melvin Anshen, "Executive Development: In-company v. University Programs," *Harvard Business Review*, Vol. 32, No. 5, September-October, 1954, pp. 83–91; Paul F. Bunker, "Characteristics of Executive Development Programs," *Special Studies No. 14*, University of Arizona, College of Business and Public Administration, January, 1958.

At the same time, candidates can be clearly informed that some *cold storage training* and deferred application are to be expected. They are to be ready when and as needed and are not to expect that vacancies will be created for them.

Problems of compensation frequently appear. If candidates devote large amounts of their time and effort to learning, they may disqualify themselves for bonuses. Job rotation may have a similar effect. Managers may contribute less to day-to-day operations if they are busy attending conferences and lectures or absent for university short courses. They may, at the same time, be forced to neglect organizational relationships, so that they lose in the competition for offices, assistants, secretaries, expense accounts, and perhaps promotions.

Those included in the management development program usually gain in prestige and recognition on this account. They can be expected to make some personal sacrifices in return for the special opportunity thus provided. Some firms give special attention to salaries of trainees and assure them of continued participation in bonus plans. Without such special attention the firms fear that likely candidates may hesitate to participate in these programs.

4.0 APPRAISAL OF DEVELOPMENT PROGRAMS

Most firms appear to take for granted the worth and effectiveness of training and development programs. They assume that education is inherently good. Because it is also expensive, many firms are currently interested in evaluating their development programs, from those involving rank-and-file employees to those designed for top-level managers.

Evaluation requires identification of criteria. They can be inferred from the policy that explains the establishment of each program. Policy may have proposed, for example, to reduce grievances by supervisory training. Analysis of training needs also defines specific purposes for training programs. The success and value of each program can be judged by comparison with these objectives, if they have been clearly defined. Often this essential is overlooked, so that no one can tell how well a program has worked because no one is clear about what the program is supposed to do.

Evaluation should consider the soundness of policy, with careful consideration of the theory on which it is based. Policy may propose to use development programs for purposes they cannot achieve. Programs cannot take the place, for example, of personal aptitudes and talent. They cannot give participants the capacity for training.

4.1 Before-and-after comparisons. Probably the most common evaluative technique is the before-and-after comparison. Participants are examined at the start of the program and after they have completed it. Evidence of change is noted. This device is more easily adapted to development programs for supervisors than to those for middle managers or executives. The long-term management development process should probably be evaluated by stages or steps. The questions to be asked concern the usefulness of each step in the process. Studies can thus appraise the identification of potential, personnel appraisals, university programs, or personal counseling.

4.2 Control groups. In all applications of before-and-after checks, evaluators must be on the alert for extraneous factors and influences that contaminate the samples. Contacts with other employees, experience on the job, unplanned self-training, night school, or correspondence courses may be responsible for many observed changes. The best protection against errors of inference at this point is the control group. Such a group, excluded from the training, is given the same tests as the training group. Care must be taken to be sure that the control group is identical in all other respects.

4.3 Yardsticks and criteria. Most studies of management development conclude that it has been beneficial. Riegel, for example, reports that such programs improve present executives and all levels of supervision, provide a firm-wide understanding of problems, help supervisors do a better job, reduce the shock when key executives are lost, and offset the disadvantages of inbreeding by promotion from within. They help to identify better potential managers and thus improve promotions.[41]

Discussions of the values and contributions as well as the shortcomings and mistakes of management development have attracted wide attention in recent years. Evaluation has attempted to test what participants have learned at various stages, the comparative value of various methods of instruction, the special contributions of university programs, and the influence of development experience on managers' careers.[42]

For job training, speed and quality of output may be useful criteria. For supervisory training and management development, major dependence has been placed on the opinions of participants and those of associates and senior members of management.[43]

McMurry has noted eight tests which he concludes must be met by any successful management training program. It must (1) train candidates for specific positions, (2) define necessary qualities and skills, (3) include only trainees with adequate potential, (4) carefully determine which qualities

---

[41] John W. Riegel, *op. cit.,* pp. 10–14.

[42] See, for example, Louis A. Allen, "Does Management Development Develop Managers?," *Personnel,* Vol. 34, No. 2, September-October, 1957, pp. 18–25; Daniel M. Goodacre, II, "The Experimental Evaluation of Management Training," *ibid.,* Vol. 33, No. 6, May, 1957, pp. 534–538; Morris A. Saritt, "Is Management Training Worth While?" *ibid.,* Vol. 34, No. 2, September-October, 1957, pp. 79–82; Kenneth R. Andrews, "Is Management Training Effective?" *Harvard Business Review,* Vol. 35, No. 1, January-February, 1957, pp. 85–94; Thomas A. Mahoney, *et al.,* "A Research Approach to Management Development," Dubuque, Iowa: William C. Brown Company, 1960.

[43] See Charles B. Hedrick, "Feedback: A Method of Evaluating and Improving Management Training," *Personnel,* Vol. 32, No. 6, July, 1955, pp. 16–29; Ludwig Huttner and Raymond A. Katzell, "Developing a Yardstick of Supervisory Performance," *Personnel,* Vol. 33, No. 4, January, 1957, pp. 371–378; John B. Miner, "Management Development and Attitude Change," *Personnel Administration,* Vol. 24, No. 3, May-June, 1961, pp. 21–26.

can be developed through training, (5) use tested and proved techniques and procedures, (6) assure qualified trainers, (7) assure adequate trainee motivation, and (8) demonstrate results of the program.[44]

One practical question that must be faced in evaluating progress in self-development by executives is that of *time*. A Twentieth Century Fund study reported in 1959 that executives spend 3.5 hours per week in study to further their careers (see Figure 19.5). How much improvement can be expected from such an allocation? This question becomes more impressive if thought

HOW MUCH TIME DO EXECUTIVES SPEND ON THE JOB - HOW MUCH TIME AT LEISURE?	
ON THE JOB	**HOURS PER WK.**
AT OFFICE OR PLACE OF BUSINESS	42.7
AT HOME: PAPER WORK, ETC.	6.8
BUSINESS ENTERTAINING	2.6
TRAVEL BETWEEN HOME AND OFFICE	5.3
BUSINESS-SOCIAL FUNCTIONS OUTSIDE HOME	2.8
BUSINESS TRAVEL	6.6
TOTAL HOURS AT WORK	66.8
LEISURE ACTIVITIES	**HOURS**
CIVIC AND POLITICAL ACTIVITIES	2.4
LITERARY AND CULTURAL ACTIVITIES	5.2
HOBBIES, SPORTS, RELAXING, ETC.	21.8
STUDY TO FURTHER CAREER	3.5
CHURCH ACTIVITIES	2.1

Figure 19.5 Executive Time Budgets
SOURCE: Reproduced by permission from *Newsletter,* Twentieth Century Fund, No. 36, Fall, 1959.

is given to the obvious trends toward ever-widening management responsibilities. Three or four hours per week may be inadequate in preparing for these changes. Some consideration has been given to a policy that proposes something like *sabbatical leaves* for managers.

[44] Robert N. McMurry, "Executive Development: Dollars Down the Drain?" *Dun's Review and Modern Industry,* Vol. 76, No. 2, August, 1960, pp. 36–38.

5.0 SUMMARY

Modern management is impressed with the need for better, more competent present and future managers. This chapter first notes the policy that explains current interest, concern and activity in management development programs. The remainder of the chapter suggests the essential characteristics of planned programs for this purpose.

Helping managers prepare for growing responsibilities and maintaining competence in their jobs is a formidable assignment, although some managers assume that on-the-job experience can meet these needs.[45]

Defining the manager job, especially in terms of future requirements, presents many problems. Section 2 of the chapter has noted current confusion

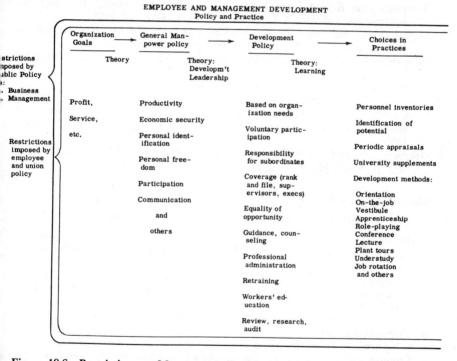

EMPLOYEE AND MANAGEMENT DEVELOPMENT
Policy and Practice

Figure 19.6   Restrictions on Management Decisions in Management Development

about the future of management and the details of prospective job specifications.

Section 3 outlines the major steps or stages in formal management development programs, with special emphasis on the identification of potential for development, maintenance of managerial inventories and forecasts of replacements, provision of development opportunities and the appraisal and counseling of participants. Section 4 suggests methods of evaluating training

[45] See "The Egghead Millionaires," *Fortune,* September, 1960, p. 174.

programs, with particular reference to management development.

Recruited, selected, developing employees and managers must be encouraged to work effectively toward accomplishment of the organization's mission. The next section of the book turns attention to the management problems of interest and incentivation.

SELECTED SUPPLEMENTARY READINGS

"The Company President—and the Impossible Job That Has To Be Done," *Acme Reporter* (official publication of the Association of Consulting Management Engineers, 347 Madison Avenue, New York 17, N.Y.) 1961 Series, Number 1, April, 1961.

Executive Development in Small Business, Washington, D.C.: Small Business Administration, 1954.

Hemphill, John K. and Lewis B. Ward, "The Executive Study," *Personnel Administration,* Vol. 21, No. 1, pp. 49–55, January-February, 1958.

Kepner, C. H., and Tregoe, B. B., "Developing Decision Makers," *Harvard Business Review,* Vol. 38, No. 5, pp. 115–125, September-October, 1960.

Livingston, Robert Teviot, *The Managers' Job,* chap. 1. New York: Columbia University Press, 1960.

Shartle, Carroll L., *Executive Performance and Leadership,* chap. 10. Englewood Cliffs, N.J.: Prentice-Hall, Inc., 1956.

Viteles, Morris S., "Human Relations and the Humanities in the Education of Business Leaders," *Personnel Psychology,* Vol. 12, pp. 1–28, No. 1, Spring, 1959.

Wikstrom, Walter S., "Identifying Comers in Management," *Management Record,* Vol. 24, No. 3, March, 1962, pp. 13–16.

SHORT CASE PROBLEM 19.1

University Training for Management Development

Mr. Yale, vice-president in charge of industrial relations for the Peeper Company, is beginning to wonder if he acted too rapidly in encouraging the firm to undertake a program of management development. He made a study of probable losses of managerial manpower during the next ten years. That study indicates that such losses will be heavy—that the trend is upward in that about six times as many men will probably be lost in the tenth year as in the first year. On the basis of this forecast, Mr. Yale has secured an authorization to undertake a formal management development program.

As his first step, he asked all executives to nominate candidates for special training and preparation. On the basis of these nominations, he has selected two men to be sent to a special university executive-development program. It is expected that, on the basis of this experience, they may make suggestions for other parts of the total management development program.

Neither of the two men thus selected wishes to attend the university program. They give several reasons: 12 weeks is too long to be away from their jobs; they are not university graduates and will not feel at home in what is essentially a graduate school atmosphere; they think their absence may adversely affect salary adjustments for them in the next year; one of them refuses to leave his family for such an extended period.

Problem: On the basis of this limited summary of the situation, what would you suggest to Mr. Yale? Does he simply have the wrong candidates? Are the men right in their objections? How would you proceed?

SHORT CASE PROBLEM 19.2

The Unhappy Developee*

A district manager in a large, geographically decentralized company is notified that he is being promoted to a policy level position at headquarters. It is a big promotion with a large salary increase. His role in the organization will be a much more powerful one, and he will be associated with the major executives of the firm.

The headquarters group who selected him for this position have carefully considered a number of possible candidates. This man stands out among them in a way which makes him the natural choice. His performance has been under observation for some time, and there is little question that he possesses the necessary qualifications, not only for this opening but for an even higher position. There is genuine satisfaction that such an outstanding candidate is available.

The man is appalled. He doesn't want the job. His goal, as he expresses it, is to be the "best damned district manager in the company." He enjoys his direct associations with operating people in the field, and he doesn't want a policy level job. He and his wife enjoy the kind of life they have created in a small city, and they dislike actively both the living conditions and the social obligations of the headquarters city.

He expresses his feelings as strongly as he can, but his objections are brushed aside. The organization's needs are such that his refusal to accept the promotion would be unthinkable. His superiors say to themselves that of course when he has settled in to the new job, he will recognize that it was the right thing. And so he makes the move.

Problem: What policy can you infer from this incident? How would you forecast the outcome in terms of both the firm and the individual?

SHORT CASE PROBLEM 19.3

Counseling on Appraisals

Bill Eakles is one of four assistant managers in the Planning Division of Jones Electronic Controls Corporation in Baltimore, Maryland. He reports to Chuck England, manager of the division. Bill has held his present position for two years. Bill and Chuck have been friends for a longer period. Both have families, and their wives and children are frequently together. Bill's office is one floor down, directly below Chuck's.

Jones Electronic has a program of annual appraisals for all managers. Each manager rates all those who report directly to him, using a linear scale.

Last year was the first time Chuck had rated Bill. Chuck's rating at that time had indicated "average" on all qualities. This year, he has rated Bill "excellent" on quantity and quality of work and on knowledge of the job. He has rated "attitude toward work" as average and "capacity to develop" as average. On two items, "initiative" and "attitude toward others," Chuck has rated Bill as "less than average."

Appraisal practice requires that the rater discuss the rating with each ratee. Chuck has asked Bill to come in for a discussion of his rating.

Problem: 1. Assume that this discussion is scheduled for our next class period. Be prepared to play the part of either Bill or Chuck in this discussion.

2. If you see objections to this procedure, be prepared to suggest a better one (for example, forced choice or field review) and to demonstrate its superiority.

* (Quoted by permission from Douglas McGregor, *The Human Side of Enterprise*, New York: McGraw-Hill Book Company, Inc., 1960, pp. 50–51.

SHORT CASE PROBLEM 19.4

Deficiency in Management Skills

State University of ————

OFFICE MEMORANDUM

FILE: Hansen, Niels
DATE: April 14, 1958

TO: Files
FROM: Professor Clyde Newcomb
RE: Program for Niels Hansen

Visit today from Mr. Oscar Swenson, president of Swirl-Clean, 4980 Cicero Avenue, Chicago, Illinois. He came in to talk about Niels Hansen, who graduated from the Business School in 1951. Hansen majored with me in Management. He graduated third from the top in the Class of '51. He went to work immediately in Swirl-Clean as an assistant in the Production Department. His earlier work in Engineering was helpful; he was promoted regularly and is now Production Manager.

In 1957, Swirl-Clean employed Kusak and Associates, New York consulting firm, to conduct a management audit. They recommended a number of changes and made specific suggestions with respect to Niels. They concluded that he is a person of great potential but is quite unsatisfactory in his present position. They believe that he is a likely candidate for the general manager job and perhaps president if he can overcome present limitations, but they recommend releasing him promptly if he does not take immediate steps to remove what they regard as obvious deficiencies.

The consultants have discovered a great deal of evidence that indicates Niels simply cannot communicate effectively. According to their report, his assistants do not understand him. The assistants' impression of his objectives and personal values is, in the opinion of consultants, almost 180 degrees away from the real Niels. He has created an impression of coldness and ruthlessness that is widely reported among employees in the division. That impression has been responsible for resignations of several senior employees and two assistant managers. Niels' reputation on this point has been reported back to several colleges, where it is creating problems in recruitment. Within the organization, at least two members of the management group have stated bluntly that they do not agree with Niels and could not work with him if he were promoted.

Mr. Swenson agrees with the report of the consulting firm. He knows Niels and agrees that he is not at all the kind of person represented by impressions of employees in his department. Mr. Swenson feels that Niels is in many respects the most competent planner and the best potential candidate for general manager available in present management. For that reason, he has proposed to Niels that Niels return here to the University, on paid leave, to develop the skills which he lacks. Mr. Swenson says the firm is willing to keep Niels here for one quarter or two next year if we can help him. I told Mr. Swenson I would discuss the problem with other members of the faculty and advise him with respect to our recommendations.

Problem: Do you think the University can do anything for Niels? Would you recommend that he come back to the University? If so, for how long? What specific education or training would you recommend for him? What courses in your present curriculum would be helpful to him in developing the skills he apparently lacks? (Consider such courses as Public Speaking, Human Relations, Psychological Aspects of Management, Industrial Relations, and any others you might suggest from outside your school or department or management).

VI. INCENTIVES IN WORK

20. *Financial Incentives: Policy*

Managers plan and create or maintain working organizations. They staff the organization with men and women selected to meet its needs and to perform the work to be done. They recruit and select with that objective in mind. They train and assist in the continuing self-improvement and development of workers—from rank-and-file recruits to experienced craftsmen, supervisors, managers, and executives—as noted in immediately preceding chapters. All these managerial activities are undertaken to permit the organization to carry out its mission by providing an appropriate setting —an effective tone and atmosphere and structure of interpersonal relationships for work.

Managers must also provide *incentives* for working. They have the responsibility to get those who are employed in the organization to do the jobs essential to the effective accomplishment of its mission. It is their job to *incentivate*—to stimulate and maintain appropriate motivation among all those who make up the personnel of the organization. Workers at all levels must somehow be persuaded to commit themselves to the jobs assigned to them and to accept the role of workers and apply their skills, energies, and efforts to individual jobs.

Much of the discussion in earlier chapters has focused on *indirect incentivation* through the development of an effective work setting—in organization, in staffing, and in assisting in individual development. In this section of the book, attention turns to direct incentivation of individuals and groups within the framework of the working organization.

In democratic societies, the principal type of personal incentivation used by managers is the *reward*. Incentivating is thus largely a process of rewarding. In some earlier periods, managers leaned heavily on negative rewards, i.e., *penalties* for failure to do the work assigned. In autocratic societies in which

439

workers were slaves, severe penalties for inadequate performance were regarded as the most effective incentives.

In early industrialized societies, the free employer could discharge workers
he regarded as unsatisfactory. As employer freedom to hire and fire was restricted, in part by the growth of unions and in part by more limited supplies
of labor, the carrot has been substituted for the whip, and rewards for excellence in working have largely replaced penalties for noncompliance or less-
than-satisfactory performance.

Of all rewards, by far the most obvious in industrial societies are those
that may be described as financial or monetary. Independent artisans, even
during the agricultural period, were paid for their contributions. Serfs also
received a sort of payment in kind in their sharing of the crops they tended
for the lord of the agricultural manor. The journeymen of the handicraft
period were "day" workers and received wages for their services. With industrialization, wages and salaries became the most common of all rewards
for work. The wage has frequently been described as the *cash nexus* between
employers and employees. The dollar wage or salary has been supplemented
by a wide range of premiums, bonuses, stock ownership, profit-sharing, stock
options and so-called "fringes" that are paid as additions to the formal wage.

This chapter is the first of five that deal with the manager's problems in
incentivation and related policy and practice. This and the following two
chapters are concerned with financial incentives: wages, salaries, more complicated methods of payment, and the fringes of employee benefits and
services.

Few managers would claim that they make the policies on wages. As in
other managerial policy, managers work within restrictions imposed by public
policy and those of employees and their unions. Policy on financial incentives
is, in other words, tripartite in development and formulation. The first section of this chapter considers public policy on wages and salaries. A second
section notes the policies of employees and unions. Section 3 outlines the
policy decisions to be made by management within the framework thus
imposed.

1.0   PUBLIC POLICY ON COMPENSATION

Managerial policy on financial compensation feels the strong influence
of public policy in this area. Wages and salaries are recognized as the largest
single segment of national income, the major source of disposable income
and hence of the demand for goods and services. Much of their impact in
the markets of the nation is immediate; it cannot be delayed. Recognition of
varying *propensities to spend* and to save has emphasized this importance
of wage and salary income.

Not all financial compensation is available for immediate expenditures.
Payments to the accounts of employees for numerous benefits, such as pensions, life and health insurance, disability, sick leave, hospitalization, and

other benefits represent *deferred income.* Nevertheless, these supplements to wages and salaries become significant sources of demand. Federal accounting recognizes this complex of payments in its measurement and reporting of income distribution. Monthly reports in *Economic Indicators,* the *Survey of Current Business,* and elsewhere show the "compensation of employees"— not merely wages and salaries—as a share of national income. Figure 20.1 provides a picture of variations in this distribution in the years since the great depression of 1929–1935.

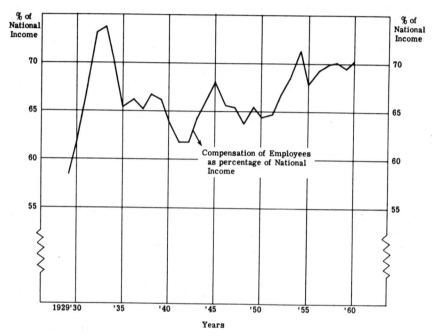

Figure 20.1   Compensation of Employees as a Percentage of National Income, 1929–1960.
SOURCE: U.S. Department of Commerce data.

The importance of personal income as a tax base is also widely recognized. Ability to pay—an elementary criterion of appropriate tax incidence—is essentially a matter of income. Direct taxation of income has become a continually more important source of revenue for both federal and state governments. This trend has continued in spite of conflicting theory that emphasizes the social importance of investment and the hazards of tax and fiscal policy that reduces both private funds available for investment and incentives for saving.

1.1   Balance of distributive shares. Government—especially at the federal level—is now charged with responsibility for directing the distribution of national income in a manner designed to encourage prosperity and growth and to prevent recession and stagnation. This objective prescribes delicate balances between income available for immediate expenditure and consumption and income to be saved and invested. The rate of growth in the national economy is closely related to and influenced by this distribution.

On the one hand, public agencies must take into account the growing investment requirements specified by a continually rising *capital-worker ratio*. In manufacturing industries, for example, each employee must be equipped with from $3,000 to $100,000 of plant facilities, machinery, and tools. Such capital equipment is continually deteriorating. It wears out and may become obsolete in only a few years. Meanwhile, as the labor force continues to grow—with the rate of growth rising—capital investment must expand to provide the necessary facilities for a million or more new workers each year.

Income allocated to investment cannot, at the same time, be made available for consumption. Yet the roots of demand for the goods and services to be produced are to be found in the income available for spending. For this reason, many of the most critical decisions for public policy concern the direction to be given to distribution of the national income. Another basic question concerns the desirable rate of growth in gross national product —two per cent, or four, or more. Another question concerns the weight to be given to maintaining high levels of employment.

Public policy recognizes that increased distributions of income to low-wage groups may have much more of an impact on immediate spending and consumption than the same amounts distributed to high wage and salaried groups. On the other hand, increases in amounts or shares distributed as personal income may encourage the purchase of luxuries—gadgets and mink coats—at the expense of saving, investment, or public defense or education.

1.2   Progress in living scales. Public policy proposes that material living scales—*the goods and services available to citizens*—shall show a persistent upward trend. Political stability is regarded as dependent on continual improvement in living scales. Citizens are more satisfied and less likely to be charmed by proposals for radical political and economic change if they can anticipate better living in the future. At the same time, in democratic societies, humanitarian considerations are regarded as requiring the reduction of poverty and dependency.

The possibility of such *continuing advances* is rarely questioned. Historic evidence supports the theory that progress in living scales faces no limits. In this country, studies of wages and their purchasing power over the century and a half for which such data are available indicate that real wages have increased at an average rate of about one per cent per year. Such growth has not been steady and uniform; it is marked by periods of slower and more rapid growth and of actual declines.[1]

1.3   Economic growth and productivity. Public policy proposes that

[1] For data and greater detail, see Dale Yoder and H. G. Heneman, Jr., *Labor Economics and Industrial Relations,* Cincinnati: South-Western Publishing Company,

wages and salaries are to participate in a continuing expansion of the national economy as measured by the gross national product. It proposes, in effect, to bake a bigger cake for all to share. International competition with respect to rates of growth has attracted wide attention. Newly industrialized nations have experienced very high rates of growth, in part because they started from low levels. Soviet Russia has made impressive progress in expanding its gross national product. Many Americans have become concerned because of our own relatively slow advances.

Recent expressions of public policy propose rapid economic growth, rising average worker productivity, and rising wages to keep pace with the increase in average productivity. This policy is subject to frequent criticism, for increases in average productivity represent the contributions of all factors of production. Current policy appears to assume, however, that proportionate contributions remain fairly stable, so that labor is entitled to its proportionate share of any increase.

Common expressions of this policy imply that wage and salary receivers should receive wage increases equal to the national average growth in productivity. However, average man-hour increases in productivity vary widely from industry to industry and firm to firm. Applications of the policy can, for this reason, create serious problems in industries in which man-hour productivity increases at less than the average rate or actually decreases.[2]

For the last fifty years, the overall annual average has been about 2.2 per cent. These conclusions relate output in constant dollar value to paid hours of work. Parallel studies by the federal Department of Commerce use a different base—hours actually worked. Department of Commerce calculations show an average annual increase since World War II of about 3.5 per cent per year, compared with 2.2 per cent for the last fifty years. These and other studies agree that the rate of increase has speeded somewhat since World War II, so that the present average may be almost 4 per cent per year.[3]

1.4 Avoiding inflation. At the same time that public policy regards

---

1959, pp. 579ff; also "Employment and Earnings Statistics for the United States, 1909–1960," *Bulletin 1312*, U.S. Bureau of Labor Statistics, 1961.

[2] See Figure 3.8, Chapter 3; "The Nation's Rapidly Rising Productivity," *Labor's Economic Review*, Vol. 3, No. 11, November, 1958; "Wages, Prices, Profits and Productivity," New York: The American Assembly, Columbia University, June, 1959; Solomon Fabricant, "Basic Facts on Productivity Change," New York: National Bureau of Economic Research, 1959.

[3] See "Indexes of Output Per Man Hour for Selected Industries," Washington, D.C.: Bureau of Labor Statistics, April, 1959; also Chapter 3, section 1.6; also John W. Kendrick, *Productivity Trends in the United States,* New York: National Bureau of Economic Research, 1961.

In 1961, member nations in the Organization for Economic Cooperation sought to secure agreement on a goal of from 4 to 5 per cent growth per year. Meanwhile, in this country, wage increases have exceeded productivity gains in short-term selected periods in many industries. T. A. Anderson cited numerous illustrations in steel, non-electrical machinery, electrical machinery, automobiles, fabricated metal products, rubber, foods, petroleum, nonferrous metals, and chemicals. See his "Employment, Growth and Price Levels," *Hearings,* Joint Economic Commitee, Washington, D.C.: Government Printing Office, 1959.

continuing increases in wages as essential to keep pace with rising productivity, it opposes such wage increases as may generate large-scale, *wage-push inflation*. Public opinion recognizes the dangers of inflation: it may create hardships for fixed-dollar-income families and citizens; inflation may wipe out the value of wage increases. At the same time, many citizens believe that a small amount of inflation is necessary to stimulate high levels of growth. They conclude that a little inflation, say a one per cent rise in price levels per year, is a reasonable price to pay for rapid growth. In general, therefore, public policy seeks to control and limit rather than to prevent inflation.

1.5 International competition. With the world-wide spread of industrialization in the years since World War II, international competition has become a matter of growing concern. As foreign nations have adopted American technologies and purchased American equipment and as they have secured additional capital, they have increased the productivity of their manpower as well as their total production. Their finished products have sometimes become available in American markets at prices lower than those for comparable domestic products. Japanese steels, photographic, optical, and electronic goods, and German cutlery and optical products illustrate these developments.

A growing concern in this country attaches to the hazards of pricing ourselves out of international markets. Public policy seeks to avoid wage increases that may exert this effect. While no legislative or other formal statements of public policy on this point can be cited, the pressure of this intention has been clearly recognized by management. A presidential communication to the steel industry in 1961, for example, expressed the hope that prices would not be increased at that time. It was widely interpreted as a request to hold wage increases to limits prescribed by existing prices.

1.6 Short-term stability. Over periods of years, wages are to increase, to share in economic growth and greater productivity. For the short term, policy seeks stability, regularity, an even, week-to-week, month to month real income. It proposes to avoid the feast and famine aspects of wage payments, the short-term boom and bust in worker income. To a large degree, this is employment policy rather than wage policy, but the two are interrelated. Thus the Fair Labor Standards Act permits extensive overtime without premium pay to industries that guarantee 2080 hours of work with pay each year.

1.7 Need basis. Public policy proposes to put a *floor under wages* that will eliminate what are regarded as *substandard rates*. Wages are to insure wage-earners minimum *standards of comfort and decency*. To implement this policy, state agencies prescribe minimum wage rates for specified occupations in 33 states and the District of Columbia, and federal legislation —the Fair Labor Standards Act of 1938—makes similar provisions for interstate industry.

It should be noted that all such legislation applies to *wage rates* rather than to *earnings*. It makes numerous assumptions: that those affected are supporting average-sized families; that they are working full weeks; that budget studies can calculate living costs at comfort and decency levels; that requirement of these minimum rates will not adversely affect employment.

Legislation for this purpose has a long history. Massachusetts passed the earliest state law in 1912. Some of the state laws set specific rates; others authorize minimum wage commissions or other agencies to determine appropriate figures from time to time.

Both federal and state legislation setting minimal rates go beyond the living wage objective. While that is the yardstick in the Fair Labor Standards Act, the federal Davis-Bacon Act of 1931 uses a different criterion. It, and several similar state laws, are *prevailing wage* acts. They require that workers on public construction be paid the prevailing rates in the locality. *Public contract* laws, illustrated by the Walsh-Healey Act of 1936, require prevailing rates on materials furnished by contract with public agencies.

Managers are well aware of the influence of the federal Wage and Hour law or Fair Labor Standards Act. It sets minimum rates of pay and requires premium rates of pay for overtime in excess of 40 hours per week. Its impact extends beyond recipients of minimal rates, for higher wage groups receive increases to maintain differentials. Minimum rates have risen from 25 cents per hour in 1938 to $1.15 per hour in 1961.[4]

Several studies have sought to evaluate the effects of public policy as expressed in minimum wage legislation. Their conclusions are not uniform. It is apparent, however, that public intervention may exert an adverse effect on employment in particular industries. To some degree, this change may result—if labor is sufficiently mobile—in a superior allocation of manpower resources in the total economy. It is clear, also, that raising minima may create inflationary pressures,[5] but they may be offset by improved utilization and management. Public policy must balance these relatively unpredictable adverse effects against the economic and humanitarian gains to be achieved by such intervention.

---

[4] Revisions in 1961 raised the minimum rates to $1.25 and increased coverage by an estimated two million employees. The 1961 legislation set a minimum rate of $1.15 for two years and $1.25 in 1963 for workers already covered. For employers covered for the first time, rates start at $1.00 and move to $1.25 after three years. For these employees, there are no overtime pay requirements for two years. For the third year, premium pay begins after 44 hours. For the fourth year, the rates increase after 42 hours. In the fifth year and thereafter, overtime must be paid for time over 40 hours per week, as for all other covered employers.

Coverage is described as including employers "engaged in interstate commerce or in the production of goods for such commerce," but numerous industries and occupations have been excluded. Extensions of coverage in 1961 were directed mainly at retail and service establishments.

[5] Donald E. Cullen, "Minimum Wage Laws," Ithaca, N.Y.: New York State School of Industrial and Labor Relations, February, 1961; Isador Lubin and Charles A. Pearce, "New York's Minimum Wage Law: The First Twenty Years," *Industrial and Labor Relations Review*, Vol. 11, No. 2, January, 1958, pp. 203–19; Arnold J. Tolles, "American Minimum Wage Laws: Their Purposes and Results," *Proceedings*, Industrial Relations Research Association, 1959, pp. 107–108.

1.8 Equal pay rules. So-called *equal pay laws* in several states and similar rules in federal legislation seek to prevent *sex differentials* in wages. They require that wages be *job rates* rather than *personal rates*. Their intention is clear. It is also clear that they may have a quite different effect from that intended. Employers, faced with this requirement in state laws, may prefer male workers. As a result, the legislation may eliminate many jobs for women. It is frequently charged that this has been the principal objective of many advocates of equal pay laws.[6]

1.9 Time, place, form of wages. Public policy intends that wages shall be paid when due. Legislation specifies, in the various states, that wages shall be paid at regular intervals (one-week or two-week), and that they shall be paid in cash or equivalent. The second of these requirements is designed to prevent payment in *scrip,* a special currency sometimes used to restrict employee expenditures to company stores. Rules frequently prohibit payment in saloons. All states have *lien laws* that give wages a preferred status among debts. The carpenter who works on a house, for example, has a wage claim that must be satisfied before the claims of other creditors for hardware, lumber, or other building materials.[7]

2.0 EMPLOYEE AND UNION POLICY

Experienced managers recognize that policy on wages is perhaps the most common subject for collective bargaining. Wages and hours are the traditional and basic areas for negotiation, so much so that many other subjects may be treated as phases or aspects of compensation. Benefits and services are frequently evaluated in terms of their financial costs and as additions to wages, and work rules may be translated to make them essentially financial matters.

Employees presumably have their personal wage and salary policies. They have in mind their intentions, which are expressed in their selections of job opportunities. Personal policies may appear to employees to justify changing jobs or employers if they regard compensation as inadequate. Employee policies may be inferred from their actions; economic analysis of labor supply expresses such inferences. For more tangible expressions of employee policy, however, union declarations and demands provide available evidence. Insofar as unions are democratic, they may be accepted as spokesmen for their members and perhaps for unorganized workers as well. In any case, their influence on managerial wage policy is more apparent and direct than that of individual workers.

Major planks in union wage platforms have been noted in Chapter 10,

[6] On this point, see Vernon Seigler, "Equal Pay for Women Laws: Are They Desirable," *Labor Law Journal,* Vol. 5, No. 10, October, 1954, pp. 663–88ff.

[7] Most firms now pay both salaried and hourly-rated employees by check. Biweekly or semimonthly payments are most common for office workers; weekly payments are general for blue-collar workers. See *Personnel Policies and Practices Report,* Par. 158, No. 15–32, 1961.

including their emphasis on *standardization* and on *wage packages* that include numerous employee benefits and services. Modern policy and practice in wage and salary administration is influenced by these proposals and by several more specific policies that deserve attention.

2.1   The policy of "more." Unquestionably, the most widely recognized union policy is one that proposes continuous increases in real wages. This persistent policy is memorialized in the classic reply attributed to Samuel Gompers, first president of the American Federation of Labor. Questioned by an irritated employer spokesman as to whether unions had any ultimate standard on which wage demands were based, Gompers is reputed to have declared that the standard was simple—"more."

Union policy proposes that wages and the purchasing power of wages shall continue to rise, so that wage earners can anticipate and achieve ever higher scales of living. To that end, more specific policy may advance several proposals, depending on the setting. Thus, in a period of rising prices, union policy may propose a close tie with costs of living. Unions may demand *escalator clauses* that require *automatic increases* in wage rates to match advances in the consumer price index. Under different circumstances, unions may seek to incorporate the gains from such clauses in the *basic wage,* so that they will not be lost if retail prices soften.

The general policy of *more* may take a different form if, in periods of prosperity, labor's share in total national income shows a tendency to decline. Then, union policy may emphasize *purchasing power* and the hazards of declining or inadequate consumer demand as a basis for increases.

2.2   Sharing productivity. As the economy expands and gross national product grows, a persistent union policy demands that labor be granted its share in such increases. This policy may take the form of negotiated *productivity increases* or *improvement clauses.* These clauses provide for automatic increases, usually annual, amounting to a stated fraction of total increases in man-hour productivity. Sometimes the proposal contemplates experience in the industry or firm as the base; employees, as members of the organization, are to receive a fixed proportion of whatever increase is achieved. Sometimes, union policy argues for an annual advance related to the average productivity increase in the national economy.

In their advocacy of this second type of productivity increase, unions must face a question about industries and firms that do not experience an average increase. Some statements of union policy suggest that policy should not be changed in such cases. They argue that the union pressure will encourage more effective management, to the benefit of the entire economy. To the argument that the policy may bankrupt some employers, unions may answer that firms so vulnerable had better go out of business. Unions may, on the other hand, recognize the hazards to their members and compromise the policy.

Union policy on sharing productivity sees no wage-push inflation inherent in such proposals. Since increases are assumed to represent only labor's share in rising output, the union position holds that no generation of pressure for higher prices is involved. Productivity increases, from this viewpoint, are only a substitute for reductions in prices to consumers.

With respect to inflation, union policy is by no means clear. Unions and their members recognize the hazards to real earnings in continuing price advances. On the other hand, unions may advocate a little inflation as necessary to insure economic growth.[8]

2.3 Stable earnings. Unions propose to increase week-to-week stability of earnings for their members through negotiated rates and working conditions. Collective agreements propose long-term stability in rates; they provide wage contracts extending over multi-year periods. Reopening clauses can be limited to adjustments for living costs and rising productivity. Throughout the same periods, clauses that regulate overtime and assure fairness in work assignments also tend to stabilize earnings.

With the same goal in mind, union policy advocates benefits—unemployment, sickness, and disability—to maintain employee income during periods of enforced idleness. In effect, policy proposes an approximation of an *annual wage.*

2.4 Fairness through standardization. Common but not universal union wage policy proposes standardized job rates, a *union scale* that assures the same rate of pay to all workers in the same job classification. In part, this policy is justified as a necessity in collective bargaining; negotiation could not extend to the setting of rates for each individual worker. In part, policy assumes that the range of performance among workers on the same job is too small to justify differentials in pay. Unions may argue that no fair basis for discrimination among such workers can be found and that variations in rates would tend to reflect favoritism and might be used to alienate individual workers from their colleagues and the union.

Some union policy, it must be recognized, favors individual adjustments in earnings based on output. Some unions—coal miners are an example— propose a guaranteed minimum with payments above the level tied to individual productivity.

2.5 Differentials in wages. Union policy has its own conflicts. Proposals to insure continuing advances and to adjust for changing living costs frequently emerge as demands for across-the-board cents-per-hour adjustments. As such, they tend to narrow wage structures, bringing lowest rates nearer to those that are highest. Unions are not unaware of the criterion of need which may appear to justify larger proportionate increases in lower wage classes. On the other hand, many of their members seek to preserve the differentials in rates that have historically marked their occupations.

Wage patterns have a strong influence on wage policy. Unions frequently seek to keep wages of their members in a consistent, long-term pattern, as compared with those in other industries or localities. Policy may propose to

[8] For a union statement, see "Policies for Economic Growth," *AFL-CIO Publication No. 87,* 1959.

equalize carpenter rates with those in another city or to maintain a 15 cent or 5 per cent premium over rates in a nearby locality.

3.0 TRIPARTITE POLICY

Managers develop compensation policy for their organizations within the constraints and restrictions imposed by public and employee-union objectives. They balance the pressures from these sources and add their own preferences to determine intended courses for their firms. Public agencies require consideration of another component: specific compensation policies imposed by legislative bodies. In private firms, managers may be guided by similar declarations by stockholders and their representatives. In many firms, on the other hand, the wage policies of stockholders must be presumed; they have not been articulated.

Manager decisions on compensation policy are further complicated by the difficulty of implementing intentions in this area. Even the most commendable policies, with wide public and employee acceptance, encounter difficulty in the applications of yardsticks and criteria. Questions arise as to what may properly be regarded as *needs*—whether these include silk hose, tobacco, entertainment, and other components of the family market basket. Similar questions may be raised with respect to *contributions,* for satisfactory objective measures are often unavailable. Attempts to combine elements of policy multiply these difficulties; what appears reasonable on the basis of need, for example, may be quite unsatisfactory on the basis of contribution.

No simple formula distinguishes the contributions of the several factors in production. Most of the so-called scientific bases for wages accept market prices as measures of relative contributions. The conclusion is inescapable; even with agreement on the broad range of compensation policy, no one can say for sure what is an accurate application to a particular job rate. Implementation involves unavoidable approximations and hence opportunities for criticism and controversy.

3.1 Compensation-incentivation theory. Not all managers, by any means, subscribe to the same theories with respect to the relationships between wages and salaries and on-the-job performance. Most managers appear to assume that the ranges for wages and salaries within which they can exercise discretion are rather narrowly limited by labor and product markets. They have no wide range of choice. Lower limits are set by *current market prices* for these services, including minimal wages set by law. Employers cannot hire and retain workers at lower rates. They cannot greatly exceed market prices because to do so would generate costs that would exclude their products in competition with those of other employers.

Managers see wages, salaries, and other financial compensation as *labor costs.* They can pay wages above market prices if they make a superior application as evidenced by reduced labor costs. If they see little possibility of such improvements in applications of labor, their range of choice with respect to rates of pay is thus restricted. Thus a manager relates wage offers to his estimates of elasticities of demand in product markets and elasticities of supplies in labor markets.

This range of discretion in compensation is also influenced by the significance of labor costs in various industries. Elasticities in demands for labor vary inversely with proportions of labor costs to total costs. In industries with high capital-worker ratios and comparatively small proportions of labor costs—petroleum and chemicals, for example—upper limits on wage offers may be quite flexible. In high-labor-cost industries, managers are likely to regard themselves as sharply restricted. Automobile production, meat packing, steel, textile products and home-building are examples of such industries. One study of changing prices and costs gives strong support for this viewpoint; labor costs per unit were found to have behaved "more like a fixed cost than a variable one."[9]

As the other side of the same coin, managers regard payments in excess of market wages as major incentives for superior performance. They offer premium wages for premium contributions. They expect the possibility of extra earnings to stimulate extra effort. Their theory of work regards the offer of higher earnings as the carrot of persuasion.

Some managers hold that market rates must provide reasonable economic security; these rates must meet the minimal material needs of workers. Without such security, employees could not be expected to give their full attention and effort to the jobs to be done. Other managers see unfulfilled personal needs as the *principal spur to effort*. They argue that workers put forth their best efforts when hard times reduce their security. They insist that insecurity—perhaps in the form of frequent cycles of extensive unemployment with reductions in earnings—is necessary to maintain a high work motivation.

In the long years in which wage theory was essentially a theory of subsistence, employers and managers regarded their action as restricted by the *natural laws* that limited income allocations to wage earners. Employers could not, in the short run, pay wages in excess of their available, liquid funds. In the long run, wage levels were set by inexorable natural law that caused supplies of labor to increase up to the limits of subsistence.

Later theory related wage payments to the productivity of workers and thus expanded the range of discretion for managers. In perfect competition, wages tended to approximate the *marginal productivity* or, as later amended, the *marginal revenue* of labor in each sharply defined labor market. The recognition of a relationship between wages and productivity implied that employees might raise wages by increasing their contributions. Managers might pay higher wages if workers increased their effectiveness. For both workers and managers, this later analysis opened the possibility of *market*

      [9] Charles L. Schultze and Joseph L. Tryon, "Prices and Costs in Manufacturing Industries," *Study Paper No. 17,* Joint Committee Print, 86th Cong., Washington, D.C.: Government Printing Office, 1960.

controls that could raise or lower wage levels. Such a viewpoint encouraged the unionization of employees and the development of business unionism in free labor markets. At the same time, it justified managerial efforts to increase output by dangling the possibility of extra earnings. Piece rates and more complicated premiums and bonuses express these traditional theories of work and incentivation.

Many managers base their policy on this viewpoint. Current theory, however, gives much less weight to natural laws and much more to the complexity of motivation in work. Modern compensation theory begins with the assumption that the employer must pay for the effort and skill contributed by members of his working organization. Free workers must be paid to work. Although levels of their performance and contribution may be influenced by many considerations other than their pay, none of these others can take the place of pay. Further, variations in the amounts and methods of payment may influence the worker's level of performance.

This viewpoint recognizes the indirect and derived nature of demand in modern work. Few workers work to satisfy their own direct demands. They do not generally eat or wear the products on which they are working. They work to produce goods or services for an employer—to satisfy his demands and specifications. They know, however, that he does not intend to use the products himself. He may produce to meet the demands of merchants, who in turn prepare themselves to satisfy customers. In such a roundabout production process, no simple substitute for wages and salaries is conceivable. Barter is impracticable. Direct personal production and consumption—the back to nature movement—is impossible with modern populations. Wages are quite realistically an essential cash nexus or link.

At this point, some managers conclude that economic need is the dominating influence on performance. They assume, therefore, that if wages can be held at levels that leave many unsatisfied needs, employees will work harder than if wage levels assure the satisfaction of all major or basic needs. Other theory, however, holds that levels of performance are raised by economic security. It argues that wages must be adequate to assure satisfaction of current needs of workers.

Modern work theory provides at least a partial resolution for this apparent contradiction. It suggests that wages and supplementary forms of financial compensation have an important but limited role in incentivation. They may set the stage for developing higher levels of motivation in work. They are basic essentials and prerequisites for additional incentives. Current theory notes that relatively high levels of financial compensation with accompanying economic security may encourage attitudes of indifference. Employees may assume that about all they need to do is just enough to get by and hold their jobs. At this point, however, within what Dubin has described as a "range of indifference," special bonuses or premiums may encourage added effort. They may be roughly compared to the trading stamps distributed by retail stores. They may have little effect, particularly if their provision is widespread. Some managers are less impressed with the effectiveness of individual premiums—available for superior performance—than with *group rewards*. They conclude that group pressures, stimulated by the possibility of extra earnings, are more effective than individual bonuses.

A considerable volume of speculation surrounds the question as to what effect the *affluent society* may have on the influence of financial compensation as an incentive to work. Affluence, it may be noted, represents a continuation and extension of a long trend. It is not an abrupt, revolutionary change. Just as rising living scales in the past have increased the influence of nonfinancial incentives, affluence may make nonfinancial considerations even more influential in the future.

3.2 Going wages. The easiest wage policy, for many managers, is one that proposes to let others make the decisions and to follow a well-beaten path by paying *going rates*. Policy proposes to keep wages and salaries in line with what others are paying. Such a policy usually holds pressures and conflict to a minimum. It takes for granted that going rates, together with related benefits and services, meet the essential needs of employees. The question of living wages or wages based on subsistence can be ignored, not because managers reject arguments for such payments, but because most market rates and benefits are well above the living wage level.

These assumptions may not be justified. Continued extensions of minimum wage regulations point to many markets in which substandard wages do not meet these requirements. Although progress has been made in reducing proportions of families with incomes at or below an acceptable level, several millions still fall in this category. Table 20.1 summarizes the facts of dollar family income as reported by the Census Bureau in January, 1961. If $3,000 of annual family income is accepted as a minimum, almost one-fourth of all families fall in the substandard category.

Managers may also assume that going rates take account of rising costs of living. They may, on the other hand, propose *escalator* provisions that adjust rates of pay to keep them tuned to changes in living costs.

In many firms, managers adopt a policy of following *key bargains* that establish the pattern for a wide range of firms and occupations. Such rates are negotiated in key industries—such as automobiles, steel, and rubber. Agreements concluded in these industries are copied as defining going rates in related labor markets.

3.3 Structures and differentials. Employer policy generally seeks to preserve the existing wage structures and the differentials that distinguish wage and salary classes. The wage and salary structure in an industry or plant is the system or hierarchy of rates, from the lowest paid common and custodial labor to the highest skilled workers and white-collar jobs. In such a structure, *differentials* represent the amounts by which each level of wages exceeds those *below* it. Thus, in a simple foundry wage structure, the rate for the lowest paid laborer may be $2.25 per hour; immediately above that

Table 20.1 Family Incomes in the United States, 1947–1959*

(In current dollars; per cent not shown where less than 0.5)

Total money income (current dollars)	1959	1958	1957	1956	1955	1954	1953	1952	1951	1950	1949	1948	1947
FAMILIES													
Number — thousands	45,062	44,202	43,714	43,445	42,843	41,934	41,202	40,832	40,578	39,929	39,303	38,624	37,237
Percent	100	100	100	100	100	100	100	100	100	100	100	100	100
Under $3,000 …	23	24	25	26	29	31	30	33	36	43	47	45	49
$3,000 to $4,999 .	22	25	26	27	30	31	32	34	35	34	32	34	31
$5,000 to $9,999 .	43	41	41	39	35	32	33	29	25	20	18	18	17
$10,000 to $14,999	9	8	6	6	5	5	4	3	3	} 3	3	3	3
$15,000 and over.	3	2	2	2	1	1	1	1	1				
Median income ..	$5,417	$5,087	$4,971	$4,783	$4,421	$4,173	$4,233	$3,890	$3,709	$3,319	$3,107	$3,187	$3,031

* SOURCE: "Incomes of Families and Persons in the United States: 1959," *Current Population Reports*, Series P-60, No. 35, January 5, 1961.

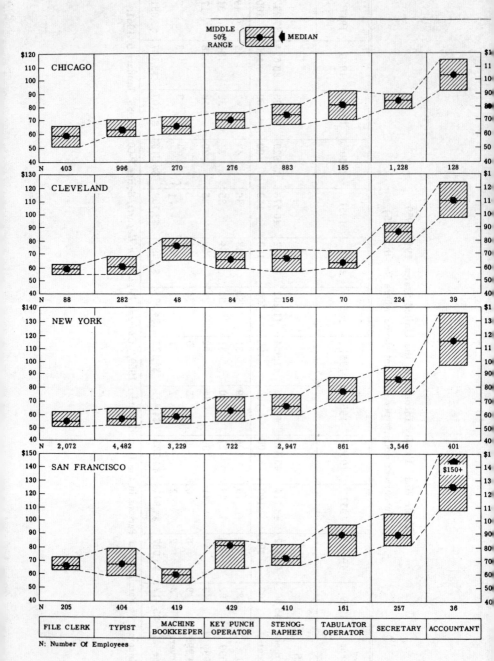

Figure 20.2 Structure of Weekly Salaries for Office Workers
SOURCE: National Industrial Conference Board, *Management Record*,
Vol. 19, No. 12, December, 1957, p. 430.

454

rate is the "shakeout and flask carrier" classification, with a rate of $2.40. The differential is the 15 cents that separates these rates.

Similar structures may be seen in every industry and in white-collar as well as in blue-collar jobs. Figure 20.2, for example, illustrates the structure and differentials in certain office jobs in several cities. Table 20.2 summarizes a generalized structure for 17 localities.

Table 20.2   Occupational Wage Structure (Median Weekly Earnings) in 17 Localities

Male Janitor's Earnings = 100

Occupation	Median Index Number	Occupation	Median Index Number
PLANT WORKERS		Elevator operators, passenger	100
—Men—		—Women—	
Tool and die makers	156	Packers, shipping	99
Engineers, stationary	148	Elevator operators, passenger	93
Electricians, maintenance	146	Janitors, porters, and cleaners	92
Machinists, maintenance	145		
Carpenters, maintenance	142	**OFFICE WORKERS**	
Machine-tool operators, tool room	142		
Mechanics, maintenance	140	—Men—	
Mechanics, automotive (main-		Clerks, accounting, class A	137
tenance)	139	Clerks, order	129
Pipefitters, maintenance	137	Tabulating machine operators	121
Painters, maintenance	136	Clerks, accounting, class B	115
Truck drivers, heavy	132	—Women—	
Shipping clerks	126	Office boys	82
Truck drivers, medium	123	Secretaries	129
Firemen, stationary boiler	123	Clerks, accounting, class A	125
Receiving clerks	121	Tabulating machine operators	113
Truck drivers, light	119	Stenographers, general	105
Helpers, trades (maintenance)	114	Clerks, accounting, class B	104
Truckers, power (forklift)	113	Switchboard operators	104
Order fillers	111	Typists, class A	101
Packers, shipping	109	Comptometer operators	101
Guards	108	Key-punch operators	99
Laborers, material handling	106	Typists, class B	91
Watchmen	101	Office girls	81

SOURCE: *The American Workers' Fact Book, 1960,* Washington, D.C.: U. S. Department of Labor, 1960, p. 107.

For many years, the total range of rates in blue-collar occupations has been narrowing. Before World War II, a common ratio of top factory rates to lowest rates in the same plants was 180 to 100. If the lowest rate was 50 cents per hour, the highest was about 90 cents per hour. In recent years, studies of the same structures indicate that the current ratio is more nearly 155 to 100.

Manager policy has generally sought to maintain differentials and oppose narrowing of these structures. Differentials are regarded as important as an incentive to work for promotion. Few workers would improve themselves enough to justify advancement, according to this theory, if higher-level jobs provided less of an increase in wages.

Wage structures create and maintain *skill differentials*. In addition, some practice creates *sex differentials:* providing lower rates of pay for women in certain jobs than for men in the same jobs. Not all employer policy favors such differentials, although some employers justify these differences, and one-third of the firms reporting to the National Office Management Association in 1960 provided higher rates for males. Advocates contend· that women do not actually perform the same work as men, in that certain heavy lifting or other parts of the job may be performed for them. In such situations, although the job title remains the same, the work must be supported by additional indirect workers—helpers who do certain parts of it. Further, employers may feel that a part of their payments for many jobs is really compensation for learning, preparing employees for advancement to more difficult jobs. Women employees in the same positions may be much more temporary in their work; they may have no intention of seeking or being available for promotions. Also, women may require more supervision and additional expense in scheduling shift arrangements.

Wage rates within particular industries may vary in various sections of the nation. Such *geographic differentials* are important to employers. Those in lower-wage sections seek to preserve them. Other employers tend to work for their elimination.[10]

3.4 Contribution. Most employer policy proposes to relate levels of pay to variations in contributions. Workers are to be paid what they have earned, that is what their participation in the total process justifies.

One frequently stated objective seeks to implement this general policy by establishing *job rates*. Each job is studied to determine how important it is in terms of what it contributes. Rates are established for each job, and all workers in the same job are to receive similar rates. This procedure is designed to protect workers against wages based on favoritism and discrimination and to encourage workers to qualify for advancement.

A variant of this policy proposes to maintain *rate ranges* for jobs. They will be set to approximate the range of possible contributions by those who hold each particular job. Within these ranges, *steps* in rates can be used to reward superior performance. They can be used for *merit increases*. Progression through the usual four or five steps in each range may be based on merit or efficiency ratings or on the recommendations of supervisors. These increases may, on the other hand, be assured by a system of *automatic progressions*, with regular increases granted each half-year or year, on the assumption that experience tends to increase the contribution of incumbents.

[10] For details on wage structures and differentials, see H. M. Douty, "Wage Structures and Administration," Institute of Industrial Relations, Los Angeles: University of California, 1954; M. W. Reder, "The Theory of Occupational Wage Differentials," *American Economic Review*, Vol. 45, No. 5, December, 1955, pp. 833–53; Jack Stieber, "Occupational Wage Differentials in the Basic Steel Industry," *Industrial and Labor Relations Review*, Vol. 12, No. 2, January, 1959, pp. 167–81.

Policies that propose to relate payments to contribution encounter the basic difficulty of measuring contribution. Some policy proposes a system of *job evaluation* that studies each job and rates its potential contribution to the total process (see Chapter 21). This process provides a measure or at least an ordering and ranking of jobs, which is, however, based on the subjective judgments of raters. Several investigations have sought to discover objective measures of effort, energy, skill, and related elements in a worker's contribution. Wickstead, for example, suggested in 1910 that work be measured in foot-pounds, but immediately admitted that he could not apply the measure to the work of writing the statement.[11] Much more recently, Harvard investigators have reported on calories as a basis of comparison. Current rates of pay, however, show little resemblance to the pattern of calorie contributions, which give top rating to the wood chopper (400–600 calories per hour) and stonemason (200–400), and give much lower ratings to housepainters and carpenters (150–200) and tailors (50–100).[12]

3.5 Fairness, equity. Employer policy generally stresses the intention that wages and salaries shall be fair. In part, fairness is related to contribution. In part, it is related to comparable payments by other employers. Fairness is a matter of opinion. No simple objective measure establishes criteria by which it is to be judged. The age-old generalization of both employer and union policy—"a fair day's pay for a fair day's work"—is both a statement of policy and a difficult puzzle.

Most employer policy—and union policy as well—recognizes two principal types of unfairness. One is *interplant inequities*. It refers to differences in rates paid for similar jobs in various firms in the same industry or locality. The other unfairness reflects *intraplant inequities* and refers to what are regarded as improper relationships between rates on various jobs in the same plant. Modern wage and salary administration has developed programs designed to correct or reduce both types of inequities. As will be noted, the most common of these practices uses some system of *job evaluation* to reduce intraplant inequities and *wage and salary surveys* with appropriate adjustments to insure equity on an interplant basis.

3.6 Preventing inflation. Some employer policy describes an intention to restrict advances in wages as a means of "holding the price line" and of resisting wage-generated inflationary pressures. In part, this policy is an expression of the general determination to limit labor costs. Employers, especially those who find their product markets invaded by a growing volume of goods produced in other nations or by competitors in this country, may be determined to hold the line on wages. Their policy on this point is not different from that which assumes that competition sets a top limit to the wages they can, should and intend to pay.

When policy goes further and contemplates determined opposition to wage

---

[11] Philip H. Wickstead, *Common Sense of Political Economy*, London: Macmillan & Co., Ltd., 1910.
[12] *Industrial Relations News*, Vol. 9, No. 19, May 9, 1959, p. 2.

increases for the purpose of preserving general price levels or restricting their advances, it expresses an interesting theory: that the employer is the protector of the public interest in prices and income distribution. Not many employers have explicitly expressed such a theory. A few, notably the large steel companies, have done so and have been encouraged in this position by representatives of the government.

3.7 Ability to pay. Some claims for wage increases have been based on the argument that the profits of employers justify additional payments to workers. Employer policy on this contention is generally negative in two ways. On the one hand, it holds that levels of wages should not be based on current ability to pay. On the other, it argues that a negative ability to pay should be a basis for refusing demands for wage increases.

On the first point, employer policy usually holds that several considerations make current profit levels an improper basis for wage adjustments. Methods of calculating profits are subject to variations; opinions would and do differ as to the amounts actually available for wage payments. Profits vary from quarter to quarter; no one would suggest the desirability of such frequent changes in rates of pay. Levels of profit vary among firms in the same business. If wages were similarly varied, some firms might lose all of their employees. Most of these arguments are unnecessary, for few spokesmen for workers would propose any such detailed linking of wages and profits.

The question as to whether inability to pay should be considered in wage adjustments is more difficult. If firms cannot pay, they presumably will not. They may be forced out of business. This is a price that neither employees nor local communities may wish to pay. Except in the most simple firms, however, no objective evidence is readily available on the reality of claims of inability to pay. The practical answer, therefore, seems to involve the degree of mutual trust. If an employer can convince workers of his inability to pay more, this consideration may influence wage demands. If employees do not trust such statements or figures, the policy can have little effect on demands.[13]

4.0 SUMMARY

Financial compensation—the payment of wages and salaries and supplementary benefits and services purchased for employees—is widely regarded as the cash nexus and the most tangible bond between an employer and his employees. The wage or salary is the most commonly described and frequently compared characteristic of jobs. Wage rates and earnings provide, without question, the most widely compiled information about employment. Next to indications of trends in employment and unemployment, levels of wages and salaries are generally accepted as the most useful indicators of health and prosperity in employment relationships.

[13] See Paul Bullock, *Standards of Wage Determination,* Los Angeles: University of California Institute of Industrial Relations, 1960.

Theories of finanical compensation are a part of the general category of work theories. They seek to provide explanations of relationships between amounts and levels and forms of financial compensation, on the one hand, and employee contributions of effort, energy, skill and thought to the missions of working organizations, on the other. Historic theory has given financial compensation the major role in influencing employee behavior on the job. In part, it has been a theory of *subsistence*. Later theory held that the possibility of increased earnings was a major influence in worker performance. Incentivation appeared largely a matter of dangling the carrot of greater income, of promising higher financial rewards for superior performance. The way to get more productivity from employees in this view is to offer to pay them for it.

Both experience and research—the latter well illustrated by the much publicized Hawthorne experiments—have forced recognition of inadequacies in any simple theory of work. Modern theory regards wages and salaries as but one variable in the equation of work. It holds that financial compensation, although always an important consideration in the minds of workers, is never a substitute for carefully planned and soundly managed employment relationships.

Management policy on wages and salaries is shaped both by public policy and employee-union policy. It is distinctly tripartite. Public interest in financial compensation is broadly based, extending from an intention to prevent substandard wages to one of maintaining the health, stability, and growth of the economy through appropriate distribution of the national income. Complex public goals include constantly rising living scales for citizens, general prosperity and economic growth, and a minimum of backsliding through inflation.

Union-employee policy is in part consistent with public policy. It proposes continuing advances in living scales, the sharing of higher productivity with workers, maintaining the stability of wage income, uniformity in job rates, and some protection of historic structures and differentials in them.

Manager policy must combine these complicated public and union intentions with those of owners. One common manager policy proposes to keep wages in line with *going rates* in the labor markets of the locality or industry. Manager policy generally emphasizes the desirable relationship between wages or salaries and contribution and proposes to reward superior performance with premium pay. At the same time, it seeks to preserve existing wage and salary structures, with *differentials* that are regarded as representing compensation for the added responsibilities and contributions of higher paid jobs. Policy recognizes employees' great interest in the *fairness* of wages. To most managers, this means that differences in wage rates should accurately reflect differences in contribution. Policy proposes to avoid or reduce wage inequities, both those within the wage and salary structure of a plant and those in which the same jobs in an industry or locality receive different rates of pay. Manager policy may incorporate a notion of employer responsibility to restrain wage-push inflation. It may also emphasize the limits of an employer's ability to meet wage demands.

To implement this complex of public, union, and private policies, current practice includes an equally varied range of wage and salary programs. Modern wage and salary administration may provide time and piece rates, special premium and bonus systems, compensation in stock or options to purchase stock, profit-sharing, a variety of job evaluation plans, and a host of fringe payments or employee benefits and services. The next chapter introduces this broad area of practice in *wage and salary administration*. Thereafter, Chapter 22 notes common provisions for employee benefits and services.

SELECTED SUPPLEMENTARY READING

Bachman, Jules, *Wage Determination,* chaps. 1 and 2. Princeton, N.J.: D. Van Nostrand Company, Inc., 1959.

Belcher, David W., *Wage and Salary Administration,* chaps. 1, 2, 3, 4, and 5. Englewood Cliffs, N.J.: Prentice-Hall, Inc., 1955.

Brinker, Paul A., "The $1 Minimum Wage Impact on 15 Oklahoma Industries," *Monthly Labor Review,* Vol. 80, No. 9, pp. 1092–1095, September, 1957.

Bullock, Paul, *Standards of Wage Determination,* pp. 1–57. Los Angeles: University of California Institute of Industrial Relations, 1960.

Johnson, David B., "Vintage Federal Wage Laws," *Labor Law Journal,* Vol. 9, No. 12, pp. 904–909ff, December, 1958.

Rothe, Harold F., "How Much Incentive in Incentive Pay?" *Supervisory Management,* Vol. 5, No. 8, pp. 11–15, August, 1960.

Samuels, Norman J., "Effects of the $1 Minimum Wage in Seven Industries" and "Effects of the $1 Minimum Wage in Three Seasonal Industries," *Monthly Labor Review,* Vol. 80, Nos. 3 and 9, pp. 323–28, 1087–1091, March and September, 1957.

Wages, Prices, Profits and Productivity. American Assembly, Columbia University, pp. 1–36, June, 1959.

SHORT CASE PROBLEM 20.1

Breaking the Bargaining Pattern

Gilson Steel is a local fabricating and supply firm, located in the "open country" far from the large steel centers. The firm has been in business many years. About a third of the employees have worked in the organization for more than ten years. Top management would like to get away from the current practice in which all negotiations on wage matters and fringes simply follow the national pattern. This practice was adopted in the years following World War II.

The firm's president feels that the key bargain system tends to divorce employees from the firm. He thinks they feel that their employer is the U. S. Steel Corporation, instead of Gilson. He argues that the local firm, which has prospered, can do more for employees than is possible in a national pattern. He says that local conditions should be taken into account and that local management knows more about what is good for employees than the big steel companies do. His basic objection to current practice, however, is his conviction that it tends to divorce employees from the local employer.

The labor relations manager has been urged to try negotiating terms at variance with the national pattern. He has been told that the firm is willing to "spend some money" to "break the pattern."

Problem: You have been invited as a consultant to help the labor relations manager. Would you accept the invitation? Do you see any general principles that may serve as guides? What would you advise?

SHORT CASE PROBLEM 20.2

The Four-Day Workweek

In December, 1961, the 7,000 members of Local 3 of the International Brotherhood of Electrical Workers who perform electrical installations in new construction in New York City began negotiation of a new contract. The existing contract expired approximately one month later. The union attracted wide public attention by announcing that contract demands would include a four-day workweek, plus a wage and benefit increase of approximately 40 cents per hour.

The established workweek consisted of five days of 6 hours each, plus an additional hour of overtime each day. Overtime was not guaranteed by employers but was firmly established by the continuing shortage of skilled electricians. Although many members of the local had only recently moved into the jurisdiction, demands had been in excess of supplies for several years. Earnings under existing contract provisions had approximated $165 per week, plus benefits estimated to cost about $40 per week and an additional $4 per man per day contribution by employers to an annuity fund.

According to spokesmen for the union, the new demand was based on prospective technological displacement. Members feared that the growing use of prefabricated components would reduce the need for on-site workers in the years ahead. Other building trade workers indicated their support of the new demands and their intention to observe picket lines if the issue resulted in a strike. It seemed clear that employer refusal to accept the I.B.E.W. demands might well precipitate a broad scale cessation of commercial construction and wide unemployment of building tradesmen.

Newspaper reports of the response of contractors suggested that union proposals would result in a hundred per cent increase in union member pay, that it would require renegotiation of construction contracts, that it was not justified by any forseeable changes in employment in the industry. Employers insisted that the growing complexity of commercial wiring had increased employment in the industry by more than 20 per cent in the preceding 15 years.

Several forecasts predicted that employers would make a futile attempt to hold the line against the union and would then, after a short strike, accept the major union proposals. Some observers predicted that the demands would have an appreciable influence in restricting future construction.

Problem: If you were employed as a manager in one of the larger contracting firms and had been asked to advise on policy in this matter, what would be the nature of your advice? You might like to know that nationally, at the time, unemployment was running at about 6.1 per cent of the labor force, also that the average factory worker's wage was about $90 per week.

What, in your opinion, is the real objective of the union and its members? Are these demands merely a far-out base for negotiating? What part do you expect state or federal negotiators to play? Is there a basic conflict in compensation theory on the part of the union and the employer-contractors? Do you expect that the union will take a strike on the issue? Should the contractors do so? Can $200 per week workers take a longer strike than those whose average pay is half that level?

What detailed outline of policy in the matter would you give your associates in the firm?

16

21. Wage and Salary Administration

Policy on financial compensation is implemented in numerous programs. As a whole, these programs constitute the managerial function generally described as *wage and salary administration*.

Even in organizations that stress direct financial incentives, wage and salary programs are seldom simple. Indeed, managers who expect the most from financial incentives generally develop complicated systems of administration to implement these policies. They pay wages and salaries, but they also augment these basic forms of financial compensation with special premiums and bonuses, incentive wage plans, numerous employee benefits and services, and perhaps with employee stock purchase or profit-sharing programs.[1]

Very large business organizations maintain special wage and salary administration units to develop and direct programs designed to implement compensation policy. Figure 21.1 is a composite job or occupational description that outlines the usual activities and responsibilities of the wage and salary administrator.

Smaller working organizations generally cannot afford such specialization. They can, however, assign responsibility to one or more members of their industrial relations staff. Not infrequently, a *wage and salary committee* maintains a general overview and supervision of financial compensation, seeking to provide uniformity in the application of policy throughout the

[1] American practice in developing complex financial incentives is by no means exceptional. Foreign firms frequently report even more complicated formulas in their wage and salary programs. In South and Central America, for example, as many as 50 variables may influence the size of the pay check.

Supervisor of:

WAGE AND SALARY ADMINISTRATION

(principal responsibility for coordinating the wage and salary program in a company)

Reported Titles

Wage and salary administrator; salary administrator; manager of salary compensation; supervisor of salary administration and organization planning; assistant personnel director.

JOB DUTIES

Principal Duties

WAGE AND SALARY ADMINISTRATION	
Time	35%

With the assistance of one or more wage and salary specialists, coordinates the evaluation of jobs for compensation purposes. Assigns jobs to labor grades or classifications. Establishes and maintains wage and salary structures. Conducts wage and salary surveys. May recommend and administer plans for incentive wage systems or supplementary compensation.

ADMINISTRATION

Consults with other managers, including members of the employee relations staff, concerning wage and

QUALIFICATIONS FOR EMPLOYMENT

Reported Education

Highest Degree Received	Per Cent	Most Frequently Reported Areas of Specialization
No degree	8	
Bachelor's	50	Economics, mathematics, sociology
Master's	42	Industrial relations, mechanical engineering, psychology, economics
Ph.D.	—	
Total	*100*	

Reported Experience

An average of four years' experience in employee relations prior to present position.

Recommended Preparation

A bachelor's degree is minimal as an educational background for this job; a master's is distinctly preferable. Appropriate major and minor fields include economics, industrial relations, business administration, psychology, and engineering. Experience should include several years in industrial relations staff jobs, with some of that experience as a staff specialist in wage and salary administration.

Figure 21.1 Extract from the Occupational Description, Supervisor of Wage and Salary Administration.
SOURCE: "Jobs in Employee Relations," *Research Study Number 38,* American Management Association, 1959, pp. 27–29.

whole. In larger organizations, wage administration may be separated from salary administration for managerial convenience.

Programs of financial compensation are not readily classified in terms of the policies they are expected to implement. Most programs have multiple purposes. Hourly rates of pay, for example, are intended not only to meet the economic needs of recipients but also, through their variation from job to job, to provide an incentive for continuing improvement and self-development. For convenience in discussion, however, programs have been divided, in the several sections of this chapter, according to their major emphasis and impact. Five major groups of programs are distinguished, including:

1. Programs designed primarily to meet economic needs and provide economic security;
2. Programs that relate earnings to productivity and contribution;
3. Programs that relate earnings to the over-all financial success of the enterprise;
4. Programs designed to assure fairness and equity in wages and salaries; and
5. Special programs of executive compensation.[2]

In addition to these five types of programs, current practice provides a variety of supplements in the form of employee benefits and services.

It may be well to note at the outset that the terms *wages* and *salaries* describe many variations in methods of payment. In popular usage, *wages* are payments to hourly rated, production workers. *Salaries* are payments to clerical, supervisory, and managerial employees. Wages are paid to those who generally have no guarantee of continuous employment throughout the week, month, or year. Salaries are compensation for workers paid on an annual or other long-term basis. Salaried workers include most of those regarded as *exempt* employees under provisions of the Fair Labor Standards Act; exempt workers have managerial responsibilities and may work overtime without premium pay.

Earnings are not the same as wages. They represent a product—the result of multiplying a rate by the number of periods or pieces for which the rate is paid. Earnings may combine several rates, as when work includes overtime. For hourly rated workers, a common measure of pay is *average weekly earnings*. Sometimes, to facilitate comparisons, overtime payments are eliminated to provide a measure of *average straight time hourly earnings* (ASTHE).

[2] For details of each of these types of programs, see David W. Belcher, *Wage and Salary Administration*, Englewood Cliffs, N.J.: Prentice-Hall, Inc., 1962; Charles W. Brennan, *Wage Administration*, Homewood, Ill.: Richard D. Irwin, Inc., 1956; Adolph Langsner and Herbert G. Zollitsch, *Wage and Salary Administration*, Cincinnati: South-Western Publishing Company, 1961; Vivienne Marquis and M. Joseph Dooher, eds., *AMA Handbook of Wage and Salary Administration*, New York: American Management Association, 1950; Lawrence C. Lovejoy, *Wage and Salary Administration*, New York: The Ronald Press Company, 1959; Jay L. Otis and Richard H. Leukart, *Job Evaluation*, Englewood Cliffs, N.J.: Prentice-Hall, Inc., 1954.

Real wages represent *the purchasing power of money payments.* They may refer to wage rates or to earnings. In either case, they are calculated by dividing dollar amounts by an appropriate cost of living or consumer price index. Sometimes changes in real wages are dramatized by relating prices to hours or minutes of work; for machinists, for example, an electric iron cost 5.5 hours in 1938, but by 1958 it cost only 2.75 hours.

Take-home pay is a measure of earnings which includes premium payments but excludes deductions for Social Security, income taxes, bonds, insurance and other such charges.

Four principal types of *wage rates* may be distinguished. Most common are *time rates*—payments per hour, per day, or per week. They are used where output cannot be readily measured or where the pace of work is controlled, as on a production line. They may be used because delays and interruptions are frequent or because work requires high quality or close tolerances. They are the usual payment for trainees. As a general rule, inspection costs are higher when employees are not paid on a time basis. About three-fourths of all workers in manufacturing are paid on an hourly basis. In non-manufacturing industries, proportions are higher.[3]

Time rates may be paid on a *flat rate* basis, meaning that all workers on the job receive the same rate. Managers may favor *rate ranges,* with a succession of rates for the same job. Progress through the several steps of such a rate range may be automatic—at specified intervals—or based on some appraisal of merit.

A second type of wage rate is the *piece rate,* which represents a uniform payment for each unit processed. Sometimes, the piece rate is modified to provide a *guaranteed hourly or weekly minimum.* Piece rates are used for jobs in which the amount of work done by an individual or group is readily measured. They require uniform working conditions, raw materials, and supporting services.

Incentive wages, of which the piece rate is the simplest form, relate earnings to productivity and may use premiums, bonuses, or a variety of rates to compensate for superior performance.

Commissions are another form of piece rate or incentive payment. They are widely used in the compensation of salesmen, where they are related to the dollar volume of sales.

In earlier practice, employees were sometimes paid in *keep* or *kind.* They received their board or lodging or a proportion of whatever they produced. Some earlier practice provided *sliding scales* that based rates of pay on the prices of products.

1.0 NEEDS AND ECONOMIC SECURITY

Public, union and manager policies generally agree on the intention to make wages adequate in terms of need. They propose to provide a high

[3] See L. Earl Lewis, "Extent of Incentive Pay in Manufacturing," *Monthly Labor Review,* Vol. 83, No. 5, May, 1960, pp. 460–63.

degree of *economic security*. They expect wage payments to keep up with rising living costs. They propose to stabilize real earnings.

Several wage and salary programs are designed rather specifically to implement policy on adequacy and security. They include cost of living adjustments, guaranteed annual wages, salaries for production workers, and family allowances. In addition to minimum wage laws (see Chap. 20, Section 1.7), several other programs, with major purposes related to other policies, make some contribution to these objectives.

1.1 Cost of Living Adjustments. Rising living costs are perhaps the most serious threat to the adequacy of wages. Managerial policy that seeks to provide employees with substantial economic security cannot ignore the impact of rising prices. More than four million employees work under programs that insure automatic *escalator adjustments* tied to the Bureau of Labor Statistics Consumer Price Index. Other employees have similar agreements that relate wage adjustments to other indexes.

Local indexes are desirable. Weights used by nation-wide indexes may not be appropriate in the individual locality. Prices in one locality may not change in the same degree as in others. Proportions of individual income expended for specific items vary greatly from one locality to another and from one income class to another. Since the family budget studies—on which current indexes are based—are those of city wage earners, the indexes should be regarded as only a very crude measure of changes in the living costs for other groups—for schoolteachers, farmers, and professional persons, for example.

Rates that have been advanced by escalator programs may be described as *C.O.L.A.*, i.e., *cost of living adjusted*. Employees frequently seek to have adjustments incorporated in base rates. Some managers strongly oppose these automatic adjustments as sources of inflationary pressure and a spiral of price increases.

Difficult problems arise when one group of employees, for example production workers, is covered by an escalator clause, while others are not. Common practice in such situations specifies *tandem adjustments,* in which the same measure of increase is applied to all employees. If union members have such provisions and office employees do not, failure to provide a similar advance for white-collar employees might be regarded as an invitation to organize.

1.2 Guaranteed Annual Wages. Policy designed to give economic security cannot focus attention on rates of pay alone. It must take into account the influence of *employment stability*. Employees must be working in order to benefit from whatever rates of pay have been established.

One type of program designed to meet this need provides *guaranteed annual wages*. Some G.A.W. plans have been established unilaterally by employers; others have been negotiated. Unions have frequently demanded such guarantees as means of forcing liberalization of unemployment insurance provisions (see Chapter 22). In essence these plans provide that permanent employees—those who have established eligibility through seniority—are assured weekly pay checks throughout the year.

Best-known guaranteed-wage plans are probably those of Geo. A. Hormel and Company, Procter and Gamble, the Nunn-Bush Shoe Company, and the Quaker Oats Company, but many other firms have experimented with them.[4]

The Fair Labor Standards Act encourages guarantees of employment. In negotiated plans that guarantee at least 1,840 hours per year, overtime need not be paid for work up to 12 hours per day or 56 hours per week, except that if total hours exceed 2,240, overtime is payable on all the excess over 40 hours per week.

Many employers and their associations, while proposing to achieve stable employment, insist that no widespread application of guaranteed annual wages is possible. They suggest that successful guarantees are feasible only in the production and distribution of non-durable goods, where employment is already stable, so that such plans are not needed. They argue that negotiated plans in other industries, especially those producing capital goods, give a false sense of security to employees. Costs of plans in such situations might be so great that production and employment would be reduced, and desirable technological change would be prevented, they insist, for investors would not put their funds into a business with such heavy liabilities.

Current plans and proposals generally limit participation to a group having established eligibility by their length of service. They usually place some limit on the total amount of the guarantee or the total liability of the employer. Some plans permit employers to transfer employees to various jobs as a means of keeping them at work.[5]

Demands for guaranteed annual wages have become less frequent with liberalization of unemployment insurance provisions and with negotiated programs of *supplemental unemployment benefits*. The latter, by bringing benefit levels to approximately 60 per cent of wages, achieve in part the objectives of guaranteed annual wages.[6]

1.3   Salaries for blue-collar workers. Stability of income has been provided in some firms by plans that make all blue-collar workers salaried employees. The Gillette Safety Razor Company instituted such a practice in

---

[4] See Henry L. Nunn, *Partners in Production*, Englewood Cliffs, N.J.: Prentice-Hall, Inc., 1961.

[5] See William Haber, "The Guaranteed Annual Wage," *Michigan Business Review*, Vol. 6, No. 1, January, 1954, pp. 26–32; J. W. Garbarino, *Guaranteed Wages*, Berkeley: University of California Institute of Industrial Relations, 1954; Emile Bouvier, *Guaranteed Annual Wage: A Modified System*, Montreal: Industrial and Labor Relations Publications, 1954.

[6] See Chapter 22, also Bureau of National Affairs, "The Guaranteed Annual Wage," Washington, D.C., 1955; Jack Chernick, "The Guaranteed Annual Wage, Employment and Economic Progress," *Industrial and Labor Relations Review*, Vol. 9, No. 3, April, 1956, pp. 469–73, also his "A Guide to the Guaranteed Wage," *Bulletin 4*, Rutgers University Institute of Management and Labor Relations, 1955.

the fall of 1955. International Business Machines announced a similar program for its 60,000 employees throughout the nation in June, 1958. Cannon Electric Company installed a similar system in its Salem, Massachusetts, and Santa Ana, California divisions in 1959.

A few reports on these programs note that absenteeism has not increased; on the contrary, it has been reduced. Somewhat the same effect is reported with respect to tardiness. Employees under these new arrangements are not penalized for illness; they receive full pay when ill.

1.4 Family Allowances. Policy that emphasizes economic security for employees has encouraged systems of *family allowances* in several European and central American nations and, until recently, in Canada. Provisions vary in detail but generally grant wage supplements based on numbers of dependent children. In some early practice, employers were required to provide these premium rates; the effect was to create instability of employment for those with larger numbers of children. Public funds now provide these supplements. No similar practice has been developed or widely proposed in the United States, but the same principle has been applied in adjusting unemployment benefits to family size in several states.

2.0 PRODUCTIVITY AND CONTRIBUTION

Perhaps the most commonly stated intention in modern wage policy is that of basing wages and salaries on the contribution of the worker. Wage and salary structures represent formal systems of rates for this purpose; they create differentials in payments assumed to represent similar differences in the contributions of jobs. *Productivity increases* or *improvement factor* adjustments also relate wages to output, but only indirectly, especially if they are scaled according to national or industry averages of advances. Employee stock-ownership and profit-sharing programs include a similar but less direct expression of this policy and are discussed in the next section of this chapter. Job evaluation programs are designed to measure the contributions of various assignments; they, also, are discussed in later sections, because they also emphasize the policy of achieving fairness and equity in payments.[7]

The most obvious programs for relating earnings to productivity are those usually described as *incentive wages.* They vary from simple piece rates to complicated arrangements that adjust the piece rate according to the level of output or time saved, either by individuals or by groups. Some of them are described as *premium plans,* because they provide higher, premium rates for higher levels of productivity. Others are called *bonus plans,* because the nature of the reward is that of special, supplementary payments.

---

[7] A prime problem is that of measuring contribution and productivity. In many jobs, that problem is complicated by the wide development and acceptance of *pseudoproductive behavior.* See Harold B. Pepinsky and Karl E. Weick, "The Simulation of Productivity in Organizations," *Personnel Administration,* Vol. 24, No. 6, November-December, 1961, pp. 18–24.

These incentive wage programs are becoming less common, largely because so much of today's production is machine-paced. Individual employees or groups can do little to speed the production line or the pace of the automatic machine. On the other hand, many employers and some unions and individual employees prefer incentive wage payments.

Plans begin by establishing a "standard" of performance for the job. That standard may be set on the basis of earlier experience or it may be determined by time study. It is assumed to represent what an average qualified jobholder can produce without injury, strain, or extra effort. Plans then provide for special added premiums or bonuses to be paid to employees who exceed this standard output.

Most plans provide earnings from 20 to 30 per cent above comparable hourly rates for the same jobs. Reports on plans newly introduced frequently describe much greater increases if standards are based on earlier experience.

By far the most popular incentive wage plans represent minor variations from straight piece rates. A survey of current practice by the editors of *Factory* found that two-thirds of all plans are of this type—either straight piece rates or *standard-hour* plans.[8] The latter translate piece work into time per unit or standard hours or minutes. In contrast, *sharing* plans that operate on a *pay-perform curve* account for only a third of current applications. In effect, this means that the trend in incentive plans is toward the simpler, more readily calculated types.

Standard-hour plans require no complicated illustration. Sometimes called *100 per cent premium* plans, they divide actual output by that regarded as standard for the minute or hour and then compensate directly for the time equivalent of production.

Most of the other current plans share the benefits of production in excess of standard with the employee on a less than one-for-one basis. They provide premium rates, but employees receive less per piece than they would on a straight piece-rate basis. Most of these plans represent modifications of the classic Halsey and Rowan plans, which are illustrated in Tables 21.1 and 21.2. The *Taylor differential piece rate* is different in that it provides a low piece rate for inefficient workers and a higher rate for those who achieve or surpass standard. It is shown in Table 21.3. Another classic, the Gantt Task and Bonus System, provides a premium piece rate for all production above standard. It is illustrated in Table 21.4. Most current plans provide a guaranteed minimum daily or weekly rate of pay. *Factory* editors observe that "The once-popular combination of low guarantee and high incentive pay is dying out." Another early principle of these plans—that employees temporarily assigned to hourly rated, non-incentive jobs are paid the base hourly rate—also seems to have lost support in present practice. Although payment of the day rate is common on jobs without time standards, practice on other jobs provides for payments that combine day rates and average earnings.

[8] "The Truth about Wage Incentives and Work Measurement Today," *Factory*, April, 1959, pp. 74–84.

16*

Table 21.1   The Halsey Plan

Employee	Units per Week	Time Taken per Piece, Hours	Time Saved per Piece, Hours	Hours Saved	Base Wage	Premium for Time Saved	Weekly Earnings
A	3.6	11.1	...	None	$80	...	$ 80
B (Standard)..	4.0	10.0	...	None	80	...	80
C	6.0	6.7	3.3	20	80	$20	100
D	8.0	5.0	5.0	40	80	40	120

Data: Normal weekly wage, $80.00 (40 hours); normal hourly rate, $2.00; normal output or production, 4 units per week, 10 hours per unit; earnings, time taken at hourly rate plus premium, guaranteed weekly wage, $80; premium, 50 per cent of time rate for time saved.

Table 21.2   The Rowan Plan

Employee	Units per Week	Time Taken per Piece, Hours	Time Saved per Piece, Hours	Per Cent Normal Time Taken per Piece	Per Cent Normal Time Saved per Piece	Hourly Rate	Weekly Earnings
A	3.6	11.1	...	111.1	...	$2.00	$ 80.00
B	4.0	10.0	...	100.0	...	2.00	80.00
C	6.0	6.7	3.3	66.7	33.3	2.66	106.40
D	8.0	5.0	5.0	50.0	50.0	3.00	120.00

Data: Normal weekly wage, $80.00 (40 hours); normal hourly wage, $2.00; normal output or production, 4 units per week, 10 hours per unit; earnings, time taken at hourly rate plus premium; guaranteed weekly wage, $80.00; premium hourly rate is base rate plus percentage of time saved.

Table 21.3   The Taylor Differential Piece-rate Plan

Employee	Units per Week	Price Rate	Weekly Earnings
A	3.6	$15.00	$ 54.00
B (Standard)	4.0	20.00	80.00
C	6.0	20.00	120.00
D	8.0	20.00	160.00

Data: Normal weekly wage, $80.00 (40 hours); standard output, 4 units per week, 10 hours per unit. Two piece rates: standard and above, $20 per piece; under standard, $15.00 per piece.

Table 21.4   The Gantt Task and Bonus System

Employee	Units per Week	Standard Hours Allowed	Wage for Time Allowed	Premium	Weekly Earnings	Labor Cost per Piece
A	3.6	36	$ 80.00	...	$ 80.00	$22.22
B	4.0	40	80.00	$16.00	96.00	24.00
C	6.0	60	120.00	24.00	144.00	24.00
D	8.0	80	160.00	32.00	192.00	24.00

Data: Guaranteed weekly wage, $80.00; standard output or production, 4 units per week, 10 hours per unit; standard time rate, $2.00 per hour; earnings, standard and above, time allowed at standard time rate plus premium; below standard, guaranteed weekly wage; premium, 20 per cent of payment for time allowed.

Figure 21.2 illustrates effects of these various plans on weekly earnings of employees, and Figure 21.3 shows how the various systems affect unit labor costs.

How effectively do these plans implement modern compensation policies? Do they attain the objectives prescribed by such policies? These are questions on which there is much heat and not too much light.

Those who oppose incentive systems charge that they are often applied to jobs for which no realistic standards have been set. Measurement of standard performance remains a source of disagreement. Adjustments in standards for changes in the jobs or in materials also occasion differences in opinion.

The simple fact that many workers dislike and distrust such arrangements limits their effectiveness. Calculations of earnings may be complex; a common observation of workers is that they really don't know how much they have earned. In many organizations, although incentive plans may create pressures for added contribution, these plans also develop employee resentment, with charges that rates and earnings are not fair and equitable.

At the same time, managements tend to expect too much of these plans. Managers forget the theory that effective incentivation is a complex rather than a simple phenomenon. It is no accident that the most satisfactory incentive wage plans are in firms in which the rest of the employee relations program is thoroughly and thoughtfully developed. Incentivation in such circumstances is not a simple assignment to the wage program; the latter is but one element in the total.

Individual incentives are probably more difficult to fit into a total program of incentivation than group incentive plans. The individual incentive provides earnings, on the average, from 20 to 30 per cent above nonincentive rates. This premium creates a substantial barrier to union efforts at standardized rates; frequent union opposition results from this characteristic of incentive plans.

At the same time, the emphasis on detailed measurement of individual output may create resentment. Some workers resent the implication that they will work at reasonable levels of effort only if their contribution is continually checked. Experience indicates that many deceitful practices, holding portions of a good day's output for another time, inaccurate reporting of production, false claims and grievances, are common with workers on incentive.

Continuing managerial discussions of loose standards and charges that workers do not appreciate improved equipment and superior planning encourage employee suspicion that managers are on the lookout for excuses to reduce incentive rates. Repeated experience with rate reductions whenever employees on incentive "earn too much" has a similar influence. Although individual status may sometimes be improved by unusually high production, the same superiority may create resentment among fellow workers. Employees on incentive may regard increased earnings as being offset by the loss of friendship and regard of co-workers.

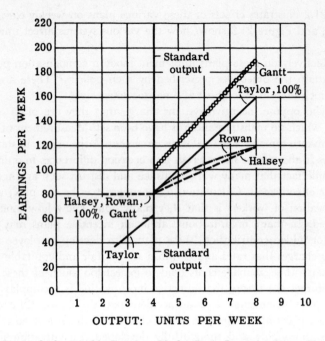

Figure 21.2 Weekly Earnings Under Basic Incentive Wage Plans

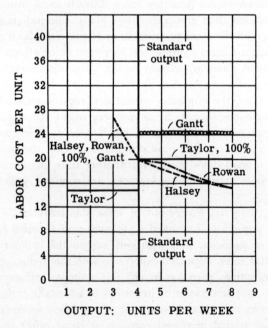

Figure 21.3 Unit Labor Costs Under Basic Incentive Wage Plans

Group incentives avoid many of these limitations. They can be expanded to include indirect workers, always a problem when they work with or serve those on incentives. Some group plans include white-collar clerical employees in a plant-wide incentive plan. In a few instances, on the other hand, systems of individual incentives have been installed in offices.[9]

3.0 STOCK OWNERSHIP AND PROFIT-SHARING

Another type of program that seeks to relate compensation to contribution encourages employees to own shares of stock in the enterprise or offers them the opportunity to participate in its profits. Most of these programs have been advanced by managers; in recent years, however, unions have proposed that employees share directly in profits. Managers see employee stock-ownership and profit-sharing as means of making employees partners in the enterprise. These programs could create common objectives for managers and managees. At the same time, they could implement the policy of relating compensation to effort, for employees could see themselves as contributing to their own prosperity.

3.1 Employee Stock Ownership. Employee stock ownership plans are not new. Some experimental arrangements—involving profit-sharing through distributions of stock—are reported as early as 1829 in Great Britain and 1842 in France. Earliest plans in this country were those of Procter and Gamble and the Illinois Central Railway, begun in 1893, and the United States Steel Corporation, instituted in 1903. Employee stock ownership plans grew in popularity until the stock market crash of 1929 effectively subdued employee interest in such securities.

Since World War II, interest in these plans has revived, in part as a means of supplementing retirement income. They offer possibilities of minimizing the effects of inflation, for values of equities tend to advance with other prices. These advantages have appealed to executives, many of whom have received options to buy stock at favorable prices. Employees have frequently welcomed a similar privilege.

Current plans are not uniform. In some, the firm helps employees buy and offers partial payment plans for that purpose. Stock may be priced at the market or may be available at a discount. Some plans require the employee-owner to give the firm first chance to buy any shares he offers to sell. Some plans guarantee the price of stock sold to employees for as long as ten

---

[9] See "Bonus and Incentive Plans for Supervisors," *Conference Board Management Record,* Vol. 18, No. 1, January, 1956, pp. 2–5; Fergus G. Chandler, "Wage Incentives in Small Business," Washington, D.C.: Small Business Administration, September, 1954; Phil Carroll, *Better Wage Incentives,* New York: McGraw–Hill Book Company, Inc., 1957; Thomas Q. Gilson and Myron J. Lefcowitz, "A Plant-wide Productivity Bonus in a Small Factory," *Industrial and Labor Relations Review,* Vol. 10, No. 2, January, 1957, pp. 284–96; R. Marriott, *Incentive Payment Systems,* London: Staples Press Ltd., 1957; "Incentive Wage Plans for White-collar Workers," *Personnel Policies and Practices Report,* Par. 190, No. 15–84, 1961, "Group Wage Incentives: Experience with the Scanlon Plan," *Industrial Relations Memo No. 141,* New York: Industrial Relations Counselors, 1962.

years. Others supplement employee payments with a contribution from the firm.

Although the precise number of such plans in operation in the United States is not clear, with estimates ranging from a few hundred to several thousand, some evidence is available from sampling studies. A 1961 study of its members by the New York Stock Exchange found that one-fifth of the members have employee stock ownership plans. About one-half of the employees eligible to participate in such plans have done so. In one type of arrangement, found in 114 of the 233 firms, employees buy stock through payroll deductions. In 79 firms, employee contributions for this purpose are augmented by matching funds. A third plan issues stock to employees as part of a profit-sharing arrangement.

Numbers of such plans and of participating employees could increase rapidly, for stock purchase plans have been held to be a form of compensation and hence subject to collective bargaining. Some unions have proposed these plans.

On the other hand, employee stock purchase plans have not become a major form of compensation. Probably not more than 3 per cent of all employees own stock in the firms in which they work. The number is not increasing rapidly. Incentive effects of stock ownership are largely taken for granted. When stock values decline, the result may adversely affect employee morale and productivity.[10]

3.2 Profit-sharing Plans. Perhaps the most obvious way to let employees benefit from contributions is to share profits. Employee profit-sharing plans have appealed to many managers as an ideal method of relating worker gains to worker contributions.

Profit-sharing has a long history both in this country and abroad, but recent plans are quite different from early, pioneering experiments. In early plans, employees simply shared in the profits, economic fortunes, and risks of their employer. Sometimes, they received their share of profits in the form of stock. In other situations, they received year-end bonuses, which might be used to purchase stock or taken as cash. In the newer plans, the profit to be shared is often that developed by a *profit-sharing trust fund*. A portion of that fund is normally invested in the stock of the firm, but larger portions are otherwise invested. A common formula puts approximately one-third in the firm's stock, another third in government bonds, and the remainder in the stocks of other firms.

Many managers see profit-sharing as one of the most effective forms of group incentives. It helps to implement policies proposing employee participation and identification. Firms with successful experience have formed a Council of Profit-Sharing Industries and a Profit-Sharing Research Founda-

---

[10] See Victor Perlo, "Peoples' Capitalism and Stock Ownership," *American Economic Review*, Volume 48, No. 3, June, 1958, pp. 337ff.; "The Workers Turn into Owners," *Business Week*, May 11, 1957, pp. 93–97; "Who Owns Stock?" *Economic Trends and Outlook*, Vol. 5, Nos. 7 and 8, July-August, 1960.

tion.[11] More than 4,800 profit-sharing plans were initiated during 1960.

Historic union opposition to profit-sharing has declined. Indeed, a major reason for anticipating an increase in such plans is the negotiation of a profit-sharing plan by the United Automobile Workers and American Motors in September, 1961. That development has special significance, also, because profit-sharing was coupled with relief from work rules regarded by the firm to be restrictive. Negotiated plans vary significantly from those advanced by managements; being negotiated they cannot be terminated on a unilateral basis.[12]

Profit-sharing plans may provide *current distribution* or *deferred distribution* of profits. The Lincoln Electric Company plan, for example, features current distribution in the form of a year-end bonus, which may amount to from a fifth of annual wages to more than one hundred per cent. Sears Roebuck, on the other hand, defers the distribution of profits, letting them accumulate to supplement retirement pay. Some plans combine current and deferred distributions.

Profit-sharing may be combined with union-management cooperative arrangements (see Chapter 13, section 3.0). Thus, for example, in the *Scanlon plan,* management and union agree on a program to increase suggestions, employee and union participation, and productivity and to share in the resulting savings. An employee bonus is calculated each month by comparison of payrolls and sales value. On the basis of experience, an expected ratio is determined. Payroll savings in excess of this ratio are shared, with employees receiving 75 per cent. In a variant of this procedure, the *Rucker plan,* a somewhat more detailed analysis is used to calculate savings, and employees receive 40 per cent.[13]

One of the effects of profit-sharing and stock ownership is a heightened employee interest in the quality and competence of management. Such plans may encourage criticisms of managerial policy and practice; over a period of years, they may exert a powerful influence in the movement toward professionalization of management.

Continued growth in profit-sharing is widely expected. Past experience in this area is not a dependable guide. Employees are far better educated and more keenly aware of industry's problems today. Many employers appear convinced that plans improve teamwork, output, and employee attitudes. Several firms with such plans report consistently impressive increases in productivity averaging 10 to 15 per cent per year, which they attribute to these arrangements.

Profit-sharing trust funds offer a somewhat more secure investment than

[11] The first is located at 337 West Madison Street, Chicago 6, and the second at 1718 Sherman Avenue, Evanston, Illinois.

[12] See, in this connection, Ted Metaxes, "Why Profit-Sharing is Booming," *Mill and Factory,* Vol. 67, No. 1, July, 1960, pp. 112–15.

[13] See, for greater detail and reports on the operation of these plans, David W. Belcher, *Wage and Salary Administration,* Englewood Cliffs, N.J.: Prentice-Hall, Inc., 1955, pp. 416–31.

the simpler, single-stock plans. These more recent adaptations, often combined with provisions for savings and retirement, have been encouraged by 1951 legislation facilitating tax savings by such plans. Gains in the asset value of employee trust funds are not taxed until the employee sells his equities. In some cases, these funds have been used to buy a controlling interest in the business. Some 20,000 plans have been submitted to the Bureau of Internal Revenue for approval.

Earlier plans tended to restrict participation to executives and supervisors. Newer plans include all employees with a specified length of service, commonly from one to five years. Most current plans permit the employee to contribute to the trust fund up to a specified maximum, generally 5 per cent of his annual earnings.

4.0 FAIRNESS AND EQUITY

A major objective in most compensation policy proposes to pay wages and salaries that are fair in comparison to those paid workers in similar jobs and in the other jobs of the same establishment. The yardstick of fairness in such policy is comparative. It checks existing wages against other wages. As noted, two principal types of unfairness or inequity are of major concern. One involves wage rates lower than those paid for comparable work in other establishments. The other inequity is one in which a given job receives less than its fair rate as compared with other job rates in the same firm.

The most common practice for avoiding interplant inequities is the *survey of wages and salaries*. It provides a formal comparison of job rates in establishments regarded as comparable. It is supplementary to numerous less formal comparisons. Unions of employees may, for example, compare rates negotiated in various contracts. Employers may compare notes on going rates in professional meetings of managers. Both may consult the reports of current rates frequently released by employment offices and other public agencies.

All these informal comparisons have serious limitations and may become subjects of controversy and conflict. Jobs with the same title may vary significantly from plant to plant. Similarly, jobs with the same title may have several rates rather than a single rate within a firm, with differentials based on experience or merit. Any unplanned sample of rates is likely to be challenged.

4.1 Wage and salary surveys. Formal wage and salary surveys attempt to avoid these difficulties. They use common job descriptions and report ranges and clusters in rates, sometimes with calculated medians or modal rates.

Most surveys do not attempt to secure wage or salary information on every job. Rather, *key jobs* are selected for pricing. They are jobs that are common and fairly uniform among the firms to be checked. They are also jobs which account for comparatively large numbers of employees. Thus, for example, the job of machinist *A* or turret-lathe operator or multiple-spindle drill-press operator might meet these requirements in certain types of manufacturing. In a survey of clerical salaries, examples of key jobs might include typist, file clerk, secretary, and comptometer operator. The number of such jobs to be surveyed depends on the coverage of the survey and the complexity of the wage structure.

Key jobs must be described in detail for the survey, for job titles may be misleading. If data are collected by personal visit, these details can be checked by observation. If the survey is conducted by mail, specific job descriptions are essential. Practice in the presentation of survey data varies. An excellent example is illustrated in Figure 21.4.[14]

4.2   Job-evaluation systems. For establishing appropriate relationships in wages and salaries among jobs within an organization, use of job evaluation is becoming standard practice. To some extent, of course, these relationships can be established by reference to the wage or salary survey. However, since jobs with the same title are likely to vary somewhat from firm to firm and since surveys generally include only key jobs, internal comparisons are desirable to assure fairness among wages and salaries.

All job evaluation systems lean heavily on job analysis and job descriptions. The job description provides information on which each job is rated or evaluated. The resulting measures of value are then translated into wage and salary rates. In some practice, jobs with similar values are grouped in *salary classes,* or *labor grades,* with rates or ranges assigned to these groups of positions.

Job evaluation does not actually price jobs. It does not provide a simple answer to the question: What is this job worth? Rather, it takes one step in that direction. It says that, compared to other jobs, a particular job has a specified comparative value. It thus places each job in its position in the whole job structure. Pricing the jobs in the structure requires additional steps.

In essence, job evaluation begins by asking the questions: What do we pay for? What are the contributions or working conditions—skills, responsibilities, difficulties, hardships, inconvenience, and unpleasantness—for which we pay wages and salaries? Once a list of such job factors is at hand, job evaluation asks more questions: How much of each of these factors does each job involve? How does each job compare with all others? Some systems of job evaluation make these questions explicit. In others, they are not actually stated, but the procedure implies them.

Employees and unions frequently participate in the job-evaluation program. Employees may be included on the committee that plans the develop-

[14] In 1961, the Federal Bureau of Labor Statistics inaugurated a new nationwide annual series of reports on professional administrative, technical, and clerical pay. The first report covered jobs in accounting, legal services, clerical, engineering, scientific, drafting, and personnel jobs. It is available as "National Survey of Professional, Administrative, Technical, and Clerical Pay," *Bulletin 1286, 1961.*

Base Hourly Rates	Number of Male Employees	Number of Female Employees	Total Number of Employees	Percent of Total Employees
$ 4.20 and over	25	0	25	2.92%
4.10 to 4.19	23	0	23	2.69
4.00 to 4.09	19	0	19	2.22
3.90 to 3.99	22	3	25	2.92
3.80 to 3.89	42	1	43	5.03
3.70 to 3.79	59	0	59	6.90
3.60 to 3.69	62	2	64	7.49
3.50 to 3.59	58	0	58	6.78
3.40 to 3.49	116	3	119	13.92
3.30 to 3.39	92	1	93	10.88
3.20 to 3.29	107	1	108	12.63
3.10 to 3.19	82	2	84	9.83
3.00 to 3.09	62	0	62	7.25
2.90 to 2.99	35	1	36	4.21
2.80 to 2.89	24	1	25	2.92
2.70 to 2.79	9	0	9	1.05
2.60 to 2.69	1	0	1	.12
under 2.60	2	0	2	.24
TOTALS	840	15	855	100.00%

TOTAL NUMBER OF COMPANIES 50

WEIGHTED AVERAGE	$ 3.40	MEDIAN	$ 3.40
FIRST QUARTILE	$ 3.19	THIRD QUARTILE	$ 3.66
10th PERCENTILE	$ 3.00	90th PERCENTILE	$ 3.91

GROUP IV JOB CLASSIFICATIONS

DRAFTSMAN

Job Titles Currently in Use: Designer; Senior Designer; Design Draftsman; Electro-Mechanical Designer; Checker-Design; Drafting Checker; Draftsman, Senior; Product Designer "A" & "B"; Tool Designer-Advanced; Designer "A"; Detailer; and Drawing Checker.

Number of Employees	Number of Firms	Weighted Average Hrly. Rate	Median Rate	1st Quartile	3rd Quartile	10th Percentile	90th Percentile
377	38	$ 3.59	$ 3.50	$ 3.32	$ 3.80	$ 3.14	$ 4.07

LABORATORY-DEVELOPMENT TECHNICIAN

Job Titles Currently in Use: Laboratory Technician, Senior; Specialist, Electronic; Senior Engineering Technician; Research Technician, Senior; Testing Engineer "D"; Special Analyst; Senior Engineering Research Technician; Experimental Mechanic "A"; Laboratory Analyst, Senior; Test Equipment Builder; Test Engineer; Research and Technical Analyst; Electronic Technician, Senior; Engineering Associate-Electronics Research; and Technician, Precision Instrument, Senior.

Number of Employees	Number of Firms	Weighted Average Hrly. Rate	Median Rate	1st Quartile	3rd Quartile	10th Percentile	90th Percentile
298	21	$ 3.29	$ 3.24	$ 3.08	$ 3.45	$ 2.93	$ 3.74

ENGINEERING AIDE

Job Titles Currently in Use: Engineering Assistant; Engineering Aide; Estimator; Associate Mechanical Engineer; Master Engineering Aide; Engineering Associate; and Research and Development Technical Aide.

Number of Employees	Number of Firms	Weighted Average Hrly. Rate	Median Rate	1st Quartile	3rd Quartile	10th Percentile	90th Percentile
166	13	$ 3.37	$ 3.37	$ 3.18	$ 3.55	$ 2.99	$ 3.75

Figure 21.4 Excerpt from a Local Wage Survey

SOURCE: Reproduced by permission of the Merchants and Manufacturers Association, Los Angeles, Calif. from "Professional Engineering Salary Survey and Technical Wage Rate Survey," May, 1960, pp. 60–61.

ment and installation of a system. They may also be members of a committee that applies the rating procedure to individual jobs.

The four principal systems of job evaluation may be listed, in the order of their complexity, as follows:

1. Ranking systems
2. Job-classification systems
3. Point or manual systems
4. Factor-comparison systems

4.21 Ranking systems. Ranking systems of job evaluation are generally used in smaller units, where all jobs are well known to job raters. They do not assign measurable scores or point values to jobs but merely establish the number of pay classes and their relative positions. In other words, they out-line a hierarchy of job groups, some of which may include many jobs and others only one or a few.

Sometimes the ranking system makes use of yardsticks which are applied to each job to assist in its appraisal. They ordinarily include a few broad qualities characteristic of all jobs in varying degrees. The distinctive characteristic of this system, however, is that it does not emphasize breaking each job down into factors. Rather, each job as a whole is ranked among all others.

Jobs may be classified among major departments, and salary grades or levels identified within each such division.

Ranking systems are best suited to small organizations in which a committee can be expected to know all jobs. Their chief advantage is simplicity.

4.22 Job-classification systems. As the designation of systems of this type suggests, they also emphasize allocation to classes of jobs. Job-classification systems begin with an over-all view of all jobs as a basis for identification of major salary or wage classes. For each class, a general specification is prepared, indicating the types of work and responsibility that will be included. Salary ranges may be tentatively specified for each class and subclass. All jobs are then fitted into these predetermined classes. A classification committee, working with job descriptions, allocates each job to its *slot*.

This system also is best suited to small units. In larger organizations, class specifications must be quite complicated if job raters are to make appropriate allocations. The specification of wage or salary levels in advance may tend to influence the *slotting* of jobs, and is an important hazard in this procedure.

In some applications of the system, classes are identified in terms of services or functions as well as levels.

4.23 Point systems. The most obvious feature of most point systems is their use of a *manual*. The manual outlines elements or factors upon which each job is to be rated and provides scales and yardsticks by which each degree of each factor is to be valued. It describes several job elements and prescribes the weighting to be applied to each such element. It includes a scale for each element, by means of which varying degrees are to be appraised. These degrees determine the number of points to be credited to the job. The total of such points establishes the *point value* of the job.

Manuals may be developed for each individual firm or agency, or firms may use a readymade system such as that of the National Metal Trades Association or the National Office Management Association. Both of these systems have been widely applied. Similarly, in the life insurance field, wide use is made of the Life Office Management Association plan.

POINTS ASSIGNED TO FACTORS AND KEY TO GRADES

Factors	1st degree	2nd degree	3rd degree	4th degree	5th degree
Skill					
1. Education	14	28	42	56	70
2. Experience	22	44	66	88	110
3. Initiative and ingenuity	14	28	42	56	70
Effort					
4. Physical demand	10	20	30	40	50
5. Mental or visual demand	5	10	15	20	25
Responsibility					
6. Equipment or process	5	10	15	20	25
7. Material or product	5	10	15	20	25
8. Safety of others	5	10	15	20	25
9. Work of others	5	10	15	20	25
Job conditions					
10. Working conditions	10	20	30	40	50
11. Unavoidable hazards	5	10	15	20	25

Fig. 21.5   Job Elements and Degree Values
(National Metal Trades Association System)

The National Metal Trades Association system for hourly rated jobs provides the list of factors and values shown in Figure 21.5. Another schedule of factors and values is provided for office employees.

The manual plays a large part in the success or failure of the point system. If job elements have not been properly selected or defined, if they are improperly weighted, or if degrees are not effectively distinguished and clearly identified, job ratings are likely to be inaccurate. In the development of a point system, the selection and weighting of elements is a major undertaking. The system has the important advantage of forcing job raters to consider individual factors, rather than the job as a whole or, what is still more objectionable, the person in a job. The system tends to simplify the rating procedure and to provide similar standards for all raters.

On the other hand, point systems introduce inflexibility that may create inequities. The listing of factors may omit some elements that are important in certain jobs. It is apparent also that arbitrary weights are attached to various degrees and to the factors by specifying maximum and minimum points. The same point systems cannot generally be used for production and office employees. Some criticism is aimed at this creation of two different sets of yardsticks.

4.24 *Factor-comparison systems.* The factor-comparison system is essentially a job evaluation specialist's method—a technique for those who are perfectionists in the comparison and appraisal of jobs. It may, indeed, give a false sense of exactness by its somewhat complicated procedure.

The method begins by selecting the major job elements or factors—usually four or more of them. These are not predetermined, as in the *manual* procedure, but are chosen on the basis of job analysis. They represent a schedule of job factors or elements found to be important in greater or lesser degree in all jobs. Among the factors most frequently named are mental requirements, skill requirements, physical requirements, responsibility, and working conditions.

A distinctive feature of factor comparison is the method of determining the weights to be applied to the job elements. In some cases, a committee carefully considers the problem and on the basis of its pooled judgment sets these weights. In a more detailed procedure, a group of ten to twenty key jobs is selected. Each of them is ranked according to each of these elements. If a committee does the ranking, averages of ranks are calculated and assigned to each job.

Each key job's current rate of pay is then analyzed to determine what per cent of the total rate is attributable to each job element. Thus, for job number 1, the first element may be assigned a value of 15%, the second, 20%; the third, 35%; and the fourth, 30%. When all key job rates have been thus analyzed, averages of the percentages thus computed are accepted as weights for the elements.

As the next step, all other jobs are appraised and assigned a value on each factor or element. This result is accomplished by comparing these jobs with the key jobs. When these values on the individual jobs have been weighted, the total point value of each job becomes available.

Among the advantages of the factor-comparison method is the fact that unlike jobs can be evaluated. The system may be applied to combinations of clerical, manual, and supervisory positions. This adaptability stems from the procedure, which describes the basic factors in very broad terms and without reference to a specific scale. Hence, "skill," for example, encompasses all kinds of skills. Factor-comparison systems benefit from the fact that the weights selected are not entirely arbitrary, but reflect existing wage and salary practice. Perhaps most important is the fact that they impose no external system of factors and weights, but derive these essentials by detailed analyses and appraisal of established practice.

On the other hand, factor-comparison systems are complicated, and installation is expensive. They may not be readily explainable to employees. They cannot be developed by an inexpert lay committee but require leadership by a competent and experienced practitioner.[15]

In current practice, largest numbers of production employees are covered by manual or point systems, but there is an apparent tendency to favor the more complicated factor-comparison system.[16] Although most of the firms queried exclude management, supervisors, and professional workers, two out of three use job evaluation for other white-collar workers. In 40 per cent of the firms, programs were established by their own personnel department; in 18 per cent, the services of outside consultants were used. About half of the respondents used area and industry surveys to provide basic financial information, while others depended on data provided by their employer associations or other organizations of managers. For these white-collar workers, 48.4 per cent of the responding firms used a point system, 22 per cent used the factor-comparison system, 4.2 per cent used job ranking, and 22.9 per cent used a combination of systems.

4.3 Limitations of job evaluation. Numerous special systems of job evaluation introduce variations away from these basic systems. Job evaluation plans have changed and are changing, in part because their coverage has been extended in many organizations to include supervisory and management jobs. White-collar workers have been more critical than most production workers. They have forced recognition of the essentially subjective quality of all job ratings.

Meanwhile, studies have indicated that, as in the rating of employees, qualities frequently overlap. As a result, numbers of factors can frequently be reduced without adverse effects on ratings. The weights assigned to various qualities are subject to question, which may account for the growing trend toward the factor-comparison system, especially for white-collar employees and for managers. Experience has clearly indicated the necessity for continuing attention and frequent revaluation of individual jobs. Experience also suggests that every system should be accompanied by an adequate grievance procedure, so that those who feel that their work has been improperly valued may be assured an unbiased review.

Unions generally offer little opposition to job evaluation, although they do not regard it as removing the need for negotiating wages and salaries. Indeed, unions have frequently suggested and encouraged the acceptance of job evaluation, for it tends to eliminate friction within their ranks. It settles

---

[15] For details of these systems, see D. W. Belcher, *Wage and Salary Administration,* Englewood Cliffs, N.J.: Prentice-Hall, Inc., 1962; Adolph Langsner and Herbert G. Zollitsch, *Wage and Salary Administration,* Cincinnati: South-Western Publishing Company, 1961; Charles Walter Lytle, *Job Evaluation Methods,* New York: The Ronald Press Company, 1954; Jay-L. Otis and Richard H. Leukart, *Job Evaluation,* 2d ed., Englewood Cliffs, N.J.: Prentice-Hall, Inc., 1954; John Patton and C. L. Littlefield, *Job Evaluation,* Homewood, Ill.: Richard D. Irwin, Inc., 1957.

[16] The *Personnel Policies and Practices Report* describes a 1961 survey of extensions of job evaluation to white-collar workers. Par. 183, No. 15–70, 1961.

issues as to relative rates on various jobs that may otherwise create difficult problems for union officers.[17]

Market pressures may create serious hazards for job evaluation. What shall be done when enough employees cannot be found at the rate of pay suggested by job evaluation? This is a rhetorical question; there is no simple nor general answer. A preliminary step might re-examine the rating for which wages or salaries appear inadequate. A second might check the entire wage structure, which may have failed to keep pace with upward trends. In some situations, temporary rates may be established, on the theory that the unusual situation will not persist.[18]

As in extensions of the job-evaluation program to supervisory and technical as well as managerial jobs, many firms have encountered special problems in applications to scientific and research positions. The usual factors, or qualities, require new definitions in such applications. Responsibility, for example, must become responsibility for discoveries and innovations rather than for numbers of subordinates or for dollars of sales. For this reason, many plans exclude these jobs, and others have developed special *maturity curve systems* with *parallel ladders* of promotion and compensation.

Maturity curves relate levels of salaries to age groups. They may include a procedure somewhat like that described as *job classification* in which assignments to several types of scientists are distinguished. For each broad classification, curves show annual salaries by age. Several such curves may be created, with one representing the upper 10 or 20 per cent of salaries, another for the lowest 10 or 20 per cent, and a third representing the central group. Each curve identifies a series of median salaries plotted above the horizontal axis, which measures salary receivers in terms of age. Salary surveys may be undertaken to create similar curves representing practice in other comparable organizations. The propriety of individual salaries is judged by comparisons with those of their peers in terms of age, rather than by attempting to measure performance against specified standards and job descriptions.

Parallel ladders create structures of salaries for scientists with salary grades comparable to those of other supervisors and managers. For the scientists, however, systematic promotion does not emphasize growing responsibility for the supervision of others. The scientist can, therefore, anticipate regular advancement without becoming an administrator.

4.4 Pricing the Job Structure. Job evaluation creates a structure or hierarchy of jobs, ordered and ranked according to their value to the organization; it does not put price tags on jobs. It may assign point values; it does not tell anyone what a point is worth. The pricing process is an added

---

[17] See, for example, Robert L. Stutz and Harold E. Smalley, "Management, Union Join in Job Evaluation," *Personnel Journal*, Vol. 34, No. 11, April, 1956, pp. 412–16.

[18] See Preston P. Le Breton, "Must Market Pressure Wreck the Company's Salary Structure?" *Personnel*, Vol. 36, No. 4, July-August, 1959, pp. 34–45; For more on special problems of salary administration in the employment of scientists, see George W. Torrence, "Maturity Curves and Salary Administration," *Management Record*, Vol. 24, No. 1, January, 1962, pp. 14–17.

step. Prices must take into account an added factor beyond the relative value of each job. That factor is the influence of supply and demand in the labor markets in which manpower must be bought and sold.

The pricing process seeks to create a wage structure to parallel the point-value structure. Thereafter, the wage structure may be raised or lowered, as a structure. The pattern and relationship of wages, however, can be preserved.

For the preliminary transition from point values to dollars, a variety of procedures may be used. A *fixed value* for each point may be established by equating the average number of points to the average rate of pay. In another procedure, point values are priced by comparison with common labor rates. Prices on all other jobs are calculated by assuming that each point has the same value in all jobs.

Any simple averaging procedure can provide only a crude estimate of the value of a point. In more common practice, point values are compared with current prices on a number—usually 12 to 20—*key jobs*. Point values are plotted against the selected wage rates, as shown in Figure 21.6. Then a trend line is fitted to the points represented by key jobs. Several methods are used in fitting these trends. A straight-line trend, such as that shown in the figure, may be fitted by inspection. Or one of the common statistical trends may be fitted by the semi-averages or least-squares methods. Thereafter, a price structure for all jobs may be established by reading appropriate rates from this *wage line*.

Such a straight-line or linear trend may not provide a satisfactory fit to the prices of jobs. It assumes that point values are fixed, that a point is worth the same amount for common labor as for the most skilled job. Frequently, when such a scatter diagram of point values and rates is prepared, the pattern is clearly curvilinear. Point values apparently increase in value as they increase in number. In such structures, a curve is fitted either by inspection or by trend-fitting statistical techniques.

Many objections are raised against such curved trend lines. It is difficult to explain them to rank-and-file employees, who may reasonably feel that a point is as valuable when it is theirs as when it appears in a more skilled job. For this reason fixed-value points are widely preferred, as is the resulting straight *wage line*.

This result can be achieved without injury to the market prices of skilled employees by use of a geometric or modified geometric scale on the ratings of individual elements. Many of the manuals used in point systems include this feature.

4.5 Labor grades. In any large organization, individual wage rates for each job may create an undesirable multiplicity of fractional dollars-and-cents rates. Ordinarily, therefore, *labor grades* are established, each grade representing a range of point values, with one wage rate or range for the entire grade. Thus, for example, if point values range from 162 to 372, as

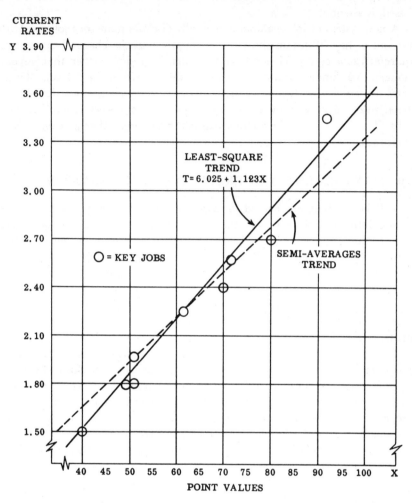

CURRENT
RATES

LEAST-SQUARE
TREND
T= 6.025 + 1.123X

O = KEY JOBS

SEMI-AVERAGES
TREND

POINT VALUES

Figure 21.6   Linear Trends Fitted to Rates and Point Values of Key Jobs

they might if the National Metal Trades Association system for male manual workers is used, this range may be divided into ten labor grades, of 21 points each. The rate for the midpoint of the grade is established for all positions in each grade.

Labor grades may be given *flat rates* or *rate ranges*. Ranges usually increase in width as rates increase. Ranges usually vary—from minimum to maximum—by about 40 per cent of the minimum.

4.6   Adjustments to New Rates. When job evaluation is used for the first time, employees may be suspicious and fearful of possible effects. Careful explanation of the whole program, including the policies on which it is based, is essential.

A new system of job evaluation generally discloses numerous job rates that are out of line. Rates on these *red circle jobs* must be changed to meet requirements of equity. Generally the change is gradual rather than revolutionary. All "under" rates are raised to their newly defined level. "Over" rates are circled for future revision. They are temporarily regarded as *personal rates,* to be continued as long as present employees remain in these jobs. If attrition is too slow, employees may be offered other jobs that justify their rates.

5.0 MANAGEMENT AND EXECUTIVE COMPENSATION

Policy to be implemented in management and executive compensation is not distinctly different from that inherent in other wage and salary administration, but somewhat greater emphasis is placed on incentivation through financial rewards. Put another way, managers appear to give less acceptance to broad, complex work theory in their compensation policy for themselves. They rely principally on dangling the carrot of greater financial rewards to stimulate superior performance. Present or deferred monetary rewards seem to be the principal answer to the question as to what makes the manager perform.

This reliance on financial incentivation has encountered some conflict with *public policy,* which appears to assume that managers will perform effectively without the broad-differentials apparent in structures of manager and executive salaries. As a result, public policy has developed income and other tax programs that tend to reduce these differentials. In response, manager policy has sought means of evading and overcoming these limitations.

Programs of executive and manager compensation show these policies. To some extent, they have applied the job evaluation procedure to manager jobs. For top positions, however, programs represent various combinations of *package payments* that combine current salaries and bonuses with a variety of deferred rewards.

5.1 Job evaluation for manager jobs. Although early job evaluation plans were limited to the jobs of hourly-rated employees, current practice extends their coverage to many managerial and some executive positions. Most current applications to managerial positions create a separate system for that purpose. They use a different group of factors for evaluation. Farwell, for example, rates managerial positions on nine types of responsibilities: responsibility for programs, projects, or operations; supervision of personnel; employee relations; customer and public contacts; internal contacts; investigation or fact finding; planning, forecasting, and scheduling; establishment of standards; and gain or loss.[19] Methods Engineering Council begins with a

---

[19] Stanley P. Farwell, "Evaluation of Managerial Positions," Chicago: Business Research Corporation, rev. ed., 1954.

lengthy list of factors which are analyzed to determine those upon which dependence can be placed. Judgment, experience, organizing and planning skill, persuasive skill, and industriousness are cited as illustrations of qualities that might be found definitive in a firm's managerial jobs.

Procedure in evaluation and in the establishment of trend lines, salary ranges, and grades is not unlike that employed in evaluating production and clerical jobs. Job structures are compared with current salaries within the firm and with those disclosed in surveys of managerial compensation. Resulting rates and ranges may be integrated with those of nonmanagerial jobs. They usually overlap these structures, so that integration is not too complicated.[20]

Pricing of managerial jobs relies on surveys and studies of salary structures, which, in turn, influence the factors in job evaluation. Studies of differentials in rates tend to find explanations in terms of size (numbers of employees), managers' span of control, and the going rates of pay for subordinates.[21]

5.2   Package Pay. Programs of executive compensation have not been successful in maintaining the historic differentials in executive pay. The structure has narrowed. Executive pay has not maintained its earlier ratio to profits. Progressive income taxes now cut deeply into executives salaries and limit opportunities for saving.

The current practice of *package payments* seeks to maintain what are regarded as essentials in the incentivation of top managers. It includes, as a base, a careful regard for the *going rate*. A number of executive and managerial salary surveys are conducted for this purpose, and data with respect to corporate salaries are available from the Securities and Exchange Commission.[22]

Many programs add to the base pay a bonus based on improvements in sales or profits or accomplishment of stated objectives.[23] In a 1961 survey

[20] See Robert E. Sibson, "Management Level Job Evaluation," *Advanced Management,* Vol. 21, No. 2, February, 1956, pp. 20–25; N. Beatrice Worthy, "Pay Levels for Professional and Administrative Personnel," *Management Record,* Vol. 23, No. 3, March, 1961, pp. 22–31.

[21] See David R. Roberts, "A General Theory of Executive Compensation Based on Statistically Tested Propositions," *Quarterly Journal of Economics,* Vol. 70, No. 2, May, 1956, pp. 270–94; A. Charnes, W. E. Cooper, and R. O. Ferguson, "Optimal Estimation of Executive Compensation by Linear Programming," *Management Science,* Vol. 1, No. 2, January, 1955, pp. 138–51; Herbert A. Simon, "The Compensation of Executives," *Sociometry,* Vol. 20, No. 1, March, 1957, pp. 32–35.

[22] See, for example, Harland Fox and Mitchell Meyer, "Top Management Compensation Trends in Manufacturing," *Management Record,* Vol. 21, No. 10, October 1959, pp. 318–21; Arch Patton, "Executive Compensation in 1960," *Harvard Business Review,* Vol. 39, No. 5, September-October, 1961, pp. 152–57, and "What is an Executive Worth?" *ibid.,* Vol. 39, No. 2, March-April, 65–73; "Executive Pay Trends Changing," *Nation's Business,* Vol. 46, No. 12, December, 1958, pp. 57ff.; N. B. Winstanley, "Practical Guides for Executive Compensation," *Advanced Management,* Vol. 24, No. 1, January, 1959, pp. 9–13.

[23] See "Incentive Bonuses for Executives," *Management Record,* Vol. 18, No. 3, March, 1956, pp. 82–84; Perrin Stryker, "The Executive Bonus," *Fortune,* December, 1956, pp. 127–31; Richard C. Smyth, "Bonus Plans for Executives," *Harvard Business Review,* Vol. 37, No. 4, July-August, 1959, pp. 71ff.

undertaken by Cresap, McCormick, and Paget, 64 per cent of the 80 reporting firms provide special incentive plans. Executives are rewarded individually; in half of the cases, performance is appraised informally.[24]

Many packages include supplements that combine profit-sharing with deferred benefits to avoid the heaviest impacts of taxes. Elements in the package may include *tax-exempt services:* a company car and driver, club memberships, and other fringes. More important components supplement current salaries with sizable contributions to a *tax-exempt trust fund* for profit-sharing. Another involves the granting of *options* to purchase stock and thus to develop capital gains (taxable at a lower rate) rather than salary income. Other common provisions pay for *insurance* against catastrophic illness and temporary or permanent disability.

Stock options have become a favorite special incentive for executives in recent years. These arrangements offer top managers the opportunity to buy stocks in the future at what is regarded as the current fair market value. Plans assume that stock market values will be directly affected by the success of management, so that these rights can become increasingly valuable. At the same time, the plans are expected to tie the executive to the firm by increasing his personal share of proprietorship. While the plans have caught on rapidly, their effects are not entirely clear. They do tend to hold managers until the option period has expired if business and market values are improving. However, much, if not most, of the stock thus acquired is not retained.[25]

6.0 SUMMARY

This chapter describes the major programs designed to implement policy on financial compensation. The preliminary section of the chapter notes the distinctive terminology that has grown up about wage and salary administration. Thereafter, sections distinguish programs in terms of major compensation policies.

It should be noted that programs discussed in this chapter represent only a part of the financial compensation of modern employees and managers. Employee benefits and services add an impressive supplement to total take-home pay. These benefits and services have become so. prominent and important in current practice that an additional chapter, directly following, notes the most common of these programs.

SELECTED SUPPLEMENTARY READINGS

Chernick, Jack, "A Guide to the Guaranteed Annual Wage," *Bulletin No. 4,* Institute of Management and Labor Relations, Rutgers University, 1955. Also his

[24] *Industrial Relations News,* Vol. 11, No. 44, November 4, 1961.
[25] See "Executive Compensation—How Much to Whom?" *Acme Reporter* (Official Publication of Association of Consulting Management Engineers, Inc.), 1959 Series, No. 3, August, 1959.

"The Guaranteed Annual Wage, Employment and Economic Progress," *Industrial and Labor Relations Review,* Vol. 9, No. 3, pp. 469–73, April, 1956.

Garbarino, Joseph W., "Wage Escalation and Wage Inflation," *Reprint No. 155,* University of California Institute of Industrial Relations, Berkeley, 1961.

Laws, Robert H., "Job Evaluation in Small Industry," *Management Aids for Small Manufacturers,* Small Business Administration, May, 1958.

Patton, Arch, *Men, Money and Motivation.* New York: McGraw-Hill Book Company, Inc., 1961.

Position Evaluation Techniques, Pamphlet No. 10, Washington, D.C.: Society for Personnel Administration, 1955.

"The Stock Option Scandal," Industrial Union Department, *Publication No. 32,* AFL-CIO, December, 1959.

Tower, James W., "Incentive Patterns of Executive Compensation," in *Addresses on Industrial Relations, 1960 Series,* Bulletin No. 28, University of Michigan Bureau of Industrial Relations, 1960.

Zinck, W. Clements, "Incentive Applications in the Small Manufacturing Plant," *Personnel Journal,* Vol. 40, No. 2, June, 1961, pp. 72–78.

SHORT CASE PROBLEM 21.1

Point Values for Skilled Jobs

"A point's a point," says the shop foreman, "but I simply can't hire or hold our skilled men with these rates." He referred to rates based on a straight wage line fitted to the point values and wage rates on a dozen key jobs. The new rates had been in effect only a short time. They were established, following job evaluation, on a unilateral basis by the employer. The wage line raised many job rates in the shop, but it reduced those at the top.

The job-evaluation program was undertaken to provide a basis for a sound wage structure throughout the shop. It was conducted by an interdepartmental committee. Comparisons of earlier rates with wage-survey data had indicated that the old structure was not in line with those of the industry. The new wage line was keyed to rates shown in the survey.

Problem: What is the source of this difficulty? Prepare a memorandum to the director of employee relations suggesting alternative methods of correcting the deficiency.

SHORT CASE PROBLEM 21.2

Job Evaluation for Bank Managers

The chairman of the board of directors of the Second National Bank has proposed that all managerial positions be included in the bank's job evaluation plan. He has talked with executives in several large business organizations in which such a practice has been found entirely possible and helpful. He proposed this action to the board at its latest meeting. The president asked that no action be taken until he could discuss it with those who would be affected.

Most of the middle-management group appear to be opposed to such a procedure. The president, while trying to remain neutral, has expressed a fear that if salaries are fitted to job evaluation, he will lose his best men. Many department heads and assistants insist that their jobs simply can't be rated on the scale used for subordinate positions. Others argue that no individual or small group can possibly know what their jobs involve. It is also argued that the qualities for which managers are paid are so varied and intangible that no systematic comparison of jobs makes sense.

The personnel manager and his staff are united in favoring the idea. The chairman of the board, through the president, has asked the personnel department to prepare a statement in favor of the development, explaining what it would do and how it would be done.

Problem: You have been assigned the responsibility for a first draft of this statement, to be directed to the rest of the personnel staff for discussion.

SHORT CASE PROBLEM 21.3

Changing Wage Plans

A change in wage plans appears to have effected a significant improvement in the productivity of employees in the welding shop of firm X. Data are summarized below. Appraise the change to discover the probability that it is merely accidental variation.

PRODUCTIVITY OF EMPLOYEES IN UNITS PER DAY

Employee	Before the Change	After the Change
A	21	21
B	24	27
C	30	32
D	37	40
E	27	27
F	26	25
G	29	32
H	22	24
I	34	36
J	33	36
K	31	34
L	21	21
M	23	25
N	25	27
O	27	27
P	24	23
Q	26	28
R	35	37
S	36	37
T	35	37
U	22	22
V	24	25
W	24	26
X	36	37
Y	29	30
Z	31	33

SHORT CASE PROBLEM 21.4

Wage Dispute Over Computation of Hours[*]

The Background: Two employees on the 3:30 to 12 midnight shift worked a ten-hour day, Monday through Saturday. On Thursday, because of a breakdown in equipment, they started at 9:30 P.M. and worked until 6:00 A.M. Friday morning.

[*] *Employee Relations and Arbitration Report,* Vol. 20, No. 24, May 31, 1960, pp. 5, 6.

They were paid for a total of 67 straight time hours. They asserted that the company had failed to compute their hours properly, and claimed they were short five hours pay. The contract provided that the workweek was to start at 12:01 A.M. Monday. It also provided that time and one-half would be paid for all hours worked over eight daily and for a sixth consecutive day, and double time would be paid for a seventh consecutive day.

The Issue: Did the company compute the hours properly?

The Union Argues: The company did not compute the hours according to the terms of the agreement. It based its computations on the 24-hour period following the start of the employees' shift, instead of computing the hours worked from the contractually established starting time of 12:01 A.M. Under the agreement, each workday commences at 12:01 A.M The company has failed to follow a consistent definition of the workday, since it has used the contract's starting time in some cases and the employees' shift starting time in others. As result of the company's improper computations, the employees were not fully paid for the hours they worked.

The Company Argues: The employees were straight shift employees scheduled to work a ten-hour day. The company concedes that the workday begins at 12:01 A.M. But it believes that an *employee's* workday begins with the start of his shift and continues for the next 24 hours. These employees worked a total of 58 hours, 40 hours at straight time, and 18 hours at time and one-half. They were properly paid for 67 straight time hours. It makes no difference whether the hours were computed on a daily or weekly basis. Any other way of computing the hours would result in pyramiding, which is prohibited by the agreement.

Problem: Use the actual arbitration case to check your judgment in this type of wage adjustment and decide the issue thus presented.

22. Employee Benefits and Services

An important part of total financial compensation, from the manager's viewpoint, is composed of the costs of employee benefits and services. They are *labor costs,* an important part of the payroll. They add an additional cost, supplementary to wages and salaries, averaging about 22 per cent of payroll in the United States and much more in some other nations. They are rather clearly here to stay; even the most recently industrialized nations make them an incentive for commitment to industrial employment.

Anyone who questions the effects of tripartite policy-making on the initiative and creativeness of management should be reassured by the growing range and numbers of these services. New benefits appear each year; many of them are suggested by unions or prescribed by government, but managers have done their part.

Dollar costs of these more or less indirect incentives are impressive, ranging from $300 to almost $2,000 per employee per year, not including the costs of similar benefits for managers and executives, which may be many times these amounts. Employee contributions to their costs represent a small fraction of the total, probably less than 5 per cent of earnings.[1]

Costs in the United States are higher in cents per hour but lower as a proportion of earnings than in most other nations. In 1960, average costs in the United States were about 47 cents per hour and about 22 to 23 per cent

---

[1] In the absence of any standard accounting for benefits, it is difficult to compare the experience of firms with respect to costs. Vacations, holidays, and rest periods appear to be among the most expensive benefits. Pensions, disability, and health and welfare programs are also expensive.

of the total payroll. In the United Kingdom, they amounted to about 17 per cent of the payroll; in Canada, 24 per cent; in the Netherlands, 30 per cent; in Japan, 40 per cent; in West Germany, 45 per cent; in Italy, 75 per cent.[2]

Popular usage describes benefits and services as *fringes,* a designation they received in World War II. In the war-time wage stabilization program, many of the usual benefits were regarded as noninflationary supplements to cash wage payments. Many benefits were well established long before that time, however, having been provided by unions and by paternalistic employers to help wage-earners meet common financial problems.

Managers are concerned about benefits and services in part because they are costly, in part because they represent important devices and practices for implementing management objectives, and in part because they create added duties and responsibilities for administrators. Administration of pension and retirement plans or those providing insurance, hospitalization or medical care requires special knowledge and competence. Much of the value of all such programs may be lost if they are not carefully planned and if employees are not advised and counseled in their use of the benefits available to them.

The broad range of benefits and services is suggested by Table 22.1, which represents a partial list of current fringes.

Section 1 of the chapter reviews the tripartite policy that explains these programs. Thereafter, sections outline the most common provisions in terms of their major purposes, noting those designed to increase employee leisure and income, to maintain and improve employee morale and identification with the organization, to advance employment security, to assist in protecting the health of employees and their families, and to prevent dependency in old age.

1.0 TRIPARTITE POLICY ON BENEFITS AND SERVICES

Managers, insofar as they administer employee benefits and services, seek to implement tripartite policy. The intentions they try to carry out are in part public, in part those advanced by employees and their unions, and in part the contributions of employers and managers. Managers do not play a dominant role in administering all benefits and services. Public agencies administer some of them; managers may do little more than comply with prescribed regulations of the programs of unemployment insurance and public old age pensions, for example. To a much more limited degree, some unions have taken over administrative responsibility for other programs; the Teamsters, for example, sometimes insist on their own pension and insurance programs, to which managers merely subscribe and contribute.

Public policy plays a leading role in explaining several important types of fringe provisions. It proposes to find the financial support for socially

[2] See, for details, *The New Competition; International Comparisons,* New York: National Industrial Conference Board, Inc., 1961.

Table 22.1 A Partial List of Employee Benefits and Services

I. For Added Leisure and Income

Call-back pay
Call-in pay
Clean-up time
Clothes-change time
Coffee breaks
Cost-of-living bonus
Downtime pay
Family allowances
Holidays
Hour limits
Jury duty pay
Leave, for illness
Leave, death of relative
Leave, for grievances
Leave, for negotiation
Leave, for voting
Lonely pay
Military bonus
Overtime pay
Portal-to-portal pay
Reporting pay
Rest pauses
Room and board allowance
Setup time
Shift differentials
Standby pay
Supper money
Travel pay
Vacations
Voting time

III. For Employment Security

Death benefits
Layoff pay
Leave for maternity
Retraining plans
Technological adjustment pay
Severance pay
Supplementary unemployment benefits
Unemployment insurance

V. For Old Age and Retirement

Deferred income plans
Old age assistance
Old age counseling
OASDI
Private pension plans
Profit sharing plans
Rest homes
Retirement counseling
Stock ownership plans

II. For Personal Identification and Participation

Anniversary awards
Athletic activities
Attendance bonus
Beauty parlor service
Cafeteria
Canteen
Car wash service
Charm school
Christmas bonus
Counseling
Credit union
Dietetic advice
Discounts
Educational aids
Financial advice
Food service
Home financing
Housing
Income tax aid
Information racks
Laundry service
Legal aid
Loan association
Moving aid
Music with work
Orchestra
Parking space
Quality bonus
Recreational programs
Savings bond aid
Safety clothes
Scholarships
Suggestion bonus
Thrift plans
Transportation aids
Year-end bonus

IV. For Health Protection

Accident insurance
Dental care
Disability insurance
Health insurance
Hospitalization
Illness insurance
Life insurance
Medical care plan
Medical examinations
Optical services
Plant nursing service
Sickness insurance
Sick benefits
Sick leave
Surgical care plan
Temporary disability insurance
Visiting nurse service
Workmen's compensation

desirable benefits at the source of most personal income. Employment, it concludes, should carry a substantial share of the costs of *maintaining* the labor force, as illustrated by the losses involved in industrial accidents or ill health or unemployment.

Public policy has long emphasized the advancement of economic security for wage and salary workers. It has exerted the major influence in providing such benefits as *unemployment insurance* and *public pensions.* Public policy has favored shorter working hours, *paid vacations,* and *premium pay* to discourage overtime. It has proposed greater leisure to facilitate increased participation in civic activities and as a protection against accidents and illness. Public policy has sought to make credit available to those who may need small loans; *credit unions* have been favored as a means to that end. Public policy has sought to relieve workers of the economic burdens resulting from industrial ill health and accidents; *workmen's compensation laws* are an expression of this policy, as are laws providing *temporary disability insurance.*

Employee-union policy has supported all of these public intentions. In addition, it has sought to make work less irksome by permitting *rest pauses* and other breaks without penalty. It has used the same practices, along with others, to increase payments to workers, as illustrated by requirements of premium pay for overtime, shift differentials, double or treble pay on Sundays and holidays, employment of standby workers, and paid vacations. Unions have sought more generous benefits for unemployment through *supplemental unemployment benefits* (SUB). Unions have advanced plans for special assistance and *retraining* for workers who become unemployed on account of automation and other changes in demands for their services. Unions have sought added protection against the hazards of illness through *paid sick leave* and a variety of *health and welfare programs.*

Although managers may sometimes appear as opposed to all fringes, they have invented and advanced many of their own. Moreover, once such benefits are offered by one firm, managers in many others may seek to provide them or improve on them in order to secure and hold the workers they need. Managers have recognized that many benefits offer possibilities of implementing their policies to improve employee morale, to encourage wider participation and understanding, and to assist employees in identifying their personal goals and interests with those of the organization. Managers have also recognized economies to be gained through group sponsorship of such services as insurance and hospitalization. Accordingly, they have sponsored private pension and retirement programs and provided recreational, counseling, legal aid, and other similar services.

2.0 ADDED LEISURE AND INCOME

Many, but by no means all of the employee benefits in this category can be traced to employee-union policy. Reductions in what are usually described as *normal* hours of work, premium pay for second and third shifts, paid holidays, vacations, and rest periods have frequently been negotiated. So have the many *work rules* represented by call-in and call-back pay and the provision of standby workers. Many of these benefits also express public policy. At the same time, they frequently implement management policy that seeks to discover the most satisfactory and efficient pattern of working hours and working conditions.

2.1   Hours of work. A variety of benefits is associated with arrangements of working hours. Most obvious is the payment of *premium rates* for *overtime* beyond what are considered *normal hours.* Here the influence of public policy is clear; federal policy has established 40 hours as the normal workweek and 8 hours as the normal work-day for interstate industry. Hours in excess of these must be compensated at time and one-half for all but *exempt* employees—normally those with supervisory and managerial responsibility and authority.

Some firms, however, offer more attractive arrangements. They may pay exempt employees overtime. A few of them have experimented with shorter work weeks and attempted to discover the *ideal work week* for the next 10 or 20 years. Additional premium pay is common for work on *holidays, weekends, Sundays,* and additional *sixth* and *seventh* days worked in the week. While time and one-half is the usual payment for overtime, most current practice pays double rates for overtime on Saturdays and holidays. All these provisions are frequently used to increase earnings rather than to assure more leisure.

Some employers regard the growth of *moonlighting* as indicating that many, if not most, workers need to or want to work longer, rather than shorter, hours. Numbers of moonlighters—workers with other jobs in addition to one full-time job—have been increasing—more than 100 per cent from 1950 to 1960. In December, 1961, there were more than three million, with 1¾ million holding more than one wage-earner job and 1¼ million who combine self-employment with a wage or salary job. Moonlighters are more common among male than among female workers and among married men than among those who are unmarried. Largest numbers are in agricultural and professional-technical occupations. The most common second jobs are in sales and service activities.[3]

Managerial policy on moonlighting is far from uniform. Although many managers express the opinion that the practice is undesirable and lowers the efficiency of workers on the primary job, most employers condone it unless it involves working for a competitor or engaging in some activity that reflects unfavorably on the primary employer.

2.2   Shift differentials. Night shifts ordinarily receive from five to ten

[3] See Jacob Schiffman, "Multiple Jobholders in December, 1960," *Monthly Labor Review,* Vol. 84, No. 10, October, 1961, pp. 1066–1073; Alan C. Filley, "Spotlight on Moonlighting," *Personnel,* Vol. 37, No. 6, November-December, 1960, pp. 45–49; "Moonlighting and Its Controls," *Management Record,* Vol. 19, No. 7, July, 1957, pp. 234ff.; Estelle Hepton, "Moonlighting in Waikiki," *ILR Research* (New York State School of Industrial and Labor Relations), Vol. 7, No. 1, Spring, 1961, pp. 3–9.

per cent more than the regular day shift. A third shift—after midnight—
usually receives the highest premium. Sometimes, this pay differential is implemented by an arrangement in which employees receive 8 hours pay for
7 or 7½ hours of work.

2.3 Paid holidays. Eight legal holidays are provided for employees in the
federal service. Analysis of union contract provisions indicates that most of
them provide for six paid holidays. One practice provides a half-holiday before Christmas and New Year's. Another less common practice gives each
employee a holiday on his birthday.[4]

2.4 Paid vacations. Formerly a type of benefit available only to salaried
employees, paid vacations are now common for all employees. Studies of collective bargaining agreements filed with the federal Department of Labor
report that more than 90 per cent of the agreements include provision for
graduated vacations, based on length of service. The most common pattern
allows paid vacations of 1 week for 1 year's service, 2 weeks for 5 years, 3
weeks for 15 years, and 4 weeks for 25 years. A trend toward liberalizing
these provisions is apparent.

2.5 Rest pauses and coffee breaks. These have become common practice
in employment. In part, they are little more than a formal recognition of
the fact that workers take such breaks and a means of establishing some
ground rules for them. Common practice provides short 10 to 15 minute
periods in mid-morning and mid-afternoon. They are less frequently formal-
ized on other shifts.

Several policies explain these provisions. Some experience suggests their
value in improving communications. They may be intended to reduce monotony on the job, improve attention to work, and increase productivity
during the rest of the working period. They provide an opportunity for employees to become acquainted and perhaps to develop greater identification
with members of their work groups. This practice has been frequently criticized as a waste of time. Some difficulty may be encountered in holding the
break within the time limits set for it. Some cynics have proposed that interest throughout the whole working day is so desultory that what is needed
is a work break![5]

2.6 Standby, downtime, and reporting pay. Current practice frequently
provides minimum guarantees of pay for short working periods. *Standby
pay* insures that an employee shall be paid for unworked time in which
he remains available at the request of a supervisor. *Downtime pay* relieves
an employee of lost-time deductions when machine failure or other interference prevents him from continuing his work. *Reporting pay* grants regular
wages for a minimum of 2 to 4 hours to employees who find upon reporting
that they have no work to do. Such a benefit is available only if they have

---

[4] For details, see *Personnel Policies and Practices Report,* Par. 7102, No. 15–146,
1961.

[5] For details, see Dena G. Weiss and Ernestine M. Moore, "Paid Rest Periods in
Major Contracts, 1959," *Monthly Labor Review,* Vol. 83, No. 9, September, 1960, pp.
958ff; *Personnel Policies and Practices Report,* Par. 291, No. 26–15, 1961.

not been properly notified. *Call-in pay* provides a minimum (usually four hours) of pay for employees who are called in for special work in addition to their normal work-day or work-week. Such compensations may also be described as *call-back pay.*

Other benefits of a similar type provide *portal-to-portal pay,* in which employees are credited with working time from their entrance to the employer's premises. Special time allowances may compensate for wash-up and changing to and from working clothes.[6]

2.7 Leaves of absence. These may be granted to employees, with or without pay. Generally, short leaves of a few days involve no loss of pay. Longer leaves are without pay, but the employee is assured that his job will be held open for him and that he will suffer no loss of seniority.

Short leaves are granted on request and are conditional on the purpose for which they are requested. Perhaps the most common are those in which an employee seeks to attend a funeral in the family or to visit relatives. Long-term leaves may be granted to employees who seek to hold public or union office. *Maternity leave* has become a common practice. Most plans permit the employee to accumulate seniority during the absence; others protect seniority at the time of the leave. Plans usually provide that the employee can return to the same or a similar job after the leave.[7]

3.0 MORALE: PERSONAL IDENTIFICATION

Managers, largely on their own initiative, have created a number of common benefits they hope will facilitate employee adjustment to and appreciation of working conditions and relationships. These aids are regarded as evidencing management's interest in each employee and management's willingness to assist him in finding solutions to personal problems. These benefits will, managers intend, encourage a reciprocal feeling of friendliness and personal identification with the interests and mission of the organization.

3.1 Employee counseling. In many larger firms, *professional counselors* assist employees in meeting the major and minor personal crises that arise. Studies of these counseling services disclose a wide range of such problems, including those of diet, absenteeism, transportation, housing, health, insurance, family difficulties, and financial strains. The most common problems are financial, marital, job, personality, and health, in that order, according to one study. Women employees make more use of these counseling services than men. A satisfactory staffing ratio provides one counselor for each 300 employees.

3.2 Legal aid. Among the professional services provided for employees,

[6] See Dena G. Weiss and Theresa L. Ellis, "Paid Time for Washup, Cleanup and Clothes Change in 1959," *Monthly Labor Review,* Vol. 83, No. 9, September, 1960, pp. 964ff.

[7] See "Maternity Leaves of Absence," *Management Record,* Vol. 21, No. 7–8, July-August, 1959, pp. 233–34.

some employers offer legal advice. Such service is usually limited to advice on relatively small problems—financial matters, traffic violations, income tax returns, wills, citizenship, and help in checking real estate and other contracts. For more complicated problems, employees may be assisted in finding satisfactory attorneys in private practice.

In most arrangements, these services are provided by the legal department of the firm. In others, outside attorneys are retained by the employer for this purpose. In some practice, the employee relations staff is authorized to hire an attorney to aid employees in specific problem situations.

3.3 Food services. For larger plants, the provision of special feeding facilities for employees is probably the most common of all services not required by legislation. More than half of the larger manufacturing firms (with 1,000 or more employees) make some formal provision for feeding both office and production employees. Most common is the employee cafeteria. It may serve only a single meal in firms operating on a one-shift basis. It may, on the other hand, serve a meal for each shift and, in addition, provide the facilities for coffee breaks or rest periods.

Food services include lunchrooms, cafeterias, lunch counters, lunch carts or rolling cafeterias, coffee-hour or rest-period eating facilities, snack-bars, coffee bars, and milk bars.

3.4 Recreational programs. Some employers have promoted a wide range of recreational activities for employees and their families. The value of such programs in encouraging identification with fellow workers and with the firm is generally taken for granted; few attempts have been made to evaluate these assumed results. Details of the programs may be developed by paid recreational directors or by committees or associations of employees.

Many types of recreational activities are provided. Indoor and outdoor sports and games (basketball, volleyball, bowling, tennis, softball, golf) are most popular for industry as a whole. Social activities (including dancing, card games, parties, banquets, and smokers) are next. Musical activities (bands, glee clubs, choruses, orchestras), arts, crafts, dramatic programs, outdoor excursions (picnicking, hunting, fishing, and gardening), family programs (parties, picnics, and Boy Scout and Girl Scout activities), libraries, study groups, and hobbies all offer opportunities for recreational planning and leadership.

3.5 Housing and transportation. Some employers have taken the initiative in building homes for their employees. The history of company housing, however, includes many chapters that warn managements to proceed with caution. Early company housing generally involved creation of the company town. Some of these villages have been highly successful, from the standpoint of both management and employees. In many cases, however, employees have objected to supervision by management and to the scrutiny of neighbors who are also fellow employees. The company town has become, in many localities, a symbol of an industrial feudalism that is widely discredited.

Some concerns have sought to avoid these difficulties by assisting employees to buy or build their own homes. Long-term credit has been made available to employees at favorable rates. Some employers have contracted with builders to erect groups of homes, thus reducing building costs. Other managements aid new employees in finding rental property. Such assistance may extend to outright wage and salary supplements for employees asked to move to a new area when new plants are opened. If firms ask employees to make such moves they may compensate for the losses incurred in selling homes and purchasing or building comparable living accommodations in the new location.

Getting employees to and from work is a major problem in many localities. Where streetcars and buses formerly provided adequate facilities, larger plants and suburban living now limit the usefulness of these forms of urban transportation.

To ease the load on public facilities, employers may stagger working schedules for various departments. This practice, however, is frequently unpopular with employees who have organized car pools and group transportation. As larger proportions of employees have come to depend on automobiles for transportation, firms have provided parking lots conveniently available to working locations. Current practice makes no charge for these facilities.

3.6 Credit for employees. Employers have long recognized the frequent needs of employees for credit. Many firms have sought to encourage saving by offering special inducements for employee participation in savings and loan associations. Others have encouraged mutual benefit associations that make small loans to members. Some firms have provided capital for these organizations and have assisted employees in consolidating their obligations and budgeting payments. In part, manager objectives were philanthropic and paternalistic. In part, they were quite practical; they provided a means of avoiding the frequent inconvenience of garnishing wages and making direct payments to creditors.

Garnishments and assignments of wages still represent a source of inconvenience. In some firms, repeated garnishments are a basis for discharge. Meanwhile, however, credit arrangements for employees have expanded and changed. The common practice in larger organizations is encouragement of a *credit union.*

The credit union is a cooperative saving and loaning association. It proposes to facilitate employee saving by providing a convenient investment in stock of the cooperative. At the same time, it makes loans to members without the high interest rates typical of small loans from banks and private lending companies.[8]

---

[8] Much of the growth of credit unions can be traced to early "loan shark" exploitation of workers in years before states provided regulatory legislation.

Credit unions may be chartered by the federal government or by states. Federal legislation to assist such voluntary associations dates from 1934. In 1960, almost 20,000 credit unions were in operation, with approximately 11 million members, assets of approximately 5 billion dollars, and reserves of 250 millions. Local units maintain

3.7 Stores, discounts. Some employers allow employees to purchase the products of the firm at discounted prices. Some firms permit employees to buy through the firm's purchasing office, but this practice is becoming less common.

In earlier practice, firms in isolated localities maintained company stores. Sometimes they paid employees in *scrip,* redeemable only at the company store. Charges of exploitation, overcharging, and manipulated employee accounts were frequent. Stores appeared to be a source of employee dissatisfaction and resentment rather than of good will. All states have outlawed payment in scrip. Stores have almost entirely disappeared.

3.8 Music and work. One benefit that creates divided reactions involves the provision of musical programs to accompany work. Manager policy frequently views it as a means of *reducing strain and monotony* and introducing rhythm in work. Employees have frequently requested music. It has some long-established relationships to work. Early sea chants timed to the reefing of sails, folk songs adapted to the loading of cotton, and other combinations of music and work have a long history. Wartime studies of music and work indicated that it was favored by a majority of both employers and employees. Music is generally welcomed by employees, especially those in monotonous jobs. Several reports indicate that music increases output. In some cases, it has appeared to improve the quality of work. Other reports, however, indicate that it may sometimes distract attention and increase spoilage.

Uhrbrock reports that employee reactions to music on the job, while mixed, show some patterns. Most factory employees react favorably to music. Different age groups react differently. Music appears to encourage increased production among young, inexperienced employees on routine jobs. Older, skilled workers in more complex jobs show no significant effects.[9]

4.0 EMPLOYMENT SECURITY

Policies of employees, their unions, the public, and many employers converge in proposing to maximize such personal and family security as can be provided by *stable employment.* The objective is to provide reasonably steady and certain income from work. Put another way, this policy proposes to relieve workers, so far as possible, from fear and worry about unemployment and the loss of jobs and income.

Similar policy generates numerous other programs, including some already described. Some programs put all employees on a *salary basis* to insure

---

a Credit Union National Association (CUNA), which negotiates surety bonds for member groups and represents their interests in state and federal legislative bodies.

For details, see the reports of the Credit Union National Association, Madison, Wisconsin, and the "Report on Credit Unions," issued each month by Reports, Incorporated, Kent, Connecticut.

[9] Richard S. Uhrbrock, "Music on the Job: Its Influence on Worker Morale and Production," *Personnel Psychology,* Vol. 14, No. 1, Spring, 1961, pp. 9–38.

weekly or monthly income. Others guarantee *annual wages.* One of the most common practices—but one that is infrequently described as a benefit—is the guarantee of *seniority* in *job rights.* Such a provision requires that employees be laid off in the reverse order of their seniority and rehired according to length of service. It permits senior employees to bump their juniors. At least one court has held that when such seniority has been negotiated, employees retain these rights, even if the contract terminates or the plant is moved.[10]

Unemployment is occasioned by a wide range of factors, from personal limitations to seasonal, cyclical, and longer-term cultural and technological change. Public policy is concerned about all types of unemployment from whatever source, but particular concern is presently attached to *persistent unemployment* in particular areas and industries and to *structural* or *technological* or *prosperity unemployment,* occasioned by changing demands for labor and the elimination of jobs.

One type of benefit that has gained wide acceptance both here and abroad is described as *severance pay* or *dismissal compensation.* Another, and the best known type of benefit in this category, is unemployment insurance. In addition to these, current practice includes *supplemental unemployment benefits* and such special retraining assistance as is provided in *technological adjustment pay.*

4.1   Severance pay. One means of cushioning the impact of job losses involves provision of *severance pay* or dismissal pay. It is provided by the employer and involves no waiting period. It thus enables the former employee to support himself while seeking another job. Some foreign legislation has made *dismissal compensation* compulsory in lieu of an extended notice of dismissal.

Current practice provides severance pay in about one-fourth of all collective agreements. Other similar programs are maintained on a unilateral basis by many employers. Some plans make a uniform payment to all employees. Most of them graduate payments according to length of service. Workers become eligible after a minimum of from one to five years employment, and grants are made to employees dismissed because jobs are eliminated by technological change, reduced business activity, shutdown, merger, or other cause beyond the control of the employee. In some cases, severance pay is granted to employees who leave for military service, those who cannot work on account of disability, those who retire, and those who are released for inefficiency. In a few plans, even employees who are discharged *for cause* (meaning serious infractions of work rules) may receive severance pay.

Amounts paid show wide variation. A fairly common pattern allows one week's pay for each year of service in excess of five years.[11]

[10] Zdanok *v.* Glidden Co., 61 ALC 1392, 1961.

[11] For current practice, see the reports of the National Industrial Conference Board as released in the *Management Record* and in "Personnel Practices in Factory and Office," *Studies in Personnel Policy.* See also the *AFL-CIO Collective Bargaining Report,* Vol. 4, No. 10, October, 1959, and subsequent reports.

4.2 Unemployment insurance. Major dependence, as a means of assuring stability in employment income, is placed on unemployment insurance. The present program in the United States dates from 1935. Unemployment insurance was instituted by the Social Security Act, which created a federal tax on employer payrolls and permitted states to recover 90 per cent of that tax if they created acceptable state programs.

Major unemployment insurance provisions of the 1935 act may be outlined as follows:

1. The law levied a tax on specified employer payrolls (defined in terms of size and industry).
2. It excluded railways (which have their own system), agriculture, and non-profit organizations and agencies.
3. It established no federal system of benefits but encouraged states to create benefit-paying facilities.
4. Employers in states that created insurance programs could credit 90 per cent of their federal tax to their states, to be used as insurance funds.
5. Coverage, eligibility for benefits, benefit amounts, and duration were left to the states.

Although details of this law have been modified, the federal-state cooperative program has been preserved. The present federal tax is 3 per cent, levied on the first $3,000 of wages. All states now have their own programs. All are administered through public employment offices directed by state divisions of employment security.

Stated public policy at the time the system was established proposed to provide benefits for those who had lost their jobs, who wanted to work, and who had established eligibility for benefits by earlier working experience. The program was also expected to counter the spiral of recession and depression by maintaining consumer demand in periods of falling employment.

4.21 Coverage. The decision as to which workers shall be covered by these provisions is left to the states. The federal government defines the coverage of its taxes for the program, but states can accept or modify that base for coverage in terms of benefits. For example, while federal taxes are levied only against employers of four or more employees, states can tax smaller units and can make benefits available to their employees. Growing numbers of states have done so. Several states now include employers of one or more, while a larger number includes employers of two or more.

The range of industries covered by these provisions has been extended from time to time. Present coverage is pictured in Figure 22.1.

In total, unemployment insurance protects approximately four-fifths of all wage and salary workers. The 1960 amendments to the federal law extended coverage to some 2.5 million ex-servicemen and to about 65,000 employees of federal instrumentalities (semipublic financial organizations). State

504

coverage was extended in the same year. By 1961, total coverage was about 46.5 millions.[12]

4.22 Benefits. Policy on *benefits* has sought to provide income to meet basic worker living costs but not enough to discourage job seeking. A gross yardstick, widely used, is 50 per cent of usual wages. However, most states have established fixed maximum payments. In periods of rising prices, these limitations quickly get out of date. They become the going rate; in 1957,

1. UNEMPLOYMENT INSURANCE COVERAGE OF WAGE AND SALARY WORKERS
OVER 46 MILLION WAGE EARNERS WERE PROTECTED BY UNEMPLOYMENT INSURANCE IN 1960

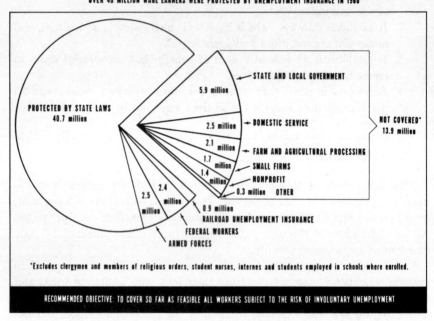

*Excludes clergymen and members of religious orders, student nurses, internes and students employed in schools where enrolled.

RECOMMENDED OBJECTIVE: TO COVER SO FAR AS FEASIBLE ALL WORKERS SUBJECT TO THE RISK OF INVOLUNTARY UNEMPLOYMENT

Figure 22.1   Coverage of Unemployment Insurance, 1961
SOURCE: "Unemployment Insurance: State Laws and Experience," Bureau of Employment Security, April, 1961.

52 per cent of all beneficiaries received the maximum rates. Six states have now established flexible maximum rates (see Figure 22.2).

Meanwhile, also, several states have increased benefit amounts by adding a variable allowance for the number of dependents.

4.23 Duration. States also determine the maximum *duration* of benefits. Maxima vary from state to state, averaging about 24 weeks. As a result, in recession periods (1958 and 1961), federal legislation has been necessary to permit temporary extensions of the benefit period and thus to take care of several millions of workers who exhausted benefit rights. Since 1958, several

[12] See Saul J. Blaustein, "The Challenge Facing the Unemployment Insurance System," *Monthly Labor Review,* Vol. 84, No. 3, 1961, pp. 242–49.

STATE   AVERAGE WEEKLY BENEFIT AMOUNT

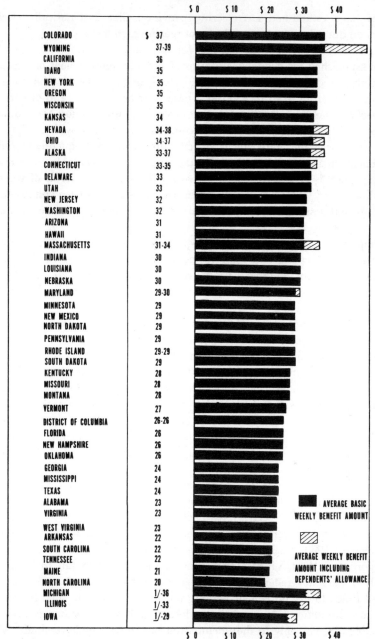

1/ AVERAGE BASIC WEEKLY BENEFIT AMOUNT NOT AVAILABLE

UNITED STATES DEPARTMENT OF LABOR
BUREAU OF EMPLOYMENT SECURITY
UNEMPLOYMENT INSURANCE SERVICE
AUGUST 1960

Figure 22.2   Average Weekly Unemployment Benefits, July 1959–
March 1960

states have established a triggering provision that automatically releases limits on duration when unemployment reaches high levels.

4.24 Eligibility. To be eligible for benefits, an employee must first have established his eligibility in terms of previous employment or earnings. Eligibility is defined in terms of the actual amount earned (the common minimum is from $150 to $300 in a base quarter), or the ratio of earnings to weekly benefits (from 20 to 50 times *weekly earnings*—most commonly 30 times weekly earnings), or by some combination of these with a stipulated number of weeks of employment. Specific provisions are frequently modified.

Benefits may be claimed only if the applicant is available for suitable work, which is generally defined as work comparable—in terms of working conditions and wages—to that in which the claimant has been employed.

Most states stipulate a *waiting period* before benefits become available, generally one week.

Employees may be disqualified for quitting without cause, for having been discharged for cause, and for refusing to accept suitable work. Disqualification may be for a stated period. In most states, strikers are entirely disqualified; in others, i.e., New York and Rhode Island, they are disqualified for a specified period.[13]

4.25 Experience rating. All states have rating arrangements designed to encourage managers to stabilize employment and to police the system. Merit rating operates through tax provisions. Employers who have smaller claims for benefit payments charged against their accounts are taxed at lower rates. These provisions have been under frequent attack from the spokesmen for labor organizations, who argue that they encourage employers to oppose liberalizing benefits. They insist that stabilization is seldom a result of employer action, since stable employment depends largely on the state of the economy, and since erratic employment is generally beyond the control of individual firms.

Merit rating and the reluctance of states to impose higher taxes have created serious problems in financing unemployment insurance. In several states, accumulated reserves have declined rapidly in recent recessions. Although the total reserves of the system amounted to about $6.6 billion at the close of 1960, Alaska was in debt and Michigan, Pennsylvania, Delaware, Oregon, and West Virginia had allowed their funds to fall to hazardous levels. Emergency federal legislation in the 1958 and 1960 recessions provided funds to extend benefit periods and to make loans to state funds.

4.26 Limitations. Unemployment insurance has unquestionably provided valuable aid, not only to the unemployed but to the whole economy. More than 5.8 million workers were assisted in 1957, 8.2 million in 1958, and 6.1 million in 1959. The program paid out $1.8 billion in 1957, $4 billion in 1958, and $2.6 billion in 1959.[14]

---

[13] See Willard A. Lewis, "Unemployment Compensation in Labor Disputes," *Management Record,* Vol. 23, No. 1, January, 1961, pp. 3ff.

[14] See Richard A. Lester, "The Economic Significance of Unemployment Com-

Many critics of the current program suggest that it should be *federalized.* They point to the divergence in taxes, benefits, duration, and disqualification in state programs. They argue that the federal government should at least establish standards of adequate service. They note the tendency of the co-operative system to generate interstate competition for minimum tax rates as a lure to employers. For the same purpose, states may apply more rigorous eligibility rules and disqualifications and restrict benefit amounts and duration. They may expect federal aid when payments threaten the adequacy of reserve funds. The tendency to increase taxes for this purpose when unemployment is at its peak defeats the purpose of cushioning the impact of recession.

Decisions must be made with respect to the present purpose and policy of the whole program. If it is to be simply an organized *system of relief,* then much of the red tape of administration can be eliminated. If it is truly an insurance system, then steps must be taken to relate benefits to premiums. If it is expected to stabilize employment by offering employers tax advantages, taxes must be more realistic. Some proposals favor interstate sharing of costs. The wage base of $3,000 is obviously outdated. And perhaps most important, public employment offices need to be sharply divorced from benefit administration so that they can specialize in finding jobs for people and people for jobs rather than administering benefits.[15]

4.3 Supplemental unemployment benefits. One answer to restrictions on amounts and duration of unemployment benefits is a negotiated system of *supplemental benefits.* Supplemental benefits first appeared as a result of United Automobile Workers-Ford Motor Company negotiations in 1955. Almost immediately they were included in contracts with the other automobile makers. They have since expanded into steel, aluminum, rubber, ocean transportation, and agricultural equipment. In addition, workers in many individual firms in other industries now participate in similar arrangements. Total coverage probably includes at least two million employees.

The plans have been criticized as a union device for encouraging more generous unemployment benefits. They have probably exerted some such influence, although that is not readily demonstrated. They establish a special fund, contributed to by employers, which is used to provide added income to idle employees who are drawing unemployment insurance benefits.

pensation," *Review of Economics and Statistics,* Vol. 42, No. 4, November, 1960, pp. 349–72.

[15] See Joseph M. Becker, S.J., "Twenty-five years of Unemployment Insurance," *Political Science Quarterly,* Vol. 75, No. 4, December, 1960, pp. 481–99, also his "The Adequacy of the Benefit Amount in Unemployment Insurance," Kalamazoo, Michigan: The W. E. Upjohn Institute for Employment Research, May, 1961; Harry Malisoff, "Simplifying Unemployment Insurance Objectives," *BIRC Publication Number 14,* Industrial Relations Section, California Institute of Technology, December, 1960, and his "The Insurance Character of Unemployment Insurance," Kalamazoo, Michigan: The W. E. Upjohn Institute for Employment Research, December, 1961; "Unemployment Insurance and the Family Finances of the Unemployed," *Report Number U–203,* Bureau of Employment Security, July, 1961.

Plans bring workers' total income to about 65 per cent of normal straight-time earnings. Eligibility to receive the supplement is based on eligibility for unemployment insurance. Duration of the supplements depends on credits accumulated by each worker and on the financial status of the fund. A maximum duration is established, usually from 39 to 52 weeks. Funds for these benefits are provided by employer contributions—commonly 5 cents per man-hour. Plans establish a specified maximum for the total of the fund; at that point employer contributions are suspended. They resume whenever the fund drops below this maximum.

Plans have created fewer problems than many observers expected and have spread, but not rapidly. They have provided a valuable element of balance in community economies. They have added from $15 to $30 to weekly benefits for individual workers, with aggregate payments averaging from $10 million to $12 million per month in the 1958 recession period.[16]

4.4 Retraining and TAP. One of the serious threats to the employment income of many workers is *structural unemployment,* the loss of jobs because of changing demands for particular occupations. It may result from changes in customs of consumption; few patrons now use the services of livery stables or millinery shops. Structural unemployment may result from changed methods of production and technological advances. Its appearance is spotty; it strikes more severely in particular industries and localities. Because its impact is especially heavy on the low-skilled, older, less educated, nonwhite workers, it may be closely related to *persistent unemployment.*

Finding new jobs for some displaced workers may not be difficult. In some installations of automation, increased business has itself provided employment, and programs of retraining have prepared employees for these opportunities. In other circumstances, especially if older workers are involved, retraining may be costly and shifts to new types of work may be difficult.

The problem is not new nor is it distinctive to the United States. European nations have developed a variety of programs to cope with it, including *area redevelopment,* assistance in *labor migration, emergency public works, vocational guidance,* and *personal rehabilitation.*[17]

In the United States, most policy proposes some form of retraining benefits. Several states have revised unemployment insurance benefits to permit their payment and extension while workers are taking retraining courses. Within individual firms, programs have advised workers who are to be displaced of plans to eliminate their jobs and of programs for assisting them in making changes. An excellent illustration is provided by the American Tele-

---

[16] For details see "Supplemental Unemployment Benefits," *AFL-CIO Collective Bargaining Report,* Vol. 3, No. 12, December, 1958; John W. McConnell, "Private Unemployment Payment Pay Plans—Economic Effects," *Monthly Labor Review,* Vol. 79, No. 3, March, 1956, pp. 300–303.

[17] See "Economic Programs for Labor Surplus Areas in Selected Countries of Western Europe," *Joint Committee Print,* Washington, D.C.: Government Printing Office, 1960.

phone and Telegraph Company's change to automatic dial operation and direct dialing in long distance calls. Retraining included both on-the-job and classroom instruction. It may help displaced employees find jobs in other firms.[18] Retraining may require changes in existing jobs—job enlargement—and retraining employees for broader responsibilities.

Among the most widely publicized retraining programs are those of Armour and Company and the Amalgamated Meat Cutters and Butcher Workers and the United Packinghouse Workers, the American Cable and Radio Corporation and the Communications Workers, the Longshoremen of the Pacific Coast and the Steamship and Stevedoring Employers, and similar programs for east coast longshoremen and those in Hawaii.[19] These plans create special *automation funds,* maintained by contributions from employers, to be used in easing the impact of technological change. They relieve pressure for opposition to changes. They guarantee employees against layoff on this account, assure them of a minimum of 35 hours per week, protect individuals against any speed-up, and provide for early retirement benefits.

A new fringe, combining long advance notice of displacement with special compensation, appeared as a result of negotiations in the meat-packing industry in 1961. Called *TAP,* for *technological adjustment pay,* it assures employees of Armour and Company who are members of the United Packinghouse Workers or the Amalgamated Meat Cutters and Butcher Workmen 90 days advance notice of shutdowns. Employees with five years of seniority are entitled to from 26 to 39 weeks of pay if other jobs are not found for them.

5.0 HEALTH AND WELFARE

Current policy proposes to protect employment income against the major health hazards of workers and their dependents. Several types of benefits have been developed for this purpose, including those that provide compensation for industrial accidents and work-connected illness, numerous forms of insurance, and medical, dental, nursing, and hospital services.

5.1 Safety programs and workmen's compensation. No accurate national summary of numbers of accidents, time lost, or total economic loss occasioned by work-connected accidents and illness is possible, because reporting systems in the states are not uniform. In most states, on-the-job accidents are re-

[18] See "Automation's Impact," *Wall Street Journal,* December 1, 1961.
[19] See Max D. Kossoris, "Working Rules in West Coast Longshoring," *Monthly Labor Review,* Vol. 84, No. 1, January, 1961, pp. 1–10; "Information and Union Comment on the 1960 Mechanization and Modernization Fund Agreement," San Francisco: International Longshoremen's and Warehousemen's Union (150 Golden Gate Ave.), November, 1960; Leonard P. Adams and Robert L. Aronson, *Workers and Industrial Change,* Ithaca, New York: Cornell University, 1959; "Industrial Relations Counselors," *Current News,* June 29, 1961 (American Cable plan); "Progress Report of Armour's Tripartite Automation Committee," *Monthly Labor Review,* Vol. 84, No. 8, August, 1961, pp. 851–57.

ported only if they occasion loss of time beyond the shift in which they occur. In some states, only compensable accidents and illness are reported, which means that the time lost must extend through a several-day waiting period in which no compensation is paid.

For purposes of comparison from plant to plant and time to time, work-connected accident and illness are frequently measured in terms of frequency and severity rates. Such rates take account of the exposure or opportunity for working accidents, that is the total number of man-hours worked. Accident frequency rates are calculated as the number of lost-time accidents per million man-hours worked. Accident-severity rates are calculated as the number of days lost per million man-hours.

In recent years, practice has also tended to note the number of disabling injuries and the total time loss occasioned by such injuries. Disabling injuries are classified as fatalities, permanent total disabilities, permanent partial disabilities, and temporary total disabilities.

Accident frequency and severity rates vary widely from one industry to another. High frequency rates are common in coal mining, other mining, lumbering, meat packing, and woodworking. High severity rates are notable in coal mining, other mining, lumbering, construction, and marine transportation.[20]

Public requirement of financial benefits for those injured on the job has encouraged a nonfinancial benefit—*safety programs.* These programs involve determined efforts to reduce both accidents and the losses they cause. They begin with the assumption that most work-connected accidents can be prevented. They search for and try to reduce the influence of personal characteristics and working conditions that cause accidents. For example, beards may offer special hazards, as may neglected fire extinguishers, loose-fitting clothes, shorts worn by attractive girl employees, neckties on machine operators, improper glasses, and careless enforcement of safety rules.

Safety programs try to discover when, where, and why accidents occur. They provide necessary safety equipment—shoes, goggles, gloves. These programs make strenuous efforts to enlist employee understanding and cooperation. Supervisors are given special training in accident prevention. Bulletin boards maintain a continuing campaign. Publications feature the safety program. Contests between departments and plants encourage all employees to watch for hazards and to avoid or censure unsafe actions.

5.11 Accident proneness. A great deal of attention has been directed to *accident proneness,* the tendency of certain employees to have more than their share of accidents. Preliminary analysis tends to relate this condition to personal characteristics, but research indicates that no simple concept of accident proneness is realistic. Many conditions, some personal and some environmental, influence the accident experience of workers. Some individuals have more than their share of accidents. Individuals also vary in their

[20] For details of numbers and costs of accidents, see the reports of the National Safety Council, especially *National Safety News* and *Accident Facts,* also frequent reports in the *Monthly Labor Review.*

accident proneness from time to time. Their proneness is, however, influenced by numerous working and living conditions as well as by personal traits.

Some prediction is possible. Repeaters appear to be those whose attention is less readily held, who are more susceptible to distraction, who are more independent and resistant to group pressures, and who usually present an appearance of great self-confidence. They are independent in attitude and less sensitive. They may be physically weak and chronically tired as well as somewhat less self-controlled. They may show tendencies toward egocentricity, anxiety, and resentment.[21]

On the other hand, environmental factors may reduce or magnify the influence of all such variables. Jobs that threaten work status or comfort, probability of layoff or shutdown, unstable family relationships, characteristics of residential areas, and adequacy of earnings may be significant factors in accident experience.[22]

5.12 Legislation. Current policy assumes that employees do not intentionally create situations that injure themselves or fellow-workers. Policy has discarded the earlier viewpoint expressed in *employers' liability laws* and the *common law rules* incorporated in this type of legislation. Employers' liability laws assumed that employees must accept the normal hazards of their jobs. These laws noted that employees are sometimes at least partially responsible for injuries to co-workers and that employees frequently contribute to the causes of accidents in which they are injured. Policy proposed to protect employers from claims arising under these conditions.

Employees, employers, and the public found many unsatisfactory results of procedure under employers' liability laws. Since employees must sue for their benefits, a large number of such cases came into court. Employers were constantly harassed with the possibility of expensive settlements. Many employees found court procedure so expensive that they settled out of court. In many cases, injured employees were left without means of support and became public charges. Most of the funds paid by employers went to lawyers, insurers, and the courts. Only about one-third of the total reached injured employees.

Policy is quite different in the *workmen's compensation laws* that have largely superseded employers' liability acts. All states have such legislation, and federal laws provide workmen's compensation for government employees, longshoremen, and harbor workers. No attempt is made to allocate responsibility or to distribute the burden of accidents on the basis of such allocations. All serious injuries are compensable. Benefits are standardized and adminis-

---

[21] See Thomas N. Jenkins, "The Accident Prone Personality: A Preliminary Study," *Personnel*, Vol. 33, No. 1, July, 1956, pp. 29–32; Anthony Davids and James T. Mahoney, "Personality Dynamics and Accident Proneness in an Industrial Setting," *Journal of Applied Psychology*, Vol. 41, No. 5, October, 1957, pp. 303–6.

[22] See Russell de Reamer, "Accident Proneness: Fact or Fiction," *Supervisory Management*, Vol. 3, No. 12, December, 1958, pp. 12–14; Paul Slivnick, Willard Kerr, and William Kosinar, "A Study of Accidents in 147 Factories," *Personnel Psychology*, Vol. 10, No. 1, Spring, 1957, pp. 43–54; Wayne K. Kirchner, "The Fallacy of Accident Proneness," *Personnel*, Vol. 38, No. 6, November-December, 1961, pp. 34–37.

tration seeks to avoid the necessity for court action. Ultimate recourse to the courts is permitted, but special administrative machinery is provided, so that complicated legal procedure is generally unnecessary. For the most part, employers hire insurance companies to assume their risks under the acts, although several laws allow them to post a bond guaranteeing payment of compensation costs in lieu of such insurance.

All states now have compensation laws. In only about half of them, however, is employer participation compulsory. In the rest, employers may elect to come under the new laws or to remain under liability provisions.

Workmen's compensation benefits are provided through insurance. Employers pay for such benefits by their purchase of insurance. Premiums are based on rates that reflect hazards. In firms where accidents are expected to be numerous or serious, rates reflect this risk. As a result, incentive is provided for the reduction and control of accidents.

The coverage provided by workmen's compensation laws is limited. Agricultural and domestic employees are generally excluded. Laws also specify what types of accidents, injuries, and illness are compensable. Some laws exclude firms with less than 15 to 20 employees, although about half the state laws cover all firms, without reference to size. States do not uniformly provide coverage for their own and other public employees, although most states provide some such coverage. *Waiting periods* range from 1 to 14 days.

Because insurance costs reflect individual employer experience, many employers have been reluctant to hire persons already partially disabled. A workman who has suffered a partial disability, as, for instance, the loss of sight in one eye, is more likely to become totally disabled than a similar employee with no such partial disability. To prevent discrimination in hiring, all but five states have created special *second-injury rules.* Employers assume responsibility for only the additional partial disability. Public funds are provided to supplement the employer's contribution and thus to provide the heavier benefit.

Most of the laws originally contemplated benefits for temporary total disability amounting to about two-thirds of the average weekly wage. These percentage maxima are restricted, however, by dollar limits. Benefits are also limited by a specified maximum number of weeks for which they can be paid and by a maximum total payment. As a result most of the actual benefit payments fall well below 50 per cent of average weekly wages. Survivors' benefits are provided.[23]

In all states, benefits include medical aid. About three-fourths of the states provide complete medical care; others specify dollar or time limits.

Laws are usually administered by state departments of labor or industrial

[23] See "State Workmen's Compensation Laws," Bulletin 212, Washington, D.C.: Department of Labor, Dec., 1961; Earl F. Cheit, "Adequacy of Workmen's Compensation," *Insurance Law Journal,* April, 1955, pp. 245ff.; also his "Benefit Levels in Workmen's Compensation," *Monthly Labor Review,* Vol. 80, No. 7, July, 1958, pp. 723–30; Monroe Berkowitz, "Trends and Problems in Workmen's Compensation," *Social Service Review,* Vol. 32, No. 2, June, 1958, pp. 167–80.

commissions. In five states, they are administered by the courts. A common practice creates special tripartite review tribunals for cases which become matters of dispute. Some 23 states include provisions for maintenance of workers during programs of vocational rehabilitation. In only a few states is this program closely integrated with the administration of benefits. As a result, many of those who should receive constructive attention are neglected.

5.2 Compensation for illness. It is clear that industrial accidents represent only one of many types of health hazards that threaten worker income. Illness is also a constant hazard. Male workers lose an average of five working days per year on account of illness; female workers lose seven. Current practice provides a number of health and welfare programs designed to minimize the economic losses arising from illness. For many types of work-connected sickness, workmen's compensation may provide benefits. For other illness, current programs provide paid sick leave, temporary disability insurance, hospitalization, insurance against catastrophic illness, medical and surgical care, and dental services. The Old Age and Survivor's Disability Insurance program has been modified to include disability benefits for covered workers.

Workmen's compensation laws provide benefits for work-connected illness. In 18 states, laws provide *schedule coverage,* which means that they cover a specified list of diseases regarded as resulting from employment. Thirty-four other laws provide *full coverage,* meaning that all such conditions are covered. In two states, no coverage of occupational diseases is included.

Weekly benefits and survivors' benefits are approximately the same as for accidents.

5.3 Temporary disability insurance. The larger share of employee disabilities are not work-related; most lost time from accidents and illness is, for this reason, not covered by workmen's compensation. To meet this hazard, legislation in four states provides *temporary disability insurance.* The federal government provides similar protection for railroad workers. In all, about 11 million workers enjoyed this protection in 1960.

Formal temporary disability plans vary in the methods by which benefits are provided. In Rhode Island and in the railroad plan, all coverage is provided by a public insurance fund. In California, New York, and New Jersey, private insurance and self-insurance may be substituted for participation in the public insurance plan. New York administers the program through its Workmen's Compensation Board. The other states administer their programs through the public employment service. Funds are provided for the most part by employee contributions, although employers contribute in New Jersey and in the federal program for interstate transportation. Benefits range from ten to 85 dollars per week, and are calculated as from one-half to two-thirds of average weekly wages.[24]

It is notable that none of this legislation has been enacted since 1950. Reports on the value and usefulness of provisions are generally favorable, but the public insurance plan in California paid out 117 per cent of its income,

[24] For details, see *Personnel Policies and Practices Report,* Par. 25.323.

and in Rhode Island, expenditures exceeded income by 4 per cent in 1959. No strong movement has developed to expand coverage by additional state laws.[25]

5.4   Paid sick leave. Legally required disability insurance provides only a relatively small portion of the total benefits paid workers to compensate for illness. Skolnick estimates that formal paid sick-leave benefits amounted to approximately 70.5 per cent of the wage loss for covered workers. Negotiated sick-leave plans paid an average of $35 per week in 1958.[26]

In 1960, about one-fifth of all collective bargaining agreements included sick-leave provisions. Employees with one year's service are granted from 2 to 20 days of paid sick leave each year. Some plans are graduated; numbers of days increase with length of service. A few plans pay employees for unused leave. Still others allow employees to accumulate unused leave up to specified maxima.

All of these benefits may be supplemented by other programs that provide *hospitalization* and *medical, surgical,* and *optical* care and a wide range of insurance. Group hospitalization and surgical-care plans now protect some 85 million workers and dependents. Medical-care plans cover about 50 million workers and family members.

Detailed provisions vary widely and are subject to constant change, generally toward making them more liberal. Hospitalization, for example, may cover all or only a part of total costs. Medical care may specify maximum dollar amounts; hospitalization generally states limits in days. Most hospitalization plans are non-contributory; employers pay total costs. Several unions maintain their own health centers.[27]

5.5   Group health programs. In addition to these various benefits, increasing numbers of employees are included in group health programs. For some, this service is provided voluntarily by employers. For others, their union maintains the necessary health centers and clinics. In other situations, medical-care programs have been negotiated and are jointly administered.

Large-scale health programs, whether conducted in the plant or provided by agreement with a local clinic, offer a wide range of health services. Many plants supplement preliminary physical examinations with later examinations at regular intervals. Some plant medical facilities provide physical examina-

---

[25] For details see Herbert M. Wilson, "A Decade of Disability Insurance," *Employment Security Review,* Vol. 23, No. 12, December, 1956, pp. 13–16; annual reports of the Bureau of Employment Security on "Significant Temporary Disability Insurance Data."

[26] See Alfred M. Skolnick, "Income-loss Protection Against Short-term Sickness, 1948–1957," *Social Security Bulletin,* January, 1959, pp. 7–14; "Sickness and Accident Benefits," *AFL-CIO Collective Bargaining Report,* Vol. 4, No. 11, November, 1959, pp. 65–68.

[27] For details, see "Major Medical Insurance: An Analysis of Evolving Patterns," Industrial Relations Memo No. 134, New York: Industrial Relations Counselors, 1957; "Hospitalization Benefits," AFL-CIO Collective Bargaining Reports, Vol. 5, Nos. 4 and 7, May-June and September, 1960; see also publications of the Foundation of Employee Health, Medical Care and Welfare, Inc., 1300 Connecticut Ave., N.W., Washington 6, D.C.

tions, give emergency medical attention, and are also available for regular consultations. Others provide the services of dentists, oculists, trained nurses; and psychiatrists on a full-time basis. Notable among significant developments in these services is the increasing attention given to psychosomatic problems.[28]

Employees have generally not abused these provisions. In one California study, for example, absences charged to sickness were actually less frequent among workers who were given paid sick leave. Workers with health insurance show more frequent illness than those without, but their hospitalization is shorter.[29]

6.0 OLD AGE AND RETIREMENT

A major source of worker concern about economic security is the possibility of dependency in old age. Workers know that they are living longer than their fathers and grandfathers. As industrialization continues, fewer families provide their own homes for the aging. The family farm has become unavailable as a spot for retirement. Involuntary retirement, disability, or death may create serious economic problems for workers or their survivors.

Current policy, seeking to insure a minimum of insecurity, has developed public, union, and individual firm programs to meet these problems. Public programs now provide both old age pensions and less formal, noncontributory assistance. Private programs provide supplementary pensions and retirement programs.

6.1 OASDI. The Social Security Act established a system of retirement benefits based on equal employer and employee contributions to public insurance reserves. Policy proposes a system of earned benefits based on contributions by employees and their employers. The system is financed by a payroll tax on the first $4,800 of annual earnings in covered employment. The current rate, paid in equal amounts by employers and employees, is $3\frac{1}{8}$ per cent. Self-employed participants pay $1\frac{1}{2}$ times the employee rate. Under current legislation, the rate will increase to $3\frac{5}{8}$ per cent in 1963, $4\frac{1}{8}$ per cent in 1966, and $4\frac{5}{8}$ per cent in 1969.

Coverage of these provisions has been frequently extended. It now includes most employees except those of religious, charitable, and educational organizations, who may, however, elect to become covered. Ministers may also elect to be covered, as may self-employed workers. Federal employees not otherwise provided with similar benefits are included. Discharged members of the uniformed military services are covered. State employees may be covered by a state-federal agreement. Professional workers are covered if they are employees and may elect coverage if self-employed.[30]

[28] See Benjamin W. Goodman, "Health Checklist for Small Plants," *Management Aids,* No. 126, Washington, D.C.: Small Business Administration, June, 1961; W. R. Spriegel and Edwin W. Mumma, "Mental Health in Industry," *Personnel Study No. 15,* University of Texas Bureau of Business Research, 1962.

[29] See Industrial Relations Counselors, Inc., *Current News,* Vol. 26, No. 8, February 23, 1961, p. 36.

[30] By 1961 amendments, medical doctors, dentists, lawyers, accountants, and other

Retirement benefits or pensions become available after covered workers achieve *fully insured* or *currently insured status,* with special eligibility rules for disabled workers. Eligibility depends on the number of quarters employed in covered employment. A worker becomes *fully insured* when covered for 40 quarters, or for one-fourth of the quarters since 1950 or since he reached the age of 21. A minimum of six quarters is required. He is *currently insured* if he has worked in covered employment at least 6 quarters in the 13 quarters before he becomes 65 or dies. Eligibility for disability benefits requires 20 quarters of coverage.

Full benefits become available to insured workers at age 65. Both male and female workers can take their benefits at age 62, but amounts are reduced. Wives of covered workers become eligible for benefits at age 62, or earlier if they have a dependent child. Eligible wives receive a benefit of 50 per cent of the husband's benefit. Dependent children also receive 50 per cent of a parent's primary benefit or 75 per cent as survivors of a deceased worker. A maximum family benefit limits all these provisions. Dependent parents of a covered worker are eligible for benefits.

Benefits are calculated in terms of a *primary benefit amount.* A benefit table (see Table 22.2) relates these benefits to average monthly wages in covered employment.

Benefits are reduced for pensioners under 72 years of age if they are earning more than $1200 per year. Benefits are reduced by $1 for each $2 earned in excess of $1200 up to $1700 and by all of the excess over $1500. This limitation does not apply after age 72.

OASDI also provides disability benefits for permanently and totally disabled workers.

The OASDI program has been frequently amended and modified. No Congress in recent years has been without several proposed amendments. The most widely discussed changes would supplement present benefits with an extensive program of medical care. The parallel Old Age Assistance program (see next section) was modified in 1960 to encourage state provision of limited medical benefits.

6.2 Old Age Assistance. The Social Security Act provides a number of *assistance* programs in addition to OASDI. They provide federal grants to states for aid to dependent children, the blind, and the permanently and totally disabled, as well as an *Old Age Assistance* program. Aid is granted on the basis of need in all the assistance programs.

Eligibility for Old Age Assistance is determined by the states, which also set the amounts of benefits. Federal participation is limited to grants to the states for a share of the costs. State eligibility standards vary widely; in some states large proportions of those over 65 are eligible and receive benefits. In

self-employed, if not covered, are permitted tax deductions for contributions to their own retirement programs. If such self-employed professionals have four or more employees, the plan must cover all of them and be fully vested. With less than four employees, the plan may be limited to the individual, but contributions cannot exceed 10 per cent of earnings or $2,500 annually.

Table 22.2 OASDI Primary Benefits and Family Maxima

Average Monthly Wage	Primary Insurance Amount	Maximum Family Benefit	Average Monthly Wage	Primary Insurance Amount	Maximum Family Benefit
$ — 54	$ 33	$ 53.00	$184—188	$ 81	$150.40
55— 56	34	54.00	189—193	82	154.40
57— 58	35	55.00	194—197	83	157.70
59— 60	36	56.00	198—202	84	161.60
61— 61	37	57.00	203—207	85	165.60
62— 63	38	58.00	208—211	86	168.80
64— 65	39	59.00	212—216	87	172.80
66— 67	40	60.00	217—221	88	176.80
68— 69	41	61.50	222—225	89	180.00
70— 70	42	63.00	226—230	90	184.00
71— 72	43	64.50	231—235	91	188.00
73— 74	44	66.00	236—239	92	191.20
75— 76	45	67.50	240—244	93	195.20
77— 78	46	69.00	245—249	94	199.20
79— 80	47	70.50	250—253	95	202.40
81— 81	48	72.00	254—258	96	206.40
82— 83	49	73.50	259—263	97	210.40
84— 85	50	75.00	264—267	98	213.60
86— 87	51	76.50	268—272	99	217.60
88— 89	52	78.00	273—277	100	221.60
90— 90	53	79.50	278—281	101	224.80
91— 92	54	81.00	282—286	102	228.80
93— 94	55	82.50	287—291	103	232.80
95— 96	56	84.00	292—295	104	236.00
97— 97	57	85.50	296—300	105	240.00
98— 99	58	87.00	301—305	106	244.00
100—101	59	88.50	306—309	107	247.20
102—102	60	90.00	310—315	108	251.20
103—104	61	91.50	315—319	109	254.00
105—106	62	93.00	320—323	110	254.00
107—107	63	94.50	324—328	111	254.00
108—109	64	96.00	329—333	112	254.00
110—113	65	97.50	334—337	113	254.00
114—118	66	99.00	338—342	114	254.00
119—122	67	100.50	343—347	115	254.00
123—127	68	102.00	348—351	116	254.00
128—132	69	105.60	352—356	117	254.00
133—136	70	108.80	357—361	118	254.00
137—141	71	112.80	362—365	119	254.00
142—146	72	116.80	366—370	120	254.00
147—150	73	120.00	371—375	121	254.00
151—155	74	124.00	376—379	122	254.00
156—160	75	128.00	380—384	123	254.00
161—164	76	131.20	385—389	124	254.00
165—169	77	135.20	390—393	125	254.00
170—174	78	139.20	394—398	126	254.00
175—178	79	142.40	399—400	127	254.00
179—183	80	146.40			

others, need must be demonstrated, and much smaller proportions are covered. Administrative rules in several states raise questions as to what policy the program seeks to implement.

The Old Age Assistance program has been frequently described as a stop-gap to meet needs that will be reduced as more employees are covered by OASDI. Actually, this has not been true; both numbers of recipients and amounts of benefits have expanded.

6.3 Private pensions. Private pension programs antedate the retirement benefits provided under the Social Security Act. When that legislation was being discussed, several proposals would have excluded firms with established private plans from its coverage. Proponents of such exemption assumed that one pension was enough, that employees would not need more and certainly would not want to contribute to more than one plan. Nevertheless, private plans have grown rapidly since that time. In part, the expansion is a result of bargained plans; pensions have been a favorite subject for negotiation. Most private plans are regarded as supplementary to OASDI. They provide the added amounts that appear necessary to give reasonable security after retirement.

Many plans represent a means of insuring that employees, including managers, will retire. They specify a compulsory retirement age. Expansion has been encouraged by a rapid development of generous retirement benefits for managers.

Coverage of private pensions extended, in 1960, to some 22 million employees. It was, at that time, growing at a rate of about one million per year. While heaviest coverage is among white collar workers, growing proportions of blue-collar workers are covered. More than 40,000 plans were operating in 1960. Many of these plans combine pensions with profit-sharing. Less than one-fourth of the coverage is provided by insured plans, but they are gaining wider acceptance, especially in small firms. Coverage of private plans now extends to about one-fourth of the labor force.[31]

Most private plans are financed by employer contributions; in about one-sixth of all plans, employees also contribute. Benefits are administered by insurance firms or by trustees of noninsured plans. For bargained plans, the most common benefit, after 30 years of service, is about $175 per month, including OASDI benefits. In general, benefits represent a higher percentage of wages and salaries for lower-paid workers. Thus for those earning $3,000 annually, total monthly benefits, including OASDI, amount to about 64 per cent of earnings. At the $6,000 salary level, benefits amount to only about 40 per cent. In most plans, workers become eligible to participate after one year of employment. Full benefits become available after 15 years in the most common pattern.[32]

---

[31] For time-to-time changes, see *Pensions and Profit-sharing Report,* for example, Par. 39.3, No. 39–3, 1961; Daniel M. Holland, "What Can We Expect from Pensions," *Harvard Business Review,* Vol. 37, No. 4, July-August, 1959, pp. 125–40.

[32] Robert Tilove, *Pension Funds and Economic Freedom,* New York: Fund for the

6.31   Vesting. Some concern is frequently expressed that private pension plans reduce the mobility of workers, holding them in jobs that make less than maximum use of their knowledge, skills, and abilities. For this reason, pressures have increased for early *vesting,* i.e., granting workers the right to take accrued credits in private pension plans with them when they move. Most private plans provide for vesting after a stated period; the most common time is 10 years. Plans may also specify a minimum age for vesting, ranging from 40 to 60 years. Vesting may be *full* or *graduated,* granting larger shares of accrued funds for additional services.[33]

The persistence of inflation has encouraged many private plans to include *variable annuities* as a part of pension planning. Variable annuities invest a portion of retirement fund assets in common stocks as a hedge against inflation. They are thus able to provide what are sometimes called *cost-of-living pensions* that increase as the price level advances.

A general trend toward broader coverage and higher benefits is clear and persistent. Retired workers need, on the average, about 60 per cent of their normal pre-retirement earnings. Current provisions fall somewhat below this standard. Managers face increasing complexities in handling pension programs. Assets of these programs have grown rapidly, from about six billion dollars in 1950 to more than 25 billion in 1960. They are expected to be more than 75 billion dollars by 1965.[34]

A federal Welfare and Pension Plans Disclosure Act was passed in 1958 and amended in 1962. It requires that administrators be bonded and that they provide detailed annual reports for plans that include as many as 26 participants. The federal Department of Labor is authorized to require such reporting and, if necessary, to subpoena records. Severe penalties are provided for mismanagement of funds, including kickbacks designed to influence administration of these plans.[35]

6.4   Retirement programs. Most pension provisions make benefits available only to those who have retired. All of the plans designate a normal retirement age. More than half of them provide for *compulsory* or *automatic* retirement at the specified age. The most common normal retirement age is 65, but automatic retirement may specify a later date, generally age 68 or 70. Retirement ages for females are frequently lower.

Republic, 1959, p. 17. For details of benefits, see Walter W. Kolodrubetz, "Normal Retirement Provisions under Collective Bargaining," *Monthly Labor Review,* Vol. 83, No. 10, October, 1960, pp. 1052ff.

[33] Elliot Romm, "Pension Planning," *Research Study 43,* American Management Association, 1960: Robert Tilove, *op. cit.,* pp. 21–22; "Pension Plans: Vesting and Retirement Age Provisions," *AFL-CIO Collective Bargaining Report,* Vol. 4, No. 9, September, 1959, pp. 49–54.

[34] See Paul P. Harbrecht, S.J., *Pension Funds and Economic Power,* New York: Twentieth Century Fund, 1959; J. Henry Richardson, *Economic and Financial Aspects of Social Security,* Toronto: University of Toronto Press, 1959.

[35] For details, see "How to Operate Under the New Disclosure Law," *Labor Report Bulletin 35,* Englewood Cliffs, N.J.: Prentice-Hall, Inc., March 22, 1962.

Provisions for retirement and particularly for compulsory retirement have solved some problems, but they have created other, new problems. Among the most important are the following:

(1) The social problem of supporting a growing number and proportion of idle, nonproductive participants. However retirement may be financed and however great the savings funds may become, the goods and services sought by those who are retired must be taken from the current stream of production. Because pensions create an added demand for goods and services not balanced by current contributions to production on the part of pensioners, these payments inevitably maintain a pressure toward inflation.

(2) Pensions are frequently inadequate to provide for the scale of living to which pensioners are accustomed.

(3) Hardship may arise in the case of individuals who reach the automatic retirement age but are in good health and have no other interests to replace their work.

(4) A serious problem has arisen from the tendency of many employers to avoid hiring new employees who are older than 45 or 50.[36]

Current policy on retirement is based on inadequate consideration of both social and individual needs. It reflects dubious generalizations about the destructive nature of the aging process. Policy has sought simple answers to a complex problem.

Future programs are likely to be more complex, mainly to take account of differences in individuals and in occupations. Both physical and mental abilities, at some stage in life, reach a peak from which some decline is inevitable. Many physical characteristics show a continuing decline from early ages. Kleemeier reports increased reaction times, reduced strength of grip, reduced visual acuity, and reduced auditory acuity—all tendencies notable after ages 20 to 30. Physical degeneration appears to be especially rapid after approximately 60 years of age.[37] On the other hand, mental abilities show no such clear-cut pattern of change. Verbal abilities decline very little.

Current policy is affected by the attitudes of some younger employees. Younger workers frequently avoid work with older employees. Youngsters may feel that their seniors block advancement and may favor compulsory retirement for this reason.

Many plans now recognize the need for flexibility in compulsory retirement. Early retirement for long-service employees is frequently permitted, as is retirement on account of disability. Flexibility in the other direction—per-

[36] See Margaret S. Gordon, "The Older Worker and Retirement Policies," *Monthly Labor Review,* Vol. 83, No. 6, June, 1960, pp. 577–85; Robert K. Burns, "Economic Aspects of Aging and Retirement," *American Journal of Sociology,* Vol. 59, No. 4, April, 1957, pp. 384–90; Jack Culley and Fred Slavick, "Employment Problems of Older Workers," *Information Series No. 1,* University of Iowa Bureau of Labor and Management, January, 1959.

[37] Robert W. Kleemeier, "Age Changes in Psychomotor Capacity and Productivity," *Studies of Aging and Retirement, No. 43,* University of Chicago Industrial Relations Center, 1954; James E. Berren, "Age in Mental Abilities," *Studies in Aging and Retirement, No. 44,* University of Chicago Industrial Relations Center, 1954.

mitting employment beyond the normal retirement age—is less common. Although automatic or compulsory retirement based solely on chronological age may be unreasonable and costly, no generally acceptable alternative has appeared.

An increasing number of private plans include provision for some relaxation of the compulsory rule. If an employee prefers to remain on the job, his request is considered by his supervisor or a committee. Continued employment usually involves deferring retirement for a specified period—ordinarily, one year—after which the procedure must be repeated. In several arrangements, if an employee wishes to continue but can't fill his present job, transfer to less arduous work is permitted. Some plans increase the amount of the pension if it is deferred by continued employment.

Special attention has been given to flexibility in the retirement of managers and executives. The Wm. Wrigley Jr. Company allows an executive to stay on with the permission of a retirement committee. But he must take one month's additional leave without pay for each added year. Meanwhile, his pension is increased for each added year of work.

Many firms now try to help employees get ready for retirement. In one plan, retirement interviews, beginning five years before retirement, stress the need for planning by employees, suggest the development of hobbies and avocations and participation in community educational and cultural activities, and assist in planning the retirement budget.[38]

7.0 SUMMARY

Tripartite policy has been the source of a wide and growing range of employee benefits and services. Managers do not administer all of them, but they have major responsibility for many and obligations for participating in several publicly-administered programs.

Many benefits are multi-purpose; they seek to further several policies. The total pattern combines somewhat diverse objectives, including the improvement of worker performance, the protection of health, additional assurances of economic security, and increased worker income. As a whole, they are intended to make work less unpleasant and more productive.

In total, their costs represent a significant addition to the payroll. Policy intends that they shall be charged against that account; it assumes that employment should be charged with benefits that appear as necessary or desirable in maintaining the work force. Because they are costly and appear as additional labor costs, critical managers have sometimes labeled them the *hidden payroll*.

The chapter has outlined an overview of these fringes, classifying them according to their major emphasis or intent.

[38] See Woodrow W. Hunter, "Pre-Retirement Education," *Geriatrics,* Vol. 15, November, 1960, pp. 793–800; Jack F. Rhode, "Fixed or Variable Retirement Ages," *Personnel Administration,* Vol. 24, No. 1, January-February, 1961, pp. 18–22.

This chapter concludes discussion of financial incentives. In the next chapter, incentivation is considered in terms of employee attitudes and morale.

SELECTED SUPPLEMENTARY READINGS *

Beaumont, Richard A., and James W. Tower, *Executive Retirement and Effective Management.* New York: Industrial Relations Counselors, Inc., 1961.

"Economic Programs for Labor Surplus Areas in Selected Countries of Western Europe," *Joint Committee Print,* 86th Cong., 2d sess., Washington, D.C.: Government Printing Office, 1960.

"Father of the twenty-five-hour-week," *Fortune,* March, 1962, pp. 189–94.

"Financing Old Age, Survivors and Disability Insurance," *A Report of the Advisory Council on Social Security Financing.* Washington, D.C.: Government Printing Office, 1959.

Hunter, Woodrow W., Pre-retirement Education, *Geriatrics,* Vol. 15, pp. 793–800, November, 1960. (Also published as *Reprint Series No. 16,* University of Michigan-Wayne University Institute of Labor and Industrial Relations, 1960.)

Lewis, H. Gregg, "Hours of Work and Hours of Leisure," *Proceedings,* Ninth Annual Meeting, December, 1956, Industrial Relations Research Associations, 1957.

"State Workmen's Compensation Laws," *Bulletin 161,* U. S. Department of Labor, Superintendent of Documents, May, 1960.

"Trends in Employee Benefits," *Industrial Relations Memo 137,* New York: Industrial Relations Counselors, Inc., March 31, 1961.

"The Issue of the Shorter Work Week," National Association of Manufacturers (Industrial Relations Division), February, 1961.

Wistert, F. M., *Fringe Benefits.* New York: Reinhold Publishing Corp., 1959.

"Workmen's Compensation—A National Problem," *Labor's Economic Review,* Vol. 6, No. 3–4, March-April, 1961.

SHORT CASE PROBLEM 22.1

*Changed Vacation Schedules**

A drug company usually closed its plant for a two-week period to permit the scheduling of essential maintenance and repair work. The shutdown was designated as a vacation period and production employees were given their vacations at this time. Employees entitled to more than two weeks were allowed to select other periods during the year for the additional vacation time. Early in 1960, the company notified the union that it would extend the shutdown period to three weeks. This was necessary, said the company, because the expansion of its manufacturing facilities had increased the amount of preventive maintenance and repair work to be done during the shutdown.

The union immediately filed a grievance claiming the company's proposed action would violate the agreement. The contract provided that existing conditions and standards could not be changed without union consent except for the purpose of improving the production or efficiency of the plant. The dispute was submitted to arbitration.

The union contended that the company did not have the right to change an existing condition of employment, namely the past practice of permitting the selec-

* From *Employee Relations and Arbitration Report,* March 20, 1961, Vol. 21, No. 19, Englewood Cliffs, N.J.: Prentice-Hall, Inc.

tion of other vacation periods by employees entitled to more than two weeks of vacation. Extending the shutdown would deprive employees of this benefit, eliminate an established past practice, and discriminate against employees in their choice of additional vacation periods. The union also claimed that much of the maintenance and repair work scheduled to be done during the shutdown could be scheduled and performed at other times throughout the year.

The company contended it had the right to extend the shutdown period without union consent, since the work performed by the maintenance employees was essentially to improve production and maintain plant efficiency.

Problem: Write out a summary of your reasoning and an award for this case.

SHORT CASE PROBLEM 22.2

Retirement Tests

Formal retirement has become an established part of employment, with growing acceptance in both public and private employment. Administration of private retirement programs is generally linked with public benefits available under the Social Security Act. How would you answer the following "retirement test" questions for those covered by the Federal Act?*

1. Your old employer has offered you a part-time job. If you take it, how can you tell how much you will receive in benefits?

2. If you start work after you have qualified for benefits, should you report this to the Social Security Administration?

3. If your estimate of earnings will permit some benefit payments to be made to you for a year, do you have to wait until the end of the year to get these payments?

4. Your wife and you together receive $110 monthly in benefits on your Social Security record, and you earn $200 a month in each month of 1961 ($2,400 in the year). What Social Security benefits will you both receive?

5. Will your earnings make any difference in the benefits payable to members of your family on your Social Security record?

6. You receive widow's benefits, and also receive benefits for your two small children. If you work, will you lose the children's benefits?

7. How can you tell whether your services in self-employment in a month are substantial?

8. How will your earnings affect your benefits after you are 72?

9. How and when do you make a report to the Social Security Administration about your annual earnings?

SHORT CASE PROBLEM 22.3

Moving Executives and Supervisors

A large retailing concern is opening a new store in another locality. Several executives and supervisors will be transferrel to the new location. Executives are considering what should be done to facilitate their moving. One suggestion is that the company pay moving expenses. Another proposes that the company give a special allowance of 10 per cent of annual salary to compensate for the unavoidable costs of moving. Other suggestions have proposed that the company assume responsibility for a proportion of the difference between the selling price of homes in the parent city and the cost of comparable new homes in the city to which executives are moving.

The company will designate those who are to move.

* From *Pension and Profit-Sharing Report,* Vol. 19, No. 63, Par. 63.2, 1961. Englewood Cliffs, N.J.: Prentice-Hall, Inc.

Problem: What type of arrangement would you recommend? What are your reasons?

SHORT CASE PROBLEM 22.4

Benefits or Discipline

The ABC (public utility) Company sends its service-truck drivers throughout the territory it serves. Truck driver Jones, after 25 years of faithful service to the company with no disciplinary actions on his record, visited a number of taverns and, driving his truck on the wrong side of the highway, struck a car and killed its three occupants. Jones was severely injured and was not expected to live.

The company took no disciplinary action at the time on account of Jones's precarious condition. The company's sick benefit and hospitalization programs have paid for six months of hospitalization and medical attention. The expiration of the six-month period is at hand. Jones is still confined to the hospital and will not be able to return to his job, in the opinion of physicians, within the foreseeable future.

Problem: What action shall be taken about Jones? Shall he be disciplined? Discharged? Should action have been taken immediately after the accident? Should he be permitted to retire on pension at once?

SHORT CASE PROBLEM 22.5

Leaves of Absence for Jail Terms

Negotiation of a new agreement is stalled because of a union demand for revised policy on leaves of absence. The employer has made what he considers a reasonable proposal. He is willing to agree that leave shall be allowed for employees forced to serve a jail sentence of less than 30 days. Representatives of the union do not regard this provision as adequate.

The situation grew out of an experience of the past year. Peter Norquist, an employee with five years of service, was divorced. He was ordered to pay what he and his friends regarded as excessive alimony. He failed to keep up his payments and, having been found to be in contempt of court, was sent to jail. He immediately requested a leave of absence which would hold his job for him and allow his seniority to accumulate while he was in jail. The employer refused the request, indicating his willingness to rehire Norquist if he returned within 30 days.

The union argues that it is grossly unfair for an employee already mistreated by the court to suffer additional injury from his employer. Further, it insists, a jail sentence for non-support is in no way comparable to one imposed because of a crime.

The employer agrees with these points. He cites the facts that accepted policy justifies discharge of an employee convicted of a crime, but that leaves are always granted for jail sentences arising out of minor offenses, such as traffic violations. He points out that Norquist might spend most of his time in jail if he fails to keep up his payments.

Problem: You have the job of preparing a statement of policy that will be acceptable to both parties, to be included in the new contract.

SHORT CASE PROBLEM 22.6

Accidents and Education

Measure the relationship between accidents and education as shown by the following tabulation prepared by the personnel department of a large organization. (Use biserial *r*.)

Education (Years)	Number of Employees Having One or More Accidents	No Accidents
6	430	120
8	370	110
10	210	410
12	180	420

SHORT CASE PROBLEM 22.7

Seniority and Accidents

Management seeks to discover the possible relationship between length of service with the company and accidents. It has prepared the following tabulation.

Employee	Accidents (Average per Year)	Years of Service	Employee	Accidents (Average per Year)	Years of Service
1	2.7	16	16	1.0	40
2	1.7	44	17	1.0	38
3	2.8	11	18	0.9	28
4	2.2	20	19	1.25	32
5	3.2	9	20	0.5	24
6	2.0	5	21	1.5	34
7	3.1	7	22	1.1	30
8	2.9	3	23	1.9	36
9	3.5	2	24	0.9	26
10	2.6	2	25	2.4	14
11	3.6	2	26	2.0	12
12	3.0	2	27	2.0	10
13	4.0	1	28	1.9	8
14	2.5	1	29	2.7	15
15	4.5	1	30	1.8	6

Problem: On the basis of this sample, do you conclude that length of service is an important factor in accidents? How would you measure and evaluate whatever relationship exists?

18

23. *Employee Morale*

Whether or not managers understand and accept modern work and organization theory, most of them have become much impressed with the importance of employee morale. They regard it as a measure of their effectiveness in incentivation. They also assume that morale is an element in incentivation, that maintaining high morale may be as influential as high wages or generous employee benefits and services. Managers actively cultivate what they regard as evidence or symptoms of satisfactory morale. They become concerned about behavior they interpret as suggesting low morale.

This point of view on the part of managers represents a major change from earlier manager attitudes. Some early captains of industry apparently couldn't have cared less about the morale of employees. They paid the piper and called the tune. Employees accepted the manager's terms when they took the job. They could be happy or satisfied with their work or not, so long as their performance was satisfactory to their employer. The manager may have been informally or even formally advised of employee reactions; he may have hoped that some employees would be pleased with assignments and would appreciate and like him. Little evidence is available on this point, but the absence of any extensive concern about employee morale is clear.

Frequent discussions of employee morale became common in American management literature after labor markets began to tighten in this country, in part as a result of restricted immigration. Greater interest developed when unions began their rapid expansion after enactment of the National Labor Relations Act in 1935. Managers learned more about the importance of employee views, feelings, and reactions from publicity on the pioneering research at the Hawthorne plant of Western Electric just before World War II.[1] In

[1] See F. J. Roethlisberger and William J. Dickson, *Management and the Workers,* Cambridge, Mass.: Harvard University Press, 1939.

that war, concern about morale of military forces became the subject of wide discussion. Just as World War I popularized the use of testing for selection, World War II spread the gospel of morale for superior performance. Just as World War I had its Committee on the Classification of Personnel, World War II contributed the *Morale Services Division* in the military services.[2]

Management concern about employee morale results in two principal types of programs. One involves the development of techniques and practices designed to discover and interpret employee feelings and reactions. Managers seek to assess the current state of morale and to compare it with the findings in similar assessments at earlier periods or in other organizations. The second type of program is designed to reduce negative reactions and to cultivate and maintain high morale.

Section 1 of this chapter notes current conceptions of employee morale and considers some major difficulties inherent in efforts to appraise it. Section 2 outlines current policy, noting the assumptions and theory that underlie and explain it. Section 3 is concerned with symptoms of negative or low morale. Section 4 outlines common practice in maintaining continual checks on morale and using such appraisals to assure continuing high levels of employee morale.

1.0 MORALE, ATTITUDES AND BEHAVIOR

Morale is a term that is widely used without careful definition. Few lay citizens hesitate to use it, but many would find it difficult to define. It describes a feeling, somewhat related to spirit, *esprit de corps,* enthusiasm, or zeal. For a group of workers, popular usage suggests that morale refers to the over-all tone, climate, and atmosphere of work, perhaps vaguely sensed by members. If workers appear to feel enthusiastic, optimistic about the group's activities and mission, and friendly to each other, they are described as having *good* or *high morale.* If they seem dissatisfied, irritated, cranky, critical, restless, and pessimistic, these reactions are described as evidence of *poor* or *low morale.*

1.1 Individual and group morale. As suggested, two fairly distinct conceptions of morale may be identified within the meanings attached to the term. From one viewpoint, morale is regarded as essentially an *individual matter.* It is described in terms of the feelings of an employee or manager toward his work; it is also a matter of work-satisfaction. It is the "sum of satisfactions" experienced by an employee as a jobholder and member of the organization. The concept relates morale to the needs of the individual and

---

[2] This sharp switch in manager attitudes is epitomized in the classic morale interview with the heating engineer in the underground boiler room. Questioned at length about his reactions to work without sunlight, in overheated workspace, without promise of promotion, he steadfastly insisted that he had no criticisms. Pressed for some suggestion for improvement, he finally admitted that a bit of forced ventilation might help. "But," he cautioned, "please don't tell Mr. Smith [the president]. He worries so about how we feel!"

to his need-satisfaction. It also gauges the individual's morale in terms of his adjustment to his job and his role in the organization.

In the industrial situation, this notion of morale is concerned with an employee's feelings toward the kind of work he does, his fellow workers, his prestige and status, and his employer. Morale is a combination or composite of these feelings, combined with reactions to his hours, earnings, supervision, the personnel policies and practices of the employer, and other working conditions.

Such a viewpoint emphasizes the worker's adjustment to his work and immediate working relationships. However, adjustment may mean much more than merely an accommodation to the job. It may involve the individual's reactions to the whole working relationship, including his particular job, his colleagues in the work group, his supervisor, his employer, and the current system of working relationships. It may include adjustment to ideas and customs and other people's feelings as well as to people and physical surroundings.

When morale is regarded as an individual phenomenon, many investigators organize these feelings around what are assumed to be the worker's *needs*. Studies of employee morale, so defined, generally begin with or derive a list of *needs categories*. Guion, for example, defines *morale* in terms of the degree to which an individual sees his personal needs as satisfied.[3] Such studies have leaned on and contributed to current theories of work, already outlined in Chapter 4. They identify such values as economic security; opportunities for personal recognition, participation, expression, and self-development; and self-respect (worth and importance of the job).[4]

Analysis in terms of individual needs has not, however, provided a simple, uniform, universal structure of values, in part because needs categories overlap. Also, the form of expression may change. Priorities in levels of needs presumably vary; when security is assured, the level of intensity with which it is regarded may decline.[5] Herzberg found that such studies listed ten major "job factors," including intrinsic aspects of the job, supervision, working conditions, wages, opportunity for advancement, security, company, social aspects of the job, communications, and benefits. On the basis of an extensive survey of morale studies, Scott, Dawis, England, and Lofquist derived a list of eight commonly identified value areas, including type of work, working conditions, promotion or advancement, wages and salaries, co-workers, supervision, communication, and identification with the firm or management.[6]

   [3] Robert M. Guion, "Industrial Morale: The Problem of Terminology," *Personnel Psychology*, Vol. 11, No. 1, 1958, pp. 59–64.
   [4] See, for example, I. C. Ross and Alvin Zander, "Need Satisfaction and Employee Turnover," *Personnel Psychology*, Vol. 10, No. 3, Fall, 1957, pp. 327–38.
   [5] See the discussion of work theory in Chapter 4; also Frederick Herzberg *et al., Job Attitudes: Review of Research and Opinion*, Pittsburgh: Psychological Service of Pittsburgh, 1957, especially pp. 39–40.
   [6] Thomas B. Scott *et al.,* "A Definition of Work Adjustment," *University of Minnesota Studies in Vocational Rehabilitation*, No. 10, University of Minnesota Industrial Relations Center, 1958. See also Oakley J. Gordon, "A Factor Analysis of

A related but somewhat different view of morale directs attention to the group rather than to the individual. It defines morale in terms of group or *social reactions* and concentrates on feelings toward social values rather than toward individual values. It places somewhat less emphasis on particular working conditions and more on feelings of *cohesiveness,* group interest and identification with the mission of the group, and optimism about the success of the whole. Thus Finlay, Sartain, and Tate conclude that morale is essentially a feeling of belonging so dominating that the worker places the group's interest above his own. Kahn and Morse regard morale as the sum of satisfactions the worker gains because of his participation in the group.[7]

From this viewpoint, the most important aspects of morale are the somewhat contagious reactions of group members to the immediate working group or crew, to fellow-workers in such groups, and to the formal and informal behavior patterns in the group. Studies of morale in the armed services disclosed interesting patterns and differences in these reactions. In modern industrial practice, interest is directed to patterns of feelings toward the work group, the whole working organization, the community, and the industrial relations system.

Current discussions of worker, supervisory, and managerial morale may not recognize a distinction between individual and group approaches. Investigations often propose to examine a broad range of individual worker reactions as well as dominant patterns among members of work groups. They seek information on the extent to which workers feel that their work meets individual needs, but they are also interested in the way members of work crews feel about their co-workers, the group, the organization and its mission, and the promise of successful achievement.

1.2   Indicators of morale. It is important to note that in both individual and group morale, the reference is to *feelings* and *spirit*. Not infrequently it is said that high or low morale can be felt, that feelings are broadcast and communicated. It must be recognized that feelings are subjective; they must be inferred from some form of objective expression and behavior. Judgments about levels of morale, therefore, rest on some such evidence—actions, expressions, oral comments, criticisms, and answers to questions. Such evidence must then be interpreted or translated into valuations of morale.

This requirement creates a persistent hazard of improper inference. Thus an employee's behavior in being consistently late to work may be attributable to his feelings with regard to the importance of his job and of being on time; it may indicate what would be widely regarded as low morale. He may exhibit the same behavior, however, because the local transportation system leaves only the most harsh alternatives. The same sort of question may be

Human Needs and Industrial Morale," *Personnel Psychology,* Vol. 8, No. 1. Spring, 1955, pp. 1–18.

[7] William W. Finlay, A. Q. Sartain, and Willis M. Tate, *Human Behavior in Industry,* New York: The McGraw-Hill Book Company, Inc., 1955, pp. 223–33; Robert Kahn and Nancy C. Morse, "The Relation of Productivity to Morale," *Fourth Annual Meeting Proceedings,* Industrial Relations Research Association, 1951, p. 70.

raised about interpretations of fighting on the job or restricting output.

Current analyses of employee morale cannot avoid this danger of misinterpretation, whether or not they recognize it. All examine what workers do and say as a means of appraising their feelings or morale. Two types of evidence have wide acceptance and usage. One is overt behavior as expressed in labor turnover, productivity, promptness, waste prevention, and other activity such as restlessness, malingering, loitering, or tardiness and absenteeism. The other type of evidence is what employees say and how they say it—their expressed opinions and reactions.

Studies like that undertaken at Hawthorne emphasize the evidence of behavior and performance. Evaluation of opinions is much more common today. Studies of opinions can be made more rapidly and more economically. They can quickly raise issues that may evoke a wide range of opinions on a variety of subjects. They can ask about issues by questions that permit an expression of the *intensity* or *seriousness* with which opinions are held.

The most common designation for these oral or written comments or opinions describes them as *attitudes,* and the most common current studies of employee morale are usually called *attitude surveys.* At this point, however, another distinction should be recognized. Attitudes are *predispositions to action,* including an important element of feeling. Feelings are presumably reflected in attitudes, but they are not identical. Here again, an element of interpretation and translation is unavoidable. *Attitude surveys* are mainly *opinion polls.* Employee morale must be inferred from these expressions of opinions, perhaps by combining them and noting patterns. Whatever the results are called, the necessity for such interpretation is inescapable.

Major attention is given, in current practice, to the assessment of *employee morale,* with particular attention to rank-and-file, shop, and office workers. Some interest has been shown in the morale of first-line supervisors, but comparatively little concern has been expressed about the morale of middle managers and those in higher echelons. The apparent assumption is that morale problems are restricted to nonsupervisory employees. However, studies that have included supervisory employees have sometimes found their morale to be less satisfactory than that of the rank-and-file workers they supervise.

Almost 50 years ago, editors of *Management Review* described a need for attitude studies directed toward managers. They noted that extensive attention had been given to the opinions of workers. They suggested that a similar "exploration of the mind of management" was in order and concluded, "The mind of management is also an integral part of the human relationships in industry." This opinion must not have gained wide acceptance, although it appears entirely reasonable. The need for checking on the attitudes and morale of managers can scarcely be less today; little has been done in the intervening years to meet it.[8]

[8] See Conrad M. Arensberg *et al., Research in Industrial Human Relations,* New York: Harper & Brothers, 1957, p. 10; "Industrial Morale" (A symposium), *Personnel Psychology,* Vol. 11, No. 1, Spring, 1958, pp. 59–94; Melany E. Baehr and

2.0 POLICY ON EMPLOYEE MORALE

Most managers are enthusiastically *for* employee morale; they agree on a policy that seeks to develop and maintain high morale. Many managers are concerned about employee morale. Policy may express this concern and indicate the intention to remove or revise whatever conditions appear to occasion low morale. To this end, policy may propose periodic studies or investigations to discover levels of and trends in employee morale. On the other hand, some managerial policy opposes formal studies of employee morale and questions the propriety and ethics of such investigations.

2.1 Development and maintenance of high morale. The most common managerial policy proposes to develop and maintain a high level of employee morale. That policy is justified by managers on the basis of a variety of philosophical and theoretical positions, some of them frequently stated and discussed, others less frequently made explicit.

To some degree, for example, this policy may express an essentially *paternalistic viewpoint*. It is a common observation that most of us want to be liked by those with whom we associate; much of our system of social control leans heavily on this human trait. While evidence here is impressionistic, it is reasonable to assume that managers seek high morale in part as a reflection of favorable feelings toward them.

The policy may, at the same time, express a degree of *insecurity on the part of managers*. They have heard criticisms of their competence and performance and of their need to earn the respect and confidence of employees. Even if they do not understand nor subscribe to such analysis, they may regard high levels of morale as worthwhile insurance.

Probably the most frequent justification of the policy holds that high morale means *improved employee contributions* and *lower labor costs*. Some theory regards morale as an important factor in motivation and the maintenance of morale as a means of incentivation. A direct morale-productivity relationship is widely assumed. Managers seek high morale as a means of magnifying the impact of the wage dollar; they propose to prevent low morale because it can exert an opposite influence.

This theory has wide acceptance, probably because it is obviously plausible. It seems rather obvious, for example, that enthusiastic employees are less likely to seek employment elsewhere; costly *labor turnover* can be avoided. Indeed, such employees may be effective aids in recruitment, with related savings. On the job, the morale-productivity connection seems so clear that high productivity is regarded as an important indicator of high morale.

Evidence on this relationship is, however, by no means conclusive. Attempts to check on it encounter the inevitable question as to the reliability of evidence and interpretation. Most of the evidence has been supplied by

Richard Renck, "The Definition and Measurement of Employee Morale," *Administrative Science Quarterly,* Vol. 3, No. 2, September, 1958, pp. 157–184; J. R. Glennon *et al.,* "A New Dimension in Measuring Morale," *Harvard Business Review,* Vol. 38, No. 1, January-February, 1960, pp. 106ff.

employee opinion polls such as those described in Section 4 of this chapter. They seem to indicate no consistent correlation between the composite or total of favorable opinions and high output. They find, however, that certain areas of favorable opinions—those with reference to the job, communications, supervision, and fellow workers—are positively correlated with output.[9]

Managers may also equate morale with *loyalty*. They may seek to develop employee loyalty to their supervisors, managers, and the firm. They frequently deplore what they regard as a lack of loyalty on the part of many employees and charge that unions have alienated employee loyalty.

This type of justification deserves critical evaluation. Both individual firm and social interests warrant recognition of the *complex nature of loyalty*. Blind, uncritical loyalty is likely to be objectionable on all counts. That type of loyalty to the firm may encourage employees to commit flagrant violations of public policy, as was evidenced in the anti-trust convictions of corporate officials in the electrical manufacturing industry in 1961. Loyalty to the work group can create similar conflicts within an organization.[10]

Further, studies suggest that unions do not necessarily reduce employee loyalty to the employer. Employees have no sharply limited, total loyalty. If they become loyal to one group, it does not follow that they take some loyalty from another. On the contrary, employees who are apparently most loyal to their union are also most loyal to their employer. They are, it appears, the kind of people who develop strong loyalties.

It may well be that loyalty is responsive; that it develops when cultivated. Managements that stress productivity and pay and ignore other aspects of employment relationships may tend to prevent the development of strong loyalties to managers and the firm.

The whole emphasis on loyalty may have serious implications for the public welfare in a democracy, whether the loyalties in question are directed toward company, union, or some other organization. Strong loyalties of this type imply a *totality of commitment* that may seriously handicap individual freedom in thought and action.[11]

[9] See Arthur H. Brayfield and Walter H. Crockett, "Employee Attitudes and Employee Performance," *Psychological Bulletin*, Vol. 52, No. 5, September, 1955, pp. 396–424; Arthur H. Brayfield and Richard V. Wills, "Interrelationships Among Measures of Job Satisfaction and General Satisfaction," *Journal of Applied Psychology*, Vol. 41, No. 4, August, 1957, pp. 201–205; Rensis Likert and Stanley E. Seashore, "Employee Attitudes and Output," *Monthly Labor Review*, Vol. 77, No. 6, June, 1954, pp. 641–49; A. Zalesnik, C. R. Christensen, and F. J. Roethlisberger, *The Motivation, Productivity and Satisfaction of Workers*, Boston: Graduate School of Business, Harvard University, 1958; Ross Stagner, "Motivational Aspects of Industrial Morale," *Personnel Psychology*, Vol. 11, No. 1, Spring, 1958, pp. 64–70; Harry C. Triandis, "A Critique and an Experimental Design for the Study of the Relationship between Productivity and Job Satisfaction," *Psychological Bulletin*, Vol. 56, 1959, pp. 309–12.
[10] See T. W. Fletcher, "The Nature of Administrative Loyalty," *Public Administration Review*, Vol. 18, Winter, 1958, pp. 37–42.
[11] Many studies have sought answers to questions about employee loyalty. Here are a few samples: Theodore V. Purcell, *Blue-Collar Man*, Cambridge, Mass.: Harvard University Press, 1960; Lois R. Dean, "Union Activity and Dual Loyalty," *Industrial*

Managers may justify their interest in improving and maintaining employee morale on the ground that high morale is good *protection against interference in management.* If morale is high, it is argued, employees will be less likely to criticize leaders and managerial policy and practice. It is the careless management, in this view, that encourages employees to organize and to support radical union demands.

Some managers conclude that levels of morale among employees are measures of the *quality* and *success of management.* They seek to maintain high morale to reassure themselves that they and their associates are doing a good job.

2.2 Continuing appraisals of morale. Policy frequently proposes to make continuing or frequent checks on morale, in part by watching for and investigating suggestions of low morale and in part by undertaking special studies of current morale at regular intervals. Managers who seek to maintain high morale are likely to be concerned about any evidence of employee dissatisfaction and ill-feeling. Work stoppages, slowdowns, unusually high levels of absenteeism or tardiness, or of labor turnover and restriction of output are among the frequently mentioned symptoms of negative morale.

In part, proposals for frequent checks on morale arise from the growing size of working organizations. Managers feel more need for these formal studies when size prevents frequent, day-to-day, personal contacts with employees. Some evidence suggests that morale may be affected by the size of the organization, that it tends to vary inversely, with lower morale in larger organizations.[12]

Some policy proposes frequent studies of employee morale on the theory that these investigations may themselves improve employee attitudes. The fact that management is interested in employee reactions and provides an opportunity for their expression may contribute to a sense of belonging and personal importance. At the same time, attitude and morale surveys may provide an opportunity for employees to express their opinions and to describe their frustrations and thus to release tensions. The morale survey, like the counseling interview, may have cathartic value. This is a possibility that deserves more study; it is not extensively supported by research or experience.

Not all managers are impressed with the importance of employee morale. Some still regard it as relatively unimportant, questioning that it has significant influence on output and doubting that it deserves the attention it has received in recent years. Some managers suggest that low morale may be more frequently correlated with high output. As one manager put it, "When

and Labor Relations Review, Vol. 7, No. 4, July, 1954, pp. 526–36; "Dual Allegiance to Union and Management" (symposium), *University of Illinois Bulletin,* Vol. 51, No. 79, July, 1954; "Dual Loyalty in Industrial Society" (symposium), *Monthly Labor Review,* Vol. 76, No. 12, December, 1953, pp. 1273–77.
    [12] See Julius E. Eitington, "Bigness and Morale," *Personnel Administration,* Vol. 20, No. 1, January-February, 1957, pp. 6–11; Sergio Talacchi, "Organization Size, Individual Attitudes and Behavior: an Empirical Study," *Administrative Science Quarterly,* Vol. 5, No. 3, December, 1960, pp. 398–420.

morale gets high, no one gets any work done." With the same viewpoint, some managers conclude that employee dissatisfaction, as expressed in continued "griping," is a good sign. Other managers suggest that they have other means of insuring productivity, that employees have to keep up with the production line, and that supervision assures efficient operation.

Still other managers, although they agree that high employee morale is desirable, oppose formal investigations of current attitudes. Three views or assumptions generally explain this conclusion. In the first, managers insist that they already know the attitudes and morale of their employees. They need no formal attitude or morale survey to give them the facts. Generally, they feel that their supervisors can and do sense and report the attitudes of workers. Generally, also, those who feel that they already know are sure that most of their employees are well-satisfied if not enthusiastic about their working relationships.

A second viewpoint usually associated with investigations of morale holds that such investigations generally destroy morale by suggesting sources of dissatisfaction. It argues that these studies suggest shortcomings and irritations by asking employees about numerous details of their work and associations. Many employees would not have thought of objections had they not been mentioned. Evidence to support this assumption is sparse, and most available evidence discredits the theory.[13]

A third source of opposition to morale studies concludes that it is useless to check on employee feelings because management can't do much to change them. This conclusion, which may at first seem quite unrealistic, has some validity in organizations in which policy-making is centralized and thus effectively divorced from local management. If the western division of a firm must accept policy and program from an eastern office that is unwilling to permit variations from these front office decisions, local management may have good reason for avoiding the whole subject. Indeed, local managers may hold more critical attitudes than rank-and-file employees.

Many managers, both in this country and abroad, have expressed concern about the propriety of asking employees what they think and how they feel. The classic expression of this view suggests, "We hire workers to work; what they think and feel is their own business." Again, some managers conclude that how the worker feels about the way they run the shop is personal; to inquire about it suggests that managers assume the right to control employee thought. The viewpoint may justify critical consideration of the depth to which opinions are probed and the areas covered in such studies. Perhaps inquiries should be confined strictly to work and working relationships.

3.0 THE SYNDROME OF NEGATIVE MORALE

Although the most formal and tangible programs in which managers seek

[13] See "Attitudes on Attitude Surveys," *Personnel Administration*, Vol. 19, No. 4, July-August, 1956, pp. 18–22.

to appraise employee morale are their attitude-opinion interviews and surveys, more attention is probably given to what are regarded as symptoms of low or negative morale. This is, in a sense, a case of the squeaking wheel getting the grease. Managers are quick to note and anxious to understand overt signs of employee disinterest, dissatisfaction, and irritation.

Some of these symptoms are widely described as *industrial unrest,* including loitering, malingering, resignations, grievances, and work stoppages. Unrest is closely akin to morale; it is usually defined as behavior expressing basic personal needs which does not, however, satisfy these needs. Other, somewhat similar behavior that is widely regarded as evidencing low morale includes greater than usual frequency of absenteeism or tardiness, disciplinary problems, and restriction of output.

These are all only symptoms. They may appear for reasons other than a low level of employee morale, although negative morale is probably similar to the fever that accompanies a wide variety of illness or maladjustment. Alert managements recognize that whether or not such behavior always indicates low morale, it always deserves careful investigation.

3.1 Lack of interest. A general lack of interest in the job is perhaps the most commonly described form of industrial unrest. An employee may be outspoken about his lack of interest; more common is a tendency to loiter, malinger, wander away from the work, with wide fluctuations in productivity. Such *inarticulate unrest* has been widely observed in situations other than the workshop. If it persists, it may become *articulate* in oral or written letters, declarations, arguments, grievances, and disputes.

Usual analysis of such behavior in the work situation describes it as expressing *fatigue* or a reaction to *monotony.* It concludes that morale may be shaped by these conditions, that fatigue may be a dimension of morale and monotony a factor in some fatigue and thus in low morale. As Cozan has noted, current interpretations of fatigue see it as expressing both physiological and psychological states. Psychological fatigue may follow from prolonged mental effort, or it may also express the strain of emotional conflicts.[14]

Fatigue may be evident in *listlessness* and *lack of interest.* One method of identifying it analyzes the measured output of workers who are free to set their own pace. Fatigue appears to be cumulative. Productivity declines with passing hours during the working day. Interruptions of work in which the individual has an opportunity to rest may result in lessened evidence of fatigue. A *fatigue curve* of output can be drawn as in Figure 23.1. The figure represents individual output in 15-minute periods throughout a work day. At the outset, the rate of work shows a tendency to increase in the warm-up period. It reaches a peak, after which it turns downward. The downward movement is interrupted by rest and lunch periods, after which there is a rise to a somewhat lower top than that achieved in the morning, followed by a continuing decline to the end of the work day.

[14] Lee W. Cozan, "A Broader Concept of Work Fatigue," *Journal of Personnel Administration and Industrial Relations,* Vol. 3, No. 1, Spring, 1957, pp. 1–6.

Monotony creates a quite different picture. The monotonous job, for an employee who expects more stimulation from his work, may be a continuing irritation. The employee becomes listless and bored, with a strong tendency toward *day-dreaming*. Attention shifts to and from the job at hand. As indicated in Figure 23.2, the curve of output for those who find the work monotonous shows numerous sharp fluctuations. In clear contrast to the fatigue curve, the rate of output tends to fall during the middle of the work period and to rise toward the close of the period. This *end spurt* is apparently an expression of relief at the prospect of release from the boredom of the job.

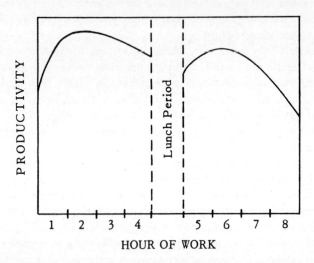

Figure 23.1   Fatigue Curve: Typical Work Curve for Motor-Skill Task
SOURCE: I.L.M. Bosticco, Technical Aids for Small Manufacturers, (Small Business Administration), *op. cit.*, p. 4.

Management practice in seeking to reduce fatigue is generally concerned with its physical expression. Perhaps the most common attack provides more frequent *rest periods*. Some practice lessens the physical activity by added mechanization or providing other assistance. The job may be *enlarged* to include a greater variety of tasks, on the theory that *job enlargement* will exercise different physical and mental functions.[15]

Attacks on monotony begin with selection and placement, in which such

---

[15] Study of energy expenditures has encouraged these adjustments. They indicate that lying relaxed expends only 1.3 calories per minute; sitting, 1.5; light assembly, 1.8; general office work in a standing position, 2.0; tool room work, 3.9; bricklaying, 4.0; mixing cement, 4.7; sawing soft wood, 6.3; lumbering and tree felling, 10.7. See I.L.M. Bosticco, "Is Worker Fatigue Costing You Dollars?", *Technical Aids for Small Manufacturers*, Washington: Small Business Administration, January-February, 1960; Louis E. Davis and Dudley Josselyn, "How Fatigue Affects Productivity," *Personnel*, Vol. 30, No. 1, July, 1953, pp. 54–59.

assignments are given to those who appear least likely to be irritated by routine. *Changing jobs* during the day may permit an escape; some employees are rotated among several jobs to break the monotony of a single assignment. Many firms and agencies have experimented with *job enlargement,* in which a number of specialized tasks are combined. Spokesmen for this attack suggest that specialization has been carried too far in routine, monotonous jobs. It has made the employee a producer rather than a designer and creator. Job

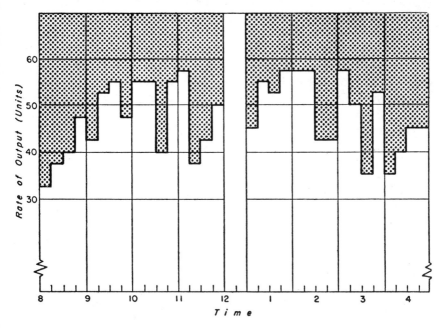

Figure 23.2   Monotony Curve of Output

enlargement may be an important part of a broad change that substitutes a working environment which the worker controls and modifies.[16]

3.2   Labor turnover. One of the oldest recognized forms of industrial unrest is labor turnover, the changes in the composition of the work force that result from the hiring, release, and replacement of employees. Some of that change, of course, cannot be regarded as expressing employee dissatisfaction with the job. Some employees are released on the initiative of the employer. Some turnover is a result of reduced demands for workers. A varying propor-

[16] See Robert H. Guest, "Job Enlargement—A Revolution in Job Design," *Personnel Administration,* Vol. 20, No. 2, March-April, 1957, pp. 9–16; Maurice D. Kilbridge, "Reduced Costs Through Job Enlargement: A Case," *Journal of Business,* Vol. 33, No. 4, October, 1960, pp. 357–62; "Turnover, Absence and Transfer Rates as Indicators of Employee Dissatisfaction with Repetitive Work," *Industrial and Labor Relations Review,* Vol. 15, No. 1, October, 1961, pp. 21–32.

tion of the total, however, represents voluntary separations—quits—which may be significant. Some quits may not indicate low morale; an employee may find it necessary to move for reasons of health, family plans, or other non-work-connected reasons.

All labor turnover above what is regarded as normal is likely to attract the attention of managers, in part because it is expensive.[17] High levels of quits have greatest significance as indicators of employee dissatisfaction.

The simplest measure of labor turnover is the *separation rate,* generally defined as the number of separations per month per 100 of the average working force. Separations include all quits, layoffs, and discharges. The average force is usually measured by adding numbers on the payroll at the beginning of the period and at the end of the period and dividing by two. Thus, if the firm began the month with 1,000 employees and ended with 2,000, the average working force would be 1,500. And if, during the period, 100 employees had severed their relationship with the firm, then the separation rate would be 6.67.

This simple measure of labor turnover takes no account of either seasonal or cyclical fluctuations. To overcome some of these limitations, some current practice calculates a *net turnover rate,* which emphasizes the number of *replacements* rather than of separations. Replacements are those employed to fill positions left vacant as a result of separations.

Nationwide separation and accession rates are reported by the Bureau of Labor Statistics and published in each issue of the *Monthly Labor Review.* Rates for quits, layoffs, total separations, new hires, and total accessions are distinguished. Each is calculated as a ratio, of which the base is the number of employees in the work force in the week nearest the 15th of the month.

Attempts to reduce turnover generally begin by refining rates for individual firms and for departments, eliminating unavoidable losses (deaths, retirement, etc.). To interpret voluntary separations, attention is directed to sources, employment experience and record, and the information contributed by *exit interviews.* Statistical analysis identifies types of employees with greatest turnover, as well as departments with the least satisfactory experience.[18]

3.3   Grievances. Grievances may be both an indication of employee dissatisfaction and a means of alleviating such dissatisfactions. Wide acceptance of formal grievance procedures has developed largely since World War II. Almost all collective agreements now include these provisions. In addition,

---

[17] See "Labour Turnover—Meaning and Measurement," *International Labour Review,* Vol. 81, No. 6, June, 1960, pp. 513–26; "Labor Turnover: Causes, Costs and Methods of Control," Los Angeles: Merchants and Manufacturers Association, 1959; Frederick J. Gaudet, "What Top Management Doesn't Know About Turnover," *Personnel,* Vol. 34, No. 5, March-April, 1958, pp. 54–59.

[18] Comparisons are usually made with published rates. It must be recognized, however, that both accession and separation rates vary widely from time to time and from industry to industry.

many firms and agencies maintain similar procedures for unorganized employees. Current practice generally limits the use of these formal procedures to issues affecting individuals or small groups of employees, excluding subjects that would involve broad renegotiation of current practice. The usual arrangement creates a three- to five-step procedure, beginning with review at the supervisor's level, followed by referral to a grievance committee and then to officers of the firm and the union. Most current practice includes a final step of terminal, binding arbitration (see Chapter 10, section 3.36).

Grievances represent situations in which employees feel that they have not been treated fairly. They are, therefore, rather direct indicators of individual morale. For white-collar workers, the most common complaints involve charges of excessive hours and unfair treatment in promotions. Among blue-collar workers, promotions and seniority are prominent, accompanied by many grievances involving job classifications and rates of pay. Blue-collar workers have more grievances per capita than white-collar employees.[19]

Practice generally emphasizes preliminary analysis of *changing numbers of grievances,* with possible trends. Experience is compared with that of other similar firms. Analysis notes the proportions that are *processed beyond the first stage,* assuming that those which go farther indicate more serious dissatisfactions. Attention is given, also, to the number that go to arbitration and to those won and lost in the arbitration stage.

3.4 Work stoppages. Strikes are one of the most spectacular forms of industrial unrest. Not all stoppages, of course, are strikes; some are lockouts, in which employers take the initiative. Usually, however, a lockout represents an employer's last gesture of authority when a strike is imminent. All work stoppages suggest the existence of serious employee dissatisfactions and criticisms.

Managers may encounter real difficulty in interpreting the behavior of strikes. Published statistics of causes are not very helpful. The monthly reporting of strikes by the federal Bureau of Labor Statistics—their numbers and the numbers of strikers, time lost, duration, cause, and outcome—may create a misleading impression of simplicity. For many years, courts have held that some purposes of strikes are legal and will be approved. Others are not. Purposes regarded as proper include the advancement of wages and the improvement of working conditions. For this reason, these issues or causes are generally included in disputes, whether or not they are basic to the conflict. Reported results of strikes are similarly questionable. Since most of them are settled by compromise, either side may claim a victory.

---

[19] For desciptions of nonnegotiated arrangements, see "Grievance Procedures for Unorganzied Employees," *BNA's Personnel Policies Forum,* Survey No. 49, October, 1958; Reid L. Shaw, "A Grievance Procedure for Non-Unionized Employees," *Personnel,* Vol. 36, No. 4, July-August, 1959, pp. 66–70; Charles C. Killingsworth, "Grievance Adjudication in Public Employment," *American Arbitration Journal,* Vol. 13, No. 1, January, 1958, pp. 3–15.

To interpret work stoppages in terms of morale, management must probe beneath these stated issues. It must understand and discount, also, several recognized patterns in strikes. They are *seasonal*, with higher levels in spring and early fall, when agreements expire. They occur more frequently when unions and employers are *inexperienced* in collective bargaining. The growing provision of *mediation* unquestionably prevents many stoppages and reduces the duration of those that occur. All statistical evidence with respect to strikes, for this reason, provides quite superficial indications of underlying employee morale.[20]

3.5 Absenteeism. Unusually high rates of absenteeism may deserve investigation as an indication of low morale. In normal, peacetime operations, hourly employees can be expected to be absent about six days per year. As a rate, this is often described as about 3 per cent. That rate is subject to wide variation, which may be attributed to personal characteristics, occupation, location, industry, weather, and other circumstances. Some employees may be described as absence-prone; they have much more absence than others, so that a minority of the work force generally accounts for the larger share of absences.

As has been noted with respect to other symptoms involving employee behavior, low morale is but one of several factors in absenteeism. One major cause of absence is illness. The common cold gets the credit for an important part of all absences. Younger workers are absent more often than those over 45 years, but their absences tend to be of shorter duration. Women have more absenteeism than men. Supervisory employees generally show lower rates than hourly-rated employees. Paid sick leave plans do not appear to increase absences if they provide for a brief *waiting period* (1 or 2 days). Absences are more common before and after holidays and on Mondays.[21]

These general patterns can be expected. Variations from them or unusually high rates of absence deserve careful investigation. Perhaps the simplest way for the unhappy, dissatisfied employee to express his feeling is to stay away.

3.6 Disciplinary problems. Disciplinary problems often suggest low morale. Employees involved may be critical and irritated; they may see little to be optimistic about. Their disregard of shop rules may well be an expression of this frustration. Unusual numbers of disciplinary cases are, therefore, a common element in the syndrome of negative morale.

Some disciplinary problems may be traced to ineffective or inadequate

[20] For more on patterns and trends in strikes, see Arthur M. Ross and Paul T. Hartman, *Changing Patterns of Industrial Conflict,* New York: John Wiley and Sons, Inc., 1960; Joseph Krislow, "Work Stoppages of Government Employees," *Quarterly Review of Economics and Business,* Vol. 1, No. 1, February, 1961, pp. 87–92.

[21] For details, see Marjorie Brookshire, *Absenteeism,* University of California at Los Angeles, Institute of Industrial Relations, 1960; Grant Canfield and David G. Soash, "Presenteeism—A Constructive View," *Personnel Journal,* Vol. 34, No. 3, July-August, 1955, pp. 94–97; Jack F. Culley, "Prevention and Control of Industrial Absenteeism," *Information Series No. 2,* University of Iowa Bureau of Labor and Management, June, 1959, Floyd C. Mann and John E. Sparling, "Changing Absence Rates," *Personnel,* Vol. 32, No. 5, March, 1956, pp. 392–408.

orientation; an employee may not know the rules. Some may be traceable to inappropriate rules. Some may arise out of the limitations of supervision. Roots of many disciplinary problems are obscure; they may reach far back into errors of selection or transfer.

Employee morale may be affected both by the rules themselves and by the manner of their enforcement. Investigation may disclose unreasonable rules; it may also encounter unfair, uneven, capricious administration. Penalties may not be appropriately related to the seriousness of offenses. Punishment for violation may not be uniform. Unfairness in discipline can be expected to have distinctly adverse effects on morale.

Management may find that it has been largely to blame for many problems in this area. Managerial laxity in the enforcement of shop discipline is documented in hundreds of arbitration reports. The responsibility for making and enforcing shop rules can be shared with employees, but it cannot be neglected without hazards to morale. Firms have sometimes found *disciplinary review boards* helpful in avoiding such hazards. Composed of employees, supervisors and managers, they consider the charges against employees and recommend suitable corrective action.

Lack of skill and understanding in the enforcement of rules and in reprimands by supervisors are a well-recognized source of employee dissatisfaction. Individual criticism, reprimands, and warnings are now widely regarded as personal matters to be handled in private. Assessment of penalties deserves thoughtful, thorough consideration, not hasty action. For many offenses, comment may include warnings of more serious penalties for subsequent violations. In all such action, the appropriate objective is to correct, to establish a relationship likely to prevent repetition. Records of all such actions must be made as a basis for future action, but common practice purges the record after a stated period without violations.[22]

One type of disciplinary problem deserves special mention, for it is now widely regarded as symptomatic of morale. Historic practice provided serious penalties for *drinking* or *drunkenness* on the job. Current opinion, however, regards chronic alcoholism as an illness and proposes medical or psychiatric treatment. If alcoholism is a common offense in any shop, the possibility that it may indicate low morale deserves serious consideration. Several firms are cooperating with medical schools in research designed to learn more about this type of illness.[23]

3.7 Restriction of output. Intentional restriction of output is an indication of worker feelings that closely approximates the definition of negative morale. In it, employees purposefully produce less than they can. They set formal limits or *bogeys,* exerting pressure on members of their crews to enforce these limits. In the most obvious of these practices, employees enforce

---

[22] Standard practice makes some common offenses *just cause* for discharge, including falsification of important records, stealing, immoral conduct (sex offenses), sabotage, and conviction on a criminal charge. In such cases, warnings are usually not required.

[23] For an interesting report on one common disciplinary problem, see Irwin Ross, "Thievery in the Plant," *Fortune,* October, 1961, pp. 140ff.

work rules that prevent efficient operation. Unions may fine or otherwise penalize co-workers who violate these rules, although the National Labor Relations Board, in 1961, ruled that such action is improper.

Featherbedding is usually regarded as involving special *make-work practices* that force the employment of unneeded workers. The printing trades and railroading are among the industries in which featherbedding has been widely discussed, but such practices appear in many others. It is only one of the common forms of restriction. Such practices are not limited to union members; they have been reported among unorganized employees as well. In some cases, they are rather obvious attempts to preserve jobs threatened by technological change. In others, they appear to have developed as a means of spreading the work and avoiding periods of unemployment.[24]

Statistical analysis may help in noting the appearance of restriction. Time-to-time comparisons of average productivity in a shop have been used for this purpose. Frequently distributions of output, illustrated in Figure 23.3, can be examined for declining averages and narrower dispersion. When such checks show a distinct narrowing, with almost all employees at the same level of output, or a distinct skewness, with few workers producing at levels well above average, the likelihood of intentional restriction is suggested and warrants investigation.

Sometimes restrictive practices can be eliminated by negotiating changes in work rules. Reference has been made to this type of adjustment in long-shoring (see Chapter 22, Section 4.4). It has been used, also, in the theater, in negotiations involving the International Alliance of Theatrical Stage Employees. The same objective was attained in the American Motors-UAW negotiations in the fall of 1961, in which profit-sharing was a part of the exchange.

With both organized and unorganized employees, managers will discover that employees may feel that they have something like a property right in their jobs, so that unilateral demands for elimination of restrictions creates powerful resistance.[25] Employees and unions may also find a justification for restrictions in the argument that they are following the example of employers in limiting total production.

4.0 SURVEYS OF MORALE

Many managers propose to make frequent checks on employee morale. They seek to discover its current levels and to compare them with those found in earlier periods. They propose to investigate any critical or unfriendly feelings, to discover why employees may not feel a strong attachment to the

[24] See Herbert R. Northrup, "Plain Facts about Featherbedding," *Personnel,* Vol. 35, No. 1, July-August, 1958, pp. 54-60.

[25] See William Gomberg, "Featherbedding: An Assertion of Property Rights," *Annals of the American Academy of Political and Social Science,* Vol. 333, January, 1961, pp. 120ff.

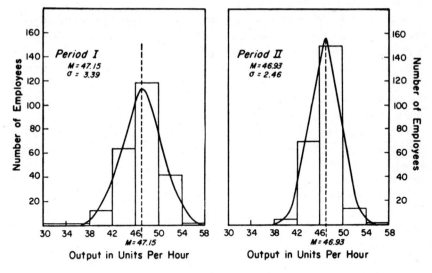

Figure 23.3 Comparative Distributions of Output in Two Periods*

* Data and essential measures may be summarized as follows.

Period I.

Production in Units	Number of Workers
30-34-	1
34-38-	1
38-42-	12
42-46-	64
46-50-	119
50-54-	42
54-58-	1
	Total 240

Mean = 47.15; σ = 3.39.

Period II.

Production in Units	Number of Workers
30-34-	0
34-38-	0
38-42-	5
42-46-	70
46-50-	150
50-54-	14
54-58-	1
	Total 240

Mean = 46.934; σ = 2.460.

organization or why they are not optimistic and enthusiastic about their own or the organization's future.

For this purpose, principal reliance is placed on polls of employee opinions, widely described as *attitude studies*.

In some earlier periods, managers depended on supervisors and friendly employees to tell them how workers were feeling. In some firms, *industrial spies* were employed. They took jobs in the plant, participated in employee discussions, and reported back to managers. In some smaller organizations, managers still lean heavily on the reports of individual employees. Perhaps the most common method of keeping informed with respect to employee morale seeks information from foremen and supervisors.

Managers in large organizations have found that more formal investigations usually provide much more information than they get from supervisors or informal visits with employees. They undertake *periodic studies,* usually once each year, using interviews or printed questionnaires. Some practice combines interviews and questionnaires, first administering a written instrument and supplementing it with subsequent interviews to gain additional detail.

When major reliance is placed on interviews, employees are usually invited to a private office, where they can talk quite informally and on a confidential basis. Interviews are somewhat *structured,* with enough direction to insure attention to areas or dimensions managers regard as of major importance. At the same time, however, employees are encouraged to introduce whatever may be of concern to them, to express their peeves and gripes. They are assured that their observations will not be identified. In some practice, these interviews are recorded for subsequent analysis. Whether recording influences the freedom with which employees voice their opinions is not clear.

Such interviews, if they are to cover a wide range of subjects, are time-consuming and costly. They require *trained interviewers,* who are not generally available except in large organizations. The records they provide for study inevitably include an important element of interpretation on the part of the interviewer. For all these reasons, most firms prefer a survey, using a written scale or questionnaire, which can be administered to all or to a sample of employees at regular intervals. When questionnaires disclose or suggest the existence of unexplained dissatisfaction, more intensive investigation may be undertaken. Carefully planned interviews may ferret out feelings not apparent from the preliminary survey.

Morale scales or questionnaires ask many questions and interpret replies to provide what is regarded as a measured evaluation of employee attitudes. They seek reactions to a variety of subjects. They may appraise the *intensity* of feeling. Responses may provide a basis for useful comparisons of common patterns among younger and older employees, those selected from various sources, those with differing experience, or employees in different departments. All employees may be asked to participate, or administration may be limited to a selected sample. The same questionnaires can be used in subsequent administrations, thus facilitating *time-to-time comparisons*. Similarly, identical questionnaires can be used in a variety of plants, permitting inter-plant comparisons.

The original cost of developing and perfecting a satisfactory questionnaire, however, makes it impractical for most small firms to create their own instrument for this purpose. For the majority of firms, such a survey must use a questionnaire prepared by one of the university centers or consulting firms. Administration of the questionnaire may also require outside assistance. Analysis and interpretation of answers for several hundred employees can best be performed in central laboratories. The standard questionnaires have their own built-in dimensions or subscales.

As noted in Section 2 of this chapter, both interviews and questionnaires propose to identify and measure patterns of employee attitudes. They begin with the assumption that attitudes provide a useful clue to morale. They further assume that *patterns in expressed opinions* can be interpreted to provide an accurate appraisal of attitudes. They rely on groups of items to create the *image of the attitude*. Ten questions, for example, may be regarded as components in a subscale defining attitudes toward supervision.

4.1 Preliminary questions. Several questions deserve attention before any formal program of attitude or morale surveys is undertaken. One question has been suggested: Should employees be queried by interview or should they use formal questionnaires? A second question concerns long-term plans. Shall this be a one-shot approach, or shall it be regarded as a continuing program, with repeated checks at regular intervals? This question is not simply answered; in some firms such surveys seem to be somewhat habit-forming. Managers frequently learn so much from the first survey that they insist on subsequent studies, in part for purposes of comparison.

Also, decision must be made as to whether an outside consulting agency is to be charged with responsibility for conducting the survey and analyzing the results. Consulting firms frequently have competent personnel and facilities for this purpose. Several colleges and universities also act in this capacity. On the other hand, some firms prefer to administer questionnaires themselves. What is best may depend to a considerable degree on numbers of employees and on the dimensions of attitudes that are to be measured. If employees distrust the employer, they may be more candid in replying to an outside agency such as a university research center. Also, if staff members are inexperienced in attitude analysis, they should probably seek professional assistance from outside the firm.

A related question concerns the identification of replies by employees. Shall their answers be signed or anonymous? It appears to make no difference if replies are addressed to an outside agency in which employees have confidence.[26] Replies may be coded to identify departments and a face sheet may provide data on age, sex, length of service, and other considerations, even if replies are unsigned.

What areas shall be included in the questions to be asked? The answer is

[26] See LaVerne Hamel and Hans G. Reif, "Should Attitude Questionnaires Be Signed?" *Personnel Psychology*, Vol. 5, No. 2, Summer, 1952, pp. 87–91. See also Marvin D. Dunnette and Herbert G. Heneman, Jr., "Influence of Scale Administrator on Employee Attitude Responses," *Journal of Applied Psychology*, Vol. 40, No. 2, 1956, pp. 73–77.

to be found in the purpose of the survey. However, another important consideration is the availability of a reliable scale or a suitable instrument. A questionnaire already developed and tested is preferable to a new, tailor-made device. As noted, the standard scale has the advantage of permitting meaningful comparisons with other similar groups of employees. Sometimes attitudes toward special policies or practices are checked by items supplementing a standard scale.

Another question concerns the number of employees to be queried. In what is perhaps the most common practice, all employees are given an opportunity to answer. However, in large organizations, a carefully selected sample, representative of the major divisions and of various ages and experience, may be almost as dependable. Costs of the survey can be reduced by this sampling procedure.

If a questionnaire is to be used, how shall it be distributed? Employees may be called together in a dining room or other assembly and asked to fill out questionnaires in such a session. This method has some advantages. It permits monitors and administrators to help those who do not understand or may not read well. It avoids consultation among employees, which might contaminate their replies.

In other practice, questionnaires are given out with pay checks, or mailed direct to employees, or sent to employees by an outside agency. They may be taken to employees by interviewers. Care is in order on this point, for results may readily reflect the circumstances under which questionnaires are filled out.

When such a survey has been planned for the first time, steps must be taken to interpret it to employees. Their unreserved participation is essential. If they are represented by unions, union officers may well be consulted at the start. Labor organizations are frequently as interested in the results as are managements and may be in a position to assist in making the survey effective.[27]

The question as to what is to be done with survey findings deserves careful consideration before any survey is undertaken. Should they be reported to managers only or should they be distributed to all supervisors and employees? Advance information that results will be broadly distributed may influence participation in the study. What will be done about criticisms and com-

---

[27] On these points see W. B. Webb and E. P. Hollander, "Comparison of Three Morale Measures: A Survey, Pooled Group Judgments, and Self-evaluations," *Journal of Applied Psychology,* Vol. 40, No. 1, February, 1956, pp. 17–20; Ronald P. Yuzuk, "The Assessment of Employee Morale," Columbus, Ohio: Ohio State University Bureau of Business Research, 1961; R. K. Burns, "Attitude Surveys and the Diagnosis of Organization Needs," in "New Approaches to Industrial Human Relations," American Management Association, *Personnel Series No. 157,* 1954; Stephen Habbe, "The Use of a Morale Index," *Management Record,* Vol. 21, No. 10, October, 1959, pp. 322–23; Robert D. Gray, "Employee Opinion Research in Management Decision Making," *Proceedings* of the first conference on Research Developments in Personnel Management, University of California at Los Angeles, 1957, pp. 26–29; Allen L. Edwards, *Techniques of Attitude Scale Construction,* New York: Appleton-Century-Crofts, Inc., 1957.

plaints? Will steps be taken to change objectionable conditions? Will employees be informed of such actions?

In what appears to be the most common policy and related practice, detailed results of such surveys are fed back to managers and supervisors, often before they are released to employees. Results are discussed in top-management echelons, after which each departmental manager discusses findings with his assistants. In such discussions, attention is given to changes suggested by survey results. Action is taken, and employees are fully informed of such action. It is frequently observed that no management should undertake such a survey unless it is ready and willing to make changes.[28]

Managers often intend not only to change offending conditions and relationships but also to effect changes in employee attitudes by such action. One of the reasons for repeated administration is the desire to check on managerial success in improving morale. Several studies have reported on these remedial programs, especially in their efforts to facilitate technological change and to reduce resistance to automation.[29]

4.2 Dimensions: subscales. Reference to two of the most widely administered scales will indicate the dimensions they cover and the nature of their inquiries. The University of Minnesota's *Triple Audit Employee Attitude Scale* provides measured reactions to supervision, communications, working conditions, advancement and promotion, and company identification. Combination of subscale items permits a measure of general morale. The *Science Research Associates Employee Inventory* includes 78 items that are analyzed to measure attitudes toward job demands, working conditions, pay, employee benefits, security, status and recognition, identification with the firm, supervision, co-workers, administration, communication, confidence in management, and opportunity for development.

The scoring of scales and their analysis to provide subscale measures may, in both cases, be performed in central offices. Results are subsequently reported to managers, generally in the form of profiles that relate departmental and over-all scores on these dimensions to comparable norms. Scales may provide an opportunity for employees to add their comments or explanations. Such open-end questions can be of great value in interpreting answers.[30]

Excellent illustrations of the need for special scales or supplements to standard instruments are provided by the current concern about employee reactions to automation and by the distinctive attitudes of engineers and

[28] See, for one report of feedback, Robert H. Milligan and John E. Osmanski, "Attitude Survey Followed Up by Feedback Sessions," *Personnel Journal*, Vol. 33, No. 3, July-August, 1954, pp. 92–96.

[29] See, for example, John R. P. French et al., "Employee Participation in a Program of Industrial Change," *Personnel*, Vol. 35, No. 3, November-December, 1958, pp. 16–29; Harry C. Triandis, "Attitude Change through Training in Industry," *Human Organization*, Vol. 17, No. 2, Summer, 1958, pp. 27–30.

[30] See Darrel E. Roach, "Dimensions of Employee Morale," *Personnel Psychology*, Vol. 11, No. 3, Autumn, 1958, pp. 419–31; R. A. Hudson Rosen and Hjalmar Rosen, "A Suggested Modification in Job Satisfaction Surveys," *Personnel Psychology*, Vol. 8, No. 3, Autumn, 1955, pp. 303–14.

Directions

Below and on the following pages you will find a number of statements about your job.

    1. Read each statement.

    2. Choose the word below the statement which *best* tells how you feel about that statement, and put an "X" in the box above that word. Do not write in answers for questions where you can just put an "X" in the box.

    3. Do this for *all* the statements.

    4. Please answer every question.

    5. If you need help in filling out the questionnaire, please raise your hand.

    6. There are no "right" or "wrong" answers. Just tell how you feel about each statement.

YOUR ANSWERS ARE SECRET. NO ONE IN THE COMPANY WILL SEE THEM

Section I

_____ 1. The lighting for my job is

    ☐ Excellent   ☐ Good   ☐ Fair   ☐ Poor   ☐ Very Poor

_____ 2. The ventilation where I work is

    ☐ Excellent   ☐ Good   ☐ Fair   ☐ Poor   ☐ Very Poor

_____ 3. The job that the top executives are doing in this Company is

    ☐ Very Poor   ☐ Poor   ☐ Fair   ☐ Good   ☐ Excellent

_____ 4. All in all, as a place to work, this Company is

    ☐ Very Poor   ☐ Poor   ☐ Fair   ☐ Good   ☐ Excellent

_____ 5. Considering the present cost of living, my pay is

    ☐ Excellent   ☐ Good   ☐ Fair   ☐ Poor   ☐ Very Poor

_____ 6. Considering everything, my working hours are

    ☐ Very Poor   ☐ Poor   ☐ Fair   ☐ Good   ☐ Excellent

_____ 7. The spirit of cooperation among employees in my department is

    ☐ Excellent   ☐ Good   ☐ Fair   ☐ Poor   ☐ Very Poor

_____ 8. The reputation of this Company in the community (how people feel and talk about this Company) is

    ☐ Excellent   ☐ Good   ☐ Fair   ☐ Poor   ☐ Very Poor

_____ 9. Considering everything, my present job is

    ☐ Very Poor   ☐ Poor   ☐ Fair   ☐ Good   ☐ Excellent

Figure 23.4   Excerpt from the Triple Audit Attitude Scale, University of Minnesota Industrial Relations Center

scientists. Hardin has reported on employee attitudes toward recent or prospective technological changes.[31]

Special studies of morale among engineers and scientists suggest that

[31] Einar Hardin, "Computer Automation, Work Environment and Employee Satisfaction: A Case Study," *Industrial and Labor Relations Review*, Vol. 13, No. 4, July, 1960, pp. 559–67; also his "The Reactions of Employees to Office Automation," *Monthly Labor Review*, Vol. 83, No. 9, September, 1960, pp. 925–32.

several added subscales can be useful, including adequacy and quality of work space, privacy, freedom from interruptions, flexibility in working hours, opportunities for publication, and participation in professional conferences.[32]

4.3 Items or Questions. Questions or items in attitude scales are of several types. Most common is the multiple-choice type, illustrated in the excerpt from the Triple Audit Scale, shown in Figure 23.4. The *Triple Audit Scale* includes 54 of these Likert-type items. As noted, these questions are supplemented by open-end or free-response questions such as "What do you like best about working for this company?" or simply "Comments."

In standard questionnaires, these items have been carefully checked and are rechecked to be sure that the meanings are clear. (Test-retest reliability of the Triple Audit Scale is 0.85.) Criticisms of tailor-made scales frequently point to the inclusion of ambiguous words or others that carry emotional tones.

4.4 Analysis and interpretation. Scoring generally provides group measures or indexes, avoiding any individual identifications. Reports may show results in terms of the percentage of favorable and unfavorable responses on each item; more frequently scores are calculated for combinations of items in subscales. In a common presentation, scores are compared with norms in a profile not unlike that in which test scores are shown.

Modern tabulating equipment has permitted numerous breakdowns or comparisons. One department is compared with others on each of the subscales; rank-and-file employees are compared with supervisors (see Figures 23.5, 23.6, and 23.7); employee reactions may be related to age, length of service, education, special training, and many other characteristics.

In all such comparisons, the standard scales have a great advantage. Since they have been administered to thousands of employees, norms can be developed for occupations, industries, and localities. Perfection of these norms requires continuing analysis, for a variety of personal characteristics may influence such norms. England and others report, for example, that age may exert a significant influence on occupational norms.[33]

5.0 SUMMARY

Historic employers and managers usually showed little concern about employee morale. Modern managers, however, are concerned in part because they regard morale as a *measure of their success* in incentivating employees. Especially since World War II, policy has generally sought to maintain high

[32] See Paul A. Brinker, "Morale Among Professional Workers: A Case Study," *Personnel Journal*, Vol. 35, No. 8, January, 1957, pp. 297–301; George A. Peters and Max Lees, "Better Incentives for Scientific Personnel," *Personnel*, Vol. 34, No. 4, January-February, 1958, pp. 59–62; T. R. Shapiro, "The Attitudes of Scientists toward their Jobs," in R. T. Livingston and S. H. Milberg, *Human Relations in Industrial Research Management*, New York: Columbia University Press, 1957, pp. 151–62.

[33] George W. England, Abraham K. Korman, and Carroll I. Stein, "Overcoming Contradictions in Attitude Survey Results: The Need for Relevant Norms," *Personnel Administration*, Vol. 24, No. 3, May-June, 1961, pp. 36–40.

GENERAL MORALE

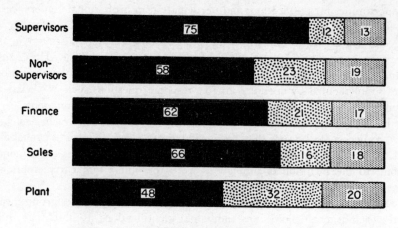

COMMUNICATIONS

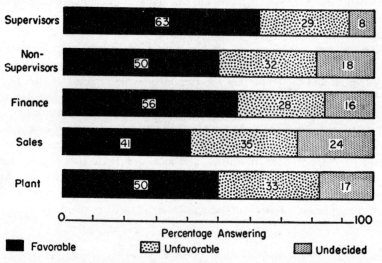

Figure 23.5 Comparisons of General Morale and Communications Scores by Groups
SOURCE: "Auditing Your Manpower Management," *Bulletin 13,* University of Minnesota Industrial Relations Center, May, 1954, p. 16.

levels of employee morale. It has frequently intended, also, to maintain continuing checks on morale and to analyze the evidence from these appraisals as a basis for changes in working relationships and conditions.

Some current conceptions of morale relate it primarily to the satisfaction of individual worker needs. Others regard morale as a social phenomenon involving the cohesiveness of work groups and attitudes with respect to the

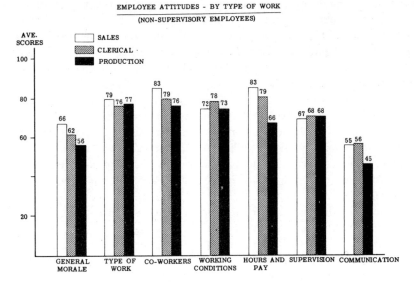

Figure 23.6 Comparison of Major Dimensions in Morale, Three Broad Occupational Groups
SOURCE: University of Minnesota Industrial Relations Center.

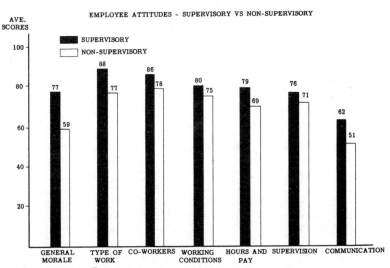

Figure 23.7 Comparison of Dimensions of Morale, Supervisory and non-Supervisory Employees
SOURCE: University of Minnesota Industrial Relations Center.

mission and success of such associations. Many managers make no distinction; they consider morale as involving both types of employee reactions.

Morale is recognized as a matter of feeling and spirit. Current practice assumes that morale can be evaluated by reference to overt expressions in *words* and *behavior*. Managers watch for activity they regard as evidencing high or low morale, particularly the latter. They also use oral and written opinion polls, described as *attitude surveys*. Employee statements and answers to questions are, in this procedure, combined and interpreted as expressing the feelings of employees.

Managerial interest in morale has focused almost entirely on employees, including rank-and-file workers and first level supervisors.

Wide use of employee opinion polls has suggested that in-plant communications exert significant influence on morale. When scales include a communications subscale, it frequently scores lowest among the several dimensions. Attitudes disclosed by surveys often indicate that employees have not been informed or have not understood. Not infrequently, analysis of employee answers also indicates that they feel sure managers have not been receiving employees loud and clear, either.

The next chapter outlines managerial interest in and concern about *employment communications*.

SELECTED SUPPLEMENTARY READINGS

Brayfield, Arthur H. and Walter H. Crockett, "Employee Attitudes and Employee Performance," *Psychological Bulletin,* Vol. 52, No. 5, pp. 396–424, September, 1955.

Brookshire, Marjorie, *Absenteeism.* Los Angeles: Institute of Industrial Relations, University of California, Los Angeles, 1960.

Craig, Alton W., "Arbitration of Labor-Management Disputes in Canada," New York State School of Industrial and Labor Relations at Cornell University, *Reprint Series No. 112,* 1962.

Dunnette, Marvin D. and Herbert G. Heneman, Jr., "Influence of Scale Administrator on Employee Attitude Responses," *Journal of Applied Psychology,* Vol. 40, No. 2, pp. 73–77, 1956.

Hardin, Einar, "Computer Automation, Work Environment and Employee Satisfaction," and "The Reaction of Employees to Office Automation," *Reprint Series Numbers 31 and 34,* Labor and Industrial Relations Center, Michigan State University, 1960–61.

"The High Cost of Labor Waste," *Fortune,* pp. 201–202, December, 1961.

Kildridge, Maurice D., "Reduced Costs Through Job Enlargement: A Case," *Journal of Business,* Vol. 33, No. 4, pp. 357–362, October, 1960.

Likert, Rensis and Stanley E. Seashore, "Employee Attitude and Output," *Monthly Labor Review,* Vol. 77, No. 6, pp. 641–649, June, 1954.

Zalesnik, A., C. R. Christensen, and F. J. Roethlisberger, *The Motivation, Productivity and Satisfaction of Workers, a Prediction Study,* Boston: Harvard University, Division of Research, Graduate School of Business, 1958.

SHORT CASE PROBLEM 23.1

Discharge for Cause

Johnson, a production employee, was granted permission to leave his job at a specified time to keep a dental appointment. He was expected to return to the job after his dentist finished with him. He left before the time specified and asked one of the other employees to "fake" his time card for him.

Johnson had been warned that his work habits were unsatisfactory, in that he left his job and visited other departments without permission. His supervisor regarded the effort to falsify his time card as sufficiently serious—in view of his earlier record—to justify discharging him.

Problem: If Johnson seeks reinstatement and you were selected as arbitrator, what general principles would you apply in deciding the question? If you want to see how another arbitrator handled the issue, see the case of the Columbia-Southern Chemical Co., 6 ALAA, section 69.412.

SHORT CASE PROBLEM 23.2

Employee Attitudes by Interview

The Diamond Pea Company is going to have a study of employee attitudes. That much was decided at the last meeting of the Board of Directors. The chairman of the board insisted on it; most of the other members were enthusiastic.

President Jones is much less pleased with the idea. Faced with the necessity of doing something, he has made the following suggestions. First, he would prefer that someone be employed to undertake a systematic interviewing procedure, which would result in individual interviews with each employee. Second, in such interviewing, he proposes that a hidden microphone be connected to a tape recorder, so that the interview can be checked by others. He does not want the employees to know that such recordings are being made. Third, if interviewing cannot be arranged, President Jones wants to use one of the questionnaire-type surveys for which the blank forms can be purchased by the company, distributed by the industrial relations division, and scored by the latter. He feels that questionnaires should be coded to indicate, in every case, the department and salary classification of the respondent. Replies would be anonymous. Finally, the president wishes to make it perfectly clear to everyone that the information provided by the returns would be confidential, for the use of management only. No report on the returns would be made to employees.

President Jones has frankly stated that he fears the survey may stir up trouble by suggesting criticisms to employees. Moreover, he doubts that employees will tell the truth about how they feel.

Problem: You are the executive vice-president. Mr. Jones has a lot of confidence in your judgment. What advice would you give him?

SHORT CASE PROBLEM 23.3

Restriction of Output

Analyze the following data to discover evidence of restriction of output. Chart them and measure the skewness of the distribution. What factor might most readily explain this condition?

Production in Units per Week	Number of Employees
20-22	10
22-24	20
24-26	120
26-28	230
28-30	10
30-32	5
32-34	5

SHORT CASE PROBLEM 23.4

Discipline and Promotions

The following tabulation presents a fourfold classification of employees so arranged as to indicate the possible relationship between disciplinary action and promotions.

Disciplinary Action	Promotional Experience	
	Promoted	Not Promoted
Non-offenders.............	73	231
Offenders.................	27	669

Problem: Do you conclude that disciplinary actions make promotions unlikely? How can you evaluate such a relationship?

SHORT CASE PROBLEM 23.5

International Cultivator Company

Organization of the International Cultivator Company provides a high degree of decentralization; so the local plant in Lisbon is largely on its own. In 1959, the general manager returned from a series of meetings in the home office with the strong conviction that he was expected to undertake some systematic investigations of employee attitudes. At the next meeting of his assistants, he broached the question. He explained that several other divisions had reported favorably on their experience with employee-attitude surveys. As a result, the home office had authorized expenditures for this purpose. He asked the advice of his associates on undertaking a somewhat similar survey.

At first, most members of the group appeared hesitant about expressing opinions on the subject. After what was almost an awkward silence, the general foreman said that he could see no serious objections, but he was not optimistic about the value of such a procedure. Other members of the group spoke briefly in support of this position. One of them was somewhat more negative. "In the first place," he said, "the best indication any management can get, so far as employee morale is concerned, is the quantity and quality of output. If we ask employees all sorts of silly questions about what they do or do not like, we can expect some silly answers. They will think up things to complain about, things they would never otherwise have dreamed of mentioning."

After this rather blunt expression of opposition, the office manager joined the discussion. He felt that employees were in general well satisfied with working conditions and relationships with their supervisors. He regarded such an experiment as somewhat dangerous, for he felt that any points on which employees appeared at all critical would be seized by the union as issues in the next negotiations.

At this point, the general manager directed a question to the director of industrial relations. "George," he said, "this is right in your bailiwick. Perhaps I should have discussed it with you before bringing it to this meeting. I'm sure we would all value your opinion."

The industrial relations director replied that he was inclined to agree with the opinions already expressed. "If we do it," he concluded, "we will have to face up to a good many criticisms of the way we are now operating. Employees will expect us to make changes. It could cost us a lot of money. We might not be willing to follow some of the suggestions. Some of the changes might not be approved by the home office."

"Let me go a step further," said he, "for I think some of our employees might quite properly object to answering the questions in a typical survey. We don't pay them to think as we do or as we think they should or even to be loyal to us. We pay them to work for us and to perform the jobs we assign. What they think about us and about other matters is their own private business."

The general manager summed up the discussion. "I feel as you do about this proposal. Also, I think we already know what our people think. We keep very close to them every day. They tell us when they don't like something. I would bet that any such study would find the morale of our employees very high. I'm going to report that we will not make such a study."

Problem: Evaluate these arguments.

SHORT CASE PROBLEM 23.6

*Proper Discipline Immediately**

The Background: A petroleum dealer ordered an *oil* shipment from a petroleum distributor. As a result of relying on the truck driver's oral instructions instead of the bill of lading, an employee pumped *gasoline* into the tank truck. Company procedure required the fuel pumper to stamp the kind and amount of petroleum on the bill of lading. It also made it standard practice to take a "flash test" on all oil pumped and to record the result and time on the back of the bill of lading. As a result, the bill of lading showed that oil had been ordered but gasoline delivered and that a flash test had been taken. But the time of the test stamped on the bill was an hour after the truck left the loading dock. Company rules make it mandatory to take such test while the truck is still on the premises. Moreover, such test cannot be given to gasoline. The error was discovered in time to prevent the gasoline from being delivered to customers. But, the next day the pump man was given a three-day suspension for negligence. Three weeks later he was discharged. The contract called for notice to the union within 48 hours of the imposition of discipline.

The Issue: Could the employer impose dual penalties for the same offense?

The Union Argues: If discipline is called for, the company is restricted to imposing one penalty based on all the facts of that one situation. Here, the company had all the necessary information or the means to acquire it. In a previous award (based on the same disciplinary notice clause), the arbitrator ruled that the employer must make up his mind on one penalty and not keep the employee up in the air while making a further investigation. This clause was not changed when the contract was renewed. And the parties agreed to abide by this interpretation even though an abnormally severe penalty might result.

The Company Argues: There is no duplication of penalties. The employer had the right to give the employee a three-day suspension for his mistake in filling the order as well as his poor work record. The discharge was based on falsification of records and a failure to make the required test within the time limit. The company did not have all the facts of the case until the day before it discharged the employee. It was only then that it found out that the time limit for the test had been violated. Moreover, it delayed in coming to a final decision because it hoped to find some mitigating circumstances allowing it to impose a lesser penalty. When none came to light, the company was justified in firing the worker.

Problem: Use this actual arbitration case, summarized here, to check your theories about employment relationships and to decide on a reasonable, nontechnical solution of the issue.

* *Employee Relations and Arbitration Report,* Vol. 21, No. 26, June 26, 1961, p. 5.

24. Employment Communications

An effective communications system is an essential ingredient of good labour-management relations. The problems involved in passing information from the management to the worker and vice versa are far from simple and many techniques have been evolved to encourage a two-way flow of facts, ideas and opinions. However, the attitudes of those conveying and receiving this information are likely to be as important as the techniques themselves. . . .[1]

Attention directed to employee and management morale inevitably raises questions about the adequacy of employment communications. Most studies of employee attitudes find that communications are a common subject of criticism. Manager attitudes often indicate a similar view. Both employees and managers frequently feel that they are left out, that they have inadequate opportunities for sharing ideas and information and for voicing their own opinions and suggestions. Rank-and-file workers often score the communications subscale or dimension in morale studies at the bottom of the list. Managers complain that they are not kept informed, that they may have to learn about developments and plans from union members or by accident at social affairs.

Modern management theory places a heavy responsibility on communications in the working organization. Communication is the flux that binds the people of an organization together. Through communication, they can attain a common viewpoint and understanding and cooperate to accomplish organizational ends and objectives. Communications keep them informed of the changing mission and of organizational progress and success. Through

[1] From the introduction to "Communications between Management and Workers in the Petroleum Industry," *International Labour Review*, Vol. 43, No. 5, May, 1961, p. 459.

communications, they are aided in understanding and maintaining a satisfactory rationale of authority and status structures.

The modern working organization requires accuracy and fidelity in its communications. Without adequate communication, the members of working organizations cannot develop enough identification with the group to cooperate at high levels. The manager's carefully planned incentives can become motivational only when their message is communicated; communication is thus a major factor in incentivation. With inaccurate communication, the whole group may be misled and disorganized.[2]

Put another way, communicating is at the very heart of the process of organizing. Since organization is a principal tool of managers, their concern about communicating is entirely reasonable. It is not remarkable that studies of manager jobs find that oral communications take up a major part of most managers' time, and that, in addition, managers face a barrage of written communications that require responses.

This chapter directs attention to the theory, policy and practice of modern management in its efforts to provide adequate communications systems for today's working organizations. Section 1 provides an overview of problems and relevant definitions. Section 2 outlines current theory and policy. Section 3 describes the common communications media. Section 4 suggests some tests that may be applied to evaluate in-plant communications.

1.0 PROBLEMS AND DEFINITIONS

Today's managers probably face more difficult problems in maintaining adequate organizational communications than their predecessors, partly because so many working organizations are large in scale and complex in nature and partly because participants expect more communication and are more critical of what they get. Modern organizations have, in many cases, combined a variety of functions, activities and processes. They have more diverse products involving greater individual and group specialization than the proprietorships and partnerships of earlier times. Today's firms and public agencies may include many more levels than earlier business structures. *Layering* interposes frictions, if not actual barriers in lines of upward and downward communications.

1.1 Problems in communications. The reality of these developments has not escaped the attention of managers. Communication has sometimes been described as "the administrator's skill." Administrators have noted their increasing difficulty in maintaining effective communication throughout the organizations they manage. Indeed, if the number of conference discussions and publications is an indicator, communication problems are among the most pressing and serious. Managers have noted their difficulties in getting

---

[2] Managers of large penal institutions have long recognized the elementary importance of communication in organizing. Limiting communications is a major means of control.

accurate messages to their outlying co-workers. They have also recognized complaints that messages were not coming through loud and clear and that opportunities were not provided for associates at all levels to advance their ideas and opinions.[3] No small part of the movement toward decentralization in large organizations has been designed to reduce communications problems.

At the same time, modern managers expect more of intra-firm communications than their earlier counterparts. Today's managers regard effective communications as a process much broader than merely transmitting orders and keeping informed with respect to the operations of individual divisions, sections, and work crews. They recognize criticisms of communications as expressing the desires of members both to be informed and to be heard. They indicate dissatisfaction with opportunities to participate and to share in the "inside information" that identifies members and distinguishes them from outsiders.

The heart of today's problems in this area of communications is one of preserving balance between extremes of under-communication and over-communication and balance between outgoing and incoming communications at all levels throughout the organization. Organizational communications should satisfy the needs of the organization and of its members without overwhelming participants. They should provide opportunity for communication without deluging participants with responsibilities for communicating. Communicating can become a burden rather than a source of satisfaction.

1.2   Varying perceptions. Members of an organization see a variety of problems in communication rather than the same, single problem. To some employees, major concern centers about the difficulty of getting a clear understanding of what is expected of them and keeping accurately informed about general changes and developments. More sophisticated workers expect communications (1) to give them clear instructions as to what they are to do; (2) to provide explanations that relate such assignments to the organization's mission and experience; and (3) to facilitate their efforts to secure the attention and interest of upper echelons long enough and often enough so that workers can feel themselves participating members in the whole.

To less thoughtful managers, the communication problem is essentially that of getting subordinates to hear and understand and execute orders. Their common complaint is that employees fail to listen carefully, to hear what they are told, to do what they have been assigned. Managers with greater understanding of modern working organizations see much more than

---

[3] See Alexander Heron's classic *Sharing Information with Employees,* Stanford, Calif.: Stanford University Press, 1942; Raymond W. Peters, *Communications within Industry,* New York: Harper & Brothers, 1950; Robert Newcomb and Marg Sammons, *Speak Up, Management,* New York: Funk & Wagnalls Company, 1951; William H. Whyte, Jr., *Is Anybody Listening?* New York: Simon and Schuster, Inc., 1952; Charles E. Redfield, *Communication in Management,* Chicago: University of Chicago Press, 1953; M. J. Dooher and V. Marquis, *Effective Communication on the Job,* New York: American Management Association, 1956; Dennis Murphy, *Better Business Communication,* New York: McGraw-Hill Book Company, Inc., 1957; Lee O. Thayer, *Administrative Communication,* Homewood, Ill.: Richard D. Irwin, Inc., 1961.

a problem of getting subordinates to listen, comprehend, and act appropriately. The problem also involves expressing managers' ideas clearly and effectively, keeping themselves informed with respect to what is happening throughout the entire organization, getting adequate reports from lower levels, learning about the reactions and opinions and suggestions of subordinates and associates, and using the communications system to shape employee attitudes and to cultivate employee ideas and suggestions.

1.3 Definitions. Communication means the exchange of thoughts, ideas, information and opinions. The term may also be used to refer to a particular message. The root of the word is the same as that of "commune" and "communion" and refers to a process of making common or mutual. The working organization requires a continuing process of communication and numerous individual communications. Hence the problem may be described either as one of communication or of communications. The broader problem is that of maintaining an effective communication process.

For convenience, that process is generally regarded as including (1) *sources* or *transmitters,* (2) a variety of *media* or *channels* that compose the *structure of communications,* and (3) *receptors* or *receivers.* Two principal subprocesses will be evident—one concerned with *transmission* and the other with *reception.* As noted, the general purpose of communication is that of giving commonality or mutuality to an idea; it is that of sharing the idea with another or others. Communication thus seeks to transmit, advance, hear, understand, or perhaps exchange ideas. The communicated idea may be a simple fact, transmitted for the information of receivers. It may be an opinion, intended in part to influence, create, or change the opinion of the receptor. It may be a suggestion, a request, or a command, designed to direct or shape the action of those to whom it is directed.

Communication, including the process as it appears in employment, may seek to advance or transmit ideas ranging from the simplest expression of feelings to complex explanations of scientific theory. Some of it indicates the transmitter's state of mind and present feeling, with little more intentional communication than the cat's purring or meow. Dogs—and foremen, supervisors, managers, and even rank-and-file employees—bark and growl when they feel like it. Pigs—to quote the classic agricultural interpretation of the communication process—grunt and rub against each other for company. Humming or singing or whistling or smiling on the job may have some similarly uncomplicated purpose.

Indeed, communication appears to be very close to the primary, creature needs of people everywhere. They communicate in part because the process of transmission is in itself pleasing and satisfying. Some such satisfaction is implicit in the common gestures of salutation, in nodding, waving, winking, and numerous other simple expressions.

Employment communication, in most of our thinking, means communication in words. It is important that we recognize several other forms. Highly important ideas and suggestions and proposals for action can be and are communicated without words, in pictures, charts, smiles, nods, head shaking, scowls, winks, and a variety of other gestures. Similarly important transmissions may take the form of direct action—shoving, slapping, touching, stroking, patting, petting, and many other similar actions.

Verbal communication is thus something of an advanced stage. The spoken or written word is a more complicated transmission than the laugh, smile or cry, as every baby demonstrates. Further, even the shortest and simplest words may be complex in their meanings when modified by non-verbal behavior, including inflections and gestures. Note the variations in intended meanings for such words as "oh" and "ah" and even "yes" or "no."

Verbal communication is complicated not only by the various meanings that may be attached to the same words but also by the frequent modification of words by inflections and gestures and the setting in which words appear. The foreman who reports that he "told" his subordinate to do something may have requested it or suggested it or ordered it. Oral communication is constantly modified, also, by the continuing *feedback process* in which ideas take shape as a result of exchanges rather than of simple one-way transmissions. Original expressions create reactions that in turn modify continuing transmissions.

1.4 Active participation. Both transmitting and receiving are active rather than passive processes. Transmitters may have a variety of reasons for transmitting; receivers must have intentions to listen and to receive if the process is to be effective. In the working organization, adequate communication requires much more than careful transmission of orders or instructions or questions. Effective communication requires adequate reception and response. It requires reception by managers. It may require explanations to supplement both orders and reports. Transmitters may seek to inform, teach, or persuade and to encourage or compliment and reward, as well as to instruct. Receivers must seek to hear, understand, comprehend, and respond to the messages intended for them.

Purpose and intent in reception may be as significant as those in transmission, for the process is incomplete without effective response. Receivers may listen carefully because they regard the incoming message as related to their welfare. They may intend to listen attentively because they see it as having personal meaning and interest to them. On the other hand, the intended receiver may prefer not to hear the message or to hear it with a meaning different from that with which it was transmitted. Receivers may give the message little attention; they may ignore it or intentionally distort it. Receivers of a message designed to teach may not care to learn. Receivers may discredit a transmitter or regard messages from a given source as biased or unimportant.[4] They may be more sensitive to the feeling of the transmitter than to the messages he transmits.[5]

[4] See Robert G. Weaver and Harold P. Zelko, "Talking Things Over on the Job," *Supervision Magazine,* May, June, and July, 1958.

[5] William C. Schutz, "Interpersonal Underworld," *Harvard Business Review,* Vol. 36, No. 4, July-August, 1958, pp. 123–35.

1.5   **Channels, media, and structures.** The organization chart is generally regarded as picturing the *formal* communication structure of the working organization. It establishes a *communications network,* with channels that are expected to carry messages both vertically and horizontally throughout the whole organization. This formal structure—so called because it is established by management and formally pictured in approved charts of the organization—creates and defines *lines of communication.* It identifies and relates transmitters and receivers and establishes an approved pattern for their exchanges. By implication and sometimes by formal declaration, it seeks to limit communication to these lines. It expects transmitters to "go through channels" and receivers to confine their attention to messages that reach them via these approved routes.

The importance of *informal* organization structures has been noted in Chapter 6. Informal communications, as Figure 6.6 has noted, may not follow the formal channels established by the organization chart. Informal communications may involve the same transmitters and receivers, but establish quite different lines among them. A single employee or supervisor may have effective channels that extend at various angles throughout the formal chart.

At least as important is the fact that relationships established by the informal communications system may provide transmission and reception that are faster, easier and, in the opinion of participants, more dependable and important than those available in the formal system. Foreman Number 51 may question what he hears directly from his superior, for example, or he may regard such messages with suspicion or consider them relatively unimportant, so long as he has his private line to the general manager. In contrast, he may regard his private, informal channels as more dependable, useful, and significant in terms of his personal interests and welfare.

2.0   THEORY AND POLICY IN COMMUNICATIONS

Current theory with respect to employment communications shows the influence of a growing volume of research and is quite different from that of earlier periods. Current policy reflects these changes. Modern policy gives great emphasis to the importance of all communication as the essential binder among the members of an organization. It assumes that only through communication can managers and employees gain and hold similar perceptions of the organizational mission and develop appropriate rationalizations of authority and status structures. Modern theory advances a number of explanations that identify factors and conditions believed to influence the effectiveness of internal communications. Some are regarded as being more influential with respect to *transmission* than to *reception,* as, for example, the clarity with which ideas are expressed, the intention and purpose of the transmission, and the technical quality and range of facilities available for transmissions. Other conditions influence *reception,* for example, the receiver's perception of, interest in, and attitude toward the source and the message.

Usually more attention has been given to factors influencing transmission than to those related to reception.

However, modern theory recognizes the reciprocal parts played by transmission and reception. It notes *semantic difficulties* that may handicap communication between individuals and groups with different backgrounds and frames of reference. It relates communication to *morale* throughout the structure. It recognizes the importance of *receiver interest* as an influence in reception. It notes numerous *barriers* to communication. It regards *rumor* and the *grapevine* as to some extent indicating unsatisfied communication needs.

2.1 Two-way communication. Both experiment and experience support the theory that one-way communication is much less effective than two-way exchanges. Clarity and understanding are facilitated by the two-way process; an order or instruction becomes more meaningful if the intended receiver has an opportunity to respond. Ambiguities can be removed and meaning explained. Even more important, the attitude of the receiver is likely to be more favorable; his perception of the transmitter is modified by the possibility of responding; his acceptance of the message is improved.

In the absence of two-way channels, reactions of receivers may become almost pathological. They may be frustrated, resentful, and critical of the transmitter. In spite of numerous transmissions directed to them, they may feel excluded, left out. The process of responding is thus recognized as an important conditioner in the whole process, and *feedback* appears as an essential throughout the organization. Modern theory concludes that when the opportunity to tranmit and to be heard is available to both parties, communication is improved. Again, modern theory holds that listening may be as important as transmitting; listening also appears as directly influenced by listening at the other end of the line. Those who feel that they are not being heard tend to be reluctant to hear.

2.2 Semantics in communications. Communication theory has long recognized the importance of different meanings attached to the same words. Transmitter and receiver may use words with quite different connotations. Variations in meaning may be slight or great, matters of degree or of radical difference. They may include strong emotional implications. Today's employment communications have been shown to be significantly influenced by such differences; studies disclose variations in the meanings attached to the same words by managers and rank-and-file workers. For example, Triandis reports significant differences in defining degrees of such job attributes as "routine," "seasonal," "professional," "executive," "easy," "active," and others.[6] Korman reports important differences among managers in their definitions of such concepts as "ask," "counsel," "appraisal," and 13 others.[7]

[6] Harry C. Triandis, "Comparative Factorial Analysis of Job Semantic Structures of Managers and Workers," *Journal of Applied Psychology,* Vol. 44, No. 5, October, 1960, pp. 297–302.
[7] Abraham K. Korman, "A Cause of Communications Failure," *Personnel Administration,* Vol. 23, No. 3, May-June, 1960, pp. 17–21.

2.3 Factor in morale. Modern theory regards the opportunity to participate in sending and receiving messages as an important consideration in morale. Both managers and employees evidence a need for communicating. Perry and Mahoney found that merely providing employees with facts about the firm does not appear to exert a significant influence on their attitudes. The extent of employee knowledge about the organization is not, in their study, significantly related to employee morale. They conclude that the philosophy and objectives of communications systems may be more significant than the sharing of information.[8] Likert reports a close relationship with morale defined as group loyalty. He says that "Communication upward, downward and between peers appears to be best in those departments which fall in the high cluster on this group-loyalty analysis and poorest in the low cluster."[9]

Bavelas and Barrett noted—from a study of internal communication patterns—that the "index of peripherality appears to be related strongly to morale." They studied a variety of patterns, illustrated in part by the diagrams in Figure 24.1. They noted that participants in peripheral positions— at the ends of communications lines—displayed apathetic, destructive, or uncooperative behavior, while those in central spots, like C in the chain and wheel patterns, indicated that they were satisfied, in high spirits, and pleased with what they had done.[10]

2.4 Skill and attitude of transmitter. Modern theory concludes that communications are influenced by both skill in transmission and the attitude of the transmitter. Current practice evidences the wide acceptance of this conclusion; perhaps more attention has been given to the quality and propriety of transmission than all the rest of the communication process. Transmission can be improved by careful attention to clarity of expression, appropriate language, and the intensity or force of the transmission. Messages can be shaped and expressed to fit the occasion and the audience. Studies of reading ease and human interest (see Section 4 of this chapter) have supported this viewpoint. Transmitters can develop helpful skills in both oral and written communication.

Attitudes of transmitters are regarded as important in part because they affect the receptivity of those to whom messages are directed. Thus, "Now hear this!" may express an appropriate attitude for those who issue military orders and instructions. The same attitude may interfere with reception in the industrial setting. Again, orders or instructions may be peremptory and arbitrary if they originate from one with recognized authority but may be much less effective if issued in the same tone by someone whose authority is questioned. An attitude that is appropriate for orders and instructions could handicap the transmission of reports and information.[11]

---

[8] Dallis Perry and Thomas A. Mahoney, "In-Plant Communications and Employee Morale," *Personnel Psychology,* Vol. 8, No. 3, Autumn, 1955, pp. 339–46.

[9] Rensis Likert, *New Patterns of Management,* New York: McGraw-Hill Book Company, Inc., 1961, p. 129.

[10] Alex Bavelas and Dermot Barrett, "An Experimental Approach to Organizational Communciation," *Personnel,* Vol. 27, No. 5, March, 1951, pp. 366–71.

[11] See David C. Phillips, "How to Make Oral Communication Interesting," *Oral*

2.5   **Interest and attitude of receivers.** As noted, the interest of receivers is now regarded as highly important as a factor in communication. Reception is a process involving positive action. Reception is tuned or selected; it listens to and sorts out and hears messages the receiver regards as of interest to him. Receivers may not be able to hear, understand and act on all the messages transmitted and in process in the communications system. To hear all of them could require more time than can be devoted to communicating. Reception must be screened. The communications "mail" must be sorted and classified. Both oral and written messages face this screening process in reception. It is

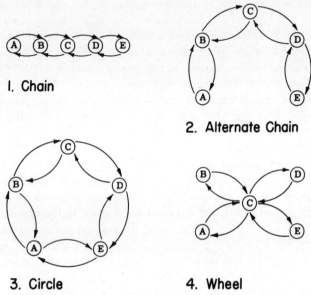

Figure 24.1   Illustrative Patterns of Communication
SOURCE: Adapted from Bavelas and Barrett, *op. cit.*

most evident in the common practice of consigning items to the wastebasket without, in many cases, opening envelopes or scanning contents.

Reception is influenced by what receivers consider important to them. They listen more attentively to messages they regard as of interest and likely to affect them. Several studies of downward communications suggest that the failure of messages to get through is largely attributable to the tendency to transmit messages of little interest and to withhold messages that would be of interest to intended receivers. Figure 24.2, for example, indicates the contrast between information sought by groups of employees and that included in downward transmisions to them. The numbers attached to items represent

Communication in Business, New York: McGraw-Hill Book Company, Inc., 1955, chap. 4.

their rank in terms of stated interest and volume of communications. The chart was constructed to help explain why employees did not know about facts and information sent along to them from higher levels of management. It appears that employees were hearing little about what they regarded as most interesting and were sent many messages they regarded as of little interest.[12]

Acceptance and understanding are affected by the receiver's attitude toward the individual message and its transmitter. Attitudes create the viewpoint with which a potential receiver regards incoming messages. They also influence the authority and credibility attached to such messages. A transmission may come through loud and clear if the receiver finds it interesting and regards the transmitter as a reliable source. Information may be regarded as

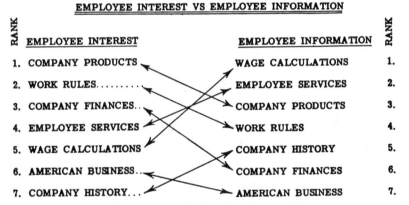

EMPLOYMENT COMMUNICATIONS:

EMPLOYEE INTEREST VS EMPLOYEE INFORMATION

RANK	EMPLOYEE INTEREST	EMPLOYEE INFORMATION	RANK
1.	COMPANY PRODUCTS	WAGE CALCULATIONS	1.
2.	WORK RULES.........	EMPLOYEE SERVICES	2.
3.	COMPANY FINANCES...	COMPANY PRODUCTS	3.
4.	EMPLOYEE SERVICES	WORK RULES	4.
5.	WAGE CALCULATIONS	COMPANY HISTORY	5.
6.	AMERICAN BUSINESS...	COMPANY FINANCES	6.
7.	COMPANY HISTORY...	AMERICAN BUSINESS	7.

Figure 24.2 Comparison of Employee Interests in Communications and Information Transmitted to Employees
SOURCE: University of Minnesota Industrial Relations Center.

unquestionable from one source and unreliable from another. The old axiom that actions speak louder than words has direct implications for the receiver's perception of the source. The transmitter who is continually complaining, for example, may find most receivers off the hook when he transmits. Lines may appear noisy, with numerous busy signals, to transmitters regarded as having little of interest to share, for experience with transmitters conditions receptivity. The biased or unreliable source cannot expect full acceptance for his expressions.

Neither employees nor managers may be proficient in reception; they may not have developed skill in listening. Frequent discussions center about the need for training in listening, particularly for managers. They may be so con-

[12] See Wayne K. Kirchner and Jerry Belenker, "What Employees Want to Know," *Personnel Journal,* Vol. 33, No. 10, March, 1955, pp. 378–79.

566 *Incentives in Work*

cerned about their own transmissions that they neglect feedback from potential receivers.[13]

2.6 Differences in media. Modern theory recognizes that both numbers and types of media may influence internal communications. Some messages benefit from direct, face-to-face, oral communications. Others, involving detailed directions or statistics, may require written media. Messages appropriate for a house organ may have little impact if published in the community newspaper.

2.7 Barriers to communication. Concern about apparent inadequacies in employment communications has encouraged study of what appear to be barriers in the process. A president, for example, cannot understand why his transmissions—involving items he feels sure should be of interest to everyone in the organization—appear to get no further than the first echelon of vice-presidents. Rogers and Roethlisberger were impressed with both barriers and gateways in the communication process. Most barriers, they found, involved a tendency to evaluate and to approve or disapprove of messages. They conclude that such barriers are interposed by receivers and can be removed by greater understanding on their part.[14]

Hatch sees these barriers as essentially filters. He pictures them as darts in communications lines connecting individuals (see Figure 24.3). Filters vary with time and experience. Some lines may be modified by several filters, each determined "by the socio-psychological distance between the two people." Hatch notes that filters can serve a useful purpose, as they presumably do when attached to cigarettes. He concludes, "If the filter is too efficient, however, nothing comes through but hot air."[15]

Layering and the greater length or span of communications in larger organizations are widely regarded as interposing barriers. Transmission must be more skillful and media more carefully selected on this account. Numbers of barriers are increased in somewhat the same proportion as are layers of intermediaries in the process. The latter may resist, stop, or absorb messages intended for retransmission. Intermediaries may become barriers rather than amplifiers or booster-stations on the line. In both upward and downward communications, intermediaries may withhold information for a variety of reasons. In messages moving upward, they may regard some information as likely to reflect unfavorably on their performance. In downward transmissions, they may seek to gain prestige and identification with management by being more informed than their subordinates.[16]

[13] See, for example, "Is Management Listening?" *Personnel Policies Forum,* Survey No. 3, Washington, D.C.: Bureau of National Affairs, May, 1951.

[14] Carl R. Rogers and F. J. Roethlisberger, "Barriers and Gateways to Communication," *Harvard Business Review,* Vol. 30, No. 4, July-August, 1952, 46–52.

[15] A. S. Hatch, "The Line Approach to Industrial Communications," in "The Personnel Function: A Progress Report," *Management Report No. 24,* New York: American Management Association, 1958.

[16] For more on barriers, see Joe Lee Jessup, "Why You and Your Boss Disagree," *Nation's Business,* May, 1960, pp. 98–102; Harold Guetzkow, "Organizational Development and Restrictions in Communication," Pittsburgh: Carnegie Institute of Technology, Graduate School of Industrial Administration, 1954.

2.8 Rumor, gossip. Modern theory holds that informal communications processes develop, at least in part, because of what members perceive as inadequacy in formal structures. When workers find it difficult, either to transmit their messages and to have them received or to hear the messages they feel should be coming to them, they tend to find other channels and media

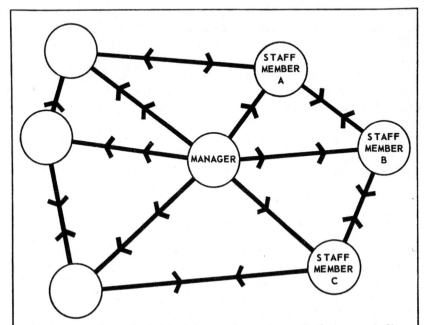

This structure is a simplified diagram of a pattern of distance and filter relationships between a manager and several staff members. The central dot represents the manager (or supervisor), and the circles on the perimeter represent six staff members. Again, lines and darts represent distances and filters, respectively. The diagram is simplified in that a filter relationship actually exists between each person in the group and every other individual. Thus, there should actually be six lines radiating from each individual—each line indicating his relationship to a different individual.

Figure 24.3   Communication Lines and Filters
SOURCE: Adapted from A. S. Hatch, *op. cit.*

that will more nearly meet their perceived needs. Informal structures develop on this account.

Rumor and gossip may be prominent in the messages carried by informal systems. If employees feel that information of interest to them is being withheld, they may seek it by informal inquiries directed to clerks, secretaries, or others. Managers may resort to similar means when they feel that they are not adequately informed through formal channels. Rumor is encouraged by attitudes that regard formal communications with suspicion or by policy that restricts information through formal channels. Distortions appear in messages that move through such informal relationships, and these distortions may affect receptivity in the formal structure.[17]

2.9   Current Policy. Many managers have, in years past, intended only to transmit orders, instructions, and the minimal information required for effective performance of individual jobs. They have, at the same time, proposed to maintain the confidential nature of information about the organization's plans and its successes and failures. Managers proposed to tell employees what to do and how to do it. The "why" of organizational mission and objectives was regarded as of importance only to owners and managers. It was privileged information to be shared within select circles and it was rarely disclosed to others, who were regarded as outside the circle. Information on how well the organization was doing—its profits and prospects—was private and secret.

Such policy generally proposed that upward communications be restricted to essential reports of progress and problems. Ideas, suggestions, and proposals were not expected from lower levels in the formal structure. Policy rarely proposed that managers give serious attention to their listening responsibilities. Rank-and-file employees, like children, were to be seen but not heard and to speak only when spoken to.

Such early communication policy expresses a long tradition with respect to the *privacy of economic information*. When most business was either a single proprietorship or partnership, the economic facts of the business appeared as essentially private information. Secretive policy was suported, also, by the assumption that effective competition required such privacy. Owners and managers concluded that what they earned, saved, or invested was their own, private business. No one else, including workers associated with their operations, had any interest in or reasonable claim on these confidential facts. Early advocates of the income tax waged a bitter battle against a similar point of view with respect to personal finances; some citizens still hold the opinion that they are justified in concealing what they conclude is concealable.

Modern communication policy in working organizations has changed in the same direction, if not to the same degree, as has today's theory. Managers have accepted the view that communication throughout the organization must be much more than a matter of managerial order giving and report receiving. They have recognized the significance of communications as essential to wide participation in and identification with organizational objectives. They relate communications to morale and to incentivation. They are concerned about informal communications, both as sources of mis-

[17] See Keith Davis, "Management Communication and the Grapevine," *Harvard Business Review*, Vol. 31, No. 5, September-October, 1953, pp. 43–49; Harry Schachter and Harvey Burdick, "A Field Experiment on Rumor Transmission and Distortion," *Journal of Abnormal and Social Psychology*, Vol. 50, No. 3, May, 1955, pp. 363–71; "How to Use the Grapevine," Washington, D.C.: Bureau of National Affairs, 1953.

information and as exerting adverse influence on transmission and reception in the formal structure.

Modern policy recognizes a variety of intentions as appropriate objectives in communication. The most common of them may be outlined as follows:

1. To maintain effective transmission and reception of orders and instructions, with adequate attention to both the quality of transmissions—in terms of clarity, meaning, and intensity—and favorable reception of these messages.

2. To insure adequate upward reporting, so that supervisors and managers are assured information required by their assigned responsibilities.

3. To assure two-way communication that can explain and interpret transmissions and develop a feeling of participation on the part of all those in the organization.

4. To encourage ideas and suggestions for more effective operation from all levels and members.

5. To relate transmissions to interests of receivers and thus to encourage receptivity and personal identification with the organization.

6. To assure the free exchange of such information and opinions as will assist all members in understanding and accepting the rationality or reasonableness of status and authority assignments throughout the structure.

7. To make available such facts and opinions as will assist members of the organization in their own development and advancement.

8. To provide an adequate formal communication structure and thus to eliminate or reduce the need for informal communications and avoid the misinformation that may be associated with rumor and gossip.

9. To maintain effective checks on internal communications and thus to evaluate the success with which each of these policies is implemented.[18]

3.0 MEDIA AND PRACTICE

To implement these policies, today's working organizations provide a wide range of communications media. Table 24.1 lists and classifies those most frequently used in formal communications. It includes, also, rumor and the grapevine, because they are so common and because they may be cultivated by management in some situations.

3.1 Face-to-face exchanges. Rank-and-file employees as well as supervisors and managers often prefer oral to written communications. They enjoy the opportunity to ask questions and to participate. Generally favorable employee reactions to the grapevine illustrate this preference. Even though that medium may actually encourage embellishment and addition, its personal

[18] For more on communications theory and policy, see Russell L. Ackoff, "Toward a Behavioral Theory of Communication," *Management Science,* Vol. 4, No. 3, April, 1958, pp. 218–34; Rex F. Harlow, "Communications for Executives," *Harvard Business Review,* Vol. 35, No. 6, November-December, 1957, pp. 145–56; John T. Dorsey, "A Communications Model for Administration," *Administrative Science Quarterly,* Vol. 2, 1957, pp. 307–24; Fred Dowling, "Communications Only Seems Simple," *Personnel Journal,* Vol. 37, No. 5, October, 1958, pp. 177–79.

Table 24.1 Media for Employment Communications

I—DOWNWARD

Oral	*Written*
1. Personal Instructions	1. Instructions and Orders
2. Lectures, Conferences, Committee Meetings	2. Letters and Memos
3. Interviews, Counseling	3. House Organs
4. Telephone, Public Address Systems, Movies, Slides	4. Bulletin Boards
5. Whistles, Bells, etc.	5. Posters
6. Social Affairs, including Union Activities	6. Handouts and Information Racks
7. Grapevine, Gossip, Rumor	7. Handbooks and Manuals
	8. Annual Reports
	9. Union Publications

II—UPWARD

Oral	*Written*
1. Face-to-Face Reports and Conversations	1. Reports
2. Interviews	2. Personal Letters
3. Telephone	3. Grievances
4. Meetings Conferences	4. Suggestion Systems
5. Social Affairs	5. Attitude and Information Surveys
6. Grapevine	6. Union Publications
7. Union Representatives and Channels	

III—HORIZONTAL

Oral	*Written*
1. Lectures, Conferences, Committee Meetings	1. Letters, Memos, Reports—Carbons, Ditto, and Mimeograph
2. Telephone, Inter-Com Systems, Movies, Slides	2. House Organ
3. Social Affairs, including Union Activities	3. Bulletin Boards and Posters
4. Grapevine, Rumor	4. Handbooks and Manuals
	5. Annual Report
	6. Union Publications

nature is attractive. The individual enjoys a relationship that places him on the inside. Managers have sometimes planted stories for circulation in these informal channels. Others have established *rumor clinics* in which members of the organization can be assured of reliable oral comments on stories reported through informal channels.

Face-to-face, oral communication is sometimes supplemented by public address systems which permit managers to speak directly to workers in the shop. Such devices are distinctly a supplement rather than a substitute; the fact that employees cannot talk back limits their usefulness.

3.2 Handbooks and house organs. Among the most widely used written media for downward transmissions are orientation materials, employee handbooks and manuals, bulletin boards, house organs or employee magazines, and financial reports to employees. Handbooks provide a summary of information with respect to employment policy, benefits and services, work rules, and background information about the employer. Table 24.2 summarizes the common subjects disclosed in one study of these employee manuals.

House organs or employee magazines represent a favorite medium for downward communication. Published weekly or monthly, by management, they usually include news on new products and company plans together with a wide range of personal items, stories about employee contests, recreation, hobbies, sports, and perhaps a personal message from the president. They may include a "letters" section in which employees can express their opinions. Earlier practice frequently included editorials expressing the opinion of management, but both messages from officials and editorials are now less frequent. The volume and cost of such publications are impressive.[19] Such management-sponsored journals are sometimes paralleled by a union publication that may facilitate upward communication screened through union officials. In a few cases, managements use the union publication to circulate information to employees.

Table 24.2   Subjects Included in Employee Handbooks

Data from "The Employee Handbook, "Los Angeles Merchants and Manufacturers Association, 1955.

Absence and attendance	Company policies
Accidents and health	Company services for employees
Addresses	Employee publications
Advancement and promotion	Employment—hiring and induction
Activities—athletic, recreational, social	Fire protection
Admittance and passes	Hours
Age	Insurance and pensions
Allowances	Military service
Apprenticeship and training	National emergency policies
Automobiles	Personal affairs
Banking facilities	Personnel policies
Benefit associations	Resignations and termination procedure
Cafeterias and lunchrooms	Salaries and wages
Clothing	Service
Collective bargaining and unions	Suggestion systems
Community relationship	Working conditions
Company data	

3.3   **Financial reports.** Many firms now provide special financial reports to employees. They include essentially the same information as that provided stockholders, with additional interpretation to make clear the meaning of balance sheet and profit and loss items and to explain the importance of taxes as well as wages and salaries. Recent practice has sometimes sought to explain and justify levels of depreciation charges and the reinvestment of income. Financial reports to employees are generally silent on a subject of wide employee interest: manager and executive salaries and benefits.

3.4   **Bulletin Boards.** Perhaps the oldest and most widely used medium for downward written communications in the factory is the bulletin board. Common practice provides one such board for each 50 to 100 employees. Few of them are attractive, and their effectiveness should be frequently checked.

[19] See "How to Play the House Organ," *Fortune,* October, 1952, pp. 144ff.

Although most managements appear to have found a means of getting items on the board, the problem of removing out-dated items has apparently resisted all attacks.

3.5 Information racks. These are essentially display stands in which pamphlets and booklets are made available to employees on a cafeteria basis. Subjects include hobbies, projects, cooking, budgeting, home economics, economics (both macro and micro), civilian defense, health, taxation, and many others. Studies have found that distribution averages about four items per month per employee and that about one-third of all employees avail themselves of the opportunity to secure reading material. Several firms now make a business of furnishing publications for reading racks. The idea is credited to General Motors and is said to have originated in 1948.[20]

3.6 Suggestion systems. In many organizations, the most obvious medium for written upward communications is the suggestion system. Employees are invited to submit their ideas and proposals. Those that appear to have merit may win substantial financial rewards. At the same time, they provide an opportunity for employees to express criticisms and relieve frustrations. Special suggestion forms are available and suggestion boxes are located throughout the plant. National Industrial Conference Board surveys report that about one-third of all reporting firms maintain suggestion systems. Rewards are generally related to resulting savings; some amount to several thousand dollars. The average has been estimated at $25.

Usually, a special committee evaluates suggestions and determines rewards. From 200 to 300 suggestions per 1,000 employees per year seems to be about average. From one-tenth to more than one-half of all suggestions receive some reward. In many firms, procedure is slow, with long delays in awards and adverse employee reactions on this account. Some firms have discontinued these provisions because they found most suggestions were in effect criticisms of supervision and management. Others have concluded that employees are reluctant about advancing suggestions that might eliminate jobs.[21]

3.7 Audio-visual supplements. Current practice recognizes the fact that a great deal of employment communication is non-verbal. Pictures, charts, graphs, movies, slide-films, flannel-boards, and many other visual aids are widely used. Gestures are formally recognized as communications devices in certain operations like the direction of crane operators, where noise or distance makes verbal communication difficult or impossible.

[20] "Information Racks: A New Communication Medium," *Studies in Personnel Policy No. 125,* National Industrial Conference Board, February, 1952 and subsequent reports; "Personnel Practices: Management Measures the Reading Rack Program," New York: *Industrial Relations News,* October, 1955; Lawrence C. Lovejoy, "How Effective is the Company Reading Rack?" *Personnel,* Vol. 34, No. 5, March-April, 1958, pp. 60–64.

[21] For more detail on suggestion systems, see Stanley J. Seimer, *Suggestion Plans in American Industry,* Syracuse, N.Y.: Syracuse University Press, 1959; "Suggestion Systems for Small- and Medium-sized Companies," *Informed Executive,* Associated Industries of Cleveland, Number 234, August 1, 1958; *Industrial Relations News,* Vol. 9, No. 11, March 18, 1961, p. 1; *Personnel Policies and Practices Report,* Par. 195, No. 15–92, 1961.

3.8 Other media. Many other media are used by managers in current attempts to carry out communications policy. *Committees* are appointed to facilitate oral and written exchanges and thus overcome weak links or barriers in the formal communications system. Managers arrange *retreats* in which selected associates meet for a day or weekend in a secluded hotel or resort to confer without the usual confusion and interruptions of offices and shops. *Dinners, picnics,* and other *social affairs* may be staged to permit extra contacts and freer exchanges. Messages may be carried by movies, slides, or souvenirs.

Many messages are sent as letters to the homes of employees or included as special *pay-check inserts.* Firms may keep printshops busy getting out pamphlets and booklets on employee benefits and services, long-term opportunities and advantages in employment, and, in some cases, social, political, and economic opinions of executives.

In-plant *public address systems,* publicized in wartime by Jack and Heintz, may be supplemented by *intercom systems* that allow a manager to visit with from one to a dozen of his associates. *Closed-circuit television* has been used to arrange something like face-to-face communications in firms that operate several plants. Teletype provides a means of rapid written exchanges in similar organizations.

Some firms have purchased time on local television stations to reach employees and their families. Managers have sometimes placed lengthy messages in the advertising columns of local papers, especially if management and union are involved in controversy. The effectiveness of such emergency transmissions is not known.

Managers have, in other words, used just about every known medium and technique, possibly excepting sign language and extra-sensory perception!

4.0 CHECKS ON IN-PLANT COMMUNICATIONS

A persistent question in all programs concerns their effectiveness. Such evidence as is available provides few conclusive answers. Experience and research provide little more than spotty information. Experience can be interpreted to provide different answers. The management that has installed regular Monday morning meetings of foremen to give them the latest word may conclude that they are excellent. A participating foreman may be less impressed. Few careful checks are recorded on even such an expensive and frequently ostentatious medium as the annual report. Despite annual expenditures of millions of dollars, few generalizations can be made about the impact of the communications dollar.

Communications policy has, however, tended to place an increasing emphasis on the intention to check on communications programs and to examine each of the three phases: transmissions, media, and reception. The determination to discover how well communications programs are serving their purposes has led to a variety of tests.

4.1 Morale studies. Within individual firms, some evidence is available from studies of employee morale. Questionnaire surveys of employee opinions usually include a communications dimension or subscale. They may ask for detailed reactions to particular practices and media. They may invite comments and explanations of answers that provide valuable evidence on transmission, media, and receptivity. They can do much more than record employee reactions to manager practice in transmission; they can suggest how

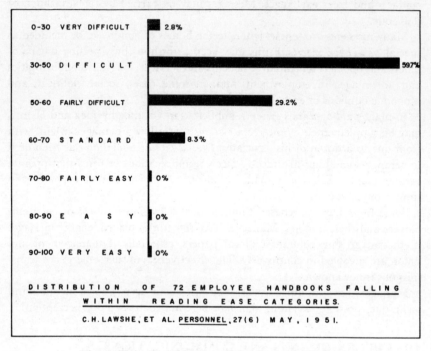

0-30 VERY DIFFICULT	2.8%
30-50 D I F F I C U L T	59.7%
50-60 FAIRLY DIFFICULT	29.2%
60-70 S T A N D A R D	8.3%
70-80 FAIRLY EASY	0%
80-90 E A S Y	0%
90-100 VERY EASY	0%

DISTRIBUTION   OF   72 EMPLOYEE   HANDBOOKS   FALLING   WITHIN   READING   EASE   CATEGORIES.

C.H. LAWSHE, ET AL. <u>PERSONNEL</u>, 27(6)   MAY, 1951.

Figure 24.4   Reading Ease of Employee Handbooks
SOURCE: Data from C. H. Lawshe, H. E. Holmes, Jr. and George M. Turmail, "An Analysis of Employee Handbooks," *Personnel*, Vol. 27, No. 6, May, 1951, pp. 478–495.

employees view upward and horizontal communication and what they see as desirable supplements to current practice.

4.2   Reading ease and interest. One approach to evaluation of communication seeks to classify written messages in terms of the ease with which they may be read and their human interest. The most frequent practice limits tests of employment communications to the first of these criteria. Lawshe and others, however, measured both the reading ease and human interest of such written materials as employee handbooks. They found that most of these publications fall in the "difficult" category with respect to readability (see Figure 24.4) and are about average in interest. Lauer and Paterson measured

0.30	31-50	51-60	61-70	71-80	81-90	91-100
x	x					
x	x					
x	x					
x	x					
x	x					
x	x					
x	x					
x	x					
x	x					

0.30	31-50	51-60	61-70	71-80	81-90	91-100
Very Difficult	*Difficult*	*Fairly Difficult*	*Standard*	*Fairly Easy*	*Easy*	*Very Easy*
College	High School or Some College	Some High School	7th or 8th Grade	6th Grade	5th Grade	4th Grade

NOTE: Each x represents the reading case score of one contract.

Fig. 24.5 Readability of Union Contracts

SOURCE: Jeanne Lauer and Donald G. Paterson, "Readability of Union Contracts," *Personnel,* Vol. 28, No. 1, July, 1951, pp. 36–40.

READING EASE OF UNION NEWSPAPERS AND FIRM HOUSE ORGANS
(ADAPTED FROM FARR, PATERSON, STONE)

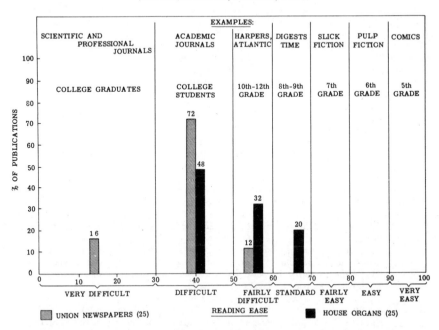

Figure 24.6 Readability of Union Newspapers and Employee House Organs

SOURCE: Data from J. N. Farr, Donald G. Paterson and C. H. Stone, "Readability and Human Interest of Management and Union Publications," *Industrial and Labor Relations Review,* Vol. 4, No. 1, October 1950, pp. 88–93.

the readibility of 20 union contracts (see Figure 24.5). As the figure indicates, all of them fell at "difficult" or "very difficult" levels. Farr, Paterson,
and Stone checked the readability of both union newspapers and employee
house organs. Their findings are shown in Figure 24.6.

Tests of reading ease have become readily available in recent years. Two
principal techniques are used, one developed by Gunning and known as the
"Fog Index" and the other popularized by Rudolph Flesch.[22] Reading ease
is correlated with the length of words and of sentences. A modification of the
earlier Flesch procedure substitutes the count of 1-syllable words for that of
total syllables in the sample of written material and permits use of the table
shown as Table 24.3.[23]

4.3 Communication audits. Many firms have experimented with a
communications audit, essentially one phase of the more inclusive industrial relations audit to be discussed in the final chapter of this book.[24] In these
audits of communications, a frequent approach measures the information
known to various groups of managers and employees and compares that information with what has been made available to them. Figure 24.7 illustrates
findings in one such analysis, which combined the scores for six firms. The
figure compares supervisors and nonsupervisors and indicates that the former
were better informed on all subject classifications except that of employee

[22] For more on the Fog Index, see Robert Gunning, "How to Improve Your Writing," *Factory Management and Maintenance,* Vol. 110, No. 6, June, 1952, pp. 134ff.;
for Flesch's approach, see Rudolph Flesch, *How to Test Readability,* New York:
Harper & Brothers, 1951. See also his "A New Readability Yardstick," *Journal of
Applied Psychology,* Vol. 32, No. 3, June, 1948, pp. 221–33.

[23] Students may wish to check on the readability of their own or other writing (not,
please, that in this text). Directions may be stated as follows:

    1. Select one or more representative 100-word samples of the writing to be
evaluated;

    2. Count the words in each sentence in the 100-word sample and calculate the
average length of sentence.

    3. Count the number of 1-syllable words in the 100-word sample.

    4. If several samples are taken, calculate an average number of words per
sentence and an average of the number of 1-syllable words per 100 words.

    5. Enter the table (Table 24.3) at the row representing average length of sen-
tences and follow across to the column representing the number of 1-syllable
words. (As noted, the number of syllables per 100 words can be used, if preferred.)

    6. The index at the juncture of the selected row and column can be translated
as follows:

        0–29 means *very difficult,* typical of college and professional literature.

        30–50 means *difficult,* requiring some high-school or college education.

        51–59 means *fairly difficult,* requiring some high-school education.

        60–69 is *standard,* the level of newspapers.

        70–79 is *fairly easy,* about the level of the 6th grade.

        80–89 is *very easy,* at the level of the 5th grade and the comics.

[24] See Harry B. Funk and C. Robert Becker, "Measuring the Effectiveness of Indus-
trial Communications," *Personnel,* Vol. 28, No. 3, November, 1952, pp. 237–40; George
S. Odiorne, "An Application of the Communications Audit," *Personnel Psychology,*
Vol. 7, No. 2, Summer, 1954, pp. 235–40; Harold P. Zelko, "How Effective are Your
Company Communications?" *Advanced Management,* Vol. 21, No. 2, February, 1956,
pp. 10–14.

Table 24.3 Flesch Reading Ease Index Table*

Number of One Syllable Words per Hundred Words (Upper Row) and Syllables per Hundred Words (Lower Row)

Average Sentence Length	34 / 218	36 / 214	38 / 210	40 / 206	42 / 202	44 / 199	46 / 195	48 / 191	50 / 187	52 / 184	54 / 180	56 / 176	58 / 172	60 / 168	62 / 165	64 / 161	66 / 157	68 / 153	70 / 149	72 / 146	74 / 142	76 / 138	78 / 134	80 / 131	82 / 127	84 / 123
9	13	17	20	23	27	29	33	36	39	42	45	49	52	56	58	61	65	68	72	74	78	81	84	87	90	94
10	12	16	19	22	26	28	32	35	38	41	44	48	51	55	57	60	64	67	71	73	77	80	83	86	89	93
11	11	15	18	21	25	27	31	34	37	40	43	47	50	54	56	59	63	66	70	72	76	79	82	85	88	92
12	10	14	17	20	24	26	30	33	36	39	42	46	49	53	55	58	62	65	69	71	75	78	81	84	87	91
13	9	13	16	19	23	25	29	32	35	38	41	45	48	52	54	57	61	64	68	70	74	77	80	83	86	90
14	8	12	15	18	22	24	28	31	34	37	40	44	47	50	53	56	60	63	67	69	73	76	79	82	85	89
15	7	11	14	17	21	23	27	30	33	36	39	43	46	49	52	55	59	62	66	68	72	75	78	81	84	88
16	6	10	13	16	20	22	26	29	32	35	38	42	45	48	51	54	58	61	65	67	71	74	77	80	83	87
17	5	9	12	15	19	21	25	28	31	34	37	41	44	47	50	53	57	60	64	66	70	73	76	79	82	86
18	4	8	11	14	18	20	24	27	30	33	36	40	43	46	49	52	56	59	63	65	69	72	75	78	81	85
19	3	7	10	13	17	19	23	26	29	32	35	39	42	45	48	51	55	58	62	64	68	71	74	77	80	83
20	2	5	9	12	16	18	22	25	28	31	34	38	41	44	47	50	54	57	60	63	66	70	73	76	79	82
21	1	4	8	11	15	17	21	24	27	30	33	37	40	43	46	49	53	56	59	62	65	69	72	75	78	81
22		3	7	10	14	16	20	23	26	29	32	36	39	42	45	48	52	55	58	61	64	68	71	74	77	80
23		2	6	9	13	15	19	22	25	28	31	35	38	41	44	47	51	54	57	60	63	67	70	73	76	79
24		1	5	8	12	14	18	21	24	27	30	34	37	40	43	46	50	53	56	59	62	66	69	72	75	78
25			4	7	11	13	16	20	23	26	29	33	36	39	42	45	49	52	55	58	61	65	68	71	74	77
26			3	6	10	12	15	19	22	25	28	32	35	38	41	44	48	51	54	57	60	64	67	70	73	76
27			2	5	9	11	14	18	21	24	27	31	34	37	40	43	47	50	53	56	59	63	66	69	72	75
28			1	4	8	10	13	17	20	23	26	30	33	36	39	42	46	49	52	55	58	62	65	68	71	74
29				3	7	9	12	16	19	22	25	29	32	35	38	41	45	48	51	54	57	61	64	67	70	73
30				2	5	8	11	15	18	21	24	27	31	34	37	40	44	47	50	53	56	60	63	66	69	72
31				1	4	7	10	14	17	20	23	26	30	33	36	39	43	46	49	52	55	59	62	65	68	71
32					3	6	9	13	16	19	22	25	29	32	35	38	42	45	48	51	54	58	61	64	67	70
33					2	5	8	12	15	18	21	24	28	31	34	37	41	44	47	50	53	57	60	63	66	69
34					1	4	7	11	14	17	20	23	27	30	33	36	40	43	46	49	52	56	59	61	65	68
35						3	6	10	13	16	19	22	26	29	32	35	38	42	45	48	51	55	58	60	64	67
36						2	5	9	12	15	18	21	25	28	31	34	37	41	44	47	50	54	57	59	63	66
37						1	4	8	11	14	17	20	24	27	30	33	36	40	43	46	49	53	56	58	62	65
38							3	7	10	13	16	19	23	26	29	32	35	39	42	45	48	52	55	57	61	64

* Reproduced by permission from James N. Farr, James J. Jenkins, and Donald G. Paterson, "Simplification of Flesch Reading Ease Formula," *Journal of Applied Psychology*, Vol. 35, No. 5, October, 1951, p. 335.

earnings. Figure 24.8 pictures a similar comparison among various classes of employees in a single firm.

A variant of the information test, or a special form, assumes that the effectiveness of internal communications may be measured in terms of the commonality of information or the *consensus* among members of the organization. Such an approach places little significance on the accuracy of

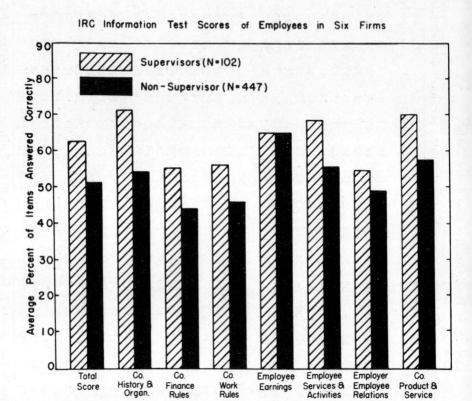

Figure 24.7 Information Test Scores: Supervisors and Employees in Six Firms
SOURCE: Data from Univeristy of Minnesota Industrial Relations Center.

common information; the test of exchanging ideas is the consistency of information, including opinions and impressions, throughout all levels and divisions of the organization. Samples of items from an instrument used in evaluating consensus are illustrated in Figure 24.9.

Other investigations have included content analyses applied to employee publications and checks of reader interest and recollection designed to discover who reads them and what features attract greatest interest and approval.

These tests of the various techniques of communication can be helpful, both in evaluating present practice and in suggesting other possible tests. On the other hand, any thorough appraisal of employment communications in a firm or agency must combine such measures and probe somewhat deeper. Policy as well as practice and results must be appraised. Question must be raised as to what management intends to accomplish in the communications structure it creates and maintains. These intentions or policies must be care-

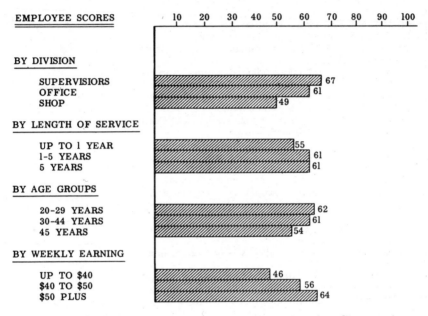

Figure 24.8 Measured Employment Information by Classes of Employees
SOURCE: Data from University of Minnesota Industrial Relations Center.

fully considered in terms of current theory. Once policies have been checked, practice and results can be compared with these intentions.

5.0 SUMMARY

Modern policy in many working organizations places heavy emphasis on intentions to emphasize multi-purpose intraorganizational communications. Current theory relates effective internal communications to many managerial goals and objectives. It views internal communications as the essential flux that binds members together and permits them to share in the ideas, ideals, goals and mission of the whole.

	Yes	No	Don't Know
2. Does the length of paid vacations increase with length of service?			
3. Are employees told about the firm's safety rules?			
4. Are employees paid when they report for work and are not needed?			
7. Does this firm have an employee magazine or paper?			
8. Does this firm have an employee stock ownership plan?			
11. Does this firm have a group health insurance plan?			
18. Does this firm have a profit-sharing plan?			
19. Does this firm have a life insurance program for its employees?			
21. Are charity collections allowed during working hours?			
27. Are notices of holidays and other important dates posted *regularly* on bulletin boards?			
29. May employees attend church services on Good Friday without a deduction in pay?			
32. Are all employees paid on the same day?			
33. May employees attend funeral services on company time?			
37. Do employees contribute to a retirement fund?			
38. Does this firm have a compulsory retirement age?			
43. Are employees paid for time spent at grievance meetings?			
49. Does an employee retain his seniority while serving in the armed forces?			
54. Are there meetings for supervisors or foremen in all departments?			
57. Have the prices of the firm's products or services gone up in the past year?			
62. Has this firm improved any of its products in the last year?			
93. Would most employees recommend this firm to their friends as a good place to work?			

Fig. 24.9 Sample Items—Communications-Consensus Scale

SOURCE: University of Minnesota Industrial Relations Center

Meanwhile, studies of employee attitudes and morale have contributed to growing managerial awareness of serious shortcomings in employment communications. Attitude studies often indicate wide dissatisfaction with internal communications. Both employees and managers frequently complain that messages do not get through or that transmissions emerge from the communications process with discrepancies and mutilations.

Problems of internal communication are almost certainly more complicated than they were when working organizations were small and simple. If communications is indeed the essential administrator's skill, he needs much more of it today than was required in the simple shop of the master craftsmen.

Meanwhile, communications problems of rank-and-file members of a working organization have also grown more complicated. They must communicate through a complex system in which numbers of messages are vastly increased. They must identify messages intended for them as well as recipients for their own communications. They have added responsibilities for screening and filtering and ignoring background noise that were not present in the craftsman's home workshop.

Analysis of communication processes generally distinguishes three phases— transmission, media and channels, and reception. Each plays an essential part in the whole. Each requires managerial consideration and planning if internal communications are to be effective in terms of policy. Reception, no less than transmission, must be worked at; it requires active thought and calculated participation. Moreover, these phases of communication influence each other —transmission is influenced by the transmitter's view of the receiver, and reception is affected by both media and the receiver's perception of the transmitter. Both transmitter and receiver must depend on media and channels; both must find open lines on which to complete their calls. Informal communications structures presumably develop in the absence of satisfactory formal provisions.

Current theory notes the essential two-way characteristic of communication; the problem of semantics in exchanging ideas; the possible influence of communication on morale, including the significance of varying communication patterns; the importance of both skill and attitude in transmissions; the manner in which interest and attitude affect receptivity; the necessity for choice among various media; the tendency of some participants to create barriers rather than to serve as amplifiers.

Current practice uses a wide range of media and both formal and informal communications systems. Techniques and devices range from simple face-to-face, oral exchanges to closed circuit television. Communication occupies a major portion of the manager's time and attention. Much of this time and effort may be wasted, for it is possible that many communication practices are quite ineffective and that others are less useful than is assumed. For this reason, current policy often proposes to check on communications programs, with special audits, measures of information and consensus, and evaluations of reading ease and reader interest.

This chapter ends the section on incentivation. Attention turns now to the functions of research and review or audit. The next chapter considers the needs and opportunities for, and the potential contributions of, research in manpower management.

SELECTED SUPPLEMENTARY READINGS

Bellows, Roger M., *Psychology of Personnel in Business and Industry,* 3rd ed., chap. 6. Englewood Cliffs, N.J.: Prentice-Hall, Inc., 1961.
England, George W., Margaret Thomas, and Donald G. Paterson, "Reliability of

the Original and the Simplified Flesch Reading-Ease Formulas," *Journal of Applied Psychology,* Vol. 37, No. 2, pp. 111–113, April, 1953.

Hatch, A. S., "The Line Approach to Industrial Communications," *Management Report Number 24,* American Management Association, 1958.

Mahoney, Thomas A., "How Management Communicates with Employees," *Personnel,* Vol. 31, No. 2, pp. 109–114, September, 1954.

McCormick, Ernest J., *Human Engineering,* chaps. 4, 5, 6, 7, and 8. New York: McGraw-Hill Book Company, Inc., 1957.

Rogers, Carl R. and F. J. Roethlisberger, "Barriers and Gateways to Communication," *Harvard Business Review,* Vol. 30, No. 4, pp. 46–52.

Schutz, William C., "The Interpersonal Underworld," *Harvard Business Review,* Vol. 36, No. 4, pp. 123–135, July-August, 1958.

SHORT CASE PROBLEM 24.1

Communications in Conflict

The problem of employment communications has come sharply to the attention of all members of top management in the Turnbull Manufacturing Company. Their employees are out on strike. They have gone out at the one time in the year when the company can't afford to delay deliveries. Cancellations of orders are expected momentarily. If orders are cancelled now, all hope of a profitable year is ended.

Communications are obviously involved in two ways. In the first place, when the dispute arose, upward communications appeared to be reassuring. The foremen and supervisors reported that rank and file regarded their union's demands as extreme and would not support the union in a strike. The strike was called, and all non-supervisory employees went out. At the end of a week, many of the foremen reported that employees to whom they talked were organizing a back-to-work movement. Two weeks later, it had not developed.

Meanwhile, in a series of negotiations, the employer has granted most of the union's demands. But the union negotiators are insistent on all of them. The employer feels that any further concessions are impossible. Officers of the firm believe that employees would accept the terms now offered if they knew of the concessions and realized the hazardous position of the firm. But they do not know how to inform employees and convince them of the sincerity of the management. Advertisements in the local newspapers have been proposed by the public relations department. The sales department suggests a house-to-house campaign. The legal department has proposed asking the mayor of the city to form a citizens' committee.

Problem: What is your reaction to these proposals? How would you approach the immediate problem? What would you suggest for the longer-term future?

SHORT CASE PROBLEM 24.2

A Communications Audit

Mr. George P. is general industrial relations director of a manufacturing firm. The firm employs 2,000 people. Mr. P. is convinced that communications within the organization are not effective, that much misunderstanding results. He feels that, as a result, rumor and gossip injure morale.

On this basis, he has asked permission to pay for a communications audit by the laboratory staff of a nearby university industrial relations center. He suggests that the problem is one faced by many other firms and that the university center can help this firm gain from the experience of others. He feels that such an audit will indicate weaknesses in the in-plant communications system and thus suggest ways of bettering it.

The comptroller of the firm is sharply opposed to this suggestion. He says that Mr. P. should be able to recognize deficiencies and weaknesses without such outside help. He insists that social scientists in a university can't be of help in a "practical" problem like this and would have no interest in it. He says that the problem is not a "scientific" problem anyway, that all it takes to solve it is common sense. He also argues that installation of a public address system would be a better investment.

Problem: Prepare an interoffice memorandum summarizing what Mr. P. might say in answer to these comments.

SHORT CASE PROBLEM 24.3

Besseler Stave and Spline Company

The firm employs more than a thousand semiskilled and skilled production workers in a large, one-floor, modern plant near Chicago, Illinois. As a small firm, years ago, it was the leading producer of umbrella frames and fancy handles in this country. When that market largely disappeared, the firm produced a wide variety of products, including buggy whips, steel traps, ear-muff frames, gas-engine mufflers, and soft steel stampings. In 1945, with obvious imagination, the firm was extensively reorganized and added several new lines, including bobby pins, beauty parlor equipment, lock washers and self-locking machine screws. At the time of the reorganization, a new employee relations program was initiated. As one part of that program, the firm provided a suggestion system, with substantial rewards for usable suggestions.

In 1958, when business was slack and budgets were being trimmed, the following suggestion was received:

SUGGESTION No. 472
Since World War II us fellows in the shop have had music with our work. We didn't ask for it, but we got it anyway. Most of the time, it comes on about an hour after we start and keeps going until we leave. Most of the men don't like it. Music may be OK for women. We can't talk to each other with jazz bands and waltzes on top of the shop noise.
I suggest we stop the music. With the music off, I suggest that we use the squawkers for messages we want to hear from the front office. You could tell us how things are going. You could let us know about new orders and prospects. We would like to know more about some of the new ideas that we hear about in the scuttlebutt. You could announce it when sledding gets tough, and maybe we could help to smooth things out. Some of us might have new ideas. Ideas for new business and for cutting costs on the stuff we are making. Some of us already know more than we are telling. We know quite a lot of tricks and would be glad to help at a time like that. Sort of like Jack and Hines.
SIGNED: Alex Steglas   *EMPLOYEE NO. 872*

Problem: The suggestion committee consists of three shop foremen, one employee who is a swedger operator, the assistant, general foreman, and a member of the industrial relations staff. The staff member acts as executive secretary, receiving suggestions and studying them in advance of committee meetings, and making recommendations for their disposition.

Assume you are acting as secretary of the committee. What would be your recommendation on this suggestion?

VII. INSIGHT, PERSPECTIVE, AND EVALUATION

25. Industrial Relations Research

Research is another of the principal tools of the manager. It can be as useful in manpower management as in other managerial responsibilities. Research is a multi-purpose tool; it can help in finding better solutions for a wide range of problems. Managers have found numerous opportunities to improve their practice and the employment relationships they direct through industrial relations research.

Large-scale firms and agencies frequently have their own personnel or industrial relations research divisions, with staff members who devote full time to continuing studies of problems suggested either by the employment relations department or by line managers and executives. In smaller organizations, managers may cooperate in joint research projects undertaken by their trade associations, local chapters of the Society for the Advancement of Management or other professional groups, or nationwide organizations. Some firms maintain close working relationships with individual faculty members or special personnel and industrial relations institutes and centers in universities. Other managers in numerous firms, large and small, attend research-reporting conferences and read and contribute to research-reporting journals to keep informed of research contributions.[1]

The trend toward professional management is marked by the increasing scope and depth of management research. Professional management is *research-minded management,* for all modern professions lean heavily on

[1] See Ernest J. McCormick, "The Use of Research in Personnel Decision Making," *Personnel Administration*, Vol. 24, No. 5, September-October, 1961, pp. 23–32.

research as the most efficient and economical method of testing theories and building a more dependable body of skills, knowledge, and understanding. Managers are becoming more sophisticated with respect to the conduct of research and the use of research contributions to management theory, policy, and practice.

Most of us anticipate improvements in management in the years ahead. Few of us regard the effectiveness of management as approximating the real possibilities in working relationships, either in achieving the missions of organizations or aiding workers to gain their personal goals. We may reasonably expect breakthroughs in our understanding of management that will mean as much to all of us as our growing knowledge of outer space and nuclear energy. Research can be expected to provide much of that added understanding. In doing so, it can also improve our education for management, for we must learn before we can teach. Professional schools of management can be expected to become *research-oriented,* as have our schools of medicine, education, and engineering.

Research is a short cut that replaces the slower, more precarious road of trial and error, i.e., experience. Research introduces *system* and *planning* and *purpose* into investigations of the problems it studies. Research is *purposive, systematic investigation, designed to test carefully considered hypotheses or answer thoughtfully framed questions.* In the language of university catalogs, research broadens horizons and expands the frontiers of knowledge.

Earlier chapters have noted the many theories that explain current policy and practice in the management of human resources and have explained the importance of theory as a basis for both policy and practice. They have detailed historic and current theories of work, organization, administration, labor movements, public intervention, and others. All such theories express hypotheses that can be tested by research as well as by experience. At the same time, research can help to appraise the wide range of policies and practices suggested by these theories. The present chapter turns to the use of research to test these and other theories and to find improved solutions for the problems managers face in their management of people.

Preceding sections of this book have provided numerous examples of research contributions to improved understanding and practice in manpower management. This chapter considers the policy that explains growing interest in research and the practice in which research is undertaken. It outlines the research process and suggests how managers can keep themselves informed with respect to the current contributions of research in the field. Section 1 describes the principal levels of research and essentials in the research method. Section 2 notes various types of studies, classified by method. Section 3 outlines major steps in the research process. Section 4 lists the principal research agencies in the industrial relations field and the most useful research-reporting publications.

1.0 NATURE OF RESEARCH

Research means *systematic investigation*. The word itself suggests re-examination, a repeated search. It looks again—and perhaps again and again. It begins with questions, inquiry, and perhaps some tentative answers. It plans and carries out investigations designed to find and test answers. Essential characteristics of research include the facts that it is (1) planned, designed investigation and analysis, (2) carried out in a systematic manner, (3) to check, verify, or disprove hunches, clues, or assumptions, and thus (4) to supplement and extend knowledge and understanding. Whatever the specific problem, whatever the design of the experiment or the nature of the investigation, these are the basic characteristics of research. Research always seeks *answers* to questions or *solutions* for problems. Sometimes this objective is described as the *testing of hypotheses,* which means that tentative answers are stated and research is used to verify or disprove them.

Research is sharply distinguished from casual observation by the research method and point of view. Research proposes to find answers to questions by *systematic investigation* and *objective* analysis. It is thus distinguished from partisan argument or debate, in which facts may be selected to prove a point or justify a predetermined answer.

Research investigates problems of varying complexity. Some questions to be answered may be relatively simple and limited in scope. Others may be complicated, deep, and broad. A local manager for the telephone company may undertake a study of secretarial wage rates in his small community. He collects data according to plan and analyzes them by job and experience to discover ranges of rates and averages for each category. The training division of a manufacturing firm designs a study to check on the comparative effectiveness of two types of job training within their business. A local employer association may ask its research division to analyze current practice in providing parking space for employees, noting the regulations and limitations imposed. A local union may employ a research assistant to compare the language of contract clauses. A university faculty member or industrial relations center or a state employment service may study the educational backgrounds of labor relations directors in the state or region or across the nation. A graduate student may compare investment policies in joint employer-union pension trust funds with those managed by employers. An association of managers may carry on a long-term investigation of the personal characteristics of successful managers. A Ph.D. thesis may try to discover negotiated solutions for featherbedding practices. A half-dozen universities may cooperate in a nationwide investigation of worker mobilities.

Such a listing of possible studies is intended to suggest the range in nature and scope and depth of management research, particularly in the management of people. Some studies are small and relatively simple. Some are vast and inclusive. Some are relatively thin; others are deep and penetrating. Some can be conducted within the walls of a library or in the files of an employer association or union. Some research gets its questions from problems encountered in daily practice. Other studies grow out of the reflections of a student impressed by the unknowns in current theory, policy, or practice. Some research involves tests of techniques and seeks answers to questions about what is being done and how well it achieves stated objectives. Other research involves tests of general theory to discover the evidence to support or disprove these plausible explanations.

1.1 Essentials in research. Not all investigations can be called research. Indeed, question can be raised about whether some of the studies mentioned in preceding paragraphs are research. Sometimes it is assumed that current surveys of practice or attitudes, for example, are not research, because they are largely compilations and classifications of existing knowledge. Sometimes, also, library studies are regarded as outside the boundaries of research, because they may investigate only what is already known and reported. Some definitions of research restrict it to empirical investigations in which researchers collect original data for analysis and interpretations. Some definitions see research as essentially experimental, involving the manipulation of variables within the confines of a laboratory. Some define research as the testing of models that describe assumed relationships among stated factors. Many graduate schools require that research for the Ph.D. thesis make a significant contribution to knowledge. They thus suggest that this requirement is essential in the definition of research.

The essential requirement of research is its *method*. Large studies or small, minor or major, having only immediate implications or very broad applicability and significance, can be regarded as research if they properly apply the methods of research. The method is *purposive;* it seeks answers to specific questions and is thus not merely an accumulation of unstructured observations. The method is *objective;* it recognizes and limits bias and prejudice in every step of the process. As a demonstration of its objectivity, it may make all its data available to competent critics so that they may reassure themselves of this quality. The method is *systematic;* it begins with a design or plan and carries out its investigation in terms of that design. The method is *analytical;* it is not limited to a simple summary of unclassified facts nor does it permit conclusions unjustified by principles of logic.[2]

1.2 Background. Research in management, including the management of employment relationships, is by no means new. In this country, the studies of Frederick Taylor, dating back to the 1880's, sought to improve efficiency in the work of both employees and managers. Taylor, together with Emerson, Gantt, and others, undertook studies of the relationship between financial compensation and employee productivity. Also, in the late years of the 19th century and the early years of the 20th, a number of industrial psychologists

---

[2] Such a restrictive statement may appear to exclude the sudden burst of insight sometimes credited with significant discoveries. Some advances in undertsanding may appear by accident. For others, the stage of planned investigation may be overshadowed by the suddenness and brilliance of discovery. See W. I. Beveridge, *The Art of Scientific Investigation,* New York: Random House, 1957, especially Chap. 3.

made important contributions. Munsterberg, Bingham, Terman, Link, Goddard, and others sought to improve selection through studies of occupational requirements and personal qualifications of streetcar motormen, telephone operators, and others.

World War I accelerated these psychological studies. The army established its Committee on the Classification of Personnel to develop and apply intelligence and trade tests to military personnel. Studies of costs of living and real wages were initiated by the National Industrial Conference Board (1916). Experiments with job analysis, work simplification, and fatigue were undertaken by the Society of Industrial Engineers (1917).

In Great Britain, the Health of Munitions Workers Committee (1915), later known as the Industrial Fatigue Board, made investigations of industrial accidents, employee health, fatigue, and related problems. It was assisted by the National Institute of Industrial Psychology and Physiology. German research turned toward means of increasing output and improving selection.

Business managers, as well as those in the public service, were impressed with the contributions of military studies. Following World War I, a number of larger business organizations began experiments with new selection procedures and training programs. Similar investigations were sponsored in the federal civil service. The first of many special university research units was established as the Industrial Relations Section at Princeton in 1922. Outstanding in the research in private industry was the five-year study undertaken in 1927 in the Hawthorne, Illinois, plant of the Western Electric Company.

World War II encouraged an even wider range of studies. Manpower shortages during the war directed attention to problems of training, development, utilization, and compensation. A Bureau of Manpower Utilization in the War Manpower Commission developed and sponsored the *Training-Within-Industry Program* (TWI) and aided in the retraining and reallocation of approximately one-third of the national labor force. Military services studied morale as related to indicators of military efficiency. *A Minimum Wartime Workweek* was established after preliminary studies of the effects of varying working hours. War Production Board studies disclosed wide variations in output among workers engaged in similar occupations, using identical equipment. Programs designed to retain employees in *essential industries* and *critical occupations* and to encourage shifts into these jobs created growing interest in manpower mobility and labor-market frictions.

Following World War II, university activity in industrial relations research was sharply increased. Numerous industrial relations research divisions, centers, and institutes were formed. Their research interests generally included problems in both labor disposition or allocation—labor-marketing processes—and manpower utilization, the broad area of manpower management. In 1942, the Social Science Research Council established a Committee on Labor Market Research to stimulate, encourage, and assist in industrial relations studies. In 1947, a national professional society, the Industrial Relations Research Association, was formed. Its membership includes representatives of employers, unions, government agencies, and university faculties.

University centers have expanded both the scope and depth of their studies. Some of them have specialized in *labor-marketing processes*, with emphasis on problems of employment, vocational counseling, placement, career guidance, training, and development. Others have maintained continuing interest in the role of government in employment relationships. They have been concerned with *social problems*—unemployment, underemployment, labor immobilities of various types, imbalance in management-union relationships, low wages, and long hours. Other university centers have directed their attention principally to problems in manpower management, including those of organization for work, recruitment, selection, promotion, training, supervisory and management development, collective bargaining, contract administration, wage and salary administration, employee benefits and services, personnel appraisals, and others. Many of the university organizations have made significant contributions in all of these areas.[3]

Many large business organizations have established their own personnel or industrial relations research divisions. Smaller firms have joined with larger business units in local employer associations that frequently maintain research units.[4]

1.3   Co-disciplinary approach. With this expansion of industrial relations research, it became apparent that day-to-day problems of industrial relations seldom fall within the area of competence and interest of a single social science. While labor-marketing problems may be largely economic, as is suggested by the development of a specialized field of *labor economics*, they are rarely purely economic.

The need for co-disciplinary attacks on many industrial relations problems has suggested that manpower management must lean heavily on the behavioral sciences for solutions and for continuing progress. Major problem areas require the viewpoint and specialized competence of various social sciences, as is suggested by references in earlier chapters. Many of the university centers now include representatives of the several behavioral sciences as members of their research faculties. Personnel and industrial relations research divisions in industry frequently follow a similar practice. Graduate

---

[3] For details, see Frank B. Miller, *Personnel Research Contributions by U. S. Universities,* Ithaca, N. Y.: Cornell University, November, 1960; C. M. Arensberg et al., *Research in Industrial Human Relations,* New York: Harper & Brothers, 1957; Neil W. Chamberlain et al., *A Decade of Industrial Relations Research,* New York: Harper & Brothers, 1958; H. G. Heneman, Jr., et. al., *Employment Relations Research,* New York: Harper & Brothers, 1960.

[4] See Robert Fitzpatrick and Clifford P. Hahn, "Personnel Research in Industry," *Personnel,* Vol. 31, No. 5, March, 1955, pp. 422–28; Cecil E. Goode, *Personnel Research Frontiers,* Chicago: Public Personnel Association, 1960; Rensis Likert, "Personnel Research Is Growing Up," *Personnel Administration,* Vol. 19, No. 5, September-October, 1956, pp. 19–21; John C. Flanagan, "Personnel Research and the Better Use of Human Resources," *Personnel,* Vol. 35, No. 2, September-October, 1958, pp. 50–59.

education for industrial relations seeks to integrate contributions of the behavioral sciences in analysis of the field's problems.[5]

1.4 Pure, basic, and applied studies. Research is *pure* when it is designed to provide understanding largely for its own sake. Pure research is thus divorced from immediately practical applications or uses. It seeks to explain for the sake of adding to the store of knowledge and understanding. It is frequently regarded as a superior type of research, in part because it may be undertaken without the incentive of financial rewards. Sometimes it is suggested that university centers should use their resources for such studies, since individual firms or agencies appear unlikely to undertake them.

In some discussions, a distinction is made between *pure* and *basic* research. *Basic research* investigates problems or answers questions that are or may be of importance in solving a variety of practical problems. One basic study, for example, sought to discover the reliability of wives' answers to questions about the work histories of their husbands—dates, wages, and reasons for change. Other basic research has compared sampling procedures as means of securing employment information, has experimented with test-scoring and item-development procedures, and has designed improved methods of comparing training programs.[6]

Applied research uses the method of scientific inquiry to find answers to immediate, practical problems. It is sharply and directly stimulated by need. It may deal with simple or complex problems. Applied research is the most common variety in management. It is readily illustrated by a personnel department's study of sources to discover which of several are most useful. Again, a labor relations director may seek an answer to the question: has our new sick leave provision resulted in greater absenteeism? Or an employer association may analyze the administration of fair employment practice rules in several communities as a guide for member practice.

Applied research includes, as one major component, what is described as *developmental research,* undertaken to improve current practice. Applied research may seek answers to difficult questions. It may involve a complex design with numerous subsidiary questions. Its distinctive mark is its immediate usefulness and applicability.

1.5 Priorities in research. Each of these types of research can contribute to progress in understanding and improvement in practice. We need all of them. Continuing advancement is retarded if they do not move along hand in hand, for each may contribute to the others. This relationship is clear in the case of basic research. It should also be noted, however, that pure research frequently has important implications—perhaps not recognized by the pure researcher—for the solution of practical problems. In the other direction, the results of applied research may provide essential data for pure research.

[5] For a critical but stimulating commentary, see Loren Baritz, *The Servants of Power,* Middletown, Conn.: Wesleyan University Press, 1960.

[6] See, for example, Einar Hardin and Gerald L. Hershey, "Accuracy of Employee Reports on Changes in Pay," *Journal of Applied Psychology,* Vol. 44, No. 4, December, 1960, pp. 269–75.

Attempts to create and maintain a hierarchy of prestige in which pure research is regarded as more important lose much of their meaning when these interrelationships are recognized. Which type of research is more important varies from time to time and place to place. A great deal of basic or applied research may be limited in its value pending a breakthrough in pure research; on the other hand, the very question that forms the heart of pure research may not be recognized until the results of numerous applied studies become available.

1.6 Segmental studies. It is worth noting, in this connection, that the size or magnitude of a study—as measured by the breadth of its questions and hypotheses and the amounts of time and financial support required—is not necessarily correlated with its potential contribution. Vast studies may be undertaken to provide answers to small questions—questions that could perhaps be answered satisfactorily in a much simpler manner. Not infrequently, also, a number of small, segmental, *additive* studies may be more effective than one large project. What is important is that the study be appropriate in method and design, so that whatever it contributes can be accepted with clear understanding and a high degree of assurance. Especially if they are designed to be additive, segmental studies can make important contributions. As a general rule, studies benefit from a reduction in size and scope; many studies undertake too much. In theses, in association projects, and in staff studies, both quality and contribution are generally improved by pruning to produce small but highly dependable segmental studies.

2.0 TYPES OF RESEARCH STUDIES

Questions can be answered and problems solved by a variety of research approaches. Few problems or hypotheses are so unique that only one systematic method of analysis is possible. For most of the problems with which research is concerned, the investigator has a choice of several approaches. Some of them are likely to be distinctly superior; their results will be more certain and dependable; they may require much less work; they may be faster; they may be better suited to the experience and competence of the investigator. A preliminary step in research involves the careful consideration of choices among types of studies. A general *law of parsimony* usually dictates that the method chosen will be that of minimum difficulty, effort, and cost, assuming adequate quality in the prospective results.

Several fairly distinctive types of research studies are widely recognized. In practice, studies often combine two or more of them.

2.1 Deductive, logical studies. In some research, the problem is defined as applying known principles or laws to new situations. An understanding is to be secured by systematic applications of accepted generalizations or principles. This method is a deductive process, reasoning from the general to the specific. The logical method is sometimes described as "armchair research," since the investigator is primarily engaged in trying to think through preliminary questions. This process is frequently a step toward some other method, for it serves to suggest hypotheses which may be tested by a variety of methods.

2.2 Historical studies. Historical studies undertake a carefully planned and structured investigation of records and documents and interviews with those who have been on the scene, thus seeking to discover precisely what appear to have been major elements and relationships in the evolutionary process under consideration. Such studies might, for example, trace the decline in managerial prerogatives or the development of industrial unionism. The essence of the historical method is its systematic investigation of what has happened and its emphasis on a time-span or longitudinal analysis. This type of study may be preliminary to some additional method, as, for example, in a study designed to discover explanations for peaceful bargaining in some firms as contrasted with numerous stoppages in others.

2.3 Case studies. Case studies provide a systematic investigation of the relationships that have been significant in a single situation or case. Thus, a study may seek to discover how and why the X company and the Y union get along so well. Or a case study may look at the experience of the Z agency with paid sick leave. The method is sharply focused and intensive; it is designed to identify and record all relevant facts in a comparatively small and sharply defined situation. Excellent illustrations are provided by the National Planning Association's series of studies of the *Causes of Industrial Peace* and by Purcell's *The Worker Speaks His Mind on Company and Union.*[7]

The clear meaning of findings in the case study is limited to the one specific situation. But a series of similarly structured case studies may point to a more general hypothesis. The case study may suggest additional studies. Case studies can, therefore, be of great value in laying the foundation for more inclusive research.

2.4 Surveys. The distinctive feature of the survey is its comprehensive view and its concentration on the collection of original data. Some descriptions of research have discredited the survey because early applications of the method sometimes emphasized empirical evidence and observation without attention to analysis or theory. Its design was overly simple. Modern practice, however, usually includes careful design and planning, together with more or less intensive analysis, in statistical or other studies. Surveys are widely used in industrial relations. Many employer associations and unions conduct regular surveys, gathering current information on wages, hours, contract provisions, and issues in negotiations. Surveys may involve sampling and other techniques that necessitate care and planning in both design and execution.

2.5 Statistical or quantitative studies. Many studies seek to measure, analyze, classify, and interpret quantitative data and are, for that reason, described as statistical. Such studies are distinguished by their emphasis upon quantification, statistical manipulation, and statistical inference. They seek

[7] Theodore V. Purcell, Cambridge, Mass.: Harvard University Press, 1953.

aggregative measures such as averages, measures of dispersion, trends and correlations. They estimate from samples and evaluate probabilities. Through comparison with the laws of chance and accident, they appraise the significance or reliability of various findings.

With modern electronic data-processing equipment, the usefulness of quantitative studies has been impressively increased. Many such studies seek to develop mathematical models that simulate behavioral processes. Potential contributions from such studies appear promising, although the method has not been widely applied to problems in the industrial relations field.[8]

2.6 **Experimental studies.** The essence of the experimental or laboratory method is the investigator's control of the variables. Observations are made under conditions of control. The investigator manipulates what he regards as factors or causes and evaluates what appear to be sequential or resulting conditions, holding other known or suspected factors under control.

Some current impressions hold that the experimental method is rarely applicable in industrial relations and, in general, in the social sciences. The essence of experimental methods is the use of controls. While it is true that there are difficulties in programs of experimental social studies undertaken on a grand scale, controls can be maintained on many smaller experimental investigations. Thus, a study in which profit sharing is introduced into one of two similar situations is entirely feasible. The creation and observation of a control group in a study of training or counseling could justify greater reliance on findings. In many situations, statistical manipulation can simulate control.

3.0 THE RESEARCH PROCESS

Management research, including research directed toward problems in the general area of manpower management, is not sharply different in its process or procedure from other *applied sciences*—for example, medicine, education, or engineering. As noted, its methods are those of all scientific research. Its point of view and objectives are similar. Although the data with which it must deal are distinctive, the manner in which data are discovered, compiled, and analyzed is not unique.

The problem must first be recognized and stated, usually as a question for which an answer is sought or an hypothesis to be tested. For most research, an intensive *literature search* is in order, to insure that the study is additive. The very essence of research is its systematic analysis, which means that studies must be carefully designed. In carrying out designs, data are collected and

---

[8] See Thomas A. Mahoney, "Mathematics in Industrial Relations: A Look Ahead," *Special Release 3*, University of Minnesota Industrial Relations Center, December, 1960; Ross Stagner, Milton Derber, and W. Ellison Chalmers, "The Dimensionality of Union-Management Relations at the Local Level," *Journal of Applied Psychology*, Vol. 43, No. 1, February, 1959, pp. 1–7; Lowell Hattery, "Electronic Computers and Personnel Administration," *Personnel Administration*, Vol. 19, No. 2, March-April, 1956, pp. 7–13; Melvin Anshen, "The Manager and the Black Box," *Harvard Business Review*, Vol. 38, No. 6, November-December, 1960, pp. 85–92.

analyzed, hypotheses are tested, and conclusions are derived. If results are to be made available to others, a report is prepared.

3.1   Selecting problems for study. Both managers and students who have have had little acquaintance with research may find it difficult to recognize the need and opportunities for studies. To the experienced investigator, such opportunities are evident and numerous, so that the problem is one of establishing personal priorities. One research consultant suggests that the ideal approach is to make every management problem a project. A 1961 seminar on "Establishing and Conducting a Company Research Program," presented by the University of Michigan Bureau of Industrial Relations, included a session on "Suggested Areas for Personnel Research," with special attention to problems in management development, employee benefits, salary administration, employee attitude studies, and analysis of selection practices.

For many managers, the question as to what to study is answered by other managers and executives. Not infrequently, line managers bring questions to the industrial relations staff for investigation. Research may be undertaken on instruction or request. In other situations, the pressure of certain problems requires immediate attention to them. In many localities, studies are undertaken by local associations of managers, and individual firms are expected to do their part. The special interests of managers may influence the direction of their studies.

Students of management are often concerned about how they can best select a subject for research. They may have to complete a research project as a part of course or degree requirements. They may be given an opportunity to undertake a study under direction as part of their training for professional careers.

Much depends, in such situations, on the nature of the assignment. Several questions should be answered to narrow the range. One concerns the *personal skills, knowledge,* and *competence of the student.* What is his background and level of sophistication in the field? What preparation has he had? How much of the basic literature does he know? What research techniques and tools is he prepared to use?

Another question is concerned with *fixed limits on time and resources.* How long can the project take and how many hours can the researcher spend on it? What institutional help is available to him? Can he travel, use the mails, have access to programming and computer assistance? Is there technical assistance that may be used, for example, in designing the study or in preparing and testing questionnaires?

A very important question concerns the *interests of the investigator.* What area of problems is of greatest interest to him? As research is essentially a learning process, interest and motivation can be expected to exert a powerful influence on the quality and value of such studies.

As a general principle—and excluding immediate problems that offer challenges in applied research—one of the most helpful sources of ideas for research will be found in a review of relevant theory. It is the very nature of theory to state plausible propositions that are not conclusively demonstrated. One of the major attributes of theory is its function of suggesting questions that should be tested. Theory is an inexhaustible source of questions, for new or modified theories are constantly appearing.

This does not imply that students should attempt a test of an inclusive general theory. It would be rather obviously unrealistic, for example, to expect a single-quarter research study to undertake a conclusive test of work theory or of learning theory. Similarly, individual research can't provide comprehensive tests of theories of staffing working organizations or of incentivation, labor movements or collective bargaining.

These *general* theories can, however, provide leads or clues to much more limited studies. What questions, for example, does a general theory of work suggest with respect to the work of office employees in a local insurance firm? Or for the office employees in the business office of the college? What questions does general learning theory raise with respect to the effectiveness of a single training technique for assemblers of gyroscopes in a small organization? What questions do general theories of labor movements raise with respect to the attitudes of local cab drivers toward their union? General theories raise questions. Such questions can be applied to limited, manageable situations. Studies can be additive and valuable without being comprehensive and conclusive on a broad scale.

3.2   Search of literature. Once a problem has been selected or accepted on assignment, many investigators find themselves anxious to collect data. They want action, to get the show on the road. They are impatient if not impulsive. For most studies, however, a thorough literature search is not only essential; it can speed the research process. The investigator needs to know what has been done with respect to the same or similar problems and how it has been done. He needs to know both the contributions and deficiencies of related studies. He can take advantage of lessons learned in earlier studies. From them, he can sharpen his own inquiry. They may have developed techniques and aids (questionnaires, schedules, tests, forms, etc.) that he can use.

Such a search of the literature is, of course, directed to the most likely research-reporting publications. For some problem areas, recent books may summarize earlier research. Textbooks may contain important leads in their footnotes. Handbooks in the specialized management fields may list important research contributions. For recent contributions, greatest dependence must be placed on the journal or periodical literature of the field.

3.3   Statement of problem. This is often a difficult step. Usually, those interested in possible studies know in a general way what they seek to learn. They have an idea of their problem. The sharpening of the question and its clear definitive specification, however, may be difficult. That is why it is frequently said that once a question is properly stated, the problem is half solved.

A search of the relevant literature can be helpful in developing an accurate statement of the problem or hypothesis. Such a search may discover how others have stated it. It may disclose deficiencies of earlier statements.

The task is to bring the study down from a general idea of what is to be investigated to a precise statement. For example, a project within a firm may seek to investigate the effectiveness of the incentive wage program. For the purposes of research, however, several terms will have to be much more sharply defined. What incentive wage program; the whole company-wide arrangement or the specific group-incentive plan of drop-forge operators? What effectiveness; the measure of individual daily product, the costs of machine up-keep and repair, the measure of spoilage, the level of unit product costs, or some combination of these and other evidences of effectiveness?

On a broader scale, a proposed project may intend to study featherbedding in industry. The final statement of the problem, however, must decide, first of all, what question or questions are to be asked about it. What is it that the research is to try to discover? Is the question one of the costs of featherbedding, or of its sources and causes, or of changes or trends in these practices, or of methods of avoiding it, or is some other question contemplated? Perhaps the answer here is that the study will investigate methods of reducing or eliminating featherbedding. Another question must then ask, What do you mean by featherbedding? By whom? Where and when?

3.4 Design: operational hypotheses. Once the problem has been precisely stated, the study must be designed. Plans must be drawn for finding answers. Developing the design is a delicate and difficult assignment; deficiencies in design generally mean that answers will not be dependable or that the study will produce answers to the wrong questions.

The design stage is one in which the researcher creates his flight plan or road map and schedule. Planning and designing the study may be regarded as comparable to the architect's function in planning a residence or factory or store. It is a step in which expertness and experience can be of great value. The study must be designed in a manner such that its findings will have a maximum of relevance and reliability.

Effective design involves careful consideration of methodology, the logical soundness of the procedure. Do the steps taken and the devices and techniques used fit the questions to be answered? Or are they, at points, like the classic student response to a question for which he doesn't know the answer? Do they, in other words, provide an excellent answer to some other question? Do they proceed logically, step by step, to build up an appropriate, consistent answer to the question or questions with which the inquiry began?

Design evaluates proposed methods before they are applied. Many serious deficiencies in studies can be avoided by such planning. In many situations, methodological design involves the testing of a detailed model. In others, the design may create a pilot study as a prelude to a more extensive investigation.[9]

[9] See Russell L. Ackoff, *The Design of Social Research*, Chicago: University of Chicago Press, 1953; Leon Festinger and Daniel Katz, *Research Methods in the Be-*

In the process of designing a study, *operational* or *working hypotheses* are substituted for the non-technical statement of the problem. Even when the question has been clearly stated, it may have to be restated to make it operationally practicable. Operational hypotheses restate questions in the specific terms in which they can be answered. Maybe, for example, the best available evidence of employee health is the record of time lost on account of illness in this firm. Again, the only usable measure of featherbedding may be output per man-hour or size of work crew. For some questions, samples may have to be substituted for complete data. Scores on specific attitude scales or subscales may be the operational evidence of employee reactions.

Design may include the advance preparation of *dummy tables,* in which data are to be recorded. With headings and stubs completed, the resulting cells in the table can be checked to see that they would, if filled in, provide precisely the answers for which they are intended. Another useful procedure involves the *pretesting* of all devices—scales, checklists, interviews, and schedules. They can be tried out in a comparable situation, with care not to contaminate the sample to be used in the major study.

If, after extensive planning and pretesting, question still remains as to possible obstacles and problems, it may be well to make a *pilot study.* Such an exploratory and experimental investigation can demonstrate the strengths and weaknesses of the proposed larger study and provide an opportunity for revised planning that might be disastrous if introduced in the middle of the major study.[10]

3.5 Data collection and analysis. In the empirical study, the next stage is presumably that of collecting and analyzing data. In many studies, they are already at hand in company or published records. This step may, on the other hand, take the investigator into the field and into the leg work of research. Data, facts, evidence are gathered and tabulated, classified and analyzed. In many studies, inexperienced investigators are shocked to discover that this stage, which they had regarded as the very heart of the project, may take far less time than thoroughgoing preliminary steps.

3.6 Testing hypotheses. If the study has been adequately designed, results will provide evidence with respect to hypotheses. Results may not be conclusive, however. They may suggest but not prove a positive or negative evaluation. Much of the time and effort spent on design is intended to make findings more dependable, but many studies end with probabilities rather than certainties.

Since the purpose of research is to test hypotheses, it is essential that appropriate tests be applied. Suppose, for example, that a small in-plant study investigates the relationship of employee attitudes to length of service.

havioral Sciences, New York: The Dryden Press, Inc., 1953; William H. Goode and Paul K. Hatt, *Methods in Social Research,* New York: McGraw-Hill Book Company, Inc., 1952.

[10] See Waldo H. Kliever, "The Design of Research Projects and Programs" in David B. Hertz and A. H. Rubenstein, eds., *Research Operations in Industry,* New York: King's Crown Press, 1953, pp. 24–51.

Data indicate that long-service employees (ten years or more) score 3 points higher on a standard scale than employees of lesser service. How shall these findings be evaluated? Do they prove the hypothesis that employee attitudes toward employment in the firm improve with continued service?

Aside from the reliability of the scale, several additional considerations must be recognized. The difference in scores may be impressive if the total range of scores is only from 5 to 10. The same difference looks much less meaningful if that range is from 70 to 160. The difference is less impressive if both groups of employees include a wide range or if overlap is extensive. Evaluation may change if evidence discloses that only 32 employees were included in the sample, which was assumed to represent all the 700 employees. It will make some difference, perhaps, if most of the long-service employees are supervisors.

The problem of testing hypotheses is essentially one of logic. It is aided greatly, however, by a variety of statistical tests.[11]

3.7 Reporting research. The results of research are usually reported. Some studies, however, appear to fade away without benefit of a formal report. Others are reported in a manner that limits communication and interpretation of their findings. One of the most common criticisms of research is the conclusion that results merely fill formidable volumes that gather dust in offices and libraries.

Few of those who are competent, interested, and active in research appear to have an equal ability to do a good job of describing, interpreting, and explaining the meaning and significance of research findings. Many reports of studies are dull and difficult reading. In-plant research can and should be reported in a form that encourages and facilitates reading and understanding by those who can use the results. In current practice, many studies open with a one- or two-page summary. They make use of charts and graphs. They conclude with a review of findings. They may detail data in one or more appendices.

If research is to have a broader impact, it must be reported in the *professional journals* (see Section 4.0). Only by such publication can the full contribution of studies advance the profession. One of the marks of the professional in such published reports is the careful, accurate assignment of credit to all those who have made significant contributions to the study.

3.8 Support for research. Intra-firm research is generally assigned to individuals or divisions that have staff and budget for this purpose. Student research may be assisted and subsidized by bureaus of business research or other funds provided by educational institutions. Larger projects usually seek foundation support, many of them from the National Science Foundation. The Social Science Research Council and the National Academy of Manage-

---

[11] See Allen L. Edwards, *Experimental Design in Psychological Research,* New York: Rinehart & Company, Inc., 1950; Russell L. Ackoff, *The Design of Social Research,* Chicago: University of Chicago Press, 1953, chaps. 6, 7, and 8.

ment are examples of agencies that may be helpful in finding foundation or other support.

3.9 Evaluation of research. The practitioner who is to use the contributions of research must be able to recognize the limitations of studies, both those undertaken within his own organization and those reported in the professional journals. Suggestions for such appraisals can be inferred from earlier sections of this chapter. A preliminary question concerns the *essentials of research,* the method used in whatever investigation has been undertaken. Reports can be checked to discover, also, the care and precision with which the problem or question or hypothesis has been stated. Questions can be raised about the selection of appropriate design and the thoroughness with which that design was observed. A *checklist* of points to be noted might include the following items:

1. Statement of the problem;
2. The known experience and competence of the investigator;
3. The significance of the study; its possible value;
4. Relationship to other studies;
5. Propriety of method; rationale;
6. Design and model;
7. Adequacy of data; sampling limitations;
8. Analysis, inferences, and tests of hypotheses;
9. Conclusions and adequacy of reporting.

Some help in appraising reported research may be gained from the experience of foundations that are continually called on to evaluate proposals for studies. Figure 25.1 summarizes the suggestions of the National Science Foundation as to information needed to evaluate requests for their support.

4.0 RESEARCH AGENCIES AND PUBLICATIONS

Those engaged in research as well as the manager who seeks to keep informed about current contributions must depend largely on professional organizations and research-reporting publications. Many of the professional associations hold regular conferences in which studies are reported, compared, and discussed. Some of the associations publish journals that report research. This section of the chapter has been prepared to help students and practitioners in identifying these sources.

4.1 Professional associations. Associations that communicate information on industrial relations research are of several types. They include:

(a) *Local personnel or industrial relations groups.* Several hundred local associations, usually city-wide in scope, have been organized in most of the middle-sized and larger metropolitan areas. Their membership is usually open to all practitioners. They meet, usually once each month, and may arrange frequent visits to the business firms represented in their membership. They include reports of research in their programs, and many of them also publish newsletters in which research findings are described.

(b) *National and regional personnel associations.* Several organizations of national scope offer membership to personnel staff members. Some of them are specialized, like the National Association of Training Directors. Others provide membership opportunities for several types of management specialists,

---

Suggestions for Preparing a Research Proposal

The Foundation does not recommend any specific form for proposals at this time. The handling of proposals is facilitated, however, if they are submitted in 15 copies on letter size paper to the National Science Foundation, Washington 25, D.C. It is also suggested that proposals cover the following points insofar as they may be applicable:

1. *Name and address of institution.*
2. *Name of principal investigator.*
3. *Title of proposed research.*
4. *Description of proposed research.* A description of the work to be undertaken, its objectives and its relation to the present state of knowledge in the field and to comparable work in progress elsewhere, together with pertinent literature citations should be included.
5. *Procedure.* This should consist of an outline of the general plan of the work, including design of experiments to be undertaken, if any, and the procedure to be followed.
6. *Facilities.* Facilities and major items of permanent equipment that are available should be described.
7. *Personnel.* A short biographical sketch and a bibliography of the principal investigator and other professional personnel should be included.
8. *Budget.* The budget should comprise an estimate of the total cost of the project and a statement of its proposed duration, with a breakdown of costs for each year. Funds requested from the Foundation should be indicated for each of the categories listed below. If there are contributions from other sources, itemize in similar categories.
   a. *Salaries.* Itemize positions, giving names of professional personnel, if selected.
   b. *Permanent equipment.* Itemize major pieces of equipment required.
   c. *Expendable equipment and supplies.*
   d. *Travel.*
   e. *Other direct costs.* Itemize other direct costs not included in *a* through *d* above, such as costs of publication and of physical facilities.
   f. *Indirect costs.* Not to exceed 15 per cent of the total of funds for direct costs requested of the Foundation, *a* through *e* above.
9. *Approval.* One copy of the proposal should be signed by the principal investigator, by the department head, and by an official authorized to sign for the institution.

Fig. 25.1   National Science Foundation Suggestions for Research Proposals
(From the Second Annual Report of the National Science Foundation, 1952, p. 52)

as do the Society for the Advancement of Management and the National Academy of Management. Some of them accept firm memberships. Some, like the Society for Personnel Administration, have emphasized public or governmental personnel problems. Some include industry, union, and academic members, as does the Industrial Relations Research Association.

Others, including the large Personnel Division of the American Management Association and the American Society of Personnel Administrators, have emphasized the problems of staff members in industry.

Some professional associations of social scientists (economists, psychologists) hold annual meetings and publish proceedings and journals that are of interest to practitioners in the industrial relations field. Some trade associations include personnel and industrial relations sections. The following list of associations may be helpful for those who wish to keep abreast of current research.

American Economic Association, Northwestern University, Evanston, Illinois.

American Labor Education Service, 1776 Broadway, New York 19, New York.

American Management Association, 1515 Broadway, New York 36, New York.

American Personnel and Guidance Association, Inc., 1534 O Street, N.W., Washington 5, D.C. (formerly the National Vocational Guidance Association).

American Psychological Association, 1515 Massachusetts Avenue N.W., Washington 5, D.C.

American Society for Personnel Administration, Marquette University, Milwaukee, Wisconsin.

American Society of Training Directors (care of Journal of Industrial Training), 160 East 48th Street, New York, New York.

American Statistical Association, 1108 16th Street N.W., Washington 6, D.C.

Chamber of Commerce of the United States, Washington 6, D.C.

Industrial Relations Counselors, Inc., 1270 Avenue of Americas, New York 20, New York.

Industrial Relations Research Association, Park and University, Temp. 3, Room 5, Madison 5, Wisconsin.

International Labour Organization, 917 15th Street N.W., Washington 6, D.C.

Metropolitan Life Insurance Company, Policyholders Service Bureau, 1 Madison Avenue, New York 10, New York.

National Association of Manufacturers, 14 West 49th Street, New York 20, New York.

National Bureau of Economic Research, 261 Madison Avenue, New York, New York.

National Industrial Conference Board, 247 Park Avenue, New York, New York.

National Office Management Association, 132 West Chelten Avenue, Philadelphia 44, Pennsylvania.

National Safety Council, 425 North Michigan Avenue, Chicago 11, Illinois.

Society for the Advancement of Management, 74 Fifth Avenue, New York 16, New York.

Society for Personnel Administration, 5505 Connecticut Ave., N.W., Washington 15, D.C.

Workers Education Bureau of America, 1525 H Street N.W., Washington 5, D.C.

4.2 Professional conferences. Many local associations and several of the national organizations listed in the preceding section hold regular conferences in which current research is reported and discussed. In addition, several universities arrange annual conferences and institutes in which current research is a major subject. These conferences are usually announced well in advance in the professional publications described in Section 4.4 of this chapter.

4.3 University centers. A growing number of American and foreign universities have created special industrial relations centers or institutes which maintain research programs, engage in cooperative research with industry, unions, and government agencies, and provide special conferences, clinics, and seminars, as well as bibliographies on major subjects.

4.4 Professional journals. A rapidly growing list of periodicals reports the research of university faculty members, research centers, public agencies, and private firms. Many of these publications have appeared within the past decade, and the emergence of several additional publications in the early 1960's attests to increasing interest and activity in industrial relations research. The following list is by no means complete. Numerous local and regional associations include reports of research in their publications. Many publications, like those of the National Safety Council and the *Journal of Industrial Medicine* limit their coverage to a small segment of the industrial relations field. For a comprehensive and strictly up-to-date list, therefore, the student or manager should consult one of the librarians in the university industrial relations centers.[12]

Publications Reporting Industrial Relations Research

1. *Administrative Science Quarterly.* Graduate School of Business and Public Administration, Cornell University, Ithaca, New York. Quarterly, since June, 1956. Broad coverage of management opinion and research reports, with a continuing emphasis on theory and philosophy. Book reviews and abstracts.

2. *Advanced Management.* Society for the Advancement of Management, 74 5th Avenue, New York 11, New York. Successor to *The Society for the Advancement of Management Journal,* the *Bulletin of the Taylor Society,* and *Modern Management.* Monthly, since 1936. Reports of managerial developments and viewpoints in all phases of management.

3. *American Journal of Sociology.* Published for the American Sociological Association by the University of Chicago Press, 5750 Ellis Avenue, Chicago 37, Illinois. Bimonthly, since 1895. Increasing attention to the broad area of industrial sociology, with frequent reports on studies of work and organization theory.

4. *American Management Association Research Reports.* American Management Association, 1515 Broadway, New York 36, New York. Irregular, since 1942. Reports of company philosophy, policy, and practice in all phases of management.

5. *Bulletin of Industrial Psychology and Personnel Practice.* Department of Labour and National Service, Melbourne, Australia. Quarterly, since 1944. Reports of research in Australia and abroad, book reviews, and abstracts of articles from numerous other foreign and domestic publications.

6. *Business Week.* McGraw-Hill Publishing Company, Inc., 330 West 42nd Street, New York. Weekly, since September 7, 1929. Journalistic review of current developments in the broad field of business.

7. *Employment Relations Abstracts.* Information Service, Inc., 10 West Warren Street, Detroit, Michigan. Semimonthly, looseleaf service, since 1950. The title from 1950 through 1959 was *Labor-Personnel Index.*

8. *Ergonomics.* Taylor and Francis, Ltd., Red Lion Court, Fleet Street, London.

---

[12] See, also, the special bibliographies prepared and circulated by the Association of Industrial Relations Librarians and the frequently revised list of periodicals in *Union Contracts and Collective Bargaining Report,* Par. 50,306.5.

Quarterly, since 1957. Coverage emphasizes human engineering, combines approaches of human biology, anatomy, physiology, and psychology with mechanical engineering.

9. *Harvard Business Review.* Harvard Graduate School of Business Administration, Soldiers Field, Boston 63, Massachusetts. Bimonthly, since October, 1922. A review of the general field of business. Frequent articles on industrial relations.

10. *Human Organization.* The Society for Applied Anthropology, New York State School of Industrial and Labor Relations, Cornell University, Ithaca, New York. Quarterly, since 1941. Intercultural approach to problems of human relations, including industrial relations.

11. *Human Relations.* Tavistock Institute of Human Relations, 68–74 Carter Lane, London, E.C. 4. Quarterly, since 1947. Self-described as a "journal of studies toward the integration of the social sciences" with frequent reports on industrial relations.

12. *Industrial and Labor Relations Review.* New York State School of Labor and Industrial Relations, Cornell University, Ithaca, New York. Quarterly, since October, 1947. Opinions and reports of studies on labor legislation, collective bargaining, and related subjects.

13. *Industrial Medicine and Surgery.* Industrial Medicine Publishing Company, 605 North.Michigan Avenue, Chicago, Illinois. Monthly, since 1932. Emphasis on health programs in industry, with reports on health hazards, occupational diseases, handicapped workers, medical services, and related subjects.

14. *Industrial Relations.* Institute of Industrial Relations, University of California, at Berkeley and at Los Angeles. Quarterly, since October, 1961. Journal of ideas and opinions as well as reports of research.

15. *Industrial Relations News.* Industrial Relations Newsletter, Inc., 230 West 41st Street, New York 36, New York. Weekly, since April, 1954. Broad reporting coverage on labor relations, labor markets, training, recruitment, safety, employee activities, legislation, and related practice.

16. *Industrial Relations Quarterly Review.* Department of Industrial Relations, Faculty of Social Sciences, Laval University, Quebec, Canada. Quarterly, since 1945. Broad coverage of research and opinion with emphasis on Canadian industrial relations. Reviews, communications, and comments.

17. *Industrial Training Abstracts.* Wayne University Press, Detroit, Michigan. Quarterly, since 1947. Abstracts articles dealing with apprentice, foreman and supervisory, safety, sales, and related types of training in industry.

18. *Industrial Welfare and Personnel Management.* Industrial Welfare Society, Inc., 48 Bryanston Square, London, W.1. Formerly *Boys' Welfare Journal, Journal of Industrial Welfare,* and *Industrial Welfare.* Monthly, since 1918. British journal reporting developments in manpower management.

19. *International Labour Review.* International Labour Office, Geneva, Switzerland. Monthly, since 1921. Special articles dealing with social and economic problems of labor. Statistical section maintains continuing series on wages, hours, and other conditions of employment.

20. *Journal of the Academy of Management.* Academy of Management, Business Administration Building, Michigan State University, East Lansing, Michigan. Three times yearly, since 1958. Reports of discussion and research in the management field.

21. *Journal of the American Society of Training Directors.* Official publication of the American Society of Training Directors, 2020 University Avenue, Madison, Wisconsin. Monthly, since January-February, 1954. Formerly (1947–

1954) the *Journal of Industrial Training*. Broad coverage of the personnel field, with, however, a special emphasis on training problems.

22. *Journal of Applied Psychology*. American Psychological Association, 1313 16th Street N.W., Washington 6, D.C. Bimonthly, since 1917. All phases of applied psychology, with numerous reports of personnel research.

23. *Journal of Industrial Engineering*. American Institute of Industrial Engineers, A. French Building, 225 North Avenue, N.W., Atlanta, Georgia. Bimonthly, since 1949. Emphasis on operations research, linear programming, work design, work sampling and measurement, wage incentives, and similar problems.

24. *Journal of Personnel Administration*. First issue, October, 1954. Official journal of the American Society for Personnel Administration.

25. *Journal of Personnel Administration and Industrial Relations*, Personnel Research Publishers, Washington, D.C. Quarterly, since January, 1954. Reports original studies and theoretical analyses in all phases of the industrial relations field.

26. *Labour Gazette*. Department of Labour of Canada, Ottawa. Monthly, since 1900. A "review of the labour-industrial situation throughout Canada." Includes articles, statistics, and reviews.

27. *Labor Law Journal*. Commerce Clearing House, Inc., 214 N. Michigan Avenue, Chicago 1, Illinois. Monthly, since October 1949. Articles generally present non-legalistic discussions of legal phases of industrial relations.

28. *Management Abstracts*. British Institute of Management, 17 Hill St., London, W.1. Since September, 1948. Abstracting articles throughout the broad field of management.

29. *Management Record*. National Industrial Conference Board, 247 Park Avenue, New York 22, New York. Monthly, since 1916. Numerous reports of both experience and research, surveys conducted by the N.I.C.B. staff, digests of symposia.

30. *Management Review*. American Management Association, 330 West 42nd Street, New York 36, New York. Monthly, since May, 1912. General coverage of all phases of management.

31. *Monthly Labor Review*. Bureau of Labor Statistics, U. S. Department of Labor, Washington, D.C. Monthly, since July, 1915. Summaries of staff studies in industrial relations. Statistical section includes continuing series on industrial disputes, employment, payrolls, and cost of living.

32. *Occupational Psychology*. National Institute of Industrial Psychology, 14 Welbeck St., London, W.1. Quarterly since 1922 (formerly the *Human Factor* and the *Journal of the National Institute of Industrial Psychology*). Reporting of research on vocational guidance, personnel administration, and industrial psychology.

33. *Personnel*. American Management Association, 330 West 42nd Street, New York 36, New York. Quarterly since January, 1919 (suspended, November, 1921), bi-monthly since April, 1927. Broad interest in entire field of industrial relations. Numerous reports of surveys, studies, experience.

34. *Personnel Administration*. Society for Personnel Administration, 715 G. St., Washington 1, D.C. Bi-monthly since 1939. Articles on all phases of personnel administration, with emphasis on practice in public agencies.

35. *Personnel Administration and Industrial Relations*. Personnel Research Publishers, Washington, D.C. Quarterly, since 1954. Reports of original studies, theoretical papers, discussions.

36. *Personnel and Guidance Journal*. Formerly *Occupations*. American Personnel

and Guidance Association, 20th and Northampton Streets, Easton, Penn. Monthly, since 1952 (and as *Occupations,* since 1921.) Emphasis on counseling, selection, placement, with occasional broader interest.

37. *Personnel Journal.* Personnel Journal, Inc., Post Office Box 239, Swarthmore, Penn. Formerly *Journal of Personnel* and formerly published by the Personnel Research Federation. Monthly, since May, 1922, except July and August. Articles include reports of experience and research, chronicle developments, and discuss controversial issues.

38. *Personnel Management.* Formerly the *Journal of the Institute of Personnel Management.* Institute of Personnel Management, Management House, 80 Fetter Lane, London, E.C. 4. Quarterly, since 1920. Theory and practice in both personnel management and labor relations.

39. *Personnel Management Abstracts.* Bureau of Industrial Relations, University of Michigan, Ann Arbor, (Formerly, until 1962, Washington, D.C.) Bi-monthly, since 1955. Abstracts of books and articles in both personnel management and labor relations.

40. *Personnel Series.* American Management Association, 330 West 42nd Street, New York 36, New York. Irregularly (several per year) since 1930. Reports of papers and discussions at A.M.A. personnel conferences. Broad coverage of the field.

41. *Personnel Psychology.* P. O. Box 6965, College Station, Durham, N.C. Quarterly, since spring, 1948. Emphasizes reports on research in psychological aspects of personnel and industrial relations.

42. *Public Personnel Review.* Civil Service Assembly of the United States and Canada, 1313 East 60th Street, Chicago, Illinois. Quarterly, since 1940. Major emphasis on personnel problems in government service.

43. *Social Science Reporter.* Rex F. Harlow, editor and publisher, 365 Guinda Street, Palo Alto, California. Semimonthly, since 1952. Current reports for executives on social science research—covering industrial relations, psychology, sociology, and co-disciplinary studies.

44. *Studies in Personnel Policy.* National Industrial Conference Board, 247 Park Avenue, New York 22, New York. Irregular, since 1937. Mainly comparisons of experience and evaluations of programs with frequent surveys of policy and practice.

45. *Supervision.* Supervision Publishing Co., Inc., 404 North Wesley Avenue. Mount Morris, Illinois. Monthly, since 1939. Popular discussion of personnel problems at the level of first-line supervision.

Many of these publications include studies of the role of government in industrial relations. For systematic reporting of legislation and administrative decisions and arbitration awards, however, major reliance must be placed on the special labor reporting services, such as the *Labor Policies and Practice Series* of the Bureau of National Affairs (1231 24th Street, N.W., Washington, D.C.); the *Labor Law Reporter* and the *Labor Law Journal* (Commerce Clearing House, 214 North Michigan Avenue, Chicago 1, Illinois); and *Union Contracts and Collective Bargaining Report, Personnel Policies and Practices Report, Employee Relations and Arbitration Report,* and *Pension and Profit Sharing Report* (all published by Prentice-Hall, Inc., Englewood Cliffs, New Jersey).

New journals, some limited to the general area of industrial relations and others concerned with the broad field of management, are appearing frequently. As the relationship of management to the behavioral sciences has received growing attention, articles of interest to students of management have become more frequent in *social science journals*. Publications that cross the lines among the various disciplines, for example, the *American Behavioral Scientist* (monthly, except July and August, Box 294, Princeton, New Jersey), could become increasingly interesting. So also may such indexing services as the *Business Methods Index*, which reports on British, Canadian, and American books, magazines, and other publications (monthly, Box 453, Ottawa, Canada).

In addition to the *Harvard Business Review* shown in the above list, several other publications of university schools of business, management, and administration frequently include articles of interest and reports of research in industrial relations. Illustrative of this group of publications are the *California Management Review* (graduate schools of business of the University of California), *Business Horizons* (Indiana University), the *Quarterly Review of Economics and Business* (University of Illinois), the *Journal of Business* (University of Chicago), *Business Topics* (Michigan State University), *The Executive* (Baker Library, Harvard Graduate School of Business), and several others that may deserve equal billing.

5.0 SUMMARY

It is to be expected that managers of the future will make increasing use of the tool of research for the advancement of both theory and practice in manpower management. Many of them may participate in research within their own organizations; others may join with other managers in the research programs of professional organizations and university centers. Managers are becoming increasingly research-oriented and more sophisticated in the conduct of studies and in the evaluation of reported studies. They are assisted in their use of research by a growing volume of research-reporting journals.

Although management research, like other research, is a major responsibility of universities and of numerous public and private agencies, individual managers have an essential role. Just as the professional practitioner in medicine maintains records and files and joins with colleagues in the analysis of data derived from their practice, managers can provide an important contribution by making their experience available for analysis. They can provide the cases and situations and experiments and findings that represent basic data for many studies.

Research in manpower management can be of many types. It can use a variety of research methods—surveys, case studies, historical studies, and others. It can benefit from the knowhow, viewpoints, and skills of various social and behavioral sciences. Research can be pure, basic, or applied. Much of it is likely to consist of small segmental studies that add their important bits to the total of growing knowledge. Some can be undertaken in the workshop; some can best be performed in the experimental laboratory.

This chapter has outlined essentials in all types of industrial relations research; studies must be purposive, objective, systematic, and analytical. It has described the principal forms of research studies. It has outlined the major steps in the conduct of research. In its closing section, it has listed the principal agencies engaged in industrial relations research and the major research-reporting publications.

In industrial relations, as in other areas of management, research has achieved growing acceptance as the most economical route to progress. In the past, much of the incentive for improvement has come from domestic competition—the desire if not the necessity to learn how to do a better job than close competitors. For the future, this incentive is supplemented—if not overshadowed—by the international competition of a different philosophy of business and management. Managers in the free societies must seek to improve their theory and practice not only to compete with others within our society but also to compete with foreign combinations of business and government. The necessity for improvement in management justifies nothing less than a crash program in management research.

The chapter that follows leans heavily on research. It is concerned with the continuing evaluation and appraisal of manpower management. Much of the evidence essential to such appraisal must be provided by research. Many of the yardsticks used in rating management can be improved by research.

SELECTED SUPPLEMENTARY READINGS

Adams, Richard N. and Jack J. Preiss, *Human Organization Research.* Homewood, Ill.: The Dorsey Press, 1960.

Bellows, Roger M., "Personnel Problems that Yield to Research," *Personnel Administration,* Vol. 19, No. 5, pp. 14–18, September-October, 1956.

Essays on Industrial Relations Research—Problems and Prospects. Ann Arbor and Detroit: Institute of Labor and Industrial Relations, University of Michigan and Wayne State University, 1961.

Fitzpatrick, Robert and Clifford P. Hahn, "Personnel Research in Industry," *Personnel,* Vol. 31, No. 5, pp. 422–28, March, 1955.

Flanagan, John C., "The World of Work: Current Research Trends," *Personnel,* Vol. 35, No. 2, pp. 50–59, September-October, 1958.

Likert, Rensis, "Personnel Research is Growing Up," *Personnel Administration,* Vol. 19, No. 5, pp. 19–21, September-October, 1956.

Mahoney, Thomas A., "Mathematics in Industrial Relations," *Special Release 3,* Industrial Relations Center, University of Minnesota, December, 1960.

Parnes, Herbert S., "Research on Labor Mobility," *Bulletin 65,* Social Science Research Council, 1954.

SHORT CASE PROBLEM 25.1

Costs of Basic Research

"Why should we pay the costs of basic research?" the comptroller wants to know. Mr. Deeson, vice-president for employee relations, has presented a plan whereby the firm would make a five-year commitment to the industrial relations center of a local university. He has indicated that the center's research program, while not devoted to answering specific questions of immediate interest to the firm, will emphasize basic research which he feels is timely and necessary.

The comptroller argues that the university should itself support basic research out of the funds available to it. He insists that officers of the firm can properly be charged with misuse of corporate funds if they make gifts to support basic research. He argues that applied studies, devoted to the solution of immediate problems of the firm, may be appropriate for support. In providing such support, the firm should insist that findings be regarded as confidential and be given only to the firm. Results of basic research, he feels, will be as useful to others, including competitors, as to the supporting firm.

Problem: Prepare an answer to the comptroller.

SHORT CASE PROBLEM 25.2

Salaries and Recognition in Research

This firm has a special research division in the employee relations department. The director of research is well known among employee relations directors and personnel managers as a leader in research. He has published results of firm studies in the periodicals of the field. The studies appear to be well designed and carefully planned, so that they have reflected favorably on the firm.

Turnover in the staff division is high and the director of employee relations research is asking for higher salaries with which to recruit new staff members. He explains the turnover as indicating dissatisfaction with salaries. The firm's president, noting that beginning salaries for graduates with the M.A. degree are higher than any other starting salaries, is reluctant about allowing any further advance. He has talked with faculty members, who tell him that their graduates are not interested in working with the director of research because they see no future in it. Personal contributions are not mentioned in published reports.

The director of research scoffs at this observation, insisting that these young staff members only do the leg-work, that they are receiving fine training for positions in which they can manage research programs of their own, and that a high turnover is inevitable. He says that the market is tight, that very few persons are being trained for this type of work, and that salaries well above those for five-year engineers are essential.

Problem: You are the vice-president in charge of employee relations. What steps would you take to insure the continuing values to be gained from employee relations research?

SHORT CASE PROBLEM 25.3

Significant Differences in Morale

Courtesy of the University of Minnesota Industrial Relations Center

Here are the tabulated calculations resulting from a chi-square test of general morale scores for 5186 production employees. The table compares two groups of employees in each category listed. The question is whether there are significant differences between the two groups with respect to their general morale scores. The chi-square tests note the frequency with which employees in each group had scored above or below the median score. They thus indicate the probability of independence of the groups being compared. For example, this hypothesis of independence was rejected with respect to females versus males.

Factors Influencing Employee Morale

Group	Result	
	Hypothesis for Independence	
	Accepted	Rejected*
Sex		
Female v. male		.001
Marital Status		
Married v. not married†	X	
Union Membership		
Non-member v. member		.05
Dependents		
0 v. 1–3	X	
0 v. 4+	X	
1–3 v. 4+		.03
Age		
16–19 v. 20–29	X	
16–19 v. 30–44	X	
45–59 v. 16–19		.001
60+ v. 16–19		.001
45–59 v. 20–29		.001
60+ v. 20–29		.001
30–44 v. 20–29		.001
45–59 v. 30–44		.001
60+ v. 30–44		.001
Education		
0–8 v. 9–12		.001
0–8 v. 13+		.001
9–12 v. 13+	X	

* Figures shown indicate the level of significance.
† "Not married" includes single, widowed, and divorced persons.

Factors Influencing Employee Morale

Group	Result	
	Hypothesis for Independence	
	Accepted	Rejected*
Length of time with company		
Less than 1 year v. 1–4		.001
Less than 1 year v. 5–14		.001
Less than 1 year v. 15–24	X	
Less than 1 year v. 25+	X	
1–4 v. 5–14	X	
1–4 v. 15–24	X	
25+ v. 1–4		.001
25+ v. 5–14		.001
5–14 v. 15–24	X	
25+ v. 15–24		.01
Length of time on job		
Less than 1 year v. 1–4		.01
Less than 1 year v. 5–14		.05
Less than 1 year v. 15–24		.05
Less than 1 year v. 25+	X	
1–4 v. 5–14	X	
1–4 v. 15–24	X	
25+ v. 1–4		.001
5–14 v. 15–24	X	
25+ v. 5–14		.001
25+ v. 15–24		.001
Shift		
Other† v. day		.001
Other v. night		.02
Night v. day		.05
Weekly take-home pay		
$ 0–34 v. $35–49		.001
$ 0–34 v. $50–74		.01
$ 0–34 v. $75–99		.05
$ 0–34 v. $100+	X	
$35–49 v. $50–74		.05
$35–49 v. $75–99		.05
$35–49 v. $100+	X	
$50–74 v. $75–99	X	
$100+ v. $50–74		.001
$100+ v. $75–99		.01
Accidents		
0 v. 1	X	
0 v. 2+	X	
1 v. 2+	X	

* Figures shown indicate the level of significance.

† "Other" includes all shifts not included under "day" or "night" shifts.

Factors Influencing Employee Morale

Group	Hypothesis for Independence	
	Accepted	Rejected*
Absences		
0 v. 1–4		.001
0 v. 10+	X	
0 v. 5–9	X	
5–9 v. 1–4		.05
1–4 v. 10+	X	
5–9 v. 10+	X	
Times Tardy		
0 v. 1–4		.001
0 v. 5–9	X	
0 v. 10+	X	
1–4 v. 5–9	X	
1–4 v. 10+	X	
5–9 v. 10+	X	
Class of Occupation		
Clerical v. Sales	X	
Clerical v. Semiskilled	X	
Clerical v. Craftsman	X	
Clerical v. Service	X	
Clerical v. Laborer	X	
Professional v. Clerical		.05
Sales v. Semiskilled	X	
Sales v. Craftsman	X	
Sales v. Service	X	
Sales v. Laborer	X	
Sales v. Professional	X	
Semiskilled v. Craftsman	X	
Service v. Semiskilled		.02
Semiskilled v. Laborer	X	
Professional v. Semiskilled		.01
Service v. Craftsman		.05
Craftsman v. Laborer		.02
Professional v. Craftsman		.02
Service v. Laborer		.001
Service v. Professional	X	
Professional v. Laborer		.001

* Figures shown indicate the level of significance.

The figures above indicate the level of significance. In comparisons of age, education, length of service, length of time on the job, shift, take-home pay, accidents, absences, times tardy, and class of occupation, the groups listed first in the rejected column had the higher proportion of favorable scores.

Problem: Assume that you are responsible for interpreting these results to a group of general managers. Write your interpretive statement.

SHORT CASE PROBLEM 25.4

Use of Lie Detector

The Meterall Company found itself facing a serious problem of theft. In the electronics industry, many of the employees are ham operators. Others are inveterate do-it-yourself craftsmen and home experimenters. Small parts, some of them already outmoded and unusable in current production, may appear to such employees as of little value to the employer but handy in their home workshops. The firm has estimated that it is losing $50,000 worth of material through theft each year.

In Department 411, this objectionable practice seemed to be completely out of control. The supervisor suspected Black, an employee of 3½ years. He asked Black whether he was taking parts home. Black said he was not. Three of Black's fellow workers, however, voluntarily reported to the supervisor that they had seen Black collecting parts just before leaving the shop. The supervisor told Black of these allegations. He again asked whether Black had removed material from the property. When Black denied having done so, the supervisor asked him to step into the plant security office and take a lie detector test. Black refused and the supervisor discharged him for his refusal.

Black filed a grievance, claiming improper discharge. After several weeks in which it was processed through four stages of the grievance procedure without satisfactory disposition, the union announced it would take the grievance to arbitration on the issue: Can an employee be discharged for refusal to take a lie detector test under these circumstances?

A week later, in a supervisory conference, several foremen suggested that the firm should make a study of practice elsewhere and present the arbitrator with results to prove that such practice is both reasonable and established.

Problem: Assume that you have the assignment to undertake such a study. Outline the steps you would take and prepare a proposal for approval by your colleagues in management.

26. The Industrial Relations Audit

President Folsum: Just as your life insurance company demands a physical examination before it will issue a policy, our examining board insists on a thorough audit of a firm's management before we advance funds for its use. We need to be reassured that our clients are enjoying healthy management before we entrust them with our resources. We need much more than a financial audit to be reassured that the balance sheet and the profit and loss statement are accurate. We need, perhaps more than anything else, to find out whether management's relationships with those who work in the organization—past, present and prospective—are strong and healthy.

Stockholder: Yes, Mr. President, that is fine. But how can anyone tell?

How effective and satisfactory are employment relationships in Sears Roebuck or International Business Machines or the Crosby Light and Power Company? Are these firms healthy in their relationships among managers and employees? Are they likely to be successful in the ends they seek to attain, because the people who make up the organization are determined to achieve organizational success? Are they firms that investors should bet on and invest in because their people are maximizing contributions of effort and energy and ideas? How can anyone tell?

One major assignment to managers requires that they discover and know —whether or not they tell—about the general health of the organizations they lead. One principal managerial function is that of *control*. Control is the function of maintaining awareness and appraisal with respect to the effectiveness of the organization and its parts in accomplishing assigned missions.

As such a definition suggests, *managerial control combines checks and measurements*. Checking is somewhat similar to the use of "go-no-go" gauges in the machine or tool shop. The manager checks to see whether programs exist and missions are accomplished. In the measurement process, control applies yardsticks to determine how well assigned functions are being performed. Perhaps, for example, policy proposes to maintain a retraining program for workers displaced by modified equipment. Responsibility for such a program has been assigned to the training division. Managers, exercising the control function, check to see whether such a program is in effect. If it is, a further extension of control may seek evidence of its effectiveness.

Managers use a variety of means and measures in control. *Reports* are perhaps the most obvious and frequent. An established reporting system brings information on a daily, weekly, or monthly basis. Thus to facilitate controls in industrial relations programs, managers are regularly informed of quits, numbers of candidates interviewed and hired, grievances filed, arbitrations won and lost, and other similar indexes. Such reports may be compared with earlier experience or with that of other firms.

Managers may lean heavily on *staff divisions* for assistance in maintaining control. The reviewing function, it will be recalled, is a major part of the assignment to such divisions.

Audits are important control devices. To provide frequent checks on the use of financial and other material resources of the organization, managers use the financial or accounting audit. For broader appraisals, many firms provide a periodic check in the form of a *management* or *administrative audit*. To check on the organization's performance in its application of human resources, a similar tool—the *industrial relations audit*—is now widely used.

Within the individual firm or agency, the industrial relations or personnel audit is the thinking manager's answer to the question: How are we doing in our management of people? It is, in a sense, management's rear-view mirror with respect to employment relationships.

Formal audits of industrial relations have achieved wide and growing acceptance. Without any legal requirement that they conduct such an audit —a financial audit may be required—large numbers of firms report that they regularly audit their entire industrial relations activities.

This final chapter considers policy and practice in these personnel and industrial relations audits. The first of the following sections is concerned with the intentions of firms that lead them to the auditing of employment relationships. Section 2 describes the usual practice in conducting audits and using the information and understanding they provide.

1.0 POLICY ON AUDITING INDUSTRIAL RELATIONS

Like other audits, the industrial relations audit provides an *opportunity to be heard*. It offers a chance to tell or show what is being attempted and accomplished in the broad expanse of manpower management. It asks and listens for answers to questions about how effectively current practices and programs are carrying out the intentions identified in general and specific policies.

The audit is an investigative, analytical, comparative process. It not only listens but looks for and discovers answers. It undertakes a systematic search. It investigates formally and in depth, as contrasted with day-to-day, informal impressions.

The industrial relations audit is much more than a survey of employee morale, with which it is sometimes confused. Attitudes and morale represent only a portion of the total of evidence to be considered. They are somewhat unique, however, for morale may be in itself an objective of policy. At the same time, its appraisal can suggest the success or failure of other programs.[1]

Auditing industrial relations assumes that a valuation or score can be placed on managerial effectiveness in managing people. It assumes that appropriate policy and programs can pay off, with evidence that can be identified and evaluated.

1.1 Changing viewpoints. These assumptions have not always enjoyed wide acceptance. In earlier periods, some line and staff managers opposed attempts at formal appraisals of manpower management. They argued that the essence of success in industrial relations is maintenance of an intangible tone and atmosphere in employment. They resented efforts to establish criteria and measures for assessing the value of thought and energy devoted to employment relationships. They particularly objected to the assessment of dollar values on staff contributions. They insisted that the most important accomplishments in the management of people defy evaluation and measurement. Early textbook suggestions that programs could benefit from regular audits were frequently challenged. Many managers, including those in charge of personnel programs, argued that the contributions of their part in management must be accepted on faith.

Current attitudes toward audits of industrial relations are quite different. The sharp change became apparent in the early 1950's. Drought, Payne, and Kaltenborn are among those who advanced specific proposals of yardsticks to be applied in such evaluations.[2] The University of Minnesota Industrial

---

[1] The industrial relations audit should not be confused with the *personnel inventory*—as it sometimes is. The latter is a cataloguing and appraisal of the skills, talents, and competence of manpower resources.

[2] Neal E. Drought, "Techniques of Measuring Personnel Effectiveness," *Personnel*, Series No. 111, New York: American Management Association, 1947; Bruce Payne, "Evaluating the Personnel Department," *Personnel Journal*, Vol. 29, No. 9, February, 1951, pp. 343–45; Howard S. Kaltenborn, "Checking the Essentials of Good Industrial Relations," *Report No. 90*, California Personnel Management Association, 1950.

Relations Center's *Triple Audit of Industrial Relations* appeared in 1951.[3] A report of its application to manufacturing firms was released in 1954.[4] Meanwhile, Saltonstall noted, in 1952, "Now that the personnel field has reached a degree of maturity, there are indications that management wants answers to the question: "How good a personnel job are we doing?"[5] He considered the problem of attaching dollar values to personnel functions and proposed a detailed reporting form, including measurable indicators that could be compared from firm to firm.

In 1956, Merrihue described an *Employee Relations Index* developed by General Electric and designed to "measure the extent to which groups of employees accept, and perform in accordance with, the objectives and policies of the company." For hourly workers, ERI combined measures of absences, separations, visits to the dispensary, suggestions, disciplinary suspensions, grievances, work stoppages, and participation in the insurance plan.[6]

Current policy relates the quality of manpower management to several indicators of organization effectiveness. Policy notes the extent to which management has been successful in encouraging the personal identification of employees with the organization and their acceptance of organizational objectives. It checks on interpretations and acceptance of general and specific policy. It notes indicators of the quality of leadership, of motivation in work, the effectiveness of supervision, and the continuing growth and development of individual employees and managers. It considers the extent to which (1) policy expresses acceptable theory and (2) practice is appropriate to such policy and theory.[7]

Changing attitudes toward auditing suggest that staff members in industrial relations have become more self-confident about their leadership, skill, and special competence. They are less worried about evaluation, because they conclude that audits will demonstrate the value of their contributions. At the same time, their changing attitudes may indicate recognition that manpower management is a responsibility of all managers; it is not simply what the staff division undertakes or accomplishes. They regard the audit as a means of gaining insights that can become the basis for im-

[3] As *Bulletin 11* of the Industrial Relations Center.
[4] As *Bulletin 13*, "Auditing Your Manpower Management."
[5] Robert Saltonstall, "Evaluating Personnel Administration," *Harvard Business Review*, Vol. 30, No. 6, November-December, 1952, pp. 93–104.
[6] For more on ERI, see Willard V. Merrihue, "General Electric's Employee Relations Index," in "Personnel Practice and Policy: The Changing Picture," *Personnel Series Number 168*, New York: American Management Association, 1956, pp. 41–51.
[7] For an excellent statement, see Rensis Likert, "Measuring Organizational Performance," *Harvard Business Review*, Vol. 36, No. 2, March-April, 1958, pp. 41–50; see also "Evaluating a P-IR Program," Bureau of National Affairs *Personnel Policies Forum, Survey No. 23*. February, 1954; Seward H. French, "Measuring Progress toward Industrial Relations Objectives," *Personnel*, Vol. 30, No. 5, March, 1954, pp. 338–47; Thomas A. Mahoney, Wallace Dohman, and Thomas Jerdee, "Applying Yardsticks to Management," *Personnel*, Vol. 33, No. 6, May, 1957, pp. 556–62; "Manpower Yardsticks," *Factory Management and Maintenance*, Vol. 115, No. 9, September, 1957, pp. 109–19; Albert H. Aaronson, "Evaluation of Personnel Operations," *Personnel Administration*, Vol. 21, No. 3, May-June, 1958, pp. 28–34.

provement throughout all management rather than a search for weaknesses in staff performance.

Several concomitant changes may have influenced the trend toward formal industrial relations audits. Some of them have been mentioned in earlier chapters. Among the most important are the following:

1. *Changing managerial philosophy and theory,* particularly that which has come to regard employee participation and identification as having a powerful influence in incentivation and on the success of working organizations.

2. *The changing role of government,* with growing intervention designed to police manpower management and to protect the interests of employees, to increase their economic security and to assure full employment.

3. *Expansion of unions* and of bilateral determination of employment policy, with frequent criticisms of managerial competence in industrial relations.

4. *Rapidly rising wages,* with higher labor costs and greater opportunities for competitive advantage in the management of people.

5. *The changing mixture of skills,* with growing proportions of technical and professional workers, who present more difficult managerial problems and who are more articulate in their criticisms of management.

6. *Increasing expenditures for industrial relations staff divisions,* with higher personnel ratios and higher salaries for industrial relations specialists.

7. *More rigorous international competition,* resulting from the widening circle of industrialization, which has destroyed much of the earlier advantage enjoyed by American firms.

8. *International criticisms* of American management, with charges that it has given inadequate consideration to the individual goals and aspirations of workers and claims of superior work-motivation for participants in socialized economies.

1.2   Initiative in auditing. The industrial relations staff division has a continuing responsibility to review policy, program, and detailed practice in employment relationships. The formal, periodic audit has often been regarded as a check on this specialized staff division. Nevertheless, industrial relations divisions frequently take the initiative in proposing periodic audits. They recognize the opportunity, in such an audit, to generate wide understanding of both policy and practice in manpower management. They hope that an audit will highlight problems in this area and that it may create awareness of the need for line cooperation with staff. The audit can focus attention, both on what is being done and what needs to be done. It gives special attention to shortcomings in theory and policy as well as in technical performance. It may, therefore, assist the staff in convincing higher echelons of the need for improved policy and practice. It can emphasize the responsibilities of line as well as staff and thus create an atmosphere conducive to improved line-staff cooperation.

Decisions to audit may originate outside the staff, for example, at the

---

executive level or in the Board of Directors. Not infrequently, proposals from such sources represent implicit criticisms or suspicions that current manpower management is not what it should be. Some special audits are proposed as means of reducing costs of industrial relations management. Regular periodic audits, however, imply no hypercritical attitude toward staff or line.

1.3 Internal or external audit. Who shall conduct the audit? Some firms and agencies prefer an *internal audit,* undertaken by regular staff members as an expansion of their reviewing activities. Others propose an *external audit,* in which current policy and practice are reviewed and evaluated by auditors specially employed for this purpose. In what is probably the most common practice, outside auditors work with resident staff members.

Perhaps the strongest arguments for internal audits are the practical considerations that competent independent auditors are scarce and that their services are expensive. Also, internal audits may be an assigned responsibility of the *central* or *corporate* industrial relations divisions in large organizations. That staff division may regularly audit the activities of individual plants, primarily to discover how closely they are following corporate policy and prescribed practice. These evaluations check, for example, on practice in promotions, training, recruitment, and the use of overtime. They may limit their evaluation to the coverage of the standard practice manual.

Values to be gained from an external audit are impressive. Competent auditors from outside bring a fresh point of view with which to appraise current policy and practice. They can contribute valuable suggestions from their experience in other organizations. They are under no obligation to defend what has been or is being done or to favor certain policies or activities. They can assure concentrated attention to the audit. Resident staff members, on the other hand, may intend to conduct the audit but put it off because of the pressures of other duties.

Perhaps the ideal arrangement is that in which independent auditors are brought in to direct and work with resident staff members in the audit.

1.4 Timing. Firms that prefer internal audits frequently report that they maintain a *continuing audit.* They propose to evaluate various functional areas of manpower management or individual plants or divisions, one after another. This policy is sharply distinguished from that which proposes *periodic audits,* generally annual, as special, distinct events. Consistently scheduled, periodic appraisals offer distinct advantages; they permit useful time-to-time comparisons and they establish the audit as expressing a clear policy that intends regular systematic appraisals.

1.5 Functional coverage. Policy determines the range of activities to be covered. Common intentions propose to evaluate much more than the activities of the staff division. Rather, the audit considers policy and practice as developed and directed by both the staff division and line managers and supervisors throughout the organization. A comprehensive audit includes every phase of manpower management, with special attention to each of the major functional areas outlined in preceding chapters.

1.6 Depth. Audits may evaluate at various levels; they may be superficial or intensive and probing. Simpler, more superficial audits generally limit their evaluations to such apparent *results* or *effects* of manpower management as labor turnover, absenteeism, tardiness, selection ratios, promotions, transfers, grievances, and over-all costs of the staff division. Indicators considered in *results audits* are assumed to represent effects of managerial policy and practice. Sound management, for example, is expected to restrict labor turnover within what are regarded as normal limits. Job training, to take another example, is evaluated in terms of the time and expense required to bring new trainees up to levels of standard job performance. Some auditors and managers regard these results as the most significant measures of manpower management. The test of the program, in this view, is in the day-to-day performance of the organization and its members.

Results audits, however, may be superficial, because the meaning of such indicators is taken for granted. High absentee rates, for example, may result from a variety of causes. Policy and practice in management may have limited influence. Again, turnover may be low because unemployment is high and employees have fewer opportunities to go elsewhere. Training times may be short because public educational programs are providing an improved foundation for in-firm supplements. Results may be satisfactory in spite of rather than because of existing programs.

Perhaps the most frequent audits are *procedural audits;* they check on each division and department to see that established procedure is being observed. The auditor's handbook, in this type of appraisal, is the *standard practice manual.* Like the traveling financial auditor, his personnel counterpart compares actual with prescribed procedure in estimating manpower requirements, developing job specifications, recruitment and selection, and on throughout the entire range of manpower management.

Policy in auditing may recognize the possibility of evaluation at several levels rather than at the single level of results. As noted in Chapter 1 and illustrated in Figure 1.1, manpower management may be regarded as having two significant dimensions. One of them involves the scope or functional range of activities—staffing, labor relations, training and development, and others. The other dimension is concerned with depth in management. On the surface, industrial relations concern is focused on *problems* and on what *appear to be results* of various programs. Management, however, involves much more than merely recognizing such problems and putting out fires. It creates and develops *programs* and the various *practices* that are combined in them. Beneath such programs are *policies*—the intentions and courses selected by policy makers as the road map and plan for operations, the reason for such programs as are undertaken. Underlying these policies is the *philosophy,* the values and preferences and ideals and ideas that appear to justify selected policies. These relationships have been discussed in Chapter 4, where it was also noted that *theories* define transitions or bridges from philosophy to policy and from policy to programs, practices, and problems.

The audit may probe much deeper than *results;* it may appraise *programs, policies, philosophy,* and *theory.* Policy on the depth of the audit must determine which of these levels will be regarded. The audit may be directed at any or all of the following levels:

1. *Results,* including both accomplishments and problems regarded as effects of current management.
2. *Programs,* including the detailed practices and procedures of which they are composed.
3. *Policies,* both explicit and implicit.
4. The *philosophy* of management, its priorities in values, goals, and objectives.
5. *Theory,* the assumed relationships and plausible explanations that explain and relate philosophies, policies, practices, and continuing problems.

1.7 Built-in auditing. Programs may be undertaken and practices adopted for a variety of reasons. Sometimes these reasons are not stated or recorded; the policy they are to implement is not explicit. Auditors encounter difficulty in evaluating programs because their purposes are obscure. With the growth of auditing, this problem has attracted increasing attention. Modern policy frequently requires that checks and tests be built into new programs, thus establishing yardsticks for future audits. New programs are related to the policy they are to implement. Expected results are spelled out in advance so that they can be compared with actual experience. Reporting procedures are specified to insure adequate information for subsequent evaluations.

2.0 PRACTICE IN AUDITING

Policy decisions with respect to coverage and depth are preliminary to the auditing procedure. Within the limitations thus defined, most audits usually begin with an appraisal of the *organizational relationships* affecting manpower management, including those of line and staff; the *qualifications* of industrial relations staff members; and the adequacy of *financial support* for various programs. They then apply a variety of *standards* or *yardsticks,* their range depending on the depth of the audit. They examine personnel records and reports. They analyze and compare and prepare an *audit report,* perhaps including recommendations for change.[8]

As noted, coverage may be intentionally restricted, particularly in internal audits, in which the work is to be done by the members of the staff division.

[8] For greater detail with respect to these practices, see Dale Yoder, H. G. Heneman, Jr., John G. Turnbull, and C. Harold Stone, "Employment Relations Audits," *Handbook of Personnel Management and Labor Relations,* New York: McGraw-Hill Book Company, Inc., 1958, sec. 24; "Evaluating Your Personnel Management," *Personnel Management Series No. 6,* United States Civil Service Commission, 1954.

For inclusive audits, coverage is as broad as the functions of manpower management and may be divided in a manner not unlike the sectional and chapter divisions of this book. Major divisions usually include:

1. Organizational relationships and policy determination.
2. Staffing, including job analysis, recruitment, selection, induction, orientation, promotion, transfer.
3. Labor relations, if employees bargain collectively.
4. Training and development.
5. Wage and salary administration.
6. Employee benefits and their administration.
7. Employee morale, internal communications, discipline, grievances.
8. Research.

This functional approach is subject to numerous variations, but such an outline suggests major areas of evaluation.[9]

2.1 Organizational relationships. At some point in every audit, attention is directed to the adequacy of organizational relationships. Questions are raised as to the number and qualifications of personnel in the industrial relations staff. Is the personnel ratio within appropriate limits? As noted, the average ratio (the number of specialized staff members per hundred employees served by that staff) is approximately 0.75. Auditors recognize that such a ratio may be adequate in older established organizations but quite inadequate in new establishments with unusual responsibilities for developing job descriptions, recruiting, orienting, and training. The average ratio, also, is based on reports from many firms that maintain limited programs; they may have no formal training or no labor relations, for example.

Questions are raised about relationships between the staff division and other managers. Are the latter performing their appropriate functions in carrying out various programs? It is apparent that most of the actual management of people in working organizations is performed by managers outside the industrial relations division. What is the relationship of the staff division to top management? What part does it play in developing policy with respect to employment relationships? It should be noted that these are not essentially questions of authority; rather they seek to discover how the organization works with and utilizes the staff group.[10]

[9] For example, the checklist of policy in *The Employee Handbook* (Los Angeles: Merchants and Manufacturers Association, 1955) lists wages and hours, employee benefits, record keeping, promotions, discipline, employee placement, health and safety, employee problems, training and employee activities. The annual audit form for a large manufacturing company includes recruitment, screening and selection, interviewing, testing, reference checks, medical examinations, skill file, referrals, orientation, promotions and upgrading, reassignments of work force, terminations and discharges, job evaluation, salary evaluation, management-union relations, supervisory conferences, employee relations, employee services and facilities, plant rules and discipline, bulletin boards, health and safety, community relations, and personnel department.

[10] See on these points Bernard Rifkind, Raymond A. Conner, and Seymour W. Chad, "Applying Work Measurement to Personnel Administration," *Public Administration Review*, Vol. 17, No. 1, Winter, 1957, pp. 14–19; Dalton E. McFarland, "The Score

While analysis of relationships between line managers and those of the industrial relations staff is prominent in audits, more sophisticated and thorough appraisals regard these as only one part of the more important total. Such audits are concerned about the propriety and effectiveness of the whole organizational structure and the relationships it creates. They ask whether, on the whole, managers are using the tool of organization skillfully. How well does the organization meet recognized requirements in terms of delegation and span of control? Does it provide rational systems of authority, status and communications? To what extent has informal organization supplemented or supplanted the formal structure?

2.2 Standards and yardsticks. Audits attempt to measure and evaluate results, programs, policies, and general philosophy to a degree determined by preliminary decisions on their depth. Three steps are essential in that process. The audit must (1) identify indicators or criteria of success or quality, (2) discover sources of reliable information with respect to these criteria, and (3) apply yardsticks or measures with which to compare these indicators with norms or other standards. Each of these steps creates problems for which only partial solutions are now available. As a result, both the usual criteria and the yardsticks that are used in measurement must be recognized as crude rather than refined, with resulting errors and uncertainties in the appraisal process.

Some of the gauges employed in the audit are essentially arbitrary. They may, for example, regard the presence of certain programs as a desirable indication and their absence as a deficiency. Failure to provide a formal industrial relations staff division may be regarded as a serious shortcoming, as may the absence of written policy on manpower management. The program that does not include formal job descriptions, job evaluation, exit interviews, career planning, consultative supervision, and some form of morale survey may be given demerits for each of these omissions.

Other criteria may be quantitative, appraised in terms of extent and degree. Labor turnover, rates of absenteeism and tardiness, numbers of grievances, and proportions settled in first and second stages of the grievance procedure are of this type, as are accident frequency rates, measures of employment stability, costs of various programs, and measures of the readability of internal written communications.

Experienced auditors refer to reported average costs to judge a firm's expenditures for the industrial relations division. They can make more dependable judgments if the staff division maintains a *functional budget,* indicating rather precisely what use is made of funds.[11] Such a budget allocates funds

on the Industrial Relations Function," *Personnel,* Vol. 35, No. 4, January-February, 1959, pp. 42–51; Stephen J. Carroll, Jr., "Measuring the Work of a Personnel Department," *Personnel,* Vol. 37, No. 4, July-August, 1960, pp. 49–56.

[11] See Dale Yoder and Roberta J. Nelson, "Industrial Relations Budgets: Yardsticks for 1959" *Personnel,* Vol. 36, No. 4, July-August, 1959; Robert H. Willey, "Quality Control of Personnel Management," *Personnel Administration,* Vol. 18, No.

to major activities rather than simply to such common accounting items as salaries, travel, entertainment, and overhead. The functional budget shows the purposes for which funds are to be expended, in terms of such items as departmental administration, recruiting, promotions and transfers, labor relations, counseling, managing benefits and services, and other similar activities.

Table 26.1 outlines the most commonly used qualitative and quantitative indicators of effectiveness, classified by major function. Such symptoms of the quality of manpower management, it should be clear, provide only a superficial impression. That they are the most commonly considered evidence does not mean that they are particularly dependable. To provide reliable evaluations, better yardsticks must be developed.

The discovery of additional criteria of *healthy manpower management* and the development of useful instruments for measuring the quality of managerial activity in industrial relations represents a major challenge to the entire management profession. In the current state of the art, we may be able to tell a sick firm from one that is reasonably healthy, but we have yet to develop a standard or widely recognized syndrome of superior industrial relations health and the measurement tools with which to recognize this condition.

In part, improved measures can be provided by standardizing practice, so that rates and costs, for example, have common meaning. This step can be taken by local, regional, and national professional associations. They can, and some of them have, undertaken studies designed to increase uniformity in calculating and reporting refined rates of absenteeism, labor turnover, and tardiness. They have worked toward uniformity in the measurement of costs for staff activities, training programs and fringe benefits. Universities can also participate, as illustrated by current practice in calculating personnel ratios and standard budgeting for industrial relations activities.[12]

Research has played an important role in improving yardsticks and discovering additional measures. Research can provide tests of the syndromes of effects and results believed to be associated with superior management of human resources. The value and dependability of industrial relations audits can be increased as research combines experiment and experience to identify improved techniques for the measurement of results and the influence of programs. Research is the logical tool for testing theories on which policies are based and programs are designed or selected.

2.3   Tests of Policies. Most sophisticated practice in auditing industrial relations gives careful attention to policies. In terms of the chart shown in Chapter 1 as Figure 1.1, an audit moves in both directions from the column of policies—toward practices, results, and problems and also toward the

6, November, 1955; "Building a Functional Personnel Budget," *Management Review,* Vol. 42, No. 9, September, 1953, pp. 508ff.

[12] See Theodore Vander Noot et al., "Comparability of Absence Rates," *Personnel Journal,* Vol. 36, No. 10, March, 1958, pp. 380–82; and the periodic reports on personnel ratios and industrial relations budgets published in *Personnel.*

Table 26.1 Qualitative and Quantitative Indicators for Industrial Relations Audits

Major Function	Qualitative Indicators	Scales or Measures
1. Policy determination, organization, and administration	Staff status for IR Written manpower policy Standard policy manual Functional budget for IR	Scalar level of IR Division Personnel ratio Functional ratios Administrative costs
2. Labor Relations: negotiation and contract administration	Labor-management committees Contract interpretations No-strike clause Management security clause	Work stoppages Time lost in stoppages Grievances Grievance settlements, by level Arbitrations Favorable arbitration decisions Costs
3. Staffing: job analysis, recruiting selection, orientation, induction promotions, transfers, etc.	Personnel inventory Replacement tables Organization planning Job descriptions and specifications Source evaluation Exit interviews Induction program	Turnover rates Selection ratios Costs Recruitment times
4. Training and Development	Training programs Supervisory and management development programs Systematic promotions Career planning Formal appraisals	Time taken in training Costs, by type Apprentice ratios
5. Incentivating: wage and salary administration, employee benefits, morale, communications	Job evaluation program Wage and salary surveys House organ Employee handbook Accident and health programs	Wage and salary differentials Benefit range and costs Unemployment insurance costs Measured morale Measured communications Absenteeism rates Suggestion ratios Readability of communications
6. Audit and Review	Formal periodic audit External audit Monthly personnel report Standard personnel records	
7. Research	Formal personnel research unit Publication of research reports Research qualified staff members	Amounts budgeted for personnel research Publications

philosophy of policy-makers. Auditors begin by noting written statements of policy and the absence or limitations of policy with respect to major industrial relations activities. The "Employee Relations Check List" described in *American Business*,[13] for example, begins by questioning the presence or absence of policy and the adequacy of existing policy.

Major tests to be applied to policies have been discussed in some detail in Section 4 of Chapter 8. Policy should be clearly stated. It should be consistent with public policy. It must be rational in terms of the best, i.e., the most thoroughly tested, theory. Specific, functional policy—in staffing, labor relations or development, for example—should be consistent with general manpower policy. General or basic manpower policy should be uniform throughout the organization. Policy must be effectively communicated.

The most difficult checks and those that require greatest competence on the part of auditors involve comparisons of policy with the philosophy of policy makers and the evaluation of policies in terms of the theories they express. This is a level of auditing that separates the men from the boys. It requires a penetrating analysis of the value systems of policy makers that can disclose rather precisely how they think and feel about major goals and objectives in employment relationships. Is a policy statement that frequently mentions the dignity of individuals and toil realistic in terms of managerial viewpoints toward the people that make up the organization? Does managerial philosophy put human values first? Does it regard wide participation in employment decisions as desirable in employment? Does management actually favor the elimination of discrimination, as suggested by written policy? Answers require far more than a superficial check of exit interviews. Many audits omit this type of evaluation.

These are important and, at the same time, difficult questions. Formal policy statements may declare the intention to maintain a high level of two-way communication throughout the organization, but managers may have no real intention of listening to what they regard as the uninformed and half-baked comments of rank-and-file employees. Stated policy may propose frequent surveys of employee morale, but managers may be quite unwilling to consider criticisms or to make changes on the basis of critical employee reactions.

Appraising the soundness of theory implicit in policy also requires a high level of competence and sophistication. The test to be applied is whether theory has achieved acceptance among those most competent to evaluate it. Is policy based on a theory of work that gives financial compensation major influence? Is such a theory justified for the types of people that make up the organization? Does policy assume, for example, that major incentivation of scientists and engineers is primarily a matter of dollar salary levels? Or does it recognize the importance of recognition and participation for such workers? Does promotion policy assume that all employees want to become

[13] See "Employee Relations Check List," *American Business*, Vol. 29, No. 3, March, 1959, p. 41.

supervisors and managers? Does policy propose to cement the bonds of the organization by careful consideration of individual reactions and attitudes? Does policy express modern or outmoded, discarded theory, possibly appropriate in earlier periods?

2.4   Tests of programs and practice. Auditors may next note the programs and practices designed to implement policies, looking for indications of the degree to which intended results have been attained. Failures to achieve intended results are recognized as continuing problems.

The primary tests of each program and practice are their propriety and effectiveness in implementing policy. Such yardsticks require an understanding of theory as well as careful consideration of results and the identification of continuing problems. Auditors may conclude that some programs simply cannot be expected to achieve the intentions in policy. They may find programs unsatisfactory regardless of results, which may be attributable to other conditions. Audits lean heavily on crude indicators of results—for example, labor turnover rates, measures of time taken in training, and the costs of various programs. At the same time, however, they consider the extent to which programs include what has come to be recognized as *standard practice*. Experience appears to have demonstrated the superiority of these techniques in carrying out various policies and meeting particular problems. Thus, for example, a *manual* system of job evaluation is regarded as standard practice in many mechanical operations, and a *vestibule school* is normally prescribed where large numbers of inexperienced, new employees must be given job training.

A wide range of *standard practices* has been described in earlier chapters. In staffing, for example, standard practice provides central employment offices, a personnel inventory, scouting for college and high school graduates, formal evaluations of sources, structured interviews and standard tests, physical examinations, and an induction program. For promotions, standard practice requires regular *periodic reviews* for all employees, the forecasting of supervisory and managerial personnel requirements, and the planning of careers. Similar standard practice can be identified for each of the other major functional areas.

2.5   Records and reports. Audits lean heavily on records and reports, which are the source of much of the information on which evaluation is based. On the other hand, reports are made and records are maintained for many purposes other than the audit. As a result, records may include a good deal of information that is not helpful in an audit, and they may not provide needed information on many points. In organizations that have gained experience with audits, some records are developed specifically to meet auditing requirements and new programs are accompanied by reporting designed to build in a basis for auditing.

In the usual practice, *reports* emphasize the purpose of providing timely, current information. They outline and describe what has happened or is happening, frequently including both qualitative and quantitative information. *Records,* in distinction, emphasize the preservation of information. They contemplate future use. They may be compiled from reports. Regular reports may be filed and thus become a part of the records of an organization.

Auditors find both reports and records helpful if not essential in their evaluation. Certainly, they will examine the weekly, monthly, and annual reports prepared by many industrial relations divisions and directed to top management. In addition, they may use *special reports* describing the operation and accomplishments of new programs and experiments.

Periodic reports—weekly, monthly, and perhaps annual—include many statistical series, of which data on employment, recruitment, accidents, illness, benefits, transfers, and promotions are illustrative. In addition, they may include general observations and comments on developments regarded as of special significance in manpower management. Table 26.2 has been prepared from a collection of periodic reports to suggest the range of data regularly included in them.

Table 26.2   Composite Industrial Relations Periodic Report

A. Preliminary Summary and Overview
   Attention directed to:
      Trends
      New developments
      Notable changes
      Special projects
      Unusual accomplishments
      New problems
   Designed to:
      Catch interest
      Encourage detailed study
      Enlist co-operation
      Focus attention
B. Employment
   1. *Numbers,* beginning and/or end of period:
      By departments
      By permanent or temporary
      By sex
      By hourly rated or salaried
   2. *Labor turnover*—separations and accessions:
      By department and/or plant
      By types of separations
      By quits, layoffs, discharges
      By avoidable vs. unavoidable
      By reasons (marriage, home duties, pregnancy, moving, military service, pensioned, death)
      Comparisons with local and national rates for the industry
   3. *Unfilled requisitions:*
      By department
      By job
C. Job Analysis, Recruiting, and Selection
   1. *Jobs analyzed or reviewed:*
      By plant or department
   2. *Applications for employment:*
      By skill class
      By sex
      By source

TABLE 26.2 (Continued)

   3. *Employment interviews*
   4. *Applicants tested*
   5. *References questioned*
   6. *Costs,* per interview (in-plant and outside) per candidate tested
D. Training
   1. *Enrollments,* by training program
       New trainees, by program
       Numbers finishing, by program
   2. *Turnover*—separations of former trainees
   3. *Costs of training,* total and per capita
       By program
E. Promotion, Transfer, and Rating
   1. *Promotions,* by department
   2. *Transfers,* by department and cause
   3. *Numbers rated,* by department
F. Labor Relations
   1. *New agreements*—in negotiation, negotiated
   2. *Amendments* negotiated
   3. *Arbitrations*—in process or concluded, by results
   4. *Grievances*—settled and in process
       By subject
       By stage in which settled
       By nature of settlement
G. Medical, Health, and Safety
   1. *Deaths* among employees
   2. *Retirements*
   3. *Physical examinations*
   4. *Medical treatment,* numbers of employees, calls
   5. *Surgical cases,* by type
   6. *Hospital calls on employees*
   7. *Home nursing visits*
   8. *Illness,* numbers of cases by department:
       By type
       By department
       By time lost
   9. *Accidents,* in plant:
       By department
       By cause
       By frequency and severity rates (possibly compared with national rates)
   10. *Workmen's Compensation,* number of cases:
       By department
       By new and recurrent cases
       By amounts of benefits
       By costs
H. Other Employee Services
   1. *Benefit plan,* membership
   2. *Benefits paid:*
       By numbers of employees
       By type (death, disability, hospitalization, surgical, maternity)
       By amounts paid
   3. *Personal loans,* numbers and amounts
   4. *Credit union:*
       Applications received
       Applications approved and disapproved
       Loans extended, numbers and amounts
   5. *Life insurance:*
       Participation (by department)
       Amount in force
       Claims

TABLE 26.2 (Continued)

6. *Pensions*—normal retirements, optional retirements, disability retirements, vested cases, benefits to survivors
7. *House organ*—circulation, costs
8. *Suggestions*—numbers received, disposition, awards
9. *Cafeteria*—meals served, dollar sales, cost, subsidy
10. *Recreation activities*—types, participation, and costs
11. *Employee store*—number of sales, dollar volume
I. Wage and Salary Administration
   1. *Rates reviewed* and *rates changed:*
      By numbers affected
      By type—merit increase, revaluation
   2. *Job evaluation*—by department or type of job
   3. *Overtime*—total hours, departments, number of employees affected, total costs
   4. *Earnings,* average weekly, by department:
      Salaried and hourly rated
      Proportions in each wage and salary class and step
   5. *Call-in* and *call-back pay,* by department with cost
   6. *Severance pay*—numbers receiving, by department total cost
   7. *Unemployment claims* filed—amounts paid
   8. *Stock purchase*—numbers. of employees, dollar amounts
J. Records and reports
   1. *Special reports* released
   2. *Personnel actions* recorded
K. Research
   1. *Projects completed*
   2. *Progress report* on continuing projects
   3. *New projects* planned or undertaken
L. Staff Administration
   1. *Staff assignments,* by name
   2. *Expenditures* for staff activities:
      By controllable vs. non-controllable
      By major activities

In addition to reports on industrial relations programs, firms and agencies maintain files of *personnel records*—in part, summaries and compilations of earlier reports and, in part, personal records with respect to the individuals who make up the organization. For each manager and employee, records detail initial application forms, results of physical examinations, interviewer's notations, test scores, periodic appraisals, transfers and promotions, disciplinary actions, releases and rehirings, wages, salaries, taxes paid, contributions, and other similar items.

Both reports and records are important sources of information for auditors. The adequacy and quality of records as well as their ready availability may be subject to evaluation and comment in the audit.

2.6 Employee reactions and opinions. Current audits tend to place heavy significance on the behavior, reactions, and comments of individual supervisors, managers, and employees. Some behavior is reported in the records—absences, tardiness, disciplinary actions, promotions, transfers, and others. Personnel appraisals may be reported in a form that describes reactions. Quits and releases provide indications of attitudes. Auditors may interview individuals to inquire about their reactions and opinions.

In many audits, a formal attitude or morale survey is included. In that procedure, described in Chapter 23, a systematic investigation discovers employee reactions to current policies and practices. Current practice in auditing may place a good deal of emphasis on such information. If firms propose to develop and maintain high levels of morale, opinions discovered in such a survey provide direct evidence of the degree of success in implementing this policy. In addition, when detailed surveys are maintained, they can provide leads for evaluating numerous other programs.

2.7   **Audit report and recommendations.** In the usual practice, auditors provide a written report of their findings, conclusions, and recommendations. The over-all form and style of these reports shows the influence of older financial audit reports. The summary usually covers most of the items mentioned in this section of the chapter. It notes strengths and weaknesses in established organizational relationships. It cites major policies—both general and specific—and may evaluate their soundness, propriety, and consistency. The larger portion of the report usually dwells on individual programs—selection, training, labor relations, and others. With respect to each of them, it compares policy with practice, results, and persistent problems and suggests explanations of shortcomings.

If audits are maintained on a regular periodic basis, many important comparisons involve references to earlier periods. The audit notes significant changes, both negative and positive.

The audit report is designed primarily to meet the needs of top managers and directors, although many such reports, in whole or in part, may be forwarded to individual departments and divisions for the information of managers, supervisors, and rank-and-file employees.

Summaries and evaluations of factual information represent the most common content of auditor's reports, but they may not be the most valuable contributions. Highly useful are comparisons with the policy, practice, and experience of other firms and agencies. Similarly significant are auditor's opinions with respect to the soundness and propriety of current policies and practice.

Some reports include recommendations. On the other hand, auditors may conclude that findings should speak for themselves, so that recommendations are unnecessary. Auditors may assume that what managers do with the information and evaluation is not for the auditor to determine. Whether or not recommendations are formal, every thorough audit report points toward action.

The value of the audit and the audit report depends largely on the competence of the auditor. If he is well qualified in terms of his experience and knowledge of both theory and practice, he can make a major contribution to the improvement of management. To be most effective, however, requires a high level of personal competence and a strictly professional attitude. With such qualifications, the auditor can exert a persistent influence on the practice of management; managers with whom he deals may find his ideals and attitudes impressive and contagious. For these reasons, the responsibility of the auditor is heavy.

3.0 SUMMARY

Formal audits of industrial relations have become common only since World War II. Their purpose is to provide an inclusive overview of manpower management in the firm or agency. Like the financial audit, they establish a time and place for managers to tell their story, in this case their story with respect to their management of people; they insure a hearing on manpower management. Like the financial audit, they also suggest that the story had better be good; it is to be checked and tested and evaluated. The audit is thus both a hearing and a check-up.

In earlier periods, proposals to evaluate manpower management were frequently regarded as improper and impractical. Opponents of such audits insisted that since management was itself an art, its results were artistic rather than tangible and measurable. Effective management, in this view, was expressed in a tone and atmosphere of employment relationships that defied appraisal.

Current thinking, however, holds that not only can manpower management be appraised and evaluated, it can also be subjected to a variety of tests and measurements *at several levels*. Firms can undertake a *procedural audit,* limited to a check of the extent to which established practice is being followed throughout the organization. They can appraise numerous tangible *results* believed to flow, at least in part, from policies and programs in manpower management. They can probe much deeper and evaluate the manpower *policies* and the *philosophy* and *theories* that underlie, explain, and are assumed to justify current policy and practice.

In current practice, the most common audits are internal, procedural, and frequently superficial. They check on the extent to which practice in managing people conforms to a standard practice manual, with which they may combine an evaluation of the most obvious evidence of satisfactory performance or results. They note a number of conditions believed to be associated with effective manpower management, typified by low labor turnover, success in hiring and retention of employees, and minimum levels of disciplinary problems and grievances. They check on the cooperation of staff and line in carrying out established programs.

More advanced practice in auditing probes much deeper. It not only considers employee reactions and opinions as significant barometers; it also examines the quality and propriety of formal programs, policies, and managerial theory and philosophy.

Auditors face many problems for which only partial solutions are available. Symptoms of health and illness in industrial relations are only partially recognized and understood. Many criteria or indicators are crude. Few precise measurements can be made with existing yardsticks. Additional criteria must be discovered and tested, and improved scales must be developed for the most commonly used indicators. These developments represent a major challenge and opportunity to students and professional practitioners and to professional associations in the industrial relations field.

As the qualifications of auditors and the quality of yardsticks continue to improve, periodic industrial relations audits can become a major means of advancing the general level of performance and the competence of managers in their management of people.

SELECTED SUPPLEMENTARY READINGS

Bellows, Roger M., *Psychology of Personnel in Business and Industry*, chap. 16. Englewood Cliffs, N.J.: Prentice-Hall, Inc., 1961.

Carroll, Stephen J., Jr., "Measuring the Work of a Personnel Department," *Personnel*, Vol. 37, No. 4, pp. 49–56, July-August, 1960. (Available as *Reprint Series: No. 24*, University of Minnesota Industrial Relations Center, 1960.)

"Essentials of A Personnel Program," *Surveys in Personnel Administration, No. 1*, Federated Employers of San Francisco (2 Pine Street), November, 1954.

"Evaluating Your Personnel Management," U.S. Civil Service Commission, *Personnel Management Series No. 6*, Washington, D.C.: Government Printing Office, October, 1954.

Saltonstall, Robert, "Evaluating Personnel Administration," *Harvard Business Review*, Vol. 30, No. 6, pp. 93–104, November-December, 1952.

Torbert, Frances, *Personnel Management in Small Companies*, Institute of Industrial Relations, University of California at Los Angeles, 1959.

SHORT CASE PROBLEM 26.1

The Scratchitoff Double Audit

Scratchitoff is a firm that has grown by leaps and bounds. In 1940, total sales amounted to $345,000. By 1950, the comparable figure was $8,500,000. In 1960, sales totaled $485,000,000, the stock was listed on a national exchange, and the firm was known both at home and abroad for its consistent application of research to production and sales problems. It was third in a list of the most preferred growth stocks. It was tenth in terms of the quantity of scientific publications by employees.

Scratchitoff inaugurated an internal audit of its employee relations in 1955. The Corporate Personnel Office in LaCrosse audited each of the plants, using a systematic procedure developed in the home office.

In 1960, Scratchitoff concluded that it might benefit from an external audit of industrial relations. For that purpose it employed Shakespeare and Associates of Palo Alto, California.

Scratchitoff had moved into electronics with the purchase of a local radio and television station. It saw opportunities to profit from manufacturing in the field and established a transistor and diode subdivision in Altadena, California. The internal audit of that division found it generally healthy but deficient in its administration of wages and salaries. The internal audit report commented favorably on the personnel ratio, close cooperation of line and staff, low labor turnover, excellent records, low absenteeism, and many similar indexes. It found, however, that the Transistor Division was far out of line with respect to wages and salaries. In wage and salary administration, the corporate office had carefully avoided setting dollar ranges or rates. It had, on the other hand, developed a general wage and salary structure. That structure created two major classifications, the one employee and supervisory and the other managerial. For employees and first line supervisors, no job rates were mentioned, because operations vary widely from plant to plant. The only specification established a supervisory rate range 30 per cent above that of employees in each work crew. The structure for managers provided no dollar ranges but required that the median of each range should be at least 25 per cent above that of the next lower classification.

In the Transistor Division, the internal audit discovered that actual payments to employees varied from the stated wages and salaries because of numerous special allowances. One employee had received almost $3,000 in travel allowances to attend meetings of the Physics and Chemistry Societies. Another was given $1,350 to permit him to take his wife to a three-day meeting in London. One employee had received $650 to repay him for clerical expenses involved in writing a paper for one of the professional associations. The total of supplementary payments—in addition to stated salaries—amounted to 12 per cent of the salary budget.

The internal audit report was quite critical of these actions. It recommended that the division be required to stop such practices at once.

Mr. Shakespeare, who is handling the Scratchitoff account himself, has the report of the internal audit before him. Since it has been presented to the board of directors, he expects to be questioned about it.

Problem: What is the proper approach of an auditor in this situation? Does professional ethics require that he agree with the internal audit? If not, what may managers reasonably expect of him?

SHORT CASE PROBLEM 26.2

Functional Budgets

The personnel manager has allowed himself to be drawn into a sharp controversy with the firm's executive vice-president. The latter suggested, in an executive committee meeting, that all departments, including staff, should prepare budgets and should be ready to justify their expenditures. He argued that all activities and programs should be justifiable on a dollars-and-cents basis.

The personnel manager took immediate issue on this point. He argued, first, that it was practically impossible to put a dollar value on many personnel programs or on the consultation and advice provided by the personnel staff. Second, and more important, he insisted that there is no good reason why every expenditure should be expected to "pay off" in dollars and cents. He cited the rug in the president's office as an example of a cost whose contribution could not be assessed and further suggested that no one had shown that there was any economic contribution from the more frequent window washing in the offices as compared with the shop. He cited the landscaping and care of the front lawn as involving expenditures no one sought to justify in terms of their contribution.

The difference of opinion now appears to be headed for the president's office for decision.

Problem: Prepare an answer to the personnel manager in which you outline the potential gains from a functional personnel budget.

SHORT CASE PROBLEM 26.3

Smith Electronic Equipment Company

Employees of the Smith Electronic Equipment Company have been on strike for four weeks.

The firm was founded by Mr. George Smith in 1940. Its products have a wide applicability in both civilian industry and military equipment. Early production was limited to products invented by Mr. Smith. Subsequently, adaptations of these early devices to a wide range of products have provided the basis for a constantly growing business. World War II resulted in a minor boom in the firm's activity. After the war, expansion continued, more or less against the desires of Mr. Smith. He has often expressed his wish that the business would not get any bigger.

In spite of this preference, numbers of employees have increased from a maximum of 26 in 1941 to 560 in 1960.

The firm enjoys a reputation for able, far-sighted management, which is based on its excellent record of profits. From the early years, in which Mr. Smith almost lost the $14,000 with which he started, net earnings have increased to a 1959 figure of $1,670,000. The growth has been fairly steady, although slight downturns appeared in 1946, 1947, and 1952.

Mr. Smith is still the sole proprietor of the business. He has not, since the very early years of the firm's existence, encountered any serious problem in financing operations. He borrowed from local banks when the new building was erected in 1950, but the loans have been repaid. He has had many proposals that stock be offered for sale, but he has preferred to maintain complete ownership. He has also been urged to make some stock available to members of his management group, but he has resisted any such suggestions.

In the early years of the firm's operations, no union represented employees. Mr. Smith was presented with a demand for recognition by the United Electrical Workers as bargaining agent in 1949. At first, he resisted the proposal. He was not convinced that the union, or any other, represented a majority of his employees. He refused to recognize the union until ordered to do so, after an election, by the National Labor Relations Board. Since that time, however, the same union has continued to represent employees and to negotiate an annual contract, which expires on March 31 of each year.

The firm's wages are neither unusually high nor particularly low as compared to those of similar jobs in the community. Union demands each year have been scaled down in the course of negotiations. Increases have followed rather closely the pattern of wage changes in other industries.

The Smith Company has no personnel or labor relations departments. Mr. Smith has preferred to maintain a membership in the local employers' association and to allow that association to handle negotiations as well as the administration of resulting agreements. To the association must go whatever credit or discredit attaches to resulting wage rates as well as numerous fringes.

Early in the spring of 1960, the business agent of the union (he is not an employee of the firm) announced that the union was planning to demand an increase of 25 cents per hour for the coming year. At the time of the announcement, forecasts of average increases indicated that they would range between 10 and 15 cents. Mr. Smith and the representatives of the employers' association with whom he discussed the matter concluded that the union was merely seeking publicity. In preliminary negotiating sessions, however, the business agent announced that he was not fooling, that employees had discussed the matter carefully and were determined to have the whole of the 25 cents. In later sessions, it appeared that the union members had discussed the level of earnings and profits in the firm and had concluded that they could get the increase and were, at least to some degree, entitled to it.

The representative of the union argued that the firm could give no reasonable excuse for not paying the increase, and that the men and women employees had contributed that much and more to the success of the venture. He stated flatly that, unless the demand was granted, the men would "hit the bricks."

Both Mr. Smith and his representatives were skeptical. They had faced union threats before, although they had not experienced a work stoppage. Mr. Smith could see no real rationale in the demand. He instructed his representative not to discuss ability to pay. He didn't cite any figures; he regarded them as irrelevant. Employees struck on the morning of April 1.

Since that time, Mr. Smith feels that he has been through more than any reasonably decent individual should have to face. His friends in the community have urged him not to give in. Other employers have told him—he believes, with complete sincerity—that such an increase would start a pattern that would be ruinous in several other firms. The military services have urged him to find a solution and get the plant into production. He has had subtle suggestions that if he can't get the men back to work, orders will have to be taken elsewhere. He has suffered indignities when he entered his office at the plant. Some anonymous threats have been made, both by mail and by phone, and his wife is almost hysterical about possible hazards to his children. The union has charged him with refusal to bargain, and a hearing on that charge is to be held shortly.

He has met with the business agent of the union twice since the strike began. At the first meeting, the union representative urged him to make an offer. Mr. Smith proposed what the employers' association representative had already suggested several times in earlier negotiations—an increase of 10 cents an hour. This was apparently entirely unsatisfactory. The business agent mentioned his responsibility to employees and suggested that their hardhips in the strike were Mr. Smith's fault.

In the second meeting, the business agent seemed more belligerent. He stated that the labor market in the locality was tight and that most of the employees had found other jobs. He intimated that they were ready for a long strike—a strike to win the full amount of their demands. He further suggested that they might not now be willing to approve a settlement for the full 25 cents.

Mr. Smith is quite concerned by the suggestion of one of his close friends—another local employer. The friend states flatly that Mr. Smith is facing a "shakedown." He says that a gift of a thousand dollars to the business agent would end the strike on Mr. Smith's terms. He urges Mr. Smith to try it.

Problem: If called in as a consultant, would you conclude that this situation is traceable primarily to practice or to policy? What yardsticks would you apply to management's action and position? What action would you recommend to Mr. Smith?

Careers in Industrial Relations

What are the opportunities for jobs and careers in industrial relations? What is the prospective future for young men and women who plan careers in personnel and labor relations? Where are the jobs? How does the interested student learn about them? What educational preparation is desirable? What are the prospects for earnings and advancement and transfer into other managerial positions?

For some students, counselors have provided helpful answers to many or all of these questions. For many other students, the questions remain unanswered. A great deal of information has become available in recent years. This appendix is designed to provide a brief summary and useful references to that information.

1.0 NUMBER AND TYPES OF JOBS

No census has provided a comprehensive count of the numbers employed in industrial relations staff positions. (Most firms that have personnel or industrial relations divisions regard them as *staff;* in some small organizations, however, they are combined with other management and not specifically designated as a staff department.) Perhaps the best guide to total numbers is the *personnel ratio,* frequently mentioned in preceding chapters. That ratio indicates that, in larger working organizations, industrial relations staff members average about 0.75 per 100 employees or 1 per 133. The average cited is for all industries; some industry groups, including banking, finance and insurance, and manufacturing have higher average ratios. Others—including public utilities, trade, and transportation—report lower averages.[1] Many younger, rapidly growing firms have much higher personnel ratios. These ratios permit a rough estimate of the total number of jobs in industrial relations. The *Occupational Outlook Handbook,* prepared by the Federal Bureau of Labor Statistics and distributed by the Government Printing Office, concluded, in 1958, that there were some 50,000 professional workers in personnel and labor relations. This estimate is almost certainly too low.

[1] For up-to-date information on these ratios, see the frequent reports of University of Minnesota studies in *Personnel,* for example Roberta J. Nelson, George W. England, and Dale Yoder, "Personnel Ratios, 1960: An Analytical Look," *Personnel,* Vol. 37, No. 6, November-December, 1960, pp. 18–28.

It is important to note that, in addition to the differences from one industry to another, size of firm exerts an influence on numbers of industrial relations staff members. Few firms with less than 100 employees have a personnel department or manager. In small firms, the specialization of management is more limited and responsibility for labor management is usually only one of several types of responsibility assigned to an individual. In some very small firms, ratios are smaller; much depends on the industry and the maturity of the firm. Younger, rapidly growing organizations, especially in finance and manufacturing, require more extensive industrial relations programs and higher ratios.

It is important, also, to recognize that the personnel ratio includes all technical and professional workers reporting to the industrial relations department. It covers many types of jobs, from professional secretaries to vice-presidents. Beginning or entrance positions are only a part of this total.

Public agencies as well as private firms include large numbers of personnel jobs. In the public service, the personnel ratio is usually about 1.0, that is 1 personnel worker per 100 employees.

Opportunities in personnel work are by no means equal for the sexes. Not more than from 5 to 10 per cent of the jobs in industrial relations staff divisions are presently held by women. Most of the jobs in which women are employed are in retailing and manufacturing.

2.0 JOB RELATIONSHIPS

The top job within the industrial relations staff division is likely to be that of *Industrial Relations Director* or *Vice-president—Industrial Relations*. (About 5 per cent of the top jobs are now given the vice-president title and this proportion appears to be growing.) The "industrial relations" title has become more popular as labor relations has asumed growing importance as a part of the total job. The older and still more common title is *Personnel Director* or *Personnel Manager*. About two-thirds of those who hold the top staff job report directly to the president or chairman of the board.[2]

Throughout the entire industrial relations staff, as in management as a whole, job titles are not standardized and uniform. For that reason, one recent study of industrial relations jobs has developed functional job titles, designed to indicate fairly specifically just what each assignment involves.[3]

In terms of these functional titles, the second echelon of jobs includes the *Personnel Director* and the *Labor Relations Director*. The former is responsible for staff relationships with employees as individuals and hence for such activities as recruiting, selection, training, promotion, transfer, release, and retirement. The Labor Relations Director is responsible for union-management relationships, particularly contract negotiation and administration. The responsibilities of the two may overlap at points, for example when the union negotiates wage adjustments and employee benefits.

The next level of management is composed of supervisors and administrators of the major industrial relations functions, including employment, placement, training, wage and salary administration, benefits and services, personnel research, safety, employee publications or communications, and health. For each of these functions,

[2] See "The Personnel-Industrial Relations Function," *Survey No. 52,* Bureau of National Affairs Personnel Policies Forum, April, 1959; also the survey, "The Personnel Executive and His Staff," *Personnel Policies and Practices Report,* Par. 1502, 1961.

[3] Dale Yoder and Roberta J. Nelson, "Jobs in Employee Relations," *Research Study No. 38,* New York: American Management Association, 1959.

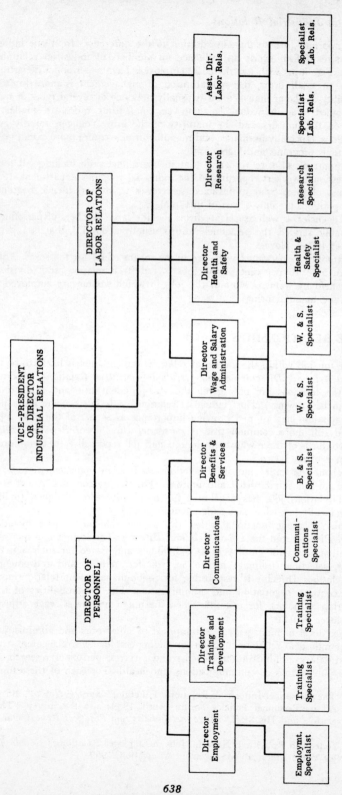

Figure A.1 Structure of Industrial Relations Staff Jobs

one or more additional scalar levels may include non-administrative specialists. They may be supported, as may higher echelons, by assistants, statisticians, secretaries, and clerical workers. The total job structure, in these functional terms, may be pictured as in Figure A1.1.[4]

Figure A1.1 represents a composite of the practice in many firms. No single firm, so far as is known, has precisely the pattern of organization suggested by the figure. In individual firms, the functions are frequently combined, so that one section of the staff is responsible for both health and safety or for a combination of health, safety, and benefits and services. In medium-sized organizations, the personnel manager may not have specialized subordinates in more than one functional area, perhaps training and development. Many firms have no labor relations director, since their employees are not organized and do not bargain collectively.[5]

2.1 Entrance jobs. Beginning jobs in industrial relations are at the assistant and specialist levels. In smaller organizations, the beginner may be employed as an assistant to the personnel manager or labor relations director. In larger organizations, beginners generally start as assistants or specialists in wage and salary administration, employment, benefit administration, communications, research, safety or training or in a position that combines two or more of these major functions.

Past practice frequently brought members into the industrial relations staff from positions in the line organization. That practice has become less common, chiefly because of the special educational requirements of industrial relations jobs. It is still a common practice in firms that provide special internship training programs. In these programs, newcomers are routed from one department to another during their first year or two, after which they are moved into one of the sections of the industrial relations division if they request that assignment.[6]

2.2 Salaries. Salaries of personnel executives range from $5,000 to more than $50,000. Annual earnings include bonuses that average about 20 per cent of salaries. As would be expected, size of firm and numbers of staff members are important factors in salaries. The top personnel executive receives, on the average, approximately one-third of the president's salary in the same organization.[7] Salaries vary by indus-

[4] For details of the duties and responsibilities of each job, alternate titles, and educational preparation, and experience, see Dale Yoder and Roberta J. Nelson, *op. cit.*

[5] For more on the responsibilities, duties, and qualifications of top managers in industrial relations, see A. L. Belcher, "How Top Management Views the Industrial Relations Function," *Personnel,* Vol. 34, No. 5, March-April, 1958, pp. 65–70; *The I. R. Executive, 1958–59,* New York: Industrial Relations News, 1959; Edith Lynch, "The Personnel Man and His Job," *Personnel,* Vol. 32, No. 6, May, 1956, pp. 487–97; "The Industrial Relations/Personnel Department: Coming of Age," *Industrial Relations News,* June, 1959; Russell L. Miller, "What Plant Managers Expect of Personnel Managers," *Personnel Administrator,* Vol. 3, No. 1, February, 1958, pp. 12–15; G. M. Oxley, "The Personnel Manager for International Operations," *Personnel,* Vol. 39, No. 6, November/December, 1961, pp. 10–16.

[6] For detailed descriptions of entrance positions, see the announcements of opportunities for personnel officers and assistants and placement officers and assistants frequently issued by the U. S. Civil Service Commission; see also "Jobs in Employee Relations," *op. cit.;* also announcements by the various state civil service offices; also the frequently excellent *Occupational Guides,* well illustrated by that for "Labor Relations Man," State of California Department of Employment, Number 297, June, 1961.

For assistance in evaluating career opportunities, see "Personnel Workers," *Occupational Briefs, No. 134,* Chicago: Science Research Associates, 1961; P. W. Maloney, "An Open Letter to the Student Seeking a Career in the Personnel Field," *Minnesota Highlights,* Vol. 2, No. 1, Winter, 1960 (available from Iota Rho Chi, care of the Industrial Relations Center, University of Minnesota); Robert Shosteck, "Careers in Labor Relations," Washington, D.C.: B'nai B'rith Vocational Service Bureau, 1953.

[7] See Dale Yoder and Roberta J. Nelson, "Salaries and Staffing Ratios in Industrial Relations, 1957," *Personnel,* Vol. 34, No. 1, July-August, 1957, pp. 18ff.

try and by region, with lower salaries in transportation, public utilities, and the government service and in southern and western sections of the nation.

Entrance salaries are about the same as for other divisions of management. Graduates with a Master's degree have been receiving $50 to $100 per month more than those with baccalaureate degrees.

2.3 Mobility and promotion. Promotions to top-level staff positions generally follow lines essentially like those shown in Figure A1.1. Candidates selected for entrance positions are expected to have the educational background on which to build competence for higher responsibilities. Because industrial relations management has made rapid strides toward professional status, staff departments assume that those who hold beginning and subordinate positions will continue their education and development and thus qualify for continuing promotions within the staff division.

One sharp break from earlier practice deserves special mention. For those who start in the industrial relations staff and have decided to make their career in that specialty, current practice avoids or sharply restricts rotation among other departments. In some earlier arrangements, staff members were transferred about in a system of job rotation, on the theory that they would thus become acquainted with several types of operations and become more effective in the employment relations field. It is now recognized, however, that the growing need for specialized competence in the industrial relations field requires continued concentration and personal growth in the field. As in all other professional occupations, the individual who does not keep up with developments loses much of his value. Job rotation tends to prevent continued professional development.[8]

Promotions are by no means confined to higher positions in the industrial relations staff. Staff members at all levels may qualify for and seek promotion into line jobs. If they have had sufficient breadth in their educational preparation and have learned to understand problems of the line, such promotions are not only possible but likely.

Indeed, the pattern of promotions to upper levels in the line appears to emphasize transfers from staff divisions to line responsibilities. Earlier practice assumed that experience in the line was essential as a qualification for promotion in the line. Many students sought direct assignment to line positions. Experience has raised serious questions about this assumption. In most firms and agencies, entrance jobs for graduates are largely in the specialized divisions—sales, finance, marketing, industrial relations, accounting, and others. The new employee may plan on a full career within the specialized field. He may, on the other hand, seek opportunities to become acquainted with other managerial functions. He may serve on committees that provide broader experience. He may ask for and be given an opportunity to work in other divisions. He makes a choice, which may come early or late in his career, between continued growth in his specialty and broader experience and responsibility within the organization. It is notable, in many of the largest and best known business firms, that former directors of personnel and industrial relations staff divisions have become presidents and executive vice-presidents.

Top levels of management are staffed with those who have made the choice to broaden assignments and responsibilities rather than to remain within the field of specialization. Beginners are brought into training programs or employed in special-

---

[8] On the trend toward professionalization in the personnel-industrial relations field, see "Professional Standards for Personnel Work," *Pamphlet No. 13,* Washington, D.C.: Society for Personnel Administration, 1956; Frank B. Miller, "Why I'm for Professionalizing," *Personnel Journal,* Vol. 38, No. 3, July-August, 1959, pp. 91ff. See also Charles A. Myers, "What about the Future of Personnel Administration?" *Personnel Administration,* Vol. 21, No. 5, September-October, 1958, pp. 5–12 (Reprint Series 2, No. 73, Department of Economics and Social Science, Massachusetts Institute of Technology); Dale Yoder, "The Outlook in Industrial Relations," *Special Release No. 1,* University of Minnesota Industrial Relations Center, July, 1959.

ized divisions. Some of them become increasingly specialized and remain in staff
assignments. Others transfer out of the original specialties and become general
managers.

Younger, more recently educated staff members have a relatively high degree of
mobility. Their superior educational backgrounds and their professional approach
to management provide a basis for assurance and competence. They can and do
transfer from one firm or agency to another much more readily than their older
counterparts, chiefly because so many older practitioners have no such breadth of
training and have not kept abreast of developments in the field.[9]

3.0 EDUCATIONAL PREPARATION

Several surveys have indicated that industrial relations managers, have, on the
average, more education than the composite of other executives. A *Harvard Business
Review* survey found that 53 per cent reported some graduate education, as compared with 43 per cent of the entire group of executives. In part, increased education is a result of the frequent employment of attorneys in labor relations divisions,
but it also results from the fact that many personnel and industrial relations managers now hold Masters degrees and some 2 per cent hold the Ph.D.[10] Perhaps most
important is the growing emphasis on professionalization in the field, which has
encouraged many personnel and industrial relations staff members to continue their
educational growth throughout their working careers.

From the study of educational attainments of present staff members and their
opinions, it seems clear that the future staff member should be educated broadly,
with at least two years' foundation in the liberal arts. In senior college and graduate
education, a broad approach to management is desirable, with specialization or
depth in industrial relations, personnel psychology, and labor economics. The
commonly favored majors, as reported in several studies, are Business, Management,
and Psychology.[11]

[9] See Edwin T. Haefele, "Some Statistics on Mobility of Personnel People," *Public
Personnel Review,* Vol. 15, No. 3, July, 1954, pp. 142–44.

[10] "Putting Executives to the Test," *Harvard Business Review,* Vol. 38, No. 4, July-
August, 1960, pp. 6–16; Dale Yoder and Roberta J. Nelson, "Jobs in Industrial Relations," *op. cit.*

[11] See Earl J. Kronenberger and P. L. Mellenbruch, "Kentucky Personnel Men
Favor Psychology and Commerce Courses," *Personnel Journal,* Vol. 36, No. 9, February, 1958, pp. 331–32. For details of educational attainment and recommended
courses, see Dale Yoder and Roberta Nelson, *Jobs in Employee Relations, op. cit.;* see
also William G. Caples, "A Survey of the Graduate Curriculum in Industrial Relations," *Annual Proceedings,* Industrial Relations Research Association, December 28–
29, 1958, pp. 224–36.

Name Index

A

Aaron, Benjamin, 226n, 230
Aaronson, Albert H., 616n
Abegglen, James C., 420n
Ackoff, Russell L., 569n, 596n, 598n
Adams, Leonard P., 509n
Adams, Richard N., 81n, 607
Adler, Mortimer J., 64n
Alfino, Anthony P., 265n
Allen, Louis A., 108n, 118n, 122, 129n, 433n
Anderson, T. A., 443n
Andrews, Kenneth R., 433n
Anshen, Melvin, 431n, 593n
Appley, Lawrence A., 50n, 157
Arensberg, Conrad M., 105n, 135, 530n, 589n
Argyris, Chris, 64n, 73, 81n, 87n, 95, 120n, 134n, 401n, 414n, 422n
Aronson, Robert L., 509n
Austin, Robert W., 419n

B

Babbage, Charles, 82
Bachman, Jules, 460
Baehr, Melany E., 530n
Baker, Alton W., 16, 126n
Bakke, E. Wight, 81n
Balinsky, Benjamin, 382
Bambrick, James J., 157
Bancroft, Gertrude, 38, 39
Barbash, Jack, 197n, 407
Baritz, Loren, 95, 590n
Barkin, Solomon, 73, 259, 261, 267
Barrett, Dermot, 563, 564n
Barton, Lewis D., 317
Bass, Bernard M., 373n
Baumback, Clifford M., 307n, 317
Bavelas, Alex, 563, 564n
Baxter, Brent, 329n
Beal, Edwin F., 200n
Beaumont, Richard A., 522

Becker, C. Robert, 576n
Becker, Joseph M., 507n
Belcher, A. L., 639n
Belcher, David W., 460, 464n, 475n, 482
Belenker, Jerry, 565n
Bellows, Roger M., 16, 93n, 296, 317, 351, 581, 607, 632
Belman, Harry S., 407
Bendix, Reinhard, 22n, 26n, 30, 65, 135, 420n
Benewitz, Maurice C., 239n
Benjamin, Roland, 358n
Benn, A. E., 140n
Bennett, C. L., 421n
Bennett, Willard E., 413n
Bennis, Warren G., 93n, 405n
Berkowitz, Monroe, 512n
Berle, Adolf, 135, 417n
Bernstein, Irving, 243n
Bernstein, Marvin K., 420n
Berren, James E., 520n
Bertotti, J. M., 35n
Berwitz, Clement J., 401n
Best, Wallace H., 377n
Beveridge, W. I., 587n
Black, James M., 8n
Blake, Robert R., 380n
Blau, Peter, 104n
Blaustein, Saul J., 504n
Bolda, R. A., 406n
Bornemann, Alfred, 417n
Bortz, Nelson M., 169n
Bosticco, I. L. M., 536n
Boulding, Kenneth E., 45n
Bouvier, Emile, 467n
Bradley, Philip D., 239n, 249
Brayfield, Arthur, 88n, 532n, 552
Brennan, Charles W., 464n
Bricker, George W., Jr., 431n
Brinker, Paul A., 460, 549n
Bromwich, Leo, 198n, 208
Brooks, Earl, 421n
Brookshire, Marjorie, 540n, 552

Subject Index

Decision-making, 59, 423
Delay, compulsory, 242
Delegation, of authority, 127
in decentralization, 128
in organization theory, 82
of policy making, 128
principle, 127
span of control, 128
Democracy, union, 215
Demotion,
defined, 303
policy on, 308
Design, in research, 596
Developee, unhappy, case problem, 437
Development, (*see also* Training, Management development),
definition, 386
evaluation, 406
facilities for, 392
identification of potential, 392, 424
management, 413
organization for, 387
policy on, 386
rank and file, 393
responsibility for, 386
Development,
selection for, 324
self-development, 393
Dictionary of Occupational Titles, 274, 280, 288, 415
Differentials,
negotiated, 203
shift, 496
wage rate, 452
D.I.G. (Diagnostic Interviewers' Guide), 332
Discharge,
cause for, 541n, 552
policy, 311
Discipline,
case problem, 555
contract clauses, 256
indicator of morale, 540
layoff as penalty, case problem, 268
managerial laxity in, 541
promotion and, case problem, 553
Disciplinary review board, 541
Disclosure, legal requirements, 225, 230, 247, 519
Disclosure and Reporting Act, 225, 247
Discounts, for employees, 501
Discrimination, in hiring, 277
Disputes, jurisdictional, 204
D.O.T. (Dictionary of Occupational Titles), 274, 280, 288, 415
Downtime, 497
Draft conventions, 177
Drunkenness, 541
Dualism, 204
Dummy tables, 597

Duplex Printing Press Company v. Deering, 279

E

Earnings,
defined, 464
in incentive wage plans, 469, 471
Economic growth, 442
Economic Indicators, 441
Education,
for decision-making, 423
for industrial relations jobs, 641
of labor force members, 42
Election, representation, 246
Elite, employer, 179
Emotional stability, tests, 339
Empathy, 401
Employee benefits (*see also* Benefits and services), 203
Employee relations, defined, 9
Employee Relations Index, 616
Employee representation plans, 150, 266
Employer associations,
administrative, 180, 264
belligerent, 179
negotiatory, 180
strike aid by, 264
types of, 179
Employers' liability laws, 511
Employment,
changing demands, 40
goals in, 3
in public service, 52
Employment agency, private, 313
Employment service, public, 314
End spurt, 536
Energy, measures, 536n
Equal pay, 446
Erdman Act, 218
E.R.I. (Employee Relations Index), 616
Erroneous inference, 333
Error, in ratings, 373
Escalator clause, 447
Escape period, 190
Ethical practices, codes, 57, 198
Ethics,
managerial, 11, 57, 419
of testing, 345
Exaction,
Lea Act provisions, 244
Taft-Hartley rule, 225
Examinations, in training programs, 405
"Exceptional employees," 306
Exclusive bargaining agent, 190
Executive (*see also* Manager),
changing requirements, 125, 128
development programs, 413
failures, 422
functions and activities, 421
recruitment, 315
skills, 422